TOM PAINE

A Political life

TOM PAINE

A Political life

JOHN KEANE

BLOOMSBURY

First published in Great Britain 1995

This paperback edition published 1996

Copyright © 1995 by John Keane

The moral right of the author has been asserted

Bloomsbury Publishing Plc, 2 Soho Square, London W1V 6HB

A CIP catalogue record for this book is
available from the British Library

ISBN 0 7475 2543 9

10 9 8 7 6 5 4 3 2 1

Printed in Great Britain by Cox & Wyman Ltd, Reading, Berkshire

For Alice
George
Leo
Rebecca

Contents

Prologue

A Citizen Extraordinary

IF ONE PURPOSE of biography is to lift individuals out of time and confer upon them a form of immortality, then the Englishman Tom Paine (1737–1809) is a natural ally of the art of preserving lives in words. More than any other public figure of the eighteenth century, Paine strikes our times like a trumpet blast from a distant world. His writings still spark disputes about matters of public importance, while his thoughts move public figures as different as Ronald Reagan and Bob Dylan, Salman Rushdie and Margaret Thatcher to quote him — as if to prove that the dead are sometimes more alive than the living.

Paine's uncanny familiarity is partly traceable to his own stupendous achievements. Despite humble beginnings, Paine's every step later generated intense public excitement. Paine reckoned that life was either a daring adventure or nothing, and for that conviction many loathed him. The dominant classes, pickled in port and privilege, certainly thought him rough and ungracious, an upstart in their world of landed wealth and courtly power. But among enemies and friends alike, Paine earned a reputation as a citizen extraordinary — as the greatest political figure of his generation.

Paine burst onto the stage of public life as a commoner. In his early years in England, he was variously employed as a corsetmaker, a ship's hand, a Methodist lay preacher, an exciseman, a teacher of English, and a writer who dabbled in public affairs. Fortune soon flung him twice into the furnace of revolution. In America, he served as a soldier, political adviser, and war correspondent. He was also the most prominent political thinker and writer during the Revolutionary struggle against the British. He was twice invited to France, where he helped draft the 1793 constitution. During the Reign of Terror, after having argued for abolishing the monarchy and preserving the life of Louis XVI, he spent nearly a year in prison, where he almost died of exhaustion and narrowly escaped the guillotine. At every turn, Paine's life was packed with excitement, drama, surprises, and some remarkable failures. His writings shocked and thrilled audiences not only in England, America, and France but also in towns as different as Dublin and Dubrovnik, Philadelphia and Warsaw, Berlin and Santo Domingo. In each place, he forged a reputation as the world's chief public defender of republican democracy — a living symbol of the modern fight for the rights of citizens against warring states and arbitrary governments, social injustice and bigotry.

These leitmotivs of Paine's life and writings obviously bind our world to his. But he is also so strikingly one of us in the thoroughly modern language he used to express himself. Eighteenth-century English prose, by contrast with its predecessors, feels surprisingly crisp. Although certain words, phrases, and sentence constructions from that period are not normally used today, eighteenth-century writing — essays, novels, pamphlets, journals, treatises — has for us a definite familiarity, as if that language and our own coexist within the boundaries of modern English.

Paine's own writing, encouraged by his reading the works of figures such as Daniel Defoe and Jonathan Swift, helped produce this familiarity. The brilliance of his quill made him a literary lion, a master of daring assertion, sly humor, and witty metaphor. Not only the message but also the modernist style of *Common Sense, Rights of Man,* and *The Age of Reason* ensured that they became the three most widely read political tracts of the eighteenth century. Their concerns still unsettle readers in our time, in no small measure because Paine, a grand master of modern prose, helped effect a revolution in political language. His books, pamphlets, letters, essays, and poetry tried to communicate complications simply. They invented a plain style crafted to capture the attention, and secure the trust, of audiences previously accustomed to being pushed about or ignored, not being written for, talked about, and taken seriously as active citizens. "As it is my design to make those that can scarcely read understand," Paine wrote, "I shall therefore avoid every literary ornament and put it in language as plain as the alphabet."

And so he usually did. Full of fire, Paine hammered out lean, lightning-quick sentences for audiences he knew well — self-educated artisans and ordinary folk like himself, for whom reading and being read to were exhilarating first-time experiences. For such folk, reading "Tommy Pain" must have resembled walking into previously unimagined political territory. In Paine's prose, they followed a confident guide, convinced that his footsteps were echoing across a landscape that no one had ever trodden before, let alone mapped. Paine described that new world of republican democracy with immense wit and seriousness. He supposed that in politics words count and that words are deeds. He further supposed that liberty is connected with prose and that people unfriendly to citizens' liberty normally wrap their power in pompous or meaningless phrases.

Paine certainly had no elaborate theory of language, and he rarely questioned his own conceited view that his writing was "plain truth," a reflection of the world as it actually is. He counted himself among the modern believers in the originally Greek idea that what makes us clever, language-using animals is our ability to rise above the contingencies of time and place and know the nature of things. Paine nevertheless pointed to modern humans' bad habit of forgetting those same circumstances. We moderns continually attribute universal importance to our own particular ways of life and we therefore have an alarming tendency to boss ourselves and others, using sticks and stones and bigoted words, into accepting our preferred version of the world. Paine despised bossing, and he had a fine ear for language masquerading as Truth. "Bastilles of the word" was Paine's phrase for needlessly haughty language, and he consequently wrote as if it were the duty of the citizen, and certainly the political thinker and writer, to be on the lookout for hubris. He prodded and poked at it wherever it appeared, his overall aim being to encourage individuals to become citizens capable of thinking, speaking, and acting clearly and confidently in public. Here Paine's didacticism dovetailed with his wider concern to take the ax to dictators and hierophants. Paine felt enormous compassion for the unjustly treated, and he despised haughty powermongers who put themselves beyond question. Paine so disliked arrogance and venality that he not only championed citizens' right to tell others what they do not want to hear. He also was prompted to show that human beings could live together on earth without earthly Gods — indeed, that we live fully only in their absence.

The precise vigor with which Paine took aim at human-made Absolutes was highly unusual in his day, and it suggests another vital reason why his life and writings continue to provoke and divide audiences two centuries later. Paine was an eighteenth-century critic with "twentieth-century" philosophic tendencies. He dared to doubt most existing Grand Ideals — his faithful belief in progress, Newtonian science, and God-given reason were among the contradictory exceptions that got him into trouble — because he was convinced that they unleashed hypocrisy and deception, bigotry and power hunger, powerlessness and violence upon the world.

Paine's early life in England made him profoundly skeptical of the view that government and religious institutions are above public suspicion. On this basis, he began his public life as a journalist, a defender of government employees' right to organize into trade unions, and a critic of the enslavement of Africans. Paine then smashed into the antiquated structures of monarchy so cherished by the governing political classes of his day. Monarchy in its various forms supposed that the body politic must be ordered hierarchically, so that every lesser unit, right down to the individual, should know its place beneath a ruler whose sanctity and power were inviolable. Paine considered the whole thing preposterous — as ludicrous as a bad play. Monarchy is "something kept behind a curtain, about which there is a great deal of bustle and fuss, and a wonderful air of seeming solemnity," he wrote. "But when, by any accident, the curtain happens to be open, and the company see what it is, they burst into laughter."

Initially, Paine worked to abolish the pseudodivinity of monarchs in the name of "the people" or "the nation," terms that he used interchangeably. Previous writers on Paine have not noticed that he soon questioned this very principle of popular sovereignty. He suspected, with good reason, that the formula of "the people" as a unified God on earth, from whom all power and wisdom emanates, was the mirror image of the old doctrine of monarchy that republicans had fought hard to replace. The formula made him nervous, especially after witnessing, firsthand, figures as different as Robespierre and George Washington attempting to abuse political power in the name of "the people."

To see "the people" as an invented fiction, prone to misuse by dictators speaking in the name of their subjects, was a bold insight. But it was perhaps not as electrifying as Paine's thunderous attacks on organized religion. Paine was certainly not the first to challenge Christianity, but the way he did so — as his enemies saw — made skepticism about every kind of organized religion a subversive living force. Paine's point was as simple as it was explosive. Talk of sacred scriptures, God's designs, and the sanctity of the church, he said, was merely talk — the talk of a few mortals bent on empowering themselves over others, whom they patronizingly labeled sinners in need of a Savior.

Such attacks on dogmas responsible for powerlessness injected great energy into Paine's activities. His life so pulsated with risk and novelty that it is difficult not to feel that Paine, whom some today might dismiss as a

dead, white European male, is alive and universally relevant, exactly because he raised enduring questions about citizens' need to guard against
organized deception and arbitrary power. His public attacks on dogma
were nevertheless not intended to push citizens into a void of confused
disbelief. Life without dogmas was possible, Paine thought, but only inasmuch as individuals cultivated their own personal morality and joined
with others as public beings. He considered all individuals of all countries
as potential citizens. As citizens, he argued, they were entitled to enjoy
certain rights but also were bound to honor certain duties within a worldwide framework of constitutional governments that maximized civil and
political freedom and guaranteed social justice. "Where liberty is, there is
my country," his good friend Benjamin Franklin once reportedly remarked to him. "Where liberty is not, there is my country," Paine quipped
in reply. Citizenship for him implied the global abolition of despotism and
injustice: "When it shall be said in any country in the world, 'My poor are
happy; neither ignorance nor distress is to be found among them; my jails
are empty of prisoners, my streets of beggars; the aged are not in want,
the taxes are not oppressive; the rational world is my friend, because I am
a friend of its happiness:' — when these things can be said," wrote Paine,
"then may that country boast of its constitution and its government."

This positive vision of what modern life could be like is strikingly contemporary. No doubt there are good reasons why Paine cannot and should
not have the first or last word in contemporary politics. Admirers of Paine
who so dogmatize his vision live in a cemetery. They end up looking like
the famous statue of Laocoön — frozen in their fight with ancient enemies, trapped in blind love for their hero, ignorant of the new forms of
good and evil developing behind their backs. Paine's eighteenth-century
vision of a decent life nevertheless retains a certain vibrance. It has survived recent genocidal wars and the anti-Communist and Islamic revolutions, and it is undoubtedly more relevant than that of Marx, the figure
most commonly identified with the nineteenth- and twentieth-century political project of bringing dignity and power to the wretched of the earth.
Not only is Paine's bold rejection of tyranny and injustice as far-reaching
as that of his nineteenth-century successor, but his practical proposals —
as the collapse of the communist utopia demonstrates — are actually
more radical than Marx's, mainly because they managed to combine
breathtaking vision, a humble respect for ordinary folk, and a sober recognition of the complexity of human affairs.

Paine was for strong, effective government but also for government limited in scope and strictly accountable to its citizens. He supported un-

bridled freedom of assembly and expression but not its licentious abuse. He favored private property and market competition but fought for the principle of guaranteed citizens' income and other tax-funded public measures to prevent society's cruel subdivision into rich and poor. And Paine, who was among the leading cosmopolitans of his era, criticized empires and backed the right of national self-determination, but only as part of a broader campaign for global integration of citizens and states. Overall, Paine devoted his life to devising methods of scattering and subdividing power, to ensuring that it was not monopolized by any single pair of hands or particular "faction." He suffered, publicly and privately, for this conviction. But there can be no doubt that he moved the world a few feet toward republican democracy — and inspired it to move a few feet farther after his death.

To trace out the life and writings of Tom Paine is thus to understand better the roots of contemporary democracy. Indeed, any appreciation of the value — and limitations — of modern republican forms of democracy is impossible without developing eyes in the back of our heads for figures like Paine. Democracy among the living, it could be said, requires democracy among the dead, in that votes must be extended to the most disfranchised of all constituencies — our silenced ancestors. Biography is one way of enfranchising dead figures such as Paine, who certainly merits the vote because he helped us to see that representative democracy and citizens' self-government is the best means by which a plurality of different, often conflicting groups can live their differences in dignity without dominating or murdering each other. Thanks in no small measure to him, democracy is nowadays viewed as a system of decision making that institutionalizes the right to be different, that celebrates intermingling and hybridity, and that thrives on change by conflict and compromise. Democracy, Paine taught us, is the enemy of enforced stereotyping — the most effective weapon yet invented against arrogant armies, pompous politicians, and power-greedy groups armed with Grand Ideals.

Paine's democratic pilgrimage made him the greatest public figure of his generation. He made more noise in the world and excited more attention than such well-known European contemporaries as Adam Smith, Jean-Jacques Rousseau, Voltaire, Immanuel Kant, Madame de Staël, Edmund Burke, and Pietro Verri. The controversies he stirred up naturally spilled onto the pages of his biographers, who currently number around fifty. The first biography, written by George Chalmers, a royalist refugee from the United States, appeared in 1791 as *The Life of Thomas Pain, Author of "The Rights of Man," with a Defence of His Writings*. Although it contains some valuable details about Paine's early life, it is not a defense of Paine, but a vicious scandalizing of his life. William Cobbett's biographer, Edward Smith, described the book as "one of the most horrible collections of abuse which even that venal day produced." And so it is. It complains about Paine's "bad grammar," and the title page of several editions contains the famous sketch of Paine, *Rights of Man* in hand, preaching to a group of apes. Chalmers — who wrote under the nom de guerre "Francis Oldys, A.M. of the University of Pennsylvania" and was paid £500 for his labors of libel by the Pitt government — even had the cheek to condemn Paine (whose father's surname was variously spelled "Payne," "Paine," and "Pain") as a dissembler who added an *e* to his name.

A second biography, published by James Cheetham shortly after Paine's death in 1809, is no better. The *Life of Thomas Paine* was among the first muckraking biographies in American literature. It was something of a scurrilous revenge on Paine, who, shortly before his death, was in the process of commencing a libel suit against Cheetham (or "Cheat 'em," as Paine called him). Cheetham's biography pictures Paine exactly as parts of America wanted to remember him and still do — as an arrogant, drunken atheist. Several nineteenth-century biographers fought hard to redress this image, making it clear in the process that biographies are not "facts" revealed in words, but are contingent interpretations, constantly subject to amendment at the hands of storytelling biographers to come. Clio Rickman, a close personal friend and regular correspondent of Paine's, was the first biographer to picture his hero in sycophantic terms. His surprisingly derivative *The Life of Thomas Paine* (1819) is marred by touches of personal vanity and paranoia; it amounts to an exercise in wielding a pen to protect an idol. Rickman was to Paine what Boswell was to Johnson. William Sherwin's *Memoirs of the Life of Thomas Paine,* published in the same year as Rickman's book, is marginally better, although it understates Paine's achievements in America and contains many unwarranted claims and conjectures. Gilbert Vale's *The Life of Thomas Paine* (1841) draws heavily on Sherwin's biography and contains some new material, but it suffers from its blinkered quest to prove Paine right on every political matter.

It was left to an American abolitionist and prominent supporter of Abraham Lincoln's in the Civil War, Moncure Conway, to write the standard two-volume biography of Paine. *The Life of Thomas Paine,* published in 1892, is still considered by every authority on Paine the key reference work. It claims to rest its case on "the simple facts, dispassionately told, of Paine's life." It is a considerable achievement, containing a great quantity of compellingly accurate material and healthy correctives to the smear campaign that had been waged against Paine for a century. Justifiably, it still enjoys the reputation of being the most valuable and fully documented sourcebook for readers of Paine's life.

The following interpretation of Paine's life nevertheless takes aim at key aspects of Conway's standard account. Things to be said against it include its numerous errors of detail and its nineteenth-century obsession (absorbed from Rickman, Sherwin, and Vale) with undoing the image of Paine as a drunken, treacherous roisterer. In too many passages, its defense of Paine is simplistic and sentimental; where Paine turns, Conway follows, swooning, summarizing Paine's achievements in superlatives:

> The first to urge extension of the principles of independence to the enslaved negro; the first to arraign monarchy, and to point out the danger of its survival in presidency; the first to propose articles of a more thorough nationality to the new-born States; the first to advocate international arbitration; the first to expose the absurdity and criminality of duelling; the first to suggest more rational ideas of marriage and divorce; the first to advocate national and international copyright; the first to plead for the animals; the first to demand justice for woman.

None of these claims is actually sustainable; they are symptomatic of the way in which Conway's account of Paine rests on stretched interpretations masquerading as facts. Conway supposes that his biography is a plain-talking "effort to bring the truth to light." This leads him to overlook the simplest of truths: that a biography is never a straightforward "factual" account of the details of a person's life, but rather it is a story, guided by a plot structure, that renders a chosen sequence of events into an intelligible narrative — one that often tells us as much about the biographer as about the person whose life is observed. In contrast to Conway's disguised sermonizing, I try to rely on techniques of modest writing, including understatement; acknowledgement of the biographer's ignorance; disclosure of confused sources and disagreement among historians; awareness that the methods of narrative storytelling adopted here are indeed reliant on interpretation and structured by plot; and, above all, recognition that Paine's life was riddled with complexity. While often admiring and defending Paine's pathbreaking achievements, I try to create an "open" rather than a "closed" text by encouraging readers to spot the plots buried in my own stories of Paine's life and to formulate their own questions and doubts about its knottiness.

The emphasis on complexity is important for two reasons. First, it is faithful to the kaleidoscopic patterns of Paine's life and work. Contrary to

Clio Rickman, his most loyal and intimate English friend, Paine was not simply "incorrupt, straightforward, sincere." Sometimes he was these things. But his life also was riddled with tensions, confusion, surprises, and unforeseen consequences. Paine's personality was complex. He loved oysters, cared little for money, despised hypocrisy, and suspected men who lived richly. He liked stirring things up, rarely knew love or sex, considered hypocrisy the homage vice pays to virtue, and did all he could to keep his private life private. He was humble and conceited, generous and dogmatic, ironic and serious. He faced dilemmas, failed to resolve problems, made misjudgments, and rarely pleased everybody.

Teasing out such tensions in biographical form is important for another reason. It makes for more challenging reading because it recognizes the need to avoid the sniping and sermonizing that has plagued every previous biography of Paine, David Freeman Hawke's *Paine* (1974) included. Hawke's biography is among the best since Conway's, but it contains weaknesses. It neglects the first half of Paine's life and harbors a surprising number of errors of detail. Its narrative clings to the minutiae of Paine's activities, often ignoring the wider dramas and developments — such as the growth of party politics in America, the French Reign of Terror, and the rise of nationalism — in which they unfolded, and without which Paine's life and political thinking cannot properly be understood. Above all, for want of any theses about Paine's significance, past and present, Hawke resorts to the technique of sniping and burdening his subject with offhand cynical remarks — to the point where readers are left wondering why Hawke ever bothered to write a biography of Paine. In contrast, this biography aims to avoid partisanship by relying on what could be called broken narrative. I try neither to rub noses with Paine nor to spit in his face, but rather to confront readers with Paine's achievements, failures, and unsolved problems — many of which (such as citizenship rights, poverty, and the scope of government power) remain our problems two centuries later. In sum, I offer readers the opportunity to ponder Paine's questions for themselves, thereby encouraging them to tinker with their own sense of reality.

The more genuinely comprehensive scope of this biography also sets it off from Conway's. During the past century, most studies of Paine have quietly deferred to Conway's standard account by concentrating on fragments of Paine's life and work. Although this has brought to light much new material, no biographer since Conway has been interested simultaneously in detailing Paine's private and public lives in England, America, France, and Belgium. In this biography, I have tried to synthesize all the available material, old and new, to develop fresh lines of inquiry into

Paine's activities. I have used previously unknown material in Russian, German, Polish, French, Dutch, Serbo-Croatian, Hungarian, Chinese, English, and Spanish. I also have given new emphasis to the novelty and influence of Paine's political thinking. Although A. J. Ayer's *Thomas Paine* (1988) and Gregory Claeys's *Thomas Paine: Social and Political Thought* (1989) both attempt, in important ways, to take stock of some of Paine's religious and political views each makes the mistake of severing and de-emphasizing the details of Paine's personal and public life from his social and political philosophy. Neither adds much to Conway's seminal account of Paine's biography, and for that reason I have tried to do what no previous account of Paine has done: to detail Paine's political ideas, to situate them in the European and American contexts of Paine's daily life, to examine how these ideas developed and how they were actually interpreted by his friends and enemies, and, finally, to restore his reputation as an original, if controversial and sometimes flawed, political thinker — which was certainly the way his contemporaries saw him.

The contextual approach to biography adopted for this purpose involves immersing readers in the detailed circumstances of a distant era, in order that they can better understand that world as it was experienced by Paine and his friends and enemies. I use the contextual approach to draw a different and more comprehensive picture of Paine's activities in America. A new account is provided of the events leading up to the publication of *Common Sense*. Paine's revolutionary analysis of the grim side of the Revolution — its encouragement of revenge, random violence, fear, and the grabbing of power and property — is highlighted. His understanding of Native Americans is treated with a fresh eye. And new evidence is marshaled to support the claim that Paine was among the earliest defenders of federalism. In formulating these and other claims, I have been guided by various reinterpretations of the American Revolution, especially Bernard Bailyn's and J. C. D. Clark's, and studies such as David A. Wilson's *Paine and Cobbett: The Transatlantic Connection* (1988); a fine doctoral dissertation by Arnold Kimsey King, "Thomas Paine in America, 1774–87" (1951); Eric Foner's *Tom Paine and Revolutionary America* (1976); and A. O. Aldridge's *Thomas Paine's American Ideology* (1984). The recently rediscovered John Hall diaries, missing since Conway's research and now held at the Library Company of Philadelphia, proved most useful, as did the impressive private collection of Paine material generously made available to me by Richard Maass and the new material concerning Paine and Robert Morris uncovered by the ongoing Robert Morris Papers project at Queens College/CUNY in Flushing, New York.

Surprisingly little is known about the long period that Paine lived in France. Conway's account of that period has become inadequate, and even such attempts to fill the gaps as A. O. Aldridge's *Man of Reason: The Life of Thomas Paine* (1960) have been overtaken by new developments. The first French biography of Paine, written by Bernard Vincent, *Thomas Paine ou la religion de la liberté* (1987), has appeared. Important new details are surfacing of Paine's extensive contributions to journals such as the *Chronique du mois* and *Le bien informé*. And exciting reinterpretations of the origins and course of the French Revolution by Keith Baker, François Furet, Monika Ozouf, Michelle Vovelle, and others arguably require a fundamental rethinking of Paine's contributions to that Revolution. I have tried to do so — for instance, by reexamining his decision to vote against the execution of the king and his reactions to the Terror, the rise of nationalism, and the militarization of the Revolution in the crucible of Anglo-French rivalry.

Finally, Paine's activities in England are here for the first time given their due weight. Conway — and every other American biographer — neglected the first half of Paine's life in England, even though such neglect arguably makes it impossible to understand Paine's later life, including his drafting of the world-shattering pamphlet *Common Sense* within a year of arriving in the American colonies from England. Conway tried to explain away our ignorance of Paine's early life by tracing everything to his contacts with the Quakers. "Had there been no Quakerism," he wrote, "there had been no Thomas Paine." Audrey Williamson's *Thomas Paine: His Life, Work and Times* (1973) correctly reacted against that reductionist explanation, but unfortunately it neither generated much new material about Paine's early years nor took account of the outbreak of new controversies in English historiography. The most recent biography to appear, Jack Fruchtman Jr.'s *Thomas Paine, Apostle of Freedom* (1994), indulges the same weaknesses. Fruchtman presents no new material; carelessly muddles details and repeats old clichés about Paine's early commitment to Quakerism and .his personal "failures"; proposes that Paine came to political writing "quite by accident"; and concludes with a strange self-contradiction: "Paine was *always* the democratic, though acerbic, journalist: an apostle of freedom" (my emphasis).

I have tried to correct at least some of these weaknesses, initially by concentrating on the task of understanding the English roots of Paine's political identity. His democratic republicanism no doubt had English antecedents — for instance, among prominent late-seventeenth-century and early-eighteenth-century figures such as Andrew Fletcher, William

Molesworth, John Trenchard, and Walter Moyle, all of them deep admirers of an older republican tradition and writers of famous tracts against the evils of standing armies, established churches, and other threats to public-spirited liberty. These English republicans, or "Commonwealthmen," defended an aristocratic concept of "people" or "country." Despite their fear of strong executive power and commitment to power sharing, they seldom or never discussed democracy, save as a negative term to describe a nightmare of anarchy. Their elitism was evident in their concern to make England great by promoting colonial expansion and fostering domestic commerce and population growth. At no time did these republicans propose universal or manhood suffrage. They believed in representation — of the independent, the well-to-do, and the literate — but not on a numerical basis. Their chief concern was to ensure that the propertied classes voted and that good men governed the country — if need be against the wishes of the huge majority of commoners.

Paine's republicanism differed in two important ways from these classical republican views. First, although he accepted the standard republican insistence on public spirit, anticlericalism, citizenship, annual parliaments, and power sharing, he pushed and dragged republicanism firmly into the modern world. After Paine, modern republican politics could no longer hide behind the dogma that a natural aristocracy of virtuous men of talent must rule over an ignorant hoi polloi hungry for property and power. Paine's brand of republicanism was dangerously democratic. It pressed for the inclusion of commoners — dairymaids, millers, fishermen, shoemakers, laborers, and servants — in the category of "the people" and considerations of "public virtue." It thereby edged republicanism toward the new principle of representative democratic government, which, Paine's good friend Thomas Jefferson later remarked, "rendered useless almost everything written before on the structures of government."

Second, unlike his predecessors', Paine's republicanism was self-taught, not bookish. The Commonwealthmen read widely about ancient republics. They admired Sparta and Rome, and their studious reflections on the decline and fall of ancient republics — attributed by them to the flouting of good laws, the decline of patriotism, and the obsession with luxury — were designed to persuade contemporary statesmen to avoid old errors and adopt right policies. Knowledge was to be the handmaiden of prudent government. Paine's republicanism was expressed through books and pamphlets, and it was certainly fueled by wide reading, of everything from the satirical prose of Jonathan Swift to Newtonian tracts on astronomy. But it requires something of a leap of imagination to see that Paine's democratic republicanism, in all its originality, did not derive primarily from books or formal education in the classics. Rather, as I try to show in the following pages, it stemmed from his firsthand experience of a maelstrom of overlapping, clashing, and colliding organizations, circles, associations, emotional commitments, personal contacts, everyday events, and stubborn intellectual currents excluded from the mainstream polite society. Out of such an English education sprang many great autodidacts — Mary Wollstonecraft, William Cobbett, William Blake, and Thomas Spence — but it was Paine, who never aspired to Oxford or Cambridge, who most effectively welded together his everyday experiences in England to become the greatest English political writer of his century.

This book was born with the help of many people and institutions. As the recipient of an Andrew Mellon Fellowship from the American Philosophical Society in Philadelphia, I was the first Paine biographer to enjoy access to its library's cataloged Gimbel Collection, whose treasures were displayed to me by Roy E. Goodman, Hildegard Stephans, Beth Carroll-Horrocks, Edward Carter II, Whitfield J. Bell, Jr., and the library's photographer, Frank Margeson. Prior to his untimely death, and even during protracted periods of illness, Edward Thompson offered me solidarity and good advice. Sir Richard Attenborough, Douglas A. Cooper, Michael Foot, David Henley, and Eric Paine, all admirers of Paine, provided various forms of support. Bernard Vincent, France's leading expert on Paine, generously offered me his time and knowledge. In Paris, Nathalie Caron guided me through the Académie des Sciences, Archives Nationales, Musée Carnavalet, and Institut d'histoire de la Révolution, to whose staff I am most grateful. Hélio Osvaldo Alves, Gregory Claeys, Neil Clayton, Ian Dyck, François Furet, Mary A. Y. Gallagher, Mark Garnett, James Green, Richard Heitzenrater, Thomas A. Hoctor, Louise Marcil Lacoste, Pat Logan, Tomaž Mastnak, Tom Nairn, Edward W. Pratt, Kenneth E. Rowe, Alfred Rubens, Nigel Sinnott, Gordon K. Thomas, Ann Thomson, Michelle Vovelle, Michael Weinzierl, and Naomi Wulf personally drew my attention to important gaps in the understanding of Paine's life. Zofia Libiszowska, Huang Yu, and Eva Dessewffy Palmai helped me with the Polish, Chinese, and Hungarian sources, respectively. Sarah Wallis and Clara Roukshina cheerfully met my requests for Russian material. Jean-Pierre Boyer uncovered new details of Paine's reception in Québec. Andries Van den Abeele fed me interesting material on Paine's contacts in Bruges. Jelena Bužančić and Vesna Pusić, herself something of a Paineite, skillfully traced details of Paine's relationship with the eighteenth-century republic of Dubrovnik, during the period when the late-twentieth-century citizens of that city suffered a military siege and vicious bombardment aimed at destroying their heritage and their lives.

My teacher C. B. Macpherson first sparked my interest in Paine and alerted me to the difficulty of categorizing him in the standard terms of modern political thought. Penelope Connell fed my thoughts about biography. Bernard Crick was instrumental in securing publishers of the manuscript. William O'Neil explained in detail how Paine suffered with the gout. Brian Jenkins enlightened me about Paine's contacts with the Constable brothers. Charles Wanostrocht and Nigel Yates provided invaluable material on eighteenth-century Sandwich. The Reverend T. S. H. Elwyn of the Baptist Historical Society furnished new documents on Paine's links with the General Baptists. In London, Alan Q. Morton of the Science Museum, Christina Scull of the Sir John Soanes Museum, and the staff at the Royal Society Library helped with material on Paine's scientific and architectural interests. Additional bibliographic help in these and other matters was given personally by staff at the British Library, the Brown University Library, the Brian O'Malley Central Library in Rotherham, the Centre for Kentish Studies, the Grantham Public Library, the Mills Memorial Library, the New York Public Library, the Public Record Office, London, the Sandwich Library, the Library Company of Philadelphia, the Trinity College Library, Dublin, the University of Virginia Library, and the Historical Society of Pennsylvania. Diane Aylward provided access to the records of the Thetford Town Council. Michael Carnell and the staff of the Thetford Library were always generous. So too were the archivists at the Norfolk Record Office in Norwich and the Suffolk Record Office in Bury St. Edmunds. Chad Goodwin, Pat Murrell, Oliver Bone of the Ancient House Museum, the Duke of Grafton, and especially David Osborne provided expert advice on how to undo the amnesia of Thetford. David Powell, Jeremy Goring, John Houghton, George Hindmarch, Colin Brent, and the staff of the Eastbourne Central Library and the Sussex Archaeological Society did the same for Lewes. Jane Weeks and John Weeks, headmaster of Thetford Grammar School, gave generously during my stays in Thetford and Bury St. Edmunds. Margaret Blunden, Alison Curtis, Martin Faulkner, Nicholas Garnham, and Geoffrey Holt were especially supportive colleagues at the University of Westminster. Bridget Cotter, a research student at the Centre for the Study of Democracy, provided vital administrative help. Bill Hamilton lived up to his reputation as an oustanding literary agent. Jennifer Josephy and Liz Calder were model editors: intelligent, literate, honest, firm, patient, cheerful, efficient. Paul Mier heartened me during the hardest times of the manuscript. My debts to Kathy O'Neil and her children are too numerous to detail.

PART I

England, 1737–1774

1

Thetford Days

Child of Violence

FROM THE HOUR of his birth, Tom Paine felt the deathly hand of the English state. Some called him a child of state violence, for the thatched cottage where he came crying into the world in Thetford, England, in the winter of 1737, stood near an execution site, on the slopes of a low, windswept hill known locally as the Wilderness.[1] Townspeople favored this name because of its wretched soil and winter winds, but also because each year, with the arrival of spring, convicted criminals were herded through the area from the borough gaol, a quarter of a mile away, up to a nearby chalk ridge resembling Golgotha. There, on Gallows Hill, within plain sight of Paine's cottage within the Wilderness, the gaol governors and town constables arranged hangings, watched by wide-eyed crowds.

The yearly ritual of Thetford executions dated back at least six centuries, to the time when the medieval gaol was first built. On Paine's birthday — Saturday, January 29, 1737 — the gaol stood on the same site that it had first occupied in the reign of King Edward I. Square-built of black flint and stretching three stories upward from its basement dungeon, the gaol symbolized the cruel punishment system in whose shadow the young Paine became an adult. From an early age, he undoubtedly knew of the building, for it was renowned as a house of horrors to which prisoners

from all over Norfolk County were brought to await trial or sentencing.
Townspeople saw the gaol as a hellish maze of bars and doors, dirt and
debauchery, which left prisoners scarred or dead. One contemporary observer likened it to the black hole of Calcutta; another considered it a
sewer of vice where the old were hardened in iniquity and the young instructed in crime.[2] Still others gossiped about its rough routines. Each
morning, it was said, prisoners were loaded with irons or forced onto the
treadmill, while at dusk, as female prisoners were flung into solitary confinement in the top floor cells, the most dangerous men were stuffed into
the low-ceilinged basement dungeon. The men were then forced by the
duty constables to lie down, head to toe, on a stone floor and to sleep, if
sleep it could be called, without either mattresses or bedding. The accused
complained constantly about the filth and poor food, while long delays in
trials and sentencing added to their misery. That is why, townspeople said,
prisoners often yearned for the courtroom — for "gaol delivery" —
which gave them momentary release into the outside world, where prisoners could hear birds twittering and feel sunlight or rain splash on their
faces, reminding them that death was not yet theirs.

The court sessions, or so-called Lent Assizes, for the county of Norfolk
were always held in Thetford during the month of March. In the year of
Paine's birth, proceedings were conducted by Sir John Willes, recently appointed as Lord Chief Justice of the Court of Common Pleas and later
satirized as a red-nosed, triple-chinned lecher in William Hogarth's painting *The Bench*. "In politicks he was a right ol' bugger," locals often said,
"but a lawy'r of great learnin' an' a judge of ability." Escorted by a livery
of forty mounted men, he had traveled from Cambridge to Thetford by
way of Newmarket, arriving in Thetford on Saturday afternoon, March 5.
His arrival in Paine's hometown was bathed in pomp, above all because
the Lord Chief Justice symbolized the power of George II's government
over outlying courts and regions. After stepping from his gilded coach,
Willes was welcomed by the splendidly dressed High Sheriff of Norfolk
and the Mayor, Henry Cocksedge. He was then escorted to his lodgings in
the King's House, where he dined privately that evening on pheasant,
spit-roasted spring lamb, and fine burgundy wine.

The arrival in Thetford of the Lord Chief Justice usually triggered a
week of town celebrations. There was an old Norfolk saying, "There no
be warm weather 'til the prison'rs are now goin' to Thetford." As if to
prove that maxim and hasten the arrival of spring, hundreds of visitors
flocked to the little town of some two thousand people to witness the spectacle of punishment. Necrophilia hung in the air. On Saturday, hours before the appearance of the Lord Chief Justice, the town grew excited.

Men and women, young and old, rich and poor rubbed shoulders for a time at the marketplace near the gaol, or lingered in small groups to watch the to-and-fro of stagecoaches at the Bell and other local inns.

Travelers often remarked that there was nothing gloomier than an English Sunday. So it was with 'Size Sunday in Thetford. By law, Sunday was a vestige of the Puritan day of enforced godliness and compulsory inactivity. The town residents and visitors were forbidden to sing or play musical instruments, dance, or play ball games, cards, or skittles. Religion and law ruled supreme, as was obvious to the handful of townspeople who watched the Lord Chief Justice walk a private path to St. Peter's Church, accompanied by the High Sheriff, the Mayor, and black-gowned members of the Thetford Corporation. There a mid-morning sermon was preached by the High Sheriff's chaplain, who emphasized in solemn tones the wrath of God and the necessity of obeying His King's laws.

Early next morning, the sobriety vanished. Booths selling ale and cider were set up, and street corners came alive. The temporary population of Thetford continued to mushroom. Accommodations in the town were always in short supply, and beds were let at inflated prices of half a guinea each, with the poorest townspeople taking in lodgers to reap some grain from the harvest. In one recorded case, a poor family had its six children sleep in one bed, three at the head and three at the foot, to earn a few shillings from a lodger. Gentlemen, taking up residence in their town houses, suffered no such discomforts. By day, they tallyhoed their hounds across the surrounding heathland and indulged in horse racing, stag hunting, and pheasant shooting. By nightfall, the same gentlemen gathered at the White Hart Inn, just down the hill from Paine's cottage on a street named Bridgegate, to drink ale, play cards, and bet on cockfights. The courtyards of other local inns had meanwhile been turned into commoners' theaters, filled to capacity every night for a week, their jesting, heckling audiences charmed and taunted with a mixture of classics and vaudeville performed by touring companies.[3]

After several days and nights of unbroken reveling, the Assizes were formally opened in the Guildhall — a short walk from the Paines' — on the morning of Thursday, March 10. The Lord Chief Justice, seated high above a packed courtroom watched over by the High Constable and the Petty Constables, read aloud his commission from the King, sealed with the Great Seal. The names of all Justices of the Peace in the county of Norfolk were then read out, and the gentlemen of the Grand Jury were administered the oath of faithfulness to their King, Church, Country, and conscience. The accused, prevented from giving evidence themselves or even knowing beforehand the charges against them, were expected to stand mute. The whole ceremony mimicked the description of the English justice system in the third part of the famous *Commentaries* of Sir William Blackstone, who himself later presided at the Thetford Lent Assizes in March 1777, three years before his death.[4] Blackstone praised the assize system as an example of "the wise oeconomy and admirable provision of our ancestors, in settling the distribution of justice in a method so well calculated for cheapness, expedition, and ease." He went on to describe the architects of the ancient system as "an illustrious train of Ancestors, who are formed by their education, interested by their property, and bound upon their conscience and honour, to be skilled in the Laws of their Country."

Ancestors of the realm loomed large in the architecture of the Guildhall courtrooms. In the smaller Nisi Prius court, where Lord Chief Justice Willes turned to the day's business, hung a fine oil painting of Justice. Its inscription read: "Judge righteously, and plead the cause of the Poor and Needy. Proverbs 31 and 9." The civil cases were heard first. Business was brisk. About two-thirds of the accused were convicted of offenses such as petty larceny, forgery, libel, and the use of unjust weights. A boy who robbed his master and a man who stole hats were ordered to be transported to the American colonies.[5] A trader convicted of dishonesty and a woman accused of being a shrew were humiliated on the ducking stool on the river Thet. The remaining convicted were ordered to be branded, put in the town pillory, publicly or privately whipped, or fined and imprisoned.

After hearing the civil cases, the Lord Chief Justice moved on to criminal business in the Crown Court, where he sat facing the Grand Jury Gallery. Behind him was a draped canopy submounted by the Royal Arms and the motto *Pro rege, lege, et grege* (For the king, the law, and the people); in the window to his right were stained-glass Royal Arms, while to his left were the Arms of the Borough of Thetford. The crowded courtroom hushed. All eyes fixed on the Lord Chief Justice, the gentlemen of the jury, and the accused, who stood motionless as their fetters were temporarily removed, their eyes sunken and glazed, convinced that the sand in their hourglass was running for the last time.

Criminal cases at the Thetford Assizes normally included burglary, stealing livestock, highway robbery, and arson. Very few were charged with murder. Crimes were as a rule ad hoc acts against property — that is, driven by material desperation and not by any widespread culture of criminality within the ranks of the poor. Sometimes the proceedings were entertaining, as when a packed courtroom watched a man capitally convicted for burglary compulsively eat oranges throughout his trial and sentencing. There were also tales of the time when the courtroom watched with amazement an accused man rob a constable in their midst, or heard the case of a boy who had picked a constable's pocket as he was arrested and was subsequently transported for fourteen years. By these standards, the criminal hearings of March 10, 1737, were uneventful. Stamped with the unsmiling authority of George II, they followed the harsh maxim of Voltaire, who had commented when visiting the area a few years before that the English were a people who murdered by law.

The nearby *Norwich Mercury* reported that in the year of Paine's birth, three of the accused were sentenced to death by the Grand Jury.[6] James Blade, age forty-one years, a former ship's carpenter apprentice, confessed to stealing money and goods to the value of twenty shillings four years earlier from the owner of the King's Head tavern in nearby Stanfield High-Green. He also confessed to keeping fairs at which members of the public played unlawful games such as pricking the girdle, thimbles and ball, and the newly invented game black joke. William Wright, "a poor stupid Creature" born at Silem in Suffolk County, was convicted of stealing a bushel of wheat from a barn and robbing a woman on the King's Highway near Dickelburgh by cutting off her pocket and escaping with one guinea, six shillings, and six pence. John Painter, about thirty-five years of age, was born of "very poor, but honest Parents" and lived near Brandon with his wife and children, working as a warrener. He was convicted of purchasing a stolen horse and stealing a parcel of tea and hiding it in a blacksmith's shop, where he was apprehended. He strongly denied the charges, insisting that the most unlawful act in his life was to poach several dozen rabbits one evening from a nearby warren.

The Lord Chief Justice ordered that each man be executed the next day. "Wretches hang that jurymen may dine," wrote Alexander Pope. And so it was in Thetford. Overnight, as the Chief Justice banqueted with the Grand Jury at the King's House, the three were held groaning in the Thetford gaol, double-ironed and handcuffed. A large yoke circled their necks, and their limbs were chained to the floor of the cell. What they thought or did overnight went unrecorded. We know only that a few minutes before eight o'clock next morning, shortly after sunrise, Blade, Wright, and Painter were escorted by the Borough Sheriff, several petty constables, a clergyman, the executioner, and his two assistants from the gaol up through the nearby Wilderness, past Paine's cottage, to the chalk ridge known as Gallows Hill.

The prisoners, dressed in the same shabby blue coats worn during their trial, looked cadaverous before the murmuring crowd bunched beside the scaffold. Prayers were said. A mournful hymn was sung by a small group in the crowd. The blue-coated men mounted the scaffold. The executioner let fall three ropes, which the assistants adjusted in turn around each prisoner's neck. The convicted joined hands. Staring into the distance, they exchanged no words. Their nightcaps were pulled down over their faces, and a black handkerchief was tied over their eyes. The crowd stilled. The clergyman called, "God bless you! God bless you!" A signal was given, and each man's shoulders were suddenly flung into convulsions. The violent breathing and choked gasps that followed went as quickly as they had come. The convicted criminals had been launched into eternity.

According to custom, the bodies were left to swing in the cold March wind for a full hour. They were then cut down and carted from the scaffold to the gaol, the dispersing crowd trailing along. John Painter's corpse was placed in a coffin, returned to his family, and later buried in a churchyard. The bodies of James Blade and William Wright were delivered to the county surgeons, who picked through their flesh and bones in the name of science, in accordance with the instructions of Lord Chief Justice Willes.

Each Lent for the next nineteen years — all of them spent in Thetford — Tom Paine likely grew conscious of the imprisonment, trial, and execution of scores of figures like Painter, Blade, and Wright. Mid-eighteenth-century punishment was an ugly sight to Paine's eyes, as it is to ours. In his youth, the field of criminal law was the most violent patch of English life. Certainly by European and world standards, Georgian England was not a murderous country. In contrast to the previous century of failed revolution, political assassinations were unknown, soldiers rarely fired on crowds, and kings lost their heads only mentally. The means of state violence were often overstretched, policing was an amateurish affair, and the resort to murder in everyday life was comparatively rare. Other forms of violence — the routine beating of wives, servants, and children, the flogging of soldiers, the brawls of drunken hirelings during election campaigns — were undoubtedly commonplace, and the ubiquity of symbolic violence, such as the seizure of overpriced bread and stone throwing against the excisemen and profiteering millers, shocked visitors to the country. But with few exceptions, even this popular symbolic violence was constrained by considerations of moral economy — that is, limited by custom to specific purposes and clearly targeted at specific objectives such as the defense of ancient liberties and the remedying of perceived injustices.

The tough application of a vicious penal code was the exception. During Paine's youth, capital statutes mushroomed, even for paltry offenses such as stealing a packet of tea, being out at night with a blackened face, purchasing a stolen horse, or stealing a few shillings. While well-to-do homicides were often acquitted or given nominal sentences, servants who pilfered from their masters or rural laborers who stole a sheep found themselves sentenced to death by hanging. England seemed destined to have laws for the rich and laws for the poor. In 1689, there had been fifty capital offenses in the country. During Paine's century, the number quadrupled, most of the additions being related (as might be expected in a burgeoning capitalist economy) to securing absolute rights of private property — against those who continued to think in old-fashioned usufructuary terms of property as the right of peacefully enjoying the use and advantages of another's property. Among the supreme ironies of the period, which Paine himself quickly grasped, was that just as Continental absolute monarchies were beginning to liberalize their statute books, England, renowned as the home of liberty and good government, was imposing Europe's most barbarous criminal code on a population that was among the least violent in the region.[7]

The Graftons

The executions at Thetford two months after Paine's birth confirmed this ironic trend. They contradict subsequent accounts of his birthplace, which has conventionally been pictured, in romantic language, as an ancient haven of poetic stillness and beauty. Francis Blomefield (1705–1752), who was educated at the same school as Paine and became the first historian of Norfolk County, introduced his account of Paine's birthplace with a strain of poetry:

> Thetford, *thy age shall introduce my rhymes,*
> *I honour all thy joys in ancient times,*
> *And wish thee happy, in what now appears*
> *The relicts of above a thousand years.*[8]

The Suffolk poet Robert Bloomfield (1766–1823), Paine's later acquaintance and critic, compounded the romance:

> *To where of old rich abbeys smil'd*
> *In all the pomp of Gothic taste*
> *By fond tradition proudly styl'd*
> *The mighty "City in the East."*[9]

And Moncure Conway, Paine's most-quoted biographer, wrote lyrically about its quaint streets, pretty landscape, historic vistas and (quoting Robert Browning) its "beauty buried everywhere." It is as if the young Paine played in the same kind of unspoiled rural utopia that inspired the idyllic prose of his contemporary, a Genevan writer whom he later read with great interest, Jean-Jacques Rousseau.

Thetford and its surrounding brecklands were actually little like that. During Paine's youth, it is true, Thetford was aptly designated "a town in the midst of a large heath," and his later love of nature undoubtedly stemmed from his familiarity with its windswept beauty. Pitted by meres, dotted with villages and houses tipped with smoking chimneys, the heath was a four-hundred-square-mile stronghold of some of the rarest English plants and insects. During the spring and summer months — or so it was said locally — the heath's bracing air and twisted lines of Scotch pines were filled with wild ducks, nightjars, lapwings, and the weird cries of the stone curlew.

The annual executions at the Thetford Assizes cast a lurid light on such romancing. So too did the presence of the Grafton family, with whose vast wealth and power the young Paine was surely familiar. A contemporary sketch of Euston Hall, the county seat of the dukes of Grafton, conveys something of their grip on the local inhabitants.[10] The estate was immense. The young Frenchman François de la Rochefoucauld, who spent a year in the area during Paine's lifetime, noted how the barrenness of parts of the estate seemed to multiply its vastness. "You cross the duke of Grafton's estate, remarkable for the great numbers of rabbits you see and foxes you don't see," reported la Rochefoucauld. "All this country, which the road crosses for eight miles, is covered only with heather, reaching out of sight in all directions; not a shrub, not a decent herb, except in the little valleys that one sees some way off, shallow and so hardly damp."[11]

Nearly forty miles in circumference, the estate dwarfed the borough of Thetford and encompassed a number of villages and hamlets, as well as perhaps the most elegant seventeenth-century church in England, St. Genevieve, where Paine's parents were married in the summer of 1734. Most visitors found the estate charming. "It lies in the open country towards the side of Norfolk not far from Thetford; a place capable of all that is pleasant and delightful in nature, and improv'd by art to every extreme that Nature is able to produce," reported Daniel Defoe on a visit several years before Paine's birth.[12] "The park and plantations are well worth your viewing: they are very expensive and sketched with great taste," observed Arthur Young during a visit in 1769. "Remark particularly the approach to the house from Bury; it is exceedingly beautiful."[13]

At the center of the Grafton estate there stood a magnificent seven-teenth-century brick house arranged around a central court with four pavilions at the corners —"after the French" as the dukes liked to tell their guests. John Evelyn, the famous diarist and expert on gardening, stayed there for a fortnight in the autumn of 1671. He noted with delight that the house was "not onely capable and roomsome, but very magnificent and commodious, as well within as without, nor lesse splendidly furnish'd."[14]

The interior, from which humble folk like Paine were excluded, con-tained painted ceilings by Antonio Verrio, a state portrait of King Charles II by Sir Peter Lely, and a conservatory adorned with maps. Showcases contained armorial plates made to order in China, a Venetian gilt table, exquisite dining chairs, mirrors, card tables, and Spanish painted cabinets. The dukes were especially proud of a painting of Charles II dancing with his sister the princess of Orange at the great ball held in the Mauritshuis, at The Hague, the night before his return to England in 1660. Downstairs and out through the front door, visitors admired the sundial in the center of the courtyard. Nearby was a walled garden with a stone seat by William Kent and a little garden house from one of his designs. From there a broad path led through the orangery past the end of the house and through the pleasure grounds to the octagonal temple, from which the Graftons watched their racehorses or expensive hounds exercising in the park amid the beeches, firs, elms, and limes.

Beside the path leading back from the temple to the house stood a dead oak, said to have been grown from an acorn from the oak in which Charles II had hid at Boscobel after the Battle of Worcester in 1651. The oak, of course, was a royalist symbol, and the thought that that dead oak pointed to the future of the English aristocracy would have been lost on the Graftons. The second duke of Grafton, Charles Fitz Roy (1683–1757), and his family formed part of a tiny class of agrarian millionaires whose point of pride was the rural palace. They felt no modesty about displaying their wealth. Like all eighteenth-century gentlemen, they were convinced that property was the very basis of civilization, that "dominion follows property" (as Bernard Mandeville famously wrote), and that the first duty of government was to preserve both. The grandeur of their estates radi-ated their confidence that they would rule forever, and history certainly seemed to be on their side.[15] From the end of the seventeenth century, technical improvements and big farming profits in wool, cattle, and corn made the possession of great estates a coveted investment. Through care-ful purchases, prudent marriages, and their control of Parliament, families like the Graftons amassed wealth far in excess of any other stratum of

English society, to the point where the shape of the rural landscape and society was altered irreversibly.

Well before Paine was born and still during his youth, large landowners throughout the country excluded certain land from common or public access. Trackways and paths were blocked off, roads redirected and swept away, without compensation. Many of the traditional common rights of grazing and wood collecting, the ancient privileges of rural folk and villagers, disappeared. The dramatic growth of rural poverty followed immediately. In Norfolk and elsewhere, such enclosure ensured the disappearance of the class of agricultural laborers eking out a precarious living on their small allotments and exercising their common right of access to their masters' property. Small proprietors — peasants or yeomen — were similarly squeezed out of existence. The dispossessed swelled the ranks of the rural poor and made their snaring and poaching presence felt in towns such as Thetford, searching for parish relief.

Although the Anglican Church and private benefactors (including the Graftons) continued to collect and distribute alms for the poor, the relief system provided by the parish authorities was constantly overburdened during Paine's youth. Especially in lean years, Thetford was stalked by migrant paupers, who were attracted to the town because of its position at the junction of several main roads. Toward the end of the eighteenth century, the desperation of the poor resulted in food riots, looting, burning, and mob violence in the Thetford area. Things had probably not yet reached this point during Paine's youth, although there is evidence that many Thetfordians felt that the fabric of society was threatened and regarded those trapped in poverty with constant suspicion. Town ordinances dating back to the sixteenth century ruled that no stranger could live in the town without the permission of the Thetford Corporation. Since these rules were easily evaded, there were occasional house-to-house searches for illegal immigrants, the idle, and the feckless. The Law of Settlement and Removal of 1662 confirmed the local parishes' responsibility for relieving the poverty of its permanent residents. From there on, the "deserving poor"— the elderly, helpless, or unavoidably unemployed — were eligible for outrelief (assistance while resident at home) or were put to useful work organized by the parish or town authorities — for instance, in the workhouse located in the lower room of the Guildhall.

Although the parishes functioned as "miniature welfare states" for the "settled" inhabitants of Thetford, the growing number of "unsettled" idle and vagrant were treated harshly.[16] The sick, poor, and old were ruthlessly driven out or bribed to leave. Unmarried pregnant women were bullied into leaving, even when in labor, in order to "pass the baby." Since it was in the financial interest of Thetford's three parishes to deny settlement certificates to nonresidents, the local authorities obtained the maximum number of removal orders. Justices of the Peace, local constables, and parish overseers of the poor cracked down hard in other ways. As Paine knew from playing in Thetford's streets, it was often a crime simply to be poor, the punishment for which was rough treatment, trial, whipping, transportation, or hanging.

It would be misleading to say that the Graftons themselves were directly responsible for creating a vulnerable underclass of rural poor in and around Thetford. The family certainly had engaged in several acts of enclosure — for example, during Paine's teenage years in the early 1750s, when the second duke of Grafton concluded that the vista from his Pink Bedroom was spoiled by the sight of Euston village. The duke proceeded to solve the problem by contracting the famous English architect Matthew Brettingham to supervise the physical resiting of the entire village and redirect the Little Ouse River to fit in with the "cleansed" rural landscape. Such megalomania was practiced elsewhere in England — Thomas Coke resited the whole Norfolk hamlet of Holkham, for instance — but the Graftons' case was exceptional, if only because they already owned all the land of the surrounding parishes and therefore did not need to enclose through recourse to Acts of Parliament. It might even be said that the bulk of the population in the Thetford area, living as they did within closed parishes protected by "my lord," was shielded by the Graftons' paternalism from the social corrosion caused by countrywide enclosure. That conclusion was reached by some contemporary observers, including Robert Bloomfield, whose poem "Autumn" waxed lyrical about the Graftons: "Lord of pure alms, and gifts that wide extend; The farmer's patron, and the poor man's friend."[17]

The prose was exaggerated, but it correctly pointed to the swollen system of patronage operated by the Graftons. The family had been persuaded of the classical theory that when masters neglect their subjects, the mob clamors for ochlocracy. They consequently took precautions by cultivating an elaborate system of patronage that bolstered their own power and divided their potential opponents, ensuring their reputation (in Edmund Burke's famous words) as the "great oaks that shade a country." The methods were less formal and escapeproof than feudal homage, more personal and comprehensive than the contractual relationships of capitalist competition, but they were hardly new. In 1574, Thetford had been granted a charter of incorporation, becoming a nominally self-governing body. It thereby gained possession of the fee farm — the right to collect taxes on behalf of the Crown and to remit only a fixed annual sum, so that any profits were retained for the use of the town. This change left Thetford wide-open to aristocratic intrigue. Thereafter, until the parliamentary reforms of 1835, it was renowned throughout the country as among the most rotten of rotten, or pocket, boroughs, in which local talent was normally prevented from climbing into national politics, high office, and high society.

Young Paine was presented a lesson in scandalously undemocratic local government, and it is not far-fetched to suppose that his belief that pride and prejudice must be continually pricked by public criticism stems from this period. It is true that Paine's contemporary the third duke of Grafton (1735–1811) was widely regarded as a Unitarian, showed liberal tendencies, and as prime minister of England during the years 1767 to 1770 was sacked by George III after pressing for more independence for the American colonies. But in and around Thetford, the Graftons' rule was virtually absolute. They dispensed a rich harvest of patronage in the form of salaried jobs, tenancies, and, through the borough, licenses, building contracts, and provisions for elections and charity dinners. Uniting in their persons practically all executive power, they acted as the satraps of the community, watching and controlling its public life, scheming to disappoint later historians by ensuring that no class of plebeians emerged to take revenge upon the patricians.

In the matter of parliamentary elections, for example, the Graftons' rule was a synonym for venality. There were occasional signs of anti-Grafton rebellion, as when the incumbent mayor, who had fallen out with the dukes, had his clothes removed by Grafton supporters during an election rally. The mayor refused to conduct the election and withdrew, taking his mayor's robes with him.[18] Such naked challenges to the parliamentary game were exceptional. Throughout the eighteenth century, the two Thetford Members of Parliament, representatives of an electoral roll of only thirty voters, elected themselves. By purchasing votes and distributing favors, the Grafton family exercised virtually undisputed control over the town. Their power of patronage peaked during Paine's first years in Thetford. Thirty years before his birth, it was said that the going rate for a Thetford vote was fifty guineas, and in 1708 one of the successful candidates, Robert Baylis, reportedly spent £3,000 to secure his return.[19] The tightening grip of the Graftons slowly brought such electoral contests to an end. Knowing the difficulty of sailing over political seas in eggshells — their fathers had reminded them of the political debacles of the 1640s —

they applied patience, time, and money to their cause. At a by-election in February 1733, Lord Charles Fitz Roy, the second duke's son, was returned. This was the last parliamentary contest for seventy years. Thereafter, all parliamentary candidates went unopposed, and a Fitz Roy was nominated at each one of the next six elections held over twenty-eight years and at eight of the subsequent sixteen elections during the years to 1826.[20]

The Graftons perfectly matched Daniel Defoe's famous description of the eighteenth-century English aristocracy as the most confident in Europe. Picturing themselves as "the great, who live profusely," they traditionally celebrated their parliamentary triumphs with a splendid dinner given for the prominent men of the borough of Thetford. In aristocratic circles, handsome dining was a measure of success. The Graftons certainly liked their guests to be up to their chins in beef, goose, and venison and up to their ears in claret, punch, and port — so much so that the young François de la Rochefoucauld expressed surprise at the decadence of the election dinner he attended:

> There were, I think, eighty of us, at two tables, each presided over by one of the new members, each magnificently waited on. Even so, we sat down at table at two o'clock and did not leave it till nine, to go dancing. Three quarters of the guests were very drunk, and everyone had had rather too much to drink. As we left the table, a great fat farmer asked me to dance a minuet, and leapt about like a twenty-year-old. The duke of Grafton's nephew, brother of one of the members, was so drunk that he was obliged to go to bed for a few hours, and then returned to the ball; and, having asked a lady to dance with him, he couldn't find her again. I have never before attended such a grand banquet, and I was very glad to judge for myself all these good Englishmen who are all very watchful of their rights, but who would give them still, I think, for a few tonnes of their port.[21]

Quakers and Anglicans

The intricate system of political jobbery operated by the Graftons ensured that every important office was a gift. The dukes were fountains of favor that watered the lives of attorneys, physicians, architects, mortgage brokers, and other middlemen. Paine's early life was certainly touched by this system, starting with his mother, Frances Cocke. Few details of her life remain, but it is certain that she came from a long line of local prominents — John Cockes was Deputy Recorder of Thetford in 1629— and that she was the daughter of Thomas Cocke, an attorney who practiced in the borough. He was required by his license to be a freeman and after several years as a Common Councilman was appointed in 1701 as the Town Clerk of Thetford, probably helped along by Grafton patronage.[22]

Frances Cocke was born in 1696/7 and grew up in the adjoining Euston Parish, in whose church, located on the Grafton estate, she later married. Her father was an Anglican, and she also became a confirmed member of the Church of England. Paine's writings rarely mention her, although later in life she expressed pride in her son's achievements, for instance by fasting every July 4 in support of his contributions to American independence from British imperialism. According to George Chalmers (Paine's first and most hostile biographer, writing under the name Francis Oldys), she was "a woman of sour temper and an eccentric character."[23] Sourness, of course, is the prerogative of survivors and eccentricity the mark of those who rebound in a cramping age, as she did by marrying rather late in life and out of her class and religion. The church register of the Suffolk parish of Euston, three miles from Thetford, is brief: "1734. Joseph Pain and Frances Cocke were married June 20th."[24]

Frances's husband, Joseph, was the son of a cordwainer named William Payne, who combined his shoemaking craft with local tenant farming. William Payne was able to produce and sell his small output of shoes in the town thanks to his admission to the list of freemen of Thetford in May 1688.[25] His farming plot, too small to take advantage of changing agricultural methods, nevertheless provided basic household needs such as milk, potatoes, and summer fruit. With no future in agriculture, his son Joseph Pain (whose surname was variously spelled Payne, Pain, and Paine) was forced to find other employment. He secured an apprenticeship and subsequently earned a living as a staymaker, working from the rented cottage in the Wilderness at the top of Bridgegate, to which he and Frances had moved a year before the birth of their son. Born in 1708, and eleven years younger than his wife, he was a fit, lively man who lived into his seventy-ninth year.[26] He took an interest in town affairs and was widely regarded as "a reputable citizen, and though poor, an honest man."[27]

Joseph Pain was raised as a practicing Quaker, but his marriage to Frances Cocke earned him the disapproval of the local Society of Friends for cooperating with the Anglican Church. "By this act of taking his wife from *the church*," claimed one observer, "Joseph Pain was, according to the rules of the Quakers, at once expelled from their community."[28] The Thetford Quakers were indeed a small, close-knit community and quietly proud of their status as the only Dissenting religion in the town. Yet there is no evidence that Joseph was looked upon as an irreclaimable offender, unworthy of being regarded as a Friend and so, in the terminology of the Quakers, "read out," or expelled. Joseph Pain was in fact registered a Quaker at burial, and it is hence more probable that his decision to marry an Anglican in her parish church was judged unorthodox and penalized by cold-shouldering, especially after Joseph and his wife chose to baptize their two children in nearby St. Cuthbert's Anglican Church. An original entry in the registry of the thirteenth-century church contains information about their second child: "Elizabeth, Daughter of Joseph Payne and Frances his wife of this parish, was born Aug't the 29th, 1738, baptized September ye 20, 1738."[29]

Much mystery still surrounds Tom Paine's baptism into the Anglican Church. It has been said that, unlike his baby sister, Elizabeth, who died in her seventh month, he went into the world as an only child and a heathen, unchristened.[30] Circumstantial evidence speaks against this view. It is probable that, within a month of his birth, Paine was baptized in the humble gray stone font of St. Cuthbert's Church. Doubt still dogs the baptism, for unfortunately that church's registers were neglected at the time. Baptism entries for the months of January, February, and March 1737 are mostly missing. An added complication is that Paine was baptized in St. Cuthbert's, despite the fact that his native parish was St. Peter's. The reason for this anomaly was that the incumbent minister, John Price, tended the churches in both parishes. This practice was not unusual in a town that had once boasted more than a dozen churches and whose remaining three churches competed for souls and tithes in a jumbled mosaic of inherited parishes.

The more important reason no written evidence of Paine's baptism remains is that the incumbent vicar, John Price, died shortly before Paine's birth. His successor, Thomas Vaughan, restored full-time ministerial services in St. Peter's only during March 1737. Paine was consequently baptized in St. Cuthbert's, and, since the high infant mortality rate (one-fifth of all English babies died in their first year) encouraged parents to have their children christened within days or weeks of their birth, a record was not kept of the baptisms during the crucial month of February 1737.[31] These are speculations, admittedly, but evidence that Paine was baptized is found in the fact that he later took several oaths of employment and was married twice by a priest, which required his prior baptism, and that around the age of twelve he was confirmed by the Bishop of Norwich on a special visit to Thetford. Although the confirmation was arranged with the help of Paine's aunt Mistress Cocke, it could not have been performed without Paine's prior baptism. According to church custom, a baptized infant made no positive personal contribution in spiritual terms. Having reached the age of reason, he or she was obliged to assume the character of a good Christian by completing, through the act of confirmation, the goodness of baptism.

In an age in which the outward display of religious belief was still a fundamental determinant of individuals' status and power, Paine was from birth a misfit. Those who insist that Quakerism was at the heart of his identity present a distorted half picture.[32] Paine was never in a straightforward sense a child of the Light. Although he absorbed much from the Quakers, it is more accurate to say that his parents' decision to compromise their religions and expose their son to the ruling state church *and* a dissenting local sect introduced him at a very young age to the peculiarly modern problem of toleration.

In the England of Paine's childhood, religious intolerance remained rampant. The Church of England, the Church of Rome, and the Puritan sects such as the Quakers were deeply antagonistic toward one another. Although each group urged toleration for its own members, few were willing to tolerate the members of other groups. Indeed, in a devoutly religious society, toleration was often seen as the greatest heresy. After all, men's and women's immortal souls were at stake, and toleration in this world was inadmissible if the price was damnation in the next. Quite aside from considerations of salvation, the heretic was also widely believed to be committing an immediate offense against God, and for that reason alone was not to be tolerated.

The Toleration Act of 1689 did not substantially change the ruling patterns of intolerance. It was a hastily drafted document that provided only the legal freedom of worship for all — Catholic, Anglican, Dissenter, and Jew alike — who accepted William and Mary as sovereigns and were prepared to accept the essentials of the Thirty-nine Articles (the confession of the Church of England). The act, it is true, granted certain special dispensations to Quakers. It not only gave them the same legal freedom of public worship as other Protestant Dissenters, but it also relieved them from subscription to any of the Thirty-nine Articles. Instead, it allowed them to subscribe to a general declaration, recognizing their conscientious objection to swear oaths and permitting them to make a simple declaration of loyalty to the new monarchs instead of swearing the Oaths of Supremacy and Allegiance.

Many Quakers remained unsatisfied. For the next half century, Quaker men and women mobilized to repeal laws that they considered discrimi-natory. The Toleration Act had not exempted them from other oaths that had to be sworn before magistrates in civil affairs, and it also continued to insist on the payment of tithes for the support of the established church. A year before Paine was born, the Quakers had resolved to act. Throughout the country — perhaps even in Thetford, although no records remain — they feverishly lobbied the King and Members of Parliament at both Westminster and in their constituencies in support of a bill to abolish the payment of tithes.[33]

The defeat of the Tithe Bill in 1736 was accompanied by a backlash of anti-Quaker petitions and public talk of the need to control elements that were troublesome and dangerous to the state. In practice, this ended the Quakers' attempt to improve the legal toleration they enjoyed and rein-forced the most intractable forms of discrimination they suffered — those rooted in everyday life. To tolerate was to permit by law, but not to en-dorse or encourage members of Dissenting minority groups, much less to provide them with the social resources vital for protecting themselves against power-hungry bigots.

Growing up in mixed-religion household, Paine was taught his first lessons in the task of combating bigotry in circumstances of diversity. Paine's family life introduced him to the paradoxical rule, vital for any po-litical community enjoying civil and political freedoms, that antagonistic religious groups can coexist peacefully only if they agree to disagree by cooperating within a secular political system — that is, accept a form of government and society that safeguards the religious preferences of all cit-izens by establishing nonreligious spaces of compromise, which in turn encourages at least some citizens to take advantage of these zones of com-promise by rejecting organized religion per se.

Paine himself took this path. Just how much his mixed religious back-ground shaped his early years and later life is a matter of contention. Yet it is clear that the supposition that Paine was one of those rare political ge-niuses who from time to time springs magically from the ranks of ordinary people is misguided.[34] Quite aside from the fact that the genius, the "favourite of nature" as Paine's German contemporary Immanuel Kant put it, comes into being only when she or he is defined as such by admir-ers, past and present (a genius is always ultimately a socially defined prod-uct, never a naturally occurring substance), time and circumstance also play key roles in the emergence of the outstanding figure who captures the imagination of others. So, for example, Paine's gut sense of morality and his native political intelligence were not inherited like seeds waiting to burst when the first showers and warm days of spring arrive. His moral capacities ultimately had religious roots. They developed within and around his home on Bridgegate, in the cross fire between Anglicanism and a Quaker community that together were to have a lasting impact on his later life and, eventually, the political shape of the modern world.

Trapped in the field of tension between state and nonstate religions, each convinced of its own Truth, Paine eventually doubted both Anglicanism and Quakerism and opted for neither, all the while absorbing some of their moral teachings and pleading for toleration of all religions and the secularization of state institutions. The militant and witty attacks on organized Christianity for which he later became internationally famous are surely traceable to his early introduction to two fundamentally opposed species of Christianity. So too are his frequent attacks, written in wonderfully florid prose, on the self-righteousness of English Quakers. "Though I reverence their philanthropy," Paine reminisced in his later years, "I can not help smiling at the conceit, that if the taste of a Quaker could have been consulted at the creation, what a silent and drab-coloured creation it would have been! Not a flower would have blossomed its gaieties, nor a bird been permitted to sing."[35]

The young Paine certainly had his moral share of official Christian doctrine. His earliest contacts with the Anglican Church were admittedly rather formal, but significant contacts they were: a baptism, a confirmation, daily prayers at school, an annual memorial service in St. Mary's Church for the founder of his school, a pious aunt, and a practicing Anglican mother who favored a Quaker husband. Under his father's influence, young Thomas also regularly attended gatherings at the tiny Quaker meetinghouse tucked away in Old Meeting Lane. Built in 1697-98, the Friends' building stood adjacent to the town lockup or cage, where minor offenders such as drunkards were held in cramped quarters at times when the main Thetford gaol was full. Quakers met in this simple building regularly until about 1865, when their dwindling community leased the meetinghouse to the Plymouth Brethren and the Salvation Army, until 1920, at which point it was sold for £750. The last photograph of the meetinghouse before its demolition highlights its simple modesty and symbolizes the belief of its members that not only theatrical performances and gambling but also gatherings for pleasure were immoral. The meetinghouse seated no more than fifty people, and its small windows ensured that the Friends witnessed testimonies of the Spirit in sullen light. The modesty of the building was complemented by the adjoining burial ground, a tomb-less graveyard containing about a dozen Friends already departed to join the Being of Beings.

Each Sunday the meetinghouse slowly filled up with frugal Friends. Most of them were workingpeople of humble means, such as carpenters and cordwainers, who thee-thoued one another at the front porch before entering: hearty men wearing big flat-brimmed hats; women who felt themselves the equal of men, all the while hiding their faces behind their fans; and children, like Tom Paine, dressed in coats with no buttons on their sleeves and pockets and no pleats at the sides. The meetings had no clear-cut beginning or end. As the national custom had it, the Thetford Friends commenced by taking their seats one by one or in family groups. During worship every individual took an equal part, and there was no appointed minister. They would remain seated in profound silence for periods stretching from several minutes to perhaps a quarter of an hour, waiting for God's strength and guidance. Then individual men and women would rise. After making a few faces and fetching a few sighs, each would recite words memorized from the Gospels. The inspiration to speak sometimes brought them to the point of quaking or trembling. Friends considered that there was no Christianity without immediate revelation, that they thought and acted through God, and that the indwelling spirit of God, resembling an inner light, inspired each individual to speak and to act. "Whosoever prays to God to enlighten 'im and proclaims the Gospel truths 'e feels," an elderly Friend might have said to us after the service, shaking our hands on the front doorstep, "let 'im be sure that God be inspiring 'im."

On Old Meeting Lane, Paine encountered men and women who practiced the art of subverting established religious and social conventions and shunned the authority of the state. The Thetford congregation, like some forty thousand other Quakers in a country whose population was between six million and seven million, were convinced that church and priest alike were unnecessary, since God Himself dwelt in each person as an Inner Light perceived as conscience or as Christ. They regarded all believers in God as brothers and sisters, scorned "hat honor," and insisted on referring to everyone, however exalted, by the familiar thee and thou. They considered it their social duty to bear each other's burdens and refused to pay tithes to the clergy or take oaths prescribed by law.

Quakers had always suffered discrimination for practicing these customs. As a boy, Paine would have been told stories of the cruel persecution of the Quakers during the previous century. He might have heard of the public whipping in the streets of Thetford of Henry Fell, a handsome thirty-year-old Quaker of medium stature with brown curly hair, condemned in 1660 as an "idle and vagrant person, and a seducer of the people" and forcibly repatriated to his last place of residence in Lancashire.[36] Paine also would have known about the Quakers' attempts to combat such persecution by conducting "the holy experiment" — emigration to the New World. And he undoubtedly heard stories of the Quaker founder and charismatic visionary, the former shoemaker's apprentice, George Fox — "dear George" as he was always known to his intimates — who in the previous century had developed this radical form of "godly" English Protestantism.

From his father's own lips, the young Paine may have heard gripping passages from the writings of Fox, including the riveting description of his own conversion from a state of profound spiritual confusion: "I fasted much and walked abroad in solitary places many days and often took my Bible and went and sat in hollow trees and lonesome places till night came on. And frequently in the night walked mournfully about by myself; for I was a man of sorrows in the times of the first workings of the Lord in me." From the descriptions provided by other Friends, the young boy probably pictured Fox as a bulky person, his long hair, outsize hat, and leather suit bringing ready recognition wherever he traveled. And Paine must have heard how the charismatic preacher had denounced the professional clergy (dubbed mere "scribes"); recommended the study and admiration of nature; condemned slavery, war, and capital punishment for crimes against property; and advised magistrates and tax assessors to "take heed of oppressing the poor." Paine must also have heard how Fox had rejected the various symbols of deference then current in speech and gesture; championed the rights of women; suffered beatings by hostile mobs and been imprisoned eight times before the mid-1670s; and concluded for his pains "that being bred at Oxford and Cambridge was not enough to fit and qualify men to be ministers of Christ."[37]

The extent of the young Paine's knowledge and acceptance of the history of Quakerism is admittedly a matter of conjecture. Did he learn to look down on theatergoers? Refuse to enjoy a game of cards? Turn his back on his peers' swearing? Like so much else of what we know about Tom Paine in his first twenty years, details of his early contact with religion are enveloped in the fog of times past. In a religious sense, young Tom is for us a diminutive, almost absent figure. His parents' and relatives' personal belongings, which would surely have contained various clues, have disappeared without a trace. There are no letters from this period written either by him or by his parents or acquaintances, no diary accounts of him by contemporaries, no detailed reminiscences by Paine himself. Later in life, he even deliberately covered his own early tracks. "Let other pens than mine dwell upon my private motives and personal thoughts of youth," he might well have said, backing up the remark with a mixture of reasons.

Paine closely guarded his early private life, partly because it left him miserable, partly to protect himself against political mudslinging, and partly because of his strong modernist inclination to look to the future and put past things behind him. His secretiveness about his early years also can be traced to his belief that public-spirited figures should be judged by their achievements, not their private lives. "The general maxim is, that measures and not men are the thing in question," he later wrote, qualifying the maxim in the same paragraph by admitting that "the circumstances of private life" must remain important when judging public figures so long as they remain prone to mask their wolfish qualities in sheep's clothing. "When hypocrisy shall be banished from the earth, the knowledge of men will be unnecessary, because their measures cannot then be fraudulent; but until that time come (which never will come) they ought, under proper limitations, to go together."[38]

Unfortunately for those inquisitive about the role of religion in his early years, Paine always considered himself free from hypocrisy and, hence, entitled to keep his lips sealed. That perception of himself as an ethical being — as having courage enough to appear as good as he really was — is nevertheless revealing. It tells something of the extent to which his soul was stamped with the Protestant principle that private and public morals should mirror one another and that individuals are best judged by their works. In addition, circumstantial evidence, together with the occasional remarks he made in his later essays and letters, details his youthful concern with religion. Such evidence confirms that through his father Paine encountered a Quaker community with an aggressive lack of deference and a deep sense of humility and affection for the simple things of life — with what Paine's contemporary and prominent eighteenth-century Quaker John Woolman called the "irresistible might of meekness."[39]

The Friends' militant modesty was constantly put to the test. "All religions are tolerated in England — in fact, though not in law," claimed the young François de la Rochefoucauld after passing through eighteenth-century Thetford.[40] Appearances were deceptive. Thetford's Quakers were on tense terms with the dominant Anglicans, whom they suspected (with good reason) of wanting to persecute them into submission. The Quakers had suffered a history of discrimination by the local population and town authorities, who found scope to apply the Conventicle Act aimed at eliminating "seditious meetings." At a young age, Paine undoubtedly felt this discrimination to be wrong, and it is hardly surprising that he sympathized with their attempts to practice mutual aid. "The Quakers," he later observed, "are remarkable for their care of the poor of their society. They are as equally remarkable for the education of their children. I am a descendant of a family of that profession . . . and I presume I may be admitted an evidence of what I assert."[41] Contrary to the well-known claims of R. H. Tawney and others,[42] the Quakers did not regard themselves as possessive individuals. Certainly, they were convinced that the spirit of God was present in each person and that no interpreter of God was required. Undoubtedly, this conviction nurtured a militant sense of themselves as individuals, reinforcing their belief in the worth and importance of each person in the face of restrictions imposed by creeds and formal services. But the Quakers did not train their pupils to the mastery of others through the mastery of self. They did not prize the qualities of the spiritual athlete locked in a solitary contest with a hostile world, as if concern with the social order was the prop of weaklings.

The Quakers reasoned to the contrary. Mutual assistance was fundamentally important to them, and not merely as a shield against discrimination. They insisted that giving recognition to the contributions of each individual required giving material assistance and loving care to each other and that such mutual aid would enable them to return in Spirit to the state of grace of the primitive Christian communities. Their pathbreaking schemes of providing accommodations, weekly allowances, legacies, and gifts of fuel and clothing to the sick and poor exemplified this conviction. The young Paine was greatly impressed. His Quakerly "feeling for the hard condition of others" (as he put it later in a letter to the town of Lewes) and his sympathies for the underdog — a corollary of the Quaker doctrine of Christian humility — radiate from his first recorded childhood memory. Paine remembered a childhood trauma in which he found himself repelled by the thought that God Almighty acted "like a passionate man that killed His son." In the first part of *The Age of Reason*, he recalled how the trauma had been triggered by a sermon given by one of his Thetford relatives:

> From the time I was capable of conceiving an idea, and acting upon it by reflection, I either doubted the truth of the christian system or thought it to be a strange affair; I scarcely knew which it was: but I well remember, when about seven or eight years of age, hearing a sermon read by a relation of mine, who was a great devotee of the church, upon the subject of what is called *Redemption by the death of the Son of God*. After the sermon was ended I went into the garden, and as I was going down the garden steps (for I per-

fectly recollect the spot) I revolted at the recollection of what I had heard, and thought to myself that it was making God Almighty act like a passionate man that killed His son when he could not revenge himself any other way; and as I was sure a man would be hanged that did such a thing, I could not see for what purpose they preached such sermons.[43]

The same sympathy for the underdog is evident in his first written prose. The earliest remaining glimpse we have of Tom Paine is an epitaph for a pet crow, which he buried in the garden of his home on Bridgegate:

> *Here lies the body of John Crow,*
> *Who once was high but now is low;*
> *Ye brother Crows take warning all,*
> *For as you rise, so must you fall.*[44]

Paine penned these lines when he was eight years old. They are important for several reasons. They reveal a young country boy with a good grasp of the pompous, pushy behavior of scavenger crows, their jet-black feathers ruffling in the wind, pecking at their prey with large black beaks, eyeing other birds nervously, nudging them aside, shrieking mournfully. The pet crow epitaph also is of interest because it reveals the first green shoots of his droll humor and poetic temperament. Most remarkable is Paine's early perception — conditioned not only by his contact with the Grafton oligarchy and the Thetford Assizes but also by his exposure to Quakerism — that even the pompous crow must inevitably climb down from its pedestal to join other humble creatures living on the earth.

Grammar School

The crow epitaph not only displays traces of the razor-sharp ability to rally human spirit against injustice for which Paine later became world famous. It also prefigures his immense capacity for writing in militant and down-to-earth language. Paine became one of the modern masters of political prose in no small measure because of the schooling he received. His half-Quaker, half-Anglican upbringing was consolidated in a literary sense when, at the age of seven, his parents sent him to Thetford Grammar School.

According to Thomas Martin, a contemporary of Paine's, the school had been "noted for the number of gentlemen's sons educated in it," but it "for many years past has been in a declining condition, without any probability of its recovering its former eminence."[45] Old endowed aca-

demic institutions throughout the country were generally suffering atro-
phy, in part because tradespeople like the Paines increasingly wanted a less
classical curriculum and more modern studies such as arithmetic, ac-
counting, French, and science. Thetford Grammar School's curriculum
reflected this change. The school prided itself on good academic standards, instructing prospective applicants that "no boy shall be admitted
but such as can read English well, and are fit to be instructed in the Accident [grammar]."[46] To raise standards in the lower school, the usher, or
assistant schoolmaster, Reverend William Knowles, taught extra classes of
arithmetic and writing for half a day on Tuesdays, Thursdays, and Satur-
days, for which each child paid a fee of 2s. 6d. Since Paine's father,
Joseph, was made a freeman of Thetford on March 31, 1737, two months
after his son's birth,[47] the family had the formal right to send young
Thomas to the school without paying the standard entrance fee of ten
shillings levied on parents of children from outside the town. It was nevertheless a sign of the precarious financial status of the Paine household
that the 2s. 6d fee, plus payments for books, quills, and ink, forced Paine's
parents to dig deep into their pockets. "My parents were not able to give
me a shilling," he later reminisced, "beyond what they gave me in education; and to do this they distressed themselves."[48] It seems probable that
Paine's aunt Mistress Cocke, who lived on nearby Heathenman Street, relieved some of the financial distress by contributing toward the costs.
"Though she lived on a small annuity," it was reported, "she imparted
much of her little income to his mother."[49]

The decision to send Paine to the school with his aunt's support seems
to have been guided by his parents' desire to give him a broad interdenom-
inational Christian education and to take advantage of the dramatic
growth of primary education in England during the eighteenth century.
The primary school movement, as it has been called, was originally fostered by Dissenters, but in Paine's youth it had become dominated by high
Anglicans and Tories, even by Jacobites some said. It offered education especially to the children of artisans and shopkeepers. It was geared toward
satisfying the growing demand for literate and numerate clerks in the expanding world of commerce, and it was run by men and women who were
fundamentally Puritan in outlook, who railed against a world of dissolute,
orgiastic recklessness, and who favored thrift, industry, and godliness.

Thetford Grammar School, five minutes' leisurely walk down Bridgegate from Paine's cottage in the Wilderness, was very much caught up in
this trend, although its origins were older. The first documentary evidence
of the school's existence dates from the beginning of the twelfth century,

and that school continued as part of ecclesiastical Thetford until the Reformation. The redistribution of church lands during this period led to the acquisition of the site by Sir Richard Fulmerston. Founded in 1566 through a bequest of Fulmerston, and subsequently administered by a trust founded through a private Act of Parliament in 1610, the school had been daily home to a long line of boys, including the noted diarist and Attorney General Roger North and the Norfolk historian and topographer Francis Blomefield.

Over the Gothic school gateway built of flint and carved gray stone tipped with green and yellow moss is the founding motto — *Loyaute me oblige* — beneath a weathered crest of two griffins with tails entwined. If those fabulous creatures with a lion's body and the head and wings of an eagle could speak of Paine's time, they would likely describe the morning prayers conducted in the cold, damp schoolroom by the old preacher (who was the curate at nearby St. Mary's Church), droning before his thirty or so assembled boy pupils the first lines of the school prayer: "Almighty and everlasting God, who govern all things in Heaven and in earth, and whose Mercy is over all thy Works, we thy suppliant creatures be here afore thee." The griffins might tell of Paine and his schoolmates taunting the school dunces and cowards, venturing on school swimming trips on warm days amid white swans in the willow-lined Little Ouse, or gobbling apples taken from the tuckshop when the master was not looking, and of their subsequent horsing or hossing (a form of corporal punishment carried out in the school yard on the horsing block, built in 1729). The griffins might also reveal the source and veracity of the whispered rumors, repeated often among Paine's later enemies, that his education "was merely and scantily English,"[50] that "he left no performances which denote juvenile vigour, or uncommon attainments," and that his reputation within the school was that of "a sharp boy, of unsettled application" and "an apt and ready scholar, although not one of the most tractable and docile."[51] The griffins would certainly tell of Paine's confessed proficiency in mathematics, his early addiction to "reading poetical authors" such as John Milton, John Bunyan, and William Shakespeare (a few of whose works were held in the school library), and his first attempts at crafting poems, including the epitaph for his pet crow and some lines on a fly being caught in a spiderweb.

The griffins would likely report as well on Paine's parents' attempts to discourage these adventures "into the field of imagination" and tell of his daunting ability to grasp the contents of books written in Latin, even though his father forbade him, according to Quaker custom, to browse through the school library's collection of Latin lexicons and works by Hieronymus, Gerardus Johannes Vossius, and others. The schoolboys were divided into two groups. The master (Isaac Coleman) taught Latin grammar to those children "as manifested ability sufficient to warrant their being instructed in this higher branch of education." The usher, Reverend William Knowles, was responsible for teaching the sons of the freemen of the borough the "elements of an ordinary English education." Paine was placed in the latter group not because he had narrow expectations "to what is useful, more than to what is ornamental: to reading, writing, and cyphering, which are so commodious to tradesmen rather than to classical knowledge, which is so decorous in gentlemen."[52] He joined the second group simply because of his father's insistence that he not be instructed in Latin. Paine later mused, "I did not learn Latin, not only because I had no inclination to learn languages, but because of the objection the Quakers have against the books in which the language is taught. But this did not prevent me from being acquainted with the subjects of all the Latin books used in the school."[53]

That recollection contained no hint that Paine actually resented the Quaker ban on learning Latin. Indeed, it is likely that he willingly embraced the firm convictions of his father and other Quakers in Thetford. His later remark that a Greek milkmaid knew more about Greek than the best Greek scholar in England[54] reflected the Quakers' belief that the ruling oligarchies in England clung to classical Latin and Greek as a means of preserving and camouflaging their power. The Quakers consequently rejected as nonsense the assumption that a young man's training for public life required him to be lashed by the tingling rod into digesting Cicero's rhetoric, the history of ancient Greece, and the rise and fall of the Roman Empire. They believed that far from building an orderly mind and polished character by making pupils' brains accomplished in structures of declension and conjugation, of rules and exceptions to rules, the study of classical languages taught unquestioning conformity to a vast web of cramping formulas. Communication through these formulas was seen by the Quakers as a means of drilling individuals on a parade ground of language, a malicious device for shaping and subordinating their wills, teaching them the bad habit of looking up to authority and down on those excluded from the charmed circles of power.

The Staymaker's Apprentice

Paine's early taste for poetry and mathematics was denied when he was removed from school at the age of twelve to serve a standard seven-year apprenticeship to his father in the staymaking trade. Joseph Pain's business on Bridgegate was part of Thetford's small manufacturing and trade economy, itself a fragment of the thriving English market economy, which boasted more small businesses and prosperous middling folk than any other European nation except the Dutch republic. Unfortunately for the Paines, Thetford stood on the margins of English business prosperity. The town had seen better days, and to some outsiders it must have resembled a sorry tumbledown place, as the duke of Portland commented after riding through the town when baby Thomas was barely able to crawl: "The town of Thetford is very poor and mean, much decayed, as I was told, of late years, many houses dropping down not worth repairing."[55]

The duke's summary was harsh, but it correctly pinpointed the long-term decline of the town. Before the Norman Conquest of England, Thetford had been one of England's largest towns, a major administrative, commercial, and industrial center with a mint and numerous churches. Its role as a regional hub had been strengthened during that period by its location on the banks of two rivers, the Thet and Little Ouse, whose waters united in the middle of town just above the old wooden Great Bridge (also known as Christopher Bridge), which young Paine crossed each day on his way to school. The location of Theodford, "the people's ford," ensured that whichever way the area was approached, pilgrims, monarchs, soldiers, traders, and other travelers were obliged to descend into town from the surrounding chain of low chalk hills known today as the East Anglian Heights. When leaving Thetford up through those hills, these same travelers were soon surrounded by the wild heathland. From the twelfth century, this breckland (as it was later called) gradually seemed to swallow up Thetford. The town went into a long-term decline, becoming, by the end of the fifteenth century, a small, impoverished market town and a remote river port of no national significance.

The town certainly continued to have regional importance. In the half century before Paine was born, the installation of simple lock gates (called staunches) and continuous dredging, straightening, and widening of the Little Ouse enabled cargo-laden barges known as lighters to moor at quays in Thetford, reinforcing its role as a trading hub in southwest Norfolk and northwest Suffolk. During Paine's teenage years, it was a distribution center for imported coal, wine, and timber destined for Euston,

Honington, Barningham, and other surrounding towns and villages. Locally produced leather, wool, and paper were sent downriver, but the greatest export was malted grain, which supplied local and national brewers and was shipped as far as Germany. Thetford also had a long tradition of specialized metalworking — whitesmiths, blacksmiths, bell founders and braziers — and it was sufficiently large to support specialized crafts. The group of sixteen freemen admitted to the borough in March 1737 included a blacksmith, a gardener, a carpenter, two publicans, an oatmeal-maker, a brazier, and a staymaker named Joseph Pain.[56]

The art of staymaking required patience, skill, and the Quakerly ability to sit for hours in busy silence, cutting and shaping woolen cloth, boning between each row of stitching, and lining the patterned stay with linen. Women of the notable classes wore stays, or corsets, stiffened with whalebone and laced at the rear, especially underneath their mantuas, a style of dress called the *robe à l'Anglaise* by foreigners. The mantua was an open, flowing robe of brightly patterned silk worn in differing widths. The slim, angular lines of its top half were dictated by the long-bodied and low-fronted stay, itself covered by a matching petticoat, a hoop tied around the waist, a linen stomacher embroidered with silk and metal thread or gems, and sleeves fitted to the elbow and finished with hanging flounces.[57]

The mantua retained its unrivaled popularity in England for nearly four decades after the late 1730s, and it is therefore puzzling that Paine's apprenticeship, which lasted nearly seven years, did not lead to a partnership with his father in the Thetford business. Paine later wrote that he felt a certain measure of restlessness in his teenage years. It has been said that he lacked "any heedful industry"[58] and that the "business of a staymaker he never liked, or indeed any occupation, which required attentive diligence and steady effort."[59] Such talk was as maliciously exaggerated as the parallel talk, among his snobbish critics, of Tom the bodicemaker and Tom the staymaker. The fact was that Paine could not remain in his father's staymaking business because it suffered an irreversible decline.

The slump in the business, ironically, was caused partly by the extended popularity of the relatively comfortable mantua, which halted the swing of the pendulum of English fashion. Before the 1730s and especially after the 1770s, that pendulum swung toward the extremes of exaggeration and fussiness, with women cast in the role of impractically dressed social ornaments. The local Thetford market for stays, in any case, had always been small. Business was so tight that at one point during the apprenticeship Paine's father sent him to make bodices with a cousin in Shipdham, a few miles from Thetford. During Paine's childhood, the

Thetford market had begun to be threatened further by competition from London and other regional towns, whose own staymakers searched for business by advertising in the local newspapers, sometimes even acting as "Manchester men," carrying their goods to shopkeepers and selling to customers directly throughout the country.

This market invasion of Joseph Pain's business was helped along by the deregulation of local business. As the Borough of Thetford slid into the hands of the Graftons, local regulations covering small businesses lapsed.[60] Controls fell into disuse, and after 1743 no new freemen were admitted in the traditional manner (that is, recruited from the ranks of apprentices or from the sons of existing freemen). The commercial and political significance of the office also changed. During the previous century and a half, the Borough of Thetford had vigorously pursued protectionist policies. It had used tolls, customs, and price controls to regulate the local markets and penalize outsiders. All businesses operating within Thetford were licensed, nonresidents were excluded whenever possible, and (according to the town's constitution of 1668) even town natives had to be freemen of the borough before they could trade.

The freemen system was designed to secure the market power of local traders, and its demise during Paine's childhood brought out the whip of market uncertainty in town affairs. As the tight trade regulations fell into disuse, competition from within the town grew fiercer. Apprentices and sons of existing freemen were no longer ensured access to local trades, and outside traders found it easier to slip through loopholes into the local market. Some artisans and traders made use of these new freedoms by diversifying into other lines of business. As well as continuing their own trades, ironmongers made cabinets, carpenters upholstered furniture, grocers sold draperies, and tallow chandlers sold medicines. Paine's father, lacking capital, could not make such a move. His son was consequently left without a guarantee of future secure employment in Thetford.

Privateering

Confronted by dead-end employment in a declining trade and eaten inside by youthful restlessness, Paine decided to run off to sea just as his seven-year apprenticeship ended. Sometime during the summer of 1756, in his twentieth year, he left his Norfolk home for London, his eyes fixed down the river Thames. In the second part of *Rights of Man*, written nearly forty years later, he recalled his decision clearly, confusing only the year of his flight: "At an early period, little more than sixteen years of age, raw and adventurous . . . I began the carver of my own fortune, and entered on board the *Terrible* privateer, Captain Death."[61]

Names like that must have whetted his wanderlust. He later wrote that "men do not, in any great numbers, turn their thoughts to the ocean, till either the country gets filled, or some peculiar advantage or necessity tempts them out. A maritime life is a kind of partial emigration."[62] What advantage or necessity did Paine see in running away to sea? The answer is unclear. Boredom with Thetford, concern about employment, and the sense that his life had passed its halfway mark (the average life expectancy at the time was a mere thirty-seven years) were probably on his mind. So too was the outbreak of the Seven Years' War (1756–63). Many English boys ached to go to sea against Bourbon France, whose military and financial power still dwarfed Georgian England and caused the English body politic to puff up with patriotism against the "French dogs."[63] It may be that Paine crudely mimicked the English posture of a plucky David battling the Bourbon Goliath, that he gloried in the name of Britain and rated pugnacity (alias love of liberty) as manly and preferable to servility. His Quaker father no doubt frowned upon such pugnacity, which makes it more likely that Paine saw his decision to board a privateer, more subtly, as an act of patriotism that would win him personal independence, money, and social respect as a *citizen*. It is even possible that his earlier exposure to the annual Thetford Assizes, the Grafton oligarchy, the tension between Anglicanism and Quakerism, grammar school education, and dead-end employment in the staymaking trade had already sparked some radical political awareness and that, accordingly, he consciously trod the path already cut by earlier eighteenth-century Commonwealthmen, who considered wartime experience on the high seas — martial spirit — a basic condition of becoming a public-spirited citizen.[64] We cannot be sure that this was young Paine's motivation, but the view that military experience ought to be at the heart of civic virtue — that the civilian and military realms must be linked if good arms and good laws were to result — was a central component of eighteenth-century European republicanism and at the heart of Paine's later concerns.

What is also certain is that Paine's yearning to expand his horizons was stimulated indirectly by the seafaring traditions of Norfolk and, more immediately, by his personal contact with the usher of Thetford Grammar School, Reverend William Knowles, who took a shine to his young pupil and related episodes from his own earlier life serving on a man-of-war. Knowles's anecdotes of seas, ships, and distant shores fed Paine's restlessness — what he later called his "raw and adventurous" mood[65] — by connecting him not only to the seafaring culture of Norfolk but also to the expanding interest in travel in eighteenth-century England, a trend that Paine eventually helped to democratize.

During the 1750s, when Paine was a teenager, the desire and ability to travel to foreign places was neither universally accessible nor evenly distributed. Although the spatial horizons of English men and women of the literate classes grew rapidly during the eighteenth century, travelers were typically aristocrats on their Grand Tour through Europe, studying languages and constitutions, collecting items for their palaces and gardens, learning about foreign habits and customs, and keeping open a weather eye for markets that could be applied at home in craft industries, manufacturing, and agriculture. The other class of travelers — the second class of noncitizen artisans like Paine — took flights of fantasy instead. This class comprised readers of books containing descriptions of far-flung countries — their exotic flora and fauna, their trading prospects and navigational hazards. Since Richard Hakluyt (1553?–1616) and Samuel Purchas (1575?–1626), travel literature had grown in popularity, and during Paine's early boyhood years sales of theological works had begun to be overtaken by travel books such as Daniel Defoe's *The Life and strange surprising Adventures of Robinson Crusoe* (1719), a romance novel based on the adventures of Alexander Selkirk, a shoemaker's son who ran away to sea on a privateer, and Jonathan Swift's *Travels into Several Remote Nations of the World* (1726), a satiric account of the travels on a merchant ship of surgeon Lemuel Gulliver.

Such travel literature helped to shape English common sense, encouraging its literate male population to feel a moral connection between the individual and the sea. The literate Englishman began to liken himself to a captain on board a ship with a small crew, the sea underneath and around him as far as the eye could see. He felt isolated from his crew and therefore virtually alone. In contrast to life at home, where monotony predominated, the Englishman saw the sea as vast, unstable, and potentially dangerous. The sea threw ships against rocks, swallowed sailors, and gave off nauseous smells. The sea therefore had to be ruled, preferably with the assistance of other English ships. Ultimately, each ship seemed alone on its vast surface, as if it were an isolated individual, and each ship was personified in its captain. His power of command seemed absolute, and the course he steered, through periods of storm and calm, felt like a command given to the sea through his crew.

Paine's conversations with Reverend Knowles at the grammar school raised his awareness of this imagery, but it did not spring to life until he came across an advertisement that appeared almost daily for two weeks in October 1756 in the pages of London's *Daily Advertiser*. It contained a glimpse of a future that would work up his hunger for adventure and at the same time provide him with a violent introduction to a type of manhood he would subsequently reject. "To cruise against the French, the *Terrible* Privateer, Captain William Death," read the advertisement. "All Gentlemen Sailors, and able-bodied Landmen, who are inclinable to try their Fortune, as well as serve their King and Country, are desired to repair on board the said Ship."[66]

Paine later confessed that he had become "heated with the false heroism" of his schoolmaster,[67] and it is therefore likely that at the time he did not realize just how perilous was the invitation to bravado, blood, and booty. When a state of war existed between countries, as it did between France and Britain at the time, the belligerent governments commissioned privately owned ships, or privateers, to prey upon the vessels of the enemy power. Most privateers sailed not for reasons of citizenship or the glory of king and country, but for profit. Merchants and other individuals also found privateering a lucrative business, and their governments encouraged it for the significant contribution "commerce destroyers" made to the financial and psychological damage heaped upon the enemy. The aim of the privateer was to capture the enemy through stealth and intimidation, without a prolonged fight and with as little damage as possible to either ship. If possible, the marauding ship would try to approach the enemy's stern. From that position, the enemy could not effectively return fire, and its steerage was most exposed to damage. Thus, the whole ship was potentially paralyzed.[68]

That was the theory. In practice, things rarely went according to plan. The privateers resembled floating gaols manned by illness and death. An estimated one-third to one-half of the men involved in skirmishes suffered imprisonment, injury, or death. The model privateersman required blind courage and love of spoils. He was a sort of half horse, half alligator with a streak of lightning in him — something of a cross between a man-of-war's crew member and a pirate. The articles of agreement that he signed clearly outlined his pay, obligations, and overall mission: to prey ruthlessly upon the vessels of the enemy power using every conceivable means. He had to endure cramped and filthy quarters for weeks on end. A privateer usually had a crew larger than it could normally accommodate because a deck crowded with armed men sometimes persuaded the captain of a potential prize to surrender more quickly. In addition, the cargo of a captured enemy ship had to be transferred to the captor ship's hold and a detail sent to board the enemy ship, where it guarded its officers and crew until the captured ship was sailed into the nearest friendly port.

Shortly after Paine signed his articles of agreement in early November 1756, the *Terrible* set sail from Execution Dock on the river Thames. Its captain's call for testing fortune and serving king and country ended in disaster. The first news of the *Terrible*'s engagement with a French privateer from St. Malo named the *Vengeance* soon reached London. According to reports in the *Daily Advertiser*, a three-hour battle "in the chops of the Channel" left the *Terrible* "much shattered." It was captured, but the battle beforehand resembled a fight between two Kilkenny cats. The victorious *Vengeance* lost its captain, its second-in-command, and two-thirds of its crew.[69] The *Terrible* suffered a gruesome fate. Only 17 of its crew survived, and more than 150 were killed, most of them by splinters sent flying from all parts of the ship by enemy cannonballs. Captain Death and every officer save one also were killed. Below deck, wounded men were left by their captors to die, slowly and painfully. Paine's friends and acquaintances — at least the few who knew of his secret decision to board the *Terrible* — feared that he was among them.

2

The Ruined Citizen

King of Prussia

TOM PAINE narrowly escaped the fate of the majority on board the *Terrible*. Hours before sailing from England, he was picked up at Execution Dock by his father, who pleaded with him to abandon his plans. Paine later reported that he was stopped from going to sea on the *Terrible* "by the affectionate and moral remonstrance of a good father."[1] How he actually felt at the time about the quashing of his first serious act of filial rebellion he did not say. Probably he was shocked, perhaps even impressed by his father's skill in tracing his whereabouts by talking to London staymakers, with whom he surmised his son had sought employment before going to sea.

Finding a job proved easy for Paine, ironically because of industrial strife. Journeyman staymakers and tailors were the first craftsmen in England to form themselves into a combination or trade union. In 1720, some seven thousand of them had organized to protest their "churlish, cruel Masters" and to raise their wages beyond the levels laid down by an Act of Parliament.[2] The tactic had met with some success and was repeated in 1744. Shortly before Paine arrived in London, groups of dissenting journeyman staymakers and tailors had again tried to organize, this time to shorten the length of their 6:00 A.M. to 8:00 P.M. workday by one hour in the evening. Ninety-five London masters had responded by refusing to hire any man unwilling to work until 8:00 P.M.[3] The confrontation gave Paine his first taste of industrial conflict. While staymakers' apprentices and assistants were paid a legally set wage and guaranteed protection against the employment of nonfreemen, combinations were illegal. The employees were also faced with dismissal without compensation in a trice, and they could be imprisoned for breaking their work contracts before the agreed time. Masters, for their part, were legally prevented from employing unqualified workers and obliged to pay the guaranteed wage. If the wage levels were exceeded, master staymakers could be fined and might even have their licenses, and so their livelihoods, confiscated.

Although the journeymen's demand for a shorter workday threatened this legal compromise, Paine appears to have had no sympathy for the action, as if his Quaker empathy with the underdog came second to his Anglican-Quaker belief in hard work. Voting with his feet, he went to work for John Morris, a reputable staymaker on Hanover Street in Long Acre, near Covent Garden. His modest wage, around 2s. 6d. a day, allowed him to rent a small, shabby room from Morris in the heart of London's nocturnal dissipations.

Like every visitor to mid-eighteenth-century Covent Garden, Paine was thunderstruck by its noise, lust, pretense, robbery, and violence. Ambling through its alleys, jostled by ironshod cart wheels and clattering hooves, a nineteen-year-old stranger from Thetford would have noticed many things: craftsmen wearing aprons of leather, sometimes of white linen; the milk order chalked on every doorpost; pickpockets loitering near the local water pumps; washerwomen hastening to begin their work; the white glove on the door knocker announcing the birth of a baby; the butchers' pile of marrowbones; the "flying barber" trimming heads for a penny; the mercury peddling newspapers and pamphlets; and oystermongers, gingerbread men, rabbit sellers, chair menders, knife grinders, and a hundred other men and women selling their wares. Covent Garden's streets were in ruinous condition, often consisting of nothing but round stones and rutted, muddy pools, and doorsteps projected hazardously across the footways. Danger was added by bullocks driven through the streets and by swarms of dogs — not the mostly quiet dog of our time, but the creature trained to defend the house, to fly at strangers, and to fight in the ring. There were also crowds of beggars, constant bawling from the shops, and a continual procession of carts, carriages, horses, and street criers. Most locals, like Paine himself, had not been locally born. There were Scots, Welsh, Irish, and migrants from all ends of England. Many had come from overseas: Scandinavians and Germans, Huguenots from France, Jews from Spain and central Europe, and Moors and other

Mediterraneans. Covent Garden's public places multiplied the variety. Near Paine's lodgings were theaters, taverns, and many of the most notorious brothels; coffeehouses where wits gathered in the afternoon and rakes gathered at night; and night houses, where those whose trade obliged them to work late into the night or to begin work early in the morning could obtain coffee and other refreshments, sometimes witnessing petty thefts and fistfights and fielding offers from prostitutes pressed by pimps.

The buzz and clang of Covent Garden stoked Paine's restlessness. So too did the long working hours and the journeyman's biting sense of dependence on his master, described by a contemporary observer as a relationship "much nearer to that of a Planter and Slave in our American Colonies than might be expected in such a country as England."[4] Weighed down by Morris's business, Paine, an only child and a headstrong young man, again plotted adventure. Within a month of the *Terrible*'s sailing from Execution Dock, and before news of its wretched fate had reached London, he had found another privateer that needed men. On January 17, 1757, the 340-ton *King of Prussia*, owned in London and commanded by Edward Menzies, "fell down the River . . . for a six Month's Cruize" with Paine on deck.[5]

After calling at Dover to pick up "16 or 20 Dutchmen," the 200-foot *King of Prussia* began its adventure from Falmouth on February 12 with 250 men on board.[6] Shortly after leaving port, Menzies conducted exercises in working the ship, preparing for battle, and cannonading targets with its 28 carriage and 24 swivel guns. We do not know whether Paine's threading and needling skills were used in repairing sails or whether he was assigned more menial tasks. Usually more lucrative than naval service, privateering attracted the best seamen available, and the normally large complement of inexperienced men like Paine did not hamper the ship's efficiency, since the majority of them were needed not for handling the vessel but for fighting. Besides, as Paine wrote later, in contradiction of the famous antidemocratic view of Plato that ignorant ship crews need knowledgeable captains, "a few able and social sailors will soon instruct . . . active landsmen in the common work of a ship."[7]

After several weeks at sea, the *King of Prussia* captured its first prize, *Le Bien Acquis*, bound for Mississippi and laden with cargo and supplies, including "1346 Casks of Flour, 60 Barrels of Gunpowder, three 24 Pounders [cannon], three 18 Pounders, 60 Bombs, Bomb-Shells, Ammunition, Soldiers Cloaths, &c."[8] The captured ship was escorted by Captain Menzies into Bristol, where, after judgment by the High Court of Admiralty, its crew was released, its cargo sold at auction, and the vessel itself fitted out as an English privateer. Shortly afterward, Paine's ship sent a second prize to Falmouth, this one a French snow (a small briglike ship with a supplementary mast) named *Le Montréal*, bound for Bordeaux from Martinique.[9]

Trouble then developed. In early April 1757, Paine became trapped in a dangerous squabble between the *King of Prussia* and another English privateer. His ship had almost captured *La Flore*, a large merchant ship sailing home to France from the West Indies, when another privateer, the *Lion* of Bristol, approached, chasing the same ship. *La Flore* quickly capitulated to the *King of Prussia*, but the *Lion*'s Captain How immediately sent out a boat to board the prize, claiming to share the victory. A perilously tense moment followed. Captain Menzies, refusing to concede that the *Lion*'s presence had helped induce the ship to surrender, trained his ship's guns on the *Lion*. It suddenly looked as though Paine and the rest of the crew might be struck down "not by cannon balls, but by splinters from inside the ship that fly in all directions."[10] Mutual threats by the captains to sink each other's boats followed, the crews taunted each other, and only after several minutes of plea bargaining did Captain How decide to save his ship and try his luck in the High Court of Admiralty. Paine's ship escorted *La Flore* to Falmouth, and the owners of the *Lion*, after pressing their claim for two years, eventually received one-fifth of *La Flore*'s value of £10,400.[11]

For nearly nine weeks, the *King of Prussia* cruised the English Channel, luckless. During such lengthy periods, battle drills, sailors' chores, and deck games occupied the crew, keeping discontent and boredom at bay. Commanders commonly awarded a bonus to the sailor who first spotted the enemy, and Paine may have spent at least some of his spare moments alone, staring at the horizon, a poem or two in his head, hoping to glimpse a sail in the distance. During the month of June, the privateer finally spotted a ship from Limerick, the *Handy*, which had been in French hands for several months.[12] Required by the king's instructions to assist all friendly vessels, Menzies overtook and captured the ship, sending her into King Road, near Bristol. He was later awarded half the *Handy*'s value — a high price for its Irish owners but considerably less than its permanent loss to a French gunboat.

Joined by the *Defiance* of Bristol and with Paine still on board, the *King of Prussia* next stalked and peacefully captured a large snow headed for Cape Breton. Both privateers then teamed up with a man-of-war, the *Tartar*, whose Captain Lockhart was renowned for his daring victories against French privateers. All three ships set out in formation "in chace of the

French Fleet."[13] Nothing came of the partnership, and in early June the *King of Prussia*, parting empty-handed from the man-of-war but still in company with the *Defiance*, tracked down *Le Saint Martin* and *Le Saint Peter*, both bound for Canada, and *La Minerve*, laden with "Wine and Provisions."[14] Paine and the rest of the crew likely enjoyed the fringe benefits of privateering, which included better fare than that aboard a naval vessel. The capture of ships such as *La Minerve* added to the usual stock of biscuits, salt beef and pork, beer and rum, oatmeal, and cheese and entitled Paine and his fellow crewmen to take clothing and effects from the prisoners, and sometimes deck cargo found aboard the prize.[15]

The *King of Prussia* ended her six months' cruise after rescuing a friendly vessel, the *Pennsylvania*, which had been attacked by a French privateer during a voyage from London to Philadelphia. Both ships docked at Dartmouth on August 20, 1757, and there is no record in any London newspaper of Paine's ship's having sailed again, although it may certainly have been sold off to another owner and renamed. The owners of the *King of Prussia* met in late November to apportion the booty. It is difficult to guess the size of the financial harvest reaped by Paine. Court costs accounted for about one-tenth of the overall value, after which the privateer's owners claimed one-half.[16] Captain, officers, and experienced seamen walked away with the largest shares of the remaining profit, leaving perhaps one-half of 1 percent of the profit for each gentleman volunteer. Paine's adventure on the *King of Prussia* probably earned him at least five pounds per month at sea, or a minimum total of thirty pounds. This amount would have seemed a fortune to a young man accustomed to subsistence living, and the relative wealth with which he ended his adventure may explain his decision not to make a second voyage. He had carved his fortune with luck standing at his side; although he had escaped harm, he might not be so fortunate next time. Besides, he could now enjoy the company of like-minded men and women in London, a conurbation of 650,000 people and the powerhouse of English politics, law, finance, fashion, and the arts and sciences.

Newtonians

Those who met him in London in this period found him pleasant, intelligent, and eager to learn. Age twenty years, he was "tall and slim, about five feet eight inches,"[17] with flashing dark eyes and thick dark brown hair pulled back into a ponytail. A soft-spoken, serious country boy with a Norfolk accent, he had some moral convictions — and money in his pocket. Among the profound ironies surrounding the greatest eighteenth-century citizen was the way war furnished him with his first material breakthrough in adult life, enabling him to build a political identity with roots in his Thetford youth. What he did not know, and could not have anticipated, was that his lucrative six months at sea, leeching off the struggle for booty unleashed by the Seven Years' War, not only confirmed his refusal of his father's authority but also furnished him with the financial means of becoming a public-spirited citizen.

Paine's personality, under construction for twenty years, was now in for a wholly unanticipated, long-term conversion to republican democracy: the principle that tyranny is the death of a state and its people, that the best polity is one in which virtue or public spirit rules and the governors concede that the governed — the men among them, at least — are free and equal citizens endowed with certain entitlements (for instance, to publicize their opinions and to organize to remedy injustices).

Paine had already tasted some elements of republican democracy during his Thetford years. He had encountered the arbitrary violence of the Lent Assizes and the shrewd rural oligarchy run by the dukes of Grafton. As a half Anglican, half Quaker, he had seen religious bigotry and social discrimination. But he also had witnessed the Quakers' interest in worldly affairs, their concern for political justice, and their morality of turning the other cheek toward adversaries. At Thetford Grammar School and in his role as staymaker's apprentice, he had probably come to think of himself as a clean-living man of the disfranchised lower middle class — a class wedged precariously between the landed aristocracy, urban merchants, and manufacturers, on one side, and the majority class of commoners who were not yet able to read and write and were treated as mere subjects, not citizens, on the other. Exactly how Paine understood his adventures on the *King of Prussia* is unclear. He surely knew in advance of the violence of privateering, and that implies that at the time of volunteering, his patriotism led him to ignore the pacifist principles of the Quakers. The lure of lucre and the thrill of standing up for the first time to paternal authority, perhaps after a heated quarrel, may well have sealed his decision. In any event, such considerations were soon to take their revenge on the banausic qualities of what he often called his "boyish days."

Disembarking from the *King of Prussia* on August 20, 1757, tanned and unkempt in appearance, Paine journeyed from Dartmouth to London, where he spent the autumn and winter months of 1757–58 in Covent Garden, living off his privateer's dividend. He did not squander his money or time; his brushes with death concentrated his desire for self-improvement.

Paine spent much time browsing London's bookshops and may have taken advantage of the new circulating libraries, such as Batho's on the Strand, to borrow books on science in exchange for a small fee. "The natural bent of my mind was to science," he later wrote. "As soon as I was able, I purchased a pair of globes, and attended the philosophical lectures of Martin and Ferguson, and became afterwards acquainted with Dr. Bevis, of . . . the Royal Society, then living in the Temple."[18] As Bevis, "an excellent astronomer," took up residence in the Middle Temple only in 1764, Paine clearly did not get to know him during this period. Although his memory probably jumbled figures and events, Paine's contact with Benjamin Martin (1704–1782) and James Ferguson (1710–1776) was undoubtedly significant, for it brought him inside the circle of two of England's most reputable itinerant lecturers, whose energies were poured into bringing Newtonian science to captivated audiences otherwise excluded by prejudice from advanced education.

Paine quickly befriended the two men. Martin, a fifty-three-year-old Surreyman, enjoyed a considerable reputation as one of London's most skilled makers of spectacles. He was a mathematician, a collector of fossils, and editor of the monthly *The General Magazine of Arts and Sciences*, which published articles on philosophy, mathematical instruments, natural history, and philology. He was also a globemaker — from whom Paine likely purchased his own globe — and two years earlier he had published *On the Construction of the Globes*. His most successful work, which Paine surely consulted, was *The Philosophical Grammar* (1735), published in four parts. During the autumn of 1757, when Paine first met him, his new four-part book *The Theory of Comets Illustrated* appeared.[19]

Ferguson was a renowned Scottish astronomer with talents in mechanics and portrait painting.[20] He was a near-neighbor and friend of Benjamin Franklin's — who was lodging on Craven Street, not far from Ferguson's globemaking shop on the Strand — and at the time Paine first met Martin, the two men were collaborating to produce a new clock later known as Ferguson's clock. Age forty-seven when Paine made an appointment to meet him, Ferguson was often in poor health and (according to a contemporary, Andrew Reid) had "a very sedate appearance, face and brow a little wrinkled; he wore a large full stuff wig, which gave him a venerable look, and made him to appear older than he really was."[21] Paine had probably read his *Astronomy Explained upon Sir Isaac Newton's Principles, and made easy to those who have not studied Mathematics*, published the previous year to considerable acclaim. He liked Ferguson's amiable, simple-living character and was impressed by his superb clarity of thought and speech.

Paine discovered through the London press that Ferguson offered private and small-group lessons, for the sum of two guineas per person, in the art of using globes, and it was in this way that the two men met. His appetite for the natural sciences whetted by the monthlong course, Paine wanted further instruction, and during the next six months he attended public lectures delivered by both Ferguson and Martin at the Globe, opposite Cecil Street on the Strand. During the autumn and winter months of 1757, according to advertisements placed in London's *Daily Advertiser*, the two lecturers examined topics ranging from the general philosophy of Sir Isaac Newton to the properties of air, the phases of the moon and the behavior of comets, the reflection and refraction of light, and pendulums.[22]

Paine's regular attendance at these lectures did more than arouse his passion for science or deepen his curiosity about the ordered beauty of the heavens cultivated at grammar school and on clear, calm nights at sea on the *King of Prussia*. It also introduced him to a new culture of political radicalism that rejected throne and altar. There was admittedly little explicit political content in these lectures. They rather resembled promotional sessions for the tenets of Newtonian science, which was explained and illustrated before large and enthusiastic audiences. Sir Isaac Newton had remained president of the Royal Society until his death in 1727, and even though his work belonged to the past, during Paine's stay in London his ideas and methods continued to influence deep-seated assumptions about the universe and to dominate the study of the mathematical and physical sciences. Itinerant lecturers like Martin and Ferguson also looked to contemporary figures such as Joseph Priestley for intellectual leadership and maintained a steady correspondence with other men of science. They often referred to Francis Bacon's phrase "Knowledge is power," as though it was their watchword in further education, and they certainly regarded the whole field of scientific knowledge as common ground fit for cultivation by the united labors of individuals for the common benefit.

Paine found himself in familiar company. The men and women who attended the lectures of Ferguson and Martin were mainly self-educated shopkeepers and artisans, many of whom leaned toward unorthodox religious views, and religious Dissenters, with strong leanings toward political radicalism. Theirs was not an appeal to an Old England of customary law, popular rights, and roast beef. These audiences were decidedly modern in outlook. Convinced of the importance of mental improvement but excluded from the port and privilege of the Universities of Oxford and Cambridge because of their sex, Dissenting views, or class background, these audiences listened intently to the illustrated discussions, pondering a wide variety of detailed topics and broad fields of inquiry, from applied mathematics and astronomy to mechanics, chemistry, and geography.

For both lecturers and audiences in the middle of the eighteenth century, a key problem was, as it had been increasingly for thinking people of the previous century, to reconcile the Christian doctrines of faith in God and spiritual conversion with the coolheaded empiricism of scientific reason. In practice, preachers and publicists troubled by this puzzle tried to resolve it by emphasizing the reasonableness of Christian ethics. The dark and irrational problems of guilt and evil were set aside, the significance of miracles was played down, talk of the terrors of hell was given up, and the need for spiritual fervor was de-emphasized. God was depersonalized and portrayed as the primum mobile. From here it was only a step toward the deism expounded by Matthew Tindal, Henry St. John Bolingbroke, and other fashionable commentators on religion.

Paine's public exposure to this secular mode of Christian reasoning likely added to his skepticism about organized religion and brought him a step closer to Dissenting politics. The study of science, Paine later wrote, lifted "the soul of an islander" beyond the ebb and flow of daily events to the world of universal forces and trends.[23] According to the Newtonian faith, there was a "natural order" of things in the world, expertly designed by God — whom Martin called "the Omnipotent Architect" — for the guidance and benefit of humanity. It was believed that the laws of this natural order could be discovered by human reason and used as standards for evaluating the ideas, conduct, and institutions of any given political order. In explaining Newtonianism, Ferguson and Martin dwelled with delight on "the infinite Goodness and Wisdom" of the world and its Author. They praised the harmony and beneficence of the "Divine Geometry of Nature," cautioned against purely mechanical views of nature, and criticized the gloomy Puritan view of a "Day of Doom" awaiting fickle "Sinners in the Hands of an Angry God." Martin even entertained his audiences with rhyming couplets:

> How blest their Eyes, which Nature's Beauties see!
> How blest their Ears, which hear her harmony!
> How blissful those who understand her Laws![24]

Many attending the lectures of Ferguson and Martin were moved by such rhetoric. They too believed that natural laws operated in the human world and that a science of government, driven by the spirit of inquiry, criticism, and human improvement, could therefore be developed and applied to every human institution. Just as there was a universal law of gravitation, binding together the physical world, so there was a universal law of benevolence, binding together human beings for the sake of their happiness and freedom. Such reasoning, in which scientific curiosity often led to moral and political criticism, was at odds with the Georgian system of oligarchical government, with its cult of monarchy, its favors and sinecures, and a legal system once described by Paine as "that of following precedents." Not surprisingly, Newtonianism met increasing hostility from the English governing class, which saw correctly the tensions between the spirit of modern scientific reason and existing institutions of government, property, and manners guided by power and tradition. The circles of Newtonians reacted by becoming breeding grounds for a new radical politics. To many in those circles, Paine included, it seemed obvious that the sciences were friends of liberty — providing indisputable proof of the rational foundations of the persistent eighteenth-century fear of a Tory and royalist "conspiracy" that would undo the beneficent consequences of the events of 1688 and again make resistance to corruption, evil, and tyranny a necessity.[25]

The Methodist Revolution

Paine's dalliance with science and politics on the fringes of the Royal Society was cut short by air in his pockets. London was expensive, and his savings ran out sooner than he had expected. Within six months of setting foot on dry land, he was confronted with the problem of how to earn a living. He took advice from his former employer, John Morris, and journeyed in the spring of 1758 into county Kent, southeast of London, in search of employment and perhaps a town where he could set up a staymaking business. He found temporary employment in the port town of Dover with an acquaintance of Morris's, a staymaker named Benjamin Grace. In the spring of the following year, after some reconnaissance and an offer of a ten-pound loan from Grace, Paine set up a small staymaking shop in the provincial town of Sandwich, seventy-five miles southeast of London. The whole world now knows the name of the town — thanks to John Montagu, the fourth earl of Sandwich, who is reputed to have demanded that slices of bread filled with cold meat be delivered to his gaming tables so that he would not be interrupted by the call to dinner. Paine's life there, by contrast, has virtually disappeared without a trace. A seventeenth-century cottage at 20 New Street today bears a modest plaque which reads: "Tom Paine's cottage c. 1759. Author of Rights of Man. Inspired the American Declaration of Independence."

According to an old local tale, Paine not only established himself as a master staymaker in Sandwich but also used his cramped lodgings adjacent to the marketplace in the town center as a part-time chapel, where he preached "as an independent, or a Methodist."[26] That Paine preached from his New Street lodgings "as an Independent" is doubtful, since the local Independents already had a regular place of worship. The Independent (Congregational) chapel, well-established by the 1640s, was in fact one of the earliest establishments of its kind in England. Its members, mainly artisans, met in an old inn, the Star, at the back of the Guildhall in the corn market, later the cattle market. The meeting house, "for the worship of God by the Congregation of Protestants Dissenting from the Church of England,"[27] had been refurbished in 1706 and again in 1753, and reportedly seated up to two hundred souls; all other records of the chapel during Paine's time in Sandwich have been lost.

The story that Paine preached in Sandwich as a Methodist is more probable, since his links with Methodism actually predated his arrival in the town. In Thetford, Paine reportedly heard John Wesley preach.[28] Wesley's journal also records that when Paine was living in Dover, Benjamin Grace, Paine's employer, took him along to the Methodist chapel on Limekiln Street, where Paine, age twenty-one, confessed himself a believer and later preached sermons to the congregations ("the hearers") who gathered in that chapel.[29] It is also known that the spirit of Methodism had already reached Sandwich before Paine. John Wesley, who annually visited the area, preached there in the early 1760s "to a dull but attentive congregation."[30] It is also probable that fellow-Methodist "assistants," reaching out from nearby Canterbury, were active in the town during the time Paine was there.[31]

The extent of Paine's involvement with Methodism is uncertain, but its existence contradicts historians' conventional image of that religion as a reactionary protest against Enlightenment reason and a movement that seduced its followers into conformism.[32] The image does not apply to Paine, whose brush with the missionary evangelism of Methodism was as important to his character as his early introduction to the moral reasoning and political disputes among Thetford's Christians.

To begin with, Methodism demonstrated to Paine, a drifter at this point in his life, the value of the field meeting, the chapel, the lay preacher, the band, and the order as prototypes of social self-organization. Methodism showed that these means could enable the lonely and insecure, especially among the poor, to feel more confident and at home within a web of intimate social relationships. In Dover, as elsewhere in

England, the establishment of a chapel was an act of open rebellion against parson and squire. Within the chapel, commoners learned self-respect, self-government, self-reliance, and organizational skills. Often they also learned to read and write and to speak "in society." In words that would soon be used by Paine himself, Methodism demonstrated the fundamental importance of civil society to poor and humble folk wanting self-empowerment. Methodism highlighted the strategic importance of lifting their spirits, nurturing their solidarity, and strengthening their resolve by exploiting and expanding, nonviolently, the available civil freedoms to build new associations on the fringes of the established church and state — just as Wesley himself had first done two decades earlier in the mining districts and manufacturing towns of England.

Paine also was touched by the Methodists' doctrine of reassurance, whose egalitarianism amplified the Quaker theme that each individual was equipped with an inner light and therefore equal before God. Methodism put forward the exhilarating view, traceable to the early seventeenth-century Dutch theologian Jacobus Arminius, that Christ's sacrifice and atonement meant that all men and women might be saved, not just the preordained elect, as John Calvin and his followers had stipulated. "You are steeped in sin, and there is nothing in you which merits God's goodness," the young Paine may have told his nervous and spellbound congregations in Dover and Sandwich, rephrasing words from the lips of other Methodist preachers he had heard in action. "Yet remember: The new light of God's grace shines equally upon the poor and the rich. God is ready to welcome you — *all of you* — as His children so long as you strive to attain His grace and live the holy life which allows you to enter into His Kingdom." These were words of hope for the downtrodden. "Bourgeois" Methodism may have tended to be, but it also fed the modern democratic revolution in mid-eighteenth-century England by offering a vision of a more equal and free community of souls living together on earth. This commitment to spiritual equality was exactly what scared figures like the duchess of Buckingham, who loathed Methodists because "it is monstrous to be told that you have a heart as sinful as the common wretches that crawl on the earth."[33] Since election was not preordained or confined to a few, replied the Methodists, neither was sin or the possibility of salvation. Methodist preachers regarded their listeners ("hearers") as individuals capable of choice and as morally responsible for their own conduct. They also invited their listeners to accept God's freely given grace and to join an earthly community of newly reborn Christians in which each person strived to do good works and to watch over the spiritual welfare of all others.

The report in Wesley's journal that Paine tried his hand at preaching suggests, finally, that the young Paine also learned something of the art of public communication for which Methodism — and he himself — quickly became famous. Methodism began as a sect within the Church of England (in the form of Wesley's "Connection"), and in various parts of the country, even before Wesley's death in 1791, it became a proselytizing arm of the Establishment. Although Wesley insisted that the movement stood within the Church of England and that it should stage its moral theaters in the early morning and at other times outside "church hours," Methodism in fact resembled a second National Church charged with the task of converting the lower classes of England and, later, the heathen hordes abroad. Its initial plebeian style must have impressed Paine, as it did observers such as Dr. Johnson, who contrasted the stodginess of Anglican sermons with the remarkable ability of the Methodist preachers to talk convincingly to lower-class audiences "in a plain and familiar manner, which is the only way to do good to the common people."[34]

Plain-talking public discourse that avoided the airs and graces of the High Church and instead wielded a Christianized rhetoric of the downtrodden frightened the Anglican hierarchy. Its supporters fought back with sticks and stones — Wesley praised the Lord that no brick hit him personally — and with razor-sharp words. The arrival of Methodism in county Kent was greeted with cries of "false prophets," and a public meeting addressed by John and Charles Wesley was broken up by a club-wielding mob assisted by forty soldiers.[35] The best-known of the contemporary anti-Methodist tracts was written by William Warburton, Lord Bishop of Gloucester. His essay entitled *The Enthusiasm of Methodists and Papists Compared* described the Methodists as pretenders to pagan trances and ecstasies, as fanatical field preachers and practitioners of bogus private confessions and public miracles. Like other enemies of Methodism, Warburton reviled its "wild and pernicious Enthusiasm." It brought dishonor to Christianity by laying aside "*cool Reason and plain Scripture*" in favor of "a FANATIC MANNER of preaching" that worked up the "Passions of weak, credulous, or distempered People."[36]

Methodism certainly was passionate and fanatical, but Paine found its power of attracting tens of thousands of ordinary souls riveting. In Thetford, it seemed that the commoners were always acted upon, treated like dirt. In Dover and Sandwich, preaching and witnessing for the first time in his life, he recognized the power of an organized public campaign that did not patronize the common classes. Methodism demonstrated that the excluded majority were a social force to be reckoned with. Methodism treated ordinary men and women as having sufficient righteousness within themselves to attain, through their own individual efforts and with the help of both God and the mutual aid provided by chapels and societies, a state of sinless perfection in this life. The doctrine had a revolutionary democratic potential, despite the curious fact that most Wesleyans of this period saw themselves not as a threat to the established order but as a catalyst for rejuvenating a sluggish church and shoring up loyalty to the king. Paine thought otherwise. Methodism convinced him that injustice could be remedied. It persuaded him that the commoners did not need to be talked down to, ignored, pushed aside, or hanged for criminal offenses. Methodism brought to light the fact that they had legitimate fears and concerns. It demonstrated that they could mount the stage of public life, make their voices heard, and be treated as the equals of others.

Family Man

How far he took these beliefs in Sandwich is unknown. We do know that the summer months of 1759 were filled with more than work and religion, and that through either the local Methodists or Mr. Richard Solly — a prominent town draper with whom he did business — Paine met Mary Lambert, known locally as "a pretty girl of modest behaviour."[37] The two soon began to court openly. Paine's choice of a lover mirrored his modest social tastes. Mary Lambert, orphaned by her mother's suicide and her father's untimely death, was employed as a waiting woman to Maria Solly, wife of Richard Solly. Paine's personal link with the Sollys no doubt reassured him that his courtship with Mary Lambert, a commoner, was respectable enough, especially because Richard Solly enjoyed a reputation as Sandwich's former mayor, an annually elected post that conferred considerable powers of patronage, including the right to nominate and elect the town's two members of Parliament.[38] But by courting a commoner, Paine nevertheless revealed his exclusion from the Georgian matrimonial market. He considered marriage to be mainly about love and not about honor, patrilineage, or fortune. Evidently the Sollys approved, for the staymaker and waiting woman announced their intention to marry at the end of September in St. Peter's Church, Sandwich. The official record of the ceremony is brief: "Thomas Pain, of the Parish of St. Peters in the Town of Sandwich in Kent, Bachelor, and Mary Lambert of the same Parish, Spinster, were Married in this Church, by Licence, this Twenty Seventh Day of September, in the Year One Thousand Seven Hundred and Fifty Nine by me, William Bunce, Rector."

The signing ceremony was witnessed by Mrs. Solly and two other Sandwich residents, John Joslin and Thomas Taylor. Virtually nothing else is known of the marriage, which, if happy, was short-lived. It certainly did not match the eighteenth-century maxim that courtship is to marriage as a witty prologue is to a dull play — that marriage is a long, dusty road to the grave. The marriage in fact conformed to the opposite, contemporary saying that love, in contrast to friendship, dies whenever it appears publicly. The young couple moved to a house on Dolphin Key, but within months Paine's staymaking business faltered. Mary became pregnant — the couple followed the lower-middle-class custom of avoiding all contraception except coitus interruptus — and early in 1760, concerned about Mary's health and their inability to make ends meet, they moved to Margate, a sizable fishing town sited on a wide, windswept bay ten miles north of Sandwich. It is uncertain whether Paine managed to establish another business there or whether Mary found comfort in Margate's reputation for fresh sea air and cold bathing, but either way, the lives of the newlyweds were overshadowed by the callous hand of ill fortune.

Sometime during their first few months in Margate, and less than a year after the wedding, Mary went into labor. For women of the poorer and artisan classes at this time, giving birth was an especially dangerous act, wrapped in symbolic rituals, from which Paine, as a man, would have been strictly excluded. Birth normally took place in a darkened and heated room made to feel as "womblike" as possible. Mary would have been surrounded the whole time by Mrs. Solly and her women acquaintances (called gossips), all of whom, according to custom, drank all the caudle (warmed wine laced with sugar and spice) available. The baby was usually delivered by a "granny midwife," an experienced and trusted community figure who was blessed with a bishop's license but who had no formal medical training. After delivery the baby was commonly swaddled (allegedly to strengthen its weak bones) and then sometimes handed over to a local wet nurse. Men were excluded from all these procedures, except when complications developed and a male surgeon might be summoned.[39]

Whether that happened during the heaving, stretching, sweating, and shrieking of Mary's labor is unrecorded. All that is known is that she and her child died during delivery. Paine kept the tragic details, like so much else in his personal life, strictly private. It has been said that Mary "died on the road of ill usage, and a premature birth," and that "the women of Sandwich are positive, that she died in the British Lying-in-Hospital, in Brownlow Street, Long Acre." Another commentator chips in with gossip about how the "old women of Thetford, England, blamed him [Paine], saying that he had demanded that his wife get out of bed too soon to cook for him."[40] All this is probably apocryphal. There is no evidence to support the veiled claim that Paine maltreated or beat his wife (although the patriarchal conventions of the time would have helped to cover up such evidence). In addition, the registers of London lying-in hospitals, including those for Brownlow Street, contain no contemporary evidence of a Mrs. Pain or a Mary Lambert. Moreover, why the "women of Sandwich," where she was allegedly no longer living, should remember her precise whereabouts three decades later (when the story was invented) remains as utterly mysterious as the alternative hypothesis that Paine's deceased wife was in fact "alive in the extreme obscurity of her retreat."[41]

At age twenty-three, Paine suddenly found himself alone, a widower in a strange town with no secure means of employment. "There is neither manhood nor policy in grief,"[42] he later observed, summarizing the stone-cold, masculine reaction that marked him publicly for the rest of his life. Manliness — freedom from what other eighteenth-century republicans called "effeminacy" — was certainly among Paine's public qualities, and it is probable that it was succored by the shock of his wife's and child's death. Paine subsequently showed little interest in women and had very few good female friends. The language of his writings, which rarely mentioned women, was gendered. Paine's common sense was that of a republican man. He later criticized old-fashioned partriarchalism and championed the resistance of adult men to the "fatherly" government of monarchy. "Is it the interest of a man to be a boy all his life?" he typically asked.[43] The question's wording is revealing of how his republicanism ignored women's right not to be ignored. He stopped short of questioning the power of "fathers" by preserving the conventional imagery of women as being (potentially) as seductive, unpredictable, and unreliable as prostitutes — as creatures "womanlishly affected" (as Paine put it) by their unvirtuous disregard for Reason.[44]

How Paine reacted inwardly to the death of his wife and child is a matter for conjecture. It is significant that he was always taciturn on paper about the few women in his life. He wrote virtually nothing about his mother, and written comments on his deceased baby sister and his wife are nonexistent. We cannot be sure whether he felt guilty, or numb with the pain of bereavement, or bitter at having been robbed of the joy of a youthful marriage, or accepting of death as a mystery of Providence — or, indeed, a sad, swirling mixture of all four emotions. How bitterly Paine wept, for how long he mourned, and how quickly he managed to subdue the chaos inside him and live again in the outer world is unclear. We know only that from the time of the death of his wife and child he was decidedly cool towards women and enjoyed the company of men. The Marquis de Sade, Paine's French contemporary, earned himself a reputation as a model libertine who gorged himself on every carefully choreographed fantasy available to his generation. Paine, by extreme contrast, was a model ascetic. After the death of Mary and his child, he lived an outwardly asexual existence and spent virtually the whole of his waking time with men. No doubt this taste for male company was whetted by the fact that politics during the second half of the eighteenth century was exclusively a man's world. But in Paine's case something deeper was at work. He seemed numbed, defensive, persecuted, perhaps pained from deep inside as if he had been punished by castration. An inner voice constantly reminded him that his wife had suffered pregnancy and childbirth and that he bore some responsibility for her tragic death.

The Exciseman

Mary Lambert's deceased father, James Lambert, had been employed as an officer in the Excise at nearby Sittingbourne. Her childhood memories of his activities, repeated in conversations with her husband, seem to have prompted Paine when in Margate to consider a career as an exciseman, a job with whose duties he was already familiar as a privateer seaman. Shortly after the death of his wife and child, Paine wrote to his father in Thetford proposing the idea. He quickly received an encouraging response. Paine sold off his effects and packed his bags, not knowing that his father's positive advice would give him firsthand experience of venal state power. He did not yet see that his career as an exciseman would teach him a lesson about its corrupt practices, inspire him to blow the whistle on the greed of politicians and administrators, and eventually drive him into the ranks of the republican critics of the monarchic state.

During the first spring days of 1761, Paine rode on horseback from Sandwich, where he had been staying temporarily, bereaved, at the home of Maria and Richard Solly, through London and on to Thetford. He lived with his parents on Bridgegate Street, preparing his case for admission to the Excise. His grandfather Thomas Cocke put him in touch with an old family friend, Mr. Henry Cocksedge, the Recorder of Thetford, who guided him during the next year through the time-consuming rites of passage into the Excise branch of the civil service. The first stage, petitioning the Board of Excise Commissioners for an order to be instructed in the arts of the exciseman, required Paine to get a birth certificate from the vicar at St. Cuthbert's Church. He also had to arrange letters of recommendation from local Thetford notables on good terms with the government and to swear an oath before a Justice of the Peace that no fee or gratuity had been given to facilitate the petition.

It is unknown exactly when Paine's written order of instruction came through, but its arrival by post several months later allowed him to proceed to the trickier second stage of the political rites of passage into the Excise. Sometime during the autumn of 1761, Paine was visited by a local supervisor in the Excise, who in accordance with Excise rules personally checked Paine's health, personal habits, intelligence, and handwriting ability. The supervisor also looked into whether he was free from debts, held views loyal to the government, and was a baptized and confirmed member of the Church of England. The supervisor then introduced Paine to a local exciseman who spent several days instructing him in the art of gauging casks of various shapes and sizes and entering the results into a notebook. Stage two ended with a formal examination administered by the supervisor. Paine's ability to write clear and comprehensible English was tested, and attention was paid to whether he had a basic grounding in simple and decimal arithmetic. His proficiency at gauging casks, entering records into a notebook, and issuing invoices and receipts also was tested. Paine measured up. He had been well tutored in these bureaucratic skills by Mr. Cocksedge, and evidently he impressed both the exciseman instructor and the supervisor, who had to be paid forty shillings and twenty shillings, respectively, for their services. A certificate of investigation was then issued by the supervisor, after which Paine secured the names of two guarantors, who agreed to stand as security, under penalty of the considerable sum of two hundred pounds, in case he improperly handled the future revenues he would collect as an exciseman.

Paine must have understood that the procedural rigors of the first two stages of petitioning were justified by the Excise commissioners as checks on corruption within a branch of the state that tempted the base instincts of its personnel precisely because their labors raised extraordinary sums of money vital to the long-term stability and day-to-day operations of government. Stage three of the petition, Paine soon learned, revealed the extent to which these vices — and the crude insistence on loyalty to political authorities — remained at the heart of the excise profession. Through Mr. Cocksedge, and possibly the duke of Grafton, contact was made with a Mr. Frankland, a Commissioner in the Excise, who set about arranging, in the shameless style of eighteenth-century nepotism, for Paine's appointment as an unattached officer or supernumerary, for which he received a small salary.

The practice of arranging appointments was widespread, as the standard exciseman's manual, which Paine may well have consulted, made quite clear.[45] The same manual also specified that after obtaining the favors of Mr. Frankland, Paine had to comply with another string of state rituals. Before a Baron or Justice of the Peace (the evidence has not survived), he had to swear that he would faithfully execute his duties and that he would never accept any fee for services other than from the Crown. He was also required to take the sacrament in the parish church of St. Cuthbert attended by Rector John Coleman, several churchwardens, and two witnesses, each of whom had to sign a certificate to that effect. Following the service, he took the required Test Oath, certifying his conviction that the consecration and administering of the sacrament of the Lord's Supper involved no transubstantiation. Then came the most important oath of all. Back before a Baron or Justice of the Peace, Paine had to demonstrate his fitness to serve as an officer of the Crown by taking the Oath of Supremacy, swearing that King George III was the lawful king of England and abjuring any allegiance to the person pretending to be James VIII of Scotland and James III of England. Considering Paine's subsequent rebellion against monarchy, the words he compulsorily uttered now strike a deeply ironic note:

I, Thomas Pain, do swear, that I do, from my Heart, Abhor, Detest, and Abjure, as impious and heretical, that damnable Doctrine and Position, that Princes excommunicated or deprived by the Pope, or any Authority of the See of Rome, may be deposed or murdered by their Subjects, or any other whatsoever. And I do declare, that no foreign Prince, Person, Prelate, State or Potentate hath, or ought to have, any Jurisdiction, Power, Superiority, Preheminence or Authority, Ecclesiastical or Spiritual, within the Realm:

So help me God.[46]

Paine then waited for the Excise Commissioners' reply. A letter informing him of his first appointment eventually reached him in Thetford in early December 1762, fourteen months after he had lodged his application for an order to be instructed.[47] The letter directed him to a position gauging brewers' casks in Grantham, in Lincolnshire. As an apprentice officer at the most junior level, Paine was probably bored stiff gauging casks. Grantham, home subsequently to a famous power-hungry Prime Minister — Baroness Margaret Thatcher, whose pomposity Paine would have found personally irritating — was a boring small town. Although its location on a main road generated a steady flow of cask-gauging work, Paine was aware that so long as he stayed there, he would remain inexperienced in other skills expected of an exciseman and that this would jeopardize his future chances of promotion. He made it known to both his supervisor and collector, his two superiors, that he was keen to be posted elsewhere. He waited patiently, spending much of his free time mixing with local Methodists — the Grantham chapel had been established following a visit to the area in the 1750s by John Wesley[48] — and socializing with patrons of the George inn, where by tradition he and other excise officers before him lodged.

The promotion did not come until early August 1764. Sometime that month, he accepted the better-paid job of collecting revenues, gauging, visiting coffee and tea dealers, and watching out for smugglers at Alford, a small market town of a few hundred inhabitants located five miles from the North Sea coast, in Lincolnshire. Paine lodged at the Windmill, run by Solomon Hansord and his wife, who set aside for him an office in a large room on the first floor with a bow window overlooking the marketplace. Local Excise offices were normally sited at inns such as the Windmill, which were not simply drinking houses but primarily centers of information, gossip, and various kinds of business. Publicans were happy to have local traders refreshing themselves at the bar after doing business with the excise officer, and many of them, like Solomon Hansord, accepted appointment from the Board of Excise Commissioners as office keepers. Hansord's duties included making appointments, receiving documents, and ensuring security of Paine's papers and the revenues he collected.

The Alford Outride, as it was called, was a one-man station, and reputedly a hard one at that. An Excise official working in the area complained that "many of the Traders in all the Districts of the said Collection lie very remote from the Residence of the respective Supervisors, that the Roads in many Places are very deep and frequently rendered impassable by being covered in Water."[49] Another official based in Alford found the going so tough that one night he packed his belongings and rode away from the town, leaving behind his notebooks adorned with one word: "Farewell." Life was especially difficult for excisemen because the area was notoriously thick with smugglers. Casks of Dutch gin were especially prized by gangs of men who operated from the shelter of local creeks, making contact with the ships hovering off the coast, laden with the liquid contraband. Disputes between sailors and smugglers were commonplace, and Paine surely heard the chilling story of a Dutch ship whose crew disappeared without a trace on a run to Alford. Their relatives had journeyed, in vain, to Alford to recover the bodies, and local opinion differed about whether the seamen had been murdered after a drunken quarrel over dividing the spoils or whether they were victims of a carefully laid murderous trap.[50]

In addition to gauging casks, assessing innkeepers and coffee and tea dealers, and collecting revenues, Paine's job also involved patrolling the local marshy flats and gently swelling wolds along the windswept coast. He was supposed to look out for smugglers and ships and inform the local constables of their movements. He was by now an accomplished horseman and had the good fortune to avoid violent tangles with smugglers. He was enthusiastic about his post and carried out his tasks diligently. The job was secure, he felt no burning homesickness for his native Thetford, and he enjoyed the open-air life of a small and friendly coastal town. Trouble nevertheless loomed. Without warning, Paine's job was soon to end unhappily, causing him personal difficulties and stoking his political sympathies.

To understand what happened requires an appreciation of the way in which, a generation before, the government of Sir Robert Walpole had reorganized the excise system. Duties were removed from most exports and from imported raw materials required by England's manufacturers, whose interests were preserved by carefully crafted protective legislation that tightened the excise screws on other branches of commerce. As always in a system of commodity production and exchange, deregulation of the market necessitated reregulation of the market, a rule that Walpole followed before Paine's posting to Lincolnshire by introducing excises and a system of bonded warehouses for commodities such as coffee, tea, and chocolate. The government's aim was to raise much-needed state revenues by expanding the system of indirect taxes. This in turn required stamping out smuggling and developing London as a free port, from which the same commodities could be reexported with little fuss and no expense to the merchant.

In practice, enormous quantities of goods such as tea, coffee, and tobacco — the goods of the café culture — continued to be smuggled into and out of the country. The government reacted harshly by expanding the number of excise officers in the hope that the illegal trade could be crushed. The tax was widely perceived as harshly restrictive of the freedom of small traders and purchasers alike. The general population reacted with a mixture of grumpy silence and astonished outrage of the kind depicted in William Hogarth's famous witty painting of an angry mob supervising the amputation of a sign overhanging an Excise office during an election campaign. At the time of Paine's appointment as an exciseman, there were virtually no other redresses possible against officials of the Crown, and many of its minor officials, including excisemen, were seen as thugs who greedily stole or wrecked property and harassed or beat up their victims without compunction. There was a widespread feeling (as the poet Andrew Marvell said) that the Excise was a thousand-eyed greedy monster devouring common folk who were mere playthings of royal officials and despotic state power.

Moncure Conway writes that the young Alford exciseman was unaffected by such grumblings,[51] but that seems improbable. Popular hostility probably greeted Paine each working day, and it is likely that he felt internally divided, as if he were a figure catapulted against his intentions into a quandary that required him daily to reconcile irreconcilables. He had committed himself to a secure profession in an age in which most people lived in fear of pauperization, many of them actually tasting it. At the same time, he had committed himself to living with the fact that his job sparked off grumblings and resistance among his "clients." Paine wrestled with this contradiction — ultimately without success — for the next ten years of his life.

It has been conventionally thought that his first attempt at a resolution of his quandary — fiddling with his notebooks — earned him the sack. Traders bitterly resented the snooping and taxing work of the Excise. It is, therefore, not surprising that excisemen commonly avoided irritating their clients by "stamping"— that is, saving time, sidestepping abuse, and even accepting bribes by writing up false reports from their office desks without actually traveling to the traders' premises and physically examining the goods being produced or imported or exported. The standard interpretation of this period of Paine's life clings to this point. It supposes that the young Norfolk exciseman began stamping soon after he was posted to Alford and that he was eventually caught doing so nearly a year after his appointment. Accused of stamping by his supervisor, William Swallow, Paine is supposed to have freely admitted his guilt by letter to his superiors on August 13, 1765. His assumption that honesty would prove to be the best policy backfired, or so it is said, and he was sacked from service by the end of the month.[52]

Several things about this standard account do not ring true. Stamping was indeed a serious offense — as reprehensible as a police constable today faking evidence in his or her notebook — and official accounts of such cases were usually elaborate. It is, therefore, of interest that neither the collector's written report nor the confession allegedly written by Paine are to be found among the records. The official entry of the case in the Excise Board's minutes is strangely brief. More telling is the related fact that seven weeks after Paine was sacked, William Swallow was removed from his supervisory post after a formal complaint about his conduct had been lodged by an unnamed informant. The reason for his removal was made clear in the detailed report of the Excise Commissioners: for the last seven months of Paine's time in Alford, Swallow, whose job was to conduct independent checks on the accuracy of Paine's calculations and reports, was in fact stamping his own reports by copying, sometimes inaccurately, from Paine's report books![53]

Equally interesting in this saga was Swallow's difficult character. The evidence suggests that he had a history of quarreling with his office keeper at the head office of the Excise in the nearby town of Horncastle. A few months before Paine had arrived in the area, for instance, Swallow had arranged the sacking of the long-serving office keeper, no further questions being asked about the cause of the friction.[54] Such bullying of junior Excise officials was commonplace, and Paine, himself a lowly official, probably learned about the incident from Solomon Hansord, his own office keeper in Alford. It is also probable that Hansord sympathized not only with his counterpart in Horncastle but also with Paine. Hansord certainly knew that Swallow was breaking the Excise rules by cribbing from Paine's notebooks, for part of his job was to keep those notebooks under lock and key when Paine was not using them. Yet he also understood that Paine was powerless to prevent his supervisor from raiding his strongbox, for to squeal would have landed Paine the serious charges of insubordination and complicity. Siding with Paine, Hansord probably had words with Swallow, and the two men likely quarreled, which would add weight to the suspicion that it was Hansord himself who had lodged an anonymous official complaint to the commissioners about Swallow before Paine's sacking. Hansord, who got along well with Paine, had reached the conclusion that Paine was being badly used and that Swallow should be disciplined or removed from his post. Swallow, getting wind of trouble, covered his tracks and tried to save his own skin by making false allegations about Paine, knowing that the Excise authorities customarily closed ranks in support of collectors and supervisors against ride officers and other lowly officials like Paine. If Paine had spoken out against Swallow, he surely would have been victimized. By keeping his mouth shut, he suffered the same fate.

London

Each year in Thetford, Paine had seen with his own eyes the crude injustice of the punishment system administered by the Georgian monarchy. His victimization at Alford was a different, more powerful experience, for it was the first occasion when he personally tasted the power of government officials to act despotically, camouflaged by official reports and backed by the unchallengeable prerogative inherent in the Crown-in-Parliament system. His sacking instantly sharpened his sense of justice in the face of corruption. It shattered at least some of his illusions about the nature of government in Britain, leaving him with the feeling that official politics was "jockeyship," and that his native land fell far short of its reputation abroad as the home of liberty and good government. Humiliated by a corrupt state, the life of the former staymaker and privateersman was again in tatters. Tail between his legs, the twenty-eight-year-old penniless failure was forced to return to Thetford, this time securing through his disappointed father's family contacts a job as a journeyman staymaker in Diss, a small town fifteen miles from Thetford.

Little evidence of his life remains from this period. An old diary mentions that he was employed by Mr. Gudgeon's workshop in Beehive Yard on Cock Street (later Denmark Street), behind the Old Beehive Inn.[55] The details are sketchy, but the lingering impression is that Paine's behavior in Diss was erratic and luckless, as if he was no longer compatible with Norfolk or staymaking. Diss was a dismal town about the size of Thetford, sited on a lake known locally as the Mere. The local industry, linen-cloth manufacturing, had so spoiled the Mere that, as Paine's contemporary Francis Blomefield pointed out, "it stinks exceedingly, and sometimes the fish rise in great numbers."[56] The stench was not Paine's only problem. He also was bored with familiarity. He seemed gripped by feelings of loss and weighed down by moments of hopelessness. It is not surprising, if convention is to be believed, that he quarreled frequently about matters such as religion with Mr. Gudgeon, his master, and with his fellow journeymen.

Living on the hope that his father could convince Mr. Cocksedge in Thetford to pull strings at the Excise Board to secure his reemployment, Paine left for London. There he ate humble pie and petitioned for reinstatement, in the knowledge that behind the scenes a deal was being struck with the Board. This was an age of mercenary politics in which few refused on principle to feather their own nests. Paine was no exception. During his early years, Britain had become a one-party system oiled by court patronage and parliamentary and ministerial favors, to the point where the Georgian state was for many a lifeline, providing those who clung on with security and prospects, if only of a humble job. Paine accordingly confessed to the "justice" of the Excise Board's decision to sack him, thanked it for being so lenient, and denied that he had ever been dishonest or intemperate. The plea, written in the language of polite society,

came from the quill of an individual who seemed shaken by the feeling
that his life was frittering away:

> London July 3, 1766
> Honourable Sirs,
> In humble obedience to your honours' letter of discharge bearing date August 29, 1765, I delivered up my commission and since that time have given you no trouble. I confess the justice of your honours' displeasure and humbly beg to add my thanks for the candour and lenity with which you at that unfortunate time indulged me. And though the nature of the report and my own confession cut off all expectations of enjoying your honours' favour then, yet I humbly hope it has not finally excluded me therefrom, upon which hope I humbly presume to entreat your honours to restore me. The time I enjoyed my former commission was short and unfortunate — an officer only a single year. No complaint of the least dishonesty or intemperance ever appeared against me; and, if I am so happy as to succeed in this, my humble petition, I will endeavour that my future conduct shall as much engage your honours' approbation as my former has merited your displeasure.
>
> > I am, your honours' most dutiful humble servant,
> > THOMAS PAINE

Paine's calculated arse kissing paid off. The Excise Board, which knew in advance of Paine's application, reacted swiftly. The following day, they entered into their records a coldly written minute: "Friday the 4th July, 1766 . . . Ordered that he be restored on a proper vacancy."[57]

Paine again waited for a posting. After returning briefly to the Alford area, where he witnessed firsthand a suicide attempt,[58] he desperately chased employment. Determined not to serve yet more time in Thetford, he scratched out an existence in London by teaching reading and writing of English, initially at an academy for the children of artisans run by Mr. Daniel Noble at Mill Yard on Leman Street, Goodman's Fields, a neighborhood of working people filled with theaters, brothels, and taverns on a scale rivaling Covent Garden. Noble's academy stood in a forest of private-enterprise schools then shooting up throughout London, all of them taking advantage of the effective breakdown of educational licensing by church and state. Such schools were frequently short-lived, but they met a need in offering boys (and sometimes girls) from craft and petit bourgeois backgrounds a practical education in skills such as writing business letters, bookkeeping, technical drawing, and arithmetic. Some of these charitable schools were run by Methodists and Methodist sympathizers for laborers' children, who were taught godliness, craft skills, and their social duties and rights. Noble's academy was one of these. He was a child of Huguenot immigrants, and had been well educated at the Kendal Academy under Caleb Rotheram (a friend of Joseph Priestley) and at Glasgow University. He had a large private library and was well known for his Dissenting sympathies and active support for civil liberties. Noble was an ordained minister who preached Arminian views (perhaps with Paine's assistance) to his congregations at the Sabbath-Keeping Baptist Church, close to the Academy.[59] Noble and his wife, Mrs. Experience Noble, were deeply concerned with education; they ran another school in the village of Peckham, south of the river Thames. It may have been they who arranged Paine's transfer, in January 1767, to a school in the parish of Kensington owned and run by Mr. Gardiner.

The teaching work Paine did during this period was considered by his contemporaries as menial. The position of private school teacher, like that of private governess, was a third-rate job lacking a decent salary — around twenty-five pounds a year, more than a poor laborer's annual wage of ten pounds, but hardly enough for an unattached individual like Paine to live on and only half of what he had earned as an exciseman. He nevertheless enjoyed his work. It convinced him of the benefits of formal education of the disadvantaged, and for some years afterward he talked often about the need to set up schools for the self-improvement of women.[60] Paine also took advantage of the cosmopolitan energy of London. He remarked of this period in his life: "Here I derived considerable information; indeed I have seldom passed five minutes of my life, however circumstanced, in which I did not acquire some knowledge."[61] He eagerly renewed contact with the circles of scientists clustered around the Royal Society, becoming acquainted for the first time with Dr. John Bevis, an expert on earthquakes and a respected astronomer "whose great abilities were well known to the learned all over Europe."[62] He also saw much of his former lecturer James Ferguson, and it was through him that he met Benjamin Franklin — a meeting that would later alter Paine's life.

It has been said that Paine held down his teaching job in Kensington for barely three months and that, still without a definite job offer from the Excise, he turned once more to preaching, even exploring the possibility (through his previous employer, Daniel Noble) of seeking ordination in the Church of England, despite not having the necessary education in Latin.[63] This story may be pure gossip, although if it were true, it would help confirm the lingering impact of his boyhood brush with Anglicanism. More reliable is the story that during this period of residence in London, Paine again flung himself into bits and pieces of itinerant preaching in the city's open fields. The Methodists, for whom he had preached in Dover and Sandwich, welcomed lay preachers in the struggle to minister especially among London's poorer folk, whose souls they thought could be saved from wickedness and whose lives could be defended in the name of humanity and civilization.[64] Paine's earlier taste of Methodism had made him aware of its deep concern for social justice, and he was again impressed by his encounter with more experienced lay preachers — coal heavers, tailors, housepainters — who taught him the art of lifting listeners out of their everyday concerns and into the realm of spiritual ecstasies through the skillful use of vivid images, plebeian phrases, and magnetizing metaphors.

Practicing the art of rhetoric in front of hurly-burly crowds did not earn Paine a living. After politely exercising his option to decline an offer, in mid-May 1767, of appointment to the Excise office at Grampound in Cornwall — he "prayed leave to wait another vacancy"[65] — Paine accepted the next offer that came his way. On February 19, 1768, the news arrived of a posting to the Sussex town of Lewes, which he duly accepted, for the salary of fifty pounds per year. Was he delighted by the offer? Did he accept grudgingly, or perhaps even with a curse from Alford still on the tip of his tongue? Was he sad to be leaving the London scene? Had he hopes of bettering himself in Lewes? Time has so faded his reactions that the only thing certain is that Paine's moorings in his native England were loosening and that his time in Lewes would set him afloat on the Atlantic, bobbing in the direction of the American colonies.

Lewes Politics

Paine found his bearings quickly in Lewes, then a small, bustling market town about twice the size of his native Thetford. He was impressed by the town's vibrant social life, which included the Society for the Encouragement of Agriculture and Manufactures, a cricket team, a busy coffeehouse, a circulating library, and a regular visiting theater group, the New Temporary Theatre, performing comic operas, farces, and Shakespearean tragedies. Lewes also was a town of Nonconformist churches. Through Methodist connections, he rented lodgings in the fifteenth-century Bull House — known locally by its distinctive gargoyles as "the house with a monkey on it" — above the snuff and tobacco shop of Samuel and Esther Ollive, who lived on the premises. Samuel Ollive had inherited the property from his father, the Reverend John Ollive, who had ministered the adjoining Westgate Chapel from 1711 to 1740. The Ollives had three sons and a daughter, Elizabeth, all of whom had been baptized in the chapel.[66]

The Ollives' business was slow, and the family was glad to supplement its earnings by taking in a lodger. The Ollives also had a commercial interest in the newly arrived gauger of excisable commodities, which included tobacco. They were members of what Adam Smith famously called the "nation of shopkeepers" and agents of an English society that was increasingly capitalist, materialist, and market oriented. But they could not fairly be described as crouching mercenaries, as English shopkeeper types "eternally tossed about between the hope of entering the ranks of the wealthier class, and the fear of being reduced to . . . proletarians or even paupers."[67] The Ollives considered themselves upright citizens, and for that reason they found themselves attracted to the young exciseman with flashing black eyes and a lively mind, a like-minded citizen in his thirty-second year who displayed an unusual degree of interest in public affairs.

To say that Paine was already something of a political animal when he moved in with the Ollives is to contradict the standard view that it was only in Lewes that he underwent a political conversion, there discovering for the first time in his life the importance of civil and political liberties and social justice, themes for which he would later become internationally famous.[68] The standard story is unconvincing. Far from being a loyal, apolitical noncitizen, Paine already had developing political senses. His time in Thetford, London, Dover, Sandwich, and Alford had seen to that. In Lewes, Paine consolidated his views, enabling him to express his political mood with greater confidence. It is possible that before accepting the Lewes posting, Paine knew something about the town's civic life, and even that he had made personal contact with the Ollives through Richard Solly, the Methodists, or the excisemen in the neighboring county of Kent, where he had lived for three years. Lack of evidence again hinders our story at this point, although it seems probable — as Paine's polite refusal to accept an Excise posting in Cornwall confirms — that he had decided to reject a boring job in a lonely spot anywhere on the map of rural Britain.

Local government politics ensured that Lewes was not that kind of place. The town had a history of Dissenting republican politics stretching back to the English Revolution of the 1640s, when its Puritan majority had vigorously supported Parliament, which had coordinated from there its political and military campaigns throughout the county of Sussex. During that period, as townspeople told Paine many times over, Lewes's two Members of Parliament had been radicals. Colonel Anthony Stapley had signed the death warrant for King Charles I in 1649, and Colonel Herbert Morley had been among the stars of the subsequent Commonwealth. After the restoration of the monarchy in 1660, Richard Cromwell, Oliver's son and political successor, had escaped with his life through the safe haven of Lewes to the Continent.

The return of the monarchy had turned Lewes into a religious battleground. Its sizable Nonconformist population had boycotted the reimposed Church of England and suffered accordingly. The town's Baptists, Congregationalists, and Presbyterians had endured house searches and fines, and quite a few of its truculent Quakers had been imprisoned. The religious Dissenters had fought back symbolically by launching annual celebrations of the fifth of November that had been (and still are) among the most spectacular in the country. Many Lewes residents lumped together Guy Fawkes and the Gunpowder Plot with the Spanish Armada and the Irish rebellion of 1641. They believed that these events symbolized the continuing threat to liberty and good government in England from Roman Catholicism at home and abroad. The Lewes Nonconformists had adopted "No Popery" as a slogan, and they had added fuel to their annual fifth of November bonfires, when the effigy of Guy Fawkes was torched, by claiming that Charles II and the Anglican Church had papist sympathies.

The new royalist government of Charles II had responded by tampering with the structures of local self-government.[69] Its aim had been to drive out militant Puritans from the nests of power, and in 1663 it had attempted exactly that by replacing the Society of Twelve, the town's pro-republican governing body, with the semifeudal Court Leet, a yearly meeting of leading royalist sympathizers empowered to appoint key town officials such as the Steward and High Constables. Yet Nonconformist influence in town politics had never been fully defeated. Indeed, by just over a century later, when Paine took up residence in Lewes, republican-minded citizens, taking advantage of the declining power and recent death (in 1768) of the local landed oligarch, the duke of Newcastle, Thomas Pelham-Holles, had rebuilt their Society of Twelve and had recovered a measure of their former power and respectability.[70]

Samuel Ollive, Paine's landlord, was a leading contributor to this revival of local government autonomy. He was a good friend of Henry Verral's, a well-respected man-about-town whose family had until recently been landlords of the White Hart tavern, the hub of the town's social life. At the time of Paine's arrival in Lewes, Ollive and Verral were active in the town's governing body, and Ollive was one of two incumbent town Constables, a position that resembled the later role of city mayor.[71] The

Constables were charged with providing civic leadership and (with the help of two appointed policemen called Headboroughs) enforcing public order. They also acted as returning officers, supervising local elections and adjudicating disputed votes under pressure from various rival factions.

The town Constables were elected annually by the Society of Twelve. The Society was a self-perpetuating circle of town notables who twice a year discussed and decided matters of general concern to Lewes inhabitants. The Society nominated various town officials, including "scavengers" responsible for keeping the town clean, "pinders" charged with the job of rounding up stray pigs and dogs, and clerks of the marketplace. The Society, or Fellowship as it was sometimes called in Paine's time, also co-opted new members and selected two High Constables. Samuel Ollive must have arranged for Paine to be co-opted into the Society, for by his signature Paine is recorded to have been a regular member of the Society during his years in Lewes. The Society normally convened at the Town Hall, sometimes in front of a general town meeting, which debated and passed resolutions on matters ranging from borough taxes to the prohibition of "any Wheelbarrow or other Wheel Carriage Sledge or Single Wheel on the foot Pavements of this Town."[72]

Occasionally, the Society assembled across the road at the White Hart tavern, a bustling stage for coach services to and from London with stabling for a hundred horses. Amid its oak-paneled walls and Tudor fireplaces, the men of the Society handled matters such as mortgages, taxes, and town affairs. On at least one occasion when Paine was present, the meeting discussed compensation for two former Constables and agreed to "make and Collect a Town Tax on all and every the Housekeepers within the Borough aforesaid at and after the rate of Three Pence in the pound."[73]

Paine's involvement in such meetings strengthened his republican outlook. It is true that the Society and the Constables they elected were dominated by men who were local town notables and that the Society therefore functioned to protect a local oligarchy from outside interferences, especially the elaborate system of patronage that until recently had been operated by the duke of Newcastle. The Society was a counterweight to what Paine later called despotism, furnishing him with his first taste of local self-government. The Society was certainly elitist — it picked and chose its members and was accountable to nobody but itself — and yet it instructed Paine in the republican democratic maxim that citizens are best cured of their deference and parochialism when they put down roots in local affairs in which they have some say.

Paine's participation in Lewes politics was not confined to the Society of Twelve. He also regularly participated in the quite separate meetings of a church body called the Vestry, held at various Lewes venues, including the old Norman-towered St. Michael's Church, just opposite Paine's lodgings. Town records show that Paine attended his first Vestry meeting on September 15, 1768, several months after his arrival in Lewes, and that he participated in at least six other such meetings during the next five years.[74] The Vestry was a powerful body linked to St. Michael's Church. It maintained the church buildings and supervised the levying of local parish taxes. The revenues it collected were redistributed in the form of assistance to needy parishioners. In effect, the Vestry operated as a rudimentary local welfare state. Its members debated, allocated, and recorded payments for a wide variety of local needs, including the provision of street lighting, the repair of roads and buildings, and small weekly payments to orphans, widows, and the poor, the sums ranging from one to five shillings. In the strange-sounding language of the eighteenth century, the job of St. Michael's Vestry was to "police" its inhabitants, not in the narrower nineteenth- and twentieth-century sense of securing law and order by means of a professionally trained and armed police force, but in the quite different, much broader and older sense of "polishing" and "civilizing" the everyday habits and living conditions of people.[75]

The Headstrong Club

Paine's political confidence was strengthened not only by his participation in the Society of Twelve and the Vestry. Over a period of six years, he was also closely involved in the social activities of the Headstrong Club at the White Hart Inn. Although doubt surrounds the actual name of the club — it may have been named the White Hart Evening Club[76]— it was a voluntary association of public-spirited Lewes citizens who met once a week to debate pressing local, national, and international matters. Enjoying mugs of local ale and a plate of oysters beforehand — Paine never cared much for roast beef, the Englishman's sacrament — he reveled in this circle. The passionate discussion laced with witty sallies and multiple toasts sharpened his debating skills. The meetings steeled his ability to reckon with opponents and to make alliances in arguments about the pressing affairs of the time.

Which topics interested Paine and his fellow Headstrong Club members? What did they consider the pressing affairs of the time? We simply do not know. All records of the club have disappeared. Although the sharp words exchanged within the oak-paneled walls of the White Hart have become a mystery, it seems reasonable to surmise that the growing crisis in the American colonies forced Paine to debate the merits of the British Empire. He would almost certainly have plodded through the controversial ten letters of John Cartwright, written in the spring of 1774 for the London *Public Advertiser* and shortly afterward published as *American Independence, the Interest and Glory of Great Britain*. Cartwright's advice most likely astonished Paine. It urged the mother government of Britain to give independence to each of its infant American colonies, concluding, "Let us then hear no more of a right in our present-constituted parliament to govern the Americans. . . . The Americans, in common with the whole race of man, have indisputably an inherent right to liberty; and to be governed by such laws as shall best provide for the continuance of that liberty, and for securing their property."[77]

Domestic issues also agitated the Headstrong Club, among whose members was William Lee, the founder and printer of the town's weekly newspaper, the *Sussex Weekly Advertiser; or, Lewes Journal*. During Paine's years in Lewes, Lee's newspaper smacked of republicanism. Amid advertisements for tooth powder, ointments, and tincture of sage for old age, it reprinted the pseudonymous attacks on the government by "Junius," whose "brilliant pen," Paine later wrote, "enraptured without convincing."[78] The *Sussex Weekly Advertiser* also featured articles supporting criticisms of the British state and its empire by contributors sporting names such as "Philanthropos," "Horatius," and "Modestus." The newspaper complained often about the way in which "Tory tormenters" had "wriggled themselves into power." It also printed a brilliant series of some forty essays by "A Forester," who insisted, saucily, that the expressions "ONE OF THE NOBILITY" and "ONE OF NO ABILITY" had become synonymous; prankishly compared English despotism to a head-shaving machine that claims its commoner victims at random; questioned the division between rich and poor; attacked all forms of superstition in the name of "liberty of the mind," "plain truth," and "common sense"; and detailed in Swiftian prose a journey to a republican island called XHWYLMNDNA, where public virtues ruled and words such as "robbery" and "murder" were unknown to its citizens.[79]

The newspaper also tracked every move of the rebel politician John Wilkes, praising him as a "great patriot."[80] The Headstrong Club no doubt argued through many issues, but the campaign by Wilkes against Parliament must have had a special pertinence, especially after Wilkes passed through Lewes during August 1770, when he may have even met Paine during a visit to the Headstrong Club. Elsewhere in the country, Wilkes's radicalism frightened off many potential supporters — for every Friend of the People there were at least a dozen Friends of Property — but in Lewes he was given a hero's welcome. Pealing bells and applauding crowds greeted Wilkes, and, according to local reports, the slogan "Wilkes and Liberty" became "all the cry."[81] Many townspeople, and perhaps Paine himself, appreciated the political novelty of Wilkes's appeal to "the people" in his fight against parliamentary corruption.[82] They may have been hazy about the details of the turmoil being generated in London after Wilkes was thrice rejected by Parliament after due election by the county of Middlesex and the overwhelmingly defeated candidate, Colonel Luttrell, was seated in his place. They also may have had reservations about the unsavory personal character of Wilkes, the opportunist demagogue. But they could not have failed to see that the cause was bigger and better than the man. The cause of John Wilkes, skillfully translated into the language of "the rights of electors," had not only spread from Middlesex County to become a national issue. By concentrating public resentment of the government behind his cause, Wilkes also had raised a dangerous chain of revolutionary questions: What were the basic rights of the people of England? What was the proper relationship between the electorate, not to mention the public at large, and its representatives? How, save at elections, could the public intervene to make its will felt within the structures of the government and constitution? And once the doors were opened to public participation, could they be slammed shut again?

Headstrong Club members no doubt saw that the same questions were surfacing, if more vigorously, in the American colonies. They must also have seen that the language of the Wilkes campaign defined the terms in which the club itself was acting as an extraparliamentary body of citizens concerned with defining the public good.[83] That recognition probably served to bond together its members, although not to the point of quelling factional disputes and heated personal disagreements. When disputes became protracted, a club member was nominated to present to the most compelling haranguer a prize called the Headstrong Book. Presumably because some contestants always drank more than their share of ale, brandy, and Madeira, and because the book, along with its proud recipient, would therefore likely end up in a muddy rut later that night, the prize was safely delivered to the winner next morning by a local messenger boy. It was then kept by the lucky victor until the following week's meeting. Paine was reputedly often judged the best debater, as the full title of the book during this period suggests: "The Headstrong Book, or Original Book of Obstinacy. Written by **** ****, of Lewes, in Sussex, and Revised and Corrected by Thomas Paine."

Club member William Lee described Paine as "a shrewd and sensible fellow" who enjoyed an unusual "depth of political knowledge."[84] Lee even wrote a mock eulogy for Paine, tongue-in-cheek but full of admiration, crowning him the "General of the Headstrong War":

> *Immortal PAINE! while mighty reasoners jar,*
> *We crown thee General of the Headstrong War;*
> *Thy logic vanquish'd error, and thy mind*
> *No bounds, but those of right and truth, confined.*
> *Thy soul of fire must sure ascend the sky,*
> *Immortal PAINE, thy fame can never die;*
> *For men like thee their names must ever save*
> *From the black edicts of the tyrant grave.*[85]

Like a coal fanned by the breath of admirers, Paine glowed in this circle. Some of his lifelong conceit and "perseverance in a good cause and obstinacy in a bad one"[86] no doubt stemmed from this period. So did some of his remarkable ability to write prose and verse. During his stays in Sandwich, Grantham, and Alford, Paine may well have experimented with writing, but in Lewes there is evidence, weighed here carefully for the first time, that he made time to practice the art of pushing words around a page — with considerable effect.

Among the oddest things about Tom Paine were his later persistent denials of having been an author during the first half of his life in England.[87] He may have grown embarrassed by the primitiveness of his early writing. He also may have covered his tracks to boost his reputation among friends by exaggerating the originality of his latest literary effort. It is possible as well that the denials were designed to shelter English family and friends against the foreign storms precipitated by his later writings. Whatever the reason, Paine's denials are droll. Equally odd are the attempts by Paine's admirers to counter his denials by projecting his later achievements back onto his early years. Such efforts have produced exaggerated nonsense, such as the claim that Paine was the author of the "Forester" essays, whose author was in fact the curate of nearby Friston and East Dean, Reverend Richard Michell.[88]

More probable, but difficult to prove, is Paine's publication of several unrelated pieces in the *Sussex Weekly Advertiser*. One letter to the printer, from "Common Sense," defended the principle of "Liberty of the Press" and concluded that it "is better to cease to exist, than to cease to be free."[89] Paine may also, or alternatively, have written two pieces under the name "Humanus," one of them proposing a new design for a fire escape and the other passionately denouncing the deportation, in an open cart, from Yorkshire to Lewes of a vagabond, who died shortly after from exposure. "Humanus" criticized those who ordered the deportation for acting contrary to "the laws of God and Nature," accused them of murder, and concluded that they "ought not to escape with impunity, even though it were the act of an unfeeling, CIVIL TYRANT."[90]

A month later, in the summer of 1771, someone named "P_____" contributed a satirical deist poem, "An Arithmetical Paraphrase on The Lord's Prayer."[91] Another biting satire, unsigned, "The Monk and the Jew. A Tale," attacked religious bigotry by describing how a Jewish traveler named Mordecai one day plunged accidentally through thin ice into the waters beneath a frozen lake. "For Heav'n's sake help!" he cried out. "Turn christian first," snapped a nearby monk. The Jew complied, only then to be sermonized as he struggled to stay afloat in the icy water. "Drag, drag me out, _____ I freeze, _____ I die," he shrieked. The priest responded with absolution:

> *"Your peace my friend is made on high;*
> *Full absolution here I give;*
> *Saint Peter will your soul receive: _____*
> *Wash'd clean from sin, and duly shriven*
> *New converts always go to heaven;*
> *No hour for death so fit as this;*
> *Thus — thus — I launch you into bliss."*
> *So said _____ the father in a trice*
> *His convert launch'd beneath the ice.*[92]

Paine's authorship of these few pieces remains doubtful. More certain is that he contributed to the Headstrong Club pieces dabbling in local affairs. Among them was an election ballad[93] and a stinging political satire, "The Trial of Farmer Short's Dog Porter." It dealt with the true story of a Sussex farmer whose dog, Porter, was ordered to be hanged by three local judges who took offense at the farmer's decision to vote for a Member of Parliament whom they disliked. Poor dog Porter had chased a hare through field and hedge. The exhausted hare had tried to escape into a pond, where it drowned. In court, the judges quibbled at length about the motives of the dog, concluding that it had indeed chased the exhausted hare to its death and was therefore guilty. Concluded Paine:

> *This logic, rhetoric, and wit,*
> *So nicely did the matter hit,*
> *That Porter, though unheard, was cast,*

And in a halter breathed his last.
The justices adjourned to dine,
And whet their logic up with wine.[94]

The satire attacked the unchecked power and pomp of the ruling oligarchy. It was quite at odds with the prevailing English consensus about rich and poor. "Mankind are happier in a state of inequality and subordination," marveled Dr. Johnson. "Poverty," droned Patrick Colquhoun, "is . . . a most necessary and indispensable ingredient in society, without which nations and communities could not exist in a state of civilization."[95] Such thoughts were the language of the mainstream during this period. Hardly anyone — not even radicals and reformers — doubted that the gap between rich and poor could be overcome. The facts seemed to speak for themselves. The wealthy ruling oligarchy were better fed, grew taller, lived longer, and literally looked down on the poor. Their deference to the rich seemed as natural as the unequal relationship between master and servant or husband and wife.

Paine lashed out at this English consensus with tongue and quill in a style that revealed his ability to fight with words. That dangerous art he had learned from London science lectures and had himself practiced on commoners' ears in the name of religion, and it was supported by his growing conviction that monarchy was a rotten form of government. The matter of queens and kings often came up at the Headstrong Club and spilled over into the social activities of its members. It was discussed during local winter outings on frozen ponds, where Paine's skill on skates earned him the nickname "The Commodore." The same topic surfaced during matches at the Lewes Bowling Green Society, where Paine and others in the Headstrong circle were paid-up members. There, on a sloping green bordered by limes, under the shadow of an old Norman castle, Paine enjoyed socializing over bowls, attended by boys who kept the wooden bowls clean and placed lighted candles by the jack at dusk so that the players could finish their game. Headstrong bowlers were serious, but so were their politics. Paine recalled that after a day on the bowling green, over tumblers of punch, Henry Verral had remarked that Frederick of Prussia "was the best fellow in the world for a king; he had so much of the devil in him." Paine replied, sharply, that "if it were necessary for a king to have so much of the devil in him, kings might very well be dispensed with."[96]

The Case of the Excise Officers

That republican sentiment slowly circulated through Paine's veins as he rode his patch as an officer of His Majesty's Excise. Lewes was a river port with a population of around four thousand people when Paine took up his duties, which extended to the small fishing village of Brighthelmston (today known as Brighton) ten miles away. The area was thick with smugglers, and Paine, armed only with his ink bottle and stick covered with figures, trod carefully. The *Sussex Weekly Advertiser* carried frequent reports of seizures of smuggled brandy, tea, and other commodities, often after skirmishes and shoot-outs between gangs of smugglers and the local excisemen protected by soldiers.[97] Smugglers knew that capture almost inevitably meant death by hanging, and they, in their turn, often meted out savage treatment to their riding-officer enemies on horseback. The reception given the exciseman by shop owners and traders was hardly friendlier, though more polite. The exciseman also was saddled with the task of measuring beer barrels in local pubs. The age was notorious for heavy drinking, egged on by the boast of many English pubs that they could get all comers drunk for a penny, get them dead drunk for two pence, and provide a straw bed for three pence. The publicans and their customers looked with little love on the suspicious exciseman, who snooped into cellars and attics and rummaged behind curtains and walls, especially given that the rich, who brewed their own ale, were exempt from taxes.

Paine's life as an excise collector was hardly enviable. As he knew from his time in Grantham and Alford, the work was locally unpopular and poorly paid. He found considerable disgruntlement among his fellow excisemen in the Sussex area, and it is therefore not difficult to imagine why, sometime during 1772, he accepted an invitation to defend them in a petition to Parliament. It is unclear who approached him, offering him a small stipend to cover his costs. It is also unclear whether there existed an organizing committee in or beyond Lewes. The initiative was understandably launched in secrecy, since the whole affair was dangerous for the excisemen involved. The action involved more than a claim for improved wages and conditions of work. It actually supposed the legality and legitimacy of efforts by employees of the Crown to organize independently of the Crown-in-Parliament, to criticize it publicly, and, in effect, to form a trade union of excisemen in all but name.

Paine set to work writing several documents in support of a pay raise during the summer months of 1772. Whether he felt nervous in his English literary debut — he was now a headstrong thirty-five-year-old man brimming with confidence — or whether his nerves were calmed by on-going discussions about the manuscript with members of the Headstrong Club or with colleagues from the Excise living and working in the area we do not know. All that is known is that several weeks before Christmas, he took leave from his job and traveled to London, where he spent the next three months interviewing Members of Parliament and lobbying others likely to be helpful in promoting the cause of the excisemen. He carried copies of a single-sheet essay called "A Letter concerning the Nottingham Officers" and a twenty-one-page pamphlet whose short title was *The Case of the Officers of Excise*.[98]

The straightforward title of the pamphlet accurately summarized the tract's aim: to convince both houses of Parliament that the excisemen urgently needed a salary increase. The case was well prepared and sprinkled with peppery rhetoric and salty common sense. Its honesty about the corruption among excisemen was as strong as its throbbing conviction that they were being unfairly pushed into the ranks of the poor. Paine complained that although the Excise netted some five million pounds per annum, the "common necessaries of life" for an excise officer and his household could not be bought with the current salary of fifty pounds a year. After taxes, charity, and accommodation expenses were deducted, Paine reasoned, the net salary dropped to around forty-six pounds. This figure plummeted further because of the substantial costs of feeding and grooming a horse, around fourteen pounds a year. Those officers who were on "footwalks" in towns and cities, Paine said, were no better off, since they incurred equivalent costs in the form of higher urban rents, rates, and taxes, and inflated costs of basic commodities. The living conditions of all officers were further pinched by the fact that they had to shoulder the costs of relocating themselves and their households when directed to a new posting, when this very mobility excluded them from taking advantage of the local networks of mutual aid that lay beyond and underneath the realm of paid work. Wrote Paine: "Most poor mechanics, or even common labourers, have some relations, or friends, who, either out of benevolence or pride, keep their children from nakedness, supply them occasionally with perhaps half a hog, a load of wood, a chaldron of coals, or something or other which abates the severity of their distress; and yet those men thus relieved will frequently earn more than the daily pay of an excise officer."

Paine's argument, interestingly, refused to portray the excisemen as saints in a sinful world, despite the fact that their miserable living conditions forced them to join "the voice of general want" that could be heard groaning throughout England. Paine was very clear. Excise officers were underpaid and often overworked; their occupation was tiring, and sometimes their lives were at risk; and since the policy of the Excise Board was to employ them during their twenties — that is, during the prime of their lives — they were for the most part trapped by the very career that they had freely chosen. All this tempted excisemen into corruption, which was not — Paine emphasized — inherent in so-called human nature. Individuals were not naturally selfish, devious, and possessive, as certain English philosophers such as Thomas Hobbes had hitherto supposed.

Certainly, Paine argued, almost every week excisemen were tempted into graft and other forms of fraudulent dealings. They regularly colluded with their clients by accepting tips, bribes, and payoffs. And in exchange for a fee, they willfully stretched a point or turned a blind eye to violations of Excise regulations. But none of this corruption was natural. While the excisemen shared the state of frailty with the rest of the human species, their present corruption was rather a consequence of their poor conditions of employment, which certainly were unnatural. Paine was adamant that "poverty and opportunity corrupt many an honest man" and that "the language of poverty strikes the heart . . . like a knell." And yet dishonesty, fraud, and laxity were curable corruptions. If those in poverty were seduced by the opportunity to defraud others while the necessity of doing so stifled their murmurs of conscience, the whole dirty business could be stopped — and the net revenues of the state greatly increased, Paine playfully asserted — by abolishing the poverty from which it stemmed. In short, the most effective method of keeping public officeholders honest was by enabling them to live honestly. Their salaries should be raised immediately.

Four thousand copies of the pamphlet, together with "A Letter concerning the Nottingham Officers," a leaflet, and a petition, were printed in William Lee's shop in Lewes. Notices were placed in the *Sussex Weekly Advertiser,* and with the help of sympathetic colleagues working from the Excise Coffee House on Broad Street in London, Paine did his best to circulate the tract among the excisemen, electors, and their Members of Parliament. Paine thought that the campaign should be directed at public opinion as well, and he did his best to contact some of the makers of this opinion. On December 21, 1772, he sent a copy of *The Case of the Officers of Excise* to Oliver Goldsmith, a well-known London-based Irish playwright whose most celebrated work, *She Stoops to Conquer,* was soon to be performed on the London stage. Paine attached a brief letter requesting "his company for an hour or two, to partake of a bottle of wine, or any thing else."[99] Paine must have been familiar with Goldsmith's chief literary works, which included a satire on English customs, *The Citizen of the World* (1762); a biography of the French deist Voltaire; and a poem lamenting the state of a society where "wealth accumulates and men decay," "The Deserted Village" (1770). By word of mouth, Paine also probably knew the popular anecdotes about Goldsmith, which described him as a vain creature with a tender heart, a simple and generous man capable of flashes of brilliance in conversation. Goldsmith replied to Paine's letter, and the two authors soon met, becoming good friends as a result.

Virtually all of the three thousand excisemen throughout the country signed a petition in support of the claim and contributed three shillings each to cover its costs. Paine's efforts nevertheless went unrewarded. The petition fell like seeds on stony ground. Although Paine received "many letters of thanks and approbation," and although he had the support of a commissioner of the Excise Board, George Lewis Scott, Parliament refused to acknowledge the point of the claim. Paine failed even to secure a Private Member's Bill on behalf of the excisemen. The pamphlet angered senior Excise officials, who for some time, wrongly, had suspected Paine of being "PALAMEDES," the republican author of a series of essays in the *Whitehall Evening Post* attacking corrupt magistrates.[100] In mid-April, he returned to Lewes, deeply disappointed, to find an official letter awaiting him. In almost every other European country, Paine would have been arrested for petitioning against the state. English standards were more civilized, but the news was still bad. He had been sacked from his post for being absent without leave. The language of the letter awaiting him was bureaucratic and the tone revengeful. The Excise commissioners clearly wanted rid of him: "Friday 8 April. Thomas Pain, Officer of Lewes 4th O. Ride Sussex Collection having quitted his Business, without obtaining the Board's Leave for so doing, and being gone off on Account of the Debts which he hath contrasted, as by Letter of the 6th instant from Edward Clifford, Supervisor, and the said Pain having been once before Discharged, Ordered that he be again discharged."[101]

Bankruptcy and Separation

Paine was indignant, but worse fortune was to follow, adding to his feelings of futility. In July 1769, about a year after taking up his post in Lewes, his landlord Samuel Ollive died.[102] To avoid embarrassment and stifle rumor, Paine moved out, possibly returning temporarily to Thetford to see his parents and vote in a bitterly contested mayoral election, in which his name appears on a list of votes cast for the winning candidate, Mr. Arnold, alongside the names of his father, Joseph Pain, and another free-man voter, William Knowles, his old schoolmaster.[103]

Within a few months after Ollive's death, Paine accepted an invitation from Esther Ollive to help run the Bull House business, which now included (according to an advertisement placed in the *Sussex Weekly Advertiser*) "*Tobacco, Snuff, Cheese, Butter,* and Home-made *Bacon,* with every article of *Grocery* (*TEA* excepted)."[104] Esther Ollive had three sons and a daughter, Elizabeth, reportedly an intelligent and pretty woman in her twentieth year, who in 1769 opened a "boarding school for young ladies" in the town.[105] Elizabeth and Paine seemed to get along well, and, encouraged by Mrs. Ollive, the two made it known to townsfolk that they would shortly be married. They made their vows next door to the Bull House, in the Westgate Chapel, where earlier in the century Elizabeth's grandfather had been minister. Since the law forbade all marriages in Nonconformist chapels, the couple had to complete their vows at St. Michael's Church just opposite. The event in the spring of 1771 was probably a happy town affair, despite the sober lasting record: "Thomas Pain of this Parish Bachelor and Elizabeth Ollive of the same Spinster were Married in this Church by Licence this Twenty Six Day of March in the Year One Thousand seven Hundred and seventy one by me Robert Austen Curate."[106]

The marriage was witnessed by Henry Verral and Thomas Ollive, Elizabeth's oldest brother. Paine's statement that he was a bachelor was false and disloyal to his first wife. Although the white lie may have been intended to quash rumors about his past personal pain, his second marriage quickly became bogged down in scurrilous gossip. Following his marriage, Paine moved back to the Bull House, where he, Elizabeth, and her mother ran the shop, with Paine working his second job as an excise-man, playing the role of handyman, and occasionally stepping into minor disputes between the Ollive household and their neighbors. One such wrangle involved the Trustees of the Dissenters' Meeting House, Westgate Chapel, who complained of "their suffering the droppings of rain" pouring from the roof of a small shed Paine had built for his horse. Paine replied courteously:

I do hereby confess myself under an obligation of paying the sum of one shilling yearly to the Trustees of the Dissenters' Meeting House, situated in the Parish of St. Michael, Lewes, as an acknowledgement for their suffering the droppings of rain which fall from a new building lately erected by me,

to fall into a yard belonging and adjoining to the north side of the said
Meeting House.
Witness my hand,
     this 18th day of July, 1772,
          Thos. Pain.[107]

The dispute was light entertainment by comparison with the icy quarrel that soon broke out with Elizabeth. Not much more than a year after
marrying, Paine was absent for several months in London, campaigning
on behalf of the Excise officers. Prolonged absences of husbands from
wives were common in Paine's time, and it is therefore surprising how
quickly the town noticed that all was not well between them. Rumors
spread that the newlyweds had never slept together, that familiarity had
bred discontent, and that sharp words were occasionally hurled like knives
in each other's direction. Some speculated that Paine's Quaker beliefs
required an initial period of celibacy (which, if true, indicated that Paine
had undergone an unexpected spiritual conversion since his previous
marriage, knowledge of which Paine concealed from everyone in Lewes,
including possibly his wife). Others said that a local doctor, John Chambers, had quizzed Paine "on his non-performance of the connubial
rights"[108] and that Paine's impotence had led him to fling himself into the
Headstrong Club, town affairs, his work, and the campaign to build a
trade union for excisemen. Still others whispered that Paine, who was
nearly twice the age of his wife, was too set in his ways, neglectful of his
wife and his business, and too bent on drinking and arguing "politick
affairs." Unaware of the death in childbirth of his first wife, no one considered whether Paine, driven by guilt and shame, had subsequently developed a coldness toward women and a liking of men's company.

That there was substance in at least one of these stories was confirmed
when the following notice appeared in windows in Lewes in the spring of
1774:

To be Sold by AUCTION, on Thursday of this Instant, [the 14th of April]
and the following Day, All the Household Furniture, Stock in Trade, and
other Effects of THOMAS PAINE, Grocer and Tobacconist, near the West-
Gate, in Lewes. Also a Horse[,] Tobacco and Snuff Mill, with all the Uten-
sils for cutting Tobacco and grinding Snuff, and two unopened Crates of
Cream-Colour Stone Ware. To begin each Day at Ten in the Morning.
N.B. The Dwelling-House, with a good Warehouse, Stable, and pleasant
Garden, to be LET, and entered on immediately.[109]

Shortly after the auctioning of his personal effects, which was the public sign of bankruptcy, Paine and his wife went their separate ways. No reason was given publicly for the parting. A surviving document mentions only that "Dissentions had arisen between the said Thos. Pain and Elizabeth his wife, and that they had agreed to live separate."[110] Paine was tight-lipped. "I *had a cause;* it is no business of anybody," he once snapped to a friend.[111] When another friend asked about the marriage, Paine grew instantly surly, saying, "I never answer impertinent questions." Considered from Elizabeth's point of view, the separation was understandable. For her, as for other workingwomen of eighteenth-century England, marriage had probably meant — alongside affection — a bargain to set up a mutually beneficial household partnership. Through marriage, she had expected to give her husband her labor and a share in the business. In return, she had expected to gain his strength, status, affection, and earning power. Yet here was a husband who probably offered her little affection; whose disappearance to London to fight for his fellow excisemen ruined their joint business; who failed consistently to earn enough for the household to survive on; and who talked, while bogged down in details, in grand generalities about the need for justice for the poor and more liberty for all.

Justice and liberty are not terms easily applicable to Paine's second marriage. It is true that he did not try to escape wedlock through the common eighteenth-century methods of murder, suicide, bigamy, jumping backward over a "besom" (a broom placed aslant in the doorway of a house), or "wife sale" (auctioning his wife for a few guineas or an ox). Paine actually agreed to a formal separation document, which specified that upon the death (twenty-six years later) of her mother, Esther, she would be entitled to her fair share of the family estate. The agreement proved virtually worthless. Eighteenth-century custom was cruel to Elizabeth, who suffered disgrace and was forced to leave Lewes, carrying a few personal effects, never to return. She went to live with her brother Thomas, a watchmaker in the village of Cranbrook, county Kent, a few miles from Lewes. According to Clio Rickman, "Mr Paine always spoke tenderly and respectfully of his wife," and although from time to time he anonymously sent her small sums of maintenance money, she never saw her husband again, dying in July 1808 in Cranbrook a year before her husband's death.[112] Helped by friends and relatives, Elizabeth managed to carve out a measure of financial independence as a dressmaker. But her fate typified an age in which common law dissolved women's identity into men's power. Since divorces were very rare, requiring a private Act of Parliament, wives lost virtually the whole of their rights. A married woman like Elizabeth was reduced to the status of a drudge. She could not even make a will without her husband's consent, and after her death he could still have it set aside. "By marriage, the husband and wife are one person," explained William Blackstone, adding that that one person was the husband. Marriage suspended women's "very being or legal existence." A character from Mary Wollstonecraft's novel *The Wrongs of Woman* bitterly agreed: "A wife being as much a man's property as his horse, or his ass, she has nothing she can call her own."[113]

Paine's story was decidedly different. His fate illustrated the old maxim that all great achievements of modern civilization have hitherto been forged by trampling on the backs of others. At the age of thirty-seven, Paine, the ruined citizen, found himself walking at the bottom of an English society in which men valued good breeding, property, and respectable occupations. Paine was of middling stock, not a gentleman of good garb and genteel learning. He had no job, let alone a steady profession, and no property; he had no more than a few quid in his pocket and had neither a wife nor children. Yet in spite of everything, he had the talents of a citizen, and he was not, like Elizabeth, a hostage to social custom. He had not capitulated to "petticoat government," and he was therefore no laughingstock. As a man, he could turn in any direction and do as he pleased.

He wielded such privilege by returning briefly to London, where he arranged an appointment to see Benjamin Franklin, the American agent general whose scientific work he had first learned about through James Ferguson. Franklin's *Causes of the American Discontents before 1768*, published six years earlier, had just been reprinted in full in the *London Chronicle* (August 30 and September 1, 1774), and it is probable that Paine was familiar with its striking conclusion that the American colonists' loyalty to the Crown was being sorely tested by growing quarrels about taxation and that the "unhappy new system of politics . . . tends to dissolve those bands of union and to sever us for ever." The amicable Franklin was renowned for spirited conversation, and the meeting convinced Paine that he had the means to change his life, as he did at the end of September 1774 by boarding a ship bound for America.

PART II

America, 1774 – 1787

3

The Empire and the Orphan

The Empire of Contradictions

WHATEVER EXCITEMENT Tom Paine felt upon boarding the *London Packet* bound for America in the autumn of 1774 was soon crushed by bouts of acute seasickness. The standard remedies of soda water, Peruvian bark, chicken broth, and fresh air on the upper decks relieved the discomfort. Shortly afterward, however, Paine was flattened by the first potentially deadly illness of his life. During the eight-week voyage from London to Philadelphia, an epidemic, probably typhus, broke out on the ship. Nearly all of the 120 passengers, a hundred of whom were indentured servants from Germany and England, came down with a "putrid fever." Although Paine traveled first class — thanks to the separation settlement from Elizabeth — it did not protect him against the vicious epidemic, which he attributed to "the impurity of the air between decks."[1]

"Ship fever," as it was then called, was normally transmitted by lice in overcrowded conditions. It struck its victims with headaches, flushed and swollen faces, sleeplessness, and intense fevers associated with violent deliriums, diarrhea, and listlessness. Since Paine suffered all these symptoms toward the end of the journey, he was denied the rush of fresh images and strange sounds and smells that greets the immigrant to a new country. When the *London Packet*, skippered by Captain John Cooke, an acquaintance of Paine's from Lewes, docked in Philadelphia on November 30,[2] Paine was exhausted, skinny, and still feverish. He was hauled gently down the gangplank to shore on a stretcher provided by Dr. John Kearsley, a local physician who had been informed in advance by Captain Cooke that a figure recommended by Benjamin Franklin was on board. Seriously ill for another week, unable even to turn in his bed, Paine somehow managed to throw off the illness. He slowly recuperated during the next month at the home of John and Mildred Keen, the brother- and sister-in-law of Captain Cooke, helped along by close medical attention from Kearsley, much rest, and Paine's own country-bred constitution.[3]

Most indentured immigrants arrived in the American colonies with neither money nor personal connections, and the majority, like the Germans and English on board Paine's ship, were obliged to work for an employer for several years. Compared with other passengers, Paine had a good head start. He had money in his pocket, no bonds of employment, and, most important, a letter of introduction from Benjamin Franklin to his son-in-law Richard Bache, dated September 30, 1774:

> The bearer Mr Thomas Paine is very well recommended to me as an ingenious worthy young man. He goes to Pennsylvania with a view of settling there. If you can put him in a way of obtaining employment as a clerk, or assistant tutor in a school, or assistant surveyor, of all of which I think him very capable, so that he may procure a subsistence at least, till he can make acquaintance and obtain a knowledge of the country, you will do well, and much oblige your affectionate father.[4]

Such prose was to open doors for Paine. It no doubt reinforced in his head the image, widespread in England among critics of the cramping effects of English society, of the American colonies as a field of opportunity and material abundance, as the only spot on the face of the earth where individual merit, not ascribed social rank, set the limits on an individual's achievements.[5] Paine was surely familiar with Franklin's view that America was destined to become the seat of a mighty, freedom-loving, and prosperous empire that would turn Britain into a province. Paine's decision to emigrate may even have been driven by Franklin's opinion. Ever since his days in Thetford, he had certainly dreamed of seeing America. "I happened when a schoolboy," he recalled, "to pick up a pleasing natural history of Virginia, and my inclination from that day of seeing the western side of the Atlantic never left me."[6]

It was understandable that a boy living at the center of a vast global archipelago of British acquisitions should want personally to explore the American colonies. What Paine did not anticipate was that America was the weakest link in this colonial chain. When Paine arrived on the western side of the Atlantic, this weakness was barely visible. The far-flung British presence seemed invincible. It comprised a patchwork quilt of colonies of diverse origins — commercial enclaves, coastal trading posts, and giant merchant companies, themselves the relics of seventeenth-century monopoly grants such as the East India Company and the Hudson's Bay Company. Dense British settlements were well established in the Caribbean islands and along the eastern seaboard of North America. British ships and subjects were trading extensively with both the native peoples of America and the Portuguese and Spanish colonies of Central and South America. In Asia, thriving commercial enclaves on the Indian coast were in British hands, together with smaller settlements in Sumatra and the Persian Gulf and a barely tolerated presence in the Chinese port of Canton. British ships were making regular expeditions into the Pacific. And along the West African coast, a huge British trade in slaves, spices, and other commodities was conducted from forts, trading posts, and other points of contact with African merchants and rulers.

Historians still debate whether and in which sense this vast mosaic constituted an empire, but many English observers of Paine's time were confident of its power and glory. In 1768, an anonymous survey titled *The Present State of the British Empire in Europe, America, Africa and Asia* concluded that this Empire was "more extensive and perhaps more powerful than any that had hitherto existed; even the great Roman Empire not excepted."[7] More fulsome praise for the empire was provided by a four-volume survey, written by several "Gentlemen" in the year of Paine's departure for America, titled *The Present State of the British Empire:* "The British Empire is arrived at that height of Power and Glory, to which none of the States and Monarchies upon Earth could even lay the like Claim. Rome, in all her Grandeur, did not equal Great Britain; either in Constitution, Dominion, Commerce, Riches, or Strength." The same survey highlighted the fundamental importance of the British "constitution" in marking off this empire as superior to all previous empires. For "the Romans could not boast of the Liberty, Rights and Privileges, and of that Security of Property and Person, which an English Subject enjoys under the Protection of the Laws." Unlike the Roman Empire, which was "founded in Blood, Plunder and Rapine and . . . Ambition," the colonies of the British Empire were "composed, in every Quarter of the Globe" by "sound Policy, and not Ambition." Their peoples all lived "under the Crown of Great Britain" and, according to the gentlemen observers, "partake of the British Constitution, tho' all or most of them differ somewhat in their Form or Manner of Government."[8]

The government, headed by George III, considered the unwritten Crown-in-Parliament constitutional system to be the backbone of the empire's body with its variety of limbs. The king and his parliamentary supporters considered themselves lords of a worldwide matrix of colonies held together by direct royal administration represented by a governor, who with his nominated council was responsible for each colony's executive government and was assisted in the making of local laws by an elected assembly. As Edmund Burke put it in his famous Speech on Conciliation before Parliament, the Crown-in-Parliament system resembled "the throne of heaven," which "superintends all the several inferior legislatures, and guides and controls them all, without annihilating any."[9]

From this heavenly throne, the British authorities regarded the people of the colonies as English and as such entitled to an English system of parliamentary monarchic government and English law. Exactly what this meant in practice was the subject of frequently bitter controversies. Only two points were clearly settled. First, it went without saying that the "rights of Englishmen" did not extend to women or to the black or native populations of either mainland America or the Caribbean, where up to 90 percent of the colonial inhabitants were drawn from Africa, not Britain. Second, the highest aim of colonial government was to ensure that the white male colonial populations enjoyed a maximum of liberty and independence, thought to be essential stimulants of trade and commerce, consonant with obedience to imperial authority, and expressed in the form of instructions to the Governors and occasional Acts of Parliament.

This system, as Paine himself soon saw, harbored several explosive contradictions. In the American colonies, African Americans, Native Americans, and women did not de jure or de facto enjoy the rights of Englishmen; few colonists considered whether these groups should be treated as anything other than the Crown's slaves or mute subjects. It was quietly assumed that they could neither learn nor speak the language of liberty, that they were in but not of the empire. A second contradiction proved more immediately explosive. The colonial elites who dominated the Assemblies — men from landowning, professional, and merchant families in the North and from the planting class in the South — were torn between loyalty to their local communities and obedience to imperial authorities. In their hearts, these elites were Englishmen. They nearly always identified with English customs and institutions, and there is little evidence that they acted in terms of a "national identity" or perceived themselves to be under siege from "foreign" rule. At the same time, they were strongly committed to local rights and privileges, especially those demanded by the mass of small propertied voters, who held them accountable for actions that appeared to violate the rights of Englishmen.[10]

This contradictory pressure on the colonial elites was exacerbated by growing imperial demands for higher taxation of the colonies. As Paine knew from firsthand experience as an exciseman, worldwide trade was regarded by the British authorities as a vital means of bolstering national finances. The British thought that state revenues could be made to flow like streams of gold from a high level of customs duties collected on colonial imports and reexports. The continuous improvement of the British balance of trade would further increase state revenues by reducing the level of foreign imports and putting the rest of Europe into Britain's debt for reexports from Britain of commodities such as American tobacco and Indian textiles. Nevertheless, the British authorities also understood that British dominance in worldwide trade was neither self-sustaining nor self-financing. The policy of maintaining the colonial territories, keeping open lanes for British shipping through the Navigation Acts, reserving colonial markets for British manufactures, and directing colonial products to Britain all required worldwide military and naval supremacy. Trade in furs, tobacco, and molasses required the deployment of ships, guns, and troops. Supremacy was a complex ambition. It had to be planned, sometimes fought for, and always paid for through taxation. All this was clear to the government of George III. The only remaining question was, Who would pay?

The Coming Revolution Against Parliament

This fundamental question moved to the center of imperial policymaking with the conclusion of the Seven Years' War in 1763. In that year, France was defeated in a costly campaign designed to secure total victory for Britain and, hence, bolt down its role as the dominant power outside Europe. According to a classical interpretation, the gains to the British of the Seven Years' War mark a definite switch from an empire based on "mercantilist" policies of trade regulation to a more aggressive imperial strategy driven by the goal of territorial expansion and the unrestrained exercise of political power.[11] This strategy of aggressive imperialism paid off, it is argued, because for the next fifty years, Britain savored world mastery, despite its eventual loss of the American colonies and its engagement in the bloody wars of the French Revolution. The end of the Seven Years' War gave Britain access to the riches of the Spanish Empire, confirmed London as the financial heart of the Western world, and ensured Britain's dominant role in Europe's trade with Asia and Africa.

The British grip on the world did indeed strengthen during this period, but the classical interpretation is overstated. Quite aside from the lack of overall planning and the striking absence of clear ideas among British ministers of what to do with their newly acquired power, there were some definite continuities in the overall assumptions, purposes, and methods of colonial rule.[12] In fact, the odd thing about the deep political storm brewing in America when Paine arrived there in late 1774 was that its causes appeared impeccably traditional. With the approval of the young King George III, George Grenville, the king's first minister, had launched a program of imperial reform that required the colonies to bear the costs of their own administration and defense. Grenville's decision to keep large British garrisons in America in 1763, to insist that they should be paid for in part by a stamp duty, and to require that the Navigation Acts be more rigidly enforced, as in the Sugar Act of 1764, all had earlier eighteenth-century precedents. So too did the decisions to reform colonial customs, to remove the Assemblies' power to decide the sources of financing the salaries of colonial judges and other officials, as Charles Townshend had proposed in 1767, and even to revise unsatisfactory colonial charters, as was attempted for Massachusetts in 1774. In each case, the British government considered that it was acting well within the bounds of established custom. It explained that it aimed to guarantee the flow of trade in the required directions, to make adequate defense provisions, and to undo the Assemblies' usurpations of their Governors' power.

Whereas in Britain no major political row attended the measures masterminded by Grenville, in America a thousand voices began to shout in protest. What was deemed reasonable in London was judged scandalous in Philadelphia. Here were the political seeds of a revolution: the emergence, wholly unplanned, of at least two distinct power blocs who interpreted the events of the world in radically divergent ways and who drew fundamentally different conclusions about the governing state power. For a growing number of urban Americans, the British government was abusing its imperial power over the American colonies. The Sugar Act, the Stamp Act, the Townshend taxes, and the Tea Act all seemed to be examples of a larger British policy of reigning in the colonies, subjecting their inhabitants daily to inquisitive customs men and arrogant redcoats armed with pistols and muskets. In particular, Britain was seen to be demanding, unfairly, that the colonies pay for the war against the French. The colonists felt that they had already paid a high price for Britain's victory; that they had lived with terror, soaring tax bills, and violence and disease that had devoured those who had been to the front; and, above all, that only the colonial Assemblies, and not Parliament, had the customary right to tax their people.

By the autumn of 1774, there was a growing feeling among the colonists that new British legislation such as the Stamp Act was unacceptable because it differed in important ways from all previous imperial legislation. To begin with, the Stamp Act of 1765 was felt to be disturbingly invasive. The legislation struck at the heart of American daily life by requiring stamp duties to be paid on a huge variety of items and activities. Colonists who bought or sold land, traded, went to church, married, read newspapers or pamphlets, drank in taverns, gambled, became apprentices, played dice or cards, took public office, or found themselves in court all felt the pinch. Second, the new taxes were beyond the means of many colonists because they had to be paid in sterling, which most Americans never saw, let alone handled. In addition, the new legislation was seen widely as an unprecedented stage in Parliament's meddling in the legal procedures of the colonies. The Stamp Act was to be enforced in special vice-admiralty courts in which judges appointed by the government, not juries, had the only say. The penalties were tough. The successful prosecution of any person avoiding payment specified by the Act meant the forfeiture of the commodities or items involved; one-third of the booty was to be granted to the person who informed on the offender, one-third to the provincial governor, and the remaining portion to the local stamp distributor.

The key irritant in the eyes of the colonists was not the altered conduct of trials or the severity of penalties but the fact that the British seemed determined to extend the doctrine of parliamentary sovereignty over colonial affairs. During the first half of the eighteenth century, parliamentary intervention in colonial matters had been conventionally limited to trade regulation, thus reinforcing the conviction among some circles of Americans that Parliament had no jurisdiction in other policy areas.[13] During the 1760s, as the Declaratory Act of 1766 confirmed, Parliament began explicitly to insist on its right to extend its sovereign powers into every nook and cranny of colonial life. The so-called Declaratory Act affirmed the principle that Parliament could do what it wanted, when it wanted, and to whom it wanted; it enjoyed the absolute power "to make laws and statutes ... to bind the colonies and people of *America* ... in all cases whatsoever." Such talk was like salt applied to fresh wounds. Not only that, but for a growing number of American colonists, Parliament's legitimate powers of legislating for the colonies did not extend to matters of taxation. They believed that taxes were not a prerogative of the government but of the people, a free gift from them, via their representatives, to the king. That is why only the representatives of the people, acting in the House of Commons, could initiate and amend money bills.

The felt violation of this principle and the sharpening sense that British power was becoming bumptious set off tremors throughout the American colonies. Many American colonists began to question whether they should render unto Caesar those things that were still Caesar's. By the time Paine arrived in Philadelphia, the local rulers of colonial America had turned their long-standing tradition of lively political debate to the related problems of relations with Britain and how to preserve their liberty. Great planters, well-heeled merchants, lawyers, large landowners from the North, churchmen, and politicians were arguing loudly about small and large problems, shaping their political rhetoric and constitutional principles into sharply written pamphlets, newspaper essays, sermons, and poems. Their assertiveness helped to legitimate the new practice of public controversies by means of a press that was as free as any in the eighteenth century. At the time of Paine's arrival in the colonies, songs, poems, newspapers, political pamphlets, doggerel, and books were pouring from the presses of American printing shops. Much of this literature supposed a theory of politics that is strikingly relevant, so much so that it feels linked to our own times in the most intimate way.[14] The colonists worked from the idea that the driving force behind every political development, the key determinant of every political controversy, is power. Power was understood as the exercise of dominion by some men over the lives of others, and it was seen as a permanent temptation in human affairs. Likened most often to the act of trespassing, power was said to have "an encroaching nature," like a beast bent on devouring its natural prey: liberty, law, or right. The key problem in human affairs, therefore, was how to preserve liberty by inventing effective checks on the wielders of power, apportioning and monitoring it, ensuring its responsible exercise.

Not all this energetic discourse on the methods of controlling power was produced by the "better sort." Indeed, one of the soul-stirring aspects of American resistance to British rule is the gradual inclusion of the lower ranks of men in the struggle to voice their concerns. Whereas high-flying political rhetoric, soaring to the level of abstract principles, was a key weapon of the colonial elite, organized crowd action was the primary weapon of ordinary folk, laying the foundation for an emergent revolutionary mythology of resistance to tyranny. Crowd action tore down the elegant homes of colonial governors, brick by brick, tarred and feathered its opponents, erected liberty poles, and paraded through the streets with effigies. Crowds disrupted concerts, captured and destroyed British customs vessels, and risked their lives by confronting redcoats with words and sticks and stones. They dumped tea in harbors, smashed windows, organized huge public meetings, hurled insults, and forced high colonial officials to resign by publicizing their corruption.

In virtually every case, the British authorities and their compradors responded with hostile talk of "mobs" and "rabbles of Negroes and boys," regardless of the color or age of the protesters involved. Hard repression, calling out the militia and regular troops to drown the fires of rebellion, was a favored tactic. Shortly after Paine was carried by stretcher into Philadelphia, some of its German-speaking inhabitants were heard to whisper, "*Gegen Demokraten, Helfen nur Soldaten*" (Against democrats, the only remedy is soldiers). What nobody could yet foresee was that crowd action in the American colonies would help turn that maxim inside out. Without knowing it, the redcoats of the British Empire were planting the seeds of a new maxim: "Gegen Soldaten, Helfen nur Demokraten."

The Philadelphia Editor

Paine finally felt well enough to explore Philadelphia in early January 1775. He was at once impressed by its liveliness. It contained a vibrant political culture of coffeehouses, public meetings, discussion circles, and publishers, and, significantly, public arguments about the British authorities were already spreading into the lower ranks of society. Paine's experiences in England had made him a political animal, and he felt at home in his new habitat. His first words overflowed with enthusiasm for his new country. "America yet inherits a large portion of her first-imported virtue," he wrote. "Degeneracy is here almost a useless word. Those who are conversant with Europe would be tempted to believe that even the air of the Atlantic disagrees with the constitution of foreign vices."[15]

He found Philadelphia a pleasant city of red brick houses, white church spires, and cobbled and dirt streets, spacious and geometrically laid out, with names like Mulberry, Walnut, and Spruce. He loved its energy and wasted no time in following up the contacts suggested by Benjamin Franklin. In the first week of January 1775, he made an appointment to see Richard Bache,[16] a Yorkshireman who was the husband of Benjamin Franklin's only daughter, Sarah. Bache was a good contact. He was a well-to-do Philadelphia marine insurance underwriter who later, thanks to the connections of his father-in-law, became chairman of the Republican Society in that city and Postmaster General of the United States. The meeting was amicable, and Bache agreed to steer Paine to-

ward the city's vibrant literary and political scene. He also offered to help
Paine either find employment as a tutor offering private lessons in geography or open a school for young ladies.[17]

Paine meanwhile rented a room at the southeast corner of Market and
Front Streets, in the heart of the city, in plain view of the auction shed of
the Philadelphia Slave Market.[18] He spent much of his spare time pondering Joseph Priestley's recently published *Experiments and Observations on Different Kinds of Air*, reading at the Philadelphia Library Company, whose
fossil collection he greatly admired, and browsing in bookshops, his favorite being Robert Aitken's on Front Street, just opposite the London
Coffee House and right next door to his lodgings. The shop contained one
of the most extensive collections of books in the province. It also housed a
printing press, from which had already sprung the first publication of the
English Bible in the American colonies.

Aitken's attention was soon drawn to the slim, tall customer with gray-
streaked, dark brown hair tied back in a short ponytail. Aitken noticed
that his customer had browsed the shop on several occasions, carefully examining one book after another, as if the shop were a library. One morning, around January 10, 1775, the bookseller, a printer who had arrived in
the colonies from Aberdeen a few years earlier, struck up a conversation
with Paine, who quickly impressed him with his energy, knowledge, and
political and literary fluency.

The eighteenth-century habit of passing an idle hour in a bookshop
was common among middle-class men, and sometimes — as the famous
meeting of James Boswell and Dr. Johnson showed — such idling produced lifelong friendships. The encounter between Aitken and Paine was
to have more dramatic effects. Although neither man knew it, their meeting was destined to change the world. A few days later, after perusing a
sample of Paine's unpublished manuscripts, which he had brought with
him across the Atlantic from Lewes, Aitken offered Paine employment as
executive editor of a forthcoming journal to be published on the premises
and to be called *The Pennsylvania Magazine; or, American Monthly Museum*.
Aitken may have handed Paine a copy of a circular, printed a year before,
in which Paine would have read that the magazine, whose first issue was to
appear in a fortnight, would have seven general divisions: original articles,
poetry, foreign essays, news, vital statistics, lists of new books, and summaries of business information and weather reports. The magazine,
Aitken told Paine, was already being offered to subscribers for one shilling,
Pennsylvania currency.[19] It was to be published on the first Wednesday of
each month, and its original contributions would "extend to the whole

circle of science, including politics and religion as objects of philosophical disquisition, but excluding controversies in both."

Aitken attached several other strings to his offer. Paine would receive an editorial salary, at a rate to be negotiated (eventually set at the modest sum of fifty pounds a year). Aitken himself reserved the right to decide the overall policy and table of contents of the magazine, and Paine, as executive editor, would handle the day-to-day editorial duties. He was to ensure that the periodical would "avoid the suspicion of party or prejudice" and to print mainly "original American productions." Disquisitions on religion, "particularly between the different denominations," would not be included. Overall, Aitken said, the periodical should have the feel of a magazine produced in the American colonies for the American colonies.[20]

Pressed by the whip hand of unemployment and keen to resume journalism, Paine accepted these conditions. He did so without a written contract and without knowing the world-shattering consequences of his decision. Aitken's stress on the need for a magazine for the American colonies was especially significant, since their relationship with the British was rapidly souring. While Paine had been aboard the *London Packet*, the British government's view of the American colonies had noticeably toughened. Parliament, newly constituted by the elections of October and November 1774, had reaffirmed its sovereign role. Both government supporters and opposition spokesmen took their cue from the no-nonsense speech from the throne delivered by King George: "You may depend," said His Royal Highness, "on my firm and steadfast resolution to withstand any attempt to weaken or impair the supreme authority of this legislature over all the dominions of my crown; the maintenance of which I consider as essential to the dignity, the safety and the welfare of the British Empire."[21]

Meanwhile, the First Continental Congress, comprising delegates from the colonies, had met in Philadelphia beginning in September 1774 to hammer out a united front in its grievances against the British government. The eight-week Congress had concluded with a vote to boycott the importation and consumption of goods from Britain, Ireland, and the British West Indies unless the British government formally pledged to honor the rights supposedly enjoyed by all Englishmen, including the rights to be free of standing armies, to choose their own political representatives, to be tried by their peers, and to tax themselves. The deadline for acceptance of the demand, December 1, 1774, the day after Paine's arrival in the colonies, had passed. Although no one yet knew it, war was just around the corner. A strike by the Americans against British commercial power had begun. An eerie sea of uncertainty was now lapping the shores of the American colonies.

Paine and Aitken clearly intended *The Pennsylvania Magazine* to take advantage of this mood. They worked day and night on the first issue, which was nearly a month late already. It finally appeared, stitched between blue paper covers, fifty-two pages in length, on January 24, 1775. Its title page was emblazoned with a table of contents and a logo comprising a sun rising from behind an olive-twined shield stacked with a globe, a book, a flower, a lyre, and an anchor, all tied together by the motto *"Juvat in sylvis habitare"* (Happy it is to live in the woods). A notice to the public, later confirmed by Aitken as having been written by Paine, likened this first issue to "the early *snow-drop*, it comes forth in a barren season, and contents itself with modestly foretelling that Choicer Flowers are preparing to appear."[22]

A preface, "To the Publisher of the Pennsylvania Magazine," also probably written by Paine, switched similes. The new magazine was likened in genteel language to a beehive of philosophers, artists, and poets. The hive "both allures the swarm, and provides room to store their sweets. Its division into cells gives every bee a province of its own; and though they all produce honey, yet perhaps they differ in their taste for flowers, and extract with greater dexterity from one than from another."[23] Lamenting the degenerate commercialism of the English magazines and the parochialism and scarcity of "channels of communication" in the colonies, Paine praised the morally uplifting powers of a free press and urged upon his readers the themes of self-improvement ("Our happiness Will Always Depend Upon Ourselves") and progress of the human species. His words revealed the faint beginnings of that sublime modernist faith in the future that was among his greatest strengths as a republican democrat and his greatest weaknesses as a political philosopher. "Improvement and the world will expire together," wrote Paine. "And till that period arrives, we may plunder the mine, but never can exhaust it!"

The belief that the world was striding forward and upward sprang from the pages of the first issue of the magazine, giving it a more subversive twist than its eclectic table of contents might have suggested. Paine's preface warned that every previous age had vainly imagined itself superior to its predecessor. He noted that those who praised the sublime perfection of their age would always be victimized by the inexorable laws of progress. That point might have been read as an attack on British hegemony, although if that motive did exist, it was heavily veiled. Readers of the first number of *The Pennsylvania Magazine* were offered a character sketch of Voltaire, a report on the habits of North American beavers, a discourse on suicide, and accounts of the generation of sound and new methods of curing "putrid Fevers." The magazine also contained "A Mathematical Question Proposed," a simple land-surveying puzzle more than likely written by Paine, and a detailed description of a new glass-framed electricity generator, signed by "Atlanticus" and almost certainly written by Paine on the basis of his attendance at lectures given by James Ferguson and Benjamin Martin in London. The first issue listed current prices in Philadelphia for commodities such as pork and beef, coffee and chocolate, butter and Madeira. It provided a summary of the previous month's meteorological conditions. A books and poetry section listed new publications, reprinted selected passages from the most recent British books (such as Lord Kames's *Sketches of the History of Man*), and offered several poems, including one on the subject of Christmas Day, 1774, by "a Young Lady of this City." Brief reports on world events were followed by extracts from letters from correspondents in Portsmouth, Plymouth, Warsaw, and Rome. The issue contained the full text of the petition of the Continental Congress to King George III, a deaths column, and "Notes to our Correspondents," including a wittily worded instruction to "R.S." not to submit any more poor quality satires. And there was a warning to another contributor that the editorial policy of *The Pennsylvania Magazine* was to accept contributions on politics and religion but to avoid disputes in both fields.

That remark was especially curious considering that during his next fifteen months as executive editor, Paine tried hard to steer the magazine toward the growing controversies about the position of the American colonies within the British Empire. Paine's duties and his influence on the policy of the magazine often have been exaggerated,[24] although his contributions were sometimes impressive. Of far greater importance, however, was the way in which Paine's involvement with *The Pennsylvania Magazine* served as a literary apprenticeship. He was allowed to experiment with different ways of writing, and his role brought him into contact with a rich variety of ideas and forms of writing that stimulated his restless mind. For the first time in America — and on a far more open and extended scale than in Lewes — Paine was given the feeling that his opinions counted and that, with some luck and hard work, the future might offer him security as a recognized commentator on public affairs.

During his time with *The Pennsylvania Magazine*, Paine published at least seventeen and perhaps as many as twenty-six essays, poems, and reports, a clear majority of which dealt with controversial social and political matters of the day. Writing either anonymously or under noms de plume such as "Atlanticus" (his favorite), "Esop," "Vox Populi," and "Justice, and Humanity," his interests embraced three types of subjects. His ongoing concern with natural science and the technical arts, deriving from his days in London, was evident in a description of a new electrical machine and in "A Mathematical Question Proposed" (January 1775); a discussion of the geological and fossil collections of the Philadelphia Library Company and the development of mining in America (February 1775); his brief report on a new method of building simulated brick houses in England (April 1775); an account of the manufacture of saltpeter (June 1775); and reports on a new type of furnace for distilling sulfur and the latest method of desalinating seawater (January 1776). His penchant for poetry, traceable to his days as a pupil at Thetford Grammar School, was evident in "Prologue, Critic and Snow-Drop" (February 1775); "Death of General Wolfe" and a satire on Catholicism's dislike of Jews in the "Monk and the Jew" (March 1775); "Cupid and Hymen" and "An Account of the Burning of Bachelor's Hall" (April 1775); "Cruelty to Animals Exposed" (May 1775); "Curious Story" (July 1775); and two songs, "Liberty Tree" (July 1775) and "Love and Glory" (September 1775).

Most important were Paine's social and political commentaries, for which he would soon become world famous. When one reads through them today, many, including "Useful and Entertaining Hints" (February 1775), leave a strong impression that he was half bored with his narrowly defined executive editorial tasks. The magazine certainly suffered from a lack of irony and biting humor, whose appearance among the lower orders, as Oscar Wilde once remarked, is both the first sign of social unrest and a key weapon in the democratic struggle against unaccountable power. There were some sparkling exceptions, such as "New Anecdotes of Alexander the Great," a biting Swiftian satire on men of power as weakling parasites; a commentary on the diary of King Charles I's favorite, Archbishop Laud, whose awareness of his own political mortality coincided with repeated nosebleeds (June 1775); and "A Whimsical Anecdote of the late Duke of Newcastle" (October 1775), a funny story about the duke and a tax collector in Lewes. These contributions were nevertheless atypical. Although the first editorial in the magazine had praised wit as a force capable of striking down "a whole regiment of heavy artillery," its absence throughout was striking. There were even passages worthy of dedication to Dr. Dryasdust. "We imagine some of our correspondents are tired of the hot weather," wrote Paine or Aitken in the July 1775 issue, "as we have received three very *cool* pieces, beginning with Hail! Hail! Hail!"

Witlessness resurfaced in subsequent issues, and sometimes Paine's own contributions were dull, as if he was not himself when writing about non-controversial subjects wrapped in the genteel prose then typical of magazines of this kind. But here and there were signs of a different Paine — not the coolly measured entreating Paine of *The Case of the Officers of Excise*, not the writer of factual pieces on scientific subjects, but a new Paine of crisp, lean, lightning-quick sentences, hammering out political point after point for an audience of self-educated artisans and ordinary folk like himself, for whom reading and being read to were new and exhilarating experiences.

This fierier Paine wrote like someone who supposed, with immense seriousness, that in politics words count, that liberty is connected with prose, and that those unfriendly to republican liberty tend to speak and write badly. Paine supposed that it was the duty of the citizen, and particularly of the political thinker and writer, to be on the lookout for pompous language, questioning it at every turn, recommending (as he sometimes put it) the "common sense" of "the reasonable freeman" as the best antidote against folly, the overall aim being to encourage citizens to think, speak, and act more clearly and confidently. The power of such writing burned on those pages of the magazine whenever Paine took the liberty of lashing out at life in England. "When I reflect on the pompous titles bestowed on unworthy men," he wrote in "Reflections on Titles" (May 1775), "I feel an indignity that instructs me to despise the absurdity." Paine added, "as all honours, even that of kings, originated from the public, the public may justly be called the true fountain of honour."[25] Elsewhere the language was more militant still. "The *Honourable* plunderer of his country, or the *Right Honourable* murderer of mankind, create such a contrast of ideas as exhibit a monster rather than a man."[26] One monster Paine had in mind was Lord Robert Clive, who at the time was revered in England for successfully pressing the jewel of India into the crown of the British Empire. Clive's exploits and British despotism made Paine angry:

Resolved on accumulating an unbounded fortune, he enters into all the schemes of war, treaty, and intrigue. The British sword is set up for sale; the heads of contending nabobs are offered at a price, and the bribe taken from both sides. Thousands of men or money are trifles in an Indian bargain. The field is an empire, and the treasure almost without end. The wretched inhabitants are glad to compound for offenses never committed, and to purchase at any rate the privilege to breathe; while he, the sole lord of their lives and fortunes, disposes of either as he pleases and prepares for Europe.[27]

Benjamin Rush

Passages of this kind may well have been read as a paraphrase of the ill treatment of America. Alert readers could have replaced the words "India" and "Lord Clive" with "America" and "General Gage," who currently commanded British troops in the American colonies. Paine's prose certainly caused a stir — even beyond the borders of Pennsylvania. Sales of *The Pennsylvania Magazine* jumped. The first issue of the magazine had around six hundred subscribers, but within a few months this figure rose to more than fifteen hundred, making it the biggest-selling periodical thus far published in America. Its sudden rise in popularity was later attributed to the poem "Death of General Wolfe." Written for the Headstrong Club when Paine was still in Lewes and published in the March 1775 issue of the magazine, the poem, according to one observer, "gave a sudden currency which few works of that kind have since had in our country."[28] The poem was an elegy to James Wolfe, who had been slain by the French on the Plains of Abraham in Quebec in 1759 when hardly more than a youth. Though a British general, he continued to be mourned as the first great hero of the American colonies. The elegy pictures Britannia wasting away "in a mouldering cave" festooned "with the feats of her favourite son." According to Mercury, who narrates the poem, Jove takes pity on Britannia and decrees, "That Wolfe should be called to the armies above, / And the charge was intrusted to me." The poem continues:

> *To the plains of Quebec with the orders I flew,*
> *He begg'd for a moment's delay;*
> *He cry'd Oh! forbear, let me victory hear,*
> *And then the command I'll obey.*
> *With a darkening film I encompass'd his eyes,*
> *And convey'd him away in an urn,*
> *Lest the fondness he bore for his own native shore*
> *Should tempt him again to return.*[29]

The poem tapped deep veins of public feeling for liberty in the American colonies, and not surprisingly, it was widely praised. It was surely known to the celebrated Philadelphia physician Benjamin Rush, when, quite by accident one afternoon in mid-March 1775, he was introduced to Paine while browsing in Aitken's bookshop. Rush was struck by Paine's sparkling black eyes and large hooked nose in the shape of Cape Cod. Paine was impressed by Rush's intelligence and humanity. The men shared certain interests — for some time, Rush had been interested in establishing a school for ladies of the colonies — and the two quickly fell into amicable talk about politics. A few days later, Rush read an essay attacking slavery, recently published in the *Pennsylvania Journal; and the Weekly Advertiser.* The author, whose identity was concealed as "Justice, and Humanity," acknowledged that although Montesquieu, William Blackstone, and other "eminent men" had already condemned slavery, the rising sense of enslavement to the British among white Americans required them to renounce their own hypocritical enslavement of African people within America.

In spirited language, the essay argued point for point against the justifications most often heard for slavery. In reply to those who claimed that slaves could legitimately be traded on the market as commodities, the author insisted on the individuality of men and women. They were "*an unnatural commodity* . . . none can lawfully buy without evidence that they are not concurring with Men-stealers; and as the true owner has a right to reclaim his goods that were stolen, and sold; so the slave, who is proper owner of his freedom, has a right to reclaim it, however often sold." Against those who claimed that there were no laws against owning slaves came the quick reply: "So men, in some cases, are lawfully put to death, deprived of their goods, without their consent; may any man, therefore, be treated so, without any conviction of desert?" The sharpest tongue was reserved for Christian justifications of slavery:

> Christians are taught to account all men their neighbours; and love their neighbours as themselves; *and do to all men as they would be done by; to do good to all men; and Man-stealing is ranked with enormous crimes.* Is the barbarous enslaving [of] our inoffensive neighbours, and treating them like wild beasts subdued by force, reconcilable with all these *Divine precepts?* Is this doing to them as we would desire they should do to us? If they could carry off and enslave some thousands of us, would we think it just? — One would almost wish they could for once; it might convince more than Reason, or the Bible.

What should be done about the slavery crimes committed against African people? "Justice, and Humanity" insisted that the emancipation of all slaves was an urgent priority. The American colonies should set the pace for the rest of the world. Old and infirm slaves, unable physically to take advantage of their freedom, should be provided for humanely by their former masters. All other freed slaves should be offered either grants of land, low-rent allotments, or gainful employment "so as all may have some property, and fruits of their labours at their own disposal."[30]

Admirers of the essay have claimed that its author deserves the honor "of being the first American abolitionist."[31] That claim is untrue, for such proposals predated Paine's arrival in America. Rush himself had already published a pamphlet calling slavery a "national crime" that would bring "national punishment."[32] The arguments of "Justice, and Humanity" were nonetheless powerful, so much so that when Rush learned through friends that Paine was the author, he became eager "to be better acquainted with him."[33] The two met on and off throughout the rest of 1775. Rush was impressed that Paine was familiar with tracts such as John Cartwright's *American Independence, the Interest and Glory of Great Britain,* which demanded the replacement of the British Empire by a free association of states endowed with British liberties and all of them recognizing the king as their sovereign head. Rush particularly noted that Paine "had realized the independance [*sic*] of the American colonies upon Great Britain, and that he considered the measure as necessary to bring the war to a speedy and successful issue."[34]

Paine's conversion to revolutionary politics was recent. During his first few months in America, he had been struck by the powerful feelings of solidarity with the British Empire: "I found the disposition of the people such, that they might have been led by a thread and governed by a reed. Their suspicion was quick and penetrating, but their attachment to Britain was obstinate, and it was at that time a kind of treason to speak against it. They disliked the ministry, but they esteemed the nation. Their idea of grievance operated without resentment, and their single object was reconciliation."[35]

Paine himself may have indulged some of this belief, and there may even have been people, such as John Adams and John Jay, who at the time suspected him of Tory sympathies.[36] That suspicion, if it did exist, was misplaced — and deeply ironic in retrospect — for although a believer in reconciliation, Paine had arrived in America thinking, along the lines of Benjamin Franklin, that America's star was rising within the empire. It was nevertheless true that during his first few months in Philadelphia, he did not suspect that something dramatic was in the cards. "I viewed the dispute as a kind of law-suit," he later recalled. "I supposed the parties would find a way either to decide or settle it. I had no thoughts of independence or of arms. The world could not then have persuaded me that I should be either a soldier or an author."[37]

The Battle of Lexington

All that changed suddenly during the spring of 1775. According to Rush, Paine's view of the deteriorating relations between the American colonies and Britain was fundamentally altered by the Battle of Lexington. At dawn on April 19, 1775, British troops commanded by Major John Pitcairn opened fire without orders on a group of American militiamen. The Americans had assembled in front of the meetinghouse on Lexington Green dressed in their country clothes of leather jerkins and broad-brimmed hats, watched by a large crowd stunned into silence by the smell of gunpowder and the redcoats' cries of "Lay down your arms, you damned rebels or you are all dead men. Disperse ye villains, ye rebels! Disperse! Lay down your arms!" Eight militiamen were killed and ten wounded. Paine was shocked and angered. He was suddenly filled with savage indignation. He felt the need to challenge and change the world. Such feelings were consolidated soon afterward by his attendance at a stormy public meeting to discuss the news in Philadelphia's State House Yard. From that time on, Rush said, Paine became obsessed with writing on the subject of Britain and the colonies. He drew the conclusion that "when the country, into which I had just set my foot, was set on fire about my ears, it was time to stir."[41]

Stir Paine did. He published several essays on the subject in *The Pennsylvania Magazine*, and the fact that they were printed there, contrary to Aitken's founding brief, indicated that the editor sensed that times were beginning to change in the American colonies. The swing of editorial policy was evident in "The Dream Interpreted," signed by "Bucks County" and possibly written by Paine. The essay was an experiment in utopian writing. It tried to feed the imaginations of American readers by re-describing their current situation in terms of a dream about a well-watered tranquil land that had once been gripped by drought and then battered by tempests. The essay drew parallels between that once-forsaken land and the present sickly condition of America, robbed of its commerce and battered by "the arrogance of kings, the infidelity of ministers, the general corruption of government, and all the cobweb artifice of courts." It also predicted that after the present British drought and tempest, America would become a green and fertile land. It would "rise with new glories from the conflict, and her fame be established in every corner of the globe."[39]

Word by word, page by page, Paine's political views about the British Empire were becoming more radical. Evidence of the shift came in the

July 1775 issue of *The Pennsylvania Magazine,* which included a piece called "Thoughts on Defensive War" signed by "A Lover of Peace." The essay was probably written by Paine after attending a service in Philadelphia's Christ Church. There, on July 7, he heard a rousing sermon, "On the Duty of Standing Fast in Our Spiritual and Temporal Liberties," delivered by Reverend Jacob Duché to the First Battalion of Philadelphia Associators. Citing the fifth chapter of Galatians, Duché had led prayers for "our dread Sovereign Lord King George." He had called upon God to teach the monarch "that his highest temporal glory must consist in preserving to a free people their undoubted birth-rights as men, and as Britons!" Duché had concluded, "In a word, my brethren — though the worst should come — though we should be deprived of all the conveniences and elegancies of life — though we should be cut off from all our usual sources of commerce, and constrained, as many of our poor brethren have already been to abandon our present comfortable habitations — let us, nevertheless, 'Stand Fast' as the Guardians of Liberty."[43]

The same day, with the sermon still ringing in his ears, Paine set about clarifying his thoughts on whether violent means could legitimately be used to defend what, for a long time, he had considered the highest earthly goal: human liberty. It was clear to him that those who take up the sword risk perishing by the sword. Yet it was equally clear that those who refuse the sword risk perishing on the cross. How was this dilemma to be resolved? Paine left no doubts: "I am thus far a Quaker, that I would gladly agree with all the world to lay aside the use of arms, and settle matters by negotiation; but unless the whole will, the matter ends, and I take up my musket and thank heaven he has put it in my power."

The realist argument against Quaker pacifism — that might always triumphs over right unless right protects itself — had a ring of urgency about it. Its pertinence was confirmed by the recent dramatic succession of events in the colonies, including the Continental Congress's appointment of George Washington to command the American troops at Boston, the news of a bloody battle at Bunker Hill, and the declaration by Congress in favor of taking up arms. Yet as much as Paine approved the resort to arms, he made it clear in "Thoughts on Defensive War" that violence was a difficult horse to ride. Violence could easily throw its rider, galloping away from its role as a means and becoming an untamed end in itself, living according to its own wild whims and desires. He drew from this the conclusion that it was fundamentally important to be clear about the ultimate purpose for which violence could be used.

Here Paine prefigured an argument that would be repeated many times in his later life and that would help define him as the first great critic of the dark side of modern revolutions. Liberty, he argued, was the only legitimate purpose violence could serve. It followed from this that a fundamental problem of modern politics was to ensure that violence always served, not dominated, that ultimate purpose. Untamed violence, he explained, had always been a measure of the barbarousness of an age, as the American colonies were now finding to their cost:

> Whoever considers the unprincipled enemy we have to cope with, will not hesitate to declare that nothing but arms or miracles can reduce them to reason and moderation. They have lost sight of the limits of humanity. The portrait of a parent red with the blood of her children is a picture fit only for the galleries of the infernals. From the House of Commons the troops of Britain have been exhorted to fight, not for the defence of their natural rights, not to repel the invasion or the insult of enemies; but on the vilest of all pretences, gold. "Ye fight for solid revenue" was vociferated in the House. Thus America *must suffer* because she has something to lose. Her crime is property.

Paine's serious thoughts on the need for a defensive war against amoral violence of the British imperialist kind concluded on a joyful note. In solidarity with the Americans' cause, Paine broke into song, exhorting the patriots to the tune of "The Gods of Greece":

> *From the east to the west blow the trumpet to arms,*
> *Thro' the land let the sound of it flee:*
> *Let the far and the near unite with a cheer,*
> *In defense of our Liberty Tree.*[41]

The lyrics were unsophisticated, but striking was Paine's newfound commitment as a writer to the American cause. As each day passed, that cause became his passion, and it came as no surprise to those who knew him that he regarded his work for Aitken's magazine with growing indifference. He appears to have published nothing in the magazine during the next two months, in part because relations between Aitken and himself became less than cordial. There had been some quarrels, for instance, when Paine had insisted on striking out some passages that were "too free" in contributions by John Witherspoon.[42] More important, he had been with Aitken for six months, the magazine was profitable, and Paine considered his apprenticeship up. Although receiving a salary at the rate of fifty pounds a year, he was still without a contract, which he now demanded.

The two men agreed verbally to submit the terms of a contract to arbitration by Reverend Jacob Duché and Francis Hopkinson. But according to Paine, Aitken got cold feet: "The bookseller getting information of what Mr. Duché's private opinion was, withdrew from the arbitration, or rather refused to go into it, as our agreement to abide by it was only verbal."[43]

The Orphan

Paine felt double-crossed and no doubt told Aitken so. A heated exchange followed, and from that moment Paine gradually withdrew his heart and soul from the magazine. Although still engaged in editorial work for Aitken — during the late summer of 1775, Paine turned down an offer from "several literary gentlemen" in Philadelphia to set up a rival magazine[44] — he spent most of his spare time hatching a plan to write a pamphlet on the subject of the American colonies and the British Empire. During August and September 1775, Paine began to make notes. Benjamin Rush, with whom he spent much time during this period, warmly encouraged him. But Rush pointed out that despite the outbreak of armed struggle, the overwhelming majority of Philadelphians were hostile to talk of an irretrievable breakdown in the relationship between the Americans and the British. Rush warned him that "there were two words which he should avoid by every means as necessary to his own safety and that of the public — *independence* and *republicanism*."[45]

The warning may have been prompted by a short and angry opinion piece called "A Serious Thought," which Paine had prepared for publication in *The Pennsylvania Journal*. In it he drew parallels between "the horrid cruelties exercised by Britain in the East Indies," the tyrannizing of whites and the manipulation and murder of Native Americans in the American colonies, and Britain's ravaging of "the hapless shores of Africa, robbing it of its unoffending inhabitants to cultivate her stolen dominions in the West." He also drew a conclusion that alarmed Rush: "When I reflect on these, I hesitate not for a moment to believe that the Almighty will finally separate America from Britain. Call it independence or what you will, if it is the cause of God and humanity it will go on."[46]

That revolutionary conclusion was now several paces ahead of current thinking on the American side of the Atlantic. There is truth in Josiah Tucker's observation that the "bickerings and discontents" in the American colonies reflected a native insolence that was rooted in the colonists' fearless love of English liberties — that the Americans were in spirit more English than the English.[47] It is also true that heated public arguments and fierce demonstrations against British troops were spreading fast. And yet — as Paine surely understood from frank discussions with Rush — nobody whose voice counted within the American colonies thought outside the existing terms of the British Empire. Americans were mesmerized by their own denials. It was as if their deep attachment to "English liberty" strengthened their urge for comfort in the bosom of an imaginary empire, despite the widespread perception that those currently in charge of the empire were daily denying them the breast.

Evidence supporting Rush's warning to Paine could be found everywhere that counted. Public opinion had in fact not altered much during the past twelve months. For example, among the delegated representatives to the First Continental Congress, which had assembled in Philadelphia a year before on September 5, 1774, the wish for reconciliation had been stated clearly. One of the delegates, John Adams, had noted in his diary how many representatives and their friends, awash with burgundy at an "elegant supper" on the opening eve of the Congress, had toasted the "Union of Britain and the Colonies on a constitutional foundation."[48] The delegates' subsequent decision to set up an "Association" — a great covenant of nonimportation, nonconsumption, and nonexportation — had been based on the same faith in the empire. The Association had opened with the statement that "the present unhappy situation" originated from "a ruinous system of colony administration adopted by the British ministry about the year 1763, evidently calculated for enslaving these colonies, and, with them, the British Empire." The delegates nevertheless had gone out of their way to reiterate to their "fellow subjects" living in Great Britain and elsewhere that they remained faithful to "the duty we owe to ourselves and posterity, to your interest and the general welfare of the British Empire." And they had concluded with an appeal to the people of Britain, urging them to get rid of their malevolent political meddlers and muddlers, to "furnish a Parliament of such wisdom, independent in public spirit, as may save the violated rights of the whole Empire from the devices of wicked ministers and evil counsellors."[49]

Almost exactly one year later — during the same month of September 1775 when Paine was writing "A Serious Thought" and making notes for his new pamphlet — the New York Assembly was respectfully petitioning the king in virtually the same language. The Assembly reminded His Majesty "that the grandeur and strength of the British Empire" depended "essentially on a restoration of harmony of affection between the mother country and her colonies."[50] Nothing much had changed during the following couple of months, not even after November 9, 1775, when news reached Philadelphia that George III had issued a proclamation declaring the colonies in a state of rebellion, threatening "condign" punishment for the rebels and blockading colonial ports. Upon hearing the news, the Pennsylvania Assembly instructed its delegates in Congress to work for a redress of grievances and "utterly to reject" any proposals that might produce further isolation from Britain. Two weeks later, the New Jersey Assembly issued its delegates similar instructions. Shortly afterward, the Maryland Convention, nervously sitting in Annapolis, instructed its delegates in Congress to work, if possible, "for a reconciliation with the mother country."[51]

Everywhere *independence* was an opprobrious word. Talk of separation, where it existed, remained behind closed doors and confined to confidential correspondence between individuals. Even Congress, caught up in preparations for war, still talked of reconciliation. On December 6, it agreed to publish its formal reply to the king's proclamation. The language was tediously conventional: "What allegiance is it that we forget? Allegiance to Parliament? We never owed — we never owned it. Allegiance to our King? Our words have ever avowed it — our conduct has ever been consistent with it. We condemn, and with arms in our hands — a resource which Freemen will never part with — we oppose the claim and exercise of unconstitutional powers, to which neither the Crown nor Parliament were [*sic*] ever entitled."[52]

Always headstrong, Paine was not intimidated by such nostalgia for the sovereign mother country. He may have been "a fool or a fanatic,"[53] but his conviction that talk of conciliation was sickly was soon to change the course of modern history. Paine began to take his cue from the popular emotions that had already been aroused by the battles of Lexington, Concord, and Bunker Hill. Paine did not foresee that these emotions were soon to be brought to the boil by the king's proclamation, the invasion of Canada, the siege of Boston, Lord Dunmore's proclamation of martial law in Virginia, and the vague rumors that an army of foreign mercenaries was being hired "to bind the colonies in all things whatsoever" by means of guns. He was simply convinced that Americans were no longer in love with Britain and that they feared a comprehensive conspiracy against their liberties. He therefore decided to reject the advice given him by Rush. If anything, Rush's warning encouraged him, strengthening his conviction that, in politics, words count and that, chosen carefully, words can sometimes disarm tyrants.

According to Rush, Paine "seized the idea" of writing a pamphlet "with avidity."[54] He set to work on the manuscript, drawing on preexisting notes, some of them perhaps even drawn from Headstrong Club discussions in Lewes. Within a fortnight — it was now the end of September 1775 — he brought a first draft of the opening section of the manuscript to Rush's house. There, line by line, he read it aloud to Rush, amending it along the way. Throughout the autumn, Paine repeated his private readings with Rush, who was impressed by Paine's skilled pen and charmed by such memorable draft sentences as this: "Nothing can be conceived of more absurd than three millions of people flocking to the American shore every time a vessel arrives from England, to know what portion of liberty they shall enjoy." In early December 1775, when the manuscript was complete, Paine circulated a copy to David Rittenhouse, the astronomer famous for his observations on the transit of Venus in 1768, and to Samuel Adams.[55] Benjamin Franklin also read and revised parts of the manuscript.[56] All three were strongly sympathetic — Franklin, who for a long time had earnestly wished the empire could remain a great political whole, may well have been converted to Paine's argument when reading through the manuscript — and after further minor changes had been made, only the problem of presentation remained.

Paine wanted to call the pamphlet *Plain Truth*. Rush persuaded him, apparently without much effort, to use a more plebeian title with an old-fashioned republican ring: *Common Sense*.[57] Finding a publisher for the pamphlet proved — considering its radicalism — surprisingly easy. Paine was opposed to asking Aitken, with whom he now had quite frosty relations.[58] It was agreed that Rush would approach Robert Bell, a Scottish-born Philadelphia publisher and auctioneer well-known for his fearless private support of independence, his wit, and crowd-pleasing auction announcements, such as "Jewels and diamonds to be sold or sacrificed by Robert Bell, humble proveditore to the sentimentalists." Bell had a proven track record as a publisher, having published William Blackstone's *Commentaries* by subscription in 1772, a feat that was widely considered "a stupendous enterprise for the times." He readily agreed to bear the risks of publishing the manuscript and began immediately with his journeyman to set the type and print the pamphlet page by page. On January 10, 1776, *Common Sense*, stitched together and priced at two shillings, "was turned upon the world like an orphan to shift for itself."[59]

4

The Birth of America

The Reception of *Common Sense*

COMMON SENSE burst from Robert Bell's Third Street press, selling on the streets and in the bookshops of Philadelphia as fast as it was printed. It has been estimated that some twelve hundred to fifteen hundred pamphlets concerned with American affairs were published between 1763 and 1783, and that in the year 1776 alone over four hundred such pamphlets appeared.[1] Some of them went through multiple editions, but according to every contemporary and subsequent observer, *Common Sense* outpaced every one of them in terms of sales and demand. No other pamphlet published in the American colonies caused such a ruckus.

The first edition sold out within two weeks. At the end of January 1776, proof of the pamphlet's sensational impact came in the form of rival second editions and a bitter dispute about their respective authenticity and future copyright. In the *Pennsylvania Packet, or, The General Advertiser* of January 29, Bell advertised a "Second Edition . . . Written by an Englishman" and in the same column denied that Paine had instructed him not to publish that edition. He accused Paine of uttering "absolute falsehoods," of engaging in "catch-penny author-craft," and of plotting to reduce the price of subsequent editions. In the same issue of the *Pennsylvania Packet*, there appeared another advertisement, inserted by the publisher, W. and T. Bradford, announcing that a "New Edition" had gone to press and that it contained "large and interesting additions . . . among which will be a seasonable and friendly admonition to the people called Quakers." In an accompanying note, "To the Public," probably written by Tom Paine, Bell was accused of taking advantage of the huge success of the first edition and pirating a second edition. A greatly enlarged edition selling at one-half of the former price also was promised. "Several hundreds," Paine added, "are already bespoke, one thousand for Virginia. A German edition is likewise in the press."[2]

The struggle over copyright between Bell and the Bradfords and Paine continued in the *Pennsylvania Packet* of February 5. In a column addressed to "Mr Anonymous," Bell stung Paine with epithets such as "puppy," "lie," and "dog." He claimed he was owed money in the form of unanticipated "charges for stitching the pamphlets." He also mocked Paine's falsely modest attempt to hide his identity as the author while at the same time "telling it in every beer house" because his head had been "whirligigged" by success. An anonymous letter published in the same issue, again probably written by Paine, detailed the dispute. Paine claimed that he had been dissuaded from his original plan to publish *Common Sense* as a series of newspaper letters. The "noisy man" Bell had been engaged anonymously by a third party and had accepted to print the pamphlet with all of his expenses guaranteed. In return, Bell had agreed to take half the profits, if there were any, the other half being paid into a fund to purchase mittens for American soldiers. According to Paine, profits had already reached thirty pounds, and for that reason Bell, turned greedy by market success, had not yet honored his promise. Paine threatened to sue Bell if he did not stop mixing profit with politics and pay up to the charity within a week; Bell refused.[3]

We do not know exactly what happened subsequently — during the winter and spring months alone, the brazen Bell published three unauthorized editions of the pamphlet — but the Bell affair was Paine's first taste of vulnerability to publishers in an era without effective laws against libel or piracy. Such disagreements with publishers always personally upset him, and they were normally worsened by his principled refusal to make a profit on his writings and his stubborn genius for stirring up personal and political disputes.

The fate of *Common Sense* nevertheless showed that production disputes rarely hampered the public reception of his works. During the spring and summer of 1776, copies of *Common Sense* poured off the presses in a never-ending stream. In Philadelphia alone, seven editions were released. One was printed by Paine, at his own expense, and delivered to the Bradfords at eight pence halfpenny each to be sold by them at "one shilling each, or

tenpence by the dozen." Two further editions were published by the Bradfords, and three were published by Bell. During January, the pamphlet was
heralded in Pennsylvania's main German-language newspaper, the *Penn-
sylvanischer Staatsbote*, and toward the end of February a German translation, *Gesunde Vernunft gerichtet an die Einwohner von Amerika*, was made
available by the printers, Melchior Steiner and Carl Cist. Both the Bradford and Bell editions were instantly reprinted in other parts of the
colonies, many of them probably without Paine's permission. As early as
the first week of February, *Common Sense* was republished by a New York
printer, and two months later an edition appeared in Boston. Editions subsequently appeared in Salem, Newport, Hartford, Lancaster, New York,
Newburyport, Norwich, Albany, and Providence.[4] During the first week of
May, copies of *Common Sense* found their way into French-speaking Québec, carried by a commission appointed by the Continental Congress that
included Benjamin Franklin and Fleury de Mesplet, a Marseilles-born
printer who was soon to become Québec's first "Paineite" defender of
press freedom.[5]

   Common Sense also appeared quickly in Europe, sometimes in shortened
or anonymous versions. "Common Sense," recalled John Adams, "was received in France and in all Europe with Rapture."[6] In May 1776, lengthy
excerpts were published in Polish translation in *Gazeta Warszawska*.[7] During the same year, the London publisher J. Almon released five printings
of it, and other reprints appeared in Edinburgh and Newcastle upon
Tyne. A French translation appeared in Rotterdam before the end of the
year. During 1777, the essay was translated and read in the German lands.[8]
New German translations continued to appear for several decades thereafter, an example being *Gesunder Menschenverstand. An die Einwohner von America gerichtet*, published during 1794 in Copenhagen by C. G. Proft and Son.
Common Sense may even have reached as far south as Dubrovnik[9] and as far
east as Russia, where Aleksandr Radischev, the first modern Russian radical and famous author of the ode "Liberty" and *A Voyage from St. Petersburg
to Moscow*, likened the pamphlet (which he thought written by Franklin) to
God's word, breathing life into the world and lighting a new path for all
humanity.[10]

   In America, *Common Sense* quickly proved to be *the* political document of
the early phase of the Revolution. Within a month of its publication, it
seemed to set important parts of America on fire. Its daredevil spirit certainly brought overnight fame to Paine, whose contribution to the public
definition of the events as a revolutionary struggle for independence was
to prove to be as great as that of George Washington on the battlefield

and Benjamin Franklin on the diplomatic front. Paine glowed with pride. In April 1776, he reported that he was certain that 120,000 copies had already been published.[11] He later estimated that "the number of copies printed and sold in America was not short of 150,000 — and is the greatest sale that any performance has ever had since the use of letters — exclusive of the run it has had in England and Ireland."[12]

Paine was not exaggerating. Enthusiasm for the pamphlet rapidly became feverish, especially within circles where opinions counted. *Common Sense* fueled the desire of some Virginia tobacco planters to repudiate their large debts to British merchants, fanned the ambitions of certain colonial leaders to boost their reputations by declaring the colonies independent, and fired the aspirations of some colonial merchants and producers to escape the trading restrictions imposed by British navigation acts. The pamphlet also stirred the officer ranks of the army. George Washington, pronouncing it "sound doctrine and unanswerable reasoning," was converted by it fully to the cause of American independence, and many other key figures in the army spoke and wrote of it enthusiastically, confirming Washington's description of it as "working a wonderful change in the minds of many men."[13] On January 22, General Horatio Gates wrote to General Charles Lee: "There is a Pamphlet come by Irwin [General William Irvine] from Philadelphia, entitled *Common Sense* — it is an excellent performance — I think our friend Franklin has been principally concern'd in the Composition."[14] Lee had already read the pamphlet before the letter from General Gates reached him, and on January 24 he wrote to Washington: "Have you seen the pamphlet *Common Sense?* I never saw such a masterly irresistible performance. It will, if I mistake not, in concurrence with the transcendent folly and wickedness of the Ministry, give the coup-de-grace to *Great Britain*."[15]

Charles Lee later claimed that Paine had "burst forth upon the world like Jove in Thunder,"[16] but, curiously, the reaction of the Continental Congress was initially less generous. *Common Sense* stunned its delegates into nervous silence, their eyes and ears open. The pamphlet was more than a month old before one of them, Joseph Hewes of North Carolina, reported home. His letter to his friend Samuel Johnston typified the Congress's irresoluteness: "The only pamphlet that has been published here for a long time I now send you. It is a Curiosity; we have not put up any to go in the Waggon, not knowing how you might relish independency. The author is not known; some say Doctor Franklin had a hand in it, he denies it."[17]

Outside the Congress, the reaction was generally far bolder. Whether intended or not, Paine had succeeded in outflanking the very body that was supposed to be the mouthpiece of the American colonists. Its effects were not universal, but converts to *Common Sense* were to be found in all walks of life, among the literate and nonliterate of virtually every village, farm, and town of the thirteen colonies. Throughout the colonies, letters to newspapers quoted *Common Sense*, excerpts were reprinted from it, and hundreds of readers lauded its style and contents. "Who is the author of *Common Sense?*" asked a Newport reader. "I can hardly refrain from adoring him. He deserves a statue of Gold."[18]

By July 1776, few people had not read or heard of its arguments. Benjamin Rush recalled, "Its effects were sudden and extensive upon the American mind. It was read by public men, repeated in clubs, spouted in Schools, and in one instance, delivered from the pulpit instead of a sermon by a clergyman in Connecticut."[19] A contemporary historian, William Gordon, agreed. He praised Paine's "stile, manner, and language," adding, "Nothing could have been better timed than this performance. . . . It has produced most astonishing effects; and been received with vast applause; read by almost every American; and recommended as a work replete with truth."[20]

Favorable reports even streamed in from outside the country. During August, Silas Deane, who at the time was the commercial agent for Congress in France, issued a report from Paris to the Committee of Secret Correspondence on the pamphlet's huge success there:

> The pamphlet called Common Sense has been translated, and has a greater run, if possible, here than in America. A person of distinction, writing to his noble friend in office, has these words: "Je pense comme vous, mon cher comte, que le *Common Sense* est une excellente ouvrage, et que son auteur est un des plus grand législateurs des millions d'écrivains, que nous connoissions; il n'est pas douteux, que si les Américains suivent le beau plan, que leur compatriote leur a tracé, ils deviendront la nation la plus florissante, et la plus heureuse, qui ait jamais existé." Thus freely do men think and write in a country long since deprived of the essentials of liberty. As I was favoured with a sight of the letter and permitted to make this extract, I thought it worth sending you as a key to the sentiments of some of the leading men.[21]

Why did *Common Sense* have such a profound impact in the American colonies? To say simply that it was the work of a genius is to beg the question. It might be said, ungenerously, that its success was due mainly to circumstantial factors, that, for example, it fell in with the prevailing tendency of the time, giving voice to political sentiments that were already in the hearts and on the minds of countless American colonists. In other words, *Common Sense* may have been the work of a journalist or political propagandist who used the standard pamphlet format to register and publicize what most people already knew.[22]

It is true that diffuse fears of tyranny had long ago been widespread among the American colonists, and that Paine therefore preached to many who were already half-converted. Paine's choice of the pamphlet form, which allowed him complete freedom of expression and cheap mass distribution, was also unoriginal. It is also a truism that there was an element of circumstantial luck working in favor of the pamphlet, which appeared in the right place at the right time. Earlier pamphlets suggesting American autonomy — the most prominent of which was John Cartwright's *American Independence, the Interest and Glory of Great Britain,* first published in 1774 — were victimized by the simple fact that they had appeared too early. And yet the idea that *Common Sense* rode high on a huge wave of public feeling ignores the way in which Paine had not only mastered the difficult art of political timing but also had the courage and insight to keep a few steps ahead of almost everybody else, daring to say publicly and differently what others had only whispered privately. "Independence a year ago could not have been publickly mentioned with impunity," wrote a Bostonian admirer of Paine to his London correspondent. "Nothing else is now talked of, and I know not what can be done by Great Britain to prevent it."[23] That observation revealed the extent to which Paine had not only divined but also *defined* his readers' views, strengthening their beliefs, detonating their prejudices, touching their hearts, changing their minds, convincing them that they must speak out and act. *Common Sense* helped spark a new spirit — youthful and reckless, obsessed with the new, willing to experiment with actualizing what had previously been considered unthinkable or impractical.

There were also things about the text itself that contributed to its huge success. The pamphlet was scurrilous, abusive, seditious, and written with enormous sparkle; it also cunningly nurtured the anti-Catholic language of Protestant Dissent, with the intention of making its readers feel in their hearts that British power in the American colonies amounted to an ancien régime riddled with feudal, monarchical, and clerical anachronisms.[24] No account of the extraordinary impact of *Common Sense* should also neglect its original attempt to transform its readers' sense of time. *Common Sense* had a gripping sense of urgency, attempting to convince its readers that these were extraordinary times and that the colonies were caught up in the throes of a profound emergency that called for urgent decisions. "The present time . . . is that peculiar time that never comes to a nation but once," warned Paine, as if he were seizing his readers by the scruff of their necks. He tried to reinforce that new sense of time by adopting a thoroughly plebeian style. Although his attack on the British was held together by complicated arguments and nuanced points, he wrote it so that it looked and sounded straightforward. Simplicity was for Paine an important attribute of the world — it was among the so-called principles of nature — and he thought that it was the duty of the political writer to mimic it. *Common Sense* was his most polished example thus far, as Thomas Jefferson noted: "No writer has exceeded Paine in ease and familiarity of style, in perspicuity of expression, happiness of elucidation, and in simple and unassuming language. In this he may be compared with Dr. Franklin; and indeed his *Common Sense* was, for a while, believed to have been written by Dr. Franklin."[25]

Monarchy

In addition to the brilliantly plain style, the striking originality of the political ideas within the text helped to magnetize American readers. *Common Sense* daringly argued several things powerfully for the first time in the American context. This originality helps to explain why, after its appearance, public discussion in the American colonies was never the same again. Conversations about politics changed direction. They became livelier and infused with an urgent sense of moral indignation. Everyone who read and was convinced by the pamphlet suddenly saw the world in a fundamentally different way. Britain and its monarchic-parliamentary institutions now seemed paltry, miserly, and aggressive. America — even the word now seemed free for the first time — seemed larger, more confident, and capable of governing itself, even serving as a model for the rest of the world.

Paine began his arguments in *Common Sense* by hurling sharp abuse at the institution of monarchy. He was not the first to do this in the American context. A decade earlier, for example, a Philadelphia stamp commissioner had complained to his London authorities that some "lower-class" Presbyterians were calling for "No King But King Jesus."[26] But Paine's more secular version of this idea was more subversive. It walloped the virtually unchallenged belief in America that the backbone of the British constitution, the Crown-in-Parliament, was the wellspring of liberty and good government. Paine also challenged the less common belief, expressed at the time by Thomas Jefferson, that the institution of the British monarchy was essentially benign but that George III should strive to "resume the exercise of his negative power, and to prevent the passage of laws by any one legislature of the empire which might bear injuriously on the rights and interests of another."[27]

Paine disagreed with the whole idea of petitioning or putting trust in "good kings." He was adamant that the institution of monarchy was rotten to the core. The British constitution was weighed down by monarchical tyranny in the person of King George III, whose origins were traceable to William the Conqueror, whom Paine described as a "French bastard landing with an armed banditti and establishing himself king of England against the consent of the natives."[28]

Paine conceded that there was something special about the British monarchy. During the English Revolution of the 1640s, the parliamentary forces had permanently humbled the monarchy, making subsequent kings afraid that they might share the fate of Charles I. But the aim of the Revolution had not been achieved: "[T]hough we have been wise enough to shut and lock a door against absolute Monarchy, we at the same time have been foolish enough to put the crown in possession of the key." The British state, while not a harsh despotism of, say, the Turkish kind, was actually on a continuum with France, Spain, Russia, and other monarchical governments, which had in common several bad qualities.

Monarchs, Paine argued, are always despots, and monarchies are always despotisms. Established originally through conquest and plunder, all monarchs suffer from a craving for absolute power. Power begets the hunger for power and, hence, a striving for the means of ensuring that that power is unchallengeable, insulated against its opponents. This power hunger has destructive effects for everyone concerned. Repeating a thought he once expressed to Henry Verral while on the Lewes bowling green, Paine pointed out that those who think they are born to reign and all others are born to obey soon grow insolent. The pride of kings throws the world into confusion and war: "Monarchy and succession have laid . . . the world in blood and ashes."

But monarchic power is not only dangerous and destructive, wrote Paine. It also is plain silly. This is partly because monarchy is a form of government suffering from a permanent legitimacy problem. It is constantly hard-pressed to give convincing reasons in public for its superiority or even its raison d'être. Paine attacked the view, still widespread in the eighteenth century, that monarchy had a basis in Christianity, and he was scathing toward all versions of the doctrine of the divine right of kings and queens. The biblical texts were unequivocal, he argued: "The will of the Almighty as declared by Gideon, and the prophet Samuel, expressly disapproves of government by kings." And again: "*Render unto Cesar the things which are Cesar's,* is the scripture doctrine of courts, yet it is no support of monarchical government, for the Jews at that time were without a king, and in a state of vassalage to the Romans."

Furthermore, Paine saw monarchy as laughable because it tends to operate in ridiculous ways. Monarchy is government based on ignorance, not wisdom, since monarchs are generally cocooned in a court of pomp and appearance, and therefore cut off from sources of information so vital to wise decision making. "The state of a king," Paine wrote, "shuts him from the world, yet the business of a king requires him to know it thoroughly." Kings attempt to camouflage their blindness in displays of pomp, fine clothing, extravagant riches, bribery, favoritism, and the insistence that their subjects pay them "idolatrous homage." But, he continued, the practice of hereditary succession, an intrinsic feature of monarchy, typically takes its revenge on such deceptions. The subjects of monarchies inherit not leaders but asses who plunge everything they handle into folly. Paine here turned the tables on Thomas Hobbes, the famous English political philosopher of the previous century, whose classic *Leviathan* (1651) spelled out the case for a form of hereditary government as the basis for a strong state capable of preventing outbreaks of violence and civil war. Paine upended this claim, insisting that hereditary power is foolish, blind, and prone to violence. "Of more worth," he concluded, "is one honest man to society, and in the sight of God, than all the crowned ruffians that ever lived."

Civil Society Against the State

Such arguments felt transgressive to many readers at the time. In a few pages, Paine lampooned the whole history of the venerated institution of monarchy, rendering its familiarity strange, making it feel distant, silly, pretentious, profligate, and unworthy of its pompous power. The trimmings of monarchic power — escorts of soldiers, splendid clothing, sparkling crowns and scepters, elaborate rites of passage, obelisks, arches, columns, fountains, and a fine palace in the heart of the leading city — suddenly seemed trivial and passé. But Paine's savaging of monarchy had a more positive and altogether original effect. *Common Sense* was the first political essay in modern times to make and defend the distinction —

now enjoying renewed popularity two centuries after Paine — between civil society and the state.

Until the publication of *Common Sense*, these two terms were coterminous. Without exception, European and American political writers used the term *civil society* to describe a type of political association that ensured good government and peaceful order by placing its members under the influence of its laws. The term *civil society* formed part of an old European tradition traceable from modern natural law back through Cicero's ideas of *societas civilis* to classical political philosophy, and above all to Aristotle, for whom civil society (*koinōnia politiké*) is that society, the *polis,* which encompasses and dominates all others.[29] In this old European tradition, *civil society* and *political community* or *state* were interchangeable terms. To be a member of a civil society was to be a member of the political community — and, hence, obliged to act in accordance with its laws, but without performing acts harmful to other citizen members of the political community.

Common Sense treated this terminology as dead language. It disconnected the civil society–state couplet so that civil society ("society" or "civilized society" were his preferred terms) and the state (more frequently he spoke of "government") were seen as different, though related, entities. According to Paine, citizens should not turn to politicians for everything. The power of government must be limited in favor of civil society, because within all individuals, who are created equal in the eyes of God, there is a natural propensity for society. This natural sociability existed before the formation of states, and it predisposes individuals to build happy relations of peaceful competition and solidarity based on reciprocal self-interest and a shared sense of mutual aid. "Society in every state is a blessing,"[30] Paine argued, quickly adding that because individuals sometimes resist the voice of conscience and common sense, government is a necessary evil. That is to say, civil society is an unqualified good, whereas "government, like dress, is the badge of lost innocence." It follows that the more perfect civil society is, the more it regulates its own affairs and the less occasion it has for government. Government, Paine concluded, is nothing more than a delegation of power for the common benefit of society. Its proper function is to secure the liberties of citizens living within civil society against their enemies at home and abroad.

Guided by this truly original idea of "civil society versus the state," Paine proposed that each American colony's nascent civil society merge into a broadly based civil society on a continental scale. "Now is the seedtime of Continental union," he wrote. "'Tis not the affair of a City, a

County, a Province, or a Kingdom; but of a Continent — of at least one eighth part of the habitable Globe." Paine went on to link this proposed transcontinental society with the idea of the rights of citizens. In Paine's view, citizens who live within civil society possess the inalienable natural right to determine for themselves how they wish to live and be governed. Listening only to the voices of reason and conscience — Paine always understood these faculties as ultimately natural entities rather than as acquired capacities — individuals must set aside forever the old assumption that kings and queens are gods to whose words everyone must listen in awe, bowing and scraping in agreement. Individuals themselves, Paine urged, can and should become earthly gods, living under a chosen government whose ultimate purpose is the enhancement of their "freedom and security."

In saying this, Paine did not accept the call of his French contemporary Jean-Jacques Rousseau for the establishment of small, self-governing city-states modeled on ancient Greece. According to Paine, vast distances, expanding populations, and the growing complexity of public affairs rendered the doctrine of face-to-face self-government obsolete, or at least in need of amendment. Modern citizens should organize themselves into local, self-governing "societies." But in large political communities, they must necessarily rely on mechanisms of *representative* government. In turn, the body of citizens should consider themselves a nation, an independent and sovereign body that speaks a certain language, shares certain customs, lives within a given territory, and is entitled to establish a state, managed by elected representatives who are under an obligation to express the will of the nation on behalf of the nation.

The recommendation that nations be seen as sovereign bodies of citizens living within a civil society guaranteed by representative government contained a glimpse of a future world order, or so Paine thought. Since no one national body of citizens could pretend to be coterminous with humankind, each nation was required to live within a global system of interlocking states and sovereign societies. Paine's vision was at odds with the view, argued in Parliament by Lord Thomas Lyttelton in reply to Edmund Burke's plea for conciliation, that parliamentary sovereignty meant "that all inferior assemblies in this Empire were only like the corporate towns in England, which had a power, like them, of making bye-laws for their own municipal government, and nothing more."[31] Like a sharpened knife, Paine's doctrine of national self-determination cut through such talk of superior and inferior assemblies. It also slashed to shreds the compromise view, defended by Joseph Galloway of Philadelphia and others, that there could be a revised, equal partnership between the American colonies and the British Parliament — for example, by establishing an American legislature that would function as something like a third house of Parliament responsible for "the general policy and affairs of the colonies."[32] Paine's doctrine implied an altogether different, revolutionary conclusion: the American nation, hitherto viewed as an inferior "municipal" entity, was now morally and legally entitled to declare itself independent of the sovereign British state and its empire.

Resisting Independence

Paine anticipated that many readers would be startled by his conclusion that "the time hath found us" and that a "government of our own is our natural right."[33] He therefore moved quickly to defend his conclusion against several possible objections. Into the faces of those who were still attached by sentiment to the British Empire Paine flung the words of John Milton, whom he had read as a boy in Thetford: "Never can true reconcilement grow where wounds of deadly hate have pierced so deep." He reminded fainthearts and waverers of the mounting violence perpetrated by the British against the American nation: "Hath your property been destroyed before your face? Are your wife and children destitute of a bed to lie on, or bread to live on? Have you lost a parent or a child by their hands, and yourself the ruined and wretched survivor?" To those who feared economic ruin as the poisonous fruit of independence, Paine shunned the old reply that lean liberty is better than fat slavery. He instead predicted that American independence would find strong support among English manufacturers and traders, who would see, correctly, that peace with trade was preferable to war with stagnation. He added that the uncertainty caused by disturbances in America was bad for commerce, which thrives on the predictability that would come from peace with independence. Besides, independence would guarantee America a free hand in Europe's markets for corn and other agricultural products: "America would have flourished as much, and probably much more, had no European power taken any notice of her. The commerce by which she hath enriched herself are the necessaries of life, and will always have a market while eating is the custom of Europe."[34]

Paine also met head-on the objection that only within the British Empire could the American colonies be protected militarily from their enemies. Paine retorted — in language that has been repeated by virtually every subsequent critic of empires and colonies — that the British had only defended America out of self-interest. He accused the British of repeatedly dragging the American continent into wars originating in Europe. America performed the role of a pawn in the power games of European kings and queens: "Any submission to, or dependence on, Great Britain, tends directly to involve this continent in European wars and quarrels, and set us at variance with nations who would otherwise seek our friendship, and against whom we have neither anger nor complaint." In any event, Paine continued, America already had sufficient technical means of defending itself, including the capacity to lead the world in ship-building and the manufacture of war materials such as rope, iron, small arms, cannon, saltpeter, and gunpowder.

Finally, Paine tried to score a geopolitical point against the military-minded critics of independence. There was something geographically and politically unnatural about America's dependence on Britain, he wrote. Distance reinforced by poor communications made the centers of government power remote from American citizens. The idea was expressed in an early draft of *Common Sense*, read to Benjamin Rush, in which Paine mocked the absurdity of "three millions of people flocking to the American shore every time a vessel arrives from England, to know what portion of liberty they shall enjoy." In the final printed version, Paine toughened the point: "To be always running three or four thousand miles with a tale or a petition, waiting four or five months for an answer, which, when obtained, requires five or six more to explain it in, will in a few years be looked upon as folly and childishness."

All these arguments for American sovereignty Paine drew together with a final stirring anthem for American citizens. "The cause of America," he urged, "is in a great measure the cause of all mankind." He painted the American cause in the boldest terms by claiming that America could now become not only the first enclave of republican liberty in the modern world but also a safe haven from which the friends of republican liberty could spread their campaign for free and equal citizenship to the rest of the world. America must strive to be the future; otherwise, it would be nothing. Paine's stunning words quickly became famous: "O! ye that love mankind! Ye that dare oppose not only the tyranny but the tyrant, stand forth! Every spot of the old world is overrun with oppression. Freedom hath been hunted round the globe. Asia and Africa have long expelled her. Europe regards her like a stranger, and England hath given her warning to depart. O! receive the fugitive, and prepare in time an asylum for mankind."

But how exactly could America become a land of republican liberty?

Through ethical appeals directed at the uncommitted in America and Britain and at America's potential allies? By means of diplomatic negotiations and behind-the-scenes bargaining? Using muskets, cannon, swords, and gunboats? Paine did not say directly. Although he probably considered all these methods necessary, *Common Sense* offered two additional strategies that mark it once again as the genuinely pathbreaking pamphlet of the opening phases of the American Revolution.

The first is today called "people power." Paine formulated it in simple terms, but the idea was profoundly original in the history of European political thought: "'Tis not in numbers but in unity that our great strength lies; yet our present numbers are sufficient to repel the force of all the world." This simple sentence contains something of a Copernican revolution in the field of politics. The power to shape the world, Paine supposed, does not derive ultimately from rulers or their monopoly of the means of violence. Rulers surrounded by spies, police, jurists, tax collectors, generals, and administrators cannot rule for very long. Power ultimately emanates from below. Rulers can rule only insofar as they have the tacit or active support of the ruled. Without it, they become impotent in the face of citizens acting together in solidarity for the achievement of their own common goals. Paine's maxim was designed to awaken the power potential of the powerless, to help them put their finger on a fundamental rule of republican democratic politics. In fact, Paine said, citizens must not be afraid of the powerful because institutions such as governments cannot rest for long on the ends of their bayonets or muskets, the lies on the tips of their tongues, or the jobs, money, or influence they dispense. If these same citizens, when faced with arbitrary exercises of power, stand erect, claim their dignity, and exercise their rights, the powerful will quickly lose their balance. Their words will become muddled, they will tumble into confusion, and they will appear to others as laughable, pathetic creatures.

Paine's confidence that independence could be won this way was not naive. He understood, again with considerable originality, that people power can be misappropriated. *Common Sense* proposed that the will to power, far from being an obsession of the strong, is also among the dangerous vices of the weak. Revolutions made by citizens acting together are always breeding grounds for power-hungry groups and self-appointed elites. It illustrated the maxim that revolutions made in the name of liberty carry within them the seeds of tyranny by pointing to the case of the seventeenth-century fisherman-turned-tyrant Tomasso Aniello, otherwise known as Massaniello. Paine explained that Massaniello, after stirring up the inhabitants of Naples in their marketplace and appealing to their basest passions through demagogic speeches directed against their Spanish conquerors, led the Neapolitans into revolt. But in the space of a day, he became their self-appointed king. Paine warned, "If we omit it now, some Massan[i]ello may hereafter arise, who, laying hold of popular disquietudes, may collect together the desperate and the discontented, and by assuming to themselves the powers of government, finally sweep away the liberties of the continent like a deluge."

Paine anticipated, correctly, that the American disturbances would produce a revolution, in the course of which there would be battles between power groups making incompatible claims to control its overall direction. With astounding prescience, he saw that modern revolutions can be likened to periods of fever and delirium, during which the body politic suffers convulsions caused by vicious power struggles and attempts by the best-organized, most ruthless revolutionists to crush their opponents and get rid of fainthearts, silent types, and other "enemies of the revolution." *Common Sense* proposed a remedy for such threats to citizens' freedom and equality. It argued for strict controls to be placed on the exercise of power by Americans during their struggle for independence. Paine's proposals were self-consciously modest ("I only presume to offer hints, not plans"), but their direction was clear and can be summarized as follows: Those who want roses must watch the thorns. Fight for independence, but tame the delirium and viciousness sparked off by that struggle by relying as much as possible on constitutional means designed to check and balance the exercise of power.

What mechanisms did Paine have in mind? He quoted from Giacinto Dragonetti's *A Treatise on Virtues and Rewards* (1769) to drive home the point that America now required "a mode of government that contained the greatest sum of individual happiness, with the least national expense." Specifically, he called for a two-tiered, federated system of state power that would privilege the rule of law and help citizens maintain respect for their civil and political liberties. In addition to the existing colonial or provincial level of government, Paine argued, America required a new "continental form of government" that would both subdivide the institutions of state power — making it harder for American Massaniellos to come to office — and create a new level of elected, accountable government that would be sovereign, in the sense that it would serve to protect the provinces and their citizens against internal and external threats.

Paine was adamant that the new federal system should dispense with all the trimmings and trappings of monarchy. In place of the unrepresentative and corrupt Crown-in-Parliament system of the British, a republican system of government should be installed. Since republicans are not immune from knavery and the seductive charms of power, the lust for its monopoly being universal, both tiers of the new American federal system must be subject to frequent, periodic elections, which would help ensure that governors do not stand above the law, suffocate the rights of citizens, or violate the spirit of the commonweal. Paine was quite specific. A "continental conference" should be held to discuss and decide the precise future form of government of the united colonies. The conference would comprise two delegates appointed by each of the thirteen colonial legislatures and five delegates elected in each of those provinces by a secret ballot among all "qualified voters."

Paine did not specify who these voters might be and why some citizens were to be considered unqualified to vote. He instead devoted his energy to urging the conference delegates to give priority to the details of building a new federal system of state power that would be founded, at the provincial level, on annually elected unicameral assemblies set up specifically to consider "domestic business." Each assembly, the offspring of the old colonial assemblies, would elect a president and be subject to the authority — in which matters Paine did not say — of the federal government, the Continental Congress. This new level of government would comprise a minimum of 390 annually elected representatives, with each province contributing at least 30. Its deliberations, covering matters of common concern to the provinces as a whole, would be subject to a three-fifths majority rule. Each year the Congress would elect a president from among the delegates of one of the thirteen provinces. And each year the provinces would take turns putting forth their own candidates for election to the presidency.

Friends and Enemies

The success of these key propositions of *Common Sense* was astonishing. Although sales of the pamphlet were extraordinary, the real measure of its success was the bitter public debates, splits, and constitutional controversies it spawned. Records of most of these disputes have disappeared with time, but the remaining traces of evidence suggest just how much excitement and opposition Paine stirred up. Nine days after the publication of *Common Sense*, Nicholas Cresswell, an English gentleman traveling through Virginia, entered the following words in his diary: "A pamphlet called 'Commonsense' makes a great noise. One of the vilest things that ever was published to the world. Full of false representations, lies, calumny and treason whose principles are to subvert all Kingly Governments and erect an Independent Republic. I believe the writer to be some Yankey Presbyterian, Member of the Congress. The sentiments are adopted by a great number of people who are indebted to Great Britain."[35]

Elsewhere, reactions were more heated. On February 1, Daniel Dulany wrote from Annapolis, Maryland, to Robert Carter denouncing the pamphlet, which he considered the work of John Adams, as full of "extravagant, nonsensical tenets." He predicted that its arguments would have "as little Influence in the other Colonies, as they have here, where they have rec'ed their merited Contempt."[36] On February 14, Colonel Landon Carter confided to his diary that the pamphlet "is quite scandalous and disgraces the American cause much." For the next two months, he expressed nothing but "detestation" of "Common Sense, which is so violent for Independency."[37] Others in high places agreed. In March, Benjamin Franklin's son, William, the Tory governor of New Jersey and a vocal opponent of independence, begrudgingly admitted to Lord George Germain, the colonial secretary, that "the Minds of a great Number of People have been much changed in that respect since the Publication of a most inflammatory Pamphlet in which the horrid Measure is strongly and artfully recommended." Franklin added that the pamphlet would have the paradoxical "one good Effect . . . of opening the Eyes of many People of Sense & Property."[38]

It did indeed have that effect. But people of "Sense and Property" became bitterly divided, and that crumbling of imperial support was bad news for the British. A typical scene of confusion erupted in the provincial congress of South Carolina, which on February 10 was debating a committee report, presented by Colonel Henry Laurens, on the reform of the provincial government. According to an eyewitness, trouble began when Colonel Christopher Gadsden, who had just returned to Charleston after leaving the Continental Congress in Philadelphia to join his regiment, strode into the assembly, brandishing a copy of *Common Sense*. Before speaking, Gadsden presented the assembly with a handmade yellow flag bearing an image of a black-brown rattlesnake in the center with the inscription "DON'T TREAD ON ME." According to the observer, Gadsden then "boldly declared himself, not only in favour of the form of government; but for the absolute Independence of America. A distinguished member [John Rutledge] . . . declared he abhorred the idea; and that he was willing to ride post, by day and night, to Philadelphia, in order to assist in re-uniting Great Britain and America: and another [Colonel Henry Laurens] called the author of Common Sense, ———."[39]

Paine probably heard about some of these attacks by word of mouth. He certainly knew about the attacks in print, which seemed almost as numerous. Within a few weeks of the publication of *Common Sense*, a ponderous pamphlet by James Chalmers called *Plain Truth* appeared, bitterly attacking Paine's arguments in the name of the English constitution, "the pride and envy of mankind." A flood of others quickly followed, the most important of which — measured in terms of its principled disagreement and permanent influence on American institutions — was a pamphlet by John Adams, *Thoughts on Government*.[40]

In correspondence, Adams had already laid into Paine: "'Common Sense,' by his crude ignorant Notion of a Government by one Assembly, will do more Mischief, in dividing the Friends of Liberty, than all the Tory Writings together. He is a keen Writer but very ignorant of the Science of Government."[41] In *Thoughts on Government*, Adams agreed with Paine's insistence on the necessity of independence and America's ability to maintain it. He also agreed that in an "extensive country," direct assembly of the whole population was out of the question and government by elected representatives was essential. But Adams strongly criticized Paine's tendency to preserve the monarchic assumption that power ultimately rests in a single sovereign body. In effect, Adams accused Paine of treating the nation or the people as a substitute for the sovereign monarch. In so doing, Paine had overlooked the fact that the people and popular assemblies, like monarchs, are avaricious and fickle, "productive of hasty results and absurd judgments." The organization of government, wrote Adams, "ought to be more complex" than a unicameral assembly. Adams's pamphlet concluded with a strong plea for a federal government of checks and balances based on a bicameral legislature, an independent judiciary of "men of learning, legal experience, and wisdom," and a veto-wielding executive, chosen annually by both houses of the legislature. The point was that Paine's "democratical" idea of concentrating all power in unicameral legislatures at the provincial and federal levels was dangerous. Power, no matter who exercised it, implied the probability of doing harm. The aim must, therefore, be to create an American republic in which the will of the people was expressed but also controlled and refined.

Apparently, the criticism flung Paine into a bad temper. Long afterward, his adverse reaction was recorded in Adams's *Autobiography*, which reveals something of Paine's lifelong conceit. Adams's faulty memory and subsequent hostility toward Paine admittedly may have led him to exaggerate the episode. But his account of Paine's unsaintly, headstrong reaction to criticism is nonetheless important, since it exposes both Paine's greatest personal strength — his ability to push forward, against all odds, in a class-ridden and undemocratic age — and his greatest personal weakness — his extraordinary knack for making enemies, weakening his own credibility and attracting ridicule. Adams recalled how shortly after the appearance of his pamphlet, Paine had hurried over to Adams's lodgings at Mrs. Yard's boardinghouse in Philadelphia. "His business was to reprehend me for publishing my pamphlet," Adams said. Paine was visibly agitated. He spent much of the evening pacing the floor of Adams's room, "remonstrating" against his published criticism and insisting that "he was afraid it would do hurt, and that it was repugnant to the plan that he had proposed, in *Common Sense*." Paine told Adams that he simply did not see the point of perpetuating the English system of a "balance between contending powers." That political system, after all, rested on a divided hierarchy of social wealth and power. In America, by contrast, the people would rule politically *and* socially. The established church, landed aristocracy, and monarchy would be no more. Why, then, should the power of the people be hamstrung by separately functioning structures of government? Who or what would a second chamber or executive represent? Surely the people did not need to be represented twice or thrice over?

Paine's attack on his critic's "repugnant" reasoning made no headway. Adams was tough with Paine. "I told him that it was true it was repugnant, and for that reason I had written it and consented to the publication of it; for I was as much afraid of his publication as he was of mine." Adams made it clear that he was in favor of separating and dividing power that its exercise could be controlled. Paine had not heeded his own warnings about Massaniellos in the American context. He seemed blasé about the dangers of "the people," or at least a majority of voters or their representatives, abusing their power. The plan for a future American republic sketched in *Common Sense* "was so democratical without any restraint or even an attempt at any equilibrium or counterpoise, that it must produce confusion and every evil work."[42]

Paine had not heard that type of criticism of his politics before. Today suspicion of power, even power exercised by "the people," is often regarded as a hallmark of democracy. It was not seen as such in Paine's day.[43] Adams saw himself as keeping apart the conflicting ideals of republicanism and democracy. Democracy, he thought, denoted the lowest orders of society, as well as the form of government in which the popular assembly ruled. As a system of government, democracy always threatened civil disorder and the restoration of order through the power of tyrants. Democracy invariably bred tyranny.

What Paine thought of this conventional wisdom about democracy is unrecorded. *Common Sense* did not use the term, and there is not a scrap of evidence that when Paine referred to "the people" or to "citizens," he literally meant every adult male and female, rich and poor, black and white, native born and immigrant. Still, the dispute with Adams had long-term significance because, whether Paine knew it or not, his stubborn appeal to undivided popular sovereignty helped to drag republican politics a few yards toward democracy, in the sense that Paine announced his intention to widen the definition of who counted as citizens. By appealing to "the rights of mankind" and likening America to "a large and young family" of citizens needing to defend themselves against a stupid burglar, Paine signaled the need to marry the ideals of republicanism and democracy, to advance republican principles against oligarchy in any form. That is why, as Adams himself noted, *Thoughts on Government* was so heartily disliked by Franklin, Paine, and other supporters of the Radical party in Pennsylvania, who considered it disguised loyalism, a wooden horse for the preservation of monarchy. The dispute not only pointed to the eventual democratization of republican politics, with Paine on the winning side. It also raised a matter that has recurred constantly in modern revolutions: whether breaking the back of the ancien régime by revolutionary means should take priority, for a time at least, over the task of taming the exercise of all power, including that exercised by the revolutionaries themselves. Looking back on the dispute, Adams considered that his views had influenced the framing of the constitutions of New York, North Carolina, Virginia, New Jersey, and other states. He conceded that "Matlack, Young, Cannon, and Paine had influence enough" to get their "democratical" plans adopted in Pennsylvania, Georgia, and Vermont. "These three States," he remarked proudly, "have since found them such systems of anarchy . . . that they have altered them and made them more conformable to my plan."[44]

Despite their bitter confrontation in private, Paine and Adams remained friends. In public, they remained loyal to the cause of independence, and Adams always used superlatives when speaking about Paine. Five days after completing a new appendix to *Common Sense* on February 14, 1776, in which the arguments against the British were repeated in tougher language, Paine set off by coach for New York, carrying letters of introduction to General Charles Lee from Adams, Benjamin Franklin, and Benjamin Rush (who described Paine as "the celebrated author of *Common Sense*"). The letter written by Adams was particularly glowing: "I took up my pen only to introduce to your acquaintance a countryman of yours, a Citizen of the World to whom a certain Heretical Pamphlet called Common Sense is imputed. His name is Paine. He is travelling to N. York for his Curiosity and wishes to See a Gentm. whose character he so highly regards."[45]

Adams's reference helped boost Paine's reputation. During their first dinner together, Paine and General Lee, two transplanted Englishmen from different class backgrounds, got along well. "I hope he will continue cramming down the throats of squeamish mortals his wholesome truths," Lee reported to Rush. "His conversation has much life. He has genius in his eyes."[46] Paine returned the compliment, praising Lee's "great fund of military knowledge" and his "sarcastic genius," a kind phrase for the cantankerous general. The phrase could as well have been applied to Paine himself and perhaps explains why the two men, whose similar temperaments always produced sparks when rubbed against each other, never nurtured their acquaintance into a genuine friendship. In any event, Paine quickly found other admirers in New York. It is probable that gossip, a step or two ahead of him, spread the news that he was the author of *Common Sense*. There was certainly much talk of the pamphlet during his stay in the city. In the first of a series of four letters to the *New York Journal and General Advertiser*, an enthusiast called "An Independent Whig" waxed eloquent: "I have just finished the second reading of that incomparable pamphlet — 'Common Sense' addressed to the inhabitants of North America. Whether like many other productions, it has more than one author is of no consequence. You can scarce put your fingers to a single page, but you are pleased, though, it may be, startled, with the sparks of original genius."[47]

That opinion spread during Paine's stay in New York, causing local tempers to boil. Late one evening in mid-March, a demonstration of about forty pro-independence patriots, led by Peter Duyckinck, chairman of the local Committee of Mechanicks, descended on the home and printing rooms of the New York publisher Samuel Loudon. Along the grapevine, the radical artisans had learned that Loudon was printing an anonymous government-sponsored reply to Paine. They suspected, correctly, that it had been written by the loyalist assistant rector of Trinity Church, Charles Inglis, who considered *Common Sense* "shocking to the ears of Americans." It was among the "most artful, insidious and pernicious pamphlets" ever printed, wrote Inglis, and it served as such "an outrageous insult on the common sense of Americans" that its effect "must infallibly prove ruinous." Inglis's reply at times degenerated into wild rhetoric. "Even Hobbes would blush to own the author for a disciple," he snapped. "He unites the violence and rage of a republican with all the enthusiasm and folly of the fanatic. . . . This author's proposal, instead of removing our grievances, would aggravate them a thousand fold. The remedy is infinitely worse than the disease. It would be like cutting off a leg, because the toe happened to ache."[48]

The demonstrators gathered outside Loudon's quickly grew impatient. "Who is the author of the pamphlet you are printing, and who gave you the manuscript?" growled Duyckinck. "I do not know the author," Loudon replied. "I received the manuscript from a gentleman of this city, whose name, in my opinion, you have no right to demand." With that reproach, the demonstrators ran amok. They pushed their way upstairs to Loudon's printing office, seized the entire edition — fifteen hundred copies in all — and marched off to a local common, where the copies were burned to cinders.[49]

Pennsylvania Politics

Back in Philadelphia, events quickened. Inspired by Paine's pamphlet, moves were made to overthrow the loyalist-dominated Assembly and to ensure that Pennsylvania's delegates to Congress supported the cause of independence. Support for a break with Britain was already strong and growing among the poor and the urban artisans, who were in the process of developing leadership and organizing to win the vote. Opposition to the Assembly and, potentially, support for independence also were developing in the western counties of Pennsylvania. This was especially true of those areas settled by the Scotch-Irish, who were described by one contemporary observer as "the most God-provoking Democrats on this side of Hell."[50]

The Scotch-Irish resented the system of unequal representation and considered the Quaker-dominated Assembly to be unsupportive of their attempts to repel attacks by the Native American population of the region. A clean break with Britain, or so they and their radical supporters thought, would inevitably widen the suffrage and strengthen representation for the peripheral counties. The Allens, Shippens, Burds, Penns, and other Quaker men of wealth and power would then be outvoted by the poor, the city artisans, and the Presbyterian middle-class yeoman farmers.[51] The conservative forces in favor of reconciliation were nevertheless formidable — and vocal. Their opening shot against *Common Sense* had been fired on January 20 by a meeting of Quaker representatives, who voted to publish a four-page leaflet acknowledging their "just and necessary subordination to the king, and those who are lawfully placed in au-

thority under him." The Quakers bemoaned the "calamities and afflictions" which now surrounded them. Their solution was suitably obscure:
"When a man's ways please the Lord, he maketh even his enemies to be at
peace with him."[52]

Paine snapped back. He described the Quaker leaders as "ye fallen,
cringing, priest and Pemberton ridden people."[53] He also tried hard to
promote splits within the Quakers' ranks. Young Friends especially showed
signs of sympathy for independence, and some dissident Quakers had already formed themselves into a body called the Free Quakers. Paine
moved to foster this trend by accusing the Quaker representatives of ille-
gitimately mixing religion and politics, of being unrepresentative of wider
Quaker opinion, and of failing to see that a permanent peace within the
American body politic required cutting out the source of unrest by separating from Britain. That meant using defensive force: "We fight neither
for revenge nor conquest; neither from pride nor passion; we are not insulting the world with our fleets and armies, nor ravaging the globe for
plunder. Beneath the shade of our own vines are we attacked; in our own
houses, and on our own lands, is the violence committed against us."
Paine backed up this point on theological grounds by accusing the Tory
Quakers of contradicting their own principles. If it was true that the Lord
grants the gift of peacemaking to men with whom he is pleased, then that
implied that the Lord was not at all pleased with the British government.
If that was so — on this point Paine's quill moved with cocksure skill —
then Quakers who lived up to their professed principles would perforce
draw the conclusion that the violent troublemakers should be opposed, in
order to please the Lord and to seek his blessing of peace on earth.[54]

The controversy surrounding *Common Sense* quickly broadened into a
bitter political struggle to define the future of Pennsylvania. For the first
time in his life, Paine found himself bobbing about in a sea of public accusations and counteraccusations, his daily life coming to resemble a
rowdy meeting at the Headstrong Club writ large. A fortnight after his
reply to the Quakers, he received a severe tongue-lashing when four
Philadelphia newspapers carried the first in a series of eight letters by
"Cato" addressed "To the People of Pennsylvania."[55]

Speaking on behalf of Pennsylvania's wealthy merchants and landed
aristocratic opponents of independence, the author tried to strike down
Common Sense with a venomous display of what roast beef Tories like Dr.
Johnson would have called "a bottom of good sense." "Cato" (everyone
suspected that the author was in fact the Reverend Dr. William Smith, an
Anglican clergyman and provost of the College of Philadelphia[56]) claimed

that "nine-tenths of the people of Pennsylvania yet abhor the doctrine" defended by Paine. "Cato" insisted that the tensions with Britain were no more serious than a lovers' quarrel. He consequently railed against talk of a constitutional convention and urged that the colonies should patiently cooperate with the forthcoming peace plans of Lord North. "Upon such a footing, we may again be happy. Our trade will be revived. Our husband-men, our mechanics, our articers will flourish. Our language, our laws and manners being the same with those of the nation with which we are again to be connected, that connection will be natural."[57]

"Cato" warned his American readers that the proponents of independence were secretly working for foreign interference in the American colonies and that this might well come in the form of armed intervention by Catholic Spain or Catholic France. The letters bitterly criticized "interested writers, and strangers intermeddling in our affairs" and ended by pouncing on the "inconsistencies and contradictions" of the core ideas of *Common Sense* on the origins of government, hereditary monarchy, the distinction between civil society and government, and the British constitution. The author's fear of "democracy" was overwhelming. "It is a mistake," he wrote, echoing not only John Adams but also Montesquieu, John Locke, Polybius, and others, "to think that . . . the abuse of power is proper only to monarchies. Other forms of government are liable to this as well." *Common Sense* had forgotten the elementary truth that democracy dangerously concentrates power in the hands of the many. It failed to see that the unwritten British constitution perfectly embodied the vital contrary principle of the separation of powers. "All power lodged, uncontrouled, in *one* or *many*," "Cato" concluded, "has been shewn to be full of danger; lodged in *two* distinct bodies, they may chance to disagree long; but the addition of a *third* turns the scale; and further additions would only be clogs."[58]

The supporters of independence in Philadelphia — Timothy Matlack, Benjamin Franklin, David Rittenhouse, and Thomas Mifflin were among the most prominent — became worried by the length and eloquence of "Cato" 's reasoning. In mid-March, a group of them sent an urgent appeal to Paine to return from New York to fence against "Cato" 's quill.[59] Paine had probably already read a reprint of at least one of the letters in the *New York Gazette,* and always itching for a political argument, he willingly accepted the invitation, along with an offer of financial support from the group of Philadelphia "private gentlemen." The money was especially welcome, for Paine forfeited a handsome sum in royalties on *Common Sense* — one thousand pounds, he estimated[60] — by donating them to the

cause of the American patriots. During his stay in New York, he had
fallen into serious debt when two of his Philadelphia printers, Steiner &
Cist and B. Towne, demanded payment for the six thousand copies they
had printed at his own expense. This pattern was often to be repeated.
Throughout his life, Paine had difficulty handling money and balancing
accounts. Reckless generosity usually got the better of him and sooner or
later caused aggravation to donor and receiver alike.

This time he was rescued by his political supporters. Sent "by the hand
of Mr Christopher Marshall 108 dollars,"[61] Paine returned to Philadelphia, where, using the stipend to find room and board, he immediately set
to work on a new series of letters, beaming with confidence. His choice of
nom de guerre, "The Forester" (which had been used before in Lewes),
sounded less pompous and more plebeian than the "Humanus," "Atlanticus," and "Vox Populi" of the previous months. The pen name also underscored his commitment to resilience and courage in adversity, to
guiding American readers past the false trails and through the dense and
tangled undergrowth of British imperialism to the open sunlit spaces of
independence. He was immediately found out. "The Forester writes with
a spirit peculiar to himself," Abigail Adams told her husband, "and leads
me to think that he has an intimate acquaintance with Common Sense."[62]

It seemed not to matter, and probably even helped his cause, for the letters — the first of which appeared on April 1 in the *Pennsylvania Packet, or,
The General Advertiser* — were a huge success.[63] Paine began by likening
"Cato" 's epistles to an attempt to catch lions in a mousetrap. Fully
"gorged with absurdity, confusion, contradiction and the most notorious
and wilful falsehoods," they were bound to be rejected by the public. He
doubted "Cato" 's talk of patiently waiting on the British "ambassadors of
peace," instead describing them as "distributors of pardons, mischief, and
insult." Paine went on to make the point that the war against the Americans was not being conducted under the prerogative of the Crown alone,
as the British had previously done. This was a war conducted "under the
authority of the whole legislative power united," and a thoroughly corrupt
one at that. Like a viper in the bosom of the Americans, the imperial legislators had to be removed. This, Paine reiterated, was the point of the
Americans' struggle for independence. It must be seen as a practical expression of the principle of the sovereignty of the people, "whose right,
power, and property . . . may make such alterations in their mode of government as the change of times and things requires."

The second reply to "Cato" contained little that was new. Paine chose
instead to humiliate "Cato" with wit and sarcasm. "Cato's manner of

writing has as much order in it as the motion of a squirrel. He frequently writes as if he knew not what to write next, just as the other jumps about, only because it cannot stand still." He also attacked "Cato"'s heartlessness. "Cato" had made the mistake of comparing the recent behavior of the British to that of "a cruel stepdame." Paine pounced, saying, "Wonderful sensibility indeed! All the havoc and desolation of unnatural war; the destruction of thousands; the burning and depopulating of towns and cities; the ruin and separation of friends and families, are just sufficient to extort from Cato, *this one* callous confession." He concluded with words that echoed the Methodism of his English youth: "'Get thee behind me,' Cato, for thou hast not the feelings of a man."

Paine's third letter accused "Cato" of spreading false alarms about foreign invasion and repeated the point made in *Common Sense* that America should have nothing to do with the violent political intrigues of Europe. Violence, Paine insisted, is intrinsic to monarchies, whereas republics tend to produce peaceful order. Monarchies are riven by the plundering pride of kings and queens. Republics tend to be stable because they are responsive to the wishes of their public-spirited citizens. "In republican governments, the leaders of the people, if improper, are removable by vote; kings only by arms: an unsuccessful vote in the first case, leaves the voter safe; but an unsuccessful attempt in the latter, is death." Paine again projected his defense of republican principles into the international arena, summarizing Jean-Jacques Rousseau's *Jugement sur le Projet pour la paix perpetuelle de l'Abbé de Saint-Pierre* (published in 1761), which he had presumably read. Paine especially urged the formation of a "European Republic," whose member nations and governments would cooperate through a supranational "General Council" and, in cases of dispute, submit themselves to arbitration procedures rather than resorting to force of arms.

Toward Independence

The third letter to "Cato" concluded with a brief essay, "To the People," which was signed by "The Forester" and designed by Paine as an election-eve address. A week later, on May 1, 1776, Pennsylvania voted for a new assembly, expanded to include representatives from the backcountry areas that enjoyed a reputation of independent thinking. The stakes were high: if the radicals in favor of independence could break the grip of the moderates and Tories, Pennsylvania's delegates to Congress would throw their weight behind the struggle for independence. Paine did not mince words in the opening sentence of his essay: "*It is not a time to trifle.* . . . Reconcilia-

tion will not now go down, even if it were offered." Since America could
be happy only under a government of its own choosing, the singular task
remaining for each and every American citizen was to struggle for independence from the British. But Americans should not tarry, for the country "hath a blank sheet to write upon. Put it not off too long." Paine added
a striking footnote, forcing a comparison of the slavery of blacks and
whites in America: "Forget not the hapless African."[64]

The Pennsylvania election resulted in a general setback for the supporters of independence and a particularly humiliating defeat for Paine's
quill. In Philadelphia, three of the four pro-independence candidates
were defeated, while in the western counties opposition to the radicals
was much stronger than expected, even though they succeeded in electing nearly all their candidates. For the time being, the Pennsylvania Assembly remained in the hands of the friends of the British Empire. Paine
grumped for a few days, then set to work drafting the fourth and final of
the Forester letters. His aim was to deliver to his critics a no-nonsense re-
buttal. He urged the supporters of American independence to think and
act more radically. "We are got wrong . . . how shall we get right?" he
asked, ruling out any future acceptance of the authority of the Assembly
and its decisions. Describing the Assembly as a "dependent faction,"
Paine supposed that it functioned as the fickle agent of the British Empire. He hinted that it should therefore be bypassed. A new constitution
should be drawn up by a convention and a new government drawing its
power and authority from the people established: "The safest asylum, especially in times of general convulsion when no settled form of government prevails, is, *the love of the people.*" In Pennsylvania, heartland of
support for the British, the strategy of persuasion had failed; that left
only the overthrow of the government, preferably by nonviolent popular
power.[65]

On May 20, 1776, the day the letter was reprinted in the *Pennsylvania
Packet*, the radical Committee of the City and Liberties of Philadelphia
held a town meeting. Huddled together in the State House Yard, more
than seven thousand people, Paine included, stood silently in soaking rain
to hear speeches denouncing the Assembly and favoring independence.
Amid sustained applause and three hearty cheers, the meeting adopted a
"Protest" drafted by Timothy Matlack, Benjamin Rush, James Cannon,
Christopher Marshall, Paine, and others, which condemned any further
exercise of power by the Assembly that "derived from our mortal enemy
the King of Great-Britain."[66] The meeting further resolved unanimously
that the Assembly, having ignored the will of the citizens, had forfeited its

right to be recognized as the government of the state. It drew the revolutionary conclusion that the Assembly, which owed its existence to the Crown, should be replaced by a government emanating from the people. For this purpose, a constitutional convention should be called, the arrangements for which would be finalized by a conference of representatives of the city and county committees.[67]

Paine had every reason to be ecstatic. Three weeks later, the Pennsylvania Assembly buckled under the radicals' pressure, with Paine applauding. In the *Pennsylvania Packet* of June 10, 1776, an article signed by "A Watchman," and probably written by him, pointed out that by trying to dam up the rising tide of independence instead of directing it, the Assembly would now be swept away by it. "You have now forfeited the confidence of the people, by despising their authority," Paine concluded. "And you have furnished them with a suspicion that in taking up arms you yielded only to the violence of the times, or that you meant to fight for your offices, and not for your country."[68] Paine was right. On the very same day of receiving notification from Virginia that its delegates had been instructed to "declare the United Colonies free and independent," the Pennsylvania Assembly voted to appoint a committee to draft new instructions for its delegates to Congress. Its support for independence was imminent.

In Congress, discussions were moving toward the same conclusion. On June 7, 1776, Richard Henry Lee, acting on instructions sent from Virginia, successfully called on Congress to vote for a continental constitution and to establish commercial alliances with other nations. He also called for a declaration of independence. Paine's influence was paramount throughout the proceedings. *Common Sense* had called for the publication of an independence "manifesto" that would summarize "the miseries we have endured, and the peaceful methods which we have ineffectually used for redress," and it was made clear that "not being able any longer to live happily or safely under the cruel disposition of the British court, we had been driven to the necessity of breaking off all connections with her."[69] After some prevarication, Paine's reasoning prevailed. Congress agreed to appoint a five-man committee chaired by Thomas Jefferson and charged with the task of drafting an independence manifesto. A three-week moratorium on debate about independence was declared, and the committee was asked to report its findings on July 1.

Thrilled by the prospects of a declaration, Paine spent most of his time buttonholing congressmen, urging them to vote yes. There is no evidence that he had a hand in drafting the Declaration of Independence.[70] In fact, he wrote little or nothing during the lull in congressional business, his only publication being a slim pamphlet reprinted in the form of a fictional dialogue between a delegate to Congress who was reticent about voting for independence and General Richard Montgomery, who had been killed the previous year at Québec.[71] Speaking from firsthand experience of heaven, Montgomery tells the wavering delegate that Providence has designated America a special role on earth as the ark of liberty. Citing John Wilkes, Lord Grafton, and other English champions of American independence, Montgomery urges that a formal declaration of independence would benefit not only Americans and the people of Britain but also all nations on earth. Resistance to the despotic British Empire in America would enable the saplings of liberty to grow to maturity everywhere.

Paine did more than keep up pressure on Congress. Since the radicals in Congress were making common cause with the radicals in Pennsylvania, he also tracked every move made by the supporters and opponents of independence in that province. As the Congressional committee disappeared behind closed doors, the Pennsylvania radicals launched plans for a constitutional convention that would aim to bring about the collapse of the nearly century-old Pennsylvania legislature. Paine was not among the 108 delegates to the provincial conference who met on June 18 at Carpenters' Hall to finalize plans for a constitutional convention. But he certainly sympathized with the radicals' call for a convention and with the delegates' call to equalize representation among the counties. He also supported their pathbreaking decision to extend the vote to all adult males who had within the past year resided in Pennsylvania and paid taxes and who abjured all allegiance to Great Britain.[72]

Paine "had no hand in forming any part" of the new constitution that was later agreed at the Constitutional Convention in mid-July, "nor knew anything of its contents till I saw it published."[73] But again, he was on good terms with a number of the key delegates and was unquestionably sympathetic to the key resolutions of the convention. Several months before the meeting, he had remarked, for the benefit of the radicals, that if citizens were "not so perfectly free as they might to be," they had "both the *right* and the *power* to place even the whole authority of the Assembly in any body of men as they please; and whosoever is hardly enough to say to the contrary is an enemy to mankind."[74]

The same point was repeated in the *Pennsylvania Gazette* a week before Congress met to consider its stance on independence. Paine ridiculed the Pennsylvania Assembly for being unable to make up its mind about independence and concluded that it had no mandate from the people to govern. He described the conservative majority of Assembly delegates as incompetent and repeated the call for a Provincial Conference to draw up a new constitution. The conservatives had "deserted the public trust in a time of the greatest danger and difficulty. Like James the Second they have abdicated the government, and by their own act of desertion and cowardice have laid the Provincial Conference under the necessity of taking instant charge of affairs."[75] The essay appeared to many as a justification of the radicals' decision to withdraw from the Assembly, which died for lack of a quorum. Paine's radical attack reverberated in Congress as well. On July 2, three of the five Pennsylvania delegates present voted with the majority of congressmen to declare the American colonies free and independent states. Two days later, after considerable debate about details, Congress approved a revised version of Jefferson's Declaration of Independence, whose second paragraph told the world that "whenever any form of government becomes destructive . . . it is the right of the people to alter or to abolish it, and to institute new government, laying its foundation on such principle and organizing its powers in such form, as to them shall seem most likely to effect their safety and happiness." America had been born. The question was whether it could draw breath to survive.

5

War

Citizens' War

THRILLED by the Declaration of Independence but sobered by the fact that the British were already resisting the decision of Congress with troops, Paine volunteered for military service with a Pennsylvania "flying" camp. The Associators, as they were called, were a ragtag volunteer army of men who enlisted for a brief period to "fly" to a battle zone, then disbanded when the battle concluded or their mutually agreed term of duty expired. In Philadelphia, Paine approached General Daniel Roberdeau, the commander of the flying camp and a wealthy merchant with outspoken republican views. Roberdeau accepted Paine's offer to act as secretary to the general, and on July 9, the day after the Declaration of Independence was proclaimed to a large public meeting in the city, Paine marched with his camp of fellow eighteenth-century guerrillas to Amboy (now Perth Amboy), New Jersey, off the southern tip of Staten Island, where the British were preparing to invade New York and cut it off from Philadelphia.

Paine spent the next two months there, watching transports and warships flying the Union Jack sail into Raritan Bay, where they dropped anchor and off-loaded troops on Staten Island. With the daily accumulation of British military and naval might, Raritan Bay was so filled with masts that it began to resemble a forest.[1] The sight was awesome. Some of the poorly disciplined, ill-equipped Pennsylvania troops became frightened and deserted, lowering the morale of those remaining. Paine tried to raise their spirits and stop the slow trickle of deserters by passing around copies of *Common Sense*. He also repeated Roberdeau's appeal to the men to fight "for your honour's sake" to repel the "sixpenny soldiers" of the British army.[2]

Toward the end of September, when the camp's term of enlistment expired, the volunteers packed up and returned home to Philadelphia, without having seen action. Paine headed in the opposite direction. After accepting forty-eight dollars for expenses (Roberdeau had offered Paine more[3]), he traveled from Amboy up to Fort Lee, an American base camp on the west side of the Hudson River, across from the northern tip of Manhattan. There he was taken on as the aide-de-camp to General Nathanael Greene, a competent officer distinguished by his portly figure and a stiff knee that forced him to walk with a pronounced limp. Greene commanded the troops at Fort Lee and Fort Washington, just opposite, on the east side of the Hudson. His assignment was a vital part of the Americans' plan to prevent the British from occupying the Hudson Valley and thereby severing New England from the other states.

For the next two months, operating from Fort Lee headquarters, Paine observed every move of the Americans and their red-coated enemies. Each day he dined with Greene and his senior officers. The opinions and information he gathered served him well as the field correspondent for the Philadelphia press. Sensing that truth would be the first casualty of the war, he reacted by producing eyewitness reports of several skirmishes, including a life-or-death clash between the troops of Lord Percy and the Pennsylvania militia just across the river on the plains of Harlem. Writing "with a wooden pen on a drumhead," Paine's published account of the battle was eagerly read in Philadelphia, in no small measure because (according to one of the American soldiers present and fighting) it gave a "handsome puff" to the American troops, patriotically listing the full name of practically each Pennsylvanian caught up in the fray. The style of his eyewitness reporting was new to the American press. The war report filed on October 28 from White Plains was typically crisp, detailed, and designed to create a sense of immediacy:

Yesterday the enemy attacked our lines at Harleam, and Mount washington at the same time with two ships; they were repulsed in both places. We have the report of Gen. Howe's being wounded (Having his leg broke) several different ways. This morning 45 Tories and some regular prisoners, passed through here on their way to Fish-Kill. Colonel Smallwood of Maryland, is

this moment come wounded to the house where I am. He is wounded in
the arm and hip, but rode here on horseback, and can walk tolerably well.[4]

Paine excelled at raising the spirits of citizens, but the facts were bitter.
George Washington's army was slowly being worn down by the British
after a series of costly engagements in the area stretching from White
Plains to Long Island. Although opinions differed as to whether the Americans' military efforts were failing because of misguided dictates from
Congress, the military might of the British, Washington's faulty tactics, or
a combination of all these things, the army was on its knees within three
months of entering the war. Then, on November 6, 1776, the British
under General Charles Cornwallis surrounded Fort Washington, capturing the whole garrison of two thousand men and all their equipment.
From a bluff on the west bank of the Hudson River, Paine stood with
Greene's officers and troops and watched the depressing spectacle with
tears in their eyes, powerless to provide support for their comrades. Within
hours, Washington ordered the immediate evacuation of Fort Lee.
Greene disobeyed, insisting that his men could repel any attack. He was
soon forced to back down. Four days later, a six-thousand-strong contingent of British troops and Hessian mercenaries launched a surprise move
against the fort, scattering Greene's men. A British officer reported that
"the rebels fled like scared rabbits" at dawn, leaving behind not only their
breakfasts on the fire but several dozen valuable heavy cannon, many
tents, and "some poor pork, a few greasy proclamations, and some of that
scoundrel Common Sense man's letters, which we can read at our leisure,
now that we have got one of the 'impregnable redoubts' of Mr. Washington to quarter in."[5]
Paine retreated with Greene's army to Hackensack. Hungry and exhausted, the bedraggled troops paused for thirty-six hours before a combination of foul weather, poor shelter, and a fast-approaching enemy forced
them to march a loop to Brunswick via Aquaconack and Newark. In
Brunswick, they were greeted by British cannon. With fireballs rocketing
past his ears, Paine sat calmly with his pen and recalled his days as a privateer. He contrasted his physical reactions to war, past and present, and
described how fighting becomes second nature to those who survive more
than one battle: "I knew the time when I thought the whistling of a cannon ball would have frightened me almost to death; but I have since tried
it, and find that I can stand it with . . . little discomposure."[6] A rather
more sober report on Paine's footslogging, provided by a patriot soldier
accompanying him, suggested that he was battle shy and better suited to

political writing than military fighting. "Paine may be a good philosopher," the soldier wrote, "but he is not a soldier — he always kept out of danger."[7]

As Greene's army backtracked through New Jersey in confusion, Paine tacitly acknowledged the truth of the remark by writing a report for the *Pennsylvania Journal; and the Weekly Advertiser.*[8] It was the closest thing to political propaganda that he ever wrote. It substituted cheerfulness for gloom, hope for despair, firmness for irresolution. There was no mention of sick troops, deserters, or the depressing magnitude of the bungling rout at Fort Lee. Paine instead chose to emphasize the shameful treatment of American civilians by the enemy, the unwillingness of General William Howe's troops to engage his opponents, and the heavy outnumbering of the Americans by the British. He rejected public allegations that the army had acted in a "pusillanimous and disgraceful" way. "Did they know that our army was at one time less than a thousand effective men, and never more than 4,000, that the number of the enemy was at least 8,000," he whistled, "they would never have censured it at all. They would have called it prudent. Posterity will call it glorious."

The American Crisis

Paine's *Pennsylvania Journal* report was superb rhetoric, for although it managed to convey the acute perils of the moment, it did so with the maximum calmness of a political writer who wanted above all to avoid arousing panic among his already fear-ridden readers. Among Paine's genuinely novel insights was his grasp of the antidemocratic effects of fear. He understood that fear is a central ingredient of despotic regimes, in which fear of power always corrupts those who are subject to it and fear of losing power always corrupts those who are exercising it. He also understood the converse of this rule: shaking off fear — the capacity of citizens to join with others in dignity and solidarity to resist its enervating miasma — is a basic condition of constructing a democratic republican order. Paine grasped that fearlessness is not a naturally occurring substance. From his perspective, it is best thought of as a special form of courage — as the will to act gracefully under pressure that develops wherever victims of political lies and bullying make a personal effort to throw off the habit of letting fear dictate their actions as citizens.

Paine was convinced that political writing could nurture this effort, as he tried to demonstrate in his next publication, *The American Crisis*. The essay was to be among his most famous and arguably among the greatest political essays in the modern English language. It was an ode to fearlessness in circumstances that alarmed a growing number of Americans. On December 1, 1776, the term of enlistment for volunteers from New Jersey and Maryland expired, and George Washington, worried by thinning ranks and plummeting morale, made the decision not to make a stand against the British. As the American troops were forced back from Brunswick to Trenton on the Delaware River, their retreat began to resemble a rout. On December 8, the Americans crossed to the west bank of the Delaware, taking with them all the ferries and boats on the river in the hope that this would halt the British on the east side of the river. The British massed menacingly on the east bank of the Delaware, and Paine, concerned that they might now be planning an attack on Philadelphia, left the army at Trenton "on the advice of several principal officers, in order to get out some publications, as the printing presses were then at a stand and the country in a state of despair."[9]

He walked alone from Trenton to Philadelphia, a distance of thirty-five miles, sleeping rough, eating irregularly, constantly looking over his shoulder, anxious that a British soldier or informant would arrest him. More bad news greeted him in the capital. He arrived to find that refugees were streaming out of the city and that Congress had fled to the safety of Baltimore. Tory supporters were preparing a hero's welcome for General Howe, and many of the remaining inhabitants of Philadelphia were disillusioned by the poor performance of the American troops. Paine reacted angrily. In conversations, he continued to describe public criticisms of the American troops as "pusillanimous and disgraceful." He skipped over the tactical blunders of the Americans and insisted that future generations would honor the "glorious" retreat of the American troops to Trenton. He even boasted that "the names of Washington and Fabius will run parallel to eternity." And, coming to the heart of the matter, he noted the "deplorable and melancholy condition the people were in, afraid to speak and almost to think, the public presses stopt, and nothing in circulation but fears and falsehoods."[10]

With morale so low in Philadelphia and support for the War of Independence already low and wavering, it was now just possible that the British could sack the capital city. That would endanger the Revolution, since the fall of Philadelphia would render vulnerable the whole of Pennsylvania, the keystone in the arch of the American states. The deteriorating situation convinced Paine of the need for a radical renewal of the spirit of independence. He settled at his desk, gathered his notes made during the past few months at the battlefront, and in what he called "a passion of patriotism" drafted the first in a series of thirteen essays — one for each state — called *The American Crisis*."[11]

Paine wrote "in a rage when our affairs were at their lowest ebb and things in the most gloomy state."[12] His quill spat venom at King George III, describing him as "a sottish, stupid, stubborn, worthless, brutish man" who resembled "a common murderer, a highwayman or a house-breaker."[13] He lunged as well at the king's American Tory sympathizers, berating them all as cowards driven by "servile, slavish, self-interested fear." *The American Crisis* insisted that the safe retreat on the battlefield is the most difficult art to perfect, and it praised the Americans' conduct of an "orderly retreat for near an hundred miles" from Fort Lee. Paine also warned of a probable British attack led by General Howe on Philadelphia but tried hard to allay his readers' fears by boasting about the strength of the regrouping American troops: "Once more we are again collected and collecting; our new army at both ends of the continent is recruiting fast, and we shall be able to open the next campaign with sixty thousand men, well armed and clothed. This is our situation, and who will may know it."

The tract reiterated Paine's view that violence must always be strictly controlled and that the Americans' war effort must not degenerate into callous narcissism. But in this crisis, he argued, pacifism was the pawn of paternalism. The offensive war of the British was unjustified murder, whereas the Americans' defensive war against British tyranny was necessarily legitimate: "if a thief breaks into my house, burns and destroys my property, and kills or threatens to kill me, or those that are in it, and to *'bind me in all cases whatsoever'* [Paine here quoted the Declaratory Act of Parliament, February 24, 1766] to his absolute will, am I to suffer it?" He went on to insist that "America will never be happy till she gets clear of foreign dominion." He warned that when victory came to the Americans, priority would be given to the peaceful expropriation of the property of loyalists, conducted in the spirit not of "revenge" but of "the soft resentment of a suffering people." In deeply patriotic language topped with references to Providence and traces of xenophobia, *The American Crisis* pushed a fateful choice into the face of its American readers. Either Americans would struggle for a glorious victory against the British through "perseverance and fortitude," or they would sink into "cowardice and submission" and suffer a calamitous fate: "a ravaged country — a de-populated city — habitations without safety, and slavery without hope — our homes turned into barracks and bawdy-houses for Hessians, and a future race to provide for, whose fathers we shall doubt of."

Paine had begun making notes for *The American Crisis* during the long retreat from Fort Lee to Trenton. He had been exhausted and alarmed by the realization that the American forces were heavily outnumbered, outgunned, and in utter disarray. Tramping through mud by day, listening each evening to the consultations of General Greene and his officers, Paine scribbled at night by the campfires. The problem of fear and how to reassure an already anxious citizenry was constantly on his mind. "I thank God that I fear not," he wrote. "I see no real cause for fear. I know our situation well, and can see the way out of it. . . . By perseverance and fortitude we have the prospect of a glorious issue. . . . By cowardice and submission the choice of a variety of evils."

Upon returning to Philadelphia, he hurriedly drew together the manuscript, then offered it to the editor of the *Pennsylvania Journal*, who published it a week before Christmas, 1776. Several days later, it appeared as an eight-page pamphlet with a print run of eighteen thousand copies. Paine made it clear to the Philadelphia publishers, the German Americans Melchior Steiner and Carl Cist, that he had offered it to them gratis on the condition that they cover their costs and keep its price to a few pence. He emphasized that the overriding aim was to circulate its message among civilians at home and troops at the battlefront. Like all his writings in this period, Paine's prose was crafted to be read out loud to people unfamiliar with the art of reading books or pamphlets. "I dwell not upon the vapours of imagination," he wrote. "I bring reason to your ears, and, in language as plain as A, B, C, hold up truth to your eyes."

The text was pirated by printers up and down the Atlantic coast.[14] How many thousands of copies were printed and reprinted and snapped up by civilians is unknown, but there is evidence that the pamphlet circulated among the underdressed and dispirited American troops preparing for battle against the superior forces of the British and Hessian army at Trenton.[15] Paine sensed that the battle would be a watershed. A British victory might well cause the Americans' struggle to collapse. The Americans, for their part, badly needed a victory to divert the British threat to Philadelphia and inject new life into their flagging fight for independence. Washington decided to meet the challenge by assembling volunteers from Philadelphia, a regiment of German immigrant units from Charles Lee's command, and a further five hundred men subcommanded by Horatio Gates — about six thousand troops in all.

In the late-afternoon light of Christmas Day, 1776, officers assembled the American troops into small squads and read to them the text of *The American Crisis*. On the eve of battle, its opening sentences must have sounded strangely primeval to the ears of men thinking about death and injury. The words soon became famous and will always remain so until the cause of citizens' freedom is extinguished: "These are the times that try men's souls. The summer soldier and the sunshine patriot will, in this crisis, shrink from the service of their country; but he that stands it *now*, deserves the love and thanks of man and woman. Tyranny, like hell, is not easily conquered; yet we have this consolation with us, that the harder the conflict, the more glorious the triumph."[16]

After nightfall, through a storm of hail and sleet, Washington's men were ferried in flat-bottomed boats across the Delaware. They inched toward Trenton, some of them leaving trails of blood in the snow from their bandaged or bare feet, their officers prodding them during halts to keep them from falling into an icy sleep from which they would never awake. By daybreak, the troops had reached the outskirts of Trenton. That day, December 26, had been chosen because, one of Washington's aides remarked, the Hessian mercenaries occupying the town were known to "make a great deal of Christmas in Germany"[17] and would probably be suffering from a surfeit of raucous dancing, schnapps, and beer. The American gamble paid handsome dividends. Colonel Johann Gottlieb Rahl, the conceited German commander at Trenton, was caught in his nightshirt and later mortally wounded in the heavy street fighting that erupted. By nightfall, the Hessians had been routed. A thousand men were taken prisoner, and, to the Americans' delight, nearly all the enemy stores, including fine German swords and forty hogsheads of rum, were captured. Trenton was won. *The American Crisis* had proved to be a literary cannon on the battlefield of independence. The grip of the British Empire on America was loosened — for a while.

War and Civility

After the victory at Trenton, Paine fixed his energies on dampening false hopes of an early American victory, while simultaneously attempting to lighten the hearts of the American revolutionaries by heaping criticism on the British. It was typical of the sober optimism of his politics during this period of war. In the second installment of *The American Crisis*, published by Steiner and Cist on January 13, 1777,[18] he warned that a chain of unborn crises lay ahead and that American citizens must try to be patient and resilient. Yet the warning was mixed with hope, for Paine also argued that the British strategy of containing the American colonies was doomed to failure.

The essay was written in the form of an open letter to a British offi-

cial — a tactic designed both to heighten the sense of distance between
the imperial governors and their subjects and to legitimate public criticism
of those same governors by subjects who in fact considered themselves
American citizens. The letter was addressed to Lord Richard Howe, the
vice admiral of the British fleet and brother of William Howe, the commander in chief of the British forces. Richard Howe had been sent to
America the previous July to negotiate with Congress, but his overtures
had been refused. A letter that he had sent to "Mr. Washington" requesting a meeting was snubbed on the grounds that it had not used "General,"
and Howe eventually met only with Washington's unyielding aides, who
ensured that the meeting was fruitless.

Paine gave Howe an equally frosty reception. Paine prefaced the letter
with a quote from the British poet Charles Churchill (1731–1764): "What's
in the name of *lord*, that I should fear / To bring my grievance to the public ear?" He then taunted Howe with the thought that the British Empire
would suffer its first humiliation in America. Paine admitted that Britain
had the upper hand in terms of weaponry — the ultimate language in
which kings like George III speak — and that its global influence was
awesome. "Blessed with all the commerce she could wish for, and furnished, by a vast extension of dominion, with the means of civilizing both
the eastern and western world, she has made no other use of both than
proudly to idolize her own 'thunder,' and rip up the bowels of whole
countries for what she could get." Britain's global power, wrote Paine, had
made war a sport. His language was militantly anti-imperialist: "The
blood of India is not yet repaid, nor the wretchedness of Africa yet requited. Of late she has enlarged her list of national cruelties by her
butcherly destruction of the Caribbs of St. Vincent's." The same pattern
of wanton brutality was daily being repeated in America, as British pillaging after Trenton demonstrated. "Your avowed purpose here," snapped
Paine, "is to kill, conquer, plunder, pardon, and enslave: and the ravages of
your army through the Jerseys have been marked with as much barbarism
as if you had openly professed yourself the prince of ruffians."

Paine's invective was tough — "Surely there must be something
strangely degenerating in the love of monarchy, that can so completely
wear a man down to an ingrate, and make him proud to lick the dust that
kings have trod upon" — and it was designed to reiterate that independence was America's natural right. He challenged Howe to grasp the
point that Americans were no longer in love with monarchy. Paine emphasized that because the hearts of American revolutionaries underlay
their struggle for independence and republican government, the British

could never win them over, let alone control or pacify them. The most powerful cannon and longest and sharpest bayonets could no longer reach the souls of Americans. In the unlikely event that the British conquered the Americans militarily, the victory would be utterly fictional. It would resemble "robbing an orchard in the night before the fruit be ripe, and running away in the morning."

In *Common Sense*, Paine had warned that the struggle for independence was fraught with unforeseen consequences, including possibly the undermining of liberty itself by populist dictatorship. Paine resumed this theme in *The American Crisis II* by telling a story of a recent meeting with a prominent Philadelphia loyalist. Paine had told him that he had reached the conclusion "that God Almighty was visibly on our side." The loyalist had reacted cynically: "We care nothing for that, you may have Him, and welcome; if we have but enough of the devil on our side, we shall do." Paine told the anecdote to warn Americans against falling into the trap of seeking revenge against their opponents. Although he repeated his earlier threat that British colonial officials would be forced into exile and their property redistributed when the war ended, Americans owed them compassion. The British and their supporters should be treated with civility. A republic that nurtured its citizens' freedom, like a hive of bees moving freely in all directions, required the binding propolis of civility. "I am not for declaring war with every man that appears not so warm as myself," wrote Paine, calling for an end to the Americans' public humiliation of the British and their sympathizers. The traditional political language of "friends" and "enemies" had no place in the radical republicanism of the revolutionaries. "It is time to have done with tarring, feathering, carting, and taking securities for their future good behaviour," Paine wrote. "Every sensible man must feel a conscious shame at seeing a poor fellow hawked for a show about the streets."

Chief Last Night

Fear and violence were not the only enemies of republican liberty. The possibility that the Revolution would destroy the liberty of Native Americans certainly occurred to Paine. A week after the second number of *The American Crisis* appeared, Paine was approached by the Pennsylvania Council of Safety to negotiate on behalf of the Pennsylvania Assembly and the Continental Congress with several tribes of Native Americans living along the west branch of the Susquehanna River.[19] The Council treated the negotiations seriously. It had been informed that the Iroquois tribes wanted to discuss their status under the new republican government. A commission of six men — four from Pennsylvania and two from Congress — was appointed to meet their representatives and to secure a treaty of alliance. Paine, brimming with energy and empty of cash, as usual, accepted the paid post of secretary to the delegation at a modest salary of $145 and traveled to Easton, a village on the Delaware about fifty miles north of Philadelphia.

The conference began on the morning of January 27, 1777. At least six chiefs from various Iroquois tribes, flanked by some seventy men, together with their wives and children, crammed into Easton's tiny Third Street Church, which had been erected by the local Lutheran German Reformed congregation and lately used as a temporary hospital for wounded and dying American soldiers. The meeting opened with the traditional "black drink" ceremony. "After shaking hands, *drinking rum,* while the organ played, we proceeded to business," the commissioners later told Congress in a report probably written by Paine.[20] He introduced himself to the gathering as "Common Sense" and quickly made an effort to learn some words and phrases of the Iroquois language. Throughout the meeting, which lasted four days, he seemed magnetized by what he saw as the natural beauty, prudence, and intelligence of the Native Americans. He considered them fine human beings, unspoiled by modern civilization and the crooked ways of British despotism — exemplars of "the natural and primitive state of man."[21]

Paine's familiarity with Native Americans actually predated the Easton conference. In the March 1775 issue of *The Pennsylvania Magazine,* he had published a long letter by William Penn on the native peoples of the American colonies. Moreover, like his friends John Adams, Benjamin Rush, and George Washington — but unlike subsequent generations of white American political figures — Paine had grown accustomed to rubbing shoulders with native people in and around Philadelphia.[22] The Easton conference was nevertheless Paine's first and only extended political contact with Native Americans. It made such an impression on him that he spoke about it for many years after. During the conference, he talked at length to Chief Last Night, who expressed awe at the "great canoes" of the British on the rivers and lakes of Canada, but who thought it unlikely that their armies could conquer the Americans on land. "The king of England is like a fish," he said. "When he is in the water he can wag his tail. — When he comes on land he lays down on his side."[23]

Such "sagacious remarks" solidified Paine's conviction that "the English government had but half the sense this Indian had."[24] That was at least a half compliment considering that the English government had no sense at all, in Paine's view. He seemed satisfied with the progress of nego-tiations, which were oiled by gifts worth a thousand dollars brought up from Philadelphia by the Americans. The talks ended on January 30 with a peace treaty signed by the chiefs and the two congressmen. "The Indi-ans seemed to be inclined to act the wise part with respect to the present dispute," concluded the commissioners' report. "If they are to be relied upon, they mean to be neuter. We have already learnt their good inten-tions."

The talks proved a failure. Congress soon rescinded the treaty on the grounds that it had been made with "certain Indians pretending to be a Deputation from the Six Indian Nations."[25] Congress seemed annoyed by the way in which the Six Nations of the Iroquois Confederacy, for reasons of physical survival and cultural dignity, had long since mastered the art of balancing one group of whites against another, regardless of whether the balance was French against British, British against Americans, or Ameri-cans against British. The number of native groups who consistently sup-ported the revolutionaries was actually small. The majority — lured by gifts and British promises of protection from land-hungry colonists — supported the other side. This made most prominent revolutionaries furi-ous. Unprepared to be seen as soft on "savages," they were quick to sacrifice their own principles of universal liberty. Washington likened Na-tive Americans to wolves — "both being beasts of prey tho' they differ in shape." John Adams called them "blood Hounds." And the Declaration of Independence denounced them as "merciless Savages."[26]

Such attitudes had murderous implications. An Englishman recently returned from America reported during this period that "white Ameri-cans have the most rancorous antipathy to the whole race of Indians." He added, "Nothing is more common than to hear them talk of extirpating them from the face of the earth, men, women and children."[27]

Paine never indulged such talk. It is true that he did not publicly de-nounce white Americans' prejudices — that would almost certainly have meant committing political suicide. It also is true that he sided with those who considered modern societies superior in matters of "agriculture, arts, science and manufactures."[28] But despite his modernist prejudices, Paine refused to join the ranks of the majority of white Americans who relied on violence, enforced exile, disease, and cultural manipulation to wreck native peoples' ways and to drive them from their land. Paine always talked about Native Americans as his "brothers."[29] He praised their love of natural liberty — symbolized by the eagle — and their stubborn refusal, expressed in several declarations of independence, to give up their autonomy to any earthly power. Like many other contemporary observers, he noted how seriously Chief Last Night and other Iroquois talked of the freedom granted them by the Great Spirit and the laughter with which they greeted talk of obedience to kings.[30] It is just possible that their animist belief in the Great Spirit reinforced Paine's own anti-Christian, deist sympathies. Paine was certainly impressed by their egalitarianism. "Among the Indians of North America," he later wrote, "there is not . . . any of those spectacles of human misery which poverty and want present to our eyes in all the towns and streets in Europe." Poverty was a creation of what "is called civilized life. It exists not in the natural state. . . . The life of an Indian is a continual holiday, compared with the poor of Europe."[31]

Paine did not exaggerate these qualities, which ensured that Native Americans were not the passive victims of government agents after land, frontiersmen after blood, or missionaries after souls. Unlike the native peoples of Mexico and the Andes, the original Americans were not transformed into a subordinate caste. Some accepted Britain's invitation to move to Canada. Most lived skillfully on the edge of American colonial life. The so-called Proclamation Line, designed in 1763 by the British to separate Europeans from native peoples, formally defined that edge, and for a time that line, running from the border between Florida and Georgia up the eastern mountains to Chaleur Bay on the Gulf of St. Lawrence, served as a safety fence, staving off white men's hunger for land. But despite valiant attempts to push encroaching European settlers back to where they were supposed to be, and though even the names of their tribes struck fear into the hearts of many white Americans, the original Americans were heavily outnumbered and vulnerable.

The ugly waves of disease and death that followed Native Americans' earliest contacts with Europeans signaled their demise. The Iroquois alone lost half of their eight thousand to ten thousand people during the last quarter of the eighteenth century.[32] During the period covering the Easton meeting, Native Americans still believed that their own nations would earn them the respect of white Americans such as Paine. Their extraordinary skill at playing off different groups of whites seemed to confirm this belief. But in the end, regardless of whether they went it alone or chose the support of the French, the Spanish, the British, or the American revolutionaries, Native Americans were delivered an unhappy fate: to totter on the borderline between physical extinction and cultural assimilation.

On Constitutions

Paine returned to Philadelphia from Easton during the first week of February 1777. Within hours, he found himself dragged into a bitter political row. During the six months that he had been on the battlefield, constitutional and social controversies in Pennsylvania had become intertwined, and a noisy power struggle resembling a revolution within the Revolution had erupted. The conflict had been triggered in late September 1776 by the promulgation, without a vote of citizens, of a new Pennsylvania constitution favorable to the interests of Philadelphia's artisans and back-country farmers. For its time, the constitution was arguably the most democratic in the world — and certainly the most daring adopted in America during the Revolutionary period. It had been drafted by such Radicals as Timothy Matlack and James Cannon and approved by the Constitutional Convention chaired by Benjamin Franklin. Their opponents, who came to be known as Republicans, Conservatives, or Anti-Constitutionalists, tried desperately, without success, to wreck the proceedings. Their objections were fundamental. Unsatisfied, they tried to obstruct the elections of November 1776 and paralyze the Assembly that met shortly afterward, despite the risk that their actions endangered the whole state at a time of great peril.

Paine worked for give-and-take. He sympathized deeply with the Radicals, but he took the view that the precarious military situation demanded that there should be a truce between the conflicting parties. In practice, that meant that the quarreling factions should call a halt to petty politics and shelter under the new constitution, at least until the danger of military defeat had passed. In a published reply to "Phocion," probably John Dickinson, who had launched a blistering conservative attack on the Radicals and called for a revised constitution, Paine explained his concern that "a little squabbling spirit should at this ill chosen time creep in and extinguish every thing that is civil or generous among us." He warned of the dangers of anarchy generated by "pride, passion, prejudice and party" and urged the Anti-Constitutionalists to give the existing democratic constitution "a fair trial, purely for the sake of discovering what ought to be retained, reformed or rejected."[33]

A conservative version of the same argument — the so-called doctrine of prescription — would later be flung back into Paine's face by supporters of Edmund Burke, but here, under wartime conditions, it served his purpose of publicly defending the principle of republican liberty with greater political equality. The constitution abolished property qualifications for voting and office holding. All white freemen age twenty-one and over who had resided in the state one year and paid taxes were eligible to vote each year for the state Assembly. Instead of stiff property qualifications for holding office, a provision in most other state constitutions, the Pennsylvania constitution asked only for "Persons most noted for Wisdom and Virtue." So that no one could monopolize office holding, as had commonly occurred during the colonial period, assemblymen could hold office for a maximum of four years in seven. And to ensure the equal worth of each male citizen's vote, the new constitution specified that representation be apportioned among the cities and counties on the basis of their numbers of taxable inhabitants.

Conservative critics of the constitution, among them men of wealth and social position such as Robert Morris, James Wilson, and John Dickinson, disliked each of these leveling measures. They also were profoundly annoyed by the requirement that all voters and officeholders swear to an oath of loyalty to the constitution. But above all, they were positively alarmed by the underlying principle of the sovereignty of the people, expressed not only in adult male suffrage but also in a unicameral assembly subject only to two checks: first, a provision that bills introduced in one session should then be printed and not acted on until the next session, a provision that could easily be suspended "on occasions of Sudden necessity" to ensure the immediate passage of a bill; second, a provision that a Council of Censors, composed of two representatives elected by the people, should pass judgment on the conduct of the Assembly every seven years. The Anti-Constitutionalists smelled mob rule in these provisions. They seized upon the framers' view — summarized by Benjamin Franklin — that a bicameral system of divided powers would resemble putting one horse in front of a cart and another behind it, each pulling in opposite directions.[34] That view, argued the Anti-Constitutionalists, would lead to misgovernment by donkeys pulling in the same direction. The so-called representatives of the sovereign People, or at least a majority faction claiming to speak for the People, would be licensed to play the role of God, to act as tyrants unchecked by any other power.

Paine's razor-sharp political senses led him to brush aside such talk as a poor excuse for privilege, just as he had done with John Adams shortly after the publication of *Common Sense*. Paine reasoned, not inaccurately, that the quantity of noise made by the Anti-Constitutionalists against the new constitution was inversely proportional to their level of genuine popularity. He described the constitution as "the political Bible of the State.

Scarcely a family was without it."[35] That was probably an exaggeration, but it did indeed have a solid basis of popular support, for whose preservation he campaigned hard against the Anti-Constitutionalists. During March 1777, he helped organize the Whig Society, which throughout the second half of the month and again in early April called publicly for the solidarity of Pennsylvania citizens with the constitution.[36] The Society was dominated by Radicals, and on April 1 it elected a Correspondence Committee comprising Paine, David Rittenhouse, James Cannon, Thomas Young, and the artist Charles Willson Peale, who was elected chairman and soon afterward became Paine's lifelong friend.[37]

Paine's election to the Correspondence Committee gave him the opportunity to reflect in detail on constitutional matters for the first time since *Common Sense*. In early June in the *Pennsylvania Journal*, replying to an earlier letter signed by "Ludlow," he reiterated the grave dangers of petty public bickering in wartime. At the same time, he conceded that since war is a breeding ground for despotism, it was important to stimulate civilized public discussion aimed at clarifying the new constitutional framework for controlling the exercise of power. He argued that the Pennsylvania constitution rested on the fundamental distinction between natural and civil rights. Natural rights, such as the right of individuals to defend their own lives against aggressors, are merely "animal rights," he said. Existing before the advent of governments and constitutions, they are inherent in each individual. But the trouble with natural rights is that although their preservation is vital for the freedom and happiness of individuals, their full exercise normally has antisocial consequences. Paine offered the example of the right of self-defense: "a man has a *natural* right to redress himself whenever he is injured, but the full exercise of this, as a *natural* right, would be dangerous to society, because it admits him a judge in his own cause."[38]

The example, traceable to Thomas Hobbes and other English natural rights theorists, was elementary, but it served to illustrate the fundamental point: individuals living together in any society can live safely and freely only by pooling and codifying their natural rights. They must enter into a contract that establishes a constitution designed to protect and enhance their civil rights within a civil society ordered by government. A constitution is a written document, based ultimately on the consent of citizens, which specifies the powers due to government and the powers due to citizens in the form of civil entitlements such as freedom of the press and the right to vote. These civil rights are not to be found as such among animals or in the natural world. They are political inventions, the product of living, breathing, communicating citizens who agree to establish rules "for the mutual good and support of each other." The civil rights specified in constitutions are therefore alterable. Through time and from place to place, they can and should be redefined and supplemented not by legislatures, whose behavior must always be within the framework of the existing constitution, but by representatives of the people, chosen specifically for that purpose after sustained public discussion of the strengths and limits of the existing constitution.

Foreign Affairs Secretary

Paine was adamant that Pennsylvania had already gone through that process — that it had, in fact, performed the revolutionary act of replacing an unwritten so-called British constitution with a written document — and that for the time being, the new republican constitution should be allowed to stand the test of time and not be scuppered. He left the matter there, turning his attention for the next eighteen months back to the war and national politics.

Peace with victory still seemed at best a remote prospect. The Americans, still facing great odds, tried hard to maintain their spirits, which lifted noticeably after Washington's success against the Hessians at Trenton and a victory over the British several days later at Princeton. Symptomatic of the change was the decision of Congress to reconvene in Philadelphia after several months of living in retreat in the crammed boardinghouses and mud-clogged streets of the village of Baltimore. On March 12, 1777, it settled back into the capital, and during the next few weeks, while Paine was doing battle with the Anti-Constitutionalists, Congress became preoccupied with formulating a foreign policy designed to help it win the war against the British.

Particularly significant was the decision by a majority of delegates that its old Committee of Secret Correspondence, which had assigned the first agents to Europe and made preliminary efforts to secure foreign aid, should be transformed into a larger and more powerful Committee for Foreign Affairs. On the same day (April 17), Congress also voted "that a secretary be appointed to the said committee, with a salary of 70 dollars a month."[39] During the same meeting, John Adams spoke in favor of Paine's appointment to the post. It was a generous move, considering their earlier quarrel. Adams acknowledged that *Common Sense* had been of "great importance in the Revolution" and that Paine, as he later put it, "had a capacity and a ready Pen." Adams added that since his old enemy "was poor and destitute, I thought we might put him into some employ-ment, where he might be usefull and earn a living."[40]

The sentiments were patronizing, but within Congress they helped for a time to snuff out opposition to Paine. The only dissenting voice was the Reverend John Witherspoon, a delegate from New Jersey and a former contributor to *The Pennsylvania Magazine* with whom Paine had once quar-reled. According to Adams, who was surprised at the good parson's heated opposition, Witherspoon attacked Paine with the claim that

> when he first came over, he was on the other side and had written pieces against the American Cause: that he had afterwards been employed by his friend Robert Aitkin [*sic*], and finding the Tide of Popularity run rapidly, he had turned about: that he was very intemperate and could not write untill he had quickened his Thoughts with large drafts of Rum and Water; that he was in short a bad Character and not fit to be placed in such a Situation.[41]

Paine was not to know that more of the same invective awaited him in American politics. Gossip about his hard drinking was a false inflation of his periodic enjoyment of moderate social drinking in a hard-drinking age, and it confirmed his long-standing conviction that "parsons were al-ways mischievous fellows when they turned politicians."[42] Witherspoon's innuendo about Paine's royalism also was groundless. It ignored his early English political education in the ways of republicanism, left unacknowl-edged the originality of *Common Sense*, and ignored the fact that British in-telligence agents had for some time been worried about Paine's "rebellious" activities.[43] Witherspoon's intervention backfired. Daniel Roberdeau, under whom Paine had served the previous year at Amboy and who had subsequently exchanged his colonel's rank for a seat in the Pennsylvania delegation, sprang to Paine's rescue. Congress was persuaded, and the nomination was carried in no small measure because Paine was already friendly with Richard Henry Lee and other delegates who were against any proposals to increase the powers of the Continental Congress. John Adams's nomination of Paine was therefore shrewd: by proposing Paine, easily the most famous critic of unaccountable government in America, to be the only figure permanently attached to a committee that showed every sign of becoming an embryonic executive power, Adams effectively si-lenced those who feared the rise of a new despotism within the Revolu-tionary movement itself. What Adams did not know was that Paine would live up to his principled commitment to open government to the point that he would call into question the behavior of Congress itself.

Paine had just turned forty. He was in excellent health, and his public reputation — reinforced by his aquiline nose, lofty forehead, sparkling eyes, and ruddy complexion — was running high in and around Congress. He was thrilled by the appointment as secretary to the Committee for Foreign Affairs, the first official acknowledgment of his literary and political achievements. Sometimes his newcomer's arrogance, born of insecurity, got the better of him, tempting him to boast that he was "Secretary for Foreign Affairs."[44] That implied responsibility for conducting negotiations and policymaking, but in fact his duties were more humble. He was mainly responsible for keeping the records of the Committee and drafting correspondence to foreign agents, such as William Bingham in Martinique and Benjamin Franklin in Paris.[45] He seemed to enjoy the work, and the small salary was welcome.[46] So too was access to sensitive documents. For eighteen months, he told Franklin in a letter,[47] he had intended to write a history of the Revolution — his working title was *Revolution of America* — pointing out that the new post promised him invaluable materials. He asked Franklin in the same letter kindly to forward him relevant volumes of parliamentary debates since 1774, as well as files of several English Whig and Tory reviews from the same period. There was only one possible difficulty with this plan to use his post for research purposes: in accepting the post, Paine had agreed to an oath of secrecy. In accordance with the modern doctrine of *raison d'état*, he was asked to swear "to disclose no matter, the knowledge of which shall be acquired in consequence of such his office, that he shall be directed to keep secret."

Paine's oath of secrecy remained unproblematic during the first year of his appointment. Routine clerical work and the pressure of events conspired to prevent him from publishing much. He may have been involved in the Whig Society's ongoing public efforts in Pennsylvania to block calls for a constitutional convention.[48] But aside from that, his only major writing for five months was the third installment of *The American Crisis*. It appeared as a nine-penny pamphlet two days after he took up his post, on the anniversary of the Battle of Lexington. It was untypical of Paine's writings inasmuch as it seemed to adopt a hard-line proto-Jacobin view of revolutionary politics as the art of waging struggles for state power by using friends to defeat enemies. Paine confessed that until recently, he had clung to the "charitable" view that American opponents of independence "were rather a mistaken than a criminal people." He had since changed his mind. "All we want to know in America is simply this," he wrote, "who is for independence, and who is not?" He was angry. "Those who are for it, will support it, and the remainder will undoubtedly see the reasonableness of paying the charges; while those who oppose or seek to betray it, must expect the more rigid fate of the jail and the gibbet."

Paine had grown up in the shadow of the jail and the gibbet, and he had subsequently come to abhor them as symbols of despotism. Had he now changed his mind? Did he actually think that despotic means could and should be used to defeat the despotism of the British kind? Was he perchance in favor of *republican* gibbets and jails? Certainly the language in which he described the enemies of the Revolution — "banditti of hungry traitors," "avaricious miscreants," power-hungry "proprietary dependents . . . content to share it with the devil" — suggest positive answers to the first two questions at least. Some of Paine's readers must have drawn that conclusion. The more discerning would have noticed that he was bluffing. His strong language was no doubt intended to shake the confidence of waverers and opponents of the American cause. But it was backed by a practical suggestion, which explicitly ruled out the use of gibbets and jails. Throughout the United States, he proposed, citizens should be required to take an oath of loyalty to the Declaration of Independence. Those who refused should be subjected to an annual tax on the estimated value of their property. Tories were to be made to pay for cavorting with the enemy — with hard cash, not their lives.[49]

The proposal was neither fully worked out nor ever fully adopted. Nevertheless, the general tactic of smoking out loyalists from the nooks and crannies of civil society by means of purgative rituals such as taking and publishing names, oath taking, and threats to confiscate property was widely practiced at the local community level, and with considerable success.[50] The tactic of rendering suspected loyalists social outcasts was designed to avoid violence and counterviolence. It confronted loyalists with two choices: conform or leave. No more than one loyalist in eight left the United States, but many more chose to switch localities. Compared with most modern revolutions, the American Revolution was comparatively lenient on its counterrevolutionaries. Physical violence and intimidation existed, and Paine, who personally disapproved of it, surely knew about it. Dr. John Kearsley, the physician who had cared for him upon his arrival in America, was himself badly injured by a Philadelphia mob in 1777 for having written a letter before the Declaration of Independence attacking the American cause. He later died from the effects. Violence of this sort was, however, rather rare. There was far less of it than might have been expected from the dramatic upheaval of the Revolution. Aside from the military clashes, organized force, even as a threat, also was comparatively rare. For this sidestepping of Revolutionary terror, Paine must be given some credit.

The Sacking of Philadelphia

From the time of the appearance of the third number of *The American Crisis* in the spring of 1777 until early autumn, Paine virtually fell silent. As the summer days lengthened, then shortened into the first autumn frosts, he became weighed down by the war, particularly with the most ominous development: the preparation of British plans to march on the capital, Philadelphia. Although at times he tried to sound cheerful ("the general face of our affairs assures us of final success," he wrote to William Bingham in Martinique[51]), he grew ever more anxious. In the first week of July, he wrote to Benjamin Franklin explaining his proposal, already discussed with David Rittenhouse, for mass-producing and launching fire-tipped arrows across the Delaware to halt the advance of the British.[52]

His alarm was justified. At the end of August, British troops landed at the head of Delaware Bay and began to march toward the capital. They advanced to Brandywine Creek, where they were met early in the morning of September 11 by Washington's army. Howe's strategy was to make a strong surprise flanking movement to destroy the "rebel" forces by a pincer attack. The plan came perilously close to success. Seven thousand five hundred troops commanded by General Charles Cornwallis closed in on the rear of the Americans after a circuitous seventy-five-mile march through the surrounding hills. Washington, surprised, ordered the Americans to retreat, encountering heavy fire. "There was," an English officer recalled, "a most infernal fire of cannons and musquetry, smoke and incessant shouting: 'Incline to the right! Incline to the left! Halt! Charge!' The balls ploughing up the ground: the trees cracking over one's head; the branches riven by the artillery; the leaves falling as in autumn."[53] More than a thousand American soldiers were killed or wounded, and four hundred were taken prisoner. The Americans might well have been annihilated had it not been for the entanglement and delay of four British battalions in thick woodland and Cornwallis's decision not to order his exhausted men to pursue the enemy after nightfall.

Paine was working in his Philadelphia office that afternoon preparing dispatches to Franklin in Paris "when the report of cannon at Brandywine interrupted my proceeding."[54] That evening he learned of the Americans' rout. He was quick to see the disastrous implication of the bad news: Philadelphia was now vulnerable to British occupation, and many citizens were "in a state of fear and dread." Working feverishly through the night, he drafted a fourth number of *The American Crisis*, revised it, and by noon the next day rushed the final version to the printer, Steiner and Cist. He "ordered 4,000 to be printed at my own private charge and given away."[55]

The four-page pamphlet was full of stirring prose. "We are not moved by the gloomy smile of a worthless king," wrote Paine to Lord Howe, "but by the ardent glow of generous patriotism. We fight not to enslave, but to set a country free, and to make room upon the earth for honest men to live in. In such a cause we are sure that we are right; and we leave to you the despairing reflection of being the tool of a miserable tyrant." Paine reminded his readers that the American forces still held the advantage of being a citizens' army operating on home soil. General Howe was daily confronted with this fact. "He has everybody to fight, we have only his *one* army to cope with, and which wastes away at every engagement: we can not only reinforce, but can redouble our numbers; he is cut off from all supplies, and must sooner or later inevitably fall into our hands."[56]

The pamphlet was circulated widely,[57] but it had little influence on the terrified Philadelphia populace, who refused to be calmed or inspired to stand up to the advancing British. As each day passed, hundreds of supporters of independence left the city. The Pennsylvania state government fled to Lancaster. Members of Congress also packed their trunks and headed for York, leaving its Secretary to the Committee for Foreign Affairs in a Philadelphia even more staunchly loyalist then before. By the evening of September 18, more than ten thousand of Philadelphia's thirty thousand inhabitants had fled for their lives. Paine was "fully persuaded that unless something was done the city would be lost." The something he had in mind was to resist the British by engaging them, if necessary, through hand-to-hand street fighting. He proposed forming a citizens' militia, raising a defense fund of fifty thousand dollars, and throwing up "works at the heads of the streets."[58]

Paine reasoned that the British would be wary of getting trapped in urban fighting, for which they were not trained. He managed to convince Colonels Bayard and Bradford of this, and even got the ear of Thomas Mifflin, a merchant and member of the Continental Congress and Governor of Pennsylvania, who was appointed Brigadier-General in May 1776 and sent by Washington to Philadelphia later that year to rouse the city for resistance to the British.[59] But considering both the close proximity of the British and the sympathy for the redcoats among many of Philadelphia's remaining inhabitants, the proposals were unrealistic. Might soon triumphed over right. British grenadiers, flanked by howitzers and twelve-pound guns and marching in procession to the quickstep tunes of their fife-and-drum bands, quickly took possession of the city. Shortly after midnight on September 19, bells warning of the enemy's approach

sounded throughout the city. Paine, leaden with despair, found the midnight panic eerie — "a beautiful still moonlight morning and the streets
as full of men, women and children as on a market day."[60] Left without alternatives, he stowed his trunk of personal belongings and Committee for
Foreign Affairs papers in a small boat sailing for Trenton. He lingered another twenty-four hours, hoping against hope. Fearing arrest and death at
the hands of the British, he then quit the city, not knowing his ultimate
destination, a refugee from war.

The Wanderer

For the next nine months, he wandered lonely as a cloud, riding the rutted
dirt back roads of America, squatting at friends' homes, dodging British
scouts and cannon fire, tracking the military campaign from close range,
grabbing whatever bits and pieces of news could reliably be obtained
about local and international politics. In early October, after seeking out
Washington's troops (they took three days to find, Paine "being unwilling
to ask questions, not knowing what company I might be in"), he witnessed
firsthand the Battle of Germantown, a one-street village five miles from
Philadelphia. In dense fog, which caused great confusion, the Americans,
who had tried to surprise the enemy with a bayonet charge, were forced to
retreat, musket balls whizzing over their heads. In tears, Paine watched
with incredulity the American troops retreating from the battlefront, accompanied by a stream of horse-drawn wagons loaded with wounded and
dead. Despite his sadness, he found himself impressed by their plucky
morale:

> Nobody hurried themselves. Every one marched his own pace. The enemy
> kept a civil distance behind, sending every now and then a shot after us,
> and receiving the same from us. . . . The army had marched the preceding
> night fourteen miles, and having full twenty to march back we . exceed-
> ingly fatigued. They appeared to me to be only sensible of a disappoint-
> ment, not a defeat, and to be more displeased at their retreating from
> Germantown, than anxious to get to their rendezvous.

Paine breakfasted the morning after the battle with General Washington, recalling that the American commander "was at the same loss with
every other to account for the accidents of the day. I remember his expressing his surprise, by saying, that at the time he supposed everything secure, and was about giving orders for the army to proceed down to
Philadelphia; that he most unexpectedly saw a part (I think of artillery)

hastily retreating." Paine tried to explain to Washington why the Americans had acted more as an armed mob than an army: "This partial retreat was, I believe, misunderstood, and soon followed by others. The fog was frequently very thick, the troops young, and unused to breaking and rallying, and our men rendered suspicious to each other, many of them being [dressed] in red." Paine then offered Washington a maxim with encouraging implications: "A new army once disordered, is difficult to manage, the attempt dangerous. To this may be added a prudence in not putting matters to too hazardous a trial the first time. Men must be taught *regular* fighting by practice and degree, and though the expedition failed, it had this good effect — that they seemed to feel themselves more important *after* it than before, as it was the first general attack they had ever made."

Paine's observation was probably right. Although the inexperienced Americans, blood-spattered and shaking, were forced to retreat through the fog, the battle was so close that the British avoided full-scale engagements during the remainder of Howe's command. The Americans were provided with a breathing space. Their morale was further boosted by a bloody but decisive victory on the Hudson River at Saratoga, where on October 17, 1777, the British, led by General John "Gentleman Johnny" Burgoyne, were trapped by the American troops. After vacillating instead of retreating to Canada, Burgoyne surrendered to the Americans, commanded by Horatio Gates. The American victory crushed Burgoyne's personal military fantasy of cutting off New England from the rest of America. News of the surrender spread throughout the country, leaving in its wake bells ringing, cannon booming joyous salutes, and a growing number of gloomy loyalists.

Meanwhile, Paine had slipped away from Germantown. Resuming his role as aide-de-camp to General Greene, he traveled on foot alone toward the American encampments at Red Bank and Mud Island, on the New Jersey side of the Delaware River. His mission was to bring to the American forces accurate details of the Battle of Germantown. He also had instructions to review the strength of the existing American blockade of the Delaware River, a blockade that the Americans considered vital for preventing the British from servicing their forces currently occupying Philadelphia. Reaching friendly forces at the confluence of the Delaware and Schuylkill Rivers, he witnessed, with that strange personal calmness bred by survival in war, the shelling of the American galley *Champion*, on which he had slept soundly the previous night. Later that day, he traveled with Colonel Christopher Greene, the commander of Red Bank, to Fort Mifflin on Mud Island, near the Pennsylvania shore. While they were making the short crossing on the Delaware River in an open, flat-bottomed boat, the British opened fire on them. Paine acted "*very* gallant," reported a traveling companion.[61] The shelling continued for the next few hours while Paine was on Mud Island going about his business. "They threw about thirty shells into it that afternoon, without doing any damage; the ground being damp and spongy, not above five or six burst; not a man was killed or wounded," he reported. That evening, tempting fate and guided by moonlight, he rowed back to the battered *Champion*, on which he slept another evening.

Paine spent the next several days edging his way on horseback, avoiding British traps, up the valley of the Delaware River to Bordentown, where he rested for a while with Colonel Joseph Kirkbride and his family. There a letter from his friend Timothy Matlack, secretary of Pennsylvania's Executive Council, awaited him. Matlack invited Paine to act as an intelligence officer responsible for providing firsthand war reports to the Pennsylvania Assembly and Executive Council. Matlack mentioned that the job would bring "a reasonable compensation" and noted the popularity of the choice. "Everyone agrees," he wrote, "that you are the proper person for the purpose."[62]

The flattery worked. During the last week of October, fully refreshed, Paine left for the American base camp, "fourteen miles from Philadelphia."[63] He reported to the Pennsylvania government that the army was trapped in mud, though in good spirits despite three days' driving rain. In a report filed to the Committee for Foreign Affairs (Paine at this point wore two hats), he urged that more American troops would be needed during the coming winter. His advice was based on several nighttime reconnaissance missions to within sight of the British lines around Philadelphia. His report sketched a plan for a draft, suggesting that those men whose lot was not drawn should contribute a dollar or two to a fund from which the drafted, or their chosen substitutes, would be paid a salary during their period of service. In the same report, Paine scoffed at the continuing British talk of "a Rebellion" in the colonies. He insisted that the Articles of Capitulation accepted in principle by the British after their defeat at Saratoga — "that the officers and men shall be transferred to England and not serve in or against North America during the present war" — implied that England and America were independent sovereign states, equally capable of negotiating and concluding agreements. Yet Paine's native skepticism of power drove him to doubt whether the British would honor the agreement. "I would not trust them an inch farther than I could see them in the present state of things," he wrote cheekily. He went on to urge Congress not to trust in the Articles, and, significantly, for the first time he turned his pen against it for not having yet made public the details of the British surrender at Saratoga. Congress had no right to use war to justify secrecy: "They do an exceedingly wrong thing by not publishing them because they subject the whole affair to suspicion."[64]

After filing his reports, Paine backtracked the country roads to the Kirkbrides' near Bordentown, where he stayed for the first two weeks of November. Unlike the total wars that followed the French Revolution, the American struggle for independence was a part-time war in which the struggle for territory and military superiority was subordinated to the battle for the hearts and minds of the population. The war allowed time off from battle, and that is why, even when the American forces were unsure of survival, let alone victory, Paine found time to recuperate from his duties without immediate fear of being dragged away by the British. The Kirkbrides lived at Bellevue farm in Bucks County on the Pennsylvania side of the Delaware River, just opposite Bordentown, New Jersey. Paine was welcomed, well fed, and generally pampered.

Joseph Kirkbride and his wife, Mary, were well-off by Bucks County standards. According to district records from the year 1776, they paid the second highest tax in the county, owning nine horses, twenty-five sheep, twenty-five head of cattle, and three Negro slaves.[65] Kirkbride greatly admired Paine, and their lifelong friendship (Paine later considered him his closest friend) was cemented by remarkably similar experiences and ideas. Kirkbride, who was six years older than Paine, had been born into a Pennsylvania Quaker family and had received an ordinary country education. He was as fond of horses and horseback riding as Paine and loved country life. He had married Mary Rogers, a non-Quaker from Allentown, but before he could be disciplined for the offense, he had joined the provincial militia, which then ensured his expulsion from the Society of Friends. Kirkbride owned a set of globes, and his scientific and philosophical interests had earned him membership in the American Philosophical Society in 1768. The two men loved to discuss religion, and Kirkbride, true to his Quaker upbringing, was a skeptic of all organized forms of worship. A mutual friend wrote of him that he had *Common Sense enough* to disbelieve most of the Common Systematic Theories of Divinity but does not seem to establish any for himself." Kirkbride was also a political animal. He had played an active role locally in the events leading up to the Declaration of Independence and was a member of the convention that had drawn up and agreed to Pennsylvania's new state constitution. At the time of Paine's visit, during the first half of November 1777, Kirkbride was an elected member of the Assembly, colonel of the First Battalion of Bucks County Associators, and in charge of recruiting soldiers and raising arms and general supplies in a county exposed to British invasion.

Paine's quiet life at the Kirkbrides' did not last long. Around the middle of November, he returned to the American base camp to join a scouting party commanded by General Greene. For four nights and days, the party reconnoitered the dangerous ground around the American forts at the mouth of the Schuylkill, hoping to ascertain British plans. During the mission, the British showed their hand. On November 16, after a week of continuous British bombardment, Fort Mifflin on Mud Island was struck down, despite fierce American resistance. The channel into Philadelphia was now wide-open, and the Americans, fearing rout, evacuated nearby Fort Mercer and burned nearly all their ships to prevent the British from capturing them. On November 18, dug in with several thousand of Greene's melancholy troops, Paine watched the British sweep across the Delaware River to occupy Fort Mercer, unopposed.

The military situation appeared to be sliding back to the gloom of the period before Trenton. As autumn disappeared beneath the first snowfall of winter, the American war effort went into hibernation. Paine returned to the Kirkbrides', convinced that the British would winter in the comforts of Philadelphia. Meanwhile, Washington, against the advice of most of his generals, marched his hungry troops into bivouac at Valley Forge, twenty miles upriver from Philadelphia, close enough to keep an eye on the British. "I was there when the army first began to build huts," Paine told Benjamin Franklin. The American troops were "like a family of beavers: every one busy; some carrying logs, others mud, and the rest fastening them together. The whole was raised in a few days, and is a curious collection of buildings in the true rustic order."[66]

Paine had a strong tendency to believe in the beneficent outcome of events, despite signs to the contrary. He found it difficult to accept that improvements are usually paid for with setbacks and that there are not always happy endings in human history. "We rub and drive on," he told Franklin, "beyond what could ever be expected, and instead of wondering why some things have not been done better, the greater wonder is we have done so well."[67] Such providentialism, as it might be called, warped his public statements during the winter of 1777–78. Valley Forge, contrary to the impression he gave, was a desperate encampment. The British had swept through several months earlier, pillaging the area of all provisions, leaving behind a wooded wilderness. Valley Forge became the low-water mark for the American army. The troops were half frozen, destitute, and infected with a skin complaint known as the itch; horses died of starvation; and there were constant rumors about dissolving the army. American army surgeon James Thacher reported that a friend had visited the camp shortly after Paine and that "while walking with General Washington, along the soldiers' huts, he heard from many voices echoing through open crevices between the logs, '*no pay, no clothes, no provisions, no rum,*' and when a miserable being was seen flitting from one hut to another, his nakedness was only covered by a dirty blanket." Thacher added, "In the darkening hour of adversity, any man who possesses less firmness than Washington, would despair of our Independence."[68]

Paine never mentioned despair. Nor was there a word about the plots to dislodge Washington as commander of the American forces. During the Valley Forge period, a bitter power struggle over his future broke out at York, the temporary seat of Congress, and at Lancaster, the home of the Pennsylvania state government.[69] Paine's silence about this so-called Conway Cabal ensured that he did not have to take sides with or against good friends such as Richard Henry Lee, Thomas Mifflin, and Benjamin Rush, each of whom had expressed serious doubts about Washington's competence as Commander-in-Chief and was urging his replacement by Horatio Gates. But Paine had another motive in remaining silent. He, along with many others, was convinced that 1778 might be the year of victory if political and military unity could be restored and a well-supplied and disciplined army placed in the field. He considered that the dismissal of Washington would have a disastrous impact on American morale at this difficult stage of the war, and that is why he did everything he could to lift drooping spirits by focusing public attention elsewhere.

From the safety of his temporary home at Bordentown, Paine busied himself with proposals, put before Commodore Haslewood, commander of the surviving American fleet anchored at Trenton, to launch rocket-propelled or manually sailed boats packed with explosives into the midst of the British fleet hovering near Philadelphia. During his two-month stay at the Kirkbrides', Paine also began to work on the fifth number of *The American Crisis*, which he later described as an attempt to deflect the "meditated blow" against Washington, despite his "want of military judgement." He confided that he "could see no possible advantage, and nothing but mischief" in whipping up controversy about Washington.[70]

For that reason, Paine may have deliberately kept away from politics — "distracting the army in parties" he called it — by spending Christmas and most of the month of January with the Kirkbrides. But with the Washington controversy fading and an early spring thaw on its way, he set off on foot to the village of York, 120 miles to the west, where Congress was then sitting, to resume his duties as Secretary to the Committee for Foreign Affairs. The job proved undemanding for the time being, since the Committee's agents in France and the West Indies could not get their reports through the iced-in and British-blocked ports of the American east coast. Sharing an office on the second floor of a small building also used by the Board of War, Paine had virtually nothing to do. Instead of taking rooms in half-empty York, he moved to nearby Lancaster, the largest inland town in America and by that time a center for refugees from occupied Philadelphia. "A very blustering blowing night even seemed to make the House shake . . . also cold, snow flurries fine moon," wrote pharmacist Christopher Marshall, a fellow exile in Lancaster, in his diary of February 12, 1778. "Just as I lock'd [the] front door to prepare for bed Thos. Payne came. So there was supper to get for him; having been thus recruited, had his bed warmed then to bed after he sat some time regaling himself."[71]

The next day, Paine was invited to stay at the home of William Henry, an inventor, merchant, and gunsmith, whose trade naturally prospered during the war. Paine accepted, moving immediately to the Henry household, which already harbored two other refugee guests — Colonel Joseph Hart of the Supreme Executive Council, and state treasurer and astronomer David Rittenhouse, both of whom Paine knew well. Henry himself had experimented with steam engine–propelled boats and knew much about chemistry. Paine found the company stimulating and felt sufficiently at home to indulge his favorite habits, including long afternoon naps. John Joseph Henry, who was at home with his parents that winter recovering from a battle wound received at Québec, later recalled their guest's laziness. The description was tainted by a dislike of Paine. "His remissness, indolence or vacuity of thought," Henry said, "caused great heart-burning among many primary characters." Although sometimes reading until the early hours of the morning, Paine normally slept late, enjoyed a leisurely breakfast, and then went for a long stroll, which he found helped to order his thoughts. After returning to his room around noon and writing down what he had composed during his stroll, he ate "an inordinate dinner." He would then retire to his room, "wrap a blanket about him, and in a large arm-chair, take a nap, of two or three hours." He would then take a second stroll, write a few more sentences, and eat a light supper. Then his favorite activity of the day: a long fireside evening discussion helped along by gossip, laughter, hard argument, and some wine.[72]

John Joseph Henry complained that Paine wrote so slowly that dust gathered on his manuscript. The complaint was unwarranted. During his stay at the Henrys', Paine completed the fifth number of *The American Crisis*. Dated March 21, 1778, the twenty-four-page pamphlet was printed in Lancaster by John Dunlap and, very much against Paine's wishes, sold for the inflated price of 2s. 6d. The pamphlet nevertheless circulated widely, in part because the high price encouraged newspapers such as the *Boston Gazette* and publishers in New Haven and Hartford to serialize or reprint it.[73]

The first part of the pamphlet kept the tradition of publicly questioning the British from below by hurling its plainly worded arguments at Sir William Howe, the commander of the British troops occupying Philadelphia. Paine was full of cheek, and his judgment that Howe and his policies were already failures was to be proven right. Paine's sarcastic advice was well written:

> Go home, sir, and endeavour to save the remains of your ruined country, by a just representation of the madness of her measures. A few moments, well applied, may yet preserve her from political destruction. I am not one of those who wish to see Europe in a flame, because I am persuaded that such an event will not shorten the war. The rupture, at present, is confined between the two powers of America and England. England finds that she cannot conquer America, and America has no wish to conquer England. You are fighting for what you can never obtain, and we defending what we never mean to part with. A few words, therefore, settle the bargain. Let England mind her own business and we will mind ours. Govern yourselves, and we will govern ourselves. You may then trade where you please unmolested by us, and we will trade where we please unmolested by you; and such articles as we can purchase of each other better than elsewhere may be mutually done. If it were possible that you could carry on the war for twenty years you must still come to this point at last, or worse, and the sooner you think of it the better it will be for you.

Paine cheekily signed the first part of the pamphlet, "I am, Sir, with every wish for an honourable peace, Your friend, enemy, and countryman, COMMON SENSE."[74]

In the second part, he wrote for his American readers, urging their solidarity as self-respecting citizens and reminding them of their duty to defend their country. The only way "to finish the war with the least possible bloodshed," he exhorted, "is to collect an army against the power of which the enemy will have no chance." He went on to propose drafting four out of every hundred men, the remaining ninety-six supporting the citizens' army with money and services. What was most striking about this second half was what was *not* said. The sufferings of the troops at Valley Forge went unmentioned, and not a word was written about the verbal campaign being waged against Washington. Paine later admitted that the purpose of this *Crisis* was to shore up Washington's reputation and to prevent party politics from ruining the war effort. Although the essay contained little more than a fleeting mention of "the unabated fortitude of a Washington," Paine's silence was tactical: to have aired publicly the private quarrel about Washington or even to have spoken his own mind might have damaged American morale and, with that, the war effort. Both the tactic and the silence smacked of a profound political dilemma of democratic republican politics: military success required secrecy, cunning, order, discipline, and unquestioning loyalty, whereas the ultimate aim of the military campaign — republican citizenship — required the rule of law and freedom of public debate among citizens jealous of their liberty and equality.

The Silas Deane Affair

The same dilemma troubled Paine many times during the War of Independence. Although this time his calculated silence was exceptional, in every other recorded case he consistently sided with the principle of publicly accountable power against its arbitrary exercise. Still in Lancaster in mid-April 1778, Paine wrote to Henry Laurens with details of the trial of two loyalists accused of passing counterfeit Continental money. The defendants' counsel contended, cleverly, that the Act of Congress making it a felony to counterfeit or knowingly circulate counterfeit money properly "emitted by Congress" referred only to that money which had been issued by Congress up to the date of the Act. One of the accused was acquitted, the other convicted only of fraud. Paine expressed his disagreement with the "misapplied lenity" of the judgment. He insisted that the words of the Act were intended "to distinguish Continental money from other money, and not one time from another time." He also expressed his strong personal disapproval of forgery, describing it variously as "a sin against all men alike," as "reprobated by all civil nations," and as "a species of treason." But, given the seriousness of the matter, Paine's conclusion was mild mannered and politically careful. He drew back from talk of revenge and of the political necessity of overturning this particular judgment. To do that, he recognized, would have involved committing the far more serious crime of violating the rule of law. Paine concluded that under battle conditions in a revolution, when the thirst for power is difficult to quench and despotism a permanent danger, the rule of law ought to be considered an indispensable brake upon the arbitrary exercise of power. Against cynics, Paine also warned that ambiguity in the meaning of law, especially in its youth, is always to be expected. He insisted that impatience with ambiguity in matters of law easily slides into impatience with law itself. He concluded, lightheartedly, "There never was but one Act (said a Member of the House of Commons) which a man might not creep out of, i.e. the Act which obliges a man to be buried in woollen."[75]

Paine not only championed the rule of law against the militaristic tendencies of revolution; he also considered fundamentally important the cultivation of public spheres of reading, listening, and arguing and public means of judging citizens who watch over their government constantly, often getting up its nose for the sake of securing citizens' freedom and equality. The principle that public authorities should be regarded as public property had been tested many times against the British, and during the year 1778 Paine continued to lash out at their military efforts to crush the Revolution. Among his prime targets was Governor George Johnstone, a British peace commissioner, who had tried to whip up public opinion against Congress and to bribe a number of its members to desert the American cause. Paine responded with a little-remembered poem written in the style of Alexander Pope's sharply satirical couplets:

> When Satan first from Heaven's bright region fell,
> And fix'd the gloomy monarch of hell,
> Sin then was honest; Pride led on the tribe;
> No Devil receiv'd — no Devil propos'd a bribe:
> But each infernal, while he fought, abhorr'd
> The meaner mongrel arts of sap and fraud;
> Brave in his guilt, he rais'd his daring arm,
> And scorn'd the heavens, unless obtain'd by storm.
>
> But Britain — Oh! how painful 'tis to tell!
> Commits a sin that makes a blush in hell;
> Low in the ruins of demolish'd pride
> She basely skulks to conquer with a bribe,
> And when detected in the rank offence,
> Throws out a threat — to turn King's evidence.[76]

Paine explained to Henry Laurens, at around the same time as the trial of the alleged counterfeiters, that his own activities as a political writer could be compared favorably to a cultivator of fresh ideas for the public. "I am a *farmer of thoughts*," he said, "and all the crops I raise I give away."[77] The metaphor accurately described his deep commitment to defending civil and political liberties and to stimulating the republican imagination — even if this meant publicly criticizing the course of the Revolution itself.

There were times, from the spring of 1778 on, when Paine's defense of civil society began to turn against the American government itself. As the war dragged on, he found himself at the center of the young republic's biggest corruption scandal. The Silas Deane affair, as it is now called, was a gripping saga, with Paine at his sharpest. The episode was a turning point in Paine's political career, and it has a remarkable familiarity two centuries later. It was something of an eighteenth-century Iran-Contra affair. The affair raised issues of state secrecy, money laundering by governments, misuse of public power, and embezzlement of public funds by private individuals. It involved secret plans for the French and Spanish governments to pay a million livres each for military purposes and to launder that large sum of money plus used weapons from French arsenals through a private business, without the knowledge of the American Congress.

In early May 1778, after months of rumors, a bundle of dispatches arrived in York containing, among other materials, two treaties with France — a commercial treaty and a treaty of alliance — and a promise that these treaties would soon be backed by French troops and ships, sent to wing America to victory. French strings were attached. The quid pro quo laid down — that the United States, if asked, must help defend France's West Indian possessions if they were attacked — had previously been criticized by Paine and others as an example of corrupt dealings among armed monarchic states. Now, backed up against the British wall, the American side generally welcomed the whole package of French proposals. Paine himself joined in the applause, above all because of his growing conviction that the war was hampering the struggle for republican government and should therefore be ended as quickly as possible — on American terms, of course. War profiteering worried him especially. He noted that virtually every debate in the Continental Congress on matters such as sumptuary controls and profiteering focused on the growing tension in American life between private greed and public virtue. Some leading revolutionaries were insisting that public virtue was of necessity dying a slow death, that the scrambling and scratching of people to satisfy their private wants and aspirations was an ineluctable feature of modern life. The point was certainly made by Robert Morris, a wealthy Philadelphia merchant and congressman. "It is inconsistent with the principles of liberty," he wrote, "to prevent a man from the free disposal of his property on such terms as he may think fit."[78]

Paine bristled at such talk. Early English experiences had made him an unswerving adherent of the republican ideal of a commonwealth of citizens guided by public virtue. Talk by avaricious men of the necessity of avarice reinforced his suspicion that American civil society could degenerate into a mercantile society dominated by class privilege, egoism, and public corruption. For Paine, power based on self-interest was the bane of republican virtue. He reserved his particular wrath for Silas Deane, who went on record to defend the view that a merchant, or anyone for that matter, could surely disbelieve the nebulous ideal of the public good and, hence, could rarely be expected "to quit the line which interest marks out for him."[79]

Deane's views were reinforced by a business career mixed with politics. Born in Connecticut in the same year as Paine, educated at Yale College, and twice married into wealth and social influence, Deane had been employed as a country shopkeeper, a schoolteacher, and a lawyer. He cut a striking figure and was accustomed to dapper living and lavish entertainment. He was among the most prominent enthusiasts of independence in Connecticut and had served twice as a delegate from that colony to Congress, where he developed a reputation as a flamboyant schemer. Deane also had co-organized the procurement and distribution of weapons and supplies to the Green Mountain Boys, who had captured the British fort at Ticonderoga in early May 1775.

That mercantile and administrative success so impressed Congress that they approached him early in 1776 to discuss the procurement of military supplies from France. Although Deane had never traveled abroad and spoke not a word of French, Congress commissioned him as their first agent ever to be sent abroad with extraordinary powers of procurement. In his formal instructions of March 1776, he was directed to do three things: first, to procure from the French government supplies of military clothing, cannon, muskets, and ammunition for an army of twenty-five thousand men; second, to purchase European goods for distribution in the revolutionaries' negotiations with Native Americans; third, with the assistance of Arthur Lee and Benjamin Franklin, to prepare the way for a treaty of commerce and alliance between Congress and France. In return, Deane was offered his travel and living expenses and a commission of 5 percent on all materials he purchased for the American war effort.[80]

Deane landed at Bordeaux in May 1776. After purchasing commodities for Native Americans, he traveled in secret to Paris, armed with letters of introduction from Franklin and masquerading as a merchant in the trade with India. Within hours of his arrival in Paris, he sought a meeting with the Comte de Vergennes, the French Minister of Foreign Affairs. What Deane did not know was that the French court had already decided that it was expedient to support the Americans. He also was unaware that the French would insist on shrouding their aid in secrecy, partly because open support for the American cause would have required additional French preparations for going to war again with England, and partly because Louis XVI and his advisers were well aware of the serious public-embarrassment potential of an ancient monarchy's open encouragement of republican rebellion against a recognized sovereign.

It is unclear whether a meeting between Deane and the French minister ever took place, but it seems that Vergennes directed him to a gentleman named Pierre Augustin Caron de Beaumarchais, with whom Arthur Lee had already had dealings. Beaumarchais, a former watchmaker's apprentice, was at that time engaged in printing a complete edition of the writings of Voltaire and also putting finishing touches to the opera *La Mariage de Figaro*, which would later make him world famous. Beaumarchais was renowned as a lively wit, an accomplished harpist and poet, and a wheeler-dealer. The latter quality led to his appointment as head of Roderique Hortalez and Company, a paper organization set up by the French government for the purpose of channeling military supplies secretly to the Americans without the direct supervision of the crown. The laundering company was capitalized to the tune of one million livres from the French and Spanish monarchies. Surplus arms and ammunition in French arsenals also were made available to the company.[81]

Deane's negotiations with Beaumarchais had an immediate effect. Within weeks, vessels laden with guns, ammunition, and other supplies set sail for America. But the glory of the mission served as a mask for the pocket-lining intrigues of the two negotiators — or so Paine thought. According to information supplied to him by Arthur Lee, who had firsthand knowledge of the operation, the French government did not expect the Americans to pay for the supplies.[82] Although Paine and Lee were later proved right, the Americans were charged inflated prices for many materials, at least some of which were gifts from Franco-Spanish sources. The French gentleman of "wit and genius," as Deane called Beaumarchais, sold the Americans muskets at half their original cost, despite the fact that they had been discarded by the French army and given to him gratis. He sent bills of lading for shipments of materials that were in fact gifts and marked up gunpowder sold to the Americans by 500 percent. The final invoice was staggering. At the end of 1777, an agent from Hortalez and Company journeyed to Philadelphia to present Congress with a final bill of 4.5 million livres, for immediate payment to Beaumarchais. An accompanying letter written by Deane confirmed that the invoice was correct in its details. Deane in effect lied not only (as was later claimed) because his nonexistent French left him in the dark when dealing with Beaumarchais. He lied primarily because he had already yielded to the temptation to profit from the transaction, to secure contracts with French officers, and to make private purchases for himself and friends in America such as Robert Morris, who told him before leaving France, "If we have but luck in getting the goods safe to America the profits will be sufficient to content us all."[83]

Deane, unaware that his negotiations with Beaumarchais were already controversial, remained in Paris doing business until the conclusion of treaty negotiations between the Americans and the French in February 1778. He received news of his recall by Congress during the first week of March 1778. On April 1, after accepting an invitation arranged through Vergennes, Deane embarked on the fleet that was bringing the new French ambassador, Conrad Alexander Gérard, to America. The fleet arrived in Philadelphia in mid-July, with Deane expecting a tumultuous welcome in recognition of his two-year service in the cause of America. Instead, his return sparked nothing but furious controversies, the bitterest of the entire period of the Revolution. The dispute reached all the way from local Pennsylvania politics to the courts of Europe, and it divided the press and Continental Congress into bitter factions along incipient party lines. Without intending it, Deane and Paine, his chief public critic, were to deliver death blows to the classical republican ideal of an undivided political community — and assist the painful and protracted birth of competitive party politics as a permanent feature of American democracy.[84]

At the time the Deane affair erupted, Congress was already exercised by several minor scandals and riven by a fundamental disagreement about the role of public virtue in the emerging American republic. Earlier in the year, for instance, it had heard that Thomas Mifflin had misused his position as quartermaster general of the army by employing government wagons to transport civilian goods for sale on the open market. Another case involved allegations that the head of the medical department, Dr. William Shippen, had knowingly sold hospital supplies to private consumers and pocketed the profits. The allegations against Deane raised the same issue of whether, and to what extent, the pursuit of self-interest within a republic is legitimate. The critics of Deane saw him as a prototype of the new breed of American men of wealth and power. In their eyes, he was someone who had prospered on wartime contracts while the bedraggled Continental army had to make do with ragged clothes, poor food and shelter, blood-blistered feet, and often no pay. "Speculation, peculation, and an insatiable thirst for riches," snapped Washington during a visit to Congress in Philadelphia soon after Deane's return there, "seem to have got the better of every other consideration and almost of every order of men."[85]

Some congressmen, worried about the decline of public spiritedness due to spreading egoism and capitalist markets, repeated this theme. Led by Samuel Adams and Richard Henry Lee, they thought of themselves as the founders and leaders of the independence movement. Frequently called the Eastern Party, they tended to be hostile to the growth of national government, and they resented the attempts of the new French minister to influence the decisions of Congress. Like Paine, they were profoundly suspicious of Deane, and they naturally demanded the inspection of his files. Deane's reactions served merely to fuel their suspicions. He claimed that he had had no time before leaving France to order his accounts and that the books had been left behind in that country. The Eastern Party fumed. Its supporters in Congress moved that he provide a written report of his Paris activities. Those siding with Deane — a pro-merchant faction led by John Jay and Gouverneur Morris, both of them delegates from New York — blocked the motion, and the inquiry ended in acid adjectives.

The affair remained hidden from civil society until December 5, 1778. On that day Deane, frustrated by the refusal of Congress to allow him to put his case in person before it, published a lengthy diatribe against his critics. He accused Richard Henry Lee and a faction in Congress of working illegally against the treaty with France and for reconciliation with Britain.[86] The tactic of labeling his opponents counterrevolutionaries backfired. Not only did Deane's claims raise the hackles of his doubters, but his diatribe also convinced his critics that there was a plot sponsored by merchants and war profiteers to corrupt the fledgling American republic. Lee, a champion of the Franco-American alliance, dubbed Deane a ringleader in a "corrupt hotbed of vice" that "has produced a tall tree of evil, the branches of which spread over [the] great part of Europe and America." He warned that "unless it is speedily cut down and thrown away, I easily foresee extensive mischief to these states, and to the cause of human nature."[87] The uproar in Congress grew louder. Henry Laurens of

South Carolina, who currently served as president of Congress, resigned in disgust, questioning Deane's "highly derogatory" slurs against Congress and "the honour and interests of these United States."[88]

Congressional supporters of Deane responded with invective of their own — initially by withdrawing the customary vote of thanks to Laurens for his services, then by electing a new president sympathetic to Deane, John Jay of New York. Paine could no longer sit still. Having followed the whole affair silently for nearly six months, he was moved to action by his friend Laurens's resignation speech, his friend Lee's talk of spreading vice, and classified information available to him as Secretary to the Committee for Foreign Affairs. For several weeks, documents that had been crossing his desk confirmed "that the stores which Silas Deane and Beaumarchais pretended they had purchased were a present from the Court of France, and came out of the King's arsenals."[89] Convinced that there was a cover-up, Paine published an open letter to Deane in mid-December in John Dunlap's *Pennsylvania Packet*. He followed it up with another eight contributions in the same newspaper during the next four weeks.[90]

Paine initially trod with care. He had decided to enter the fray, he said, "to preserve the honour of Congress," and he claimed that threats of violence had been issued against him to help him change his mind on the matter.[91] Uncowed, he criticized Deane as unfit for public service, citing his erratic behavior and "over-strained desire to be believed." Paine also revealed his key doubt about the veracity of Deane's story: "Would anybody have supposed that a gentleman in the character of a commercial agent, and afterwards in that of a public minister, would return home after seeing himself both recalled and superseded, and not bring with him his papers and vouchers?" That question instantly ruffled feathers among Deane's supporters. Among them was General Benedict Arnold's aide-de-camp, Matthew Clarkson, who accused Paine of lying.[92] Paine snapped at Clarkson's talk of "gross misrepresentation of the facts." He also threatened to prosecute him for libel but wisely sidestepped legal wranglings by announcing, on Christmas Eve, 1778, that he would soon lay "the facts fairly, with his usual candour, before the public."[93]

The promised attack on Deane caused a minor sensation. For the first time during his stay in America, Paine leathered an American patriot, charging him with profiteering, hubris, secrecy, and war trading. Paine was astonished by the level of hostility directed at him. Many accused him of fracturing the body politic by deliberately promoting party divisions.[94] Some inferred that he was an enemy of the Revolution. Many were shocked by his boldness. "There is something in this concealment of papers that looks like an embezzlement," Paine wrote. He went on to link Deane's congressional activities to "mercantile connections." He pointed the finger especially at Robert Morris, until recently a delegate from Pennsylvania, accusing him of misuse of public office. As chairman of a committee purchasing military supplies, Paine said, Morris had directed contracts worth over half a million dollars to his own company of Willing and Morris, as well as contracts to friends, among them Deane. Paine called for a public inquiry — initiating a great American tradition — into whether Morris's private dealings were compatible with the public interest.

By broadening the attack, Paine sparked a broadened reply. His enemies thought his prose didactic to the point of being bombastic, and Morris, insisting that his business was his business, reacted sharply in an open letter: "If Mr. Deane had any commerce that was inconsistent with his public station, he must answer for it, as I did not, by becoming a Delegate for the State of Pennsylvania, relinquish my right of forming mercantile connections, I was unquestionably at liberty to form such with Mr. Deane."[95] Friends applauded Morris's toughness. Thomas Mifflin told him that their mutual enemy resembled a crazed Ottoman warrior: "Paine, like the enthusiastic madmen of the East, was determined to run the *muck* — he sallied forth, stabbed three or four slightly, met with you, but missing his arm fell a victim to his own stroke; and by attempting too much will enjoy a most mortifying and general contempt."[96] Paine, who always loved a political fight, hit back. Restating his charges of embezzlement and general corruption, he invited visitors to his office to inspect a report, "in handwriting which Mr. Deane is well acquainted with," that proved beyond a doubt that the war materials he claimed to have purchased "were promised and engaged . . . as a present . . . before he ever arrived in France."[97]

The American earth suddenly rumbled under Paine's feet. Reports circulated that Paine had "got a beating from an Officer, it is said for having wrote the piece."[98] His enemies began to portray him as a traitor of the Revolution. They were quick to point out that his seemingly innocent offer to the public of classified information violated the oath of secrecy he had signed when accepting the position of Secretary to the Committee for Foreign Affairs. How could Paine offer classified information on arms dealings as well as swear "to disclose no matter, the knowledge of which shall be acquired in consequence of such his office, that he shall be directed to keep secret"? Whispers about Paine's anti-French opinions added poison to the allegations. In the third year of the Revolution, a growing number of American patriots considered France, the enemy of the Americans' chief enemy, their closest friend in the field of foreign affairs — an ally without which they could not militarily defeat the British. They consequently jumped to the conclusion that Paine's contributions to the Deane affair impugned the honor of the French government and undermined the Franco-American alliance. Paine was seen to be thrusting a dagger into the heart of the only alliance that could save America. The new French envoy to America, Gérard, added to that impression. Worried that Paine's allegations might embarrass French government pretensions to neutrality in the American war, he decided that whatever the facts, Paine had to be silenced. He wrote to Paine to express his suspicion that he was working for the anti-French faction in Congress led by Samuel Adams and Richard Henry Lee. Gérard concluded by insisting that Paine publicly retract his noxious allegations about Deane.[99]

Paine refused to back down. On January 2, 1779, he replied, convinced more than ever that liberty entails the right to tell others what they don't want to hear. Paine tried to reassure Gérard that his suspicion was groundless, that Paine was drawing a clear and principled distinction between the French gift of supplies to the Americans and Deane's fraudulent misuse of his public authority. "My design," Paine wrote, "was and is to place the merit of these supplies where I think the merit is most due, that is in the disposition of the French nation to help us." Gérard's call for a retraction went unheeded, but he seemed satisfied by Paine's promise to be "more explicit on the subject" in a forthcoming essay, apparently interpreting this as a promised retraction.[100]

Gérard wrote that same day to thank Paine for his reassurances.[101] Gérard remained calm until he opened his *Pennsylvania Packet* on the morning of January 5, only to find Paine still on the attack. An hour later, moved by pride, anger, and political embarrassment, Gérard lodged a curtly written protest to Congress, urging it "to take measures suitable to the circumstance" to remedy what he described as Paine's "indiscreet assertions."[102] The next episode in the unfolding drama arrived more quickly than anybody expected. Pressured by talk of indiscretion and faced with the unpalatable option of falling silent, Paine offered Congress his resignation as Secretary to the Committee for Foreign Affairs.

Congress reacted by summoning Paine and his publisher, John Dunlap, to appear before it at eleven o'clock on Wednesday, January 7, 1779. The proceedings began with Dunlap being asked whether he had published pieces by Thomas Paine. He nodded and was asked to leave the legislature. Paine was then called in. John Jay, the president, picked up a copy of the *Pennsylvania Packet* and said with an icy stare, "Here is Mr.

Dunlap's paper of December 29. In it is a piece entitled 'Common Sense to the Public on Mr. Deane's affairs'; I am directed by Congress to ask you if you are the author." Paine, standing expressionless, replied, "Yes, sir, I am the author of that piece." Jay put the same question about two later pieces on the same subject and received the same reply. "You may withdraw," he said, then ruling that nothing more needed to be added to the discussion. The instant Paine was ushered out the door of Independence Hall, John Penn of North Carolina moved that "Thomas Paine be discharged from the office of secretary of the Committee for Foreign Affairs." Seconded by Gouverneur Morris, the motion flung Congress into a rage. After several hours' bitter discussion, Morris's motion was lost when put to the vote, "the states being equally divided," Paine reported.[103]

Paine wasted no time resuming the offensive. Later that day, January 7, he submitted a memorandum to Congress that pushed it to the precipice of an even bitterer disagreement about the fundamental principle of state secrets. Paine's memorandum challenged head-on the maxim that in politics a little sincerity is dangerous and a great deal of it absolutely fatal. Worded in tough, proud prose, the memorandum directly accused Congress of unjustly guillotining his case without making public the charge against him:

> I cannot in duty to my character as a freeman submit to be censured unheard. I have evidence which I presume will justify me. And I entreat this House to consider how great their reproach will be should it be told that they passed a sentence upon me without hearing me, and that a copy of the charge against me was refused to me; and likewise how much that reproach will be aggravated should I afterwards prove the censure of this House to be a libel, grounded upon a mistake which they refused fully to inquire into.[104]

Paine's argument confronted Congress with an unprecedented charge. In effect, he was saying that Congress, in disregarding the rule of law, was acting as arbitrarily as a despotic monarchy. Paine also confronted Congress with an entirely new issue: whether to confer upon him the dubious distinction of being the first senior public official to be impeached by an American government.

For the next ten days, Congress wrestled with these issues behind closed doors. Paine's enemies bit to draw blood. Their rhetoric would be repeated many times in his later life. Gouverneur Morris highlighted "the threatening letter" written to Congress by Paine, whom he described as a contemptible figure stuffed with "mad assertions," a rough-cut commoner

who was nothing better than a "mere adventurer *from England,* without fortune, without family or connections, ignorant even of grammar." According to Morris, who was a believer in the sovereignty of the legislature, not
of the people, Congress had every right in the world to censure one of its
loose-tongued employees. "What!" he shouted above the heads of heckling colleagues, "are we reduced to such a situation, that our servants shall
abuse the confidence reposed in them, shall beard us with insolent men-
aces, and we shall fear to discuss them without granting a trial forsooth?"
The key point, said Morris, was that Paine was seeking to defame and
usurp the sovereign powers of Congress. He had craftily maneuvered to
fabricate the impression abroad that he wrote on behalf of Congress. The
damage so created must be undone by sacking him from his post. That
would make clear where sovereign power lay. "And what are we?" he concluded rhetorically. "The sovereign power, who appointed, and who when
he no longer pleases us, may remove him. Nothing more is desired. We do
not wish to punish him."[105]

By insisting that Paine was a state employee, not an ordinary citizen,
Morris tried to muzzle those delegates who emphasized that Congress had
no right to discipline or punish a citizen unheard. The tactic seemed to
work. After the opening day's frosty discussions of the affair, Paine's
friends warned him that Congress would likely vote to sack him. Paine denied his enemies that pleasure. He chose to avoid a repetition of the personal humiliation he had suffered fourteen years earlier in Alford and to
ensure that the principle of free public discussion was not sacrificed at the
stake of state power by hand-delivering a letter of resignation to Congress
before the opening of business on January 8. The tone and direction of
the letter were unrepentant. Emphasizing his basic right as a "freeman" to
"yield up to no power whatever," he denied any wrongdoing: "I have betrayed no trust because I have constantly employed that trust to the public
good. I have revealed no secrets because I have told nothing that was, or I
conceive ought to be a secret. I have convicted Mr. Deane of error, and in
so doing I hope I have done my duty."[106]

The letter sparked further acrimony. The bitter arguments dragged on
another week, postponing official acceptance of his resignation. Several of
Paine's critics even turned the powers of interrogation of Congress
against Congress itself, launching something of a witch-hunt among its
delegates to clarify how Paine had discovered from the top-secret *Journals
of the Continental Congress* that he had been denied a formal hearing. After
the secretary of Congress, Charles Thomson, made it clear that the *Journals* had never left his hands and that Paine could not have seen them, an

embarrassed Henry Laurens was forced to confess that he had spoken to
Paine during the preceding days' controversies. The pro-Deane faction
made further gains by winning unanimous approval for a proposal that
John Jay write a letter, to be released to the newspapers, in which Jay reassured the French minister that Congress had rejected Paine's claims, including his various attempts (such as his warning against entangling
alliances in *Common Sense*) to "injure the reputation" of France and America and to "impair their mutual confidence."[107]

A final blow against Paine was delivered on January 16. After an entire
day of wrangling about the ex-secretary, Congress agreed that all public
papers in his possession should be returned to Congress. But the remaining issue of whether to override Paine's resignation formally by dismissing
him from his post was resolved with great difficulty. Votes in Congress
were normally cast by states, but on this occasion John Penn successfully
moved that the votes of individuals be recorded. Every delegate from New
York and the whole of the South — except Richard Henry Lee and Laurens, who was absent — voted to dismiss Paine. Every Pennsylvanian and
every New Englander supported the acceptance of his resignation. Since
no delegates from New Jersey were present, the states found themselves
deadlocked. Under the house rules, a tied vote defeated a motion, and
Congress had no option but to accept Paine's resignation. When he received the final salary installment of $250 ten weeks later, Paine's official
ties with Congress were cut forever.

6

Public Insults

Public Abuse

MONTHS after resigning as Secretary to the Continental Congress's Committee for Foreign Affairs, Tom Paine still felt the crushing controversy triggered by his attack on Silas Deane. Trouble stalked him constantly. He responded by becoming a loner, hatching plans privately about what steps to take next, calculating which friends, acquaintances, and enemies to avoid. In mid-January, he confessed to Henry Laurens, "I think it convenient to absent myself from the company even of my most intimate friends."[1] Two weeks later, he wrote to George Washington about his anchoritic existence: "I have been out no where for near these two months . . . lest I should be asked questions improper to be answered, or subject myself to conversation that might have been unpleasant."[2] To his friend Benjamin Franklin, in early March 1779 he confessed, in a rare moment of humility, that since his resignation, he had "had a most exceeding rough time" and that his official political career was now in tatters: "I have lately met with a turn, which, sooner or later, happens to all men in popular life, that is, I fell, all at once, from high credit to disgrace, and the worst word was thought too good for me."[3]

Denigration, such as that accompanying the publication of *Common Sense*, was not a stranger to Paine. Long before the fight with Deane, he had been aware, as he told his friend Richard Henry Lee, that the citizen who sets out to cause public controversy "must always expect to be privately undermined in some quarter or another."[4] The period following his resignation from Congress was nevertheless different, and more difficult, essentially because of the huge number of public insults hurled in his direction. Nathaniel Scudder reported from New Jersey that many people expected that the insults would win Paine a seat in Congress. That was wishful thinking, as was pointed out by John Armstrong of Pennsylvania, where Paine was better known: "Poor Payne, not the most prudent man in the world, is execrated by a number and much out of the books of Congress."[5]

Under the leadership of Gouverneur Morris, Congress sought to humiliate him. On January 12, 1779, it unanimously passed a resolution criticizing Paine's revelations and insisted that there was "indisputable evidence" that Louis XVI "did not preface his alliance with any supplies whatever." During the next two days, it reaffirmed its support for the alliance with the French court "of his most Christian Majesty" and adopted a resolution endorsing the claims of Pierre Auguste Caron de Beaumarchais. After getting rid of Paine, Congress continued to abuse him. John Jay continually referred to him as among the "enemies of the common cause."[6] Opinion hardened when Paine used a press review of a congressional pamphlet on the Revolution to lay into Gouverneur Morris and Henry Drayton,[7] and especially after he decided to sting Congress with a series of eight letters. He again attacked Deane's "dark incendiary conduct." He accused Deane's supporters in Congress of sheltering him from public criticism and even raised the question of "whether an extensive trading company had not been formed between Mr. Deane and certain members of Congress." Above all, Paine criticized Congress for refusing to release papers concerning his conduct. He acknowledged its right, as his former employer, to dismiss him, but he denied its right to do so without a public inquiry. He concluded, "The character of no Person can be constitutionally secure, where a formal judgment can be discretionarily produced and published and the grounds and proceedings on which that judgment is founded withheld, or subject to future and private alterations." Many delegates found his pestering either irritating or unpatriotic, especially after April 13, when Paine, walking in the footsteps of John Wilkes, published in the *Pennsylvania Packet* the names of members of Congress who had voted for and against the resolution to dismiss him.[8]

Talk of his unfaithfulness to the new republic was arguably unwarranted. It was certainly sinister, since it served to oil uglier forms of public assault on his integrity. For the first time in his life, Paine tasted physical violence in the streets of Philadelphia. "The poor fellow got a beating," Francis Lightfoot Lee reported during the height of the Deane affair.[9]

After he resigned, the street attacks continued. One such incident was recorded by John Joseph Henry, who reported that Paine was assaulted late one evening by a crowd of gentlemen on their way home from a dinner party hosted by James Mease, Clothier-General of the American army and rumored to be a chief among the shadowy band of speculators and profiteers high up in the ranks of the army. "You may readily suppose," Henry reported, "that the excellent wine of Mr. Mease exhilarated the company." Turning a corner, one of the drunken gentlemen spotted Paine walking toward them. "There comes Common Sense," he said. "Damn him, I shall common-sense him," another said. As Paine passed the group, a foot went out and tripped him. He was then pushed "on his back into the gutter, which at that time was very offensive and filthy."[10]

Paine took the abuse calmly. Convinced that he was right, it served only to thicken his skin. He grew more aloof, as if determined to play the role of a saint of the new republican politics born of the Revolution. "I have not supported a party for the sake of a party," he told his readers, "but a public right for a public good."[11] His sense of humor sharpened as well. Among friends his favorite tale was an Irish anecdote about a man in Dublin accused of robbing the Treasury. Protesting his innocence — the parallel with Silas Deane was obvious — the accused sent for a lawyer who warned him, "If you *have* robbed the Treasury, you will not be hanged, but if you have *not* robbed it, the circumstances are so strong against you, that you must expect to suffer." Upon hearing the advice, the accused was delighted. "Sir," he said, "I have money enough to bribe the _____." The lawyer, shaking his hand, also was pleased. "Oh, my dear good friend," he said, "take care what you say. I understand your case exceedingly well, 'tis a very clear one, and you may depend upon being honorable acquitted."

Laughter sparked by satire helped keep Paine afloat, but his patience was further tested when certain newspapers compounded the public insults. The worst outcome of the Deane affair for Paine personally was the continual harassment he suffered from unnamed enemies. Sporting such noms de guerre as "Plain Truth," "Cato," and "Philalethes" — who accused him of telling twenty extravagant lies[12] — they not only questioned his integrity but also tossed him abuse and veiled threats, accusing him of undermining the old monarchic doctrine of sovereign, secretive state power to campaign publicly for the principle of freedom of information *against* a revolutionary government. During July 1779, someone writing under the nom de guerre "Cato" viciously attacked him in the *Pennsylvania Evening Post*. Paine was accused of worming his way into notoriety by abusing others. It was said that he had been appointed to "a confidential office by a faction who laboured to undermine the great Fabius himself [Washington], the Saviour of his country." "Cato" insisted that Paine's treachery had been compounded by his attempts to block French supplies to the American troops. The unnamed author then reeled off a string of baiting questions and answers crafted to incite gossip. The first question — "Who was an Englishman?" — was followed by the only honest reply: "Tom _____." Subsequent questions and answers were worded more viciously than any Paine had ever read: " 'Who was a Tory?' 'Tom P_____.' . . . 'Who betrayed state affairs?' 'Tom P_____.' 'For whom did he betray them?' '_____.' . . . 'Who maintains Tom P_____?' 'Nobody knows.' 'Who is paid by the enemy?' 'Nobody knows.' 'Who best deserves it?' 'Tom P_____.' "[13]

A week later, the same newspaper stepped up the vilification. A poem beginning sarcastically with "Hail mighty Thomas!" ended with an account of Paine's birth in Thetford, suggesting that "no mere mortal mother did thee bear." Paine was described as the lowest of the low, as the excreted offspring of the god of the underworld:

> . . . *as Minerva, queen of sense uncommon,*
> *Owed not her birth to goddess or to woman;*
> *But softly crept from out her father's soull,*
> *At a small crack in't when the moon was full;*
> *So you, great Common Sense, did surely come*
> *From out the crack in grisly Pluto's bum.*[14]

Rumors and Whispers

Throughout the summer of 1779, such hearsay tugged constantly at Paine's coattails. Hearsay, one of the oldest and most primitive methods of communication, normally takes on a life of its own during revolutions. Nourished by rumors and whispers, it strides through conversations, newspapers, and other media of opinion. It tramples reputations, shatters or hardens opinions, and unpredictably triggers bitter disputes.[15] Hearsay has harsh effects, as Paine quickly found out, and that explains why, during the course of revolutions, hearsay often triggers resistance to hearsay. Hearsay brings into play the best weapon yet invented to combat its spuriousness: a free press that enables citizens to contest whispers, stop rumors in their tracks, probe monopolies of opinion, and ask questions that do not necessarily have straightforward answers.

Paine's Philadelphia friends, such as Timothy Matlack, Charles Willson Peale, and David Rittenhouse, well understood this antidote to malicious gossip. During July 1779, they managed to convince Paine to end his period of hibernation and return to public life with their full support through the press. Venomous articles were still appearing in *The Pennsylvania Evening Post*. In a piece titled "The Galled Horse Winces," Paine was again taunted by "Cato," who wrote, "Thomas you seem to be in a passion. Has Cato ruffled the smooth surface of your temper?"[16] Two days before, a similar taunt had been issued by "A Friend to Cato and to Truth," who had accused Paine of "hatred to everything produced in favour of the liberty of these states" and likened him to a used drum: "the more you have been thumped and beaten, the greater noise you have made." The author had only one piece of advice: "Go home, thou scoundrel, to thy native soil, And in a garret labor, starve, and toil."[17] "Cato" was equally abusive: "Go, wretch, hide thy pitiful head in oblivion. Crawl not from thy den but with boding bats and the night owl; and when thou presents thyself unto the gazing moon, shew her a spectacle of horror. To the whips, the stings, the scorpions of guilt, I leave thee."[18]

Paine's friends and supporters hit back. They challenged the practice, conventional at the time, of publishing anonymous ad hominem attacks on public figures. Two hours after the appearance of the piece likening Paine to a much-beaten drum, they convinced Paine to visit the office of Benjamin Towne, the editor of *The Pennsylvania Evening Post*. Paine asked to know the identity of "Cato" and his friend but went away empty-handed. Towne insisted that he was sworn to secrecy out of respect for his author and that "nothing but a halter could extort it from him."[19] In an age in which civil society still sanctioned rough justice, exactly this threat was applied by Paine's sympathizers. Whether their threats were serious or merely symbolic is unknown, but the sight of a crowd brandishing a noose outside Towne's editorial offices quickly convinced him to divulge that the culprit was Whitehead Humphreys, a local iron and steel merchant known for his offensive manners and support for the conservatives.

That evening the same crowd, headed by the painter Charles Willson Peale, William Bonam, a tallow chandler, and Alexander Boyd, an army major, gathered at the home of Humphreys, singing ditties and chanting slogans. Informed by the servants that Humphreys was not at home, some members of the crowd grew impatient and forced their way into the house. According to a lodger, Humphreys's sister was insulted and "dangerously wounded . . . in the head."[20] At that moment, Humphreys returned. He flew into a rage and soon appeared on his front porch, each hand wrapped around a pistol. "What do you want?" he shouted. Someone in the crowd replied, "We want you, and we will have you." Seconds of murmuring passed. Humphreys stood firm. He shouted that if anyone dared enter his premises, he "would instantly put him to death." The crowd stood firm. Some drew pistols and began to wave them in the air. A shoot-out seemed imminent. It was defused, to everyone's surprise, after someone began flinging names at Humphreys — "Friend of the Tories," "Uncommon Sense," "Liar" — with Humphreys himself rebounding the abuse by calling the crowd "lawless banditti."[21]

There followed twenty tense minutes of exchanged insults and a threat, clothed in laughter, to melt down the premises from which he conducted his iron and steel business. Humphreys then wheedled the crowd into agreeing to allow him to meet its leaders the next morning at ten o'clock at the London Coffee House to talk through the matter. Both parties were on time. Coffee was ordered. Humphreys, flanked by several prominent conservatives — including Silas Deane, John Nixon, and James Wilson — opened with the insistence that he had every right to publish his opinions under any name about any matter as he saw fit. The "Cato" articles were read aloud, and Paine was harangued as "a disturber of the public peace, a spreader of falsehoods and sower of dissension among the people." At one point, after invective about Paine's "scribbling," alleged calumny, and wavering support for the Revolution, someone proposed a vote on whether Paine "was a friend to America."[22] Violence was again narrowly averted. Paine's supporters then lectured Humphreys on the principle of "liberty of the press." They stressed that they were not seeking to muzzle the press. They explained that they were instead concerned that he understand that his citizen's right to express his opinions freely implied the duty not to misuse that right. "Liberty of the press," they said, did not mean "licentiousness of the press." The use of the press to malign others and undermine their liberties, whether anonymously or not, was inconsistent with the principle of press freedom. Humphreys sat silently. The showdown ended peacefully and earned a small victory for Paine. After one further crack at Paine in print, Humphreys fell silent.

A few days after the London Coffee House meeting, Paine's supporters renewed their offensive by organizing a public rally in support of his reputation. According to press reports, on July 27, at nine o'clock in the morning, a general town meeting of "several thousand" people in the State House Yard resolved "that Mr. Thomas Paine is considered by this meeting as a friend to the American cause, and therefore . . . we will support and defend him, so long as his conduct shall continue to prove him to be a friend to this country."[23]

Men of Wealth

Encomiums of this kind freed Paine for a time from obloquy, enabling him to return to the stage of public affairs. His daily life quickly became hectic. Sitting on committees, writing reports, and meeting almost daily with friends, Paine became preoccupied, from the end of the summer through to the following spring of 1780, with the widening gap between rich and poor effected by the Revolution. After resigning from Congress and collecting his last payment, the poverty of unemployment shadowed him personally. Though publicly active, he worried constantly about falling into destitution. In his campaign on behalf of excisemen, conducted from Lewes, he had stressed the exorbitant cost of keeping a horse. Those days in England, he told his friend Henry Laurens, now seemed opulent: "I think I have a right to ride a horse of my own, but I cannot now even afford to hire one, which is a situation I never was in before."[24]

On the day of his resignation from Congress, Paine had had the chance to throw off the nagging worry of poverty by accepting a handsome bribe from the French government. The strange offer was put to him during a private supper in York with an emissary from the French ambassador, Conrad Alexandre Gérard.[25] It was repeated several times afterward, and a week later Paine, puzzled by Gérard's motives, accepted an invitation to visit him for afternoon tea. Paine admitted after the visit that he had felt some embarrassment because others might have thought that he was soliciting a pension or pardon. In fact, toward the end of that afternoon tea, Gérard, flanked by M. de Mirales, the unofficial Spanish representative in Philadelphia, had tried to bribe him, offering him a handsome salary of one thousand dollars a year to write and publish articles in support of the Franco-American alliance against the British. "Monsieur Paine," Gérard said in his thick French accent, "I have always had a great respect for you, and should be glad of some opportunity of showing you more solid marks of my friendship." Paine flatly refused the offer. He was sure that the principle at stake — the freedom of political writers to express their views independently of any party or government — was inviolable, even if this meant personal pauperization. A month earlier, Paine had likened hack writers who "write on any subject for bread, or in any service for pay," to prostitutes driven by poverty to rent out their bodies to clients.[26] His view had not changed after tea with Gérard. "Any service I can render to either of the countries in alliance, or to both," Paine replied politely, "I ever have done and shall do, and Mr. Gérard's *esteem* will be the only recompense I shall desire."[27] Later, in a letter to Congress, Paine suggested, graciously, that he refused the proffered salary because its aim was to muzzle him: "I thought it my duty to decline it; as it was accompanied with a condition which I conceived had a tendency to prevent the information I have since given [concerning Silas Deane], and shall yet give to the country on public affairs."[28]

These were the defiant words of a poor publicist with rich republican morals. They left Paine with no alternative but to accept a menial clerical job in the office of Owen Biddle, a prominent radical sympathizer, Quaker, and merchant engaged in buying grain and hay for the American army.[29] The job lasted only until the end of the summer, and the small salary helped to pay Paine's room and board on Market Street and other minor pleasures: snuff, the daily glass or two of rum or brandy, the repair of his boots, the odd meal in a local coffeehouse. Paine never fully shed the Quaker style of life he had first lived in small-town Thetford, and during this period he lived and looked like an ascetic, in no small measure because the value of his small salary was daily eroded by galloping inflation. During the spring and summer of 1779, prices for basic commodities such as bread and salt soared, hitting hard the lower ranks of artisans, rural and urban laborers, ordinary soldiers, and the old, the sick, and other people without employment. During a three-week period in May, according to one delegate to Congress, prices increased 100 percent.[30] The problem was exacerbated by the loss of market value of the paper dollar — the phrase "not worth a Continental" stems from this period — which came to be worth less than a copper penny. As Paine knew well in his clerk's job, prices quoted in dollars rocketed, while salaries and wages paid in the same currency were corroded from within. Everyone in possession of dollars suffered, in effect paying a tax on their dollars proportionate to the time it was in their possession. "Like a hackney coach," observed a contributor to the *Pennsylvania Packet*, "it must be paid for by the hour."[31]

What could be done about this hyperinflation? Congress, lacking the authority to impose direct taxes, was unable to exercise any effective control over the value of its currency, which declined with every issue of paper money. Others resorted to rough treatment to solve the problem. In Philadelphia, Levi Hollingsworth, a prominent merchant in the business of shipping flour to Maryland, was physically threatened by a crowd that minced no words. Threats against the wealthy class also appeared in the press, in the taverns, and on the streets, and within the ranks of the militia there was growing speculation that the poorer classes might be forced to break into supplies of flour and grain held by certain merchants.[32]

The merchants of Philadelphia and other cities normally said that their high prices were the effect rather than the cause of inflation. In any case, they added, all government efforts at regulating prices would be stillborn because the circulation of hard currencies — the French livre, for example — would ensure that purchasers with such currencies in their pockets would always be willing to pay the higher market price for the goods under consideration. Inflation was an unstoppable maelstrom. Trapped in its swirl, even hard currencies would lose their value, albeit at a slower rate than paper dollars. Bad money would always drive good money from the marketplace.

Paine thought these claims spurious. They functioned, in his view, as masks to hide the selfish property interests of the merchants. Paine's humble upbringing, his early experience of the Graftons' oligarchy, and his defense of the excisemen combined to make him forever suspicious of men of wealth. That suspicion had been revived by the public fracas with Silas Deane, the epitome of a private man with shabby morals. It is of great interest that in the same week that Paine first attacked Deane publicly, he had been developing a parallel attack on men of wealth in an important series of theoretical essays — subsequently forgotten or ignored by most observers — in the pages of the *Pennsylvania Packet*.[33] Paine tried to cut men of wealth down to size. He argued that living, breathing labor, not property, is the ultimate source of material wealth: "Where there are none to labour, and but few to consume, land and property is not riches." He also warned of the dangers to a republic posed by the greed for power of the propertied class, emphasizing that citizens jealous of their civil and political rights, and not men of wealth, form the backbone of any republic, particularly one fighting for its life: "Property alone cannot defend a country against invading enemies. Houses and lands cannot fight; sheep and oxen cannot be taught the musket; therefore the defence must be personal, and that which equally unites all must be something equally the property of all, viz. an equal share of freedom, independent of the varieties of wealth."

If, as Paine thought, regimes become corrupt when the propertied rich manipulate the laws to grind down the poor, then a young republic like America could easily suffer the same fate, especially if its citizens fell under the influence of self-interested men of property. "A rich man makes a bonny traitor,"[34] he told his friend Joseph Reed, quoting James I. If that was so, then republican principles must be extended to the sphere of economic life. Men of wealth must be tamed by public ethics. Property and its corresponding "liberal" values must be subject to the universal "civic humanist" rule of civil and political rights. That would not fully eliminate disparities of wealth. But the availability of rights to all adult, male citizens, not just to property owners, would ensure ongoing controversies about how to divide that which is divisible. Such controversies would ensure that existing patterns of wealth and inequality would never be seen as natural, as reflecting the will of God, or as a brutal fact of economic life.

Paine was no believer in self-regulating "free markets." He was not an "ideological spokesman for the bourgeoisie."[35] He certainly believed — in this he was remarkably modern — that market mechanisms for structuring decisions about investment, production, and consumption through anonymous monetary exchanges could never be eliminated from the heart of civil societies without destroying their vitality and what Paine sometimes called "civil independent pride." Industry, commerce, and agriculture regulated by means of money-based private exchanges were essential for a free civil society, if only to protect it from meddlesome state power. But — the qualification was of the utmost importance to Paine — he refused to draw from this the conclusion that the various institutions of civil society should be ruled by impersonal "market forces." Within this sphere, individuals should not be treated as private entrepreneurs whose talents and powers are presumed to be natural and whose conduct is guided by the bourgeois principle of differential cash rewards for workers and owners of property. He was adamant that market exchanges must be controlled and nurtured politically. A self-regulating market is undesirable. It motivates individuals not on the basis of commitment to serve and be served by their fellow citizens, but through a mixture of greed and fear. Market competition encourages citizens to see each other as threats and as sources of private self-enrichment.

A self-regulating market, or so Paine argued, also is unworkable. It could never exist for long without paralyzing itself and wiping out its social preconditions — for instance, by generating inflation, widening the gap between men of wealth and others, and pauperizing whole layers of society. Paine therefore concluded that the actual or optimal shape of market transactions within a republic must always be crafted by political and legal regulations. A republic requires nonmarket support mechanisms such as public discussion, voluntary associations, taxation schemes, judgments by elected, public-spirited civil magistrates, and government controls. Such nonmarket mechanisms enable producing and exchanging individuals to aim at cash results, but only insofar as they see that the cash so generated is subject to redistribution out of a desire to contribute to a free and equal civil society. The best system of government, in short, is one that nurtures its citizens' civil and political liberties and mutual aid by means of a civil society structured by restricted and regulated market exchanges.[36]

Paine first tested these theoretical ideas on the problem of runaway inflation. In opposition to the merchants' view, Paine pointed out that unchecked prices in effect acted as a tax on ordinary citizens, siphoning money from them as "price-takers" to the "price-makers," or men of wealth. To remedy such inequity, he argued, prices should be regulated by governments. Since Congress had refused to do so on the grounds that this was a matter for individual states, price controls should be imposed by the various state assemblies. Paine's position quickly became known in Philadelphia circles and beyond. It won support at a public meeting in the State House Yard on May 27, 1779. The meeting elected him (along with Timothy Matlack, David Rittenhouse, Charles Willson Peale, and several other prominent Philadelphians) to serve on the two citizens' committees set up to investigate the business activities of Robert Morris, another man of wealth who later earned the title "Financier of the Revolution."[37]

The public meeting heard speeches against "monopolizers and forestallers" bent on "getting rich" by "sucking the blood" of citizens. It passed several resolutions to "encourage fair and honest commerce." The committees set about investigating the rumor that Morris had made large profits selling flour to the French navy at inflated prices and that he had similarly profited on the cargo of flour carried by the French ship *Victorieux*, which had docked at Philadelphia at the end of April. Both citizens' committees exonerated Morris of the charges. But with an eye to the publicity effects of their inquiry, the printed report of Paine's committee concluded with a toughly worded admonition, probably written by Paine: "Tho', as a merchant, he may be strictly within rules, yet when he considers the many public and honorary stations he has filled and the times he lives in, he must feel himself some what out of character."[38]

A week later, after several further raucous public meetings in the State House Yard, Paine was elected to two new committees.[39] One set itself the task of supervising a scheme for controlling the price of salt and flour in the capital city. The other was empowered to draw up a plan for freezing the supply of Continental currency and raising taxes in Pennsylvania through house-to-house canvassing to collect three years' contributions in advance. Both schemes caused considerable public outcry, especially among the wealthy and their supporters. The squawking reaction of Benjamin Rush, Paine's onetime friend and supporter, typified those who feared that the committees would deliver American politics into the hands of popular power. "Poor Pennsylvania! Most miserable spot on the Globe," wrote Rush. "They call it a Democracy — a Mobocracy in my opinion would be more proper. All our laws breathe the spirit of town meetings. My family and my business now engross all my time and attention. My Country I have long ago left to the care of Timy. Matlack, Tom Paine — Charles Willson Peale and Co."[40]

That kind of reaction helped kill both schemes. Most merchants and many artisans, driven by self-interest, simply refused to comply with price controls. Paine was nonplussed by the absurd outcomes. Inflation continued to run wild. During this period, Paine later complained, he had to pay "three hundred paper dollars for one pair of worsted stockings." If anything, price controls fostered "dearness and famine instead of plenty and cheapness" because producers slowed down their production and withheld it from the market in anticipation of later price deregulation and, thus, enhanced profits. Price controls also had the paradoxical effect of dramatically increasing unofficial, or black-market, prices for the commodities made scarce by price controls. "The consequence was that no salt was brought to market, and the price rose to thirty-six shillings per bushel," reported Paine. "The price before the war was only one shilling and sixpence per bushel; and we regulated the price of flour (farina) till there was none in the market, and the people were glad to procure it at any price."[41] The other scheme for raising state taxes and calling on Congress to cease printing paper money was stillborn. The so-called Citizens' Plan, drafted by Paine, championed the idea of taxes as gifts from citizens to governments.[42] It proposed that government revenues be increased and put on a sounder basis by calling on citizens voluntarily to pay their taxes in hard currency in advance, the contributions then being credited against their future individual tax assessments. The Executive Council of the state government of Pennsylvania initially welcomed the proposal. But the plan was wrecked by a congressional decision to issue another forty million dollars in Continental currency, thereby ensuring that inflation continued on its destructive course.

Slavery — Again

A serious illness prevented Paine from campaigning against Congress's decision to issue more currency and devising new methods of protecting citizens against the acid of inflation. His more general concern with crafting a theory of political economy aimed at the difficult process of transition from despotism to republican democracy also had to be shelved. During the middle of August 1779, for the second time in his life — he was smitten first during his journey to America — he was flattened by a fever. It confined him to bed for several weeks, and then for another week after a relapse. Friends like Timothy Matlack and David Rittenhouse paid him frequent visits and sent their servants to look after him in his room on Market Street. But the physical and emotional stress of the past year had finally struck, leaving Paine miserable. The first blush of revolutionary idealism had turned pale. "I know but one kind of life I am fit for," he wrote to his friend Henry Laurens, "and that is a thinking one, and, of course, a writing one — but I have confined myself so much of late, taken so little exercise, and lived so very sparingly, that unless I alter my way of life it will alter me."[43] He again complained of falling into poverty. Scratching out an existence as a salaried clerk paid in Continental dollars had been difficult, and in any case the job had ended during his illness. Unemployed, Paine again began to search desperately for new sources of income.

He hatched a plan to publish by subscription his collected works in two volumes. Supplies of printing paper were virtually exhausted in Philadelphia, and the plan consequently came to nothing. Paine then sought support for the plan from the Pennsylvania government. During the autumn of 1779, he wrote twice to the Supreme Executive Council of Pennsylvania requesting for that purpose a "loan of fifteen hundred pounds for which I will give bond payable within a year."[44] No funds were forthcoming, but the Pennsylvania government, now dominated by the Radicals after their sweeping victory in the October elections, was at least reminded of his plight. Paine soon cheered up. In early November, after looking into his financial situation, the Assembly voted to appoint Paine as its clerk. He was pleasantly surprised by the posting, and the moderate salary and warm welcome extended him by Assembly delegates further helped him throw off the spell of "idleness, uneasiness and hopeless thinking"[45] that had dogged him since his illness.

For the next few months, his desk was so pelted with paper that there was little spare time for lugubriousness. "As for myself," he confided to Henry Laurens three weeks after his appointment, "thank God, I am well and feel much pleasanter than I did — the clerkship is not much but it is something like business."[46] He must have found some of the routine "business" — minutes of meetings and committee reports — deadly boring.[47] Mostly, he spent long days in his tiny office carefully reading, certifying, and publicizing the vigorous program of reform legislation pushed through the Assembly by the Radical majority. From mid-November 1779 until the first week of June 1780, practically every issue of the *Pennsylvania Gazette* included at least one full text, and often two, of bills certified by

Paine as clerk of the Assembly. The legislation was wide-ranging, encompassing matters such as stripping proprietors of their public lands and quitrents, the incorporation of the American Philosophical Society, reform of the Anglican-dominated College of Philadelphia, and the outlawing of slavery.

The new law — the first in the world — to commence the abolition of slavery was for many delegates the prized jewel in the legislative program. Paine, in his capacity as clerk of the Assembly, certainly proofread a draft of the legislation. It may be that he actually had a hand in the formulation of its preamble.[48] According to one story, Paine was approached by George Bryan, a well-known Presbyterian and member of the radical group within the Assembly, who had been campaigning hard for two years for an abolition law. Bryan called slavery "the opprobrium of America" and knew that Paine shared his view that God would hardly tolerate the hypocrisy of those who enslaved others while fighting to secure their own liberty. Bryan was a bibliophile with a particular interest in the history of resistance to slavery. He remembered well that Paine, shortly after arriving in America, had published a piece in the *Pennsylvania Journal* lashing out against the African slave trade. Bryan knew that a few weeks after the appearance of Paine's essay, and partly inspired by it, the first antislavery society in any country had been formed on April 14, 1775, by a meeting at the Sun Tavern on Second Street in Philadelphia. The founding members, drawn mainly from the Society of Friends, had decided to call themselves The Society for the Relief of Free Negroes unlawfully held in Bondage. The preamble of their constitution, Bryan recalled, had repeated Paine's argument that freedom for white Americans required freedom for black Americans. It had concluded that "loosing the bonds of wickedness and setting the oppressed free, is evidently a duty incumbent on all professors of Christianity, but more especially at a time when justice, liberty, and the laws of the land are the general topics among most ranks and stations of men."[49]

Bryan wanted to give legal force to this type of campaign. Yet he knew that his own campaign within the Assembly was vigorously opposed by the slave owners and merchants of the state. That is why, according to the story, he looked on Paine as a useful pen with prose capable of changing their minds, or at least dampening their opposition. The task was formidable, given the extent to which slavery and the Atlantic slave trade had become ingrained in American social life. At this stage of the Revolution, there were about half a million slaves in the thirteen states: 200,000 in Virginia, 100,000 in South Carolina, 70,000 or 80,000 each in North Carolina and Maryland, approximately 25,000 in New York, 10,000 in New

Jersey, 6,000 in Pennsylvania and Connecticut, 5,000 in Massachusetts, and 4,000 in Rhode Island.[50] African-American men and women were engaged in skilled crafts and trades, drudge work and field gangs, cultivating cotton and other crops. Their forced labor formed part of an interdependent Atlantic economy linking together Caribbean sugar plantations, Pennsylvania farmers, and New England fishermen with the textile workers of Nantes, the iron manufacturers of Birmingham, and the poorest English farm laborer's wife who took sugar in her tea. The size of the Atlantic slave trade was monstrous. In the eighteenth century, it has been estimated, exports of Africans in the Atlantic slave trade exceeded 6 million, nearly three times the number confiscated and shipped out from 1450 to 1700. Nearly half of these eighteenth-century slaves were transported by Englishmen or Anglo-Americans.[51]

The bill championed by George Bryan in the Pennsylvania legislature was designed to break this pattern of exploitation. There had certainly been earlier attempts in the American colonies to deal legally with the stark contradiction that slavery posed for republican governments based on principles of natural rights. In 1767, for example, the Massachusetts General Court had debated and defeated a bill "to prevent the unwarrantable & unusual Practice . . . of inslaving Mankind in the Province." During 1774, the Continental Congress had included in the second article of the Continental Association a pledge not only to forswear further traffic in slaves but also to hire no vessels and sell no goods "to those who are concerned in it." In the same year, the Rhode Island Assembly had banned the importation of slaves into its territory.[52]

The Pennsylvania Assembly bill was more radical than any of these initiatives. For the first time anywhere, it legislated not for the restriction of the slave trade, but for the eventual abolition of the institution of slavery itself. The preamble, full of cosmopolitan sentiment and deist language, bubbled with the novelty:

WHEN we contemplate our abhorrence of that condition, to which the arms and tyranny of Great-Britain were exerted to reduce us, we are unavoidably led to a serious and grateful sense of the manifold blessings which we have undeservedly received from the hand of that Being from whom every good and perfect gift cometh. Impressed with these ideas, we conceive that it is our duty, and we rejoice that it is in our power, to extend a portion of that freedom to others, which hath been extended to us. . . . It is not for us to inquire, why, in the creation of mankind, the inhabitants of the several parts of the earth were distinguished by a difference in feature or complexion. It is sufficient to know, that all are the work of an Almighty Hand.[53]

Bryan and other supporters of the bill were forced to make compromises to the slave owners and merchants to secure its passage into law. In its final version, passed on March 1, 1780, slave owners in the state of Pennsylvania were no longer legally entitled to command for life the services of children born of slaves. After reaching the age of twenty-eight years, these children of slaves would be free. The law further specified that up to the age of twenty-eight years, children of slaves should enjoy rights of relief from despotic masters and mistresses and be valued as the equals of apprentices and indentured servants. The legislation disappointed many abolitionists. The first draft of the bill had stipulated emancipation at the age of twenty-one — twenty-eight years was a long time to wait for freedom when the average life expectancy was often lower than this. Moreover, the legislation did not specify an ultimate time limit for the outright abolition of slavery. The law nevertheless hardened the political commitment to prohibiting the further importation of slaves. It also signaled that in a republic, black slavery was a historical anomaly and should ultimately be abolished.

"We Want Rousing"

Paine was disappointed by the watered-down legislation, although he may have drawn some consolation from knowing that its preamble was substantially more radical — and more inspiring than the current American military campaign. Soon after the law's passage, he found time to return to *The American Crisis* series, which had been neglected for nearly eighteen months. On February 26, he completed the eighth number. Addressed to "the People of England," it reiterated the old point that "whether America shall be independent or not" remained the life-or-death question. But, for the first time, Paine warned the English that they could expect soon to feel the tremors of the American war on their own soil. The successes of John Paul Jones — a personal friend of Paine's who some months earlier had commanded a naval expedition into British coastal waters with the aim of bringing the war home to the enemy — were a taste of things to come. Jones's victories against British vessels, Paine argued, demonstrated that until now, the English had been leading sheltered lives:

> To you every thing has been foreign but the taxes to support it. You knew
> not what it was to be alarmed at midnight with an armed enemy in the
> streets. You were strangers to the distressing scene of a family in flight, and

to the thousand restless cares and tender sorrows that incessantly arose. To see women and children wandering in the severity of winter, with the broken remains of a well furnished house, and seeking shelter in every crib and hut, were matters that you had no conception of. You knew not what it was to stand by and see your goods chopped for fuel, and your beds ripped to pieces to make packages for plunder.[54]

The pathos was designed less to convince English readers — how many copies of the pamphlet actually reached English shores is unknown — than to lift the spirits of his American readers. With the Deane affair behind him, Paine was again gripped by anxiety about the course of the war. Nothing but bad news was reaching Philadelphia from every direction. George Washington reported that the harsh winter months had further demoralized his half-starved troops. He confessed that many "have been four or five days without meat entirely and short of bread, and none but on very scanty supplies. Some for their preservation have been compelled to maraud and rob from the Inhabitants, and I have it not in my power to punish or to repress the practice."[55] Paine's friend Nathanael Greene similarly reported that the troops under his command were "more than half naked and two-thirds starved."[56] Some commanders in the field abandoned hope. Many began to tremble or panic about the growing impatience and rising incidence of mutiny within their ranks. "A hungry army will soon be a seditious one," warned Paine.[57] Around the end of May 1780, Washington wrote to Joseph Reed of the Pennsylvania Council to propose that the state's executive be granted emergency powers to deal with the desperate situation. Within minutes of the letter's arrival, the doors of the Assembly chamber were locked, and Paine, profoundly moved, read aloud its contents to a sea of despairing faces. "I assure you," wrote Washington, "every Idea you can form of our distresses, will fall short of the reality. . . . This is not a time for formality or ceremony. The crisis in every point of view is extraordinary and extraordinary expedients are necessary."[58] Shortly afterward came news of the disastrous loss of Charleston to the British.

Toward the end of March 1780, British land and sea forces commanded by Lieutenant General Henry Clinton had gradually surrounded Charleston and choked off its contact with the outside world. The Americans had refused to surrender and dug in, hoping that the British would withdraw to avoid serious bloodshed. A group of American women pleaded with the British commanders for restraint, seeking permission "to go into town to take leave of their sons." The British replied with night-

and-day bombardment. The shelling was so merciless that at one point Clinton reprimanded his artillery commander for allowing his men to fire their guns so indiscriminately. It was, he said, "absurd, impolitic, inhuman to burn a town you mean to occupy." On May 12, the town surrendered. More than four thousand men, including a thousand sailors, were taken prisoner. Huge quantities of ammunition and weapons fell into British hands. British losses during the siege were around three hundred men, a number of whom were killed, or so Paine heard from reports, when a captured musket was flung, still loaded, into a shed where gunpowder was stored. The consequent explosion mutilated those nearby to such an extent that it was impossible to "make out a single human figure."[59]

Paine steeled himself against further news from Charleston, issuing a flurry of letters and proposals. To Blair McClenaghan, a prominent Philadelphia merchant, he described the seriousness of the situation: "Charleston is without doubt totally gone, and though the fate of America does not depend upon it yet the loss of the garrison is such a formidable blow that unless some very sudden and spirited exertions be made the distress that will follow will be long and heavy."[60] In a long letter, which took him two days to draft, he outlined to Joseph Reed, president of the Supreme Executive Council of Pennsylvania, a new plan for drafting male citizens into the army.[61] He insisted that yet another watershed had been reached in the struggle against the British and that bold, imaginative steps were required. "We want rousing," he wrote. He proposed that all able-bodied adult men had a duty to defend their government and that all of them should be registered within their own towns and villages into groups of thirty volunteers. Each registrant would then be asked to make a donation of, say, three dollars to their local support fund. When the time came for the group to offer up a soldier to the army, a volunteer would step forward, or one would be decided by lot. In each case, the new citizen-soldier would receive in full the money paid into the support fund by the group.

But where would the money come from to furnish the overhead for the newly expanded army? Paine insisted that the rich must dip into their pockets. They would likely do so out of self-interest, he told McClenaghan. Property was always the object of a conquest, and therefore "it is the rich that will suffer most by the ravages of an Enemy."[62] To Reed, Paine expressed the same point: "Something must be done, and that something, to give it popularity, must begin with men of property."[63] Paine recommended new property taxes on loyalists and urged Philadelphia's traders and merchants to establish an army support fund, to which he personally contributed five hundred dollars from what he had saved from his pay from the state treasury, pledging a further "mite" of five hundred dollars if the fund proved inadequate.

The proposal was introduced by McClenaghan at a meeting of Philadelphia merchants at the London Coffee House on June 8. The merchants resolved to encourage enlistments by establishing a subscription fund, into which McClenaghan, Robert Morris, and others present paid sizable sums. Shortly after official news of the bombing and capture of Charleston reached Philadelphia, the same group reconvened at the City Tavern to discuss the urgent need to bolster state revenues. The men voted to broaden the original fund into a bank with funds earmarked for supplying the army with wages, arms, and equipment. McClenaghan and Morris each subscribed £10,000, and ninety other gentlemen each subscribed amounts between £1,000 and £6,000.[64] The plan eventually netted pledges of around £300,000, which was used to create the first bank in America, the Bank of Pennsylvania. Congress pledged to underwrite the new bank, and Paine, whose five hundred dollars seems to have been politely returned to him on the grounds that he was already poor enough, was delighted with the speed at which its funds were directed toward the war effort. "By means of this bank," he later reported proudly, "the army was supplied through the campaign and being at the same time recruited was enabled to maintain its ground."[65]

Paine's proposals for funding the army of citizens by means of citizens' donations and progressive taxation of the rich rested on his long-standing belief, first outlined in *Common Sense*, that governments are powerless without the support of the governed. He agreed with Washington's estimate of the seriousness of the situation, but he disagreed with the strategy of declaring martial law. "The ability of any government," he told McClenaghan, "is nothing more than the abilities of individuals collected."[66] The implication of that view was that the struggle to invent and define American public opinion remained the first priority. That is why Paine moved fast to block any propaganda gains to the British from their victory in Charleston with another pamphlet in *The American Crisis* series. On June 9, the ninth number appeared, bursting with defiance. It maintained that the fall of Charleston, a town of secondary importance to the overall British strategy, was nothing like a final blow to the Americans, since it had failed to convince the population of the need to capitulate. "America ever *is* what she *thinks* herself to be," Paine reminded his readers. He pointed to two developments in the state of Pennsylvania — the marked growth of voluntary donations in support of the army and the steps being taken by men of wealth to establish a new bank — that proved that the Americans' courage remained unbroken. In contrast to the British oligarchy, he concluded, "the cause of America stands not on the will of a few but on the broad foundation of property and popularity."[67]

Thoughts of Europe

Paine now seemed his old ebullient self. Fully recovered from the fracas with Silas Deane, his thoughts were razor sharp, his quill quick and militant, his resilience toughened by setbacks. He was held aloft for a time by news that he had been awarded the honorary degree of Master of Arts at the Fourth of July celebrations at the newly created University of Pennsylvania.[68] The former pupil of Thetford Grammar School seemed pleased — but not delighted — by the honor. Paine always carried his academic laurels lightly. He rarely mentioned his honorary degree from the University of Pennsylvania in private conversation and referred to it only once in writing.[69] Friends close to Paine found his indifference puzzling. Some speculated that he found the academic honor incompatible with his self-image as a writer for the people. Others thought he might have been embarrassed by an award that resembled a political gift from an institution enjoying close links with the Radical-dominated Assembly. All of them noted how quickly his contentment evaporated and how, during the summer of 1780, he became unsettled, as if he were wrestling with his soul to decide his future role in the American struggle for independence.

The pangs of uncertainty were not new. They had first appeared the previous autumn of 1779, during his extended illness, when he had moaned privately about rough treatment by the Revolution and talked of leaving America for France. He also had expressed the view, whose cosmopolitanism some in America considered treacherous, that he was above all else a citizen of the world, not a citizen of the new American republic. During his relapse, he had even written to Henry Laurens to say that "perhaps America would feel the less obligation to me, did she know, that it was neither the place nor the people but the Cause itself that irresistibly engaged me in its support; for I should have acted the same part in any other country could the same circumstances have arisen there which have happened here."[70]

Around the time of his Master of Arts award, Paine hatched the idea of supporting the wider cause. He would secretly return to England. There, hidden within the entrails of the empire, he would whet the English appetite for liberty. He would make the people see that the bloody struggle for American independence was being waged in defense of the originally English principle of liberty, for which the empire supposedly still stood. Although the plan ultimately proved to be the most fraught of Paine's career, his reasons were well thought out. He noted that the Americans' cause was still poorly understood in Europe, especially in England, where "delusions" and a "rancorous spirit" still plagued the public. He was convinced that dissolving English ignorance was now a vital condition of American success. For that purpose, he thought, the press, the unpredictable "Engine . . . in the affairs of government,"[71] could be used to great advantage by adding to the mounting social pressures on the English government. In private discussions, Paine also noted evidence of the growing dangers of foreign invasion and domestic upheaval in England. He knew that the previous summer, following the Spanish declaration of war on Britain, a combined French and Spanish fleet of sixty-six ships had entered the English Channel, causing considerable alarm throughout the country. He also was aware that there were continuing outbursts of sympathy for the Americans within the Whiggish opposition — and even reports of British troops and officers refusing to march aboard the transports bound for America.

The seeds of the thesis that there could be a republican revolution in England had been planted in the second number of *The American Crisis*. There Paine had told Lord William Howe that the Americans could more easily effect a revolution in England than the British could conquer America. "A few thousand men landed in England with the declared design of deposing the present king, bringing his ministers to trial, and setting up the Duke of Gloucester in his stead," he had boasted, "would assuredly carry their point."[72] Three and a half years later, the same thesis became his daily obsession. Paine quickly firmed up his plans. He would pose as an Englishman returning from a tour of America. Once admitted to England, he would use his publishing contacts to take advantage of the "free and open" press. He could then write as "a person possessed of a knowledge of America, and capable of fixing it in the minds of the people of England." The ultimate aim, Paine said, was to produce a "general disposition for peace"[73] by circulating a pamphlet whose impact in England would be as explosive as that of *Common Sense* in America.

All of Paine's friends were either horrified at the plan or stunned by its absurdity. Some, Nathanael Greene among them, tried to convince him that it was too dangerous. Greene told him that he should think twice about the scheme and not forget his vital public role in America. An astonished Joseph Reed "thought it both difficult and dangerous."[74] Always headstrong, Paine silently brushed aside such objections. With the plan clearly sketched in his head, he requested a year's unpaid leave of absence from his post in the Pennsylvania Assembly, covering his tracks by claiming that he needed to "collect and furnish myself with materials for a history of the Revolution."[75] The Assembly saw through the alibi. Surmising that the plan was too dangerous, and inclined to coolness about Paine in any case (the Conservatives had just won a surprising victory in Pennsylvania elections), the Assembly refused him permission and moved quickly to appoint another clerk, Samuel Sterrett. Paine resigned at once and immediately booked a passage to England, hoping to board either the *Franklin* or the *Shelalah,* both of which were preparing to sail from Philadelphia. He had saved enough money for the journey from his clerk's job, and nothing, it seemed, could prevent him from cutting through the Atlantic winter storms to his native England.

Quite unexpectedly, two stones blocked his path to the docks. One was the personal intervention of Greene, who during a long afternoon conversation at Paine's lodgings on Front Street expressed (so Paine reported) "some apprehension." Greene then wrote within a matter of days to Paine from Annapolis "strongly dissuading" him from making the journey.[76] The second stone frightened Paine, fully convincing him that Greene's advice was not exaggerated. During the last week of September 1780, Major John André, Adjutant-General to the British army, was apprehended in Tarrytown while traveling in civilian disguise down the Hudson Valley to New York. His captors, three men variously described as "militiamen," "volunteers," "bushmen," and "American prowlers, or skinners," found incriminating papers stuffed inside his shoes. André, convinced that the men were loyalists, made the mistake of admitting that he was a British officer. He then tried, but failed, to bribe the men, who promptly arrested him. André wrote immediately to George Washington, asking no clemency but a gentlemanly manner of death. On Sunday, October 1, 1780, in the Old Dutch Church in Sleepy Hollow at Tappan (often called Orangeburg), André was brought before a court-martial presided over by Paine's friend Greene. André was charged with espionage — with entering enemy territory, forsaking his uniform for a civilian disguise, and bearing incriminating papers. The court found André guilty and sentenced him to execution, which Washington ordered to take place on the following day near the center of the American encampment, in full view of its regiments.

A French Alternative

This was the first spy trial on American soil since the British execution of the young revolutionary Nathan Hale, a Connecticut schoolteacher. Paine was shaken by André's death. Knowing that he himself risked exactly the same fate in England, the politically shrewd Paine abandoned his plans, set about clearing his desk in the Assembly, and planned a safer alternative.

It was only a matter of weeks before that alternative — a mission to France — materialized. The Continental Congress had for some time been discussing whether and how new forms of support for the war effort might be solicited in France. Paine too had become convinced of the need for a new, openly negotiated agreement with the French. He campaigned hard for an agreement by lobbying the delegates to Congress and publishing at his own expense *The Crisis Extraordinary* during the month of October 1780. The sixteen-page pamphlet repeated a sentence used four months earlier by George Washington in a letter to Congress describing the serious underfunding of the American army. "The crisis, in every point of view, is extraordinary," Washington had groaned.[77] Paine agreed. Americans, he thought, had every right as citizens to regard taxation as a free gift to their government. But these dark times required citizens to give more generously. Wading through a swamp of taxation figures, he made the accountant's point that it would be three times cheaper to win the war by increasing taxes in America than to lose the war and succumb to the gross tax hunger of the British. He despaired that "the people generally do not understand the insufficiency of the taxes to carry on the war" and called for swift action to rouse their generosity and remedy the problem through new tax legislation.[78]

Paine's argument was partly intended as a rap on the knuckles of the Pennsylvania Assembly, which at that very moment was deadlocked over a new money bill. Its speaker, the well-known Lutheran John Muhlenberg, had urged Paine to write something against the Assembly's refusal to levy the new levels of taxation requested by Congress. *The Crisis Extraordinary* was well aimed. Muhlenberg arranged for the Assembly to purchase ten dozen copies and to distribute them to its delegates.[79] Paine reported that although the case he presented traveled "a tedious course of difficult business, and over an untrodden path," the pamphlet had some effect. Muhlenberg told him over dinner a few evenings after the publication of *The Crisis Extraordinary* that "all opposition had ceased and the House which before had been equally divided had that day been unanimous"[80] in accepting Congress's demand for higher taxation.

The Crisis Extraordinary also turned heads toward Paine just at the moment when Congress was discussing where to raise hard cash to continue the war effort. Paine himself was convinced that America again needed an injection of French cash. He drafted a letter to the French Foreign Minister, Comte de Vergennes, "stating undisguisedly the true case: and concluding with the request, whether France could not, either as a subsidy or a loan, supply the United States with a million sterling, and continue that supply, annually, during the war."[81] Paine showed the letter to the secretary to the French minister, M. Marbois, who was unenthusiastic, and then to Ralph Izard, former commissioner of Congress to Tuscany and now a Congressman from South Carolina. Izard promised that he would attempt to raise the matter in the legislature. The promise sparked considerable congressional debate, some of it referring to *The Crisis Extraordinary* and to Paine's letter to the Comte de Vergennes. The delegates finally agreed on November 22 to request a special hard cash loan of 25 million livres from Louis XVI. A fortnight later, after accusations that the existing envoy in Paris, Benjamin Franklin, had lost touch with American affairs, the delegates resolved to send a special envoy to Paris to plead the American case. Alexander Hamilton, a member of Washington's staff, was nominated for the delicate mission but declined on the ground that he was "not sufficiently known to Congress to unite their suffrages in his favour."[82] Instead an offer was extended to another Washington aide, John Laurens, the twenty-six-year-old son of Paine's close friend Henry Laurens.

John Laurens had met Paine nearly three years earlier at Washington's headquarters, and the two men liked each other.[83] Paine, always attracted to quick-witted men, found the young Laurens a brilliant mind and an eloquent conversationalist and debater. Laurens despised slavery. He always incited vigorous discussion at dinner parties by proposing that black Americans should earn their emancipation by being drafted into the army, with those surviving the Revolution to be set free. Laurens spoke good French and was familiar with English affairs — he had studied law in Geneva and later moved to London, where he had completed his studies in law at the Middle Temple. He also was absorbed in the military campaigns of the Revolution. He was an admirer of Washington, for whom he had served as an aide from the early campaigns of the war. Laurens had been dispatched to defend Charleston, where he was taken prisoner by the conquering British army. Shortly after his safe release through a swap of prisoners, Laurens received a letter offering him the mission to Paris. Before accepting, he took the unusual step of paying a visit to Paine to express his reservations about the journey. "Colonel Laurens was exceedingly averse to going," reported Paine, confessing that "though he was well acquainted with the military, he was not with the political line, and proposed my going with him as secretary."[84]

Things were probably not so cut-and-dried. It is certainly possible that Paine invited himself along. He was, after all, itching to return to Europe to publish or do something substantial to defeat the British. Whatever the case, he wasted no time preparing for the journey. He abandoned plans to start a newspaper in Philadelphia, losing money on seventy reams of paper that he had already purchased from Québec with the help of Ralph Izard. He sold his belongings, collected his final salary of forty-four pounds from the Assembly, paid off his debts, and purchased, with the cash left over, ninety dollars in bills of exchange in preparation for the journey. He also tried to brush up on his knowledge of the French political scene by meeting with as many Frenchmen as possible. A fortnight before Christmas, 1780, he agreed to a morning interview with Marquis de Chastellux, who at the time was visiting Philadelphia and had expressed a keen desire to meet "that author so celebrated in America, and throughout Europe, by his excellent work, entitled *Common Sense*, and several other political pamphlets." Chastellux was a distinguished member of the French Academy, a former friend of Voltaire's, and major general in the French army. His diary note for December 14 revealed a shocked fascination with the condition of Paine's room, cluttered with the neglected mess of an expectant traveler: "I discovered, at his apartments, all the attributes of a man of letters; a room pretty much in disorder, dusty furniture, and a large table covered with books lying open, and manuscripts begun. His person was in a correspondent dress, nor did his physiognomy belie the spirit that reigns throughout his works."

Chastellux commented astutely on Paine's status as an independent political writer. He was fascinated by Paine's unusual role as critic of government and defender of civil society and its citizens: "His existence at Philadelphia is similar to that of those political writers in England, who have obtained nothing, and have neither credit enough in the State, nor sufficient political weight to obtain a part in the affairs of government. Their works are read with more curiosity than confidence, their projects being regarded as the play of imagination, than as well concerted plans." Although Chastellux liked Paine and enjoyed his company — "our conversation was agreeable and animated" — he concluded that Paine was less a politician and more a maker and unmaker of public opinion: "As his patriotism and his talents are unquestionable, it is natural to conclude that the vivacity of his imagination and the independence of his character, render him more calculated for reasoning on affairs, than for conditioning them."[85]

Others thought so too, but with less respect than Chastellux felt for Paine. In Congress, as Paine's departure for France grew imminent, his involvement in the mission came under heavy fire. The Deane affair had not been forgotten. John Witherspoon led the assault, which hardened Paine's conviction that he was a man of sour grapes who would "never forgive me for publishing *Common Sense* and going a step beyond him in Literary reputation."[86] Witherspoon and others repeated the old charge that Paine was unfaithful to the Revolution, that he was a mere free rider on its back, a craven figure who joined the cause only when it was safe to do so. Rumors also mushroomed outside Congress. Sarah Franklin Bache, Benjamin Franklin's daughter, whom Paine knew well, wrote from Philadelphia to her father on January 14, 1781: "There never was a man less beloved in a place than Paine is in this, having at different times disputed with everybody. The most rational thing he could have done would have been to have died the instant he had finished his *Common Sense*, for he never again will have it in his power to leave the world with so much credit."[87] A few days later, vitriolic words were flung at Paine at the American Philosophical Society, where for some time his possible membership had been actively discussed. A proposal by Dr. James Hutchinson, a respected Philadelphia physician who later became Surgeon-General of Pennsylvania, that Paine be admitted as a member of the society was blocked after a tense discussion. Eight candidates were short-listed, seven of whom, including Chastellux, were accepted automatically. Paine, a signatory of the original Act incorporating the society (on March 15, 1780), was one of two odd men out.[88]

With knives at his back, Paine resolved to leave Philadelphia fast. He withdrew his request to act as secretary to Laurens, telling him that he now wanted to cover his own costs and travel only as his private companion. Paine explained that this would be the best way of dealing with the "contention" stirred up by the likes of Witherspoon.[89] By paying his own way, Paine no doubt also thought that he could avoid irritating his old friend Benjamin Franklin, who must have seen Laurens's mission as an implied vote of no confidence by Congress in his current activities in Paris. Paine's place was filled by a twenty-three-year-old officer, Major William Jackson, who joined Laurens and Paine in mid-January in Philadelphia to plan their journey. Paine seemed philosophical. A few days before departure, he wrote to Nathanael Greene: "I leave America with the perfect satisfaction of having been to her an honest, faithful and affectionate friend." The parting words contained remorse as well: "I go away with the hope of returning to spend better or more agreeable days with her than those which are past."[90]

Shortly after the farewell, Paine, Jackson, Laurens, and an unknown French officer journeyed to Washington's headquarters in New Jersey. There they spent three days being briefed by him about the military campaign and the supplies to be requested from the French. The winter was harsh, and their difficult final journey overland to Boston ended in temporary disappointment. The *Alliance,* the suitably named gunboat that was to ferry them to France, still had no crew, despite promises by the local authorities. Laurens complained loudly for more than three weeks until enough hands were assembled on deck. On Sunday evening, February 11, the *Alliance,* "barely in condition,"[91] sailed from Boston harbor under the command of Captain John Barry. Renowned as the first American naval officer to have captured a British ship during the Revolution, Barry was a shrewd seaman who soon added to his reputation with a quick and daring voyage across the North Atlantic.

7

The Federalist

French Mission

TOM PAINE was glad to leave behind the sniping of his American critics. As the *Alliance* glided out of Boston harbor, however, he felt twinges of anxiety about the dangerous journey to come. He still suffered the occasional bad dream about his previous crossing of the Atlantic. His anxiety was compounded by the possibility that the diplomatic and military importance of the voyage through Atlantic waters thick with enemy ships would end in failure or disaster. Just before boarding the *Alliance*, Paine also had heard the chilling news that the *Shelalah*, on which he had tried to book a passage, had been lost at sea, with all hands presumed drowned.

His fears became real on the fifth night out from Boston. Two hundred miles south of Newfoundland, around nine in the evening, the *Alliance* entered a vast flotilla of drifting icebergs. The black shroud of the moonless, cloud-covered sky added to the confusion. Captain John Barry at first thought that the ship had run aground. After several fraught soundings with the lead and line, the ship heaving and listing wildly, he concluded that the real danger was that the ship would break up after a chance collision with the massive icebergs now towering over it. At eleven o'clock that evening, a huge fist of ice gashed the portside quarter gallery; John Laurens narrowly escaped the crush. Shortly afterward, the wind began to howl, ripping one of the mainsails in half. Some crew members began to pray. Paine, in the clutches of mild panic, was no longer sure that the ship, now drifting aimlessly, could survive: "The sea, in whatever direction it could be seen, appeared a tumultuous assemblage of floating rolling rocks, which we could not avoid and against which there was no defense."[1]

For seven hours, icebergs and waves crashed against the *Alliance* without its captain, crew, or passengers knowing the size of the iceberg flotilla or the direction in which the gale was hounding them. The fury continued until just before daybreak, when the ship began to roll more easily, the ocean gently lapping the hull, watched by a ship of shaken survivors stunned into reverent silence by their good luck. A few days later, after running repairs to the ship and rotated sleep, Captain Barry, nourished by escape from the clutches of death, maneuvered the *Alliance* into "a glorious breeze which carried us from nine to twelve miles an hour for seven days."[2] Just south of Greenland, two enemy ships were sighted. Barry ordered their chase, distributed arms to every man on board, including Paine, and placed Colonel Laurens in charge. The skirmish ended abruptly when the pursued ships turned on the *Alliance*. Finding it impossible to sail in tandem, the enemy ships' captains prudently called off the chase.

The following day, another clump of enemy ships was spotted, and once again the *Alliance*, dutiful of the law of privateering on the high seas — nothing ventured, nothing gained — let loose. Barry and his crew bore down fast on the smallest ship, a Scottish ten-gun cutter named the *Russel*, bound for Glasgow. The cutter retreated, leaving the *Alliance* a free hand with the larger Venetian cargo ship laden with glass bottles, pepper, indigo, and other merchandise. Barry and his crew approached the Venetian ship from its aft — Paine had practiced the technique many times on the *King of Prussia* — managing to board and disarm its several frightened watchmen without a shot being fired. The Venetian crew and captain, all found to be in irons but in good condition, were released and the ship returned to them gratis after Barry determined that it had been pirated contrary to the rights of neutral nations. Paine glowed with pride at the thought that he was sailing under the American flag: "The opportunity of doing an act of humanity like this, must to every mind capable of enjoying the chief of human pleasures, that of relieving insulted distress, be esteemed preferable to the richest prize that could have been taken."[3]

For reasons of revolutionary pride or personal embarrassment, Paine failed to mention that during the skirmish, the *Alliance* had captured a British twelve-gun boat, the *Alert*, whose captain and crew were later imprisoned and with whose captain, the Comte de Noailles, Paine had reportedly dueled.[4] The *Alliance* reached the French coast in a near-record

twenty-three days, but head winds and thick fog prevented it from docking
at L'Orient, on the southern shores of Brittany, for another three days.
The entourage headed by Laurens was greeted by the town commandant,
who, Paine remarked, "paid me great compliments on what he called the
great success and spirit of my publications." Finding that fame had pre-
ceded him on his first visit to France, Paine was especially pleased to have
set foot on terra firma after a month at sea. He enjoyed sampling the local
oysters, goat cheese, and cider wine but seemed less impressed by the town
of L'Orient. Among Brittany's largest towns, it enjoyed an immense natural harbor protected from the Atlantic Ocean by the Île de Groix. L'Orient had been founded a century earlier as a port from which the
Compagnie des Indes — the French equivalent of the English East India
Company — conducted its trade in exotic wealth imported from the rest
of the world. Paine's description of the town was confined to a brief and
chipper sentence: "L'Orient is a clean agreeable town, the streets straight
but not in general at right angles."[5]

Paine was unable to speak more than a few syllables of French, and
wary of English spies, he naturally gravitated toward the several Americans resident in the town. From one of them, Benjamin Franklin's grand-
nephew Jonathan Williams, a merchant, Paine accepted an invitation to
journey overland one hundred miles southeast to the regional center of
Nantes, leaving Laurens and his secretary, William Jackson, to set off directly for Paris. The journey was easy, and Paine got along well with
Williams, who liked him "as a companion because he is a pleasant as well
as a sensible man."[6] In Nantes, Paine was given a reception befitting a
hero from the rising American mirage to the west.[7] He must have been
puzzled by the way in which the authorities of the French monarchy
seemed to welcome him warmly wherever he traveled, despite the fact
that their treatment of him as their enemy's enemy, and therefore as their
friend, implied support for his radical republicanism. The loveliest ironies
are unintended, and so must have been the irony attending the official reception for him in Nantes. Paine, dressed in foul-smelling clothes, hirsute,
and suffering from a case of itch contracted during the month at sea,
stood proudly amid several dozen prominent citizens, listening in silence
to the welcoming speech of the mayor of Nantes, who surely must have
harbored thoughts that Paine was subversive in more than appearance.

Following tunes played by a pipe-and-drum band and smiles and hand-
shakes from curious well-wishers, Paine was escorted by his interpreter,
Elkanah Watson, to nearby lodgings. There the forty-four-year-old revolutionary was led straight to a bathtub. Watson, a hostile opponent of

Paine's writings, recalled forty years later in his memoirs that he had found him "coarse and uncouth in his manners, loathsome in his appearance, and a disgusting egotist; rejoicing most in talking of himself, and reading the effusions of his own mind." His practical advice to Paine was to yield to a scrubbing brush and soap: "I took the liberty, on his asking for the loan of a clean shirt, of speaking to him frankly of his dirty appearance and brimstone odor; and prevailed upon him to stew for an hour, in a hot bath." Paine resisted, perhaps because he worried that his itch would worsen upon contact with water, or perhaps because after a month without bathing, the idea of a bath simply did not appeal, especially given the fresh smells and sights of France now tingling his senses. Watson persisted, this time offering his guest a bribe of a full pile of recent English newspapers. "He at once consented," recalled Watson, "and accompanied me to the bath, where I instructed the keeper in French (which Paine did not understand) gradually to increase the heat of the water, until 'le Monsieur etait bien bouilli.'" Absorbed for more than two hours in news from home, Paine was none the wiser until helped by the keeper from the bath, parboiled clean.[8]

Little is known about Paine's activities during the next several months. After journeying to Paris by horse-drawn coach to rendezvous with Laurens and Jackson, as planned, he took up lodgings in the village of Passy, on the highway from Paris to Versailles, close to Laurens and Jackson and within walking distance of the magnificent Hôtel Valentinois, the residence of Benjamin Franklin. In this little American quarter of fine views and terraces and gardens leading down to the Seine, Paine set to work as Laurens's unofficial secretary, drafting letters to French and American officials, filing correspondence, talking politics, exchanging gossip, and helping to plan the Americans' next moves.[9] While Paine had been in Nantes, Laurens, tutored by Franklin, had begun his rounds through the court of Louis XVI. He had met the French foreign minister, Comte de Vergennes, Jacques Necker, various key ministers, and the King himself, making the case whenever the opportunity arose for loans, gifts, and urgently needed supplies for the American revolutionaries. Reports on the competence of Laurens in these negotiations vary. His secondhand knowledge and outright unfamiliarity with the courtly intrigues of French politics crippled him at times. At a social occasion for gentlemen and ladies attached to the court, Paine was told, the inexperienced Laurens had even collared Louis XVI to press the American case for generous aid, with bystanding guests shocked at the display of atrocious social manners of the foreigner fresh from the battlefield.

Laurens certainly got off to a bad start with Vergennes. After their first meeting to discuss the American request, Vergennes "exclaimed vehemently against the exorbitance of the demand." He issued a warning through Franklin that unless Laurens polished his manners, he would no longer be received in official circles. Vergennes later denounced Laurens as a young man suffering "inexperience in affairs."[10] Franklin remained publicly silent, working behind the scenes to smooth ruffled feathers. And Paine, having braved the Atlantic on a mission that he knew could well help to topple the British Empire in America, kept a brave face, loyally praising the "address and alacrity"[11] of Laurens, all the while sweating at his desk to ensure that written communications from him were fluent, precise, and persuasive.

During the two and a half months it took to conclude negotiations, Paine kept a low public profile. Contrary to Lamartine, the king never "showered Paine with his favours."[12] In fact, Paine mainly stuck close to his hotel, getting by in public places in poor pidgin English and, during his spare moments, contemplating his future. The news that the French were prepared to send a powerful fleet to the American coast during the summer, to guarantee a loan of ten million livres, to make gifts of hard cash totaling six million livres, and to ship large quantities of clothing, arms, and ammunition to America proved to be bittersweet for Paine. He was visibly delighted by the success, but the news confronted him with unsettling questions about what he would do with his life next. Foremost in his mind was the disturbing thought that his days in America were numbered. Each day, he weighed two possibilities. One was to remain temporarily in Europe to write a pamphlet for publication in London, after which he would return on a French frigate along with the last installment of cash for the Americans.[13] The second possibility, he confessed one evening over dinner with Laurens, involved not returning to America at all: "I told Colonel Laurens that though I had every wish it was possible a man could feel for the success of the cause which America was engaged in, yet such had been the treatment I had received, and such the hardship and difficulties I had experienced year after year, that I had no heart to return back and was resolved not to do it."[14]

Laurens exploded. Paine's story was that Laurens had a "passionate attachment" to him and that Laurens wanted him for personal support on the journey in case any personal misfortune struck him down. Paine backed down. In the second half of May, from temporary accommodations in St. Germain, he wrote a note to William Temple Franklin asking him to forward his "spurs and great coat" from Passy.[15] Young Captain

Jackson was sent to Amsterdam to supervise a shipment of French cash to America, and a few days later, on the first day of June, Paine and Laurens boarded the seventy-two-gun French frigate *la Résolute* at Brest, bound for Philadelphia. Escorted by several gunboats and two brigs (the *Cibelle* and *Olimpe*) packed with clothing and military supplies, *la Résolute,* itself weighed down by 2.5 million silver livres packed in double casks, made slow progress. Paine complained that the convoy "experienced every contrariety"[16] and that the journey seemed endless. The convoy sailed a circuitous zigzag route to avoid interception by the enemy. The pace was further slowed by a change of plans midway across the Atlantic. Learning from a passing friendly vessel, the *Minerva,* that the French navy had failed to clear the Delaware capes of British warships, Laurens ordered that the convoy alter its course and head for the safer port of Boston. The ships finally arrived in Boston on the afternoon of August 26, 1781, the return trip having taken eighty-six days, three times longer than the outbound journey.[17]

Homelessness

The cargo unloaded on the Boston wharves arrived too late to be of any direct use to the American war effort. The morale boost it provided was nonetheless important. As sixteen teams of oxen guarded by two American regiments slowly hauled the supplies toward Philadelphia, George Washington prepared for the campaign that shortly afterward resulted in the surrender of General Charles Cornwallis in Virginia. The information that both naval and financial aid were on the way was relayed to the American commander by a team of galloping couriers, and the effect on his confidence was probably considerable. The cargo had an even more powerful, if unintended, effect. It had been earmarked by the French as a direct gift to Washington, but Congress, intent on keeping the military under civil control, ordered the supplies to be turned over to the Board of War and the cash to Robert Morris, the new Superintendent of Finance, who used the funds four months later as capital stock to convert the Bank of Philadelphia into the powerful Bank of North America.[18]

Paine received no public recognition of his role in the dangerous French mission. Its conclusion struck him as humiliating. After resting briefly in Boston, he and Laurens hired a sulky and set off southward ahead of the land convoy, with Laurens itching to join Washington's campaign. Not far from Providence, the sulky broke down, whereupon Laurens borrowed horses from Rhode Island friends and scrambled toward Yorktown, where Washington's troops were gathering. Left behind with a servant, two horses, and a mere six guineas in his pocket to cover his expenses during the remaining three-hundred-mile journey to Philadelphia, Paine felt utterly forlorn. At Bordentown, he had to borrow a dollar to get across the Delaware River by ferry. His plan to join Laurens in Yorktown was done in by empty pockets.[19]

Paine slipped into Philadelphia virtually unnoticed. Traveling had made him wiser, but miserable. The feeling that nobody cared wounded his pride, fueled his immodesty, and noticeably cooled his warm feelings for America. For the next few months, his mood swung erratically between self-pity and arrogance, resentment of his poverty and grumblings about delayed generosity from others. Part of the problem was that America had changed in his absence. The Articles of Confederation had been ratified, and a more conservative group was now in control of Congress. Robert Morris, the new Superintendent of Finance, had been granted broad powers to bring the chaotic financial situation under control. And there was a pronounced rise in the level of public optimism about the outcome of the military struggle against the British.

The feeling that the British were in deep military trouble understandably bothered Paine, particularly because it raised fundamental questions about his future role as a political writer in "normal" peacetime conditions. For the first time in his life, he began to tread the path of permanent insecurity later experienced by every modern political writer enjoying a healthy measure of civil and political freedom. Marquis de Chastellux, during his visit to Paine's lodgings a year earlier, had spotted the novelty of his situation: "His existence at Philadelphia is similar to that of those political writers in England, who have obtained nothing, and have neither credit enough in the State, nor sufficient political weight to obtain a part in the affairs of government. Their works are read with more curiosity than confidence, their projects being regarded as the play of imagination, than as well concerted plans."[20]

Chastellux made it sound as if these new-style political writers were losers, but in fact Paine, from his days in Lewes, had deliberately explored the role as a matter of principle. He openly shunned the classical republican, ultimately platonic view of the political thinker as a foot servant of government power. He was among the first modern political writers to experiment with the art of writing democratically and for democratic ends. He hammered out a colloquial style that eschewed meaningless sentences, purple passages, and general humbug because he considered that the highest duty of political writers was to irritate their country's government. Rather than keeping things running quietly and smoothly, they should encourage subjects to become pugnacious citizens. In other words, the fundamental aim of the political writer was to defend citizens against arbitrary exercises of power in the spheres of civil society and the state. That duty to question publicly the powerful and the power hungry implied that every writer was destined at some point to be called a traitor — or to be ignored or flung to the sidelines of power, where extended bouts of self-doubt and material poverty would see to it that the writer worried about more immediate matters.

Having already been attacked as a traitor, it was now Paine's turn to suffer official rejection and its side effects — biting poverty and nagging self-doubt. A few days after arriving in Philadelphia, he wrote to Thomas McKean, president of Congress, offering his services as a courier running information between Congress and the battlefront. McKean never replied. Paine meanwhile had been forced to spend the money entrusted to him by John Laurens on pressing needs. He also had to borrow extra funds from acquaintances — including an assistant judge from South Carolina named Burke — to pay for his room and board on Second Street. In desperation, he even began to hatch plans to beg a passage to Holland, where at least, he told several acquaintances, "I was sure of being safe, and could not be worse off."[21]

When the glorious news of the surrender of the British at Yorktown reached Philadelphia around October 20, 1781, Paine was unemployed, broke, depressed. He recalled,

> I now felt myself worse off than ever. My intention of getting out a publication in Europe was prevented by my speedy return from that country. The money I had taken with me and which had been saved out of my salary as Clerk of the Assembly was expended. The design of Col. Laurens in placing me as Secretary had been frustrated, and the Clerkship of the House, which though of but little worth, was better than nothing, was in other hands; and I had the mortification of knowing that all this arose from an anxiety to serve in, and promote the cause of a country, whose circumstances were then rising into prosperity, and who, though she owed nothing of that prosperity to me appeared every day careless of whatever related to my personal interest.[22]

There was no way of knowing that the victory at Yorktown meant the end of the war, but the sense that the Americans were now tightening their grip on American soil prompted celebrations throughout the country. During November, with the British bottled up on Manhattan Island, Washington paraded through the streets of Philadelphia, confident that the coming winter would be the least troublesome since he had taken command of the Continental army. Paine observed the parade from his room on Second Street, opposite the Quaker Meeting House, and for the next few days and nights he watched the city come alive. Its houses were festooned with ribbons and flags, its wide streets filled with off-duty militia and clumps of chattering citizens. At night the town sparkled with candlelit windows, fireworks displays, and strings of wild tavern toasts and lavish victory balls.

Paine outwardly shared the euphoria, but the abandon of Philadelphia tightened his inner resentment. It certainly toughened his resolve to remedy the injustices of his poverty. On November 30, the seventh anniversary of his arrival in America, he decided to write to Washington, who was spending the winter in Philadelphia, to confess "the secret of my own situation." Paine bitterly described the misery of his unemployment, which stemmed, he claimed, from his exposure of Silas Deane and, indirectly, from his principled policy, stretching back to the time when he lived in England, of forgoing personal gain by redirecting royalties from his works to public causes. He accused American officials of "cold and inattentive" behavior and asked Washington, as Commander in Chief, to use his authority and detachment from party politics to pressure them into remedying his distress. Paine reaffirmed his deep love of America but repeated his threat to leave the country permanently for Europe, where perhaps he could work for the New World in the Old: "In this situation I cannot go on, and as I have no inclination to differ with the country or to tell the story of her neglect, it is my design to get to Europe, either to France or Holland. I have literary fame, and I am sure I cannot experience worse fortune than I have here."[23]

Robert Morris

Paine seemed untroubled by the possibility that he might be offered a government stipend that would contradict, if only symbolically, his yearning for independence as a political writer. He reported that Washington became "affectionately interested" in his case.[24] Washington "concerted with a friend or two" (probably Robert Morris and the French minister at Philadelphia, Chevalier de la Luzerne), suggesting that Paine's poverty be cured through a short-term grant of money or some form of employment until a long-term solution, perhaps a grant of land, could be arranged when the war finally ended. The contact with la Luzerne yielded quick, if modest, cash results.[25]

The links with Robert Morris, now the most powerful man in the United States after Washington, matured more slowly. Paine had already made contact with him in mid-September upon returning from France. A few days after unpacking his trunk, Paine had been summoned to the Office of Finance, where Morris "proposed that for the Service of the Country he should write and publish such Pieces respecting the propriety, Necessity and Utility of Taxation as might be likely to promote the Public Service of America."[26] Paine immediately wrote to Morris with a plan for supporting the army by raising taxes in Philadelphia. Morris reciprocated by calling a conference to discuss the plan with top militia officers and the president of the Supreme Executive Council of Pennsylvania.[27]

During the autumn of 1781, the two men met socially five or six times. Morris clearly bore no grudge against Paine for his involvement, two years earlier, in the Philadelphia citizens' committees that had publicly criticized Morris and other men of wealth for their profiteering. Morris and Paine enjoyed each other's company. Although they did not see eye to eye on many political matters, they both had a tenuous commitment to the anti-statist agrarian traditions then prevalent in America. Paine also shared Morris's hard money attitudes, his concern about the impact of inflation on the middle and lower classes, and his cosmopolitan belief that commerce and economic growth were the midwives of a new world order in which war would have no place. Paine borrowed books and newspapers from Morris, and the strange pair thrived on their spirited conversations, even more so after Morris confessed to Paine, upon reading the latest reports, that "he had been totally deceived in Deane" and that he now "looked upon him to be a bad man, and his reputation totally ruined."[28]

For some weeks, Morris continued to hear out Paine's repeated complaints of enduring neglect by governments in America. During a long afternoon fireside conversation at the Office of Finance on January 26, 1782, Morris reiterated that he wished the best for Paine. He again praised the magical powers of Paine's pen, but he restated that he had "nothing in my power at present to Offer as a Compensation for his services."[29] The two friends continued to meet. They were often joined by Morris's chief assistant and Paine's old enemy Gouverneur Morris, who, Paine noted, now "hopped round upon one leg," confessed that he and others had been duped by Silas Deane, and "complimented me on my quick sight, — and by God, says he, nothing carries a man through the world like honesty."[30]

Unknown to Paine, the two Morrises had already worked out a plan for employing him. On February 10, 1782, it was formalized as a written agreement with Washington and Robert Livingston, Secretary of Foreign Affairs. For the very modest salary of eight hundred dollars a year, paid out of a secret service fund primed by Robert Morris, Paine would be quietly employed for the purpose of "informing the People and rousing them into Action."[31] Shortly afterward, the two Morrises told Paine the details of the secret plan. They explained to him that their overall aim was to see to it that the American army was well fed and clothed and that it was paid a decent wage for its struggle to defeat the British. This required tax increases. "We want the aid of an able pen to urge the Legislatures of the several States to grant sufficient taxes," they told Paine, quickly adding that the plan had to be breathtakingly bold to break the current resistance to tax increases at the level of the state legislatures. That resistance could be overcome, they proposed, if priority was given to the development of a new federal level of government — they described it as "a new confederation" — equipped with the independent power to tax American citizens. In effect, this would require the dramatic strengthening of the current powers of Congress by securing a new constitution supported by American citizens. For this purpose, Paine would be paid to "prepare the minds of the people for such restraints and such taxes and imposts, as are absolutely necessary for their own welfare."[32]

Paine cautiously jumped at the offer. During an evening gathering at the Office of Finance, sharing a bottle of Madeira with Washington, the two Morrises, and Livingston, Paine confirmed that he was "well disposed to the undertaking." He was assured that he would be asked to write only in support of "upright measures" and that in any case he could veto any proposed topic or ignore any editorial comments on his manuscripts. Paine asked for his salary to be backdated so as to clear the debts amassed during his expedition to France. We do not know what was decided because the men agreed that the arrangement would be kept strictly confidential since, as Gouverneur Morris put it, "a Salary publickly and avowedly given for the above Purpose would injure the Effect of Mr. Paine's Publications, and subject him to injurious personal Reflections."[33]

The word nevertheless quickly got about. A month after the contract was signed, Joseph Reed wrote to Nathanael Greene describing Paine as "a hireling writer pensioned with £300 per annum, payable by General Washington out of the Secret Service money."[34] It is highly possible, for two reasons, that it was Paine himself who broke the secret. The more obvious reason was his strong sense of vindication. His services at last were being acknowledged officially without strings attached. His writer's veto

A detail from *The Bench*, by William Hogarth, featuring Sir John Willes, Lord Chief Justice of the Court of Common-Pleas.

Euston Hall, the seat of the Duke of Grafton. (*Engraving by R. Acon; courtesy of the Thetford Library*)

A rare early nineteenth-century sketch by Joseph Wilkinson of Thetford Grammar School. *(Courtesy of David Osborne)*

A 1764 drawing by W. Scott of the Lewes Town Hall, where Paine attended public meetings. *Courtesy of the Sussex Archaeological Society, Lewes)*

John Wilkes Esquire, by William Hogarth

Benjamin Rush

Blood-stained title page of the first pamphlet version of *The American Crisis I,* published in late December 1776. *(Courtesy of the American Philosophical Society Library)*

The *American* CRISIS.

NUMBER I.

By the Author of COMMON SENSE.

THESE are the times that try men's fouls: The fummer foldier and the funfhine patriot will, in this crifis, fhrink from the fervice of his country; but he that ftands it NOW, deferves the love and thanks of man and woman. Tyranny, like hell, is not eafily conquered; yet we have this confolation with us, that the harder the conflict, the more glorious the triumph. What we obtain too cheap, we efteem too lightly :---'Tis dearnefs only that gives every thing its value. Heaven knows how to fet a proper price upon its goods; and it would be ftrange in-deed, if fo celeftial an article as FREEDOM fhould not be highly rated. Britain, with an army to enforce her tyranny, has declared, that fhe has a right *(not only to* TAX*)* but " *to* " BIND *us in* ALL CASES WHATSOEVER," and if being *bound in that manner* is not flavery, then is there not fuch a thing as flavery upon earth. Even the expreffion is impious, for fo unlimited a power can belong only to GOD.

WHETHER the Independence of the Continent was de-clared too foon, or delayed too long, I will not now enter into as an argument; my own fimple opinion is, that had it been eight months earlier, it would have been much bet-ter. We did not make a proper ufe of laft winter, neither could we, while we were in a dependent ftate. However, the fault, if it were one, was all our own **.* But no great deal is loft yet; all that Howe has been doing for this month paft is rather a ravage than a conqueft, which the fpirit of the Jerfies a year ago would have quickly repulfed, and which time and a little refolution will foon recover.

I have as little fuperftition in me as any man living, but my

---
* " The prefent winter" (meaning the laft) " is worth an " age, if rightly employed, but if loft, or neglected, the whole " Continent will partake of the evil; and there is no punifh-" ment that man does not deferve, be he who, or what, or " where he will, that may be the means of facrificing a feafon " fo precious and ufeful."   COMMON SENSE.

George Washington, flanked by General Nathanael Greene, left, and Paine, observing the fall of Fort Washington, New York, from Fort Lee Palisades, November 16, 1776. *(Painting by Paul Ortlip; courtesy of the Fort Lee Historical Park and Fort Lee Chamber of Commerce, Fort Lee, New Jersey)*

The Yorkshire Stingo, Marylebone, circa 1770. *(Courtesy of the Institution of Civil Engineers)*

The earliest surviving mezzotint, erroneously entitled *Edward Payne Esqr.,* by James Watson, 1783, after an original portrait of Paine by C. W. Peale. *(Courtesy of the American Philosophical Society Library)*

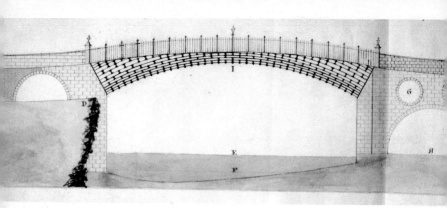

Anonymous sketches of a Paine-style cast-iron bridge for the River Wear, near Sunderland, late 1791. (*Courtesy of Sir John Soanes Museum*)

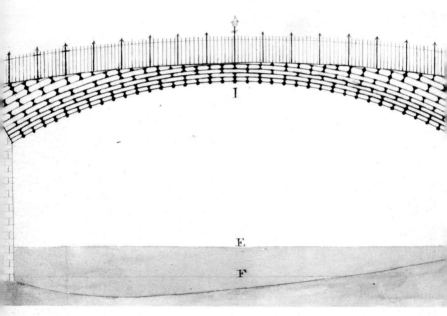

Gouverneur Morris. (*Courtesy of the Thetford Library*)

George Chalmers ("Francis Oldys"), by H. Edridge. (*Courtesy of the American Philosophical Society Library*)

Title-page image of the tenth edition of George Chalmers's *Life of Thomas Pain* (London, 1793). The caption reads "'Hear and improve', he pertly cries: 'I come to make all nations wise'."

Mad Tom, or the Man of Rights, by Hannibal Scratch, 1791. *(Courtesy of the American Philosophical Society Library)*

over his paymasters would guarantee his independence, and he therefore thought it unlikely that his acceptance of the job would turn him into a craven party hack. "I am ... under no difficulty of accepting the proposal," he told Robert Morris, "because I will know that it is not only out of friendship to me, but out of Justice to me," adding some bombast about the importance to world history of his activities in Revolutionary America: "I have the honest pride of thinking and ranking myself among the founders of a new Independent World, and I should suffer exceedingly to be put out of that track."[35]

United States of America

The less obvious reason Paine probably felt no embarrassment at leaking the arrangement was his conviction that it would provide him with a secure platform from which to argue publicly for an entirely novel idea: the success of the Revolution required Americans to craft, for the first time anywhere in the world, a two-tiered, federated system of republican government elected by and responsible to its citizens. Although he was soon to become the best-known exponent of the idea, Paine was certainly not the father of American federalist proposals. He was aware that between the adoption of the Articles of Confederation in 1778 and their approval by the states in 1781, many delegates to Congress and many officeholders in the central government had reached the conclusion that the current constitutional belt was too loosely buckled. He noted how the outcry about congressional weakness had, if anything, grown after the approval of the Articles, and it may be that soon after returning from France, he had read a series of vigorous essays by Alexander Hamilton, who had argued openly what many in and around Congress thought privately: in unitary states, the primary danger was that the sovereign would have too much power over the governed, whereas in confederal systems such as America, the danger was "directly the reverse" — in other words, "that the common sovereign" would "not have power sufficient to unite the different members together, and direct the common forces to the interest and happiness of the whole."[36]

Paine himself had first signaled the same danger two summers before in several letters, published in the *Pennsylvania Gazette*, on the dispute about rights to fish the Newfoundland banks. At the time, Paine rejected the British view that the Americans should surrender their Newfoundland fishing rights as a condition of peace. The British view, curiously, had been supported by a pro-French faction in Congress backed by the French ambassador, Conrad Alexandre Gérard, who believed that American insistence on fishing rights in the North Atlantic would make the Americans commercial competitors with France and that the insistence would, in any case, annoy the British and thus prolong the war. Paine laid into both the British and the French. He was adamant that Congress should not budge. It should regard the fishing rights that previously had been enjoyed by the colonists as now belonging exclusively to the United States. The fisheries could help empower the country by providing employment, stimulating interstate and foreign trade, and strengthening its naval forces. Without the fisheries, he argued, Congress would have at its disposal scarcely any fleet for protecting American shores.[37]

The issue had been debated in Congress for five months. Paine's proposal had been supported by the New England delegates and other friends of the "Eastern Party," but in mid-August 1779 it had been thrown out. The setback had toughened his resolve to campaign harder for empowering Congress. The next opportunity arose in the bitter land claims controversy that racked the young confederation during the second half of 1780. Although the draft Articles of Confederation contained elaborate proposals for settling boundary disputes between states and among conflicting private land claims, the document specified that "no state shall be deprived of territory for the benefit of the United States."[38] Maryland refused to accept the clause, partly because its delegates feared the future power of Virginia, which was claiming dominion over a vast territory to the west and northwest of the Allegheny Mountains, and partly because many of the Maryland leaders had interests in land companies hovering over Virginia's claimed territory. For both reasons, Maryland made it clear that it would not ratify the Articles until the land-claiming states relinquished their claims to Congress for the benefit of all states. Maryland held out for more than three years. It was supported by other "landless" states such as Pennsylvania and New Jersey and by several powerful groups of land speculators, including the Indiana Company, which wanted the lands nationalized and had its eyes on nearly three thousand square miles of territory claimed by Virginia.

During the autumn of 1780, Paine sprang to the defense of Maryland and the Indiana Company. After months of careful thought and reading, he was sure that Congress should succeed to Crown rights in all lands unoccupied by white Americans, and indeed that Congress should assume Crown prerogatives in doubtful cases, especially those resting on bogus titles secured through "purchase" from Native Americans. The disputed lands, Paine thought, should be understood as "a national fund for the benefit of all," and Congress, which should supervise their sale to private hands, should use the revenues so reaped to remedy the national debt.

Paine said all this — and remained silent about Native Americans' struggle against land sales — in a new pamphlet advertised on December 30, 1780, as *Public Good, Being an Examination into the Claim of Virginia to the vacant western Territory, And of the Right of The United States to the Same; To which is added, Proposals for laying off a new State; To be applied as a Fund for carrying on the War, or redeeming the national Debt.*[39] Its arguments angered some of Paine's Virginia friends, including Thomas Jefferson and Richard Henry Lee. James Madison reacted vitriolically, condemning *Public Good* as riddled with "calumny and influence."[40] There were also poisonous rumors that Paine was a "mercenary party scribbler" and hireling of the Indiana Company, and it was even claimed, by "Caractacus" and others, that he was complicit in bribery by virtue of having received a grant of twelve thousand acres for writing the pamphlet.[41]

Paine was understandably embarrassed when, shortly after *Public Good* appeared, he was listed as the owner of three hundred shares in the Indiana Company.[42] On past performance, he might have been expected to decline the offer. But for reasons that are not altogether clear, he did not. Instead, he sat quietly on the offer for nearly two years before applying for a title deed, all the time insisting that the company share offer was a gift that in no way violated his unswerving republican commitment to the public good. "If there is any one circumstance in my character which distinguishes itself from the rest," he said in a formal reply to "Caractacus," "it is *personal disinterestedness*, and an anxiety to serve a public cause in preference to myself."[43]

In the same reply, Paine related how he had been approached during the summer of 1779 by several Indiana Company executives, including Major Trent, who had explained to him their grievances and "offered me any compensation I would require." Paine had refused on principle. Eighteen months later, he continued, he had been again visited by the same Indiana Company executives, who had persuaded him to borrow documents that had soon convinced him of the injustice of Virginia's claim on the western territories. Paine explained that as soon as *Public Good* had been published, "I returned the materials which the company had put into my hands, and they unanimously ordered a deed to be made out to me for what they call a voters share." He had set off for France shortly afterward and had subsequently forgotten about the shares until reminded of their existence during April 1782. According to Paine, he then felt obliged to instruct the Indiana Company to announce publicly that he was a shareholder. That course of action was fully consistent with his commitment to republican principles. "From me the states have received the unremitted service of seven years, and to them I have not been the expence of a private soldier," he concluded. "I have done every thing *of* myself and *from* myself. The interest of the heart alone has carried me through a thousand things which others would have failed in or staggered at."

Such confessions of public spirit by America's best-known political writer helped quell any major uproar. So did the farsighted and constitutional proposals sketched in *Public Good*. Paine predicted that sooner or later new states would be formed and would apply to join the current union. Since "new emigrants will have something to learn when they first come to America," he cautioned the existing confederation to admit new member states slowly. He further proposed that upon admission, the new states' representatives in Congress should initially have merely observer status. There they could "sit, hear and debate on all questions and matters, but not vote on any till after the expiration of seven years." Paine made it clear that this proposal, which later became the accepted method of admitting new state members, did not presuppose that Congress should stay as it was. To the contrary, *Public Good* expressed profound unease at the present confederalist consensus. It argued instead for a new "Continental convention" for the purpose of drawing up a new federal constitution. In Paine's view, the division and extent of the powers of Congress, currently restricted to matters of peace and treaty making, needed fundamentally to be rethought. A stronger, more effective central government was sorely needed in America. "The internal control and dictatorial powers of Congress," he wrote, in words first sketched in *Common Sense*, "are not sufficiently defined." The lesson of the land claims controversy was clear. The powers of Congress "appear to be too much in some cases and too little in others; and therefore, to have them marked out legally will give additional energy to the whole, and a new confidence to the several parts."

The bargain struck with Robert Morris in early 1782 enabled Paine to step up such attacks on the confederalist dogma. Since his involvement in the fisheries and land claims affairs, the level of indebtedness of the confederation had rocketed dangerously. Paper currency had almost stopped circulating. The consequent shortage of hard currency, which was now the standard medium of exchange, made debt repayment in hard cash ever more expensive and difficult. With no hard currency to repay interest, borrowing also became virtually impossible. Meanwhile, with the army poorly supplied and unpaid, fears grew that army discontent and collusion among angry creditors might result in attempts to seize govern-ment and set up a dictatorship. It was obvious to Paine that in the face of these threats, credit-seeking expeditions to France could never be more than a stopgap measure. The fiscal problems of the United States re-quired bolder solutions. Congress in particular now needed a steady source of revenue with which to pay the interest due domestic and foreign creditors and to meet its current obligations to the military and civil branches of the central government.

But where could this money be found? Paine was sure that Congress now required its own power of taxation. He therefore welcomed a pro-posed amendment to the Articles of Confederation authorizing Congress to levy, for an indefinite period, a duty of 5 percent on the value of all goods imported into the country. The revenues so generated were to be used to repay the war debt, but the opposition to the amendment was fierce. Paine quickly lined up behind those who wanted to break the old pattern of central government's fiscal subservience to the states. Twenty-four hours before signing a formal agreement with Morris, he wrote ea-gerly to his new employer:

> I shall get out a piece tomorrow on the King of England's speech, and I
> have sent to all the printers to secure a place in the Wednesday Papers. As I
> have not time to enter on the whole business of Revenue in tomorrow's
> piece, I shall dispose it so as to endeavour to create an animated disposition
> in the Country — and shall follow it with another piece in the next week's
> papers on the subject of Revenue, of which I shall give notice.[44]

It had been almost fourteen months since Paine had published any-thing, and not surprisingly his writing — incorrectly described by most observers as *The American Crisis X* — brimmed with enthusiasm. He began by trashing the "snivelling hypocrisy" of King George III's bellicose speech at the opening of Parliament, all the while warning American readers that the nation could not win the war "without trouble and ex-pense."[45] The trouble caused by rising expenses was explained a fortnight later in an essay addressed "To the People of America. On the Expences, Arrangements and Disbursements for carrying on the War, and finishing it with Honour and Advantage." It was a spirited defense of citizens' duty to pay taxes to Congress. It tried on every argument. Those currently peti-tioning for reduced taxes should support a congressional tax, Paine said, because that was the only way in the long run to reduce its borrowing and high interest charges. A federal tax specifically earmarked for military spending, he continued, would defuse discontent within the ranks of the

underclothed, underfed, unpaid army. It would thereby bring greater justice to a country whose citizens already had the highest standard of living
in the world. A federal tax also would be less confusing to citizens, certainly compared with the currently jumbled state taxation system. That
system operated potentially as "a cloak for fraud" because the revenues it
harvested at the state level were eaten up simultaneously by domestic and
military spending by the state and confederal governments. The current
system thereby enabled elected representatives to hoodwink taxpayers by
avoiding hypothecation and fiddling with accounts and spending plans. A
federal tax, Paine argued, would be more publicly transparent and accountable. It would serve the additional purpose of reminding Americans
why they had formed a union of states in the first place. "Each state is to
the United States what each individual is to the state he lives in," he thundered. The reformed taxation system should reflect this basic principle.
Ultimately, he said, a federal tax would be a wise insurance policy. "When
we think or talk about taxes," he wrote, "we ought to recollect that we lie
down in peace and sleep in safety; that we can follow our farms or stores
or other occupations, in prosperous tranquillity; and that these inestimable blessings are procured to us by the taxes that we pay."[46]

A few days after the essay appeared in the *Pennsylvania Gazette*, Paine invited George Washington and Robert Morris to "spend a part of an
evening at my apartment, and eat a few Oysters or a crust of Bread and
Cheese." The meeting went well. Paine loved oysters and serious conversation, and he was pleased by his employers' warm reaction to his contributions. He divulged that he was preparing two further pieces, one of
which sparked much discussion. A few days later, Paine showed Morris "a
piece he intended to publish concerning the protection of our commerce." Morris "advised some alterations and thought he had best publish it as anonymous." Paine quickly forwarded a revised version of the
article, saying, "If you think it a convenient publication, being a better
judge of the Subject than myself, I will get it into Dunlap's paper of Tuesday Morning." Two days later, Morris summoned Paine to his office "in
order to remark some things to him concerning the commerce of the
country."[47] The coded exchanges centered on a manuscript arguing that
one of the principal aims of current British foreign policy was to strangle
the potentially profitable American commerce with France. The article
proposed tough action. The merchants and governments of Delaware
and Pennsylvania were advised to clear the Delaware estuary of British
ships. The French were urged to use warships to cut off New York's sizable trade with Britain and to protect American vessels sailing the At-

lantic. Morris correctly spotted that Paine's argument was a backdoor defense of the proposed 5 percent import duty. Congress would obviously benefit from its own tax on expanding transatlantic commerce, whose security could be coordinated only by Congress and not by individual states. Morris, who felt torn between the fear of upsetting the peace negotiations and the hope of strengthening Congress, continued to express misgivings about the political timing of the piece. Soon afterward, however, Paine went ahead and published it in the *Pennsylvania Packet* under the signature "An Alliance Man."[48]

In the meantime, "Common Sense" had issued another stirring call for the payment of taxes. This time Paine tried to convince his readers that the Revolution had showered them with prosperity. The subtext read, Americans! Fear not federalism! Give generously to Congress! The words beamed with the optimism of an alchemist. "We began with paper," he wrote, "and we end with gold and silver. We set out with parties, and we are approaching to unity. The strength, the property, and even the fashion of the country, are confederated in her support. Like robust and healthy youth, she hath shook off the agues of the winter, and steps forward with constitutional bloom and vigour."[49]

The crafted rhetoric brought wry smiles to the faces of Paine's critics. Here was the delicious irony of Thomas Paine, now the world's most famous critic of the modern taxation state, pressing the case, as a salaried state employee, for *increased* taxes.[50] More astute observers spotted the injustice of the indictment. Paine had not fallen into confusion. Here was not a turncoat radical who had once opposed excessive taxes and now kowtowed to his tax-hungry paymasters. Each one of Paine's essays during the late winter of 1782 developed a consistent line of criticism of the American confederation. Each essay was, in fact, an opening shot in a wider political campaign to strengthen the federal dimension of American politics.

During this period, Paine emphasized the need to be clear about the form of government demanding taxes from its population. He reminded his readers that despotisms cannot legitimately tax their subjects because they rob them of their security and freedom. Where there is no political and civil freedom, taxation is theft. Things are different in a free republic. Government is visible and accountable to its citizens, who consequently have nothing to fear from their representatives, who are entrusted with payments of money, on a mutually agreeable basis, to fund the operations of government. In keeping with an old English custom, Paine considered taxation a gift of the governed to the governors. But he also thought that taxation was not just a gift. It was a duty of citizens living democratically in a republic — a compulsory but willingly given grant to government in exchange for their security and happiness.

In the essays written for Washington and Morris, Paine reiterated that this general principle still applied to American governments. But — here he took a stride beyond most of his contemporaries — he was sure that the dalliance with confederalism was over. The current national debt and the size and complexity of continental affairs required a two-tiered system of taxation, including a new and clearly defined federal tax set by Congress and collected by the states. Paine did not trouble himself with the "inconveniences" of federal systems — for instance, the ways in which they produce ceaseless "boundary disputes" about matters such as legal jurisdiction, taxation, and the *jus belli*.[51] Nor did he deal directly with the objection — later heard during the ratification of the Constitution in 1787 — that a federal system would sap the participatory energies of citizens and siphon power into a small circle of citizens elected by the rest.[52] Paine instead dreamed of one great American federal system, which would be superior to any previous republic in terms of its citizens' wealth and power. The new federation would be a prototype of the emerging federated world order to come. It would be a political system set above all the existing transatlantic powers in its capacity to dictate the terms of the future relationship between the Old World and the New. The new federal system, he thought, also would produce a variety of quick-ripening fruits at home. Massive debt would be brought under control, and Congress would prove to be more effective and popular, in no small measure because the jumbled taxation system would be simplified. "It has been our error, as well as our misfortune," Paine concluded, "to blend the affairs of each state, especially in money matters, with those of the United States; whereas it is our case, convenience and interest, to keep them separate."[53]

Revolutionary Compassion

For a time, Paine's preoccupation with federalism softened his self-pity. He felt less wounded in part because his writing for Congress brought him into frequent contact with the inner circles of American governmental power. He met Washington and Morris every week on average, and he also saw much of Robert Livingston, the tall, slim Secretary of Foreign Affairs, whose aristocratic manners were dulled by creeping deafness at the age of thirty-five. The two got along well, especially because Livingston — who in the not-too-distant future would subsidize Robert Fulton's pathbreaking experiments with steamboats — stoked Paine's long-standing enthusiasm for practical science.

Livingston and Paine considered themselves devout republicans. They loved to argue points of principle and test them out on real-world examples. During the spring of 1782, they were forced to do so on the public controversy surrounding the case of Captain Charles Asgill, a nineteen-year-old British prisoner of war who had just been sentenced to death by Washington in reprisal for an earlier British atrocity. In April 1782, a New Jersey militia officer, Captain Joshua Huddy, who had been captured by the British, was removed from prison, taken by an officer named Lippin-cut to the Jersey shore, where he was taunted, beaten, and left to swing by the neck in the wind. He was later found by the American forces. They cut his corpse loose and buried him with full military honors. Despite American protests, the British refused to hand over Lippincut. Washington replied by ordering the execution of an equal-ranking, randomly selected British prisoner of war.

Paine and Livingston shared Washington's indignation, but the two men interpreted the atrocity differently. The disagreement between the politician and the political writer was telling. Livingston was mainly troubled by the fact that Asgill, who had been taken prisoner at Yorktown and had suffered the misfortune of being selected by lot for execution, was technically protected under the Articles of Capitulation from retaliatory treatment. Livingston expressed concern about the diplomatic damage to the United States that would follow Asgill's execution. Paine instead thought through the matter in terms of political principles. While acknowledging Livingston's concern, he tried to convince Livingston that the revenge death sentence against Asgill ought to be repugnant. Paine objected to Washington's stance on ethical grounds. According to Paine, the Revolutionary principles of civilized freedom and political equality were flatly contradicted by violent acts of revenge against opponents labeled as enemies. Livingston listened, cupping his ear. We do not know whether he found Paine's argument persuasive, but he did go on to convince Paine to write on the subject, and on the last day of May 1782, a short essay titled "To Sir Guy Carleton" appeared.

Still shadowed by memories of Thetford's gaol and gibbets, Paine protested loudly. "It is the nature of compassion to associate with misfortune," he began. He went on to explain the details of the case and then cried murder at both the British officer in charge, Lippincut, and Sir Guy Carleton, who had recently replaced Sir Henry Clinton in New York as commander in chief of the British army in North America and who would soon be reappointed governor of Canada. Paine contrasted "the horridness of revenge" practiced in battle by Native Americans with the British practice of "horridness of diversion," a much worse crime in which death itself was turned into a sport. His sharpest words were reserved for Carleton, whom he demanded should hand over Lippincut for trial: "Within the grave of your own mind lies buried the fate of Asgill. He becomes the corpse of your will, or the survivor of your justice. Deliver up the one, and you save the other; withhold the one, and the other dies by your choice."[54]

The piece had a bloodthirsty tone, but Paine made it clear that he was against sportive murders in war and reprisal murders as well. Both were insensitive to "the value of another's life." Paine was not a pacifist. He recognized that in politics "turning the other cheek" can be a devilishly self-contradictory ethic that enables the strong to outfox or destroy the weak. Yet he was also convinced that an ethic of "an eye for an eye, a tooth for a tooth" was dangerous, especially in politics, where its literal application invariably leads to mutual reprisals and escalating violence, thereby hardening the hearts of the combatants, destroying their civility, and forcing freedom into exile, condemning it to tramp other lands as a poor and hungry refugee. Therefore, the use of violent means to defend liberty was only the lesser of two evils. Paine put the point in a letter to Washington. He explained his opposition to Asgill's execution and recommended that his reprieve be used to increase the moral pressure on the British to deliver up their accused. "I am fully persuaded," he wrote, "that a suspension of his fate, still holding it *in terrorem*, will operate on a greater quantity of their passions and vices, and restrain them more than his execution would do."[55]

The appeal was published widely but with little effect. The public's ears proved deafer than Livingston's. Congress demurred, the British refused to budge, and only after an official protest from the court of France, whose honor was involved in the affair, was Captain Asgill released, the murderer of Joshua Huddy still unpunished. Paine's lack of clout during the whole affair reminded him just how much in recent years his positive influence on American politics had slipped. Although employed at the center of American politics, Paine found himself in the curious position of being at its margins. How damaging that was to his confidence as a political writer was evident during a huge gala thrown by the French minister, la Luzerne, in mid-July 1782.[56] Honoring the birth of the dauphin of France, a thousand prominent state politicians, army officers, and respectable Philadelphians — a cross section of the parvenus produced by the Revolution — were sent printed invitations, Paine included.

The hot and humid evening attracted an inquisitive, sometimes spell-bound crowd of ten thousand citizens, who gathered to eye the guests as they arrived, alone or in clumps of twos, fives, and tens, on foot, on horseback, or in sulkies. No previous social occasion in the "Quaker City" matched the splendor, and, according to reports, many of the invited guests were left breathless or dizzy. All evening, the rotund and shortsighted la Luzerne moved gracefully among his guests. According to some of them, the ladies of Philadelphia adored him as "one of the most amiable, politest, easiest behaved men"; the gentlemen respected him "both as a private and public man"; and gossips, adding to his reputation for mild eccentricity, told how he slept on an iron bed to outwit bed-bugs.[57] La Luzerne was above all a shrewd political animal, a rare French diplomat who had grafted down-to-earth republicanism onto his aristocratic background, enabling him to bridge the political abyss between the French monarchy and the American Congress — thereby driving away the dark clouds of anti-French suspicion produced by his predecessor, Gérard.

All evening la Luzerne charmed his guests, showering them with music, dancing, and a brilliant fireworks display. Just before midnight, they were invited to eat their way through a sumptuous banquet prepared by thirty chefs on loan from the French army. Most guests were charmed into silence. One observer recalled that they "looked and behaved more as if they were *worshiping* than *eating.*" Not so with Paine. He declined to dance with any ladies and, unused to frilly pomp, moved uneasily among the crowd, nagged by the feeling that he no longer belonged in America. He showed no sexual interest in the ladies in his company — sex had been just a word ever since the tragic death of Mary Lambert, his first wife — and he wavered between polite conversation and grumpy boredom. According to Benjamin Rush, he "appeared a solitary character walking among the artificial bowers in the gardens." He also "retired frequently from company to analyze his thoughts and to enjoy the repast of his own original ideas."[58]

Letter to the Abbé Raynal

Paine's anomie worsened through the summer. He dealt with it by retreating to the Library Company of Philadelphia to research and write an extended commentary on some aspects of the history of the American Revolution. Paine had often talked of writing such a history. Future generations of Americans, he used to say, would require an accurate account of their infant years, since their remembrance of things past would serve, whenever necessary, as a powerful weapon against those who sought by stealth or force to violate the country's founding principles.

The commentary had never materialized. The weight and flux of events and the difficulty of analyzing a moving target whose longer-term significance was not yet clear had all conspired against the plan. Now things were different. Paine's current isolation, combined with growing confidence that victory over the British was imminent and that the military phase of the Revolution was nearing an end, drew Paine back to the history project. A pirated English translation of Abbé Raynal's *Révolution d'Amérique,* reprinted by Robert Bell in Philadelphia in the autumn of 1781, proved to be the catalyst. Soon after its appearance in Philadelphia — Paine initially read a copy borrowed from Robert Morris — he decided to summarize his reflections on the American Revolution in the form of a reply to Raynal. He claimed, plausibly, that the reply would provide him with the opportunity "of throwing out a Publication that should reach Europe."[59] But it was also clear that Paine had an ulterior motive. He was convinced that the American revolutionaries should finish off the job by bringing the Revolution home to Europe, initially through political writing, and he thought that by tackling a prominent French writer and compiler of popular history, he just might build his reputation in France sufficiently to open doors in that country, which would be most useful were he to emigrate from America to foment dissent against despotism in the Old World.

Letter to the Abbé Raynal, on the Affairs of North America was among the most eloquent, tightly argued, and insightful of Paine's essays. It was certainly the longest. He had made jottings on the subject ever since returning from France, and he had shown an early draft of the manuscript to Robert Morris. During the summer of 1782, struggling to cure his own depression, he moved into high gear, delivering the one-hundred-page manuscript to the Philadelphia printer Melchior Steiner on August 21, 1782.

The pamphlet disputed many details of Raynal's account and queried his view that the American Revolution, like previous revolutions in history, was a temporary upheaval generated by exaggerated anxieties about piffling taxation increases. Paine objected to Raynal's use of the term *revolution* in its classical sense of a cyclical process, which — like the rotation of the moon around the earth — ends where it starts. Wielding the term in a brand-new way, Paine argued that the American events were revolutionary in that they had irreversibly altered both the structure of government and the popularly shared principles and perceptions according to which

its power was now exercised: "Our style and manner of thinking have undergone a revolution more extraordinary than the political revolution of
the country. We see with other eyes; we hear with other ears; and think
with other thoughts, than those we formerly used. We can look back on
our own prejudices, as if they had been the prejudices of other people."

Paine then tackled head-on Raynal's view that the Franco-American
alliance was unnatural and certain to corrupt one or both partners. Raynal had sympathy for monarchy, but he also believed that the American
colonies had a right to be independent. Paine spotted the confusion. He
acknowledged Raynal's worry that France — a despotic monarchy, in
Paine's terms — remained for many on both sides of the Atlantic a solid
symbol of the Old World, while America, a free republic, was now widely
seen as the dawn breeze of the New World of republican citizenship. Raynal had cause to worry, Paine went on, because the days of European
monarchies, including the benign French and bellicose British variants,
were indeed numbered. Thanks to the American Revolution, the delicate
plant of liberty and equality of citizens had taken root in American soil,
from whence its seeds would be carried by the winds of political change to
Canada, France, England, other parts of Europe, and the rest of the
globe.

Picturing himself as a sower of liberty's seeds, Paine was among the
first modern political thinkers to universalize a single revolution. He set
the compass for later revolutionaries who considered their own revolutions as important for the whole world by portraying the American Revolution as the harbinger of world citizenship and peace on earth. In
conversations with, for example, Benjamin Franklin and Oliver Goldsmith, Paine had often toyed with the idea of the "universal citizen" and
sometimes even described himself as "a citizen of the world." The reply
to Raynal highlighted the theme of universal citizenship for the first time.
The American Revolution, he said with more fervor than foresight, had
set in motion "a new system of extended civilization" marked by representative government and an international civil society "whose mind rises
above the atmosphere of local thoughts, and considers mankind, of whatever nation or profession they may be, as the work of one Creator."

Paine made it clear that the civilizing process still had enemies. Britain
remained an untamed bull in the china shop of peace. Prejudice, the
enemy of human goodwill and liberty, continued, "like a spider," to spin
cobwebs in the dark corners of individuals' minds. But, he asked, were
there not forces, aside from the American Revolution, working against ignorance and war? Commerce, he answered, was among the most power-

ful forces shrinking the world and binding together its nations as never before. The peaceful unifying effects of commerce *within* nations had been noted by others, Paine admitted, but few had yet seen the parallel civilizing effects of commerce *among* nations of the world. Commerce on a global scale — for instance, between countries like France and the United States specializing in the production and export of certain commodities — had made clear that the sea was the world's highway and that war among states was senselessly destructive. World trade also was beginning to multiply citizens' wants. Taste buds and fashions were slowly becoming cosmopolitan. This necessitated their satisfaction through the tighter integration of national economies. International business, "in itself a moral nullity," was having the paradoxical effect of laying the foundation for a new cosmopolitan morality of freedom and equality of citizens in all lands.

Modern science and literature were having similar effects, Paine commented. Literature, his own political writing included, was ensuring that "distant nations became capable of conversation" instead of suffering "the awkwardness of strangers, and the moroseness of suspicion." The highest praise, as might have been expected of the former pupil of Benjamin Martin and James Ferguson and admirer of Benjamin Franklin, was reserved for science. Partisan of no country, science "has liberally opened a temple where all may meet. Her influence on the mind, like the sun on the chilled earth, has long been preparing it for higher civilization and further improvement." In effect, Paine's message was this: Practitioners of science in all countries unite! You have nothing to lose but your seats in the international temple of knowledge. Observe, explain, speculate, experiment, invent! Make the world a better place! Persuade the citizens of all nations to question their prejudices! Urge them to overcome their ignorance and to surrender their animosity to the virtuous forces of enlightenment, mutual respect, and self-government.[60]

The idea that commerce, literature, and science were universally civilizing forces was not original. Paine swam comfortably in the cosmopolitan waters of the Enlightenment, although his account of the shrinking world in terms of civil society and representative government on a global scale was novel. Not surprisingly, the pro-American *Letter to the Abbé Raynal* was greeted respectfully in America. A half-dollar second edition soon appeared in Philadelphia, and a cheaper edition was reprinted by Benjamin Edes and Sons in Boston.[61] Fifty copies were shipped to George Washington "for the use of the army." Robert Morris sent copies of the "excellent Pamphlet" to contacts such as Daniel of St. Thomas Jenifer, Maryland's superintendent of revenue, while Charles Thomson, secretary of Congress, was forwarded thirteen dozen "to be sent as occasion might offer to the several governments."[62] For some reason, Thomson did not accept them. The international reception of the pamphlet was boosted by Paine's distribution of free copies. He admitted at the time to giving away nearly five hundred copies, including fifty copies each to Robert Livingston for distribution in the West Indies and to American ministers in Europe. Paine's hopes were bolstered by news that reprints of the pamphlet were soon to appear in London and Dublin and that it was receiving excellent reviews in France, where two translations were published during 1783. "I have lately travelled much," reported an American touring that country, "and find him everywhere. His letter to the Abbé Raynal has sealed his fame." The traveler concluded, "Even those who are jealous of, and envy him, acknowledge that the point of his pen has been as formidable in politics as the point of the sword in the field."[63] La Luzerne was impressed as well. Shortly after five different French versions had appeared in Paris, he wrote to Paine, warmly congratulating him and enclosing a gift of fifty guineas.[64]

Twelfth Crisis

The friendly French reception prompted Paine to think once more about emigrating to France. Refreshed by several weeks' vacation at the home of Colonel and Mrs. Kirkbride in Bordentown, he returned to Philadelphia, and during the first week of October 1782, he wrote to Robert Livingston with his latest thoughts on leaving America. News had just arrived in Philadelphia that the new Shelburne ministry intended to continue Lord North's policy of prosecuting war against the Americans and refusing their claim to sovereignty. Prime Minister Shelburne's speech in Parliament, which was widely reported in the English and American press, had made this crystal clear: "The sun of Great Britain will set whenever she acknowledges the independence of America. . . . The independence of America would end in the ruin of England."

Such obduracy convinced Paine more than ever that the struggle for American independence had to be brought home to Britain. A few months earlier, he had thundered at the British ministry that America refused either to give up its alliance with the French and Spanish or to lift the threat of invasion they together posed. "Let the world and Britain know," he had snapped, "that we are neither to be bought nor sold; that our mind is great and fixed; our prospect clear; and that we will support our character as firmly as our independence."[65] Passages in *Letter to the Abbé Raynal* were equally militant: "A total reformation is wanted in England. She wants an expanded mind — a heart which embraces the universe. Instead of shutting herself up in an island, and quarrelling with the world, she would derive more lasting happiness, and acquire more real riches, by generously mixing with it, and bravely saying, I am the enemy of none." Now, in an open letter to Shelburne published at the end of October as the twelfth number of *The American Crisis*, Paine took aim at Britons. "The scene of active politics," he wrote, "is in my opinion, transferred from America to Europe." He predicted that France, currently America's key European ally, would be used as a base from which American expectations "must be put into practice" in the Old World."[66]

While writing the piece, Paine received the shocking news that his friend John Laurens had just been killed, "in a trifling skirmish in South Carolina, attempting to prevent the Enemy from plundering the Country of rice," as George Washington reported to Marquis de Lafayette.[67] Paine tore into Shelburne's "jargon of inconsistency" with prose more venomous than usual:

> Alas! are those people who call themselves Englishmen, of so little internal consequence, that when America is gone, or shuts her eyes upon them, their sun is set, they can shine no more, but grope about in obscurity, and contract into insignificant animals? Was America, then, the giant of the empire, and England only her dwarf in waiting! Is the case so strangely altered, that those who once thought we could not live without them, are now brought to declare that they cannot exist without us?

Paine bellowed his conclusion: "But England will be ruined, says Lord Shelburne, if America is independent. Then I say, is England already ruined, for America is already independent."

Paine accused Shelburne of weak-kneed parochialism. He insisted that most Americans now viewed the war as absurdly barbaric: "We can look round and see the remains of burnt and destroyed houses, once the fair fruit of hard industry, and now the striking monuments of British brutality. We walk over the dead whom we loved, in every part of America, and remember by whom they fell. There is scarcely a village but brings to life some melancholy thought, and reminds us of what we have suffered, and of those we have lost by the inhumanity of Britain." Paine also reminded Shelburne that the commoners of Britain were groaning under the despotism of George III:

The British army in America care not how long the war lasts. They enjoy an easy and indolent life. They fatten on the folly of one country and the spoils of another; and, between their plunder and their prey, may go home rich. But the case is very different with the labouring farmer, the working tradesman, and the necessitous poor in England, the sweat of whose brow goes day after day to feed, in prodigality and sloth, the army that is robbing both them and us.[68]

Paine implied that these underclasses might soon actively oppose the war. When that happened, the British state would find itself in the worst of all possible worlds: bankrupt, unpopular at home, and humiliated in global politics.

In some quarters of America, the twelfth number of *The American Crisis* was greeted eagerly. Nathanael Greene gushed over Paine: "Your fame for your writings will be immortal."[69] But Paine was upset to hear that his open letter to Shelburne irritated two old friends, Benjamin Franklin and Henry Laurens, who were at that time trying to negotiate a peace deal with the English government. Laurens castigated the piece as ill timed and said he felt "sorry for some things in it."[70] Franklin was tougher still. Although defending America, he implicitly contradicted Paine's belief that the American Revolution could be extended to Europe. He told a member of the team of English negotiators then in Paris, "This rude way of writing in America will seem very strong on your side. Indeed it is true you have no idea in England of the animosity that has prevailed with us, owing to reiterated cruelties and ill treatment." He instructed the same Englishman to be silent about Paine's diatribe: "I should think now that we are studying peace and conciliation that you had as good not send to England that printed paper addressed to Lord Shelburne."[71]

Rhode Island Lightning Rod

Meanwhile, Paine had been summoned by Robert Morris to the Office of Finance to discuss their next round of political campaigning for federalism. Their decision to intervene in the looming Rhode Island crisis came easily. More than a year had passed since Congress had requested the power to impose a 5 percent duty on all goods imported to America. The measure required unanimous agreement of the states, which remained querulous, despite the campaign waged by Morris and others to convince their legislators that the tax was a vital condition of ensuring the survival of the fledgling American republic.

The opponents of the measure cried tyranny. Using the language of English "Country" politics, they emphasized their hatred of centralized power and fear of corruption, pensioners, and placemen. Wielding agrarian pen names such as "A Farmer," "A Freeholder," and "A Countryman," they argued that the measure was unjust because commercial states with no unsettled land, such as Rhode Island, would be unfairly taxed. They thought of the states' existing powers in zero-sum terms — more in the pockets of Congress automatically meant less in the hands of the states — and they were convinced that the claimed powers were both unnecessary and a ruse for eroding the states' powers. Powerful analogies were drawn between the tyranny of the British and that of Congress, and it was said (quotations from Montesquieu were in vogue) that the new despotism, combining the powers to tax and to spend, would unwisely merge the executive and legislative powers of government.[72]

Such opposition to the congressional tax was boosted by the outright rejection of the proposal by the Rhode Island legislature on November 1, 1782. Unless Rhode Island changed its mind, the initiative would fall stone-dead.[73] Paine entered the fray with gusto. During the third week of November, he wrote Morris a long letter explaining his plans for doing battle with the citizens and representatives of the "perverse sister," as Morris called Rhode Island. Paine described a forthcoming series of three letters, the first of which was already in the hands of the printer. "The second," he continued, "will be on the convenience and equality of the Tax. . . . My third Number will be particularly calculated to enforce the necessity of a stronger union, for at present we hang so loosely together that we are in danger of hanging one another." Paine was adamant that the confederacy was in crisis: "All these embarrassments are ascribable to the loose and almost disjointed Condition of the Union. The states severally not knowing what each other will do are unwilling to do any thing themselves." He proposed to Morris that the current crisis triggered by Rhode Island's obstinacy could only be resolved by means of a two-tiered system of government, in which the powers of the federal level were divided between executive and legislative functions. The executive would exercise "the right of War and peace, all foreign Affairs, the direction of the Army and Navy when we have one." The legislature, comprising "3 to 5 persons from each state," would regulate all matters requiring the coordination of the various states' laws, including "the regulation of the Post office, the regulation of Commerce and consequently of all Taxes to be raised by Commerce to, or from, foreign parts."[74]

Paine told Morris that he would write under a name other than "Common Sense," since that would help deny the Rhode Island states' rights supporters a national audience. The letters were supposed to function as a lightning rod — attracting sparks that might otherwise start fires in other fields of the confederacy. They certainly had their intended effect. Writing as "A Friend to Rhode-Island and the Union," Paine opened the series in a matter-of-fact way by patiently explaining to his readers the purpose and details of the proposed congressional tax. The old exciseman was on home soil. "The common cry has been, Why don't Congress borrow? — Why don't Congress borrow? — But who in the name of heaven will lend if you do not take care to pay, and fix on permanent funds for that purpose, and nicely and faithfully fulfil the obligation." He denied that the measure would give Congress prerogative powers, since it would be rescinded as soon as the war debts were paid off and since, in any case, there was "no such thing in America as power of any kind, independent of the people."[75]

The second letter contained original reflections on the term *sovereignty*. According to Paine, the sovereignty of political power had traditionally been considered to be indivisible. He was right. For early modern theorists of sovereignty, figures such as Jean Bodin and Thomas Hobbes, the people resemble a body crying out for a head. This sovereign head is indivisible and all-powerful. In times of public calamity, it is entitled to eliminate the "Worms within the Entrails" (Hobbes) of the body politic. The sovereign is an earthly god who enjoys the right to muzzle and blindfold its subjects and to speak and act on their behalf. It is constantly on the lookout for the state's enemies at home and abroad, and it must perforce rule both secretively and deceptively. Arcane maneuvers and pompous, noisy displays of power are the two faces of the sovereign head: not only must those who rule the people dissimulate their power — by ensuring that they know and see while keeping their subjects in the dark — they must also ensure that these same subjects live in awe of the magnificence of the state. The sovereign thrives on simulation. It must adorn itself with visible signs of its invincibility — with splendid clothing, glittering crowns and scepters, escorts of soldiers, obelisks, arches, fountains, and palaces in the heart of the leading city.

Paine tore into this originally monarchic tradition of political thinking. He objected to the way in which it overvalued unified power and treated "the people" as mere dross. But he did more than upend the top-down image of power presented by the traditional theory of sovereignty. For the first time in his life, he began to pick apart the republican assumption that "the people," like a heavenly God brought to earth, are the unified source of all political authority. America, said Paine in his second letter, was cutting a path into the political unknown by radically questioning the conventional understanding of citizenship. "Every man in America," he wrote, "stands in a two-fold order of citizenship. He is a citizen of the State he lives in, and of the United States; and without justly and truly supporting his citizenship in the latter, he will inevitably sacrifice the former." Americans needed to think of themselves as subdivided citizens of a subdivided polity. Each citizen could only become a citizen by means of a divided loyalty: "By his rank in the one, he is made secure with his neighbours; by the other, with the world. The one protects his domestic safety and property from internal robbers and injustice; the other his foreign and remote property from piracy and invasion and puts him on a rank with other nations."[76]

Paine refused to see the proposed relationship between the state and federal tiers of power in zero-sum terms. Each level would in fact thrive in the presence of the other. He insisted, again contrary to his Rhode Island critics, that the federation, by dividing and placing clear limits on the jurisdiction of the two tiers of government, would tame the arrogance of those representatives who exercised power. While prepared for Rhode Island consumption, these claims whetted appetites in and around Philadelphia. In early December, Paine was happy to hear that Congress, after furious debate and powerful support from Alexander Hamilton, had appointed a delegation to visit Rhode Island to pressure its leaders into accepting the new tax. On December 6 he dropped in on Robert Morris and "offered . . . if needfull to go thither." He mentioned that he had a number of acquaintances in Providence — the former Rhode Island delegate James Mitchell Varnum was among them — who might prove to be helpful contacts. A day later, he proposed again to Morris that a compromise formula was needed — in politics, "the way to obtain something is to give something"— and that Congress should amend its decision. He urged it to limit its legislation to a two-year program and allow a review of the impost after twelve months. Two days later, Morris, impressed by these arguments, "sent for Mr. Paine and encouraged him to go to Rhode Island respecting the impost."[77]

Offered a small sum of money by Morris to cover his expenses, Paine hired a horse from a New Jersey acquaintance and set off for Providence on December 10, two weeks in advance of the congressional delegation headed by Abner Nash of North Carolina, Samuel Osgood of Massachusetts, and Paine's Pennsylvania friend Thomas Mifflin. Paine was unaware that half a day's ride from Philadelphia, the congressional party turned back after hearing that the state of Virginia had repealed its ratification of the tax. Even if he had known the news, Paine would likely have carried on alone, determined to act as a lightning rod. The manuscript of the third letter to Rhode Island's citizens was tucked in his saddlebags, and soon after he arrived in Providence, Varnum arranged for its publication in the *Providence Gazette*. Paine held to his line that Rhode Islanders' solidarity with other citizens of the Union was reasonable, this time pointing out that America was the only country in the world without a duty on foreign imports. He added that if Congress went ahead without Rhode Island, the citizens of that state would find that their merchants would take advantage of market conditions and inflate the prices of their duty-free commodities to those of other states having to pay import duties. Rhode Island would pay the tax indirectly — into the pockets of the merchant class. The Rhode Island legislature would, in any case, be required to pay a substitute tax to Congress, which would mean that Rhode Island citizens would end up paying *double* the proposed tax. Paine also had a crack at sowers of political dissension who take perverse delight in mismeasuring the importance of things. Just like those who "see the fate of empires in the snuff of a candle," political troublemakers invent public quarrels, dissemble, and misuse their civil liberties. "The United States constitute one extended family, one imperial Commonwealth," he wrote, "the greatest and most equal in its rights and government of any ever known in the world: And while its principles permit the free exercise of debate, its manners ought to restrain every licentious abuse of it."[78]

The rhetoric made his opponents in Providence restive about the cuckoo in their nest. The *Providence Gazette* was bombarded with hostile letters. Paine, whose authorship was now an open secret, was accused of carpetbagging. Gossips on the streets of Providence concluded that his interference as a "mercenary writer" was all the more objectionable because the congressional measure had only one aim: to line the pockets of Congress and destroy the sovereignty of tiny Rhode Island.[79] The campaign against Paine was led by David Howell, a well-known Rhode Island delegate in cahoots with wealthy merchants of Providence. Howell reported that Paine was being "handled without mittens — His cause and character, I think have both rather suffered by his Tour this way."[80] The newspaper brawl and personal tension on the streets of the capital rose to the point where Paine sometimes feared for his safety. On January 23, in a letter to Robert Morris, he confessed that he had "thoughts of returning" and complained that Howell and his supporters were "endeavouring to prevent the publication of any more of my pieces."[81]

Paine hit back with three more letters in as many weeks. His tone was noticeably tougher and more sarcastic. In the fourth letter, he accused the local commercial interests of shirking their taxation duty: "The landed interest and the rental of houses have already their share of direct taxes, but commerce has contributed nothing." Keen to isolate them politically, he insisted that they were damaging the confederation. He also warned of a possible trade embargo on Rhode Island if its delegates refused to ratify the proposal.[82] The fifth letter lashed out more strongly still at the tiny merchant class of Providence. He accused them of resorting to "the yell and the war-whoop, in the place of reason, argument and good order," and of misusing the language of patriotism to cover up their privileged class selfishness. When they spoke of "liberty," Paine snapped, they actually meant the license to be selfish — to avoid taxes and to consume their wealth in private. Their opposition to the tax on commerce was unjust, since "he, who, not relishing the native liquour of his country, can indulge himself in foreign wines, or can afford to wear the fineries of foreign manufacture, is as proper an object of taxation as he who works a cider-press, or keeps a cow, or tills a few acres of land."[83]

In the sixth and final letter, published in the *Providence Gazette* on February 1, 1783, Paine's blast against the "bubble, fraud and avarice" of his opponents read like a swan song. It was clear from what he called the "wild declamation, idle and frothy rhapsody" that the Rhode Island legislature was unwilling to budge.[84] The long silence of Robert Morris — from whom Paine had not received a word for nearly a month — also disheartened him. He surmised, correctly, that Morris too had become discouraged, but he did not yet know the more depressing news that Morris, seeing no way out of the present doldrums, had tendered his resignation as Superintendent of Finance and that, for much the same reason, the Secretary of Foreign Affairs, Robert Livingston, was attempting to do the same. Paine also was unaware that the states of Maryland, North Carolina, and South Carolina had joined Rhode Island and Virginia as opponents of the impost. With the first spring spell of mild South Atlantic winds, his mission a failure, Paine packed his belongings and rode toward Philadelphia. After brief stopovers with Major General Horatio Gates at his camp on the Hudson and the Kirkbrides in Bordentown, he arrived home on March 20, 1783. So ended the first episode in his long and vexed campaign to remold the young American republic into a federal state — a campaign whose success ultimately required the Constitutional Convention of 1787 to put an end to bitter squabbling and half-cocked approaches to strengthening the Union.

8

The Woes of Peace

The Refugee

THE DAY after returning to Philadelphia, Paine had a debriefing dinner with Robert Livingston, Robert Morris, and Gouverneur Morris.
The men discussed "the want of a better cemented union,"[1] but nothing
was born of the meeting. On March 24, 1783, Morris recorded in his diary
that Paine had "called to congratulate on peace."[2] The day before, a
French ship sent by Marquis de Lafayette had brought the news that a
preliminary peace agreement had been signed by the United States,
France, and Great Britain. On April 11, the end of the war was officially
announced, and Philadelphia went wild with public and private celebrations.[3]

When in Rhode Island, Paine had probably planned carefully what he
would say in *The Last Crisis*, which appeared on April 19, the eighth anniversary of the Battle of Lexington. The words bubbled from the pages.
"'The times that tried men's souls,' are over," Paine began, alluding to the
famous first number of *The American Crisis*, "and the greatest and completest revolution the world ever knew, gloriously and happily accomplished." He again underlined the novelty and global potential of the
Revolution: "America . . . has it in her choice to do, and to live as happily
as she pleases. The world is in her hands. She has no foreign power to monopolize her commerce, perplex her legislation, or control her prosperity."
But then came several warnings. Paine likened the Revolution to a storm,

to a "long and raging hurricane" which had left behind a trail of destruction, especially in the manners of society. The Revolutionary War had destroyed civility and hardened the hearts of Americans. "The continual spectacle of woe blunts the finer feelings, and the necessity of bearing with the sight, renders it familiar." The Revolution had produced a certain moral de-skilling. Citizens, he complained, were now less inclined to see the need for individuals freely to make moral judgments and more likely to talk of the "necessity" of things.

Paine did not say how this "de-moralization" could be undone. But in swiping again at states' rights fundamentalists, he implied that the rebirth of public spirit now required Americans to pour their energies into the struggle for a federated union. "It is with confederated states as with individuals in society; something must be yielded up to make the whole secure," he wrote. He ended with an intriguing remark about how the American Revolution had turned him into a political writer.[4] The struggle against the British had clearly catapulted him to fame. For the past seven years, he had devoted his life to the Revolution, with huge success. "Common Sense" had become a household name. Now, in the face of victory and peace, his reputation threatened to slip beneath the horizon of public recognition. Thomas Paine, the writer made famous by the Revolution, was in danger of becoming a nobody. Victory might ruin him — or at least fling him into a pit of confusion about his role as a political writer. As it did.

During the spring of 1783, Paine was consumed with uncertainty about the future. In two recently discovered confidential letters he poured out his woes. "I have the honor of being ranked among the founders of an Empire which does not afford me a home," he told one friend. "I am truly weary of my situation. It is to me like a dungeon without prospects," he confessed to Robert Livingston. "My hopes have nothing to rest on, and I feel myself left in a Condition as dishonourable to the country as it is distressing to me." He admitted that during the war, he had managed to deal with various personal insecurities. Now, with the outbreak of peace, anxiety about his place in the world closed in on him like a hungry wolf. "I look round and see a large and thriving world towards whose freedom and prosperity I have freely and honourably contributed, and yet I see no prospect for myself to live in it," he told Livingston. "The Country that ought to have been to me a home, has scarcely been an Asylum. I sometimes ask myself what am I better off than a refugee, and that of the most extraordinary kind, a refugee from the Country I have befriended."[5]

The specter of unemployment deepened his dolefulness. "Trade I do not understand," the former staymaker complained. "Land I have none, or what is equal to none."[6] Poverty began to clutch and claw at his humble habits, especially after Livingston told him that he would soon resign as Secretary of Foreign Affairs. That meant Paine's own salary would soon be terminated. During the month of May 1783, he was forced to leave his Second Street lodgings and move in with the Kirkbride family in Bordentown. From there he launched yet another campaign for financial support, this time from Congress. Paine knew of the precedents: Thomas Hobbes, the seventeenth-century English exponent of counterrevolution, had received a one-hundred-pound annual pension from Charles II; Dr. Johnson, Paine's contemporary, survived well on a grant from the Crown; Alexander Pope had been offered a handsome pension by a minister of the King. Yet Paine faced two serious obstacles. First, he had trodden on so many toes during the Deane affair that his enemies, though proven wrong, remained cool toward him. The more immediate problem was that Congress had no secure source of revenues and could therefore not supply Paine with funds, even if the delegates were strongly in favor of an emolument, which at this stage they were not. This second obstacle was reinforced by the fact that thousands of American troops remained unpaid and a policy for their decommissioning and pension was still unformulated. On top of that, the public reputation of Congress was slipping. Most states busily flouted at least some of its resolutions, and attendance at its sessions was becoming patchy. It too had begun to suffer a postwar identity crisis.

After consulting Livingston, who went ahead with his resignation on June 4, Paine nevertheless decided to press for a congressional pension. There seemed no other option. He told Livingston that he had forgone royalties on all his works and had lost control of "the profits which the London Booksellers are making out of the publications." A rich philanthropist willing to support but not interfere with his work was nowhere to be found. He also told Livingston that he was too proud to beg from the public, no matter how deeply they dug into their pockets. "A person in Market Street who is only a substantial trademan told me he would freely give fifty pounds, and old Ludwick the Baker [Christopher Ludwig, superintendent of bakers for the Continental army] offered me £25 — but I should not like to have a subscription hawked about the country as if it was for charity."[7]

On June 7, he penned a deftly worded letter to Elias Boudinot, president of Congress, outlining his case for financial support. He acknowledged that priority should be given to the claims of ex-servicemen but emphasized that with the conclusion of the war, they at least had some-thing to fall back on. He had not a farthing. "For besides the general prin-ciple of right, and their own privileges, they had estates and fortunes to defend, and by the event of the war they now have them to enjoy. They are at home in every sense of the word. But with me it is otherwise. I had no other inducement than principle, and have now nothing else to enjoy." In the humblest words he could muster, Paine asked to be made at home. He proposed that Congress accept from him "an account of such services as I have rendered to America and the circumstances under which they were performed." Otherwise, he pleaded, he would probably have to leave America in search of other means of support.[8]

The letter seemed to get a positive reaction, but a whirlpool of events dragged down the appeal. Without discussion, Congress agreed to refer Paine's letter to a subcommittee composed of Hawkins, Clarke, and Pe-ters, with whom Paine was scheduled to meet on June 23. Two days before that meeting, Pennsylvania troops surrounded the State House, where Congress was meeting, to protest the refusal of the state's Executive Council to settle their long-standing pay claim. The siege nearly turned violent. The troops agreed to let both the Executive Council and Con-gress leave the building and pass through their lines, amid shouts of abuse. Irritated by the whole affair, Congress decided immediately to relocate in Prince Town (Princeton), a country village forty miles from Philadelphia. That snubbing of the Executive Council fanned the old coals of contro-versy about federalism. Paine added to the heat by accepting an invita-tion, probably from Robert Morris, to draft a conciliatory petition urging Congress to return to Philadelphia. A draft of the petition went to several people, including Joseph Reed, who heavily amended it, removing the ref-erences to the 5 percent impost. Paine suspected Reed of wanting to wreck the compromise petition for narrowly party-political ends. He stuck to his draft and sent it to Benjamin Rush, asking him to circulate it throughout Philadelphia.[9]

The petition, which cheerfully reassured Congress that it had the sup-port of the citizens of Pennsylvania, was titled "The Address of the Citi-zens of Philadelphia, and of the Liberties Thereof — to His Excellency, the President, and Congress of the United States." Left unsigned by Paine, it was published with the names of its thousand or so signatories in the *Pennsylvania Gazette* on August 6, 1783. It won strong support from nearly all leading figures in Philadelphia, but Congress, feeling under siege, remained grumpy.

Paine had no choice but to wait — for the rest of his life, it turned out.

Several times he sought a hearing before Congress, but it was not until August that the subcommittee headed by Hawkins issued a report recommending indirect financial support for Paine. The report urged his appointment as historiographer to the United States at a salary to be determined later. It stated that "a just and impartial account of our interest for public Freedom and happiness should be handed down to posterity." It urged that the compiler of this official history should be a figure "governed by the most disinterested principle of public good, totally uninfluenced by party of every kind." The report highlighted how Paine had given a great deal to the United States "without having sought, received or stipulated for any honors, advantages, or emoluments for himself." It concluded that "a History of the American revolution compiled by Mr. Paine is certainly to be desired."[10]

The report annoyed and depressed Paine. He had certainly talked in the past of writing a history of the Revolution, but in the present context Congress's offer seemed to him an insult. It smacked of America's "cold conduct" toward its own writers, and it failed to understand that as a political writer, Paine needed material support now, not in the future. The report also misstated the potential size of his claim. Paine estimated his overall costs during the Revolution at around five thousand or six thousand guineas. Congress did not appreciate that Paine wanted compensation for services rendered in the past so that he could get on with new projects — above all, writing on behalf of the American Revolution in Europe, the weak link in the chain of despotism.

Congress's offer also bothered Paine ethically. By offering him a salary rather than a grant of government-owned land, which he wanted, Congress was placing him in the awkward position of publicly accepting taxpayers' money at the very moment he was agitating publicly for increased taxes. That conflict of interest had not arisen, or so Paine thought, when he had been employed by Robert Morris, for whom he had agreed to write only what he wanted to write, uncensored and in secret, on the margins of state power. If he now accepted Congress's offer, he would be plunged into the absurdity of publicly defending Congress on a public salary, and that conflict of interest would be compounded by the fact that he was being asked to write history as a salaried official. In another report to Congress, written during September 1783 and sent to George Washington for comments, he queried the legitimacy of the proposed official history written by a state employee. Memory, he insisted, should never be entrusted to the pens of political power: "For Congress to reserve to themselves the least appearance of influence over an historian, by annexing thereto a yearly salary subject to their own control, will endanger the reputation of both the historian and the history."

Paine politely thanked Congress for its offer, then turned it down. He added pointedly that the proposed yearly salary was insufficient, since it would not even cover the cost of gathering the necessary materials in America and abroad. He concluded with yet another delicately worded request for financial support: "From a disposition to serve others, I neglected myself for years together. If, then, the part I have chosen and acted has been of any benefit to America, it remains unacknowledged." He also repeated his threat to emigrate. The next move of Congress would determine whether "unconfined by dependence" he would "remain in the rank of a citizen of America, or whether I must wish her well and say to her, Adieu."[11]

Rocky Hill

Paine's haggling with Congress was cut short by illness. An epidemic of scarlet fever, or scarlet anginosa as it was then called, had appeared among Philadelphia's children in midsummer and then worked its way slowly into the adult population. During the first week of October, he was struck down with fever, biting sore throat, and wild vomiting that lasted overnight. He felt great thirst, a rash of tiny red spots soon covered his body, and severe back and chest pains left him panting for air. He felt poorly for a week, after which he moved from his lodgings at Colonel Biddle's to the Kirkbrides' farm in Bordentown, where he convalesced for more than a month.[12]

There his spirits were lifted by an offer from Washington to visit him at his Rocky Hill country mansion headquarters near Prince Town. During the first week of November, he took up residence there, delighted. The next three weeks proved to be a happy, pampered interlude. The two men, waited on hand and foot by aides and servants, already knew each other and got along well, chatting about politics and exercising their natural curiosity, even engaging in a curious scientific experiment with natural gas. "We had several times been told," Paine recalled, "that the river or creek that runs near the bottom of Rocky Hill . . . might be set on fire, for that was the term the country people used." Paine and several of Washington's aides offered divergent interpretations of the phenomenon. Paine summarized a long evening's argument: "Their opinion was that, on disturbing the bottom of the river, some bituminous matter arose to the surface, which took fire when the light was put to it." Paine had a different view.

"I, on the contrary, supposed that a quantity of inflammable air was let loose, which ascended through the water and took fire above the surface."

Both sides accepted Washington's proposal that the dispute should be resolved by means of an experiment at dusk on Guy Fawkes Day, appropriately enough. A flat-bottomed scow, poled by soldiers, was launched onto the river, with Washington sitting at one end and Paine at the other, his empiricist's eyes gleaming. "Each of us had a roll of cartridge paper," Paine recalled, "which we lighted and held over the water about two or three inches from the surface when the soldiers began disturbing the bottom of the river with poles." Paine had the satisfaction of being proven right:

> When the mud at the bottom was disturbed by the poles, the air bubbles rose fast, and I saw the fire take from General Washington's light and descend from thence to the surface of the water, in a similar manner as when a lighted candle is held so as to touch the smoke of a candle, just blown out the smoke will take fire and the fire will descend and light up the candle. This was demonstrative evidence that what was called setting the river on fire was setting on fire the inflammable air that arose out of the mud.[13]

There were other light-headed moments at Rocky Hill, as when Paine found himself chuckling at a joke cracked by Washington. On their way to church one unusually mild Sunday morning, Paine asked to drop off his heavy winter coat at the nearby house of a friend. Returning two hours later, Paine learned that the servant who had received the coat had shortly afterward run off with both the coat and his master's best silver plate. The moral, quipped Washington, was that Paine should next time know that "it was necessary to watch as well as pray." Washington then offered one of his own coats to Paine, whose delight showed by his wearing it for several years before passing it on to a friend, instructing him to take good care of a garment that had once been owned by General Washington.[14]

Something of the emerging myth of Washington as the charismatic Hero Protector of America was evident in this episode. There was no doubt that Paine was deeply enamored of Washington. Simply being around the general boosted his spirits, making him feel at the heart of American events. During his stay at Rocky Hill, the news reached Washington that the last British garrisons would shortly evacuate New York now that the final peace treaty had been concluded. On November 25, 1783, Paine traveled on horseback, alongside Washington, to New York, entering the city as the last of the British troops embarked. Later that day, Paine proudly rode with Washington at the head of a joyous parade of

American officers, citizens on horseback, and citizens on foot, eight abreast, through cheering crowds celebrating the triumph of republican principles over the military despotism of the past decade. That evening Paine joined Washington at a grand public dinner of New York citizens and officers, peppered with the booming of thirteen cannon outside the hall and the traditional thirteen toasts, with glasses lifted high.[15]

A few days later, in the Fraunces Tavern on Pearl Street, where he was lodging at Mrs. Hamilton's, Paine witnessed the emotional departure from New York City of Washington for his favorite retreat, Mount Vernon. Another guest recorded,

> We had been assembled but a few minutes when His Excellency entered the room. His emotion, too strong to be concealed, seemed to be reciprocated by every officer present. After partaking of a slight refreshment, in almost breathless silence, the General filled his glass with wine, and turning to his officers, he said: "With a heart full of love and gratitude, I now take leave of you. I most devoutly wish that your latter days may be as prosperous and happy as your former ones have been glorious and honorable."

Following the toast, Washington left the tavern, passing silently through an honor guard down to Whitehall, at the foot of Broadway, where a barge awaited him to ferry him across the Hudson. The same guest, evidently spellbound by his master, continued: "We all followed in mournful silence to the wharf, where a prodigious crowd had assembled to witness the departure of the man who, under God, had been the great agent in establishing the glory and independence of the United States. As soon as he was seated, the barge put off into the river, and when out in the stream, our great and beloved General waved his hat, and bid us a silent adieu."[16]

Small Gifts

Washington's departure stirred up Paine's sense of homelessness. He wrote a mournful letter to James Duane, a prominent jurist and Mayor of New York City, complaining yet again of his treatment: "I candidly tell you I am tired of having no home, especially in a country where, everybody will allow, I have deserved one." He confided to Duane that Congress was unlikely to offer him a penny and that he was now faced with only two remaining options: "to apply to the States individually, the other is, to go to Europe, for as matters are now circumstanced it is impossible I can continue here." He asked Duane to do all within his powers to explore the first option. Describing himself as "a friend who has not yet been to

America the expense of a private soldier," Paine said he would be satisfied with a small allotment of the property that the New York government was currently expropriating from royalists and Tories.[17]

It would be four months before Paine received a reply, during which time Paine, grumpy and restless, resumed his campaign for American federalism. On December 9, the eighth anniversary of the Battle of Lexington, where the first blood of the Revolution had been shed, Paine completed an article for the *Pennsylvania Gazette*, signing it "Common Sense," his wartime pen name. It was a quick-moving, sharp-edged reply to a speech in the Westminster Parliament and a pamphlet (*Observations on the Commerce of the American States with Europe and the West Indies* [Philadelphia, 1783]) by John Holroyd, Earl of Sheffield, who, according to Paine, had two key aims: "to allure Americans to purchase British manufactures; and ... to spirit up the British Parliament to prohibit citizens of the United States from trading to the West India islands." The second aim had already been realized, Paine pointed out, with the slapping of a British embargo on all American goods traveling to the West Indies in other than British-registered ships. Such discrimination at the hands of British commerce and government, Paine predicted, would continue as long as the American states continued to bicker among themselves. Flinging the words of Lord Sheffield back into the faces of American opponents of federalism — "It will be a long time before the American states can be brought to act as a nation, neither are they to be feared as such by us" — Paine slammed the Rhode Island political class for its "injudicious, uncandid and indecent opposition" to the import duty proposal of the previous winter. He implied, as Alexis de Tocqueville later said openly, that republican democracies have very confused, sometimes erroneous ideas about foreign policy, generally tackling external problems only for internal reasons. Paine repeated his call for "a well-centred power in the United States" as the remedy for the present "medley of individual nothings, subject to the sport of foreign nations." The federal principle was clear: "it is only by acting in union, that the usurpations of foreign nations on the freedom of trade can be counteracted, and security extended to the commerce of America."[18]

After leaving New York City for Bordentown shortly after Christmas, Paine kept up his campaign against the supporters of confederalism, whom he now labeled "the hot-headed Whigs." He accused them of geopolitical ignorance, of being unrealistic, of not facing up to the realities of power, and of expecting "more than can or ought to be done and which if attempted will probably undo the government and place it in other hands."[19] Such invective was the only highlight of a long, cold winter spent cooped up on his newly acquired property in Bordentown hamlet. We are ignorant about his purchase of a horse, named Button, and a small house and tiny patch of meadow, but he probably acquired them during his visit with Washington at Rocky Hill, using an honorarium of twenty-four hundred livres received from Chevalier de la Luzerne for his past year's publications in support of Franco-American relations.[20]

The Bordentown purchase seemed sensible at the time. His application to Congress was stalled, and he had no long-term prospects of a secure income. Besides, he already knew the area well, having stayed there at least a dozen times with the Kirkbride family. The novelty of the investment and any thoughts he had of settling there permanently were killed off by the harsh winter. In a letter written in mid-February, he complained of having been "shut up here by the frost" for three weeks. His whining remarks about "want of amusement" revealed just how much he had outgrown his native Thetford in favor of the hurly-burly of urban life and politics.[21] Although Paine revelled in the beauty of nature, he always wilted when living in isolation. He thrived on civilized company willing to talk politics. He read books, but he was not a bookish man, preferring instead to read newspapers, magazines, and pamphlets, especially when he had company to discuss their contents. He had little talent for repairing and running a farm, was a bad cook, and hated cleaning. He certainly had little feel for country life.

He survived the winter by spending a great deal of time with his neighbors the Kirkbrides. Except for a daily afternoon walk through the snow to and from the local tavern run by Deborah Applegate, he passed the remaining time napping, complaining about not being able to write because of "a fit of gout," or writing letters, most of them filled with hopes of moving permanently to the state of New York. He lambasted Philadelphia as "a place neither of science nor society" and again bemoaned the rotten treatment of writers in modern America, certainly compared to ancient times. "The countries the most famous and the most respected of antiquity," wrote Paine, "are those which distinguished themselves by promoting and patronizing science, and on the contrary those which neglected or discouraged it are universally denominated rude and barbarous." By modern standards, he continued, America was rude:

> The patronage which Britain has shown to Arts, Science and Literature has given her a better established and lasting rank in the world than she ever acquired by her arms. And Russia is a modern instance of the effect which

the encouragement of those things produces both as to the internal improvement of a country and the character it raises abroad. The reign of
Louis the fourteenth is more distinguished by being the Era of science and
literature in France than by any other circumstance of those days.[22]

What irony! Considering Paine's disquisitions against despotism, the
glowing reference to the monarchic states of Britain, Russia, and France
openly contradicted his contempt for their corrupting powers of patronage — what he had elsewhere called their "countenance to flatterers and
partizans."[23] Momentarily, it seemed not to matter to him that power
could misshape knowledge for its own selfish ends — or that despotic
power had a history of pressing the practitioners of literature, the arts,
and science into its service, for the purpose of embellishing the state and
rooting out civil society. The contradiction was symptomatic of Paine's
current frustration and consequent willingness to try out any argument on
the American authorities in support of his claim for remuneration.

What he did not know when snowbound and miserable in Bordentown
was that his friends James Duane and Lewis Morris had steered legislation
through the New York Senate that awarded Paine sequestered property in
that state. The news reached him in early April. Wasting no time, he rode
Button, cantering on spring air, to inspect the choice of two sites offered
him unanimously by the Senate. He decided, after taking advice from
New York friends, on a three-hundred-acre site and farmhouse in New
Rochelle, a seaside township thirty miles northeast of New York City. The
farm site had formerly been owned and occupied by Frederick DaVoe, a
prosperous French-speaking Huguenot descendant who had been caught
red-handed escorting British infantry through the area. DaVoe and his
family had fled to Canada days before the conclusion of the Revolutionary War, and soon afterward their properties in the area had been confiscated.[24]

The land was officially handed over to Paine in a quiet local ceremony
on June 16, 1784. The New York legislature's ode to Paine was read aloud:
"His literary works ... inspired the citizens of this state with unanimity,
confirmed their confidence in the rectitude of their cause, and have ultimately contributed to the freedom, sovereignty and independence of the
United States."[25] Paine was pleased with the gift but not satisfied. He had
no desire to settle into a farmer's life. He was not even prepared to live in
a sleepy hollow like New Rochelle. Scattered over ten square miles and at
least a full day's teeth-jarring journey by horse or oxcart from New York
City, New Rochelle was in fact a district without a village. It contained

only a scattering of farms and houses, several taverns and churches, and a
population of perhaps three hundred people, mostly Anglican royalists of
Huguenot descent.

Paine also was unsatisfied with New Rochelle because he was now in
serious need of a cash income. Admittedly, that could have come from
renting or selling the farm. Paine told Washington that he thought the
property was "worth at least a thousand guineas,"[26] but any attempt at this
stage to sell it off would have laid him open to public charges of mercenary behavior. Paine was both too principled and too much a political animal to risk that happening. He responded by arranging for his friend
Lewis Morris to manage the property and by carrying forward his personal campaign for a grant, stipend, or pension from the political authorities. He calculated, wisely, that his best chance of success was with the
state legislatures. This strategy of concentrating on the states had the advantage of keeping him financially independent of Congress, thus mini-
mizing rumors that he campaigned for federalism only because he was in
the pay of fledgling federal authorities. "Should the method succeed, I
shall stand perfectly clear of Congress," he told Washington. "Whatever I
may then say on the necessity of strengthening the union, and enlarging
its powers, will come from me with a much better grace."[27]

For a time, the method of pressuring other state legislatures along the
lines of the New York precedent looked promising. Before his posting to
Paris to replace Franklin as the American minister, Thomas Jefferson
spoke vigorously on Paine's behalf in Virginia. Washington took the
trouble of corresponding about the matter with James Madison, Richard
Henry Lee, Governor Patrick Henry, and others in the state. To Madison,
Washington wrote, "Can nothing be done in our Assembly for poor
Paine? Must the merits, and Services of *Common Sense* continue to glide
down the stream of time, unrewarded by this Country?" He continued,
"His writings certainly have had a powerful effect upon the public mind;
ought they not then to meet an adequate return? He is poor! He is cha-
greened! and almost, if not altogether, in despair of relief."[28]

Two weeks later, Madison introduced legislation in the Virginia Assembly to provide Paine with a parcel of land that would have been worth
"about £4,000, or upward" on the market. The bill was defeated on the
third reading after a strong speech by Arthur Lee. Lee had not forgotten
Paine's attack on Virginia in *Public Good* and, as Madison told Jefferson,
"put a negative on every form which could be given to the proposed remuneration."[29] Washington retaliated by getting in touch with the president of Pennsylvania's Executive Council, John Dickinson, who sent a

note to the Pennsylvania Assembly reminding it of Washington's concern and urging it to make "a suitable acknowledgement" of Paine's "eminent services and a proper provision towards a continuance of them in an independent manner." After four months of slow marching, the Pennsylvania Assembly agreed on April 9, 1785, to award Paine a "temporary recompense" of five hundred pounds, preferring to keep the stipend low until Congress had reached a decision.[30]

Washington was clearly Paine's key ally. He kept up the pressure on Congress, which shortly after the Pennsylvania decision agreed to set up a new committee, headed by Elbridge Gerry, to examine Paine's case. Through the summer of 1785, the committee moved at a snail's pace. It eventually resolved on August 26 that "Mr. Paine is entitled to a liberal gratification from the United States."[31] The amorphous ruling stoked Paine's indignation, prompting him to jump the gun. Emptied of patience and fed up with trumpery, he wrote to Congress announcing his "intention after an absence of now almost eleven years to return to Europe as soon as I have regulated my private affairs which will be in about two months."[32]

A month and a half later, having heard not a word, he told Congress that after eleven years of service to America, he was owed at least six thousand dollars in "private expenses."[33] He reminded Congress of the rules covering compensation, claimed a thousand dollars owing to him from his time as Secretary to the Committee for Foreign Affairs, and displayed his wounds to the congressional committee in desperate, almost pathetic terms: "I must declare to the Committee that it hurts me exceedingly to find, that after a service of so many years, and through such a perilous scene, I am now treated and higgled with as if I had no feelings to suffer or honour to preserve."[34]

Gerry, who was on good terms with Paine, begged his patience and warned him to stop bleating.[35] But on September 28, Gerry's motion in favor of a payment of six thousand dollars was defeated on the floor of Congress by a two-thirds majority; only Pennsylvania, Georgia, Virginia, and Maryland supported him. Gerry managed to secure a compromise agreement that a new committee should be formed to consider a reduced payment to Paine. A week later, on October 3, a majority of delegates voted to give Paine three thousand dollars. The decision effectively ended Paine's campaign for material support among the states, whose delegates took the view that they did not now need to supplement the gift already bestowed on him by Congress.

The congressional grant was a small triumph. By American standards, it was a gift of unprecedented generosity. Paine had not only set a standard for honoring literary figures by subsequent American governments. He also had been awarded comparatively more than almost any other writer would ever receive from a federal or state government. Measured against Paine's humble needs, the combined gifts also were impressive. The New Rochelle farm, which he soon rented to a tenant farmer, and the cash grants from Congress and the Pennsylvania Assembly were more than adequate to pay off his debts. They also offered him a comfortable standard of living as a separated man without children in a country with serious debts and thousands of unpaid soldiers grumbling about postwar conditions.

Bank of North America

Paine did not see things that way. The delayed gifts were for him less than gifts. His ungratefulness was fueled by the fact that his heart was no longer in America and that the whole pension affair had gradually pushed him into spiritual exile. In early September 1785, signs of homesickness even appeared with the delivery of a letter from his aging mother and father in Thetford. "I had, a few days ago, the great pleasure and happiness of a letter from you, the first and only one I have received since the beginning of the war in 1775 to the present time," he replied, gushing. "Never hearing from you or of you, or of any of my relations, I had determined coming to England the ensuing winter, and I yet hope to have the happiness of seeing you once more after so long a separation."[36]

Before departing from America, Paine buried himself for the last time in efforts to federalize the American polity. For a pro-federalist society of ex–army officers, called the Cincinnati, Paine wrote a patriotic song. The society, named after the Roman warrior/farmer Cincinnatus, had been formed during the summer of 1783, shortly before the Continental army had been disbanded. Its activities soon aroused suspicion among some republican advocates of states' rights, who thought that it was working to restore aristocracy in America. Paine saw things quite differently, as he revealed in the song praising the Cincinnati.[37] He shared its members' perception of the society as a national fund-raising body aiming to support the widows and children of those killed during the Revolutionary War. He also saw its activities as prototypical of the sort of social initiatives now required to build a federated civil society marked by freedom of association, social justice, and solidarity among citizens of the various states.

The same defense of the spirit of "federalism from below" was evident in Paine's support for the Bank of North America during a vicious public controversy about its future. The controversy erupted during the autumn of 1785. The bank had been founded by Robert Morris four years earlier, in 1781, when both the state of Pennsylvania and the Continental Congress had granted it a charter.[38] At the time, Paine had been in France, but the hard cash John Laurens and he had secured there had provided the bulk of the bank's seed capital, evidently with Paine's approval. Under the influence of Morris, he believed that the bank was a vital condition of a federal economy and civil society that ran "underneath" and beyond the boundaries of the existing states. Morris had explained its founding purposes in similar terms. Its aims, he wrote, were to "facilitate the management of the finances of the United States," to "afford to the individual[s] of all the states a medium for their intercourse with each other," and "to increase both the internal and external commerce of North America."[39]

Within two years of its founding, these aims were severely tested. Peace plunged America into a severe economic crisis. In Paine's home state, money became scarce, land values plummeted, and protests erupted among social groups feeling the pinch. Farmers and artisans in particular campaigned publicly for a dramatic increase in the supply of paper money. The directors and stockholders of the Bank of North America jibbed at such proposals. Public feeling against it rose sharply, and the deadlock was broken only when the Pennsylvania Assembly — again in the hands of a Radical majority — authorized the issuance of £150,000 worth of paper bills and paper credit. The bank refused to accept the paper money, and the Radicals introduced legislation to destroy the bank by repealing its charter. A committee of inquiry condemned the bank for trading in favor of both its foreign shareholders and its domestic stockholders, and on April 4, 1785, the Pennsylvania bill passed a second reading in the House. Five months later, on September 13, the charter was repealed, leaving the Bank of North America to hobble along under its congressional charter, its European investors complaining of American bad faith and large American depositors withdrawing their investments in huge sums.

Sensing that the collapse of the bank was imminent, Paine leaped to its defense in a letter to Thomas Fitzsimmons, a like-minded Irish-born officer in the Revolution and delegate to Congress. The letter was written a few days after the bill to dissolve the bank's charter had been introduced, and it was eventually printed in the *Pennsylvania Gazette* just before Christmas, 1785. Paine explained the eight-month delay in publication by saying that he had been pushed into the bank controversy because several pieces on the subject had been falsely attributed to him and, above all, because he found the attack on the bank by the Pennsylvania Assembly "an ill-digested, precipitate, impolitic, faithless piece of business, in which party and prejudice is put for patriotism."[40]

Paine had no qualms about biting the hand that had just fed him a five-hundred-pound stipend. During the next two years, he published no less than nine substantial letters on the subject of the bank in the *Pennsylvania Packet* and the *Pennsylvania Gazette*, as well as a major pamphlet, *Dissertations on Government; the Affairs of the Bank; and Paper Money*. Each one of these ventures into the field of political economy sided with the view that paper money was not real money. Money, said Paine, had "something in it sacred that is not to be sported with, or trusted to the airy bubble of paper currency." The sacredness of money consisted of the fact that it was a material expression of human labor power. It was best considered "as the fruit of many years' industry, as the reward of labour, sweat and toil." Inasmuch as money was also exchangeable for labor, it could provide — given its fair distribution among citizens — access to goods and services for those social groups excluded from employment by age, bereavement, or illness. Money serves as "the widow's dowry and children's portion, and as the means of procuring the necessaries and alleviating the afflictions of life, and making old age a scene of rest."

This view of money implied that paper money was a contradiction in terms. He minced no words: "I remember a German farmer expressing as much in a few words as the whole subject requires; *'money is money, and paper is paper.'*" Paper money he denounced as "both the bubble and the iniquity of the day," and he trashed talk of the powers of paper money, as in the claim that currency was a measure of a country's wealth or the belief that paper money was a key ingredient in the military victory against the British. Paper money was simply nothing in itself. It was best described as mere "bills of credit" — that is, as *anticipated* real wealth that had not yet been produced. For that reason, Paine likened the issuance of paper money to the foolish action of property owners who mortgaged their estates and left their heirs to pay off the mortgage. In effect, the arbitrary printing of paper money encouraged both the current owners of money and civil society at large to think that they were wealthier than they actually were. To the extent that it so fooled them, it diminished the prestige of actual hard currency.

Paine's objection to paper money had directly political implications. Any government's whimsical or calculated issuance of paper money, he claimed, was an unwarranted interference with the natural process of

producing and circulating wealth by means of hard currency. Governments' power of printing money had as much despotic potential as their
power of taxing their subjects without consent. "The assumed authority
of any assembly in making paper money, or paper of any kind, a legal tender, or in other language, a compulsive payment . . . is a most presumptuous attempt at arbitrary power." The point was sometimes repeated in
tougher language, as when Paine roared that "all tender laws are tyranni-
cal and unjust, and calculated to support fraud and oppression." This line
of reasoning implied that the power to issue and control the supply of real
money must be independent of the government and that it should properly be exercised by the legally guaranteed banking institutions of civil
society. The current attack on the Bank of North America, Paine concluded, was utterly misconceived, and he was sure that it would devalue
confidence in the currency in circulation. Paine likened the opponents of
the bank to blurry-eyed hunters who "aimed at the pidgeon and shot the
crow — they fired at the bank and hit their own paper."[41]

The complaint that banks are institutions of vested interest and private
aggrandizement is commonplace today. Paine — to our astonishment
and to the surprise of many of his contemporaries — proposed the opposite view. He certainly feared the accumulation of private monopolies of
wealth and power within civil society. For that reason, paradoxically, he
was convinced that private banks were a vital check on "governing too
much" and a necessary condition of free and equal citizenship in a self-
directing civil society. He considered that the repeal of the Bank of North
America's charter would play into the hands of mean-spirited entrepreneurs — he singled out the example of George Emlen, a rich Philadelphia moneylender — who profited from paper currency. Self-serving
individuals and groups such as "unscrupulous traders who buy up great
holdings on credit, agitate for increased issues of paper money, and pay
their debts with depreciated currency which they get at little price"[42]
would run amok. The profiteers would wreck the public spirit and shared
freedoms so essential to the republic. The point for Paine was that by preventing the circulation of paper currency gained cheaply, the Bank of
North America would reduce and control the (potential) market power of
such speculators and profiteers. More positively — here Paine borrowed
from Adam Smith's *An Inquiry into the Nature and Causes of the Wealth of Nations* (1776) — the bank could increase the rate of circulation of genuine
money. It would attract domestic and foreign investors with otherwise
idle capital and extend loans to a wider variety of investors throughout
the Union. It would thereby stimulate the growth of national wealth, as

well as "socialize" investment in two senses. More capital would be made available to more manufacturers, farmers, and merchants. The bank also would fund improvements in "navigation, building bridges, opening roads . . . and other matters of public benefit."[43] The resulting growth of national wealth would thereby tend to be distributed more equally among citizens of all states within the federation. The bank, in short, would function as a catalyst for the development, from below, of a dynamic and federal civil society of producing and exchanging, but public-spirited, citizens.

Paine gave the example, familiar to his contemporaries, of farmers coming to city markets to sell their produce, only to find themselves confronted by selfish monopsonists (powerful circles or cartels of merchants able to flex their market muscles by purchasing the farmers' produce at discounted prices with either real or paper currency). With the help of the Bank of North America, Paine argued, farmers would in future guard themselves against such market injustice by taking advantage of the more openly competitive markets that would result from spreading investment more equally among a greater number of merchants. Those farmers wanting to become merchants could also be given access to the required capital on terms agreed on by the bank. The example was carefully designed to attract support from farmers in western Pennsylvania, the stronghold of Radical opposition to the bank, which they viewed as a tool of eastern corporate enterprise. Not many Radicals agreed with Paine, and within their circles his defense of the bank earned him hearty abuse. He especially ruffled their feathers by publicly attacking the Pennsylvania Assembly after its Radical majority rescinded the bank's charter on September 13, 1785, by a margin of fifty votes to twelve.

Paine spent the autumn pondering the situation. He carefully read a pro-bank pamphlet arguing that Congress, under the Articles of Confederation, had a constitutional right to charter a bank. The pamphlet had been commissioned by the bank itself and written by James Wilson, the most brilliant legal scholar in Pennsylvania.[44] Paine made notes and discussed the issue numerous times with Robert Morris, Gouverneur Morris, and Benjamin Franklin, who had just returned from France. The issue was potentially embarrassing for Paine, since he had been a strong supporter of the Radicals and still had many friends in their ranks. Yet he also took personal pride in the bank, and he claimed often in private discussions that his mission to France counted him among the prime movers in its foundation. In addition, he was firmly convinced of the political economy arguments in favor of the bank, and he was disturbed by the high-handedness of the Radicals — their willingness to use state power to tear up the bank's charter even though it had not violated its terms. Assembling favorite arguments that he had tried out privately, Paine decided to snub his orthodox Radical friends and convince the Assembly to change its mind. When the Assembly went into Christmas recess, he managed to draft *Dissertations on Government; the Affairs of the Bank; and Paper Money.* The manuscript was sent to the printer on February 18, 1786, and bound copies were available six days later, in time to greet the returning members of the Assembly.

The great debate on the Bank of North America resumed on March 27. Paine, by now a master of the art of political timing, published a short letter in the *Pennsylvania Packet* to coincide with the resumption. "Nothing is more certain," he wrote, "than that if the bank was destroyed, the market for country produce would be monopolized by a few monied men, who would command the price as they pleased."[45] Paine sat quietly in the public gallery for the duration of the four-day debate, taking notes. Tempers ran high, as Paine's friends George Clymer, Robert Morris, and Thomas Fitzsimmons did battle on the floor of the Assembly with John Smilie, William Findley, and Robert Whitehill, the key Radical opponents of the bank. Paine jotted down in his notebook that nothing "that has been agitated before the legislature of Pennsylvania ever drew together such crowded audiences."[46] On numerous occasions, he had to bite his tongue as the agitation turned in his direction. His rowdiest critic on the floor of the Assembly was Smilie, the most vocal delegate opposed to the bank. Smilie sneered several times at Paine in the gallery, denouncing him as "an author who . . . is unprincipled, hires out his pen for pay, and who, in walking the market place, without money in his pocket, finds a five shilling bill, steps into a tavern, procures with it a dinner, &c and then exclaims, this paper money, after all, if it be not money, is to me victuals and drink."[47]

The invective was unfounded. No evidence has been found that Paine was paid by the bank, and at the time Robert Morris even went out of his way to refute such suggestions.[48] The attacks nevertheless forced Paine to explain publicly the cash settlements and working arrangements he had secured with Congress in recent years. He claimed that he had no personal or private interest whatsoever in the bank, admitting only that "from the first establishment of the bank, to the present hour, I have been its friend and advocate."[49] He struck back at Smilie, the spokesman for the backcountry farmers of Pennsylvania, as one "who loves to talk about what he does not understand,"[50] and he reiterated that he had not used the bank to make profit. "I have kept cash at the bank," he said, "and the bank is at this time in account to me between eight and nine hundred pounds, for money which I brought from New York, and deposited there ever since last September, and for which I do not receive a single farthing interest. This money the country has had the use of, and I think it safer under the care of the bank, until I have occasion to call for it, than in my own custody."[51]

The high-handedness of Smilie and his Radical friends also came in for criticism. For the first time in his political career, Paine publicly attacked what might be called republican fundamentalism. He pointed out that in contrast to despotisms, in which sovereign power resides in one or a few hands, republics are distinguished by the fact that "sovereign power, or the power over which there is no control, and which controls all others, remains where nature placed it — in the people." This principle of popular sovereignty, Paine continued, quoting the Pennsylvania Bill of Rights, implied that no fraction of the people or their elected representatives could legitimately rule over the remainder without their permission. And yet — here Paine conceded a point first made against him by John Adams after the publication of *Common Sense* — the same principle of popular sovereignty paradoxically made manipulation of "the people" *by* "the people" probable. Two generations before Alexis de Tocqueville's famous discourse on the same subject, Paine pointed to the practical danger of a tyranny of the majority inherent in the principle of popular sovereignty. In the name of the people, elected representatives could exercise what Paine called "the despotism of numbers." Lusting for power, the ultimate aphrodisiac, representatives of majorities acting in the name of the people could oppress minorities. The poor could tyrannize the rich; the propertyless could assault the propertied; or one party of citizens could rule arbitrarily over all others, just as the Radicals were now attempting to do on the question of the bank.

Paine considered popular despotism to be both more dangerous and potentially more effective than its old-fashioned counterpart, precisely because of its lip service to the people. Power seemingly exercised by and for the people would be less controvertible and more licentious. The problem was how to prevent republican governments from building a throne from which they ruled despotically, all the while honoring the people. An active, independent press could help, but other antidotes were needed. Paine recognized that periodic elections were by themselves insufficient — the damage could well be done between elections — and he also ruled out violent insurrection as a dangerous, self-contradictory alternative. He proposed instead that the power of governments in republics be subjected constantly to judicial scrutiny. "When party operates to produce party laws," he wrote, "a single house is a single person and subject to the haste, rashness and passion of individual sovereignty." There was a clear need for what he called "a court of justice and trial by jury," which would have the task of checking a legislative body, ensuring that it governed within the limits of the constitution. Governments could then be taken to court and instructed to alter their ways. If they refused, they would be removed, and new elections would be held on the understanding that the incoming government could not violate the court's ruling. Paine strongly criticized the view, which he considered "truly of the despotic kind," that "every succeeding assembly has an equal power over every transaction, as well as law, done by a former assembly." Legislation should be limited in duration, he said, and he suggested a limit of thirty years, "the mean time" of one generation. "As we are not to live forever ourselves, and other generations are to follow us," he argued, "we have neither the power nor the right to govern them, or to say how they shall govern themselves." Yet within the space of a generation, no government was licensed to rip up an existing contract with specific individuals or groups. Contracts between government and civil society would be meaningless unless they were mutually acknowledged. Conversely, their annulment could be carried out only by mutual consent of the contracting parties or (in the case of businesses) by bankruptcy.[52]

This line of thinking was new to Paine's writings. It provided a clear answer to the specific question of whether a charter granted by a legislature to a corporate body such as the Bank of North America could be revoked by a succeeding legislature if the terms of the charter had not been violated. Paine's enemies were hardly satisfied. Taking satisfaction in the Assembly's decision, by a majority of thirty-nine votes to thirty, to confirm its deregistration of the bank, they dumped abuse on him. John Smilie, writing as "Atticus" in the *Pennsylvania Packet*, published a series of four letters attacking Paine as a figure of "little talent" whose prose, dotted with "numerous absurdities and glaring contradictions," displayed the "smell of the cask" and "the cause of the faction." Paine was a political writer "who, having reaped a recompense more adequate to his deserts, prostitutes his pen to the ruin of his country."[53] David Claypoole, editor of the *Pennsylvania Packet*, Paine's preferred newspaper for a decade, refused to publish his articles on the subject. Paine responded by reminding him that privately owned newspapers are "a public matter." Paine then lectured him on the distinction between editorial power and liberty of the press:

"If the freedom of the press is to be determined by the judgement of the printer of a Newspaper in preference to that of the people, who when they read will judge for themselves, the[n] freedom is on a very sandy foundation."[54]

The dining tables and merchants' offices of Philadelphia buzzed with gossip that Paine had sold out the republican spirit. Some said that he had become a Janus-faced pseudoradical. Others accused him of becoming a janissary of the rich. Peter Markoe, a Philadelphia writer, turned the gossip into a scathing poem:

> Janus *is our own, who props a bank, altho' he scorn'd a throne;*
> *And, should his breast with just resentment burn,*
> *Would scorn a bank and prop a throne in turn;*
> *But should both bank and throne reject the job;*
> *Would damn them both and idolize the mob.*[55]

During the summer and autumn of 1786, the Bank of North America controversy daily tapped Paine on the shoulder, scowling at him wherever he set foot in public, just as had happened during the fracas with Silas Deane. His friends again feared for his safety, as John Hall, a young mechanic recently arrived in America from England, recorded in his diary: "Mr. Paine not returned. We sent to all the places we could suppose him to be at and no tidings of him. We became very unhappy fearing his political enemies should have shown him foul play. Went to bed at 10 and about 2 a knocking at the door proves Mr. Paine."[56]

The controversy caused quarrels with his oldest and dearest friends. Toward the end of November, during an afternoon visit to the home of Captain Coltman, with whom he had sailed on the *London Packet* from England to America, a bitter argument about the bank erupted. There had been recent elections in Pennsylvania, and the incoming Conservatives, snatching victory by the narrowest of margins, were preparing a new charter for the bank. Paine was pleased, but he told Coltman, as he had just told Congressman Thomas Fitzsimmons in a letter, that he had warned the Conservatives "not to touch any part of the plan of finance this year."[57] Coltman replied, in a conversation "in which words were very high," that Paine's various articles on the bank had damaged the cause of liberty in America. Paine, red in the face at an instant, "swore by G-d, let who would, it was a lie." The two friends then fell uncontrollably into a bitter personal quarrel for "a considerable time." Paine stormed off, refusing to stay for dinner. The angry, twitching Coltman continued to be exercised by "politics and the bank, and what he thought the misconduct of Mr. Paine in his being out and in with the several parties." A mutual friend, who had also been invited for dinner, then proceeded to argue in support of the departed guest, whereupon Coltman "grew warm, and said he knew now he could not eat his dinner."[58]

Paine loved nothing better than a good political fight, but such scrimmages with friends like Coltman sickened him inside. In his heart, he had always disliked personal conflict. He was a commoner with a Norfolk accent, but he still valued the aristocratic civility for which the English were and are renowned, and he therefore considered private strife embarrassing, and certainly unbefitting of life within a republic. During March 1787, Paine had the satisfaction of witnessing the rechartering of the Bank of North America, its capital fixed at $2 million and its length of charter restricted to fourteen years.[59] He also attended meetings of the newly founded Society for Political Inquiries convened by Benjamin Franklin in Philadelphia. The discussion circle, whose charter read like a declaration of independence against the intellectual imperialism of Europe, had around thirty-five members, who met weekly in Franklin's library. Paine reacted glumly to the company. Although producing a discussion paper on the subject of the incorporation of towns, he reportedly "never opened his mouth."[60] Evidently, the fights with Coltman, Smilie, and others had snapped something inside him. He concluded that he had had enough of America. For the second time, he had been pecked and clawed by his enemies, and he could now see no end to it. His sense of having been misunderstood and victimized hardened, capping his desire to return to the Old World. Only his detailed travel plans now needed to be fixed.

PART III

France and England, 1787−1802

9

Rights of Man

Building Rainbows

TOM PAINE'S fascination with bridges soon decided his plans to return to Europe. During a bout of restlessness toward the end of 1785, he dreamed of designing and erecting a single-span, three-hundred-foot wooden bridge across the Harlem River in New York. Wooden bridge building was coming into vogue at the time. Until the Treaty of Paris, signed by Great Britain and America on September 3, 1783, the largest American trees had been reserved for British warship builders. Felling for home use was strictly regulated. With the removal of this constraint and the simultaneous collapse of the American export market in wooden ships, proposals, often by shipwrights, for large wooden bridges suddenly proliferated, leading within a generation to America's world mastery of wooden bridge design and construction.

Paine was intrigued by the trend, but his interest in bridges was driven by motives deeper than fashion. He was initially struck by their double meaning. Bridges were for him combinations of architectural beauty and practicality; works of genius that could also be breathtaking in their simplicity; an essential human means of moving through nature, though foreign to nature; and a human device for mastering nature without disturbing its power or destroying its beauty. Paine saw architecture as the rising spirit of an epoch translated into space. He was especially fascinated by the modernism of bridges. Bridges overcome insularity by widening the horizons of public mobility and expectation. Like rainbows, bridges link the familiar with the unfamiliar, the tried and tested with the unknown. Those crossing bridges inevitably pass from the secure to the temporarily insecure. They cross a chasm that induces a sense of momentary danger and the experience of being temporarily in suspension, high above the continuous flow of time. Upon crossing that abyss cut with waters that divide human beings and potentially sweep them toward oblivion, the traveler passes into safety, joining others previously known or unknown.

Paine never spelled out these ideas clearly. He was instead preoccupied with the practical task of designing bridges that would attract sponsors willing to back their construction. His bridge-building fantasy began to materialize during mid-November 1785, when he employed another English émigré, John Hall, as a practical assistant. Hall was a self-educated artisan like Paine who had arrived in America from Leicester, England, early in August, bearing letters of introduction to the author of *Common Sense*. Hall's employment record was impressive. He had worked for three years (1778–1780) as a "Clerk and Draughtsman" with the leading English steam engine manufacturers, Boulton and Watt. He had subsequently been employed to build and install steam engines at the new Snedshill works of the famous ironmaster John Wilkinson, at the Coalbrookdale Company's nearby Ketley works, at Banks and Onions's great cannon foundry and boring mill at Brosely in Shropshire, and at the Rotherham, Yorkshire, mills of the prominent cannon founders Samuel Walker and Company. Hall's official record contained only one blemish: Boulton and Watt had complained of his bad habit of "introducing his own inventions" and had pointed out to his prospective employers that this habit had been "the principal cause of complaint against him."[1]

Paine found this bad habit attractive — so much so that during the next few years, Hall's engineering skills and experience proved to be crucial in Paine's daily life. Hall's diary, recently rediscovered, provides most of the known details about Paine's first bridge models, which Hall affectionately referred to as "saints." Hall noted in his diary that Paine first called on him in Bordentown on November 16, 1785. "Had a Letter from Mr. Pain by his Boy Informing us of his coming this day," wrote Hall. "Between 3 & 4 oclock Mr Pain, Colonel Kerbright [*sic*] and an other Gentleman came to our door in a Waggon. Went all up stairs and partook of a Beef Steak."[2] The meeting proved amicable and productive, and within a month Hall, plied with cups of tea and watered-down wine, was working hard on Paine's first wooden bridge model at the Bordentown farm.[3]

Hall's reputation as a steam engine specialist attracted numerous visitors, including the early steamboat pioneer John Fitch.[4] Such interruptions added to the mounting sense of urgency and importance of the project shared by Paine and Hall. Paine became engrossed in the work, especially after a cast-iron model of the same bridge was begun. In early June 1786, Paine shipped both the wooden and cast-iron models on a stage boat to Benjamin Franklin in Philadelphia for inspection. "The European method of bridge architecture, by piers and arches, is not adapted to many of the rivers in America on account of the ice in winter," he told Franklin in an accompanying letter. "The construction of those I have the honour of presenting to you is designed to obviate this difficulty by leaving the whole passage of the river clear of the incumbrance of piers." Paine added, "My first design in the wooden model was for a bridge over the Harlem River, for my good friend General Morris of Morrisania . . . but I cannot help thinking that it might be carried across the Schuylkill."[5]

Paine correctly anticipated that the Harlem Bridge project was a nonstarter. The project soon collapsed under the weight of bereavement in the Morris family and objections by Gouverneur Morris, upon whose newly inherited property on the Harlem River, Morrisania, the bridge was to have been erected. Morris regarded the whole idea of a bridge that would bring a highway to New York past his estate as "by no means desirable . . . a bridge will bring trouble and cost instead of pleasure and profit, not to mention the danger of being robbed by stragglers."[6] The failure prompted Paine, the providentialist, to set his sights on a much more important goal: a wrought-iron, single-span bridge to cross the Schuylkill River in Philadelphia. No fixed bridge existed there, owing to the width (four hundred to five hundred feet) and depth of the river, although plans for multispan wooden bridges were under consideration. During the hot and steamy summer of 1786, Paine lobbied the Pennsylvania Council about his plans, and on September 22, praise and open-ended promises in hand, Paine invited Hall, who had returned to Philadelphia, to join him at Colonel Joseph Kirkbride's to begin work on a third model for a bridge designed specifically to span the Schuylkill.[7]

Hall joined him a week later. Together for the next three months, they fell into what foreman Paine called a "working fit."[8] The team included several assistants, one of whom Paine referred to as "my boy Joe," whose age and skin color are unknown. The pressure to get things right fast was great, especially after Paine was informed of a rival project championed by the Pennsylvania Agricultural Society, which began to petition the state assembly for an act of incorporation to erect a bridge on piers over the Schuylkill. Paine's response was scathing. He told the prominent Pennsylvania congressman Thomas Fitzsimmons that if that project was given government backing, "the sinking of piers will sink more money than they have any idea of and will not stand when done."[9] Paine hoped that his objections would stall any official decision and thus enable his own project to be pushed quickly to completion. Hall's diary presents a good picture of the pace at which the men worked on the new bridge model — and of the personal frictions it inevitably caused:

> Thursday December 14 1786. This day employed in raising and putting on the abutments again and fitting them. The smyth made the nuts of screws to go easier. Then set the ribs at proper distance and after dinner I and Jackaway put on some temporary pieces on the frame of wood to hold it straight and when Mr Pain came they then tied it on its wooden frame with strong cords. I then saw that it had bulged full on one side and hollow on the other. I told him of it and he said it was done by me. I denied that and words arose very high. I at length swore by God that it was straight as when I left it. He replied as positively the contrary and I think myself ill used in this affair.[10]

A few days before Christmas, with deep snow already on the ground, the miniature "saint" was packed onto a sled and pulled by horse to Benjamin Franklin's house, where friends, including David Rittenhouse, were treated to a private viewing. The thirteen-foot wrought-iron model was put on display in the Committee Room of the statehouse, where it was inspected by the representatives, one of whom "thought it pretty, others strong," and later by miscellaneous "philosophers, mechanics, statesmen and even tailors." Hall spoke eagerly of the model as a potential contribution "to the world's present wonders," and Paine was excited by the prospect of legislation to establish a public bridge-building company funded mainly by private capital.[11] Both men were too optimistic. By March 1787, it had become clear that the Pennsylvania government would continue to drag its feet and that various potential patrons of the model were highly dubious about an invention that might fling them into bankruptcy. Nervousness about Paine's design was compounded by concerns about the current state of the American iron industry, which at that point in time, as Rittenhouse told Paine, was probably incapable of cheaply producing good quality iron in quantities sufficient for a structure of that magnitude.[12]

Parisian Experiments

With the exception of chain bridges, it was to be half a century before America turned to iron bridge construction. The Schuylkill was finally crossed in 1798–1805 with a three-span wooden bridge. During heated design-related arguments with Hall, Paine had once or twice threatened to take his project to France.[13] Now, beaten by politicians' skepticism and investors' fear of bankruptcy, he concluded that he had no other option but to abandon the Schuylkill project and return to Europe. He thought that he would have a good chance of convincing the experts there of the importance of his bridge design and of getting the funds needed for a full-scale trial. He made arrangements to go first to America's ally France and then to England, where he would visit his parents in Thetford. On March 31, 1787, he wrote to Benjamin Franklin, asking him for the second time in his life for a letter of introduction, this time to influential French academicians and politicians.[14] Franklin obliged, and among the several glowing letters he wrote was one to François de la Rochefoucauld:

> The bearer of this letter is Mr. Paine, the author of a famous piece entitled "Common Sense," published here with great effect on the minds of people at the beginning of the revolution. He is an ingenious, honest man; and as such I beg leave to recommend him to your civilities. He carries with him the model of a bridge of a new construction, his own invention, concerning which I intended to have recommended him to M. Peyronnet, but I hear he is no more. You can easily procure Mr. Paine a sight of the models and drawings of the collection appertaining to the Ponts et Chaussées; they must afford him useful lights on the subject. We want a bridge over our river Schuylkill, and we have no artist here regularly bred to that kind of architecture.[15]

Paine gathered his belongings, packed up the wrought-iron model bridge, and shipped it off to New York. He saw Hall for the last time in Trenton on April 20. The close friends shared a drink in Whight's Tavern, where Paine, dressed in a red greatcoat, repaid his petty debts and invited Hall to kill time before his stagecoach arrived by going for a ride in a chaise. For half an hour, they talked politics, until the coach for New York arrived. Hall reported, "I then shook hands and wished him a good voyage and parted."[16]

The fellow "saintmakers" were not to see each other again for nearly five years. Paine's ship sailed from New York for France on April 26 and

arrived at Le Havre-de-Grâce exactly one month later. He bubbled about
being on French soil. He described the Seine Valley between Le Havre-
de-Grâce and Rouen as "the richest I ever saw. The crops are abundant,
and the cultivation in nice and beautiful order. Everything appeared to be
in fulness; the people are very stout, the women exceedingly fair, and the
horses of a vast size and very fat. I saw several at Havre that were seventeen hands high." After a day's sight-seeing at the parliament buildings
and palaces of the dukes of Normandy in Rouen, he pushed on to Paris,
with the bridge following separately. "There is great curiosity here to see
it," Paine reported to Franklin from Paris on June 22, "as bridges have
lately been a capital subject. A new Bridge is begun over the Seine, opposite the Palais de Bourbon and the Place de Louis Quinze. It is about the
breadth of the Schuylkill, and the Abbe Morley tells me, will cost five millions of livres. It is on piers."[17]

Paine presented his model bridge and accompanying plans to the
French Academy of Sciences in Paris on July 21. A commission of three
men — Jean-Baptiste Le Roy, Jean Charles de Borda, and Charles
Bossut — was set up to report on them. Although Paine hoped Franklin's
references to Le Roy and two other academy members, La Rochefoucauld
and Mme Helvétius, would help,[18] he waited anxiously for news. On August 15, he wrote to George Clymer in Philadelphia, asking him to pass on
a draft copy of the report that had just reached Paine's hands. His mood
was exuberant:

> The enclosed for Dr. Franklin is from his friend Mr. Le Roy, of the Acad-
> emy of Sciences, respecting the bridge, and the causes that have delayed
> completing the report. An arch of 4 or 5 hundred feet is such an unprece-
> dented thing, and will so much attract notice in the northern part of Eu-
> rope, that the Academy is cautious in what manner to express their final
> opinion. It is, I find, their custom to give reasons for their opinion, and this
> embarrasses them more than the opinion itself.

Paine highlighted the academy's positive points:

> That the model is strong, and that a bridge constructed on the same prin-
> ciples will also be strong, they appear to be well agreed in, but to what par-
> ticular causes to assign the strength they are not agreed in. The Committee
> was directed by the Academy to examine all the models and plans for iron
> bridges that had been proposed in France, and they unanimously gave the
> preference to our own, as being the simplest, strongest, and lightest. They
> have likewise agreed on some material points.[19]

Three days later, on August 18, 1787, Paine conveyed his excitement more briefly to Thomas Jefferson, then American minister in Paris: "The committee have among themselves finally agreed on their report . . . it will be read in the Academy on Wednesday. The report goes pretty well to support the principles of the construction, with their reasons for that opinion."[20]

Paine's optimism blinded him to the caution of his potential backers. The report in fact was not presented until the academy's meeting on August 29, which also considered another iron bridge model presented by a Paris ironworker named Clément. The report, written and presented by Le Roy, also noted the existence of several other models, but no details were provided and there was no comparative study awarding a contract to Paine, as he had implied to Clymer.[21] Paine's remark to Clymer that the academy had found his long-span arch design unprecedented also was exaggerated. There had been a spate of long-span arch designs in both iron and wood from French engineers in the decade prior to his arrival in Paris.[22] Some contemporaries, including some experts of the Royal Academy of Sciences, undoubtedly considered the long-span iron arch designs by Montpetit, Racle, and Aubry to be more soundly based than Paine's design, which to them probably looked like more of an anticlimax than a pathbreaking wonder, as he was claiming.

The academy report was nevertheless surprisingly favorable. Le Roy's friendship with Franklin undoubtedly helped; so did Paine's status as the leading American political writer and the fact that the committee comprised academic physicists and mathematicians, rather than practical-minded engineers or risk-conscious capitalists. After noting briefly the existence of other plans and the fact that an iron arch had already been constructed at Coalbrookdale, in England, Le Roy described the main features of Paine's model. Since the members of the academy had the model "before their eyes," some details were unfortunately omitted. The report was positive about the lightness and strength of the bridge. It added that the expansion effects of heat and cold would not be serious but pointed out that Paine should pay attention to the problems of torsion and wind resistance, both of which could be prevented by splaying the bridge toward the abutments — a French idea that recurred constantly right up to the time of the Tour d'Eiffel. Finally, Le Roy's report recommended the construction of a test rib on a one-half, one-third, or one-quarter scale. It drew together its judgments in a bright conclusion: "From all the above we conclude that Mr. Paine's iron bridge is ingeniously conceived; that its construction is simple, sound, and fit to provide the strength necessary to withstand effects arising from loading; and that it is worthy of a trial."[23]

Paine was half satisfied. To obtain official backing, he had to seek and win approval from the Council of the Ponts et Chaussées, whose well-known president, Jean Perronet, was not yet dead, as Franklin had thought. Paine managed to get an audience with him but found him unsympathetic. In earlier reports, on a design by Montpetit, Perronet had already made abundantly clear his objections to iron bridges.[24] He probably repeated these to Paine, telling him that he saw no justification for using iron when good building stone was so plentiful in France and that if stone could not be afforded, wood was the best substitute. Perronet also emphasized that stone was tried and tested, that it was comparatively cheap, that unlike iron it could be obtained in long blocks with stout cross sections, and that its durability could be improved further by wrapping it in lead or copper.

Paine's suspicion that he had been stonewalled was confirmed when Perronet revealed his own hand in the Parisian game of bridge contracts. Shortly after meeting with Paine, Perronet received funding for his Pont de la Concorde, with five masonry arches over the Seine on the west side of Paris. He busily made plans to begin construction sometime during 1788. In the meantime, several other Seine bridge projects were announced by entrepreneurs, and for a time — the details are scanty — Paine harbored hopes that his design might yet be used for one of them. One contender, Montpetit, had long been proposing an iron bridge over the Seine. During the period 1779–1783, he had offered alternatives of a single 600-foot span, two 300-foot spans, or three 200-foot spans, and in the summer of 1788 he came back into the picture by publishing a summary of his work, which emphasized his more than thirty years' experience in the field. Since Montpetit was the local expert on iron bridges and had his reputation and ideas to defend, it is unlikely that Paine was involved with him. No more probable was Paine's cooperation with his old enemy Pierre-Augustin Caron de Beaumarchais, who during the year 1787 was working with the architect François-Joseph Bélanger on a scheme for a wooden arched bridge on cast-iron columnar piers at the east end of town, on the site of the future Pont d'Austerlitz. Whether Beaumarchais seriously considered Paine's iron arch as an alternative is unclear. In any case, Paine's French hopes were damaged beyond repair by the inventor of a timber-bending process, Migneron de Brocqueville, who in January 1788 published a letter that favorably described the timber arch Seine design and ridiculed the whole idea of a long, single-span, wrought-iron arch that Paine had presented to the Royal Academy of Sciences.[25]

English Hopes

With the exception of Perronet's bridge, which received government backing, every other scheme for bridging the Seine fell through because of the deepening crisis of the French regime. Although Paine stayed hopeful, it dawned on him gradually that it might be easier to realize an iron bridge or even a large-scale trial in England than in France. After receiving the favorable report from the French Academy of Sciences, he sent his model to the botanist Sir Joseph Banks, president of the Royal Society in England. Soon after September 1787, he followed the model across the Channel to London.

Few details remain of this brief first return to England, although we know that during that same month, Paine journeyed to Thetford and arranged for his mother to receive a regular allowance of nine shillings a week, his father having died in mid-November of the previous year. Paine was an anchor in his mother's life, and the homecoming was probably tearful. Thirteen years had passed, during which time Paine had received only one letter from his parents. Since 1776, his proud mother told him, she had fasted on July 4 in support of her son's contributions to the Americans' struggle against the British. Paine was probably spoiled as well by Miss Cocke — whom he described affectionately as "my dear aunt" — and he spent time catching up with friends in Thetford and relatives, including Elizabeth Hustler, in nearby Bury St. Edmunds.[26]

During several weeks in Thetford, the bridge plans were temporarily set aside. Politics and the "clamour of war" were again on his mind. The one surviving letter written from Thetford in this period also suggests that he felt like an alien in his native England. "While the English boast of the freedom of their government," he wrote, "that government is the oppressor of freedom in all other countries, and France its protectress."[27] His scathing attack on the political hypocrisy of the English government triggered a bout of homesickness for America and even dampened his hopes for the success of his bridge model, which he left temporarily in the care of Banks. He was particularly worried that the renewed outbreak of war between France and England would destroy investors' confidence and trigger cutthroat competition among bridge designers that would destroy every iron bridge project, including his own. "It is very possible," he reported to his American friend George Clymer, "that after all the pains I have taken, and the money I have expended, that some counterworking project will set itself up, and in the hope of great gain, or great interest, will attempt schemes, that after some less pains will end in no bridge at all."[28]

The melancholy soon evaporated. In the spring of 1788, Paine was introduced to Peter Whiteside, an entrepreneur with a reputation for risk taking and, some said, shiftiness. Paine convinced him to back the project financially and to help him secure a patent for the bridge. English born, Whiteside had become a wealthy Philadelphian through American army contracts during the War of Independence and had been sent back to Europe by George Washington to improve "commercial relations." Whiteside and Paine secured an informal deal during the early summer. On June 15, Paine wrote to Jefferson to tell him that he was applying for a patent. On August 10, savoring newspaper reports of the aftermath of the previous year's Philadelphia Convention, he told his good friend Edmund Burke that he was temporarily turning his back on European politics, and that he would "rather erect the largest arch in the world than be the greatest Emperor in it."[29] On September 9 he sent Jefferson further news of the project:

> The model has the good fortune of preserving in England the reputation which it received from the Academy of Sciences. It is a favourite hobby horse with all who have seen it; and every one who has talked with me on the subject advised me to endeavour to obtain a Patent, as it is only by that means that I can secure to myself the direction and management. For this purpose I went, in company with Mr. Whiteside to the office . . . told them who I was, and made an affidavit that the construction was my own invention. This was the only step I took in the business. Last Wednesday I received a Patent for England, the next day a Patent for Scotland, and I am to have one for Ireland.[30]

The patent, number 1667, dated August 26, 1788, formally witnessed by Whiteside, and — a luscious irony — sworn under the sign of "His most Excellent Majesty King George the Third, by His Letters Patent under the Great Seal of Great Britain," was relatively brief and contained no diagrams. The main clauses described how the design of the single-span bridge was inspired by observations of a spider's circular web and by the conviction "that when nature empowered this insect to make a web she also instructed her in the strongest mechanical method of constructing it." The document detailed the proposed use of curved bars, metal tubes, and nuts and bolts and emphasized that bridges of various sizes, suitably enameled with melted glass to protect them against rust, could be prefabricated and transported in sections "to any part of the world to be erected."[31]

Quite a number of the techniques trumpeted in the patent application as original — from tubular supports to methods of prefabrication — had been picked up by Paine in Paris from the many ideas being exhibited and discussed there at the time of his arrival. Paine was nevertheless justified in fetching these ideas from across the Channel and patenting them, since no one else had done so. But there remained the problem of finding hard cash to realize the scheme. In the letter to Jefferson on September 9, Paine spoke of the need to attract the support of "the practical Iron Men." He clearly had his eyes on the powerful Rotherham manufacturer, Thomas Walker and partners. "The Iron Works in Yorkshire belonging to the Walkers near to Sheffield are the most eminent in England in point of establishment and property," he told Jefferson. "The proprietors are reputed to be worth two hundred thousand pounds and consequently capable of giving energy to any great undertaking." Paine divulged that he had been earwigging the firm. "A friend of theirs who had seen the model wrote to them on the subject, and two of them came to London last Friday to see it and talk with me on the business." Paine was quietly confident: "Their opinion is very decided that it can be executed either in wrought or cast iron, and I am to go down to their works next week to erect an experiment arch."[32]

By late October, work had begun at the Walkers' works at Masborough. Paine had the practical assistance of their foreman, Billy Yates, whom he described as "an excellent mechanic who fell into all my ideas with great ease and penetration" and whom he later called "President of the Board of Works."[33] Paine intended to build a 250-foot experimental arch, but work proceeded much more slowly than expected. Harsh winter weather set in early, making it impossible to work outside. The intended size of the prototype also meant that it could not easily be built indoors. And the construction work was temporarily halted and then resumed in cut-down form after Paine heard that the former local member of Parliament and nephew to the late Sir George Savile, Mr. Foljambe, was keen on erecting an iron bridge locally. "He lives about three miles from the works," reported Paine eagerly, "and the river Don runs in front of his house, over which there is an old ill-constructed bridge which he wants to remove. These circumstances determined me to begin an arch of 90 feet with an elevation of five feet."[34]

Two weeks before Christmas, 1788, the small bridge over the river Don was half completed. "The work goes on with great success and in appearance exceeds both the model and the drawing," Paine reported. He added proudly that Foljambe was delighted with its "elegance and beauty" and that there had been a stream of prominent visitors to the site, including Lord William Wentworth Fitzwilliam and Edmund Burke.[35]

Whether the bridge was ever erected over the Don is unknown. During April 1789, Paine and Yates supervised the erection of a three-ton rib arch, which was framed with wood and, Paine later told John Hall, test-loaded for twelve months with six tons of scrap iron.[36] He wrote long preliminary accounts, which have been newly discovered, of the erection and test and forwarded them on May 25, 1789, to Sir Joseph Banks for submission to the Royal Society and to Sir George Staunton for submission to the Society of Arts. In June, Banks informed him that his report had been read and accepted by the Royal Society, but for some reason Staunton, an Irish baronet with diplomatic experience in Indian and Chinese affairs, delayed sending his copy to the Society of Arts until April 1790.[37] The completed section of the bridge remained on display at Masborough. The last recorded viewing of it was by John Byng, whose journal entry for June 11, 1789, reads simply, "In Mr. Walker's work-yard we survey'd an arch of an iron bridge just cast."[38]

It is possible that the project was stillborn for financial reasons, neither Whiteside (who was at the point of bankruptcy) nor Foljambe being willing to foot the bill for completing the remaining work. Paine was consequently forced to think again. He responded by drawing up plans with the Walkers for a larger demonstration arch, to be erected in London, where it would provide more direct evidence than a written paper of the value of his system and might influence authorities and financiers to erect an iron bridge over the Thames. The scheme, Paine told Jefferson, had the added advantage of being a money earner in crowded London: "For, if only a fifth of the persons, at a half penny each, pass over a new bridge as now pass over the old ones the tolls will pay 25 per cent besides what will arise from carriages and horses."[39] By midsummer 1789, the terms of agreement with the Walkers were made public. Paine reported:

> The Walkers are to find all the materials, and fit and frame them ready for erecting, put them on board a vessel and send them to London. I am to undertake all expense from that time and to compleat the erecting. We intend first to exhibit it and afterwards put it up for sale, or dispose of it by private contract, and after paying the expenses of each party the remainder to be equally divided — one half theirs, the other mine. My principal object in this plan is to open the way for a Bridge over the Thames.[40]

Paine figured that he could raise enough capital to mount the exhibition, that he would go for broke in the hope of recouping his costs later. He had American collateral — "one thousand dollars stock in the Bank of

Philadelphia [*sic*], and two years interest due upon it last April, £180 in the hands of General Morris; £40 with Mr. Constable of New York; a house at Bordentown, and a farm at New Rochelle."[41] He was, in any case, too accustomed to living on the breadline to trouble much about financial embarrassment. He borrowed £200 from Jefferson and soon persuaded two American merchants named Cleggett and Murdoch to pay off a debt of £620, for which he had been dunned by the assignees of Whiteside, who had just been flung into the debtors' section of London's Fleet Prison. By September, Paine had found an additional backer — Benjamin Vaughan (1751–1835), wealthy son of a West Indian merchant and friend of Benjamin Franklin's.

The main problem now to be solved was to find a prominent site for the bridge prototype, whose manufacture by Yates at the Walkers' plant went without a hitch. "I had thought of Soho Square, where Sir Joseph Banks lives, but he is now in Lincolnshire," Paine reported to Jefferson.[42] He was eventually forced to settle for something less, as the correspondence of this period shows. Paine wrote to George Washington on May 1, 1790, telling him that shortly he would be sending him the key to the Bastille (a gift from Lafayette) and describing the state of the bridge: "I have manufactured a bridge (a single arch) of one hundred and ten feet span, and five feet high from the chord of the arch. It is now on board a vessel coming from Yorkshire to London, where it is to be erected. I see nothing yet to disappoint my hopes of its being advantageous to me. It is this only which keeps me in Europe, and happy I shall be, when I have it in my power to return to America." In a follow-up letter to Washington on May 31, he remained half optimistic: "My bridge is arrived and I have engaged a place to erect it in. A little time will determine its fate, but I yet see no cause to doubt of its success, though it is very probable that a war, should it break out, will as in all new things, prevent its progress so far as regards profits."[43]

Some have claimed, incorrectly, that the bridge was erected during June 1790.[44] In fact, the abutments were probably only started in June, whereas the actual erection of the ironwork did not begin until August, while completion of the decking took until at least to the end of September. The site ultimately chosen by Paine was a field next to a public house called the Yorkshire Stingo, halfway between Paddington and Marylebone. The spot was well chosen, for Paine clearly had his eyes on maximum publicity. The Yorkshire Stingo was famous for its locally brewed strong ale, a bowling green — which Paine was to use with his friends — and an annual May Day fair. A public house by this name had existed for more than a century on this spot, which was on the south side of what is now Marylebone Road, almost opposite the south end of Lisson Grove. The area was then known as Lisson Green, and Marylebone Road was part of the New Road, which had been built in the mid-eighteenth century to link Paddington and Islington. It served as a busy outer ring road to northwest London and was a center for all sorts of entertainments. Marylebone Gardens had been the most famous amusement center in the area until it was closed down because of public disturbances. Further along the road, the Queen's Head and Artichoke specialized in cream teas and bumblepuppy, a game with a tennis ball attached by string to a post. The Adam and Eve offered trapball and syllabub, a prized sweet made of cream or milk curdled with wine and sometimes whipped or solidified with gelatin, while the Jew's Harp offered skittles and beer.

Paine and his foreman, "an American Mr. Buel, a most excellent Mechanic,"[45] took up residence at the Yorkshire Stingo, and the work of erecting the 110-foot bridge in the adjoining field began by the end of May 1790. Paine reported progress in two letters to Thomas Walker. On August 8, the bridge was half erected:

> Every thing joints well and seemed well and, what is somewhat extraordinary, it has every body's good word. I have three carpenters and two labourers but I have unfortunately lost the aid of Mr. Buel. The first morning we began erecting (Tuesday), it being raining and slippery, he fell from the scaffold, and his leg taking one of the cross bars of the centre tore the flesh of it up seven or eight inches like the flap of a saddle. Luckily no bones were broke or fractured. A surgeon was very near at hand who sewed the wound up or rather sewed the flesh down again to the place. He is now doing well, having now neither pain nor fever. He can move his leg in bed very freely but he has not yet been out of it. This, of consequence, has confined me to the work from morning till night. I come home sometimes pretty well tired.[46]

During the last week of August, Paine reported that the weather had been bad, but not bad enough to prevent the team of four or five carpenters from nearly completing the work of flooring the bridge with four-inch timbers. He enclosed a detailed sketch, which has unfortunately been lost, and concluded bumptiously: "I am always discovering some new faculty in myself — either good or bad — and I find I can look after workmen much better than I thought I could."[47] During the last week of September, the Walkers' neighbor, Lord Fitzwilliam, who had taken a keen interest in the original trial rib at Masborough, inquired about the bridge exhibition.

On September 28, Thomas Walker informed him that recent press descriptions of the bridge were misleading and that in fact it was "of the catenarian form, of 110 feet span and 5 feet high" and weighed nearly 36 1/2 tons. Walker concluded, "The bridge is now erected for public exhibition at the Yorkshire Stingo Bowling Green, Lesson [sic] Green, London."[48]

Despite its expensive flooring and light appearance and Paine's glowing descriptions of its popularity, the experimental bridge turned out to be a flop. There was certainly a long line of intrigued visitors to the site, including a politely interested party from the Royal Society led by Banks. At one point, Paine even considered charging admission to the site. But many of the visitors who really mattered were tight-lipped, among them Davies Giddy — who was soon to become rich and famous as Davies Gilbert, President of the Royal Society — who inspected the site in April 1791, noting in his journal only that the bridge had a catenarian curve.[49] Others, including the following anonymous visitor, were openly hostile:

> I am afraid there is not sufficient quantity of iron in it and, as wrought iron is more subject to be corroded by rust than cast iron, I think it would have been more durable to have constructed it wholly of cast iron, increasing the quantity except the binding bolts which are cased in cast iron. I think he has also made a choice of too small a portion of a circle, as a larger portion of a smaller circle and greater depth in the ribs would have greatly added to its strength.[50]

Reticence among would-be investors, the biggest obstacle Paine had always faced, finally delivered its verdict of silence. There was a marked lack of commentary and discussion within the general and technical press, and nobody stepped forward from the ranks of the bridge's admirers offering a bag of money for its erection. Ultimately, the main value of the Lisson Green bridge was its practical demonstration of design faults to be avoided in the future. It proved a stepping-stone to more adventurous times, which enabled more capable engineers, such as John Rennie, who probably inspected Paine's model, to produce more marketable designs.[51] The most important consequence of the exhibition was the impetus it gave to plans for a long-span bridge over the river Wear at Sunderland, where Rowland Burdon (one of the two Members of Parliament for the county of Durham) had intended to erect a masonry arch with a span of about 200 feet. In 1791, he was offered an alternative design for a 200-foot-span iron bridge in the Paine style; almost certainly, the offer was made by the Walkers, who took Paine's model to Burdon's home at Castle Eden in 1791. He rejected the proposal, presumably because of his attachment to stone and the criticisms leveled at the Lisson Green bridge. Burdon subsequently changed his mind. During 1792, he began to doubt both the trumpeted practicality and the cheapness of his proposed masonry arch, to the point where he reconsidered the use of iron. With the help of the Walkers, a local ex-schoolmaster named Thomas Wilson, and advice from various well-wishers, he went on to commission a cast-iron arch with a nominal span of 240 feet — the world's longest at the time of its completion in 1796.

Although some sections of the Sunderland Bridge were probably reworked from the dismantled ribs of the Lisson Green arch,[52] there was otherwise no link between the Sunderland Bridge and Paine's models. Paine's subsequent writings make it clear that he was not personally connected with the Sunderland Bridge work at any stage and that he only heard much later that his model had been shown to Burdon. By the autumn of 1791, he had lost interest in the Lisson Green arch. He confessed to John Hall, who had just returned to England and had visited the Yorkshire Stingo site, only to be disappointed at not finding the bridge at the center of public attention, that his efforts had failed: "The Bridge has been put up, but being on wood butments they yielded, and it is now taken down."[53]

During October, as the arch began slowly to rust in the dew and drizzle of the approaching winter, the ironwork was repossessed by the Walkers. It was dismantled and taken back by barge to Rotherham, where it gathered further rust. Meanwhile, Paine returned to politics. On November 25, he told Hall, "At present I am engaged on my political Bridge. I shall bring out a new work . . . soon after New Year. It will produce something one way or other."[54]

Reflections on Revolution

The new two-part work Paine had in mind, *Rights of Man,* was destined to become the best-selling book in the history of publishing. Paine had begun to make jottings for its first part shortly after arriving in Europe in search of a backer for his bridge. He was struck immediately by how "American" were his own reactions to European political events. "My heart and myself are 3000 miles apart," he wrote to Kitty Nicholson Few, a friend in New York. "I had rather see my horse Button in his own stable, or eating the grass of Bordentown or Morrisania, than see all the pomp and show of Europe."[55] He intuitively welcomed the French disturbances during 1788 and 1789, interpreting them as the outbreak of the American

Revolution in Europe. "A share in two revolutions is living to some purpose," he told Washington excitedly. "We hear good things from France," he told Jefferson, "and I sincerely wish them all well and happy."[56] He described the regime of Louis XVI as the "protectress of freedom in all countries"[57] and expressed to his friends and acquaintances every confidence in the course of domestic French politics. "With respect to the French revolution," he wrote to Benjamin Rush, "be assured that every thing is going on right. Little inconveniences, the necessary consequence of pulling down and building up, may arise; but even these are much less than ought to have been expected."[58]

Paine's sympathy for the first phase of the French Revolution was reinforced by an unusual view of the French monarchy as a force for radical political change. Given his scathing attacks on monarchy in general since the publication of *Common Sense*, he might have been expected to be equally tough on the court of Louis XVI. Not so. Louis XVI, Paine argued, was not understandable in the traditional terms of modern political thinking. His friend Edmund Burke liked to repeat these terms by observing that "those who have been once intoxicated with power, and have derived any kind of emolument from it, even though but for one year, can never willingly abandon it."[59] Paine was sure that language did not apply to the French monarchy during this period. Louis XVI was not just another power-thirsty despot driven by visions of grand victories through conquest at home and abroad — a politician so infatuated with state power that he was unwilling to share it with others. Paine was convinced that there was something different about Louis XVI, that the house of Bourbon was not driven by lust for political power, and that instead it was engaged in a pathbreaking attempt to dismantle French despotism. Louis XVI was practicing the difficult art of unscrewing the lids of the ancien régime by forging new compromises and retreating from unworkable positions. He was a politician of retreat, a figure who understood as well as anybody that the existing monarchic despotism was unworkable and who was therefore inching his own regime across a long and slippery tightrope toward a crowned republic. "The King has not felt himself so easy of several years as at present," Paine told Burke, describing in vivid detail a public rally to greet the humbled monarch outside the Hotel de Ville:

The Crowd was immense, but orderly and well arranged, and every one armed with something. Those who had no Muskets or Swords, got what they could. Scythes, Sickles, Carpenters Chissels and Iron Spikes fixed upon Sticks, Blacksmiths with Sledge Hammers . . . When the King alighted at the Hotel de Ville, he had to pass through an Alley of Men, who crossed ⋀ them over his head under which he had to pass, impressed perhaps with the apprehension that some one was to fall upon his head. I mention this, to shew how natural it is that he should now feel himself tranquil.[60]

Paine made exactly the same point during the spring of 1790 in an appeal to George Washington:

I beg leave to suggest to your Excellency the propriety of congratulating the King and Queen of France (for they have been our friends) and the National Assembly, on the happy example they are giving to Europe. You will see, by the King's speech, which I inclose, that he prides himself on being at the head of the revolution; and I am certain that such a congratulation will be well received, and have a good effect.[61]

Paine shared this vision of a reforming "republican monarch" with his contemporary Comte de Mirabeau, who simultaneously was trying secretly to convince the king that he should stop mourning the loss of aristocratic society. That society, with its nobility, privileged corps, and parliaments, had constantly hindered royal authority, argued Mirabeau. Surely the king could adjust to new forms of interference originating from outside the court. Surely the king could even take advantage of the Revolution by assuming leadership of the nation.

The advice went unheeded; Paine's hopes were to be dashed. But for the time being, his enthusiasm for French developments contrasted starkly with his scathing remarks about politics on the other side of the Channel. He found the whole English political scene dismal. "It is a matter worth considering," he told the Marquis of Lansdowne when staying with his mother in Thetford in September 1787, "that while the English boast of the freedom of their government, that government is the oppressor of freedom in all other countries."[62] With the outbreak of war yet again between Britain and France, his opinions toughened. He welcomed the prospect of France, Spain, Russia, and the Hapsburgs forming an alliance against John Bull, whose "viciousness" in matters of foreign policy he found mirrored in the arrogant presumption that Britain was "the Queen of Isles, the pride of Nations, the Arbitress of Europe, perhaps of the world." In conversation, Paine was adamant that such arrogance needed to be satirized: "If Swift was alive, he would say — 'Spit on such Patriotism.'"[63]

Paine also played up the news of King George III's madness. His plunge into insanity symbolized the decadence of the British body politic as a whole, and Paine watched with keen interest the subsequent tussle between Parliament and the court as to who should decide and approve the accession to the throne by the Prince of Wales during his father's illness. Paine highlighted the confusion that resulted from the absence of a written constitution — the absence had become a very strange thing for American eyes — and he slammed the whole political system for its class bias and unaccountability. "The English Nation is composed of two orders of men — Peers and Commoners," he told Thomas Walker during negotiations about their bridge. He then asked Walker a pointed question: "Is not Parliament composed of two houses one of which is itself hereditary and over which the people have no control and in the establishment of which they have no election, and the other house the representatives of only a small part of the Nation? How then can the Rights of the People be asserted and supported . . . ?"[64]

That question was central to the unfolding struggle in France, and it so exercised Paine during a sojourn in Paris from November 1789 until the following March — despite his preoccupation with bridge designs and contracts — that he began to draft a long commentary on the French Revolution. He found intellectual nourishment at the lively soirees hosted by Sophie de Grouchy and Marquis de Condorcet at the Hotel de la Monnaie, where Paine was among the favorite frequent guests on a list that included people such as Adam Smith, Benjamin Franklin, Cesare Beccaria, and Thomas Jefferson.[65]

On January 12, 1790 the swashbuckling political figure Marquis de Lafayette wrote to George Washington that his friend Thomas Paine was "writing for you a brochure in which you will see a portion of my adventures."[66] Lafayette referred here to the mounting public tension on the streets of Paris between his supporters and the radical Jacobins. At the time that Paine was busily drafting his manuscript, Lafayette was among the most cunning and influential revolutionary politicians in France. Founder of political clubs in Paris, member of the National Assembly (also called the Constituent Assembly), and soon to become commander of the capital's newly established local militia, the Paris National Guard, Lafayette wielded enormous power. With good reason, the first two years of the French Revolution (1789–1791) have been called "The Years of Lafayette"[67] because during that period Lafayette and his supporters, usually called the Patriot Party or the Fayettistes, used the National Assembly to institute a series of radical reforms of the French state and society.

Church lands were nationalized. The royal veto was suspended. Various feudal taxes and laws were abolished. The country was reorganized into eighty-three departments, and approval was won for a unicameral legislature.

Paine watched the Fayettistes draw back from the full democratic implications of these reforms. Like their Whig counterparts in Britain, Lafayette and his supporters advocated a system of constitutional monarchy, a liberal order in which the power of king, corporate bodies, and church were limited in favor of the parliament, with the bulk of the population still without the vote. During October 1789, the Fayettistes maneuvered the National Assembly into accepting a decree limiting the vote to citizens who paid direct taxes worth a minimum of three days' labor. They also convinced the Assembly to pass a law restricting those voters eligible for national political office to men who paid annual direct taxes equivalent to a *marc d'argent*, a silver mark worth about fifty-four days' labor.

The legislation caused a storm of political controversy. It had the effect of dividing the nation into active and passive citizens, the latter entitled to full civil rights but only limited political rights. On the floor of the National Assembly, Robespierre rose to attack the legislation, and in the new Paris municipal institutions, the district and communal assemblies, a bitter fight for the extension of democracy erupted, led by politicians such as Jacques Pierre Brissot de Warville and Marquis de Condorcet, Paine's future Girondin allies.[68] During January 1790, when Paine was sketching the first passages of *Rights of Man*, clashes between the Fayettistes and the radicals erupted when the National Assembly reaffirmed its support for the *marc d'argent* franchise. Condorcet attacked the Assembly, describing the legislation as "dangerous for liberty" and predicting that its incorporation into the constitution would "establish a legal inequality against those you have declared equal in rights."[69] Protests in the Cordeliers district, the heart of democratic radicalism, were met with threats of repression, and on January 22 Lafayette took three thousand troops into the district to arrest the notorious journalist Jean-Paul Marat. The president of the Cordeliers district, Georges-Jacques Danton, refused to surrender Marat. Although street fighting was avoided, the confrontation was not forgotten. The seal of loyalty between the radical democrats and the political leadership of the Fayettistes was broken.[70]

Five days before the Cordeliers events, the Paris scene heavy with tension, Paine wrote a friendly letter to Edmund Burke detailing the course of the Revolution and predicting its spread beyond the borders of France.

"There is no foreign Court, not even Prussia," wrote Paine, "that could now be fond of attacking France; they are afraid of their Armies and their Subjects catching the Contagion. Here are reports of Matters beginning to work in Bohemia, and in Rome. . . . Something is beginning in Poland, just enough to make the people begin to think."[71]

Little did Paine know that his firsthand account of events on the streets of Paris was destined to fuel one of the bitterest political controversies in British politics. Although Burke seems not to have replied, his feelings about the French Revolution hardened upon receiving his friend's letter. Burke was stunned by Paine's positive remarks about the demotion of Louis XVI to a subordinate executive of the National Assembly, horrified at Paine's sneering at the aristocracy and his ready acceptance of the sequestration of church property, and startled by Paine's eager anticipation of the outbreak of revolution in other regions of Europe. Burke consequently stopped thinking of the Revolution as a sequence of spontaneous happenings with limited effects, instead considering it part of a systematic plan to propagate a false philosophy and to wreck the foundations of European civilization.[72] Burke was alarmed by the strong parallels between Paine's sympathy for the Revolution and a recently published sermon in support of the French National Assembly delivered by Dr. Richard Price to the annual meeting of the London Revolution Society on November 4, 1789, at the Dissenters' meetinghouse in Old Jewry. Price had begun his *A Discourse on the Love of Our Country* with a text from Psalm 122: "Our feet shall stand within thy gates, O Jerusalem." After commending truth, liberty, and virtue as the "three chief blessings of human nature," Price had insisted to those gathered that "our first concern, as lovers of our country, must be to enlighten it." He had proposed to greet George III's recovery from illness with the demand that the king should henceforth "consider yourself as more properly the *Servant* than the *Sovereign* of your people." Price had concluded with a spirited defense of thirty million French people "demanding liberty with an irresistible voice; their king led in triumph, and an arbitrary monarch surrendering himself to his subjects."[73]

Burke noted that the bulk of Price's sermon — like Paine's letter — was devoted not to the French events but to flaws in the British constitution. He suspected that both men were bent on fomenting civil resistance in England. Burke was most annoyed by Price's claim that English liberties dated from 1688, when the Glorious Revolution had endowed the English people with three fundamental rights: "the right to liberty of conscience in religious matters"; "the right to resist power when abused"; and "the right to choose our own governors; to cashier them for misconduct;

and to frame a government for ourselves." Burke surmised, correctly, that this argument had more to do with the execution of Charles I, the American Declaration of Independence, and the storming of the Bastille than with the events of 1688, whose principles, Burke thought, were embodied in the statute called the Declaration of Rights, an Act that specified the rights and duties of subjects and affirmed the principle of hereditary succession. What alarmed Burke, in short, were the attempts by Price and Paine to link English politics to the American and French Revolutions — to spread talk, as Paine had put it, of "the contagion" of revolution.

Burke set to work on a public reply to both men on the subject of the French events. On February 12, 1790, Burke's publisher promised in an advertisement in *St. James's Chronicle* that a book titled *Reflections on the Revolution in France, and on the Proceedings in Certain Societies in London relative to that Event* would "speedily be published." The birth of the book proved to be more protracted. In writing about a moving target and wrestling with his own passion for civil liberties, Burke remained less than satisfied with the manuscript, which he continued to fiddle with through the spring and summer. In the last week of March, back in London and living at 31 King Street, near Soho Square, Paine, who had been told in Paris of Burke's forthcoming book, straightaway visited the opposition bookseller, Debrets, on Piccadilly. He reported, "He [Debrets] informed me that Mr. Burke's pamphlet was in the press (he is not the publisher), that he believed Mr. Burke was much at a loss how to go on; that he had revised some of the sheets, six, seven, and one nine times!"[74]

Paine told a number of friends, including Charles James Fox, the leading member of the parliamentary opposition, that he had concluded from Burke's silence that the book was hostile to the French Revolution and that he therefore intended to rework his own manuscript into a public reply to Burke. Paine waited. He busied himself with the bridge project and long conversations about the emerging controversy between Britain and Spain over possession of Nootka Sound, on Vancouver Island. He was in a cocky mood and itched for a political fight about the future of Britain. *The General Evening Post* in London had already reported him as saying that he looked forward to Burke's essay, boasting that "he would answer it in *four days*."[75] He reported in mid-April, "I met Dr. Lawrence, an intimate friend of Mr. Burke, a few days ago, to whom I said, 'I am exceedingly sorry to see a friend of ours so exceedingly wrong.'" Lawrence replied, "Time will show if he is," to which Paine quipped, "He is . . . already wrong with respect to time past."[76] Paine's confidence was boosted further by the receipt of a package containing the key to the Bastille and a framed drawing of a crowd demolishing the Bastille, sent to him by Lafayette with instructions to pass the package on to George Washington as a gift to the American people. Paine wrote excitedly to Washington on May 1, telling him that "this early trophy of the spoils of despotism, and the first ripe fruits of American principles transplanted into Europe," would shortly be forwarded. In the same letter, Paine predicted the triumph of the Revolution across the Channel, likening it to a process in the natural world: "I have not the least doubt of the final and complete success of the French Revolution. Little ebbings and flowings, for and against, the natural companions of revolutions, sometimes appear, but the full current of it is, in my opinion, as fixed as the Gulf Stream."[77]

Burke more or less completed the book during September, but he continued to make further revisions for another month. As he did, Paine, who had journeyed to Paris to carry the American flag in the public celebration of the new French constitution, guessed that the birth of the published manuscript was imminent. He packed his trunk and crossed the Channel to London during the last week of October. *Reflections on the Revolution in France,* the rhetorical masterpiece of modern counterrevolutionary writing, finally appeared in London's bookshops on November 1. It caused a minor sensation. Paine was among its first avid purchasers, one of 5,500 during the first seventeen days, 12,000 by the end of the month, and 19,000 within the first year. *Reflections* was quickly translated into French, the first 2,500 copies in that language selling out in two days, followed by another 13,500 within three months. Italian and German translations were published during 1791, and reprinted English-language editions appeared later that year in America and Ireland.[78]

In England, Burke had deliberately written for readers in the class described by Paine as "Peers." His primary aim, Burke said, was to awaken politically those who would not like "to have their mansions pulled down and pillaged, their persons abused, insulted, and destroyed; their title-deeds brought out and burned before their faces."[79] The exact same propertied class and its supporters responded warmly. Burke received scores of congratulatory letters from such notable figures as Richard Cumberland, Lord Loughborough, the bishop of St. David's, General John Burgoyne, and Sir Gilbert Elliot. Horace Walpole said Burke's work was "far superior to what was expected even by his warmest admirers. I have read it twice, and though of 350 pages, I wish I could repeat every page by heart."[80] Mrs. Elizabeth Montagu described it as "admirable, excellent, incomparable,"[81] and so did members of the Convocation of the University of Oxford, who awarded the degree of LL.D. to Burke "in Consideration of his very able Representation of the true Principles of our Constitution Ecclesiastical and Civil."[82]

Reflections had the effect, unintended by Burke, of driving a wedge through the official political spectrum, splitting it into the friends and enemies of the French Revolution, or into what would soon be called the Left and the Right. Burke had thought of his tract as a manifesto for the oppositional Whig Party. He had campaigned strenuously for this group within Parliament against George III's policy of repression in America and, more recently, for the impeachment of Governor General Warren Hastings, whom he personally had accused of extortion and judicial murder in India. Burke was known as a great orator with a powerful pen, and his reputation as one of the chief supporters of the traditional Whig suspicion of the Crown's meddling in the liberties of the British people made him into something of a loose cannon in and around Parliament. *Reflections* confirmed this reputation. Not only did it apparently overturn Burke's own famous principle, spelled out two decades earlier, that in all disputes between rulers and the people, the presumption must always be on balance against the abuse of power and in favor of the people.[83] *Reflections* also produced the strangest realignment of parliamentary forces. Burke suddenly found himself caught up in the odd position of being lavishly praised by his enemies and bitterly attacked by his friends. "Read it," exclaimed his old foe George III. "It will do you good! — do you good! Every gentleman should read it."[84] Whiggish friends were less than impressed. Charles James Fox, a great admirer of Burke and the king's avowed enemy and bitter critic, considered the case presented by Burke against the French Revolution in "very bad taste."[85] A few months later, Burke retaliated in Parliament by denouncing his avowed "pupil" Fox. "There is no loss of friendship," Fox spluttered from his bench. "I regret to say there is," snapped Burke. "I have done my duty though I have lost my friend. Our friendship is at an end."[86]

At the Angel Inn

The long-standing friendship between Paine and Burke also was about to be struck down. As *Reflections on the Revolution in France* warmed the hearts of the ruling political class throughout Britain, Paine took up lodgings at the Angel Inn in Islington, with the intention of reading and writing in silence. It is doubtful whether Islington village, tucked away from the bustle and filth of central London, provided much writer's calm. William Hogarth's painting of the inn, with its clutter of rowdy commoners, whinnying horses, laughing children, and drunken gentlemen, suggests that Paine's residence there was anything but tranquil. There were probably other disruptions. Paine began extending his Paris manuscript on or around November 4. That was the anniversary of the Glorious Revolution, whose pompous displays of fireworks surely irritated him, if only because they bolstered his long-held conviction (shared with Daniel Defoe and others) that the Glorious Revolution was a fake revolution and that before 1066 the Anglo-Saxons had been blessed with representative government and liberty, whereas the Norman Invasion had destroyed both and established despotism.[87] Paine's serenity at the Angel Inn was probably also interrupted by the chants of ragged street children, with their "Please to remember, the fifth of November." Peering through his window out onto the street, Paine studied their crudely made effigies of Guy Fawkes. He was reminded of his years in Lewes, unaware that within two years, his own roughly made effigy would replace that of Guy Fawkes as a national symbol of sedition.

Paine set about studying Burke's *Reflections* and at least a handful of his Whiggish respondents. He was especially pushed and pulled by Burke's eloquent reasoning. He either half agreed with or found wholly compelling a surprising number of Burke's points. For example, Burke's strictures on the necessity of "a jealous, ever-waking vigilance, to guard the treasure of our liberty, not only from invasion, but from decay and corruption" were beyond question. Paine found convincing as well Burke's observation that in Europe the era of "generous loyalty to rank and sex" was crumbling, and that elsewhere there was "a hollow murmuring under ground . . . that threatens a general earthquake in the political world." Granting the originality of the American Revolution, he did not find farfetched Burke's observation that the French events constituted an unprecedented "revolution in sentiments, manners, and moral opinions" and that that was why "the French revolution is the most astonishing that has hitherto happened in the world."

Paine also found himself nagged by several of Burke's own worries. "The worst of these politics of revolution," wrote Burke, "is this; they temper and harden the breast, in order to prepare it for the desperate strokes which are sometimes used in extreme occasions." Paine himself had made precisely the same point frequently during the American Revolution. That Revolution had also taught Paine some hard lessons in the political art of recognizing and respecting what Burke called "difficulty." Burke castigated the "degenerate fondness for tricking short-cuts, and little fallacious facilities, that has in so many parts of the world created governments with arbitrary powers." Despite his providentialism, Paine sympathized with that point. Its corollary, that an "amicable conflict with difficulty obliges us to an intimate acquaintance with our object, and compels us to consider it in all its relations," Paine had always considered vitally important in the struggle for liberty and justice.

Reflections on the Revolution in France no doubt sharpened Paine's own sense of the life-or-death importance of the current dramas across the Channel, and that is why the book so profoundly angered him. He was certainly upset by the oblique ad hominem attacks on his own work. Burke criticized the abstractions of the "new doctors of the rights of men" and the naïveté of the "political Men of Letters" who supported the Revolution. He derided those who misguidedly "think that government may vary like modes of dress," that sentence recalling Paine's by then famous remark in *Common Sense* that "government, like dress, is the badge of lost innocence." Burke also patronized the artisan class from which Paine himself had sprung in Thetford. "The occupation of an hair-dresser, or of a working tallow-chandler, cannot be a matter of honour to any person — to say nothing of a number of other more servile employments," sneered Burke. "Such descriptions of men ought not to suffer oppression from the state; but the state suffers oppression, if such as they, either individually or collectively, are permitted to rule." Burke also implicitly poured scorn on Paine's cosmopolitanism, accusing figures like him of sedition and in need of "the most severe quarantine." "Their attachment to their country itself," he wrote, "is only so far as it agrees with some of their fleeting projects."

More galling was the substance of Burke's political argument. Paine read with interest his acknowledgment of the profligate spending, excessively unequal distribution of wealth, and unspecified "abuses" of the ancien régime. But he was shocked by Burke's coldness toward the Revolution. Burke charged the Fayettistes, in a revealing metaphor, with doing irreparable damage to the perfectly sound foundations and walls of the "noble and venerable castle" of the French monarchy. "You might have repaired those walls; you might have built on those old foundations," Burke snapped, then issued them a summons for crimes including murder. "Amidst assassination, massacre, and confiscation, perpetrated or meditated," he wrote, "they are forming plans for the good order of future society." Burke's description of the Revolution sometimes bordered on the hysterical. It was, he said, a "strange chaos of levity and ferocity" marked by "all sorts of crimes jumbled together with all sorts of follies." The Revolution had unleashed "insolent irreligion in opinions," including the heresy that "a king is but a man; a queen is but a woman." It also had authorized "treasons, robberies, rapes, assassinations, slaughters, and burnings" throughout France.

Burke made it clear that he was unprepared to countenance anything of the sort spreading across the Channel. He had nothing but praise for the existing Crown-in-Parliament regime of George III. Paine observed that Burke hardly mentioned the upheavals of the 1640s (he euphemistically called them "the time of our civil troubles in England"). Paine also noted the occultism of Burke's attempt to establish the so-called Glorious Revolution, and particularly the Declaration of Rights of February 1689, as the unbreakable cornerstone of the British unwritten constitution. "So far is it from being true, that we acquired a right by the Revolution to elect our kings," Burke wrote, "that if we had possessed it before, the English nation did at that time most solemnly renounce and abdicate it, for themselves and for all their posterity for ever." Burke blathered constantly about "the antient fundamental principles of our government" and it was therefore not surprising that his political conclusions were conservative. "The very idea of the fabrication of a new government," he wrote, "is enough to fill us with disgust and horror."

Paine was particularly shocked by Burke's stated aim of protecting what he called "masculine morality" from the clattering hooves of the "swinish multitude." Burke stressed his preference for the existing patterns of inequality. He had no kind words for the class of commoners, at whom he flung quotations from Ecclesiasticus: "How can he get wisdom that holdeth the plough, and that glorieth in the goad; that driveth oxen; and is occupied in their labours; and whose talk is of bullocks?" Burke openly championed the powers of "large proprietors" like the Graftons. He described them as the wise guardians of "manly, moral, regulated liberty" and as ultimately "the ballast in the vessel of the commonwealth." He had no doubt that these proprietors would easily withstand any challenge from the noisy "insects" called heretics. "Because half a dozen grasshoppers under a fern make the field ring with their importunate chink, whilst thousands of great cattle, reposed beneath the shadow of the British oak, chew the cud and are silent, pray do not imagine," Burke wrote, "that those who make the noise are the only inhabitants of the field . . . or that, after all, they are other than the little shrivelled, meagre, hopping, though loud and troublesome insects of the hour."

Burke naturally disapproved of the ideals of republican self-government. He attacked "the delusive gypsey predictions of a 'right to choose our governors'" because he considered that the state or civil society

(Burke used the terms interchangeably, in their premodern, pre-Paine sense) should be viewed as the offspring of time-out-of-mind conventions, which should never be tampered with for the sake of foolish utopias. The key point for Burke was that attempts to bring the American and French Revolutions home to Britain would fail. He was confident that "the English nation" or "the people of England" (he too relied on grand abstractions) would "not ape the fashions they have never tried; nor go back to those which they have found mischievous on trial. They look upon the legal hereditary succession of their crown as among their rights, not as among their wrongs; as a benefit, not as a grievance; as a security for their liberty, not as a badge of servitude." "Englishmen" were by nature prejudiced in favor of the past. They were creatures of humble deference and gradual change, if change there had to be. They knew nothing of the swinish "rights of man" or of throat-cutting "democracy." "We fear God," wrote Burke daringly. "We look up with awe to kings; with affection to parliaments; with duty to magistrates; with reverence to priests; and with respect to nobility."[88]

Reflections was a stunning performance of political rhetoric. The volume of praise for the book was staggering. Within two months of publication, *Reflections* had provoked at least seventeen sympathetic printed replies, which made Paine aware that he had to reply to its lucid images and passionate arguments, its erudite manner and imperative tone, in a manner that literally transformed the language of political debate in Britain about the French Revolution. What was needed was another *Common Sense*.

Readers who concentrate on the substantive themes of *Rights of Man* — who treat it as if it were just like any other text of modern political philosophy — miss half of what is really interesting about it. At the Angel Inn, Paine deliberately set out to expose the pseudoelegance of Burke's argument by answering him with an entirely different style of writing. *Rights of Man* sparkled with diamond-hard prose written in a colloquial style. It avoided purple passages, sentences without meaning, and general humbug. Paine explained that he aimed to test "the manner in which a work, written in a style of thinking and expression different to what had been customary in England, would be received."[89] Paine consequently paid close attention to techniques such as the choice of idiom, the rhythm of the prose, and the pattern of sentence construction, all of which aimed to subvert the conventionally pompous prose of Burke's tract. Republican democracy was for Paine too serious a matter to be entrusted to governments and ruling classes. He was convinced that since Burke and other supporters of the status quo wrapped their sophistry in pompous obscurity, the fight for extending the rights of citizenship re-quired a new style of political writing — a fresh syntax of politics that could be spoken and understood by the most humble of folk. The ad-vance of republican democracy into the world required the replacement of what Paine called "the vassalage class of manners"[90] with a new demo-cratic republican code of literary manners suited to ordinary men and women who were assumed to be capable of literary alertness and public reflection and judgment. A democratic revolution in politics, in other words, required a prior democratic revolution in prose.

What kind of literary revolution did Paine have in mind? "As it is my design to make those that can scarcely read understand," he wrote, "I shall therefore avoid every literary ornament and put it in language as plain as the alphabet."[91] That remark was and still is often accepted at face value by his sympathizers. Charles James Fox reportedly said that *Rights of Man* "seems as clear and simple as the first rule in arithmetic."[92] Subsequent academic analysts of the book similarly back up Paine's own view of the earthiness of his prose by emphasizing his down-to-earth, feet-on-the-ground empiricism.[93] Paine is said to have shunned the subtlety of style and sensitivity to language displayed by Burke in favor of "honest" language that merely drew an undistorted picture of the facts of the world.

This "realist" use of language, it is said, is evident in Paine's frequent use of terms drawn from the theater. The eighteenth century, as he knew from Thetford, abounded with ballad operas, farces, pantomimes, and other such theatrical performances. Their growing popularity tempted Paine to use stage terms to criticize courts and aristocracies and to impli-cate Burke in their illusions. So *Rights of Man* attacked the British unwrit-ten constitution as a form of comic entertainment and pointed to "the puppet-show of state and aristocracy." It also criticized the secrecy sur-rounding despotic governments as "the Pantomime of Hush" and empha-sized that although courtiers sometimes cursed monarchy behind its back, "they are in the condition of men who get their living by a show, and to whom the folly of that show is so familiar that they ridicule it." In a simi-lar vein, or so it is said, Paine accused Burke of fancifully interpreting re-ality by means of "tragic paintings . . . very well calculated for theatrical representation, where facts are manufactured for the sake of show, and ac-commodated to produce, through the weakness of sympathy, a weeping effect." And again: "I cannot consider Mr. Burke's book in scarcely any other light than a dramatic performance; and he must, I think, have con-sidered it in the same light himself, by the poetical liberties he has taken of omitting some facts, distorting others, and making the whole machinery bend to produce a stage effect."[94]

The chief difficulty with this emphasis on the "factual" quality of *Rights of Man*, and with taking at face value Paine's claim to have avoided any word "which describes nothing" and consequently "means nothing" and to have provided "a clear idea of what government is, or ought to be,"[95] is that the text was a masterful exercise in the use of rhetoric to hide rhetoric, a brilliant effort at simulated or virtual realism. Like any other political text, *Rights of Man* drew invisibly on a repertoire of devices aimed at seducing its readers. The brilliance of this tract — Paine built upon a tradition of English political writing stretching back to figures such as John Bunyan — was that it read as if it had been written by a commoner whose manners were rough and ungracious. Its author presented himself as a burping, farting rebel in an age cut by knife-sharp divisions of courtly respectability, wealth, and power. *Rights of Man* assumed prior knowledge of no authority but the Bible and the Book of Common Prayer. It side-stepped Latin and French phrases or provided simultaneous translations in the rare passages where they were used. It redeployed imagery from the daily life of commoners and renounced pompous language designed to impress cultivated readers. *Rights of Man* was designed to appeal to public audiences of self-educated artisans like himself, working people, and lesser professionals who could in turn narrate its arguments to the illiterate or half-literate. The point was to outflank Burke by replacing the accepted courtly standards of literary excellence with the vulgar and quotable language of common speech — without losing sight of the twin goals of publicly airing fundamental political issues in a serious way and publicly questioning a political class accountable only to itself.

Despotism and War

Paine worked feverishly, often at night by candlelight in his room. His quill crafted forty thousand words — the first part of *Rights of Man*[96] — in less than three months. Paine's subject was Burke's, but the image of the world drawn by Paine was altogether different. He pictured the late-eighteenth-century world as a bleak house of despotism. With the notable exception of America, Paine grumbled, the world is bullied by rapscallion rulers bent on barbarizing their subjects. This despotism — Paine took aim especially at the monarchy of George III — makes individuals afraid to think and suspicious of others. The public exercise of reason is considered as treason, and individuals' natural rights (to free speech, public assembly, and freedom of religious affiliation, for instance) are hounded to the four corners of the earth.

In this "uncivilized" and overgoverned world, citizens become caught in an endless labyrinth of political institutions that prevent them from scrutinizing the principles, good or bad, upon which existing laws are founded. Despotism breeds a culture of despotism. A thousand little rooms of unfreedom spring up in each castle of despotism, whose lines of power crisscross and boss every individual subject, even to the point of corrupting his or her language. Subjects become dependent on the every-day whims and designs of political despots and on their appointees and bureaucracies, who treat them as dumb and submissive animals, fit only for herding through a "wilderness of turnpike gates." Paine argued that despotism is a demented form of government (he meant this literally in the case of George III) that makes its subjects wretched. Despotic states tear individuals away from their true selves and from each other; they be-come degraded by a system of political alienation. Despotism turns the world upside down: potential citizens become sycophantic subjects, causes and effects appear reversed, and states and rulers claim to be the real source of property, power, and prestige.

For a long time, Paine had been convinced that despotism was a cor-rupt form of government, but in *Rights of Man* he spelled out its negative consequences. He emphasized how despotic states foster the power of men over women and children within households. Despotic states presup-pose despotic households, in which the arbitrary exercise of power by fa-thers — who, for instance, bequeath property to their firstborn sons — reinforces what Paine called "family tyranny and injustice." Fur-thermore, despotic states produce class divisions within civil society by loading its members with extortionate rates of taxation. The greedy hand of state power, never satisfied, constantly robs society of the fruits of its labors and invents alibis for the never-ending collection of taxes. The point is reached where the propertyless, who have no access to state power, are impoverished and oppressed. The rich become richer, and des-perate, sometimes violent struggles between classes erupt.

Paine also considered that war between states has its roots in despo-tism. His correspondence during the months before lodging at the Angel Inn predicted that the French events would cause panic among the ruling classes of various European despotisms and that they in turn would try to choke the Revolution to death by making war directly on France and its allies. Alarmed by this possible scenario of counterrevolution and war, Paine found himself struck repeatedly by the same questions: Why is war treated as the inevitable lot of human beings? Surely its roots are not traceable to God, who after all loves his creatures. And if war is not caused by the supposedly wicked nature of individuals (Paine disagreed with Thomas Hobbes and others in the English tradition), could it be that war is in fact a product of wicked institutions, such as top-heavy, despotic states?

These questions are today so obvious that their originality is often over-looked. Until the eighteenth century, war had been regarded by those who studied it as a sad necessity. Although there had been a long string of laments for the butchery and destructiveness of war, discourses on the na-ture of war, and even a category of books, such as Homer's *Iliad* and Tac-itus's *Germania,* that may be said to have inspired wars, war was treated as human fate. War was considered as natural as thunder and lightning, an inevitable part of the lottery of human life on earth, a sticky web that the gods had spun to trap men and women into periodically experiencing the dubious joy of victory mixed with fear, pain, and bloody defeat. Dur-ing the eighteenth century, this presumption of the inevitability of war crumbled. A long revolution in the European understanding of war broke out. War began to be studied by writers who distinguished between the causes and the pretexts of war. Its roots in the fabric of social and political life were investigated, and the possibility emerged, or so these writers thought, that war could be avoided, not just postponed to a more oppor-tune time. War came to be regarded as a thoroughly human affair for which there are thoroughly human remedies. Some writers thought more radically still, suggesting that a certain type of political system — a demo-cratic republic — would be less prone to war and that, therefore, a global fight for republican democratic institutions was the best antidote to war.[97]

Rights of Man proved to be the first shocking and most influential ex-ample of this line of thinking. Others before Paine — Jean-Jacques Rousseau and the Abbé de St. Pierre, for example — had hinted at the possible inverse link between republican democracy and war, but it was Paine who examined the connection with a degree of intellectual fire and political insight unknown to his predecessors. He portrayed despotism as an Augean stable of plots and quarrels, secrecy and dissembling. Despo-tism means gunrunning, jostling armies, and puddles of blood. The rea-son was simple: despots caught up in a system of jostling and elbowing states are compelled to prepare for war with their neighbors. They do so by plundering the pockets and lives of their subjects, since that is the most effective way of raising and feeding armies and making their subjects afraid, obedient, and willing to pay taxes. Wars between despotic states thereby tend to increase rulers' lust for power over their populations. War, wrote Paine, is "the art of *conquering at home*."[98]

"The Spring Is Begun"

"When all the land is in ruin," remarked Paine's contemporary Friedrich von Schiller, "we shall have to make peace."[99] Paine agreed. He refused to see this weeping mess of family tyranny, poverty, despotism, and war as inevitable. He understood from his time in America, and perhaps even from first-hand experience as a privateer, that war is among the greatest of all agents of change, that it wipes out banalities, quickens the pace of life, and, above all, strips away illusions and brings realities to the surface. Ever the providentialist, Paine restated his belief that the downfall of despotism was as certain as winter giving way to spring and then to summer, and that the present times resembled budding trees in February. "Though the vegetable sleep will continue longer on some trees and plants than on others, and though some of them may not *blossom* for two or three years," he wrote, "all will be in leaf in the summer, except those which are *rotten*." Paine admitted that, by definition, the future was uncertain. But he insisted that "spring is begun"[100] and that "political summer" was surely on its way.

The remaining question for Paine was whether the approaching republican democratic revolutions in Europe could be made through "reason and accommodation" rather than through the blind "convulsions" that rightly concerned Burke. Pointing to the successful example of the American Revolution, Paine stressed repeatedly the need for peacefully resisting despotic governments. William Cowper, an English contemporary, remarked in his well-known *The Task* (1785) that "war's a game, which, were their subjects wise, Kings would not play at," and Paine certainly agreed. As in *Common Sense,* he offered the seemingly naive suggestion that if and when citizens in sufficient numbers keep their nerve, claim their dignity, and act gracefully under pressure, despotic power loses its authority, its force becoming ineffective, even laughable. "What is there in the world but man?" asked Paine, quickly warning of the necessity "at all times to watch against the attempted encroachment of power, and to prevent its running to excess." The key point was that government is effective and legitimate only when guided by the right of the governed to self-government. Burke's talk of obedience and deference to power was nonsense. The power of states, Paine argued, should be delegated, on trust, only by actively consenting individuals who can legitimately retrieve this power at any time by withdrawing their consent. No group or institution has the right to bind and control how and by whom the world is to be governed. Citizens must never be confounded with their governments, and "man has no property in man." All individuals — male and female, black and white, rich and poor, young and old — are born with equal natural rights.

These "rights of man" are ultimately God-given. They predispose citizens to act freely and live peacefully for their own comfort and happiness, without injuring or trespassing on the natural rights of others. Natural rights can never be relinquished by individuals, not even when it becomes necessary to supplement them with civil rights — such as the right to a fair trial or the right to vote in periodic elections — which serve to make natural rights constitutionally safe and sound, guaranteeing their exercise against collective infringements. For Paine, natural rights provide an Archimedean point, a "fixed and steady principle" for measuring the legitimacy of states. Natural rights, by definition, cannot be annihilated, transferred, or divided, and — here Paine savaged Burke and other monarchists of his day — no generation can deny them to their heirs. Every age and every generation must be free to act for itself. The presumption that it can govern beyond the grave is despotic, a silly relic from the time when kings and queens assumed their immortality by disposing of their crowns and their subjects by will upon their deathbeds. "The idea of hereditary legislators," wrote Paine scathingly, is as "inconsistent as that of hereditary judges, or hereditary juries; and as absurd as an hereditary mathematician, or an hereditary wise man; as absurd as an hereditary poet laureate." The dead and the unborn ought to have no authority, for in politics tradition, at least as Burke understood it, counts for nothing. Only the living can exercise the rights of man.

Such reasoning led Paine to reject the old monarchist doctrine of Charles Stuart and others that the only right the people have is the right to be governed, that all the people have to do with laws is to obey them. He insisted, in language perhaps more defiant than any previous or subsequent English political writer, that governments cannot be understood as a compact between the governors and the governed, as Burke claimed, because rights-bearing, free and equal citizens naturally precede all governments. It follows that governments are legitimate or "civilized" only when they have been formed through the explicit consent of individuals and when this consent is expressed continuously through parliamentary, representative mechanisms that are protected by a written constitution. Civilized governments are constitutional governments, empowered by the active consent of naturally free and equal individuals. These governments have no rights, but only duties before their citizens. Governments ought, therefore, to be creatures of their constitutions, which specify matters such as the duration of parliaments, the frequency of elections, the mode of representation, the powers of the judiciary, the conditions under which war can be declared, and the levying and spending of public funds. Government without a constitution is equivalent to power without right. The British idea of an unwritten constitution is nonsense: "A constitution . . . is to a government, what the laws made afterwards by that government are to a court of judicature," wrote Paine. "The court of judicature does not make laws, neither can it alter them; it only acts in conformity to the laws made: and the government is in like manner governed by the constitution."

Paine did not deal with the objection that the judicial interpreters of constitutions might become powers unto themselves. Instead he emphasized (as he had done in Pennsylvania) that governments cannot legitimately amend or abolish their constitutions, for that would directly violate the trust and consent of their citizens. Citizens are the source of sovereignty, and any challenge to the principle that actively represented consent is the basis of law is despotism — government accountable only to itself.

Paine harbored no illusions about the efficacy of written constitutions. He certainly considered them vital means of controlling state power in matters such as freedom of the press, the powers of the judiciary, and the duration of parliaments. Yet written statements alone do not secure the rights of citizens. That is why citizens need public spaces in which to act freely at a distance from government. *Rights of Man* reiterated the earlier argument of *Common Sense* that the institutional division between civil society and government is fundamental, this time emphasizing two new reasons why free and equal individuals living together on earth "naturally" desire cooperative forms of social life independent of state institutions.

First, individuals' material wants usually exceed their individual powers. This means that they are incapable of satisfying their diverse wants without relying on the help and labors of others. Consequently, as Paine put it, they are driven, "as naturally as gravitation acts to a centre," to establish commercial exchanges guided by the mutual interest of individuals pursuing various trades and pursuits. This commercial interdependence of individuals — Paine thought in terms of a mainly preindustrial economy based on perfect competition among small-scale enterprises and artisans — is reinforced, he argued, by "a system of social affections." Our deep yearning for solidarity with others is a *natural* affection. It is not a *historical* invention. Paradoxically, it is replenished daily by individuals' pursuit of their interests in the market. Paine certainly feared the loss of public spirit due to the uncontrolled growth of commerce and manufacturing. But he did not doubt that suitably regulated market activity, combined with a love for others, would lead individuals to live together harmoniously within a civil society based on the rules of mutual respect, the satisfaction of interest, and the safety, freedom, and equality of individuals.

In the second part of *Rights of Man,* Paine recognized that social life can be corrupted and that this has political effects on citizens. In times past, Paine observed, social life was constantly disfigured by political conquerors armed with brutal weapons, repressive laws, and ideologies of "political superstition." In the present age, social life is stifled by despotic states aiming to divide it, destroy its natural cohesion, and stir up fear and discontent among its subjects. For this reason, Paine described despotic government as a kind of fungus growing out of a corrupt civil society. The metaphor revealed his long-standing doubt that "the people" were immediately, spontaneously ready to govern themselves. Ever since his early days in England, Paine had thought of his own political writings as contributions to the self-education and political enfranchisement of the commoners. That did not mean that he automatically favored universal adult suffrage. Royall Tyler, a Bostonian novelist who visited him in London before the publication of part one of *Rights of Man,* reported that Paine's enthusiasm for *democratic* republicanism was still dampened by doubts about majority rule. Tyler heard Paine insist, before a gathering of friends, that "the minority, in all deliberative bodies, ought, in all cases, to govern the majority." His friends' eyes were riveted on the old revolutionary dressed in a snuff-colored coat, olive velvet vest, drab breeches, coarse hose, buckled shoes, and a bobtailed wig. "You must grant me," Paine continued, "that the proportion of men of sense, to the ignorant among mankind, is at least as twenty, thirty, or even forty-nine, to an hundred. The majority of mankind are consequently most prone to errour; and if we atchieve the right, the minority ought in all cases to govern."[101]

Tyler's anecdote helps explain why *Rights of Man* recommends caution in the overturning of long-standing despotic governments, whose mischief, Paine argues, is more easily begun than ended. The leap toward republican democracy is perilous, for despotism, which divides citizens into rich and poor and accustoms everybody to living in toadyish ways, has a nasty habit of ruling from its grave. The principles of equal natural rights, active consent of the governed, and respect for society must therefore be established sufficiently well within the population before any revolution can successfully establish a republican democracy. That in turn implies that governments have an important "civilizing" function during the transition from despotism to civilized society. If (parts of) civil society have been disfigured by despotic states, then governments aiming to protect the collective interests of civil society have a charter to "explode ignorance and preclude imposition." The transition to republican democracy — Paine spoke from his experiences in Lewes — requires in particular the building up of welfare institutions catering to the social rights of citizens. The elderly, the widowed, women, newly married couples, the poor and the unemployed, disbanded soldiers, and children, who would be required to attend school, must all be provided with state transfer payments. These would be paid for through general taxation and considered "not of the nature of a charity, but of a right."

Paine's welfare proposals were among the boldest versions of the developing eighteenth-century concern with "policing."[102] Like his contemporaries, Paine failed to consider whether a transitional welfare state would in practice contradict the ultimate aim of limiting the power of government in favor of a self-governing civil society. He thought, ultimately, that the sovereign nation state could become nothing more than the elected manager and guarantor of the "universal peace, civilization and commerce"[103] of civil society. In contrast to labyrinthine, spendthrift, secretive, and bellicose despotic states, republican democratic governments would be simple and efficient, cheap, open, and peaceful. These governments' obligations to society would be well-defined, and society itself would be protected from the state through constitutionally guaranteed mechanisms of representation. Citizens would understand clearly the workings of their state. Nothing would be hidden from the eyes of civil society. The constitutionally limited state would be as visible as it would be accessible to its citizens. Its operations, as a consequence, would have widespread support. This "national association acting on the principles of society" would be needed only to supply to citizens the public services that civil society could not conveniently supply for itself. Paine was convinced that once citizens' desire for social life is aroused, despotic states will quickly crumble into ruins. Here was Paine's new "law": the more civil society develops confidence in its capacity for self-government, the less need there is for state institutions and laws. "The instant formal government is abolished," Paine wrote, "society begins to act. A general association takes place, and common interest produces common security."

"Common security" meant for Paine not just tranquillity within any single nation-state but also peace among all nation-states and their citizens. He argued that the best antidote to war is the formation of an international confederation of nationally independent and peacefully interacting civil societies that keeps an eye on the international system of nation-states, taming their bellicose urges. Paine was certain that democratic republican states, guided by civil societies held together by reciprocal interests and mutual affection, would make for a new global order freed from the curse of war. War, the keystone of despotism, would collapse, for the simple reason that citizens living in democratic republics would have no reason to go to war. Paine explained that when the rulers of a state act as if they own the state and its subjects, it is the simplest thing in the world to declare war on other states. By contrast, when citizens themselves have to decide whether war is to be declared, and then have to pay for it personally with their money and their lives, it is only natural — given their cosmopolitanism, their natural cooperativeness and sociability — that they will think twice and recoil from war, opting instead for the "cordial unison" of civilized societies and representative government.

Public Commotions

Paine finished the first part of *Rights of Man* on his fifty-fourth birthday, January 29, 1791. Released from weeks of hard writing, he celebrated in a downstairs lounge room of the Angel Inn, with several bottles of wine, followed by brandy, with his closest London friend, Clio Rickman, the well-known publisher. Around midnight, Paine clambered upstairs, collapsed into bed, and slept until noon. Shortly after waking, he took up his quill for the last time on the manuscript, sketching a dedication to his friend George Washington. Paine had cultivated the art of writing satirical dedications, but this one to Washington was deliberately reverent in tone:

SIR,

I present you a small treatise in defense of those principles of freedom which your exemplary virtue hath so eminently contributed to establish. That the Rights of Man may become as universal as your benevolence can wish, and that you may enjoy the happiness of seeing the New World regenerate the Old, is the prayer of

Sir,
Your much obliged, and
Obedient humble servant,
THOMAS PAINE

The next day, Paine passed the manuscript to the well-known London publisher Joseph Johnson, who set about printing it in time for the opening of Parliament and Washington's birthday on February 22. As the unbound copies piled up in the printing shop, Johnson was visited repeatedly by government agents. Although Johnson had already published replies to Burke's *Reflections* by Thomas Christie, Mary Wollstonecraft, and Capel Lofft, he sensed, correctly, that Paine's manuscript would attract far more attention and bitter controversy than all of them combined. Fearing the book police, and unnerved by the prospect of arrest and bankruptcy, Johnson suppressed the book on the very day of its scheduled publication.

Alarmed by the prospect that the work would be stillborn, Paine reacted fast. He agreed to a deal with another publisher, J. S. Jordan on Fleet Street, and with the help of friends and a horse and cart delivered to him Johnson's printed, unbound sheets. Paine scurried around for money to pay for the work. He managed to borrow forty pounds from George Lewis Scott, an old friend from the Excise days.[104] He then packed his trunk for Paris, where he planned to arrange a French translation, and entrusted final arrangements with the London publisher to three good friends, William Godwin, Thomas Brand Hollis, and Thomas Holcroft. Prior to leaving, Paine passed on several bound copies of the original Johnson edition into private hands, but only a few of these have survived. The British Museum has a copy on its shelves, bound in burgundy leather and wedged ignominiously among an assortment of pamphlets by various authors, including Burke's *Reflections on the Revolution in France*. Two centuries later, it is hard to imagine the public fuss whipped up by Jordan's three-shilling edition of this small book, which appeared on March 13, 1791, three weeks later than Paine had originally planned.

For the first time in his writing career, Paine had the pleasure of watching one of his own publications become an instant international bestseller. "Pain's wild rebellious burst proclaims her rights aloud," wrote his contemporary William Wordsworth, in punning allusion to the book's international impact.[105] He was not exercising poetic license. Translations of both parts of *Rights of Man* quickly appeared in France, Holland, and the German lands. Georg Forster, the sharpest German voice protesting the French ancien régime, criticized those who dismissed the Revolution as a mere passing spectacle ("eine Freiheitskomödie"), praised *Rights of Man* as a "wonderful work," and reported that both Burke's and Paine's masterpieces locally had "thousands of readers."[106] The work was also warmly received as *Excerpta ex T.P.* in Hungarian Transylvania, thanks to the local support of Jacobinist radicals and the efforts of the translator, Janos Körmöczi, future professor of mathematics and physics at the Unitarian College in Kolozsvár.[107]

The biggest commotion caused by *Rights of Man* was in Britain, just as Paine had intended. Although many of its key points had already been argued in earlier American writings, its impact in Britain was sensational. The book's defense of the French Revolution and its attempt to beard the British lion in its den sparked the fieriest public row about political principles since the 1640s. *Rights of Man* refuted the old myth that the English were incapable of writing or reading political philosophy. It proved to be one of those rare books of great political insight that outlive their time and place of birth. In Britain, *Rights of Man* made Paine the most controversial public figure of the day. It also brought him suffering. The official response was icy and unbending. For the first time in his life, Paine began to be shadowed constantly by propaganda, gossip, and government agents. He also tasted fear, punishing silence, and the outlawing of freedom of speech. "Truth . . . is always ultimately victorious," Paine wrote, but the bitter fact was that telling it helped to damage his political career.

Many readers were shocked by his rumbustious vulgarity. Charles Harrington Elliot denounced Paine as the flotsam of an age "productive of aspiring, half-bred caitiffs." Sir Brooke Boothby said that Paine "writes in defiance of grammar, as if syntax were an aristocratical invention." Boothby concluded that Paine had "the natural eloquence of a night-cellar" and that he found Paine's book "written in a kind of specious jargon, well enough calculated to impose upon the vulgar."[108]

Vulgar (from *vulgus*, meaning "common people") it certainly was. The very title — *Rights of Man* — recalled a well-known poem in praise of an unknown tenant farmer and ex-miner who had been ill-treated by his landlords. The commoner, nicknamed Jack the Blaster, had protested a decade earlier by digging a cave for himself and living rough by the seaside at Marsden Bay in northeast England. The protest quickly attracted great public attention. Visitors flocked to the cave. Among them was Thomas Spence, Paine's subsequent acquaintance, who was so moved by Jack the Blaster's resistance that he wrote the following lines in chalk above his host's fireplace:

> *Ye landlords vile, whose man's peace mar,*
> *Come levy rents here if you can;*
> *Your stewards and lawyers I defy,*
> *And live with all the RIGHTS OF MAN.*[109]

Paine saw himself as defending, in plain prose, Jack the Blasters everywhere, and it was therefore not surprising that *Rights of Man* triggered strong protests against the "vulgarity" of the author. The gentleman-author Isaac Hunt expressed alarm at Paine's "coarse and rustic" style, fearing that the language of "the Transatlantic Republican" might "seduce his illiterate and unskilled" readers, who "may be easily duped to think seditiously, and of course to act rebelliously according to his wishes."[110] *The Monthly Review,* though mainly friendly toward Paine's politics, complained about his "desultory, uncouth, and inelegant" style. "His wit is coarse, and sometimes disgraced by wretched puns; and his language, though energetic, is awkward, ungrammatical, and often debased by vulgar phraseology."[111] Samuel Romilly reported to M. Dumond that Paine's book "is written in his own wild but forcible style; inaccurate in point of grammar, flat where he attempts wit, and often ridiculous when he indulges himself in metaphors."[112] Horace Walpole remarked, astutely, that Paine's style "is so coarse, that you would think he means to degrade the language as much as the government."[113]

Walpole understandably expressed alarm when "vast numbers of Paine's pamphlet were distributed both to regiments and ships" on the second anniversary of the fall of the Bastille.[114] No book had ever sold like it. Jordan published a new edition three days after his first. It sold out within several hours. On March 30, a third edition appeared, followed by a fourth edition on April 14, then a fifth and a sixth during the month of May, by which time 50,000 copies had been sold. The figures were breathtaking by contemporary standards. Sir Walter Scott, the most popular novelist a generation after Paine, sold 10,000 copies of *Rob Roy* in a fortnight, but this figure was only marginally higher than sales of popular successes a generation before Paine. At the time of publication of *Rights of Man,* the average size of an edition was about 1,250 for a novel, 750 for more general works.[115] *Rights of Man* broke every extant publishing record. Sales were unaffected by the high price of three shillings. If anything, the price appeared to upend the law of supply and demand by accelerating sales. Paine himself estimated that in Britain the sales of the complete edition of *Rights of Man* reached "between four and five hundred thousand" copies within ten years of publication, making it the most widely read book of all time, in any language.[116]

At the time, there were around ten million people living on mainland Britain, of whom perhaps a maximum of four million were able to read. Based on those figures, one reader in ten purchased a copy of *Rights of Man.* Even that figure is misleadingly low if pirated and serialized editions are taken into account and if it is considered that in a society with a wretched standard of living, books were for most readers still occasional

luxuries. Paine's book no doubt was circulated and talked about among
the literate public, and it is highly probable that every single one of them
had at least heard of it. More astonishing was the fact that *Rights of Man*
was read aloud and talked about to the illiterate on an unheard-of scale.
Not only did the book touch virtually the whole of the reading public; it
also helped transform the meaning of the public by broadening and deepening its existing boundaries.

Paine's supporters were rhapsodic. The vast sales proved to them that
even though more than seventy books and pamphlets were eventually
written in reply to Burke's *Reflections,* many of them addressed to exactly
the same audience as Paine's, it was Paine who had dealt by far the biggest
wallop to the European political establishment. "Tammy Paine the buik
has penned," wrote the Scottish weaver and poet Alexander Wilson, "And
lent the courts a lounder."[117] Thomas Holcroft, who had helped the book
through Jordan's press, excitedly wrote to William Godwin as soon as he
set hands on a copy, reassuring him that it had not been censored in any
way: "I have got it. Verbatim except the addition of a short preface, which
as you have not seen, I send you my copy — Not a single castration (Laud
be unto God and J. S. Jordan!) can I discover — Hey for the New
Jerusalem! The millennium! And peace and eternal beatitude be unto the
soul of Thomas Paine."[118]

A measure of the radical success of the book was the heated discussion
it provoked at a meeting of the respectable Society for Constitutional Information in London. On March 23, after much disputation, it voted its
thanks to Paine "for his most masterly book." Wild cheers erupted, and an
old song with new lyrics — "God save the RIGHTS OF MAN! Let Despots, if
they can, Them overthrow" — was sung defiantly by certain members.[119]
But the controversy among the Whiggish membership cut deeply. Some
found Paine's style offensive. Horne Tooke, under pressure from Paine's
critics, confessed that *Rights of Man* contained morally dubious passages
but explained that, after all, there were passages in the Bible "which a
man would not choose to read before his wife and daughters."[120] Others
spotted a political contradiction in the Society's endorsement of Paine.
"There was certainly an apparent inconsistency," Batley remarked, "in
recommending a book which affirms we have no constitution, by a society
instituted, as I conceive, for the preservation of one."[121]

The political authorities in Britain spotted the same difficulty. But although the book made them nervous, they held back for the time being.
At the end of April, the *Gazetteer and London Daily Advertiser* reported that
there had been "a consultation of the law officers to determine whether

the author could be prosecuted" but that the "intention of doing so, whether in their power or not, has since been entirely dropped."[122] Why the government of George III desisted from legal action is a matter of opinion. Its restraint has been traced to the fact that Paine had tempered his arguments so skillfully that it would have been difficult for the state to make a charge of sedition stick in the courts.[123] That explanation ignores the point that prosecution would have been easy to fix by means of a handpicked special jury hostile to Paine's radicalism. The likely reasons for leaving Paine untouched lie elsewhere. The government probably counted on a measure of self-censorship on the part of Paine's supporters and Paineite booksellers, apparently with some initial success. "I have got it," reported Thomas Holcroft. "But mum — we don't sell it — Oh, no — Ears and eggs."[124]

The authorities also were convinced that the high price of three shillings charged by Jordan — the same price charged by Burke's publisher for *Reflections* — would restrict the readership of Paine's vulgar tract to the comfortably living, prudent class who read Burke. "Reprehensible as that book was (extremely so, in my opinion)," the Attorney General later recalled, "yet it was ushered into the world under circumstances that led me to believe that it could be confined to the judicious readers."[125] Any attempt to prosecute the author and ban the book might for this reason have backfired: to prosecute would almost certainly have provided free publicity for the book, expanding the potential market and increasing the probability that cheaper editions would be printed for the lower classes, who would likely handle the book carelessly. Better to leave sleeping donkeys doze — and much better still not to provoke their ignorant, loudmouthed master into action.

Then, finally, was the important fact that for more than reasons of personal friendship, Paine had dedicated *Rights of Man* to the president of the United States. Paine calculated, shrewdly, that embarrassment would surround any attempt by British authorities to arrest Paine for sedition, since the government of George III now considered Anglo-American cooperation a priority. Washington, who was working hard to smooth British feathers in the hope of securing a commercial treaty between the two countries, seems to have been annoyed by Paine's cunning attempt to divide and rule politicians. Indeed, Paine's attempt to use Washington to protect himself from George III so soured relations with the president that nearly a year passed before he responded to Paine's dedication and gift of fifty copies of *Rights of Man*. The gift had been sent to the president shortly after publication, along with an enthusiastic letter in which Paine reiterated his belief that in Europe "the ardour of Seventy-six is capable of renewing itself."[126] Washington's precise reaction to such talk went unrecorded, but it is clear from Washington's eventual reply that frost had settled on the president's feelings for Paine:

> The duties of my office, which at all times, especially during the Session of Congress, require an unremitting attention, naturally become more pressing towards the close of it; and as that body have resolved to rise to-morrow, and as I have determined, in case they should, to set out for Mount Vernon on the next day, you will readily conclude that the present is a busy moment with me; and to that I am persuaded your goodness will impute my not entering into the several points touched upon in your letter. Let it suffice, therefore, at this time, to say, that I rejoice in the information of your personal prosperity, and, as no one can feel a greater interest in the happiness of mankind than I do, that it is the first wish of my heart, that the enlightened policy of the present age may diffuse to all men those blessings, to which they are entitled, and lay the foundation of happiness for future generations. With great esteem etc.[127]

Fingers of Death

Shielded for the moment from prosecution by the hesitations of the British government, and aware that "the high price precluded the generality of people from purchasing,"[128] Paine moved to authorize cheap editions of *Rights of Man*. Within weeks of Jordan's first edition, requests to print popular editions poured in from all over Britain — from Sheffield, Rotherham, Chester, Leicester, several towns in Scotland — while James Mackintosh, author of *Vindiciae Gallicae: Defence of the French Revolution and Its English Admirers* (1792) tendered a request from a Warwickshire publisher to print ten thousand copies. Paine consented to every request, waiving royalties without exception. But the extraordinary response from publishers around the country served to convince him that there was room for a bigger publishing venture with potentially huge political dividends. Around April 1, 1791, he decided "to print a very numerous edition in London, under my own direction, by which means the work would be more perfect, and the price be reduced lower than it could be by *printing* small editions in the country, of only a few thousands each."[129]

The decision to step up the attack on the British monarchy was driven by Paine's hunch that the European political tide was running in his favor.

He scampered across the Channel to Paris in mid-April, spending a fort-night there in lodgings with a Mr. Hodges, an American acquaintance from previous visits.[130] He called on Gouverneur Morris daily and visited French friends and other American acquaintances. Most who recorded their encounters were appalled by his habit of angling conversations in directions where he hoped to shine. Such conceit revealed something of his lingering insecurity, but many found it abominable. Etiènne Dumont wrote: "I could easily excuse, in an American, his prejudices against England. But his egregious conceit and presumptuous self-sufficiency quite disgusted me. He was drunk with vanity. If you believed him, it was he who had done everything in America. He was an absolute caricature of the vainest of Frenchmen." The rest of Dumont's story may be apoc-ryphal or simply descriptive of Paine's scurrilous efforts to unsettle the minds of friends and foes alike. "He fancied that his book upon the rights of man ought to be substituted for every other book in the world," said Dumont. "And he told us as roundly that, if it were in his power to annihi-late every library in existence, he would do so without hesitation in order to eradicate the errors they contained, and commence with *Rights of Man* a new era of ideas and principles. He knew all his own writings by heart, but he knew nothing else."[131] Others were less charitable still toward the American rodomontade. Hodges, his roommate, forced to endure Paine's bad household manners, spoke of Paine behind his back, to Gouverneur Morris, "as being a little mad." Morris himself thought that that was "not improbable," and although the two renewed their uneasy friendship daily, there was a noticeable rise in the level of veiled mutual animosity, espe-cially after Morris told Paine that he had found as many "good things" in Burke's *Reflections* as in Paine's *Rights of Man*.[132]

Paine meanwhile followed closely the gathering momentum of the French Revolution. In Versailles, where he lodged during May and the first half of June, he began to sketch a plan of a sequel to *Rights of Man*.[133] It was to be another literary assault on European despotism with the working title *Kingship*. Spring had come early that year, and the days were so pleasantly warm and sprinkled with whiffs of cherry and lilac blossoms that the contrasting turmoil on the streets of Paris felt somehow ominous. Paine grasped that this spring of 1791 was unlike any previous European spring. He surmised that the French Revolution was a turning point in the region's history and that events in France and elsewhere were now rushing headlong into an unknown future. What he did not yet grasp was that his-tory had earmarked the Revolution as a weird laboratory producing, for the first time ever, a strange compound of contradictory trends — both good and evil — that would later make their mark on the politics of all modern countries.

Paine was sure that the French Revolution would be a rerun of the American Revolution. He was besotted with the accelerating collapse of the ancien régime and convinced (as he had told Washington) of the spread to France of "the ardour of Seventy-six." The conviction enabled Paine to spot one — but only one — face of modern revolutions. He saw that revolutions are always transformative experiences, adventures of the heart and soul. Triggered by revolts from below and serious disagreements at the summits of power, revolutions are explosive dramas that bring fundamental changes in state structures, property relations, and the cultural patterns of daily life. Paine saw that citizens initially feel strengthened by revolutions and find that their old feelings of inner emptiness temporarily disappear. Astonished, they discover boundless energy within themselves and experience joy in their determination to act to change the world. During the earliest phases of a revolution, there is consequently much talk of freedom, democracy, and the rights and powers of the people. Struggles for political democracy, civil liberties, social and economic equality, and personal rights thrive. Participation in the daily events of the revolution becomes for many citizens a giddy exploration of unknown territory.

Considering his earlier American warnings, Paine was unusually slow to see the unintended dark side of the French Revolution. Ever since that revolution, it has become clear that during the course of revolutions, the forces of change usually fragment. The people are split by heated disputes about principles and strategies. Name-calling begins, and talk of betrayal and acts of vengeance proliferate. The turbulent thrill experienced at the outbreak of revolutions withers. Civility evaporates. Disappointment, accusation, and frustration feed power struggles among various political factions, and minority groups of professional revolutionaries possessed of great initiative, organizational talent, and carefully elaborated ideologies make their appearance. Radicals accuse moderates of betrayal and claim to represent their citizens' interests best. But these same citizens are soon supplanted, often through a reign of violence and terror carried out in the name of defending the spirit of the revolution. Violence begets violence. Revolutions suck the blood from their own children, until societies reach the limits of their endurance. Grumbling and unrest spreads, and the air is filled with rumors of plots and coups d'état, until dictators, inheriting the ruins, seize the chance of governing over the maelstrom of confusion, decadence, and demoralization.

Paine first saw this ugly face of modern revolutions during his brief stay in Paris in the summer of 1791. Shortly after dawn on June 21, his friend Lafayette burst into his room in Versailles before he was out of bed, shouting excitedly in broken English, "The birds are flown! The birds are flown!" Paine propped himself up on one elbow. "Tis well," he replied gingerly," I hope there will be no attempt to recall them."[134] Dressing quickly, Paine clambered downstairs and into the street to find crowds gathering to protest the escape into hiding of King Louis XVI and his family. There Paine met Thomas Christie, a young businessman temporarily living in Paris, and later that morning, joined by a mutual friend, they strolled about the city, mingling among the crowds. Insurrection was in the air. "You see the absurdity of monarchical governments," Paine remarked. "Here will be a whole nation disturbed by the folly of one man."[135]

The trio walked on to the Tuileries, where clumps of curious citizens were lining up, peacefully, to inspect the nooks and crannies of the royal apartments, occupied until a few hours ago by the king and queen. Nearby, Paine and his friends came across a group of several hundred citizens gathered to hear a public reading of a proclamation from the National Assembly, which sought to reassure the nation that nothing, not even the escape of the king and queen, would be allowed to stand in the way of the proposed new constitution for France.

The crowd listened intently, hushed, their heads bared respectfully, their hands grasping hats decorated with the tricolor cockade. When the public reading ended, Christie reported, "in an instant all hats were on," with one exception. Rudely awakened that morning, Paine had clambered excitedly downstairs, leaving behind his cockaded hat. Trouble erupted instantly. Paine was called a royalist by an angry figure in the crowd. One section of the crowd immediately swirled around his feet. It pounced on him, tore at his clothes, punched and kicked him. Someone then shouted, "Aristocrat! A la lanterne!" Others joined in, chanting, "Aristocrat! A la lanterne! Aristocrat! A la lanterne!" Three burly men began to haul Paine toward the nearest lamppost in preparation for his hanging.[136]

Whether at that moment Paine froze with fear, just as he had in Thetford whenever he set eyes on the cadaverous faces of men about to be hanged, is unrecorded. We know only that on this midsummer afternoon near the Tuileries, he was lucky indeed. As if by a miracle, Paine was rescued with the help of Christie, who spoke good French, and an unidentified figure who stepped out of the heart of the crowd. He may have been a government agent, as was the custom, displaying the symbols of his office, all the while attempting to soothe the crowd, pleading with them to see reason and to observe due process, to release the accused, and to hold a proper trial.

Paine's miraculous release was due in no small measure to his defenders' eloquent pleas to acquit "un Américain." Accused locals were often less lucky. Pleas frequently ricocheted, causing the crowd to puff up with anger and push aside the pleader, forcing him back into the crowd, trembling and pale with fear. The crowd, shouting that the accused must be *lanterné,* promptly dragged him or her to the nearest lamppost. A rope was laced over its top bracket and its looped end placed over the head of the accused, who then gasped, spluttered, and grunted into a motionless, blowsy dangle. The head was then severed from the body with a scythe or butcher's knife, and the body was eviscerated. Pikes were tipped with the head, the heart, and various other bloody organs, and a procession through the streets set off, the roped corpse dragging behind it. The procession, a carnival of taunts and laughter, threats and gallows humor, toured the major public places of the city of Paris, as well as sites of special significance to the victim. Onlookers shouted insults at the victim or turned away, fainting or vomiting in alleyways. The procession normally ended with various bits and pieces of the corpse placed on semipermanent display on walls, windowsills, and gates, in full view of passersby.

Thanks to his "American" nationality and smooth-tongued defenders, Paine escaped this grim choreography with minor bruises and scratches, apparently uncomprehending of the nature and extent of such violent street theater (*scènes de horreur*). The French Revolution unleashed several new forms of revolutionary violence onto French society; the violence of crowds during this period was among the first of them. The strange thing is that Paine discounted stories of large-scale, uncontrolled, or planned bloodletting. He took offense at Burke's talk of "bands of cruel ruffians and assassins, reeking with blood," who displayed "all the unutterable abominations of the furies of hell."[137] He preferred instead to see the violence of this period as sporadic and likely soon to peter out. By seeing things in this way, Paine not only understated the premeditated patterns of violence at this stage of the Revolution. He also misidentified the social origins of its perpetrators. He repeated the widely shared prejudice — born in the Great Fear precipitated by the peasant insurrections during 1789 — that the violence was traceable to the wandering mobs (*les gens sans aveu*) comprising petty criminals, vagabonds, the unemployed, and idle good-for-nothings, all of whom supposedly went on the rampage for loot. Although it is true that the revolutionary crowds were mainly composed of red-capped, striped-trousered *sans culottes*, the perpetrators of violence were in fact drawn from the most stable, law-abiding sectors of French society — craftsmen, petty traders, journeymen, workshop masters, and shopkeepers — all of whom protested the need for cheap and plentiful food in the face of exorbitant prices and worsening shortages, and who consequently directed their anger, fear, and sense of uprootedness *at* the vagabondish mob.[138]

Paine seemed blind to these complications, to the point where his account of the early stages of the Revolution borders on fanciful apologetics. It was as if he wanted the Revolution against monarchy to succeed at all costs and believed that whatever those costs, providence would excuse them, with a smile. Shortly after the fingers of death had clawed at his bruised body, he wrote to Marquis de Condorcet and his associates, virtually explaining away what had just happened. "During the early period of a revolution," he commented, "mistakes are likely enough to be committed — mistakes in principle or in practise; or perhaps, mistakes both in principle and practise." He went on to attribute the violence to insufficient enlightenment, which the passage of events would remedy. Ignorance induced by monarchy was the source of the so-called mistakes. "When men are in the early stage of freedom," he observed, "they are not all sufficiently instructed to be able to inform one another mutually of their several opinions, and so they become the victims of a sort of timidity that hinders them from reaching at a single bound that elevation which they have the *right* to attain." Paine concluded on his usual note of providentialism: "We have witnessed symptoms of this imperfection at the beginning of the present Revolution. Fortunately, they were manifested before the Constitution was fully established, so that whatever defects were apparent could be corrected."

In the same letter, Paine waxed eloquent about the future course of the Revolution and affirmed support for its republican trends. He described himself as a "citizen of a land that recognizes no majesty but that of the people, no government except that of its own representatives, and no sovereignty except that of the laws." He again denounced monarchy — "*the despotic rule of one individual*, though that individual be a madman, a tyrant, or a hypocrite" — as a blight upon humanity. And he reiterated his political cosmopolitanism by criticizing the pseudorepublican aristocracies of Holland, Berne, Genoa, and Venice and by denouncing despotism in "Spain, Russia, Germany, Turkey and the whole of Asia." He concluded, "That I may live to see the freedom of these lands is my ardent desire."[139]

Le Républicain

Constantly searching for routes across political frontiers, and convinced more than ever that the European struggle for republican government depended on the success of the French Revolution, Paine offered his services to Condorcet and his circle. He guessed, correctly, that the Revolution, driven increasingly by popular protest, was beginning to take a republican turn. During 1789, virtually all respectable authorities, writers, and politicians wanted to retain the monarchy; the number of deputies who were not monarchists, for example, could have been counted on one hand. There were only marginal gains for republicans the following year. Certain clubs, societies, and papers sharing antimonarchical opinions had sprung up. Republican sentiments were evident in publications such as Camille Desmoulins's *Revolutions de France et de Brabant* and Jean-Paul Marat's *l'Ami du peuple* and prominent in the *Bouche de Fer*, a journal edited by Nicolas de Bonneville, a prominent publicist and acquaintance of Paine's. The spirit of republicanism also was associated with public figures such as Abbé Claude Fauchet, whose lectures in the *grand cirque* of the Palais-Royal sometimes attracted audiences of four thousand or five thousand Parisians, riveted to rhetorical speeches delivered with a Calvinistic fervor. Such efforts at popularizing republicanism were supplemented by the propagandist work of the so-called Popular and Fraternal Societies formed during the winter of 1790–91, many of them under the patronage of Marat.

All these initiatives were suddenly leavened by the king's flight to Varennes. The unprecedented public protests opened the mouth of republicanism, and the words it uttered suddenly ceased to sound fantastic. Popular revulsion against the king mushroomed overnight. A huge poster reading *"Maison à louer"* (House to Let) was slapped by protesters onto the gates of the Tuileries palace. Angry crowds roamed the streets of Paris smashing shop windows and inn signs bearing the fleur-de-lis or the king's name.

The upsurge in antimonarchism produced new dangers. There was now a distinct possibility that the escape of the king would encourage France's enemies to take advantage of the power vacuum and plot to crush the Revolution through war. Widespread rumors that the escape had been engineered by an Austrian committee presided over by the queen seemed to make that a real possibility. To demand the king's forfeiture of the crown (*déchéance*) on the ground of insanity — the only condition hitherto provided in the constitution — seemed to many to be a recipe for actually encouraging foreign intervention. And yet — here was the nub — the king had absconded, and popular feeling now demanded that he be deposed, a course of action that would instantly throw the constitution into the melting pot. "If the king escapes," Gouverneur Morris told Paine, "it means war; if not, a republic."[140] The only remaining alternative, it seemed, was to make the king a prisoner on the throne, provisionally suspending him from his royal functions. But that would amount to an experiment with kingless government, which was, to say the least, a treacherous path into unknown political territory.

Paine strode into this conundrum with giant steps, republican sword swinging. During the last week of June, he joined with four friends to found the Société des republicains, whose stated purpose was "to enlighten minds about republicanism." Each of the French participants spoke good English, all were republicans, and, within two years, all would be dead, either by the guillotine or their own hands. Jacques Pierre Brissot de Warville was a thirty-seven-year-old journalist and member of the Assembly; Etiènne Chavière was fifty-four years old and shortly to become Minister of Finance; Achille François du Châtelet was a thirty-two-year-old idealistic aristocrat who agreed to act, for the time being, as Paine's translator; and Marquis de Condorcet was a forty-eight-year-old aristocrat and member of the Assembly. The five knew that they had to act swiftly to take advantage of the crisis, and that they did. Paine explained, "This society opposed the restoration of Louis, not so much on account of his personal offenses, as in order to overthrow the monarchy, and to erect on its ruins the republican system and an equal representation."[141]

The club started a journal, *Le Républicain*, edited by Condorcet and assisted by two of Paine's friends, Nicolas de Bonneville, a journalist and printer, and François Xavier Lanthenas, who would later act as French translator of nearly all of Paine's writings. The journal lasted four issues and included among its pages a reprinted version of Paine's earlier letter to Condorcet and his associates expressing interest in founding a republican society. Paine meanwhile worked feverishly on a republican manifesto, addressed to his French "brethren and fellow-citizens." He completed it in one day and had it translated by Châtelet and printed by Bonneville the next.

In the early hours of July 1, he and Châtelet wandered through the streets of Paris — brush and glue, hammer and nails in hand — plastering the broadsheet onto selected street walls, ending their mission by nailing several copies to the massive wooden doors of the hall (*manège*) where the National Assembly was to meet later that morning. Paine was strident:

"An office which is the reward of birth, and which may consequently devolve on a madman, an imbecile or a tyrant, is, in the very nature of things, an absurdity." He argued that the flight of the king was tantamount to abdication and that the nation should no longer trust him. Paine's earlier praise for the king as leader of the Revolution had vanished. For the first time, the king was described irreverently as "simply Louis Capet" and accused of incompetence. "The facts show," the poster read, "that, if he is not a hypocrite or traitor, he must be a madman or an imbecile, and, in any case, entirely unfitted to discharge the function confided to him by the people." Paine reminded his readers that the greatness of a nation was measured not by the pomp and power of its king but by "the people's sense of its own dignity." He added that Louis Capet need not fear for his safety, for France would not spoil her glorious achievement by taking revenge on "a miserable creature who is conscious of his own dishonour." The issue was clear: "France, which has now attained the age of reason, should no longer be deceived by mere words, and should also reflect . . . on the peril to which the government of a king subjects a people, even when he happens to be in himself a very paltry and despicable individual."[142]

The manifesto stirred up debate in the Assembly, yet it won few supporters among the deputies, the great majority of whom were by policy, if not conviction, on the side of monarchical government. A deputy who had angrily ripped down the poster from the Assembly door denounced Châtelet and Paine for publishing seditious statements. Emmanuel-Joseph Sieyès, the spokesman for constitutional monarchy, launched a controversy with Paine in the pages of the *Gazette Nationale, ou Le Moniteur Universel*.[143] Couched in flattering language, Sieyès insisted that republicanism had no monopoly of the principle of public-spirited representative government, that France had adopted an "elective monarchy," and that radical talk of republicanism was therefore redundant. It was not sentiment or habit that kept him a monarchist, he explained, but the conviction that "there is more liberty for the individual citizen under a monarchy than under a republic."[144] Such sentiments were ever more out of touch with opinion on the streets, and nearly all newspapers and pamphlets denounced Louis's conduct, demanding his replacement by some other form of executive power. Few ventured to use the word *république*, but after the king's return on June 26, awareness grew that there was now a constitutional crisis and that a dangerous breach had opened up between public opinion and the constitutional prejudices of the government.

The tide of events was beginning to flow fast in Paine's favor. He kept up the pressure, explaining to Sieyès in the pages of *Le Moniteur* why "against the *whole hell of monarchy* . . . I have declared war." He played up his disgust for "the calamities, the exactions, the wars, and the massacres" caused by the institution of monarchy, adding that he had no personal hatred for the world's monarchs and that indeed he lived for the day when they would all enjoy "the happy and honourable state of plain individuals."[145] At a dinner for Americans in Paris hosted by William Short to celebrate Independence Day, Gouverneur Morris reported Paine to be "inflated to the eyes and big with a litter of revolutions."[146] Four days later, convinced that the American Revolution was taking root in France, Paine returned to London, charged with hopes that the Revolution would spread to England and other regions of Britain, and perhaps even to Ireland.

Twisting John Bull's Ears

The London political scene was at the boil. Enormous excitement surrounded Paine's return. He was no longer the casually known author of *Common Sense* but a riveting public figure flanked by controversy. London newspapers buzzed with gossip about his doings. "Paine is writing a new pamphlet to be entitled *Kingship* and its object is to demonstrate the inutility of kings," reported *The Oracle* on July 8, 1791. "It is to appear in November, in French, German, Spanish, Italian, and English at the same time, as persons are translating it into the four first languages as he advances in writing it. Such is the rage for disseminating democratic principles!" The Polish envoy in London, Franciszek Bukaty, reported that Paine's name was widely linked with preparations for the forthcoming English celebrations of Bastille Day and that riots were expected.[147] Paine meanwhile reported in a letter to George Washington that in England and Ireland, *Rights of Man* was selling wildly, like no other book ever published on the subject of government. He vowed, with a touch of his usual conceit, not to let it go to his head and to remain true to the Revolutionary spirit of 1776. "The same fate follows me here as I *at first* experienced in America, strong friends and violent enemies," he said. "But as I have got the ear of the country, I shall go on, and at least show them, what is a novelty here, that there can be a person beyond the reach of corruption."[148]

For a growing number of opponents, Paine was in fact corruption personified. Several days after arriving in London, news reached him of serious public disturbances in Birmingham. When friends of Paine's and French Revolution supporters arranged to hold a dinner there on July 14 to celebrate the storming of the Bastille, royalist mobs attacked the homes of prominent republican democrats, including Joseph Priestley, whose scientific equipment, library, and personal papers were destroyed. Rioting lasted two days, until the dragoons restored order. The events signaled the spread of controversies about *Rights of Man* beyond the metropolis. Paine responded by announcing his intention to arrange the printing of a cheap popular edition "just sufficient to bring in the price of the printing and paper, as I did by *Common Sense.*"[149]

The government of George III tried to limit the potential damage by commissioning a hostile biography written by "Francis Oldys." It extended to Paine the honor of being the first major publicist in modern times to be savaged by a government muckraking campaign waged publicly through the press. The biography sold well — the first edition was reprinted five times within several months — and it probably hardened the views of Paine's English and American enemies. Beyond those circles, it is impossible to know with any certainty whether and to what extent the diatribe against Paine was effective, although much of the dirt that stuck to him subsequently — the stories about the truant staymaker, neglectful husband, lapsed Christian and atheist, failed shopkeeper, and dishonest exciseman — are traceable to Oldys's scribblings.

The author was in fact a Scotsman named George Chalmers, a trained lawyer and London-based writer who was sickened by Paine's democratic republicanism. Chalmers was deeply loyal to the Crown. He had returned from a sojourn in the American colonies a bitter enemy of all politicians sympathetic to the American cause. He had publicly attacked Burke in 1777, and he had repeated his criticisms five years later in *The Deformities of Fox and Burke.* Chalmers had a job with the Board of Trade, and although Paine and his supporters dismissed him as a mere clerk, he had earned respect for his analysis of patterns of British trade in *Estimate of the Comparative Strength of Great Britain,* which was reprinted several times after its publication in 1782. He also had achieved a reputation in London as a literary man. He had assembled a large personal library, had written a study of Shakespeare and a biography of Daniel Defoe, and had edited Defoe's collected works. Chalmers was by no means a hack — as Paine's subsequent defenders claimed — but a friend and supporter of the government who found Paine's vulgarity unbearable. The *Life of Thomas Paine; the Author of Rights of Men, with a Defence of His Writings* dredged up previously obscure details of Paine's life, gave little credit to him, and railed against his poor English. Like a pedantic schoolmaster, Chalmers devoted nearly half of his biography to a sentence-by-sentence analysis of the incorrect syntax and bowdlerized grammar of *Rights of Man* — as if English lessons could discredit Paine or cure him of his radical democratic sentiments.

Paine bit his tongue, planned his next moves, and hoped others would come to his defense. A few eventually did, but most printed reactions were lukewarm. "This pamphlet is, in high degree, uncandid and abusive," remarked an anonymous commentator. "However, the incidents which it contains seem to have been collected with care and assiduity, and to rest, as to their authenticity, on the evidence of dates and records. It should be remembered, likewise, that the particulars have not been contradicted, either by Mr. PAINE, or by any of his numerous admirers."[150] Paine's silence in the face of ad hominem taunts typified his secretive attitude toward his private life. In America, during the Silas Deane affair, he had learned the political dangers of being drawn publicly into personality clashes. He also believed, as a matter of republican principle, that within a civil society, private matters are distinct from public affairs, that the personal is not exclusively political, and that the two should not be conflated. From mid-July 1791, he tried to live by this principle by canceling his plans to travel to Ireland, which likely would have caused a sensation in both countries, and living in seclusion on the outskirts of London. He stayed at the home of his old friend Clio Rickman at 7 Upper Mary-le-Bone Street, at the top end of what is today Great Portland Street. He passed the days in relative isolation, occasionally making day trips to meet the well-known radical Horne Tooke at his home in Wimbledon.

Paine's doings had everything of the decadence of the man of letters about them. "Mr. Paine's life in London," reported his host, "was a quiet round of philosophical leisure and enjoyment. It was occupied in writing, in a small epistolary correspondence, in walking about with me to visit friends, occasionally lounging at coffee-houses and public places, or being visited by a select few." The string of visitors was impressively long and distinguished, reflecting Paine's cosmopolitan past and his tightening grip on the imagination of the burgeoning political opposition to the British Crown. Rickman continued:

Lord Edward Fitzgerald; the French and American ambassadors, Mr. Sharp the engraver, Romney the painter, Mrs. Wolstonecraft [*sic*], Joel Barlow, Mr. Hull, Mr. Christie, Dr. Priestley, Dr. Towers, Colonel Oswald, the walking Stewart, Captain Sampson Perry, Mr. Tuffin, Mr. William Chopin, Captain De Stark, Mr. Horne Tooke, &c.&c. were among the number of his friends and acquaintance. At this time he read but little, took his nap after dinner, and played with my family at some game in the evening, as chess, dominos, and drafts, but never at cards; in recitations, singing, music, &c.; or passed it in conversation: the part he took in the latter was always enlightened, full of information, entertainment, and anecdote. Occasionally we visited enlightened friends, indulged in domestic jaunts, and recreations from home, frequently lounging at the White Bear, Piccadilly, with his old friend the walking Stewart, and other clever travellers from France, and different parts of Europe and America.[151]

"The walking Stewart," a veteran of many hikes across the Continent and famous for having once walked from London to Edinburgh simply to ask a personally troubling question of the writer and critic Dr. Samuel Johnson, was only one of a number of eccentrics with whom Paine kept company during this period. In between afternoons at his desk, working on drafts of his essay on kingship, he moved to and fro through the nooks and crannies of London's civil society, often in unconventional company. Rickman recalled an exotic scene at a dinner party thrown by Thomas Christie, who was in London on business. Paine, scrubbed and clean-smelling, his graying hair brushed back and gathered in the customary ponytail, was among the invited all-male guests. Dressed in a blue waistcoat, brown jacket and breeches, leather riding boots, and frilled white lace under his neck, he found himself seated at the dinner table between Horne Tooke and the famous "indisputably feminine" Frenchman Madame d'Eon. "I am now in the most extraordinary situation in which ever man was placed," remarked the smooth conversationalist Tooke, unaware that d'Eon was a man. "On the left of me sits a gentleman, who, brought up in obscurity, has proved himself the greatest political writer in the world, and has made more noise in it, and excited more attention and obtained more fame, than any man ever did." Tooke paused, then gracefully continued. "On the right of me sits a lady, who has been employed in public situations at different courts; who had high rank in the army, was greatly skilled in horsemanship, who has fought several duels, and at the small sword had no equal; who for fifty years past, all Europe has recognised in the character and dress of a gentleman." D'Eon replied wittily in elegant Parisian English, with Tooke looking puzzled and Paine — who loved the company of men — visibly amused: "Ah! Zeese are very extra ordinary tings, indeed, Monsieur Tooke, and proves zat you did not know what was at ze bottom."[152]

Though adopting a low profile, Paine kept his political eyes and ears wide-open. He gobbled up news of the first black revolution in Santo Domingo, which he keenly supported, and spent a considerable amount of time answering the dozens of letters that actually required "half a dozen clerks."[153] Occasionally, he resurfaced into the public domain. On August 20, he appeared at a public meeting, organized by the Friends of Universal Peace and Liberty at the Thatched-House Tavern on St. James's Street just off Piccadilly. A hundred jolly supporters of the French Revolution crowded into the tavern to hear Tooke, the chairman of the meeting, introduce Paine, who was in excellent form.

The atmosphere was electric as Paine rose to speak from a prepared text. "Friends and Fellow Citizens," he began. "At a moment like the present, when wilful misrepresentations are industriously spread by the partisans of arbitrary power, and the advocates of passive obedience and court government, we think it incumbent on us to declare to the world our principles, and the motives of our conduct." Raucous applause erupted. Paine continued: "We congratulate the French nation for having laid the axe to the root of tyranny, and for erecting government on the sacred *hereditary rights of man* — rights which appertain to ALL." Wild clapping again followed. For the rest of the half-hour speech, the audience punctuated Paine's sentences with laughter, applause, and earnest concentration. Paine poked fun at despots everywhere, the toughest tongue-lashing being reserved for the class-ridden decadence of Britain. "We are oppressed with a heavy national debt, a burden of taxes, and an expensive administration of government, beyond those of any people in the world," he barked. "We have also a very numerous poor; and we hold that the moral obligation of providing for old age, helpless infancy, and poverty, is far superior to that of supplying the invented wants of courtly extravagance, ambition and intrigue." Paine repeated his favorite thesis that every nation was entitled to govern itself and ended his speech with an appeal to the friends of universal peace and liberty to campaign hard for the rights of commoners against the rotting Crown-in-Parliament system. "We have nothing to apprehend from the poor," he called above the hubble-bubble of his audience. "And we fear not proud oppression, for we have truth on our side."[154]

A few days after the Thatched-House Tavern meeting, Burke published his reply to the first part of *Rights of Man*. His *Appeal from the New, to the Old Whigs* struck Paine as a silent dismissal. In a mere dozen pages, it brushed aside his arguments to reach a conclusion that was both ominous and prophetic. "I will not attempt in the smallest degree to refute them," wrote Burke. "This will probably be done (if such writings shall be thought to deserve any other than the refutation of criminal justice) by others."[155] Paine was unmoved by such talk of prosecution. Privately, he boasted that the English authorities "have already tried all the under-plots of abuse and scurrility without effect; and have managed those in general so badly as to make the work and the author the more famous."[156] He also noted, accurately and with great satisfaction, that he now occupied center stage of the political scene. "I have so far got the ear of John Bull," he told fellow "saintmaker" John Hall, "that he will read what I write — which is more than ever was done before to the same extent."[157] He found proof of this influence in the extraordinary sales of *Rights of Man*, which now topped seventeen thousand in England and Scotland and more than forty thousand in Ireland. The successes may have gone to his head, but he clearly grasped the dangers now stalking him. "The Government Gentry begin to threaten," he observed while putting the finishing touches on the kingship essay, his aim being to fight his way out of trouble by making his arguments more radical than in *Rights of Man*. Less than two months before Christmas, 1791, his mood was utterly defiant: "I see that *great rogues* escape by the excess of their crimes, and, perhaps, it may be the same in honest cases."[158]

The plans for a cheap popular edition of *Rights of Man* and its sequel were part of this political gamble. Until now, Paine had deliberately drawn back from proposals by sympathetic publishers for widening the availability of the book, reasoning that that would be a premature and dangerous provocation of the already nervous political authorities — "the wise mad folks at St. James," as he called them. The point was to create public opinion from below, and that took time. At the end of November, he confided to Hall that he thought the time was ripe and that he wanted to print a hundred thousand copies of each work, retailing them at the cost of sixpence apiece.[159]

He meanwhile became convinced that the best means of increasing public pressure on the British government would be to title his forthcoming book *Rights of Man, Part the Second*. There were serious last-minute hitches with publishers. "If you wished to be hanged or inured in a prison all your life," Joseph Johnson was advised by a friend who had read an incomplete draft of the manuscript, "publish this book."[160] Both Johnson and J. S. Jordan refused to allow their names to appear on the title page, for fear of prosecution and imprisonment. They both told Paine that they were in principle agreeable to the much safer arrangement of selling the volume, at a considerable profit, through their respective bookshops. Thomas Christie temporarily solved the problem by persuading an admirer of Paine's writings, Thomas Chapman, to publish the work. He set about typesetting the manuscript at the end of October, hoping to publish it just before Christmas, when members of Parliament were to assemble in London in time for the opening of the new parliamentary session on the last day of the year.

Everything went wrong. Paine lingered over the last fifteen or so pages of the manuscript, fiddling with details. The deadline for provoking heated discussion in the opening session of Parliament passed, and it was not until six weeks later that he was satisfied with perhaps the most moving conclusion that he had ever written:

> It is now towards the middle of February. Were I to take a turn into the country, the trees would present a leafless winterly appearance. As people are apt to pluck twigs as they walk along, I perhaps might do the same, and by chance might observe, that a *single bud* on that twig had begun to swell. I should reason very unnaturally, or rather not reason at all, to suppose *this* was the *only* bud in England which had this appearance. Instead of deciding thus, I should instantly conclude, that the same appearance was beginning, or about to begin, everywhere; and though the vegetable sleep will continue longer on some trees and plants than on others, and though some of them may not *blossom* for two or three years, all will be in leaf in the summer, except those which are *rotten*. What pace the political summer may keep with the natural, no human foresight can determine. It is, however, not difficult to perceive that the spring is begun.[161]

Sensing that the book would have a sensational impact, Chapman waited patiently for these words, in the meantime typesetting the completed parts of the manuscript. All the while, he bargained with Paine for control over the copyright. Paine became irritated by Chapman's persistence. After only skimming the manuscript, he offered Paine the sum of a hundred guineas in exchange for the copyright. Paine refused. Chapman then increased the offer to five hundred guineas and, when that was refused, raised it again to the fantastic sum of one thousand guineas. Paine insisted to Chapman that the work should not be treated as a mere commodity, subject to the whims and greed of the market, that after all political principles were at stake. He did not tell Chapman to his face that he had learned from experience that without control over the copyright, the chances were high that the wording of the text would be altered to suit the needs of the publisher and his imagined audience. The wrangling worsened when Chapman showed signs of reticence. Chapman later claimed that when he finally found time to read carefully through the proofs one afternoon, he was suddenly struck by "a dangerous tendency" in the work and that he became convinced that it would be treated as seditious libel by the authorities. "I therefore immediately concluded in my mind not to proceed any farther in the work."[162]

Chapman was now stuck with the remaining problem of how to inform Paine of his decision at this eleventh hour. He flushed with embarrassment, so much so that after writing a note to Paine breaking the bad news, he resolved to withhold it overnight, "fearful I should not have courage in the morning to deliver up the copy." Chapman knew that although Paine would undoubtedly find a substitute publisher, the delay of the book would have potentially serious political consequences. It would catapult Paine, whom he personally liked and respected, into a paroxysm of anger. And word would circulate among the radical opposition that Chapman was a pigeon-hearted publisher.

Chapman sweated, guilt-ridden. He thought luck had come his way when around six o'clock that evening, Paine called on him and his wife — in a half-drunken state. The three ate bread and cheese together, quickly falling into a heated argument about religion, "a favourite subject with him when intoxicated." Voices were raised. Chapman stood his ground, telling Paine that "he had no more Principle than a Post, or Religion than a Ruffian." An explosion followed. "The subject of debate ran very high; he opposed everything with great virulence, till at length he came to personal abuse, very much so," recalled Chapman. "An observation was made by Mrs. Chapman, late in the evening, I believe near ten o'clock, at which Mr. Paine was particularly offended; rising up in a great passion he said he had not been so personally affronted in the whole course of his life before." Paine was so enraged that he told Chapman to go to hell and to advance no "further in his work."

Chapman thought he was off the hook. Early next morning, his guilt lessened, he delivered the manuscript to Paine's house on Mary-le-Bone Street. A few hours later, still unaware that he had been double-crossed, Paine humbly visited Chapman's print shop, where he "made many apologies for what he had said; he said that it was the effect of liquor, and hoped that I would pass it over, and proceed with the work." Chapman haughtily refused Paine's apology. Paine's political suspicion was aroused instantly. It seemed incredible to him that a publisher who had offered a thousand guineas for control over Paine's hand would suddenly take offense at a bit of abuse from his inebriated tongue. Chapman's later story that he had suddenly been struck by the "dangerous tendency" of the text also seemed fraudulent to Paine, who drew the conclusion that the book police had leaned on Chapman, threatening to ruin his livelihood if he proceeded any further with the publication.[163]

Helped by a few close friends, including Mr. Crowther, Paine moved to preempt any attempt by the police to confiscate the manuscript or the sheets already printed. Within hours, he had negotiated a deal with Jordan, who after some resistance agreed to take over the already-printed stock and publish the completed work in return for the right to sell a portion of the print run of five thousand copies. Johnson chipped in with an agreement to underwrite the costs of publication in return for the same right. Paine agreed to cover both men legally by forwarding an open letter to Jordan:

February 16, 1792

Sir,

Should any person, under the sanction of any kind of authority, enquire of you respecting the author and publisher of the *Rights of Man,* you will please to mention me as the author and publisher of that work, and show to such person this letter. I will, as soon as I am made acquainted with it, appear and answer for the work personally.

Your humble servant,

THOMAS PAINE

That afternoon, the second part of *Rights of Man* was released. Jordan's press continued to work around the clock, and within the next two weeks another four printings came off the press. The brightest and most powerful political skyrocket in English history had been launched.

Within a matter of days, the "quiet round of philosophical leisure and enjoyment" that Paine had been enjoying in London was ripped apart. The government, anxious to keep an eye on him, dispatched a spy, Charles Ross, to watch the activities at the Rickmans'.[164] A further sign of things to come surfaced in the political quarrels he had with Gouverneur Morris, whom Paine visited frequently for six weeks during the early spring of 1792. Morris had just arrived in London en route to Paris, where at the end of March he would take up his new appointment by President Washington as minister to France. Paine had already told Jefferson that he considered Morris's appointment "*most unfortunate.*"[165] He thought that Morris was a reactionary, which was true. Morris told Paine that this time he had gone far too far and that he would soon pay the price. Morris spoke openly in favor of preserving the French monarchy. Behind the back of the United States Senate, which had ratified his appointment, he had even drafted and urged the carrying out of a secret plan to rescue the king from the Tuileries. He complained constantly to Paine about the mindless mobbery and violence of the Revolution across the Channel, but

Paine argued back, insisting with a laugh (said Morris) that "the riots and outrages in France are nothing at all." Morris replied that he was certain that Paine did "not believe what he says" and that it was therefore "not worthwhile to contest such declarations." But he warned, "He seems cocksure of bringing about a revolution in Great Britain, and I think it quite as likely that he will be promoted to the pillory."[166]

The fight between Morris and Paine sparked by *Rights of Man* mirrored the spreading dispute throughout the country between the forces of conservatism and radical change. Defenders of the status quo were sure in their hearts that men are created unequal and that the less equal owe obedience to their superiors precisely because the Creator has endowed them with his own sacred authority. They believed in the inviolable authority of that class whom Burke (in *Reflections*) called the "natural aristocracy" — those men "bred in a place of estimation" who "take a large view . . . in a large society," enjoy the "leisure to read, to reflect, to converse," and are "habituated in armies to command and to obey." Yet these same believers in natural aristocracy were now gripped by the feeling that the French events were ballooning into a vast, barbaric, fearsome force of destruction that, if left unopposed, might well destroy existing civilized societies.

British supporters of the Revolution were convinced, by contrast, that the final source of all earthly authority was the people — whether they included women and servants was usually not clear — who were created equal and therefore entitled to choose who should govern them. The radicals were convinced that the French events would efface older frontiers, traditions, and political institutions, which had prevailed for centuries, and that they were not just a French affair. They interpreted the Revolution as one big revolutionary agitation stretching back across the Atlantic to the American Declaration of Independence and extending forward in time and outward in space to include the current British crisis. The radicals were certain that old public loyalties and confidence in existing state authority were waning fast. They were convinced that for many people, the existing laws seemed unjust and deference to superiors was a form of humiliation. The supporters and sympathizers of the Revolution thought of themselves as witnesses to an age of "democratic revolution"[167] whose aim was to create a more equal and open, more humane and improving form of government and society. Paine summarized these radical feelings with a simple scathing maxim: "A certain writer, of some antiquity, says: 'When I was a child, I thought as a child; but when I became a man, I put away childish things.'"[168]

Prominent public organizations differed about whether or to what extent the "childish things" of the existing system should be put aside. Emblematic of the times was the serious split that developed during March and April 1792 in the ranks of the Society for Constitutional Information, which had been formed in 1784 to advance the Whiggish cause of liberal reforms, all the while affirming its allegiance to the settlement of 1688. Things changed quickly after November 4, 1791, when Paine was guest of honor at a Society meeting. "Thanks were given him for his *Rights of Man*, when his health was drank," it was reported. Paine responded with a recital of *The Revolution of the World* and, several months later, with a donation of one thousand pounds, "to apply it to such purposes they shall see proper." Some society members were unimpressed. Reverend Christopher Wyvill, a Yorkshire gentleman supporter of the society, warned in his correspondence with moderates throughout the country of "Mr. Paine's ill-timed, and . . . pernicious counsels." Wyvill's defense of the wealthy classes did not mince words: "It is unfortunate for the public cause, that Mr Paine took such unconstitutional ground, and has formed a party for the Republic among the lower classes of the people, by holding out to them the prospect of plundering the rich."[169]

Appeals to the class instincts of "moderate men" failed to hold the society together. The moderates soon lost control to the likes of dramatist Thomas Holcroft, Major John Cartwright, Horne Tooke, and the Jacobin attorney John Frost, all of whom were militant supporters of Paine's. The anti-Paine defenders of the Crown-in-Parliament system left the society in a huff to form a new society deliberately misnamed the Friends of the People, who wanted reforms to save the present system from the clamors of men and women of lower station. The remaining members of the Society for Constitutional Information then toughened their stance in favor of democratization. On May 18, Paine wrote to their chairman thanking the society for its support of his work and informing them that since he was reliably informed that the Crown planned to push ahead with his prosecution, he had resolved to defend the principle of liberty of the press by getting out fast a cheap edition of both parts of *Rights of Man*.[170] The society resolved, on the same day it received Paine's letter, to oppose the rumored prosecution, to circulate Paine's letter nationally, and to thank Paine for his "patriotic disinterestedness." It further voted to "contribute its utmost aid towards supporting the Rights of the Nation, and the Freedom of the Press, and him who has so essentially and successfully contributed to both." It concluded defiantly, "The right of investigating principles and systems of Government is one of these Rights; and . . . the Works of any Author, which cannot be refuted by reason, cannot, on the principles of good government, or of common sense, be made the subject of prosecution."[171]

The society's chairman forwarded copies of its resolutions and Paine's letter to its network of branches, including the Lewes branch, to whom Paine then wrote an open letter in time for its branch meeting. Paine recalled that since his "departure from Lewes, fortune or providence has thrown me into a line of action which my first setting out in life could not possibly have suggested to me." He reassured the citizens of Lewes that he remained as ardent a supporter of "the principles of liberty" as when he had resided there. And he underlined his continuing preoccupation with social injustice, or what he termed "the hard condition of others": "My situation among you as an officer of the revenue, for more than six years, enabled me to see into the numerous and various distresses which the weight of taxes even at that time of day occasioned."[172]

Paine's preoccupation with inequalities of wealth and liberties echoed throughout the membership of the newly founded, politically more influential London Corresponding Society. It had been organized by Thomas Hardy, a master shoemaker who owned a London shop employing half a dozen skilled craftsmen, shortly after the publication of the second part of *Rights of Man*. Hardy had tracked the events of the American Revolution with deep sympathy. Having seen the failure of upper-class efforts to reform Parliament a dozen years earlier, he, together with Horne Tooke and John Frost, set about organizing a more popular initiative backed by "tradesmen, shopkeepers and mechanics." The short-term aim was to agitate for a widened franchise, but Hardy and other members of the society took the view that this would require an attack on the parasitic aristocracy and, hence, an assault on the unequal property relations in civil society. In a letter to a Scottish correspondent, Hardy explained how he and his friends had discussed "the low and miserable conditions the people of this nation were reduced to" and had traced this injustice to "the avaricious extortions of that haughty, voluptuous and luxurious class of beings who wanted us to possess no more knowledge than to believe all things were created for the use of that small group of worthless individuals."[173]

The London Corresponding Society set about winning popular support for its attack on the existing property order by networking with provincial societies and (from May 1792) with the Jacobin Club in Paris. Through these tunnels in the subsoil of the existing civil society, it published and distributed pamphlets, handbills, and a cheap edition of *Rights of Man*. From the point of view of the ruling powers, such public solidarity with Paine's efforts to foment discussion about the rights of citizens within the lower ranks was the most dangerous of trends. It was this, and not the French events, that gave them nightmares. As the English spring turned to summer and then faded into autumn, the effects of *Rights of Man* began to be felt at the grassroots level. Throughout the British Isles, Paine's name became identical with the agitation, at a depth and with an intensity unheard-of since the failed revolution of the 1640s, if ever, for the extension of democracy — and for the struggle for independence in Ireland. The leading spokeswoman for counterrevolution, Hannah More, explained her fears of mounting "insurrection, infidelity and vice." She observed that the friends and supporters of Paine "load asses with their pernicious pamphlets and . . . get them dropped, not only in cottages, and in highways, but into mines and coal-pits."[174] Paine's six-penny book was held in the hands of crofters in Scotland, tin miners in Cornwall, shepherds in Cumbria, and shoemakers in Norwich. It was reported that in the Staffordshire potteries of Newcastle "almost every hand" and in Sheffield "every cutler" owned a copy.[175]

There were few places in Britain untouched by Paine's fearsome reputation. "The Northern parts of Wales," moaned a government correspondent, who perhaps knew something of Paine's Sandwich days, "are infested by itinerant Methodist preachers who descant on the Rights of Man and attack Kingly Government."[176] Someone from Dundee in Scotland reported that "all the inhabitants of this city have assuredly lost their heads! Would you believe that there is a question of nothing less than planting the tree of Liberty in the neighbouring towns of Forsar and Brechin? Oh! I hope that some of these planters will adorn another tree! Meanwhile, they are doing much evil. Can you imagine that a single person has sold here more than 1,000 copies of T. Payne's pamphlet."[177] Similar reports circulated from elsewhere in Scotland, including Glasgow, where during 1792 *Rights of Man* fueled public clamors for the reform of Parliament and the widening of the franchise. "The city of Glasgow alone counts 15,000 individuals gathered for that purpose," stated one report. "It is added that the celebrated work of Thomas Payne . . . is being circulated throughout all Scotland, at a very low price, & that 10,000 copies per week are being sold."[178]

Estimates of the volume of sales — and the meaning of the figures — during the months after the release of part two of *Rights of Man* are again difficult to assess. In America, perhaps 100,000 copies of the two-part edition were eventually sold.[179] The impressive reception reflected the lingering fame of "Common Sense" and the excitement and sympathy sparked by the French Revolution, whose progress was tracked closely by newspapers in every state. Despite the renewal of war in Europe and British efforts to choke the French struggle to death, liberty, it was said in Boston, now had "another feather in her cap."[180] In the same town, where the reception of *Rights of Man* was enthusiastic but not atypical, a "Civic Feast" commemorated the "rapid succession of victories which attend the arms of the republicans of France." Parades were held, followed by splendid barbecues at which huge roasted oxen were consumed by "citizen Mechanicks" and others. A collection was taken to free prisoners in the city's jail, and Oliver's Dock was renamed Liberty Square. In some local newspaper columns, "Mr." and "Mrs." or "Miss" were replaced by "Citizen" and "Citess"; the *Boston Gazette* and the *Massachusetts Mercury* hotly disputed the use of "Civess" or "Citess." Wearing of the French cockade became fashionable, and revolutionary songs were popular, usually linked to toasts to Tom Paine and the hope that the "rights of man" would "never subside till arbitrary power is hunted out of the world."[181]

Elsewhere in America — for instance, among the captains of the ship of state — *Rights of Man* caused friction and renewed fights about the meaning of the American Revolution. Shortly after English editions of part one had reached American shores, Secretary of State Thomas Jefferson, at the request of John Beckley, sent a copy to a Philadelphia printer, who planned to republish it. Jefferson enclosed a note saying that he was "extremely pleased" that "something is at length to be publickly said against the political heresies which have sprung up among us. I have no doubt our citizens will rally a second time round the standard of Common Sense."

In early May 1791, Jefferson was shocked to find that his off-the-cuff remarks had been included in the preface of the republished American edition. Some grew instantly angry. Jefferson's remarks about heretics were widely taken to be a criticism of Paine's old enemy John Adams, and a column of anonymous critics, led by "Publicola," later considered to be John Quincy Adams, struck back. Throughout the summer of 1791, American newspaper readers were treated to an extraordinary public debate about the future of republican politics. Some newspaper editors quickly took sides in the conflict. First among them was John Fenno, editor of the *Gazette of the United States*, soon to become the flagship of the Federalist Party press. Jefferson responded by complaining to Paine's friend William Short, in France, about Fenno's "torypaper," whose design, he said, was to "make way for a king, lords and commons." At the same time, Jefferson predicted that American citizens, following Paine's lead, would refuse to subscribe to Fenno's aristocratic sentiments, remaining "to a man, firm as a rock in their republican-ism."[182]

If the American reception was noisy, the response in Britain was ri-otous. In England, Wales, and Scotland, sales of the second part of *Rights of Man* probably totaled some 200,000 copies within a year of its publica-tion. The figures were phenomenal, but doubts persist about their reliabil-ity because of the unknown number of abridged and unabridged editions issued by local clubs and societies in these regions and because parts one and two circulated in both single and combined editions during 1792. There is little doubt, however, that "no single piece of nonce literature . . . had ever approached such a circulation,"[183] especially on the bloodstained soil of Ireland, where demand for the book was arguably greatest.

The fantastic Irish response was understandable in a country in which Protestants, comprising 10 percent of the population, owned 90 percent of the land; controlled the established church, army, and courts; and exer-cised government power with their heads bowed faithfully beneath the British Crown. The governing formula was a recipe for permanent crisis. "The suspicion that England governs Ireland for the purpose of keeping her low, to prevent her becoming her rival in trade and manufactures," Paine noted, "will always operate to hold Ireland in a state of sentimental hostility with England."[184] *Rights of Man* not only exploited and expanded this anti-imperial sentiment, but it also gave its champions courage by providing an earthy republican democratic language to hurl in the direc-tion of the Crown and its Irish compradors. *Rights of Man* was received enthusiastically by the tiny minority of disgruntled Protestants and mem-bers of the Opposition. It also captured readers among Ulster Presbyterians, or Dissenters, whose religious beliefs inclined them toward republicanism. The moderate Society of United Irishmen, founded in 1791 by "protes-tants of the middling ranks" in support of parliamentary reform, made Paine an honorary member.[185] But the book had the most sensational im-pact in the communities of Irish Catholic peasants, whose antipathy for Britain and bitter grievances — such as concern about rack rents, falling real wages, and the tithe — were already driving them into desperate acts of violence and defiance of authority. In towns and hamlets stretching from the provinces of Connaught to Wexford, peasants reportedly began to debate *Rights of Man* in taverns, streets, and marketplaces. Later, still under the influence of the book, they formed themselves into citizens' armies, whose enlistees affirmed a militant republican catechism: "I be-lieve in a revolution founded on the rights of man, in the natural and im-prescriptable right of *all* Irish citizens to the land."[186]

Enemy of State

Such talk frightened the government of William Pitt, forcing it to face up to three related trends. First, the growing radicalization of the French Revolution dashed all remaining hopes that Britain would profit from France's turmoil by remaining neutral. Second, and closely related, the expansionist fervor of the French regime forced the disturbing conclusion that the French Revolution was now a threat to the geopolitical balance of power in Europe and to British interests in particular. Finally, in England, Wales, Scotland, and Ireland, there were growing signs of cooperation between extraparliamentary radicalism and the revolutionary forces in France. No great leap of imagination was needed to see that these three overlapping trends were revolutionary. That is why, during the course of 1792, the Pitt regime decided that the situation constituted an emergency and that it should act, if necessary using the armed forces of the state, to root out the Paineite disease.

Since an essential part of this crisis management strategy was to demonize Paine himself, the contemporary reports from the government side need to be read with a certain skepticism. We do know that during the summer of 1792, the Secretary at War dispatched the Deputy Adjutant-General to tour parts of the country to map the patterns of sedition and measure the reliability of the troops, should they need to be sent into action. In Sheffield, the Deputy Adjutant-General reported that "the seditious doctrines of Paine and the factious people who are endeavouring to disturb the peace of the country had extended to a degree very much beyond my conception." He described Sheffield as the "centre of all their seditious machinations" and reported that some twenty-five hundred "of the lowest mechanics" had already joined the most prominent reform grouping, the Society for Constitutional Information. "Here they read the most violent publications," he said, "and comment on them, as well as on their correspondence not only with the dependent Societies in the towns and villages in the vicinity, but with those . . . in other parts of the kingdom."[187]

Meanwhile, on May 21, 1792, Pitt's government issued a proclamation against "wicked and seditious writings." Magistrates up and down the country were ordered to search out the authors and printers of such materials and to submit details so gathered to the king's ministers, "it being our determination . . . to carry the laws vigorously into execution against such offenders." Without saying so directly, the proclamation was in fact designed to suppress Paine's book. Four days later in Parliament, Fox pressed

Prime Minister Pitt to explain the rationale of the proclamation. "Principles had been laid down by Mr. Paine," he replied, "which struck at hereditary nobility, and which went to the destruction of monarchy and religion, and the total subversion of the established form of government." Cries of "shame," "damn Paine," and "traitor" punctuated the follow-up question: Why, then, had the government shilly-shallied so long? Pitt's friend and adviser, the Scotsman Henry Dundas, rose to answer that the seditious passages were found only in the recently published second part of *Rights of Man*. The government, he continued, had now established beyond a doubt that these passages were being "sedulously inculcated throughout the kingdom," and that was why it would now crack down on sedition through the courts. Dundas reiterated that the exercise of emergency powers became necessary only when "societies were seen forming themselves upon those principles that alarm was excited, and preventative measures adopted." Before the House of Commons, he waved a specimen of subversion — a copy of a petition sponsored by a Sheffield workingmen's group. Here was proof, Dundas concluded, that "when great bodies of men in large manufacturing towns adopted and circulated doctrines so pernicious in their tendency, and so subversive of the constitution and government of the country," a Royal Proclamation was absolutely necessary.[188]

Using the proclamation as a shield and a sword, the government carefully sponsored meetings throughout the country to proselytize against Paine. Local clergy and magistrates delivered addresses loyal to the Crown and against Paine, and societies of gentry were formed "to preserve inviolable the GLORIOUS CONSTITUTION OF OLD ENGLAND."[189] The government also laundered payments to publishers in an attempt to flood the minds of the reading public with anti-Paine propaganda. Chalmers's hostile biography was not an isolated example. A Portsmouth printer was paid the substantial sum of £175, in several installments, to publish twenty-two thousand copies of a pamphlet titled *Strictures on Thomas Paine's Works and Character*. Payment was authorized by the Secretary of the Treasury and paid through Admiral Sir Andrew Hamond from the secret service fund.[190]

The government arguably contradicted its case by widening and deepening the very public sphere that it was dedicated to keeping a no-entry zone for commoners. It tried to suppress this contradiction by closing down public places where commoners met and cracking down on Paineite publishers. The Royal Proclamation set off official hunts against heresy from one end of the country to another. Government spies were assigned to the popular societies to monitor and obstruct their activities. Billstickers were imprisoned for posting notices in favor of Paineite reforms. Bookshops selling *Rights of Man* were visited and harassed by agents of the book police, and sometimes arrested, prosecuted, fined, or imprisoned. Richard Phillips, who published the pro-reform *Leicester Herald,* was convicted for a year and a half for allegedly selling the book.[191] Public places frequented by Paine's sympathizers were carefully monitored and sometimes harassed. In the villages of Northamptonshire, house-to-house loyalty canvasses were conducted. In Wiltshire, "traitorous expressions" earned a schoolmaster the sack. Ipswich magistrates forcibly broke up an alehouse "Disputing Club" comprising "very Inferior People" chattering about Paine and citizens' rights. John Frost, the attorney activist in the London Corresponding Society, was arrested and sentenced to the pillory and to eighteen months' imprisonment on the pretext of a remark —"I am for equality. . . . Why, no kings!" — uttered in a Mary-le-Bone coffeehouse. And during the autumn of 1792, Manchester publicans were pressed to prevent Paineites from frequenting their taverns. Those who refused were warned that their licenses would be withdrawn. Nearly two hundred publicans consequently signed a declaration refusing the use of their tavern meeting rooms to "any CLUB or societies . . . that have a tendency to put in force what those INFERNALS so *ardently and devoutly wish for,* namely, the DESTRUCTION OF THIS COUNTRY."[192]

Then there was the government strategy of getting at Paine personally. The government tried everything after the publication of the second part of *Rights of Man* to make him scurry through darkened late-night alleyways, to corrode his self-confidence with the acid of fear, and to disturb his nights with sweaty nightmares — and even thoughts of murder. Paine's personal troubles began in April, when he was picked up at the entrance of the London Tavern, famous for its turtle soup and immense wine cellars, and charged with failing to pay off a debt of two hundred pounds due the creditors of Peter Whiteside, his former bridge-building backer. Paine was carted off to a sponging house and locked up until the following day, when Joseph Johnson and another bookseller bailed him out. The government made sure that the incident was reported in the press to cause Paine maximum embarrassment and to give authorities the maximum space in which to take their next steps.

On May 21, 1792, the Pitt government fired a more lethal shot at Paine: a summons to appear in court in just over a fortnight on charges of seditious libel. The summons, issued on the same day as the Royal Proclamation, appeared to signal the government's desire to get its hands on the throat of political dissent, but in retrospect it was designed to force Paine into exile. The authorities reasoned that a midsummer show trial was too risky, in that it might antagonize the democratic opposition to the point of taking openly revolutionary action. The public execution or transportation of Paine might spark the same explosion — as would his transformation into a martyr by long-term imprisonment on English soil. The most effective strategy, the government reasoned in secret, was to let the Damoclean sword of state power hang for a while by a thin thread over Paine's head.

Paine's daily life now resembled that of a latter-day dissident. Government spies tailed him constantly on London's streets, sending back a stream of reports to the Home Secretary's office. Those parts of the press that functioned as government mouthpieces pelted him with abuse. "It is earnestly recommended to Mad Tom," snarled the *Times*, "that he should embark for France, and there be naturalized into the regular confusion of democracy."[193] Broadsheets containing "intercepted correspondence from Satan to Citizen Paine" pictured him as a three-headed, fire-breathing monster named "Tom Stich."[194] Open letters, often identically worded but signed with different pen names, were circulated through taverns and alehouses. "Brother Weavers and Artificers," thundered "a gentleman" to the inhabitants of Manchester and Salford, "Do not let us be humbugged by Mr. Paine, who tells us a great many *Truths*, in his book, in order to shove off his *Lies*."[195] Dozens of sermons and satires directed at Paine were published, many of them written anonymously for commoners by upper-class foes masquerading as commoners. Sometimes their loyalist message was lighthearted, designed to trigger gin-soaked laughter; at other times, the language and plot were as crudely propagandist as *Liberty and Equality; Treated of in a Short History*. Printed for the author, "A Poor Man to His Equals," the pamphlet featured a Paineite figure, Mac'Serpent, who after being arrested underwent a change of heart and sat down with a squire in a pub "ordering . . . a Bucket full of Strong Beer for us, in which we drank CHURCH and KING, and OLD ENGLAND for ever."[196]

Government-sponsored meetings also mushroomed. The Association for Preserving Liberty and Property Against Republicans and Levellers waged a campaign against what it called "seditious and treasonable Libels." Royalist meetings concluded with belched slogans such as "Long live the King! God save the King!" or claret-soaked ditties sung to the popular tunes of "Bow! Wow! Wow!" or "The Roast Beef of Old England":

> *Unite then, ye Britons, unite in applause,*
> *To the men who stand forth for our rights and our laws,*
> *And from runagate Tray[t]ors defend our good cause,*
> *Then, up with the cause of old England,*
> *And down with the tricks of Tom Paine.*

Posters were hung on London walls. "Shall we trust to TOM the STAY-MAKER, and his bungling *French* Journeymen, to amend our Constitution? . . . Shall we commit our Property, Liberties, and Religion, to those who have robbed their own Church, murdered their Clergy, and denied their God?" snarled some government agent named "John Bull to His Brethren."[197] Then there was the tactic of probing Paine's personal life. The government's favorite ploy was to circulate printed copies of a letter, supposedly written two decades earlier, to Elizabeth Ollive from Paine's mother, alleging that her son was guilty of unpaid loans, "vile treatment" of his second wife, and "undutiful behaviour to the tenderest of parents."[198]

More worrisome for Paine were the signs of growing hostility among local magistrates, squires, parsons, and other members of the respectable classes — and their growing willingness to resort to violence against him. Their genteel nastiness surfaced in their sponsorship of the ugly practice of executing effigies of Paine. A barometer of this mood swing was the crackdown on Dissenters and reformers in Cambridge. On June 22, 1792, the university sent a loyal address to King George III, and during the following months officially sponsored riots and attacks on Dissenting meeting places took place. A group of more than a hundred publicans declared their willingness to gather and submit reports of activities "of a treasonable or seditious tendency" to the local magistrates. A local branch of the Association for Preserving Liberty and Property Against Republicans and Levellers was founded, and on the cold and snowy last day of the year, an effigy of Paine was burned on Market Hill.[199]

Reports of symbolic violence against Paine streamed in from all over the country. William Wilberforce, the Member of Parliament for Yorkshire, reported that a loyalist crowd had paraded through the main streets of Leeds, "carrying an image of Tom Paine upon a pole, with a rope round his neck which was held by a man behind, who continually lashed the effigy with a carter's whip. The effigy was at last burned in the marketplace, the market-bell tolling slowly. . . . A smile sat on every face. . . . 'God Save the King' resounded in the streets."[200] Reports of Guy Fawkes–style parades and demonstrations probably reached Paine's ears. From Lenewade Bridge, near his native Thetford, came news that "the Effigy of Tom Paine and a fox's skin was hung on a Gibbet and afterwards burnt. A Barrel of Beer was given on the occasion."[201] Sometimes the demonstrations were charged with weighty splendor. A report from a town not far from Grantham, where Paine had lived for nearly a year, read:

The effigy of Thomas Paine was, with great solemnity, drawn on a sledge from Lincoln Castle to the gallows, and then hanged, amidst a vast multitude of spectators. After being suspended the usual time it was taken to the Castle-hill and there hung on a gibbet post erected for the purpose. In the evening a large fire was made under the effigy, which . . . was consumed to ashes, amidst the acclamations of many hundreds of people, accompanied with a grand band of music playing "God Save the King."[202]

At other times, the occasions had a primitive folkish dramatic quality. Before an audience of West Yorkshire mine workers, a Heckmondwike mill owner dressed up as Paine had himself "discovered" reading *Rights of Man* behind a heap of coal. The horse-nosed mask he was wearing was then "arrested" and placed on a straw effigy in the town square. After ritual denunciations of Paine, the effigy was dragged around the town and then summarily "executed."[203]

Caution should be exercised when pondering the mixture of motives of those who participated in public actions against Paine. They were by no means straightforwardly royalist. There were clearly some who believed in their loyalist hearts that Paine stood for the weakening of English civilization. Others found themselves pleasurably attracted to the spectacle or were pushed by peer pressure into going through the motions of protest. The prospect of earning a few shillings from the local notable to wave a placard or shoot at or torch an effigy of the world-famous political radical attracted still others. A prosperous lawyer from the small weaving township of Ripponden in the Pennines noted in his diary that he paid ten shillings and sixpence each to certain locals "who carried about Tom Payne's Effigy and shot at it." Money sometimes bred fickleness, as in a Suffolk village, where a wealthy parish rector offered two guineas to a number of poor people to burn Paine's effigy. "They readily accepted the offer and performed the business," reported the *Morning Chronicle*. "An intelligent gentleman offered the same people two guineas more to burn the jolly rector in effigy, to which they as readily assented."[204] Still others — curiously — participated in the crucifixions because they could not see any other way in which to publicize the name of Paine in order to spark off local controversies about the merits of his radical political case, which they themselves favored, in spite of the threatening local silence.

Whatever the motives, the ritual killings always had their ugly side. Some of the parades and demonstrations were marked by bloodthirstiness, as at Littletown, where a wooden cutout figure resembling Paine was smashed to bits by the angry town executioner, whose hands bled after wielding the sledgehammer so ferociously.[205] Such scenes revealed the potential for violence in the European country many considered the paragon of political stability and liberty. Paine tried various ways of sheltering from the gathering storm of incivility. Shortly after the publication of the second part of *Rights of Man,* Joseph Johnson convinced him to spend a period of seclusion in the village of Bromley, ten miles southeast of London, at the home of a mutual friend, William Sharp, the engraver. Johnson handled the arrangements for Paine, who, according to one report, was utterly preoccupied with matters political and — his nerves on edge — bibbing his way through bottles of brandy and gin. "They went in a hackney coach," reported a friend, Henry Fuseli, "for such a vehicle could contain them, with all the movables which Paine possessed. On their arrival at the new abode, Paine discovered that half a bottle of brandy was left behind; now brandy, being important to Paine, he urged Johnson to drive back and fetch it. 'No, Mr. Paine,' said he, 'it would not be right to spend eight shillings in coach-hire, to regain one shilling's-worth of brandy.' "[206]

Paine settled for the local gin and water and Sharp paid for his room and board, "for the purpose of concealing his character and name there." Paine kept out of sight of the villagers. His landlord reported that he "behaved quietly, without complaining of his fare" and "went seldom into the town, but walked much into the fields, and often in the garden behind the house."[207] Appearances were deceptive. Far from relaxing and keeping politics at arm's length, Paine in fact worked feverishly at his desk for a month. During that time, he sketched notes describing his reactions to the brewing storm generated by the second part of *Rights of Man.* He also drafted a defiant address, which was read at the end of May at the Jacobin Club in Paris.[208]

The sojourn in Bromley was cut short on May 14 by the news that J. S. Jordan, publisher of the original edition of *Rights of Man,* had been served a summons to appear at the Court of King's Bench. Paine hurried to London to persuade Jordan to put up a fight. He offered him his attorney, Thomas Erskine, and proposed to bear the costs of defense himself.

Cutting his losses, Jordan declined and pleaded guilty. Paine's response was generous: "I make no objection against him for it. I believe that his idea by the word *guilty,* was no other than declaring himself to be the publisher, without any regard to the merits or demerits of the work."[209] He was less generous toward the Attorney General, Sir Archibald Macdonald, to whom he wrote at the end of May. Paine insisted on Jordan's innocence and accused Macdonald of conniving with Edmund Burke — "a masked pensioner at £1500 per annum for about ten years" — to suppress *Rights of Man*. Paine also called for a national convention to draw up a written constitution and urged the Attorney General to review the existing jury system. Jury service and trial by jury, Paine argued, were essential ingredients of republican democracy. But the current practice of packing juries with rich and powerful men twisted the principle into an absurd "tyranny of juries" over the accused. "Though the gentlemen of London may be very expert in understanding their particular professions and occupations, and how to make business contracts with government beneficial to themselves as individuals," he snapped, "the rest of the nation may not be disposed to consider them sufficiently qualified nor authorized to determine for the whole nation on plans of reform, and on systems and principles of government."[210]

Paine responded to his own summons a few days later by lashing out angrily at the government. On June 6, he forwarded a mischievous letter to the tough-minded Home Secretary, Henry Dundas, whom Paine scathingly described as "a man rolling in luxury at the expense of the nation." In the same open letter, Paine ignored friendly advice not to refer to George III as "king or Madjesty," in punning allusion to his mental condition, and cheekily signed the letter "I am, Mr. Dundas, Not your obedient humble servant, But the contrary."[211]

Two days later (the timing was not accidental), Dundas showed his hand by announcing the postponement of the trial until December. What appeared as a reprieve was in fact another turn in a longer political strategy of slowly tightening the screws on Paine to the point where he would either buckle or emigrate. But giving up was for him simply out of the question. He had been pushed so far by events into a head-on confrontation with the government that capitulation would have destroyed his sense of personal integrity and ruined his growing public reputation. In any case, capitulation was unthinkable, he believed, because the revolution in Britain was on its way. He certainly acted the part. Like a public hero pushed into a corner, his time on earth running short, Paine decided to perform some daring — yet deliberately understated — acts. With the usual pinch of conceit, he informed the press that he was "very quietly sitting to MR. ROMNEY, the painter." The sitting was fixed by Clio Rickman, who worked hard for Paine's consent. Rickman was pleased with the resulting portrait. It showed Paine's long face, his characteristic aquiline nose, and his deep-set eyes, more alive than in any previous or subsequent portrait or sketch. Rickman considered it "perhaps the greatest likeness ever taken by any painter" and was delighted with William Sharp's decision to make an engraving of it, which soon sold widely throughout the country.[212]

Paine meanwhile needled the government deeper by calling openly on Britons to support the French Revolution. From May 1792, he openly identified with the leading journal of the French Girondins, the sophisticated *La Chronique du mois*, and, according to the *Times*, he was among the "frequent associates" of Charles Maurice de Talleyrand, the unofficial French ambassador who had been dispatched by the National Assembly to foster better diplomatic relations between the two countries.[213] Paine also published at a breathtaking pace. In public life, he told friends, civility is germinated by words and killed by threats. He drafted parts of a pamphlet, which later appeared as *Letter Addressed to the Addressers on the Late Proclamation*. He may also have published, writing under the name "Vindex," a tract in support of the abolition of slavery titled *Old Truths and Established Facts, being an Answer to a very new pamphlet indeed!*[214] In mid-June 1792, he penned two letters to Lord Onslow Cranley, who had publicly welcomed the "most gracious Proclamation against the enemies of our happy Constitution" and whom Paine described tartly as one of a parasitic class of men "living in indolence and luxury, on the labours of the public."[215] On July 4, in a letter to the Society for Constitutional Information, Paine announced that the six-penny edition of the first part of *Rights of Man* "is circulating for the benefit and information of the POOR." He divulged that a similarly priced edition of the second part was in press and asked that the society become trustees of the thousand-pound royalties so far generated on the book, "to apply it to such purposes as they shall see proper."[216]

The society declined the offer, and Paine, displaying his usual principled selflessness, spent the money on circulating cheap, nonprofit editions of *Rights of Man*. As the government closed in on him, he remained adamant that publishing profits ought to be plowed back into political projects for extending the boundaries of citizenship. "As we have now got the stone to roll," he wrote to Thomas Walker, "it must be kept going by cheap publications. This will embarrass the Court gentry more than anything else, because it is a ground they are not used to."[217]

It was true that the "Court gentry" were unused to arguing their case publicly with the ranks of the commoners. Yet by the end of the summer of 1792, whatever embarrassment they felt had hardened into a desire for revenge. The proclamation against "wicked and seditious writings" began to be enforced rigidly. Magistrates' reports on suspected cases of sedition poured in from all over the country. The book police grew more active, and the number of court convictions of varying severity mushroomed. Government-sponsored meetings called to denounce Paine flourished, and the practice of laundering payments to publishers of anti-Paine material continued unabated. Spies swarmed around antigovernment public meetings, and taverns and coffeehouses frequented by Paineites were more tightly monitored than ever before. Paine himself was tailed constantly on the street, and his movements in and out of the Rickmans' on Mary-le-Bone Street were watched constantly by government agents. The tide of press gossip and sarcasm continued to rise, and Paine's effigy was executed a hundred times over.

Paine's friends became alarmed at the growing repression. Paine himself seemed to become unusually introspective. At the end of the first week of September, his bridge-building friend John Hall reported him morose: "Mr. Pain called. . . . Does not seem to talk much. Rather on a reserve, of the prospect of political affairs."[218] Exactly one week later, his trial at the Guildhall now looming, his friend William Blake tried to convince him — according to one story — that the reign of terror placed his life in serious danger. Blake had just been told of the rumor that a warrant had been issued for Paine's arrest. His advice was brief: "You must not go home, or you are a dead man!"[219]

The warning may have been groundless, or even deliberately exaggerated, but Paine, who was rattled but still sensible, took the advice. On the evening of September 13 — he resolved to travel under the cover of dark because "it was necessary to take precautions for his personal safety" — he headed for the Channel with two companions, the London Corresponding Society attorney John Frost and Achille Audibert, a municipal officer of Calais. Attempting to give government agents the slip, the coach wound a circuitous route through Rochester, Sandwich, and Deal, the threesome finally alighting safety in Dover, where they checked into the York Hotel. Then followed a hair-raising episode. As Paine and his companions were depositing their trunks in their room, men claiming to be Excise officials entered, forcing them to remain in the room and demanding that they empty their pockets and hand over the keys to their trunks. Paine grew apprehensive, fearing this was the arrest predicted by Blake. The officials rummaged through Paine's trunk, dragging out onto the floor every paper and letter, sealed and unsealed. Paine protested. He drew the officials' attention to "the bad policy, as well as the illegality, of Custom House officers seizing papers and letters, which were things that did not come under their cognizance." The chief official snapped that the Royal Proclamation gave them the authority to act as they wished. He then proceeded to examine in detail Paine's papers and to rip open two sealed envelopes containing letters written by Charles Pinckney, the American minister in London. The official, irritated by now, insisted on confiscating the papers and letters. Paine again protested, blocking the doorway. The two glared at one another until the official agreed to make a list of the documents before removing them from the hotel room.

An hour passed before the siege ended — in surprise. The Excise official, evidently acting under orders from elsewhere in the building, returned to Paine's room with all his papers, except for a copy of the Attorney General's summons and the proofs of *Letter Addressed to the Addressers on the Late Proclamation*, the originals of which Paine had left behind with its London copublishers, Clio Rickman and H. D. Symonds. The official hesitated. He explained that the seizure was in accordance with the Royal Proclamation, which to Paine's great surprise he then proceeded to denounce as "ill-founded," politely offering to repack Paine's trunk. The offer was accepted. The keys were handed to Paine, who finally understood that the government's aim was not to inflict harm but to force him into permanent exile.[220]

Dawn had come, and a crowd of local townspeople, informed of the minor drama at the York Hotel, gathered to witness Paine's departure from England. The three travelers, red-eyed and mentally fatigued by their all-night ordeal, stumbled with their trunks down a pebbled track onto the narrow pier. As they boarded the packet bound for Calais, the crowd puffed with hatred, singling out Paine for rough-tongued treatment. "On the Quay," reported *The London Chronicle*, "he trembled every joint; one man came up to him, and said, "Tom, you d____d scoundrel, do you think to escape without a ducking?" Others in the crowd threatened to apply a "cheap coat of tar and feather." Pale and shaking, Paine clambered aboard and went immediately below deck. As the ship was towed out into open waters, there being hardly a breath of wind, the crowd continued to hiss and to pelt Paine with ridicule. "Had we remained much longer," recalled a passenger, "they would have pelted him with stones from the beach."[221]

10

Executing a King

The Guildhall Trial

THE HOSTILE FAREWELL to Paine at Dover was matched by the government's resolve to prevent him from ever returning to bedevil England. Having successfully hounded their most dangerous opponent across the Channel into exile, the government of George III pushed ahead with plans to celebrate its victory with a glorious display of political sovereignty. It knew that a show trial and his conviction in absentia would seal his fate as political brewmaster in the British Isles, leaving him with a permanent warrant for his arrest and probable execution should he return.

Paine was aware that he had been pushed into retreat. He fired several parting shots from across the Channel. Shortly after arriving in Calais, he wrote a strongly worded letter to the Home Secretary, Henry Dundas, detailing his treatment in Dover, urging Dundas to "take measures for preventing the like in future," praising the ultimately civil behavior of the Excise officers, and drawing a parallel between the pointless bullying of private individuals by governments and those same governments' bullying of their own nations into war.[1]

Just over a month before his trial, and now in Paris, Paine wrote another stinging letter, this time to Sir Archibald Macdonald, the Attorney General. The tone was defiant. Paine claimed, with some disingenuity, that were it not for more important business in France, he would have stayed to defend himself, even at the price of prosecution. He predicted, accurately, that the government would pack the jury at his forthcoming trial and that this would reveal in advance the government's real intention: to put the citizens of England on trial and to suppress their indefeasible right "to investigate systems and principles of government." Paine boasted that his conviction would have as much personal significance as the government's obtaining a verdict against "the Man in the Moon." He also argued, cockily, that a symbolic conviction against the people of England would backfire on the ruling class. The likes of Macdonald should watch out, for a show trial would prove that "the Government of England is as great, if not the greatest, perfection of fraud and corruption that ever took place since governments began." That in turn might well concentrate the current popular disturbances into an upheaval that would lead to the sort of revenge on corrupt rulers now displayed in French politics. Paine was deliberately exaggerating, but the serious conclusion he drew expressed his long-standing belief that not even England, supposedly the home of European liberty, could withstand the impact of the modern republican democratic revolution. "The time, Sir, is becoming too serious to play with court prosecutions, and sport with national rights. The terrible examples that have taken place here . . . ought to have some weight with men in your situation."[2]

Those words must have irritated Macdonald. They certainly strengthened his resolve to proceed with the case, which began at the Guildhall in London on a drizzly mid-December morning in 1792. For the occasion, the Crown had handpicked a special jury — all wealthy, plump, and respectable men filled with icy hostility toward Paine. The recent revolutionary events in France had left them in a state of deep shock. Probably their noses could smell the blood of the September massacres, their brains were pressed by thoughts of the king's coming trial, and their ears still echoed the cries of plebeians storming the Bastille and the taunts accompanying the king's slow march from Versailles to the Tuileries.

The charge against Paine was propagating "seditious libel," and it was introduced to the court by the Honourable Spencer Perceval (who seventeen years later would become Prime Minister of England). Paine was described as a traitor to his country and a drunken roisterer who had actively supported both the American and French Revolutions and had vilified Parliament, king, and the precious settlement of 1688. The courtroom hushed. Perceval began:

Thomas Paine late of London, . . . being a wicked, malicious, seditious, and ill-disposed person . . . and most . . . seditiously and maliciously . . . contriving and intending to . . . traduce and vilify the late happy revolution providentially brought about . . . under . . . His Highness William, heretofore Prince of Orange, and afterwards King of England . . . did write and publish . . . a certain false . . . seditious libel of and concerning the said late happy revolution . . . and . . . our present Lord the king . . . and . . . the parliament of this kingdom, entitled *Rights of Man, Part the Second*.

Shortly after Perceval's summary of the charge, Thomas Erskine, Attorney General to the Prince of Wales, rose to his feet to defend Paine. Erskine's task was virtually impossible, considering the hostility of the prosecution and jury and the fact that, even before the trial had begun, Erskine himself had been pilloried throughout the Tory press as a cohort of Paine's and a fellow traveler of the French Revolution. But Erskine was renowned as a brilliant legal mind and an eloquent orator who liked to deliver long addresses. This one on December 18, 1792, was no exception. It lasted more than four hours. Each word was recorded painstakingly by Mr. Gurney, the principal shorthand writer in London at that time, and the whole text was later published in several editions, which are today deposited in the vaults of the British Library.

Summarized, Erskine's argument was that the charge of seditious libel against Paine was unjustified because it violated a key principle of the British constitution — the principle of the liberty of the press. Erskine attacked the view, defended by Sir William Blackstone, Chief Justice William Mansfield, and Tory writers such as Jonathan Swift and Dr. Johnson, that Parliament is always the sovereign power. Erskine criticized the principle of state sovereignty. In effect, he accepted the First Amendment to the United States Constitution (concluded on December 15, 1791), which specified that "Congress shall make no law . . . abridging the freedom of speech or of the press." In matters of publishing, Erskine argued, Parliament's power is limited by the right of individuals freely to speak and publish their views. Each individual naturally requires the oxygen of publicity. The government of citizens' tongues, brains, and eyes is inadmissible. Liberty of the press is a natural right, given by God. It cannot be infringed by any earthly power, and certainly not by corrupt governments wanting to save their own skin. "Every man," Erskine emphasized, "may analyze the principles of its constitution, point out its errors and defects, examine and publish its corruptions, warn his fellow citizens against their ruinous consequences." Erskine went further. Quoting Paine, he denied that freedom of individual expression by means of a free press would lead to rebellion and disorder. Civil disputes conducted in ink would not end in bloody civil war. On the contrary, rapacious governments are the primary cause of civil disorder, whereas government based on public discussion among citizens with a conscience is naturally peaceful, if noisy. A free press, like the spear of Telephus, could heal the wounds it inflicts on the body politic: "Let men communicate their thoughts with freedom, and their indignation fly off like a fire spread on the surface; like gunpowder scattered, they kindle, they communicate; but the explosion is neither loud nor dangerous: — keep them under restraint, it is subterranean fire, whose agitation is unseen till it bursts into earthquake or volcano."

These republican arguments inspired by Paine left the jury cold. The prosecution rose to reply, but Mr. Campbell, the foreman of the jury, interrupted to explain that he had been instructed by his brother jurors to save time by delivering an immediate verdict — guilty. According to reports, several people in the courtroom instantly hissed the verdict. Cries of "take them into custody" were heard. Panic ensued, and the friends of Erskine, who had received many anonymous threatening letters prior to the trial, feared for his life. They bustled him out onto the steps of the Guildhall, where, to everybody's surprise, a crowd of several thousand supporters had gathered, chanting "Paine for ever!"; "Erskine and the Rights of Juries!"; and "Paine and the liberty of the press!"

Some members of the Whiggish and Radical crowd proposed to unhitch the horses from Erskine's carriage and draw him by hand to his home in Serjeant's Inn. Erskine declined the offer, stating that he was exhausted by the day's business and that he would be most honored if his kind supporters permitted his horses to remain harnessed to his carriage. His polite request was in vain. The crowd pressed forward. The horses were unharnessed, the traces were seized, and Erskine's carriage was hauled manually through the narrow streets amid loud applause. As the procession entered Cheapside, the crowd swelled. The street was filled with more cries of "Paine and the Liberty of the Press." Windows were flung open. Women, waving handkerchiefs, called out, "God bless you Erskine; God bless you my dear Erskine." At some windows, and in the street, some gentlemen, some of them sober, shouted "Damn Tom Paine, but Erskine for ever and the Liberty of the Press." The throng became so great at Fleet market that the procession was detained for fifteen minutes. Eventually, it arrived at Serjeant's Inn, which by that time was overflowing with supporters. Erskine alighted from his carriage, made a low bow, and entered his house amid thunderous applause from the large crowd, which dispersed peaceably within a few minutes.[3]

Fatigued with Kissing

The popular support for Paine in London was impressive, but not as spectacular as the rapturous welcome he received in Calais on September 13
after crossing the Channel from Dover. It rained hard, and Paine —
soaked to the skin, cheeks and nose reddened by the cold — appeared
tired out by the long journey from London and the ordeal in Dover. "He is
the very picture of a journeyman tailor who has been drunk and playing
at nine-pins for the first three days of the week, and is returning to his
work on Thursday," remarked a snobbish gentleman who traveled on the
same packet with him. Paine's companion John Frost described the welcome extended to the commoners' hero:

> All the soldiers on duty were drawn up; the officer of the guard embraced
> him on landing, and presented him with the national cockade, which a
> handsome young woman, who was standing by, begged the honour of fix-
> ing in his hat, and returned it to him, expressing a hope that he would con-
> tinue his exertions in the behalf of Liberty, France, and the Rights of Man.
> A salute was then fired from the battery to announce to the people of
> Calais the arrival of their new representative.[4]

In early September 1792, while doing battle with the government of
George III, Paine had learned that he had been offered citizenship of
France and soon elected Calais's representative to the forthcoming National Convention. Bearing the mark of Girondin free-mindedness, the
final draft of the constitution of 1791 had provided for the possibility,
under special conditions, that any foreigner wishing to reside in France
and willing to take the civic oath could be granted naturalization by the
assembly.[5] On the eve of elections to the convention, the playwright Marie
Joseph de Chénier urged that French citizenship be granted unconditionally to distinguished foreign writers whose works had "sapped the foundations of tyranny, and prepared the road to liberty." On August 26, M.E.
Guadet, the formidable Girondin debater from Bordeaux, submitted a
proposed list of candidates before the Legislative Assembly. Some of
Chénier's suggestions had been dropped and several new names added by
Guadet, who read aloud the names of six Englishmen: William Wilberforce, Joseph Priestley, Thomas Clarkson, James Mackintosh, David
Williams, and Thomas Paine. All the nominees accepted their honorary
citizenship and, with that, eligibility for election to the convention. Only
two of the new French citizens — Priestley and Paine — were sufficiently

well-known to the electors to be nominated and approved. Priestley declined, having decided already to emigrate to the United States. Paine, under intense pressure in his native country and passionately concerned that the French Revolution succeed, accepted election and took his seat in the convention. He was nominated by no less than four departments, deciding after taking advice to accept the nomination from Pas-de-Calais.[6]

The new member for Calais had not anticipated the rapturous welcome awaiting him in his constituency. After being presented with the national cockade by the officer in charge, Paine made his way to an inn on the Rue de l'Égalite. "Vive Thomas Paine! Vive la Nation!" cried the joyful citizens who lined the road from the quay, braving the rain in the hope of catching a glimpse or shaking the hand of their new representative. After registering at the inn and depositing his trunk, Paine was escorted by a procession to the town hall. More cannon boomed as the mayor of Calais embraced Paine "with the greatest affection." He then delivered a short welcoming speech in front of a large admiring crowd. Achille Audibert whispered the translation to Paine, who afterward rose to the occasion by placing his hand on his heart and vowing in a brief reply "that his life should be devoted to their cause." After a splendid lunch and a late-afternoon nap, the new Calais representative was escorted to the town meeting hall, where "a vast concourse of people" had gathered officially to celebrate his election. Paine squeezed his way with "the greatest difficulty" through the buzzing crowd to the podium, all eyes upon him. Seated beneath a bust of Comte de Mirabeau draped with the American, French, and British flags, Paine listened intently to the speeches leading up to the official announcement of his election as deputy to the National Convention. "For some minutes after this ceremony," someone reported, "nothing was heard but 'Vive la Nation! Vive THOMAS PAINE!'"[7]

Paine lingered for several days in Calais, meeting local citizens and municipal officials, learning from scratch the role of political representative, his translator Audibert constantly at his side. On September 16, Paine and Frost left for Paris, stopping overnight in Abbeville, Amiens, and Clermont. In each town, Paine was showered with a "flattering reception" and greeted "with elaborate ceremonies."[8] He was in excellent spirits by the time he reached Paris on September 19, although Frost said, "I believe he is rather fatigued with the kissing." The grandest embrace was yet to come. After registering at White's Hotel Philadelphia in the passage des Petits Pères, Paine and Frost headed straight for the Legislative Assembly, whose final session was drawing to an end. As he entered the great hall, Paine was spotted by the Minister of Finance, Pierre Joseph Cambon, who rushed forward to kiss him, the galleries and deputies erupting into cheers and cries of "Vive Thomas Paine!"

Paine could not have known that Cambon's kiss sealed a murderous political contract. With his ears half-blocked by his tongue's ignorance of French, his eyes were initially blind to the sinister side of the Revolution. He saw only political jubilation everywhere. He was supremely confident and proud to be at the heart of French politics. On the morning of the opening of the Convention on September 20, Paine paid a visit to Gouverneur Morris, passing on the letters from Charles Pinckney that had nearly been confiscated in Dover. The two friendly archenemies quickly fell into a heated discussion about the course of the Revolution, with Paine scoffing at Morris's prediction that the Austrian and Prussian armies of counterrevolution would march on Paris in a fortnight.[9] As it happened — the news would not reach the streets of the capital for another forty-eight hours — Paine was right. By one of the great coincidences of history, the day on which the National Convention convened to elect its officers was also the day on which the national army — to cries of "Vive la Nation!" — fought its way to its first great victory. "Here and today," remarked Paine's contemporary Johann Wolfgang von Goethe, who was on the battlefield at Valmy, "begins a new age in the history of the world. Some day you will be able to say — I was there."[10]

The same excitement would have bubbled from the well-wishers and 750 deputies to the Convention that day in Paris had the news reached the city in time. Instead, strong winds and driving rain helped to solemnize the procession as it snaked its way toward the new parliament building. The member for Calais was an atypical representative. At fifty-five years of age, he was among the oldest sixth of the procession, although still a sapling compared to the "father of the House," old Longqueue of Chartres, who was seventy-four. A staymaker by trade, Paine also was one of only a handful of workingmen and artisans who were deputies, the vast majority of whom were lawyers, businessmen, professors, teachers, and doctors. Finally, whereas most deputies were from the district, town, or village in which they had been born or grown up, Paine was only one of two foreigners. The other honorary citizen deputy was Anacharsis Cloots, a rich and flamboyant baron from the duchy of Cleves, near the Dutch frontier, who called himself the "voice of humanity" (*orateur du genre humain*) and later the "voice of the trousered classes" (*orateur des sans-culottes*). Cloots urged his constituents to wage political battle against "European tyranny" (*la tyrannie européenne*), and to this end he set a personal example through his close contacts with the revolutionaries in Holland. As an extreme supporter of so-called dechristianization, he later insulted the Christians of his constituency by presenting the Convention with a copy of his *Certainty of the Proofs of Mohammedanism*. He later fell out of favor with Robespierre and was guillotined.[11]

The politicians of the first French republic filed into the Pavillon de l'Horloge, whose entrance was marked UNITÉ and surmounted by a cap of liberty in red serge. The delegates entered through the great door and past the grand staircase into the *salle des séances*. The deputies' seats were ramped in a great semicircle against one side of the hall, nine deep at the ends and six deep in the middle. Opposite them, at floor level, were the bar, the secretaries' tables, the speaker's desk, and the president's chair, from a design by Jacques Louis David. The public galleries stretched from behind the deputies' seats to each end of the hall, whose walls were decorated with busts of the classical republican heroes — Plato, Solon, Lycurgus, and Demosthenes from Greece; Cincinnatus, Brutus, Valerius Publicola, and Camillus from Rome.

The icons were arguably misleading, since the central questions facing the Convention were not classical but modern. The king of the French nation had been suspended, but since France was not yet a republic, what kind of regime was it or could it become? The new constitution of 1791, enacted before the suspension of the king, was still in force, but whether it remained valid was arguable, to say the least. Ministers had been appointed, but could they still be considered constitutional executives? Should Louis himself be brought to trial, given that the agents and accomplices of the royal counterrevolution were already dead or in exile? Should he be executed, as some had suggested in whispers?

The Convention moved quickly to debate the issues. After deciding a number of procedural matters, including the election of Jérôme Pétion de Villeneuve, the mayor of Paris, as president of the Convention, the deputies, sitting in profound silence, hearts thumping, listened to the radical proposition put to it: "That royalty be abolished in France." The motion was carried unanimously, amid passionate applause. Paine sat through the debate, riveted to the translation provided by a fellow English-speaking deputy, Étienne Goupilleau. Paine "gave his voice" to the decision, Gouverneur Morris noted in his diary that day, later adding, prophetically, that "history informs us that the passage of dethroned monarchs is short from the prison to the grave."[12] On the second full day of business, as news of the French victory at Valmy filtered in, the Convention decreed that "in future the acts of the assembly shall be dated, *First Year of the French Republic*." Three days later, after a stirring debate about the dangers of federalism, it was agreed — without the American federalist's support — that "the French Republic is one and indivisible." Without formally dissolving the existing monarchical constitution, the Convention had carried France into the realm of what had until recently been unthinkable, proclaiming it the first great European republic. All that remained was to enact a republican form of government.

The Specter of Jacobinism

The mood of the bulk of the French population was hardly reflected in these bold steps of the Convention. Paine had heard that the peasantry, who constituted a huge majority of the electorate, were at this point generally satisfied with what they had received from the Revolution. They were unprepared to fight for the restoration of the monarchy, it is true, but they also were unprepared either to undergo recruitment into the French armies to fight abroad or to become embroiled in what were perceived as Parisian political controversies. They wanted to be left alone to enjoy their newfound freedom from feudal charges and to cultivate their newly acquired land. None of this mattered. As the business of the Convention unfolded, so too did the maxim that majorities begin revolutions, while minorities — and minorities of minorities — carry on the revolution by sweeping the rest of the population along with it.

Paine had first witnessed this characteristic of modern revolutions in America during the Silas Deane affair. He tasted a bitterer form of it during the Convention debate on the judiciary sparked by the delegate Georges-Jacques Danton. With astonishing boldness, Danton plunged the deputies into an uproar by insisting that the removal of the king had left untouched the monarchy's power bases, especially the legal institutions that served to protect the aristocracy. He called for the proper election of judges: "Those who have made it their profession to act as judges of men are like priests; both of them have everlastingly deceived the people. Justice ought to be dispensed in accordance with the simple laws of reason." The implication was clear: "Let the people choose at its pleasure men of talent deserving of its confidence."[13]

Paine requested the floor. With Goupilleau standing beside him at the speaker's desk, nervously translating his spoken English paragraphs into French, Paine argued that the control of political power required a trained, educated, and disinterested judiciary. Thorough knowledge of the law and the practical ability to apply it in cases of dispute could never be acquired by "the people" or by their "political representatives." The rule of law required "impersonality." The process of interpreting and administering laws should not be left in the hands of constantly altering legislatures subject to the push and pull of elections and personalities vying for government power.

Buried in Paine's remarks was the lesson, acquired in Pennsylvania during the American Revolution from the time of publication of *Common Sense*, that unchecked legislatures were potentially as despotic as unchecked monarchs. The lesson was ignored by the Convention, which voted strongly in favor of Danton's motion. At least one member of the public gallery, an Englishman, reported that Paine's speech was "not fortunate."[14] Paine returned to his seat, aware that something was not quite right but not realizing how deep was the political crack emerging within the ranks of the deputies.

After the leaden reply to Danton, Paine tried to draw the delegates together by appealing for unity in the name of the world-historic struggle of the French revolutionaries, as he had done numerous times in his American pamphlets and addresses. In *Lettre de Thomas Paine au Peuple François*, published by his friend Nicolas de Bonneville on September 25, 1792, the fifth day of the Convention, Paine reminded his fellow citizens that "liberty cannot be purchased by a wish." He also noted the spread of republican democratic revolutions across frontiers and predicted the breakdown of the conventional state system that "divided patriotism by spots of earth, and limited citizenship to the soil, like vegetation." The future growth of active citizenship across frontiers, Paine wrote, depended heavily on the success of the French Revolution and its armies. France should be honored to be in the vanguard of citizenship, but "liberty and equality are blessings too great to be the inheritance of France alone. It is an honor to her to be their first champion."

Paine lashed out in the pamphlet at despots of all countries in the militant cosmopolitan language that was now central to his political identity: "O! ye Austrians, ye Prussians! ye who now turn your bayonets against us, it is for you, it is for all Europe, it is for all mankind, and not for France alone, that she raises the standard of Liberty and Equality!" In passing, Paine argued the interesting point that despots are always caught off balance by citizen-based armies and citizens' power — despots "have only been accustomed to make war upon each other, and they know, from system and practise, how to calculate the probable success of despot against despot; and here their knowledge and their experience end" — but the conclusion he drew seemed oddly flat, to the point of being naive: "In entering on this great scene, greater than any nation has yet been called to act in, let us say to the agitated mind, be calm." His final appeal to civility, understandable given the growing acrimony within and without the Convention, no doubt struck many deputies as either parsonic or laughable: "Let us punish by instruction, rather than by revenge. Let us begin the new era by a greatness of friendship, and hail the approach of union and success."[15]

These words fell like seeds on parched soil. The Convention simply did not hear, preoccupied as it was with its own internal disputes. During their early meetings, the deputies had sat randomly in the Pavillon de l'Horloge, where they pleased. But observers noted that as the sessions proceeded, regular groupings of so-called Jacobins to the left and Girondins to the right of the president's chair began to form, with the uncommitted deputies sitting in the center front seats and a small group of so-called Mountaineers sitting in the higher seats at one end of the hall. The membership of this political configuration was initially not fixed. Individual deputies altered their seating habits, and even within the crystallizing blocs dissension was rife. But as the days passed, the blocs hardened to the point that Paine, who spoke only a few words of French and had friends among all sections of the Convention, became aware of being caught in a dangerous bind.

The leaders of the majority Girondins, as they came to be called, were men with friends of leisure and property. They believed in private property and market competition and were convinced that every political question could be settled by appeals to conscience and reason. They had learned their republican politics from news of the American events filtered through debating societies and Sunday suppers in Bordeaux, Marseilles, and other regional towns, and they continued dining together in Paris, although they never felt especially comfortable amid its pomp and frills. Within and around the Convention, they practiced the art of political nepotism, and convinced of their own superior talents, they nurtured their ambition of monopolizing the government of the country. But they made few attempts to capture or influence the lower circles and clubs of extraparliamentary political life in Paris; these were left to their politically more astute rivals, the Jacobins.

In social background and overall aims, the Jacobin leaders differed little from their Girondin opponents. They were republicans who were no less humanitarian and idealistic, and they emphatically believed, as did the Girondins, that the Revolution, the war, and the Convention were of fundamental historical importance. Their differences with the majority Girondins centered on their deeper concern for the common people.

They also were less patient with political shibboleths, and they were more willing to gamble politically, to make tough political calculations, and to execute decisions with ruthless energy, speed, and even violence. Their taste for tough action on behalf of the people made them impatient with the drawn-out process of constitution making. That impatience built up into resentment when it became clear that the Girondins would dominate the committee assigned the task of drafting a new republican constitution.

The committee set up by the Convention on September 29 consisted of four Girondins — Jacques Pierre Brissot de Warville (who was later replaced by Charles Barbaroux), Pierre Vergniaud, Armand Gensonné, and Pétion; two Jacobins — Bertrand Barère de Vieuzac and Danton; an adviser from across the Channel, David Williams, a Girondin sympathizer who did not attend committee meetings but submitted his *Observations* on how to improve the constitution of 1791; and three avowedly nonparty men — Marquis de Condorcet, Emmanuel-Joseph Sieyès, and Paine, who were considered political philosophers knowledgeable about constitution making. Paine reported that of those three, "I was elected the second person in number of votes, the Abbé Sieyès being the first."[16] Of the independents, who dominated the proceedings, Sieyès was the least effective committee member, fastidiousness or fear holding him back from contributing to what he foresaw to be a document biased in favor of one party. Condorcet coordinated the bulk of the discussions and did most of the drafting. In this he was assisted by Paine, who, despite his ignorance of French, found time to have lengthy discussions in English with Condorcet and to produce an important memoir on the subject.

The draft constitution presented to the Convention on February 15, 1793, was a flop. It proved to be deeply unpopular with both parties. Long and refined to the point of clumsiness — it contained 368 articles and ran to 85 pages — it bore the deep imprint of Anne-Robert-Jacques Turgot's teachings on Condorcet's philosophic mind. It much more resembled a philosophical tract than a constitution. The draft also proved unpopular because it took so long to produce that others grew impatient and began to draft their own versions. The drafting process ultimately took more than four months, not least because an invitation issued on October 19 resulted in the submission of hundreds of proposals from amateur constitution makers, all of which, in the new climate of republicanism, were painstakingly perused.

After presenting the draft document, the committee adjourned, and another two months elapsed while critics studied the result. By the time Condorcet received questions from the assembly on April 17, 1793, the word was out that the Jacobin Club had instructed a rival committee to draft an alternative constitution. Worse, the Convention itself decided to set up another committee to review the many private submissions from budding legislators. Even worse, in mid-March in the Vendée, the coastal region situated between the mouth of the Loire and La Rochelle, an armed popular uprising took place against the government, and some of its officials were murdered. The Girondins were further devastated by news of a disastrous military campaign in Belgium. Not surprisingly, the draft constitution encountered heavy resistance. By May 29, when Paris itself was in the first throes of an anti-Girondin insurrection, the Convention had dealt with only 6 of the 368 articles.

During the debate on the Condorcet constitution, Paine aired his views by writing to Danton to express his concern about its unnecessary length and abstractness. He recalled how he and Condorcet had agreed that the new Pennsylvania constitution of 1776 would be the model for France's constitution. Condorcet's document had accordingly proposed the creation of a popularly elected one-chamber assembly and an executive council also chosen by the people. Paine largely approved and considered that Condorcet had not repeated the errors of the 1791 constitution prepared by the old National Assembly. "The late constitution," he wrote, "sacrificed too much to ceremony, and the impolitic apprehension of giving umbrage to foreign courts." But Paine expressed surprise and veiled disapproval of the length and complexity of the eighty-five-page document. The political situation required something different: a briefly worded, fundamental law that could be appropriated and adapted by other European nations in their struggle against despotism. "France is now in a situation to be the orator of Europe," he told Danton. The Condorcet constitution rested on a serious misjudgment of the political situation, which badly needed publicity on behalf of the Revolution, not philosophical treatises. France required a constitution that would enable it to "speak for other nations who cannot yet speak for themselves. She must put thoughts into their minds, arguments into their mouths, by showing the reason that has induced her to abolish the old system of monarchical government, and to establish the representative."[17]

Paine's confession to Danton was probably painful to write, for he had been friends with Condorcet for nearly three years. In no sense was their disagreement traceable to their respective capacities for philosophical reflection. Indeed, their political and intellectual temperaments and interests were virtually identical. The men shared a fondness for mathematics and abstract political thinking, and like Paine, Condorcet considered himself "a stranger to all parties, concerned with judging men and measures with my reason, not with my passions." The key difference was that Paine was a highly astute political animal well practiced in the art of making difficult judgments under difficult conditions, whereas Condorcet tended to look at the Revolution as a mathematical puzzle to be solved by the formula of natural and civil rights. He seemed numbed, even dizzied by the transformation of the abstraction *le peuple* into an armed, angry, and argumentative citizenry bent on changing the world. His main practical response was to escape back into the world of mathematical harmony by drafting a perfect constitution governed by reason and reason alone. Condorcet thereby failed to see what Paine now saw clearly — that a political earthquake had begun and that the days of the Girondin grip on political power were now numbered. Within a year, under enormous political pressure, Condorcet would pay for his naïveté, ending his life by suicide.

Paine's decision to speak out to Danton signaled his recognition of a shift of power toward the Jacobins and of the radicalization of the Revolution under popular pressure. He had been jolted into awareness of this shift by the delegate Georges Couthon's speech to the Convention on October 12, cynically announcing his conversion to Jacobinism. Couthon said softly:

> It is no good making pretences: you can take it from an old man, though a young republican, that there are two parties in the Convention. One consists of persons of extremist principles, limited resources, and anarchical tendencies; the other consists of shrewd, cunning, and extremely ambitious intriguers. The Girondins are for the republic, because that is the national mandate: but they are also for aristocracy, because they want to keep their influence, and to have at their disposal the appointments, the emoluments, and the financial resources of the republic.

Couthon went on to defend the central role of the Jacobin Club in resisting this new aristocracy: "Here the revolution was planned, here it was carried through. Jacobins and deputies stand together. He who deserts the club is a traitor, worthy only of the execration of his country."[18]

Punishing a King

Militant calls for a struggle against a treacherous new aristocracy always have polarizing effects during revolutions. Couthon's speech certainly worked in this way, especially because it came from the lips of a man who was severely disabled with rheumatism and rarely spoke before the Convention. On the day of his speech, Couthon had wheeled himself in his chair to and from the Jacobin Club. Sweating and exhausted, he had been carried in the arms of friends into the Convention to the speaker's desk, with all deputies in a state of suspended hush. Couthon's dramatic intervention set the scene for an almighty struggle over the single most divisive conflict to come — the punishment of the king — in which Paine would play a politically central, but personally disastrous, role.

As the armies invading the fledgling French republic were pushed back and the fear that a kingless France would be easy prey correspondingly dissolved, knives were drawn within the Convention. It was now faced with two related fundamental questions: Could the king be put on trial? Could he be tried by the Convention itself?

On November 7, an elaborate response to these questions was prepared for the Convention by Mailhe. He argued that the principle, laid down in the 1791 constitution, that "the person of the king is inviolable and sacred" was in fact subject to two restrictions. First, Mailhe spotted a tension within the constitution between the principles of the inviolability of the king and the accountability of his ministers. The constitution specified that the king's ministers were responsible for certain acts, in which cases the king was inviolable, whereas in other areas the same ministers were not accountable because the king himself was solely responsible and, hence, his inviolability no longer applied. Second, and more fundamentally, Mailhe recommended that the deputies distinguish between the old Legislative Assembly, which had been subordinate to the constitution and therefore incompetent to judge the king, and the Convention, which was the sovereign people in council and therefore a power higher than the constitution. The nation, being sovereign, was not bound to recognize royal prerogatives, he said. It was therefore entitled to treat the king as an ordinary citizen, to judge him as a citizen for acts committed prior or subsequent to his abdication. The Convention was bound by no forms of law. It might well have arranged for the trial and execution of the king at any time during the previous few months. It could order the same treatment now or at any time in the future.

The Convention was impressed. It arranged the translation of Mailhe's report into many languages and ordered its circulation throughout the departments and within the ranks of the revolutionary armies. The report undoubtedly fueled public speculation about the future of the king. It triggered a spate of pamphlets not seen in Paris since the outbreak of the Revolution and focused the minds of the deputies on the most important decision that they would make. For the next two months, seven hours a day, the Convention spent its time debating and dividing over the question. Paine, who always had a remarkable sense of the drama and historical significance of events, was riveted by the seriousness of the sessions. He noted how their near solemnity was reinforced by the president's frequent appeals to both the deputies and the public gallery to use their reason and to refrain from applauding and remonstrating.

Paine often sat next to Danton and wasted no time plunging himself into the deep divisions over whether the king should or should not be tried. It had been agreed that the terms of the debate would be limited by placing before the president two large urns, marked "CONTRE" and "POUR," into which the names of those who wished to speak would be placed and randomly drawn out in turn. This technique of ordering discussion failed to reduce the number of conflicting political positions produced by the debate; if anything, it accentuated those divisions.

Louis-Antoine-Léon de Saint-Just, the junior member of the Convention, insisted that Louis had never been a commoner, but always a king, and that since kingship was in itself a crime ("*on ne peut point regner innocemment,*" he said), he should be executed without a trial, which would prove unnecessary and expensive. At the opposite extreme were those speakers (such as Lefort and Morisson) who thought that nothing more should be done now that Louis was deposed or (such as Claude Fauchet and Rouzet) considered that capital punishment was contrary to the laws of nature as well as foolish, since allowing the heart of Louis to continue to beat would serve as a warning to all existing European despots and all future pretenders to the throne. Paine staked out a position between these extremes, although he clearly leaned to the latter view, even though it was fast losing ground.

Toward the end of November, the old maxim that the fecundity of the unexpected is more powerful than any statesmen suddenly rang true. Paine learned through private sources of the existence of a potentially explosive scandal. He was told that a locksmith named Gamain had passed on information to Jean Marie Roland de la Patière that a secret safe (*armoire de fer*) existed in the king's former private room in the Tuileries. Apparently, Gamain had been summoned by the king in May 1792 to construct the *armoire de fer* and, upon completing his contract, had fallen violently ill. Convinced that he had been poisoned, Gamain took revenge by presenting himself to Roland and revealing the story, which proved to be true. When Roland visited the palace with the locksmith, the iron chest was opened, and it was found to contain some 650 pages of private pa-

pers. They included scenarios for the king's flight, correspondence between William Pitt and Charles Calonne, details of Comte de Mirabeau's
schemes for royalist propaganda, and suggestions for the bribery of several popular leaders on the eve of the August 10 revolution.

Paine knew that when this information was revealed to the Convention, it would prove scandalous. It would dramatically reinforce the case
against the king and almost certainly magnify the deputies' demand for
his punishment, perhaps even his execution. Paine reacted quickly. He
wrote and had translated into French a speech titled "On the Propriety of
Bringing Louis XVI to Trial." Its deft arguments were shrewdly moderate.
"I think it necessary," he began, "that Louis XVI should be tried; not that
this advice is suggested by a spirit of vengeance, but because this measure
appears to me just, lawful, and conformable to sound policy." Paine sidestepped the constitutional arguments supporting his case. He implicitly
accepted Mailhe's own case and dismissed in an instant the chatter about
the king's supposed "inviolability" as an instance of the "burlesque." Instead, he chose to concentrate on the geopolitical reasons to try Louis.
Paine predicted that just as the investigation and trial of arrested thieves
often leads to the discovery of the wider gang to which they belong, so the
trial of the king would expose his involvement in the European conspiracy
of "crowned brigands." He pointed out, for example, that the trial could
help to reveal publicly the extent of George III's support for figures such
as the Landgrave of Hesse, whom he described as a "detestable dealer in
human flesh . . . paid with the produce of the taxes imposed on the English people."

Paine then pointed to a geopolitical maxim: democratic republics, he
argued, cannot thrive or even survive if despotisms are breathing down
their necks. The degree of civil and political liberty within a country is inversely proportional to the military pressures exerted on its borders. The
purpose of a trial was thus not only to expose the nature of monarchic
corruption but also to publicize the republican claims of the French Revolution, spawn the growth of a European struggle for civil society and democratic government, and help to reduce and eventually eradicate the
military tensions that choked off republican democracy. "France is now a
Republic; she has completed her revolution," wrote Paine, quickly adding
a touch of pessimism: "but she cannot earn all its advantages so long as
she is surrounded with despotic governments. Their armies and their marine oblige her also to keep troops and ships in readiness. It is therefore
her immediate interest that all nations shall be as free as herself; that revolutions shall be universal."

Throughout the address, Paine studiously avoided questions about the possible form of punishment of Louis, should he be found guilty. He considered such speculation premature and incompatible with the principle of a right to a fair and open trial, in which he certainly believed. More important, Paine tried in his address to avoid demonizing the king because he was convinced that cutting off the head of the king might seduce the Revolution into thinking, wrongly, that the body of despotism would then automatically wither and die. In addition, as he had pointed out in the case of Charles Asgill during the American Revolution, drops of blood spilled during a revolution can merge to form rivers, washing away the civility so vital to republican liberty. If the king were guillotined, why not also his ministers, their aides, their clients, and, finally, their accomplices and friends? An "avidity to punish is always dangerous to liberty," he warned. It always leads a nation "to stretch, to misinterpret, and to misapply even the best of laws." The remedy against that tendency, argued Paine, was clear: "He that would make his own liberty secure must guard even his enemy from oppression; for if he violates this duty he establishes a precedent that will reach to himself." Paine went on to insist that the king "should continue to enjoy good health," meaning that he should not be allowed to commit suicide or to die in prison, which would fuel suspicion that he had been poisoned. Paine also emphasized, against all the demonizing controversy about "inviolability," the thoroughly mortal aspects of the king, whom he described, ignoring his earlier praise, as "a weak and narrow-minded man, badly reared, like all his kind, given, it is said, to frequent excesses of drunkenness." He concluded that the Convention should concentrate on the business of securing the republic. Under no circumstances should it be fooled into primitively ad hominem judgments: "Louis XVI considered as an individual, is an object beneath the notice of the Republic."

Many other deputies did not think so. As the *armoire de fer* revelation took effect, pressure mounted for the execution of the king. Two demagogic speeches by Robespierre, delivered two weeks after Paine's address, accelerated the trend. In effect, Robespierre cried, "Those who talk of fair trials and the rule of law are unprincipled. Down with the prejudices of the ancien régime! Away with the enemies of the Revolution! Louis declared war on the Revolution, he has been defeated, and now it is the duty of the Convention to see that revolutionary justice is done. It must be done! Royalty must be abolished!" Paine cringed. A few days later, on December 10, Robert Lindet presented to the Convention the report of the commission investigating "the crimes imputed to Louis Capet." It documented with meticulous care how Louis had plotted and marched a course of counterrevolution. The courage of those in favor of revenge grew.

The next day, the king was transported in a closed carriage to the Tuileries, bundled into the Convention, and interrogated for nearly three hours. According to an engraving by Pelegrini, Paine sat within a few feet of the king.[19] President Barère prefaced his questions to the king with the solemn reminder to Paine and the other deputies that the eyes of Europe and future generations were upon them. Profound silence filled the assembly. Plainly dressed in an olive silk coat, the young king sat calmly. Without any counsel, he improvised every answer to a long list of tough and embarrassing questions, which he had not been shown beforehand. Unlike Charles I, he did not dispute the competence of the Convention to try him. Nor did he attempt to appeal over the heads of the Convention to the people. That was not his style. He answered every question and requested no extra time. Always calm and collected, Louis offered simple, unsmiling responses. Sometimes the effect was disarming; at other times, his cunning was hardly believable. When asked about documents in his own handwriting, he denied all knowledge of them. He sidestepped questions about the *armoire de fer* and claimed with a straight face that he had forgotten all about a number of other sensitive matters. On only one occasion did his understated calmness slip. When accused of shedding the blood of Frenchmen, he raised his voice and, with tears in his eyes, indignantly replied to Barère: "No, Sir! I have never shed the blood of Frenchmen."

Paine watched in silence as the king and his defenders were escorted from the Convention. Life instantly returned to the assembly, with some Jacobin deputies calling for an immediate consideration of the verdict. The majority, who saw no reason for hurrying, voted for stalling the decision. This gave time to the Girondins, with whom Paine had so far been identified and who were increasingly isolated, enabling them to call for a plebiscite of the departments. The proposed appeal to the sovereign people was not based on principles. Supporters of referenda are never more trusting of "the people" than when the latter agree with their views. Following this rule, the Girondins' move was purely tactical, designed to outflank their Jacobin opponents. The Girondin minority hoped, and the Jacobin minority feared, that by appealing to the departments, the unexpressed royalism of the countryside would surface, forcing those favoring vengeance and execution to back down.

Paine feverishly worked night and day for a third option. He slept little, ate sporadically, and talked nothing but politics. He was not in favor of the execution of the king, but he also was not in favor of a plebiscite. He feared that donkey voting would result from an ill-worded question manipulated by party factions. Above all, he was certain that a plebiscite would openly contradict the role of the Convention, whose task, after all, was to decide the shape and method of implementation of a new constitution for France. Representatives elected to represent the people in highly complex matters should get on with their job of representing their citizens. Accordingly, Paine worked to convince as many deputies as possible that the Convention should decide Louis Capet's fate. Presuming that the deputies could be convinced of his guilt, Paine hoped that he also could convince them to opt for clemency. He worked on a plan to send the king and his family to America, discussing it with Gouverneur Morris, Edmond Genet, the newly announced ambassador to the United States, and Pierre Lebrun, the minister of foreign affairs. Paine spent a whole evening at Lebrun's residence listening to Brissot and others discuss ways of dealing with the growing threats to the king's life. When asked by Genet what effect the execution of the king would have in America, Paine answered, "Bad, very bad."[20]

That curt remark captured well Paine's clear proposal for compromise, which won him respect in circles otherwise hostile to his point of view. Toward the middle of January 1793, an article in a leading Jacobin newspaper on the subject of press freedom compared him favorably with Jean-Jacques Rousseau. "If we silence today the Vilettes and the Gauthiers," said the author, referring to two reactionary journalists, "tomorrow silence will be paid on the Thomas Paines, the J. J. Rousseaus; for a policy which begins by closing the mouths of servile and cowardly pamphleteers because they can do harm, will end by depriving of utterance the generous defenders of the rights of man, because they do not know how to flatter or to compromise with principles."[21] Such praise worked to deepen interest in Paine's next address to the Convention, written in English and printed and read to the deputies in French on January 15, 1793, as *Opinion de Thomas Payne sur l'affaire de Louis Capet, adressée au Président de la Convention nationale. Imprimée par ordre de la Convention nationale.*

The address was a valiant last attempt to rescue the king from the guillotine. "Citizen President," Paine began. "My hatred and abhorrence of monarchy are sufficiently known . . . but my compassion for the unfortunate, whether friend or enemy, is equally lively and sincere." Paine emphasized his heartfelt abhorrence of monarchy not because he wanted to reinforce the mood of the deputies or to enhance his reputation among them. He instead calculated that antiroyalist sentiment could be used to embarrass those in favor of the king's execution, causing them to think twice and even to change their minds about the wisdom of a violent adieu to monarchy in their country. His reasoning was subtle. He reminded the Convention that amorality and violence are traits of monarchic despotism. He shrewdly recalled for his Jacobin opponents a speech given recently at the Jacobin Club, in which Autheine had said, "Make me a king to-day, and I shall be a robber tomorrow." Paine drew from this the pointed implication that "the kingly trade is no less destructive of all morality in the human breast, than the trade of an executioner is destructive of its sensibility."

Paine went on to warn, as he had done in *Rights of Man*, that despotisms have a nasty habit of ruling from the grave. In effect, he told the Jacobins that their lust for revenge against the king was despotic behavior. "Monarchical governments have trained the human race, and inured it to the sanguinary arts and refinements of punishment; and it is exactly the same punishment which has so long shocked the sight and tormented the patience of the people, that now, in their turn, they practise in revenge upon their oppressors." The moral was clear: the Convention was duty-bound to avoid bloodletting and to find another, more effective — republican democratic — way of dealing with a king who was surely guilty of considerable crimes. Paine prodded the conscience of the Jacobins by skillfully referring to a speech in the old National Assembly given by Robespierre on the need to abolish the death penalty. He then urged the deputies as a whole to do everything to ensure that France throw off the yoke of monarchy without defiling itself in the impurities of its own blood: "It becomes us to be strictly on our guard against the abomination and perversity of monarchical examples: as France has been the first of European nations to abolish royalty, let her also be the first to abolish the punishment of death, and to find out a milder and more effectual substitute."

What, then, could be done with the king and his family? Reminding the deputies that he considered himself a citizen of both France and the United States, and by implication that he could therefore speak with some authority on the matter, Paine proposed that Louis Capet be exiled to the United States. He pointed to a precedent for this nonviolent compromise — the late-seventeenth-century banishment into exile of the Stuart family, who subsequently "sank into obscurity, confounded itself with the multitude, and is at length extinct." Louis's banishment to republican America would clearly be different, since there he could fully grasp what he, as a politician of retreat, already sensed. There, "far removed from the miseries and crimes of royalty, he may learn, from the constant aspect of public prosperity, that the true system of government consists not in kings, but in fair, equal and honorable representation."

For all its tactical and intellectual brilliance, Paine's address was out of step with the mood of the majority of deputies. Revenge was rife, and certainly the majority of deputies were not in favor of the Girondin proposal to go back to the country in a referendum. Barère once again spoke for the nonparty majority when he emphasized the prudence with which deputies had considered the fate of the king and said that it would therefore be both superfluous and cowardly to hold a referendum on a matter on which the Convention had been empowered to decide. "It is for you to vote, before the statue of Brutus, before your country, before the whole world," he concluded. "It is by judging the last king of the French that the National Convention will enter into the fields of fame."[22]

And so on January 15 the voting began. There were three questions: Is Louis guilty? Do you wish your decision to be referred to the people? What form of punishment does Louis deserve? It was agreed that voting was compulsory, that absent members could submit their votes in writing, and that those present should announce their votes aloud from the tribune, giving reasons for their decision if they so wished. There was virtually unanimous agreement that the king was guilty. Nearly two-thirds of the deputies, Paine among them, voted in support of the Jacobin view that a referendum on the form of punishment should not be held. Paine supported the Jacobin position not because he wanted to bring matters to a head, but for the entirely opposite reason that it would minimize the chances of the king's execution. Exactly what form the punishment should take was the most difficult question to resolve. It was complicated by a prior dispute about the size of the majority required to carry the decision. Danton set the pace by insisting that the fate of the king should be decided in exactly the same way as other matters concerning the republic had been: by a simple majority. The proposal was adopted. The Girondins, who until now had reasoned that no decision would be better than a Jacobin decision, grew nervous.

Voting on the final question began at eight in the evening on January 16, 1793, continuing nonstop for twenty-four hours. The hall was transformed into something of a macabre house of entertainment. As deputy after deputy mounted the tribune to make his statement and cast his vote, a half-whispering, half-festive public crowd gathered at one end of the hall and in the public galleries to witness the possible entry of death into the

Convention. Men of all classes rubbed shoulders, some of them gawking foreigners bent on witnessing history being made, others chatting and sipping brandy or wine, sometimes hushing as a deputy explained his vote. Exhausted deputies napped, waiting for their turn to vote. Ladies in charming negligees, some of them pricking cards with pins to keep count of the votes, ate oranges and ices and drank liqueurs. Friends and acquaintances sent and received greetings, and now and again speculation ran through the crowd that a scrutineer had attempted to slip away a vote in order to save the troubled king.

The crowd heard a string of morbid verdicts. Some deputies uttered only one word when casting their vote: death. Others spluttered obituaries. Barère said, "As a classical author said, the tree of liberty grows only when it is watered by the blood of all species of tyrants. The law says death, and I am only its voice." Anacharsis Cloots, the only other foreign deputy, issued a toughly worded verdict: "Louis is guilty of high treason [lèse majesté]. What punishment have his crimes merited? I answer, in the name of the human race, death."

Paine's turn to vote came at midday on January 17. When his name was called, his heart thumped and limbs numbed. Fatigued, he walked slowly to the tribune. He steadied himself, paused, hands behind his back, and spoke slowly in practiced French: "I vote for the confinement of Louis until the end of the war, and for his perpetual banishment after the war."[23]

Several other deputies followed suit. The philosopher Bançal referred to Paine in his brief speech calling for imprisonment: "I think that this judgement will be that not of kings, who prefer a dead king to a humbled king, but the judgement of the nations and of posterity, because it is that of Thomas Paine, the most deadly enemy of kings and royalty, whose vote is for me the anticipation of posterity." Another deputy waxed eloquent about him: "By the example of Thomas Paine, whose vote is not suspect, by the example of that illustrious stranger, friend of the people, enemy of kings and royalty, and zealous defender of republican liberty, I vote for imprisonment during the war, and banishment at the peace." Still another expressed his support in more modest language: "I rely on the opinion of Thomas Paine, and I vote like him for imprisonment."

Paine's plea for clemency was defeated — by one vote. When the final results were announced later that evening, 287 had voted with Paine either for imprisonment or exile, sometimes substituting death in case of foreign invasion, while 72 had voted for death with a plea of clemency (sursis); on the other side, 361 deputies — the slimmest possible majority — had voted unconditionally for death. The opponents of the decision, including

Paine himself, scurried to delay, amend, or quash the decision. With the Jacobins clamoring loudly that political justice necessitated the immediate execution of the king, Paine worked through the night of January 18 preparing another address to the Convention, which he hoped would undo the decision, which he thought morally and politically unwise, when it was once again put to a vote.

The address was translated and read the next day by Bançal, and it caused an uproar. Bançal began reading: "The decision come to in the Convention yesterday in favor of death has filled me with genuine sorrow." Jean-Paul Marat interrupted, shouting: "I deny the right of Thomas Paine to vote on such a subject; as he is a Quaker, of course his religious views run counter to the infliction of capital punishment." Paine was indeed the son of a Quaker, but that allegation was untrue, even if rhetorically effective, for Paine's reasons for preserving Louis's life, traceable to Thetford, were wholly secular and political, as his friends and supporters knew. Bançal continued, amid heckling: "Liberty and humanity have ever been the words that best expressed my thoughts, and it is my conviction that the union of these two principles, in all cases, tends more than anything also to insure the grandeur of a nation." The heckling turned into sinister murmurs when Paine spoke openly against the Jacobins. He accused them of acting "from a spirit of revenge rather than from a spirit of justice" and predicted that the execution of the king would backfire geopolitically against France. "France's sole ally is the United States of America," read Bançal, his voice barely audible above the hubbub. "It is the only nation upon which France can depend for a supply of naval stores, because all the kingdoms of northern Europe are either now waging war against her, or shortly will be."

Bançal paused, then continued, taking advantage of a temporary lull in the uproar: "Should you come, then, to the resolution of putting Louis to death, you will excite the heartfelt sorrow of your ally." Pandemonium broke out. Thuriot angrily shouted down Bançal: "The words you are reading are not those of Thomas Paine." Marat added to the uproar: "I denounce the translator. Such opinions are not Thomas Paine's. The translation is incorrect." Another deputy, Garran, fought for control of the floor and sprang to Bançal's defense: "It is a correct translation of the original, which I have read."

The angry confusion threatened violence. Paine rushed toward the tribune to try to halt the slide toward utter confusion. Standing beside Bançal, he testified that the preceding words were indeed his own. Uproar returned to hubbub, and Bançal resumed to draw Paine's conclusion: "Do not, I beseech you bestow upon the English tyrant the satisfaction of learning that the man who helped America, the land of my love, to burst her fetters, has died on the scaffold." In a flash, Marat leaped from his seat, ran to the middle of the chamber, and shouted, "Paine's reason for voting against the death penalty is that he is a Quaker." Paine exploded, his French instantly improved by anger: "I have been influenced in my vote by public policy as well as by moral reasons."[24]

The retort failed to save the king. That afternoon, on January 19, Louis's final hope of life was killed by a final vote, 380 to 310. Two days later, at about ten in the morning, the king was brought in a closed blue-topped carriage through lines of armed citizens and red-coated, black-hatted soldiers to the Place de la Revolution, where a cold mist still hung over the huge crowd waiting to witness the end. Paine, protesting against the decision and sickened by the sight of bloodied and wrenched bodies dangling in the wind ever since his days in Thetford, was not present. After five minutes in prayer, drums beating constantly, Louis was escorted from the carriage to the scaffold, which he mounted, assisted by a priest. When he reached his destination, the king raised his arm to signal the drummers to be silent and said in a loud voice: "My people, I die an inno-cent man" (*Peuple, je meurs innocent*). Whatever words he subsequently ut-tered were drowned by the defiant rat-a-tat of kettledrums. Only the men who pinioned him heard Louis's last words: "I hope that my blood may secure the happiness of the French people." A second later, the blade fell, blood spurted over the scaffold, and the executioner held aloft the severed head, the crowd chanting in unison, "*Vive la nation!*"

Exile in Saint-Denis

The body and severed head of the king were buried that day in the ceme-tery of the Madeleine. Orders were given that the grave should be dug to a depth of ten feet, as if that unusual distance between surface and casket would ensure that the hand of the Bourbon monarchy would forever be prevented from touching the living. Paine himself doubted whether despotism could be abolished by so simple an act and so little earth. He foresaw that the Convention's decision to execute the king involved much more than disposing of the monarch. He saw that the weeks of strife within the Convention had had as much to do with party politics and the struggle for state power as with "revolutionary justice." From this, he pri-vately drew the chilling conclusion that the violence practiced on the king would likely be turned on those deputies and citizens who had opposed the decision. In fact, before coming into exile, he had told a friend, John King: "If the French kill their king, it will be a signal for my departure, for I will not abide among such sanguinary men."[25]

As each day passed, "sanguinary men" tightened their grip on the Revolution. Paine found it impossible to escape. Unable to travel to England, where he would have been arrested and executed, or to return to America because of the dangers of being apprehended by British ships, he had no option for the time being but to stay put in France and quietly retreat from French politics. There was no doubt that he badly needed rest after the grueling dramas of the past four months. The constant stream of visitors to consult his opinions on French and international politics added to his exhaustion. Clio Rickman, who had just been convicted for selling Paine's works in England and had fled to Paris to escape prison, described the magnetism of Paine within the English-speaking community centered on White's Hotel, where Paine was living. At one point, said Rickman, Paine tried to silence the hubbub by moving to a hotel near the Rue de Richelieu. Word quickly got out, and the flow of callers actually increased to the point where, uncharacteristically, Paine insisted on appointments. "He was so plagued and interrupted by numerous visitors, and sometimes by adventurers," reported Rickman, "that in order to have some time to himself he appropriated two mornings in a week for his levee days. To this . . . he was extremely adverse, from the fuss and formality attending it, but he was nevertheless obliged to adopt it."[26]

Paine responded by going into internal exile. He moved to the country, to the village of Saint-Denis, situated some nine kilometers north of Paris and famous as the cradle of Gothic architecture. There, in comparative peace and quiet, he occupied part of the hotel where Madame de Pompadour once stayed. He rose early, usually around seven, soon afterward breakfasting with several English residents, including his friends William Choppin and William Johnson, whom he had first met in London. Paine had long, animated discussions over breakfasts of coffee and toasted bread with a fellow resident, M. La Borde, a former military officer who was interested in mechanics and geometry, subjects that were among Paine's favorites. After breakfast, Paine usually wandered alone for an hour or two in the well-designed, spacious hotel gardens, lost in thought. Afterward, he played "chess, whist, piquet, or cribbage" and "marbles, scotch hops, battledores," talked about his childhood, or exchanged anecdotes. He then retired to his bedroom, where he remained in solitude until dinner, working at his desk, "up to his knees in letters and papers of various descriptions."[27]

The flow of visitors continued. By prior arrangement, he was joined by numerous dinner guests, including Brissot, Bançal, and General Francisco Miranda, together with a number of English and American associates such as Mary Wollstonecraft, Thomas Christie, Joel Barlow, and Captain Imlay.[28] Some were unimpressed. "He is better in print than in the flesh," reported Georg Forster in mid-May 1793. "He has all the wit and egoism of the model Englishman. His blazing-red face dotted with purple blotches make him ugly, although he appears inspired and his eyes are full of fire."[29] Rickman, always faithful, described dinners at the hotel as occasions when those fiery eyes often burned: "His conversation was often witty and cheerful, always acute and improving, but never frivolous." From time to time, Paine received invitations to dinners elsewhere, which he liked to accept. An evening attended by Wollstonecraft saw Paine again in good spirits: "For above four hours he kept every one in astonishment and admiration of his memory, his keen observation of men and manners, his numberless anecdotes of the American Indians, of the American war, of Franklin, Washington, and even of his Majesty, of whom he told several curious facts of humour and benevolence. His remarks on genius and taste can never be forgotten by those present."[30]

The time spent at Saint-Denis was a period of pensiveness and physical recuperation, evidenced by his willingness, for the first time in his life, to describe his surroundings with delighted precision. He clearly felt affection for this haven in an increasingly heartless world of French politics. He wrote, "My apartments consisted of three rooms; the first for wood, water, etc.; the next was the bedroom; and beyond it the sitting-room, which looked into the garden through a glass door; and on the outside there was a small landing place railed in, and a flight of narrow stairs almost hidden by the vines that grew over it, by which I could descend into the garden, without going down stairs through the house." Saint-Denis seemed to stir memories of his childhood in Thetford, filling him with the initial delight of a country boy returning to his native region:

The house, which was enclosed by a wall and gateway from the street, was a good deal like an old mansion farmhouse. The courtyard was like a farmyard, stocked with fowls — ducks, turkeys, and geese; which for amusement, we used to feed out of the parlor window on the ground floor. There were some hutches for rabbits, and a sty with two pigs. Beyond was a garden of more than an acre of ground, well laid out, and stocked with excellent fruit trees. The orange, apricot, and greengage plums, were the best I ever tasted.[31]

For several months, playing games of cribbage and chess, feeding fowl, tasting homegrown oranges, and contributing to animated dinner conversations proved to be relaxing diversions from politics. But despite everything, Paine could not quite manage to free himself from the clutches of the Revolution. The newspaper accounts reaching him each day, together with the verbal reports delivered to him by his guests, reminded him of the quickening pace, polarization, and violence of events. Four days after the execution of the king, Edmond Louis Alexis de Dubois de Crancé, the chief military strategist in the republican army, brought forward a plan for the recruitment of 300,000 volunteers and the creation of eight armies, totaling more than half a million men. Several of these armies were to be used for an offensive against Prussia and Austria, some were to defend the southern frontiers, and the rest were to be detailed for an invasion of England.

On February 1, 1793, as the foundations of the *grande armée* began to be laid, war was declared on England in the name of the French republic. The call for troops in Paris was answered enthusiastically, especially in the backstreets of the city. But in the Atlantic coastal department of the Vendée, a major armed uprising against recruitment broke out on March 10. The activists had mixed motives. Their ranks included farmers who refused to sell their grain for depreciated paper money; women who believed that the Blues (as they called the republican troops) would eat their infants; priests who feared the secular trends in French society; squires burning to avenge the king's death; and peasants opposed to sending off their sons to fight for a government they disliked and against an enemy they had never seen. The net effect of this motley opposition was to shatter the remaining power and confidence of the Girondin-led government. A charter summarizing the demands of the opponents of recruitment was presented to the Convention on March 23. It read like a program of the existing frightened civil society against an unrepresentative, despotic state: "No enlistment, no forced labour [*corvée*], no requisitioning, no taxation without local consent, no searching of houses, and complete freedom of worship, speech, and publication."

By the time those words were read to the deputies, the Girondins within the assembly were panicking. They supported a move decreeing the death penalty for all arms-bearing rebels and the confiscation of all their possessions. Local detachments of the National Guard and troops from the Belgian front were deployed against the resistance, but the crisis undid the remaining power of Girondin partisans and nominees throughout the country. By early April, they were fast losing their remaining influence in the executive and administrative branches of government. News from the military front was equally disastrous for the Girondins. The army's expedition into Holland had failed, the Brabant had again fallen into enemy hands, and, on April 5, the commander of the republican army, General Charles Dumouriez, deserted his troops in a cloud of bullets fired by them at him as he galloped to safety behind enemy lines. Meanwhile, in Paris, the Jacobin forces had effectively wrenched power from the Convention. The "sovereign people," armed and organized and under Jacobin control, moved with ease through the clubs, popular societies, presses, and sectional meetings denouncing the Girondins, guns, knives, and matches at the ready. At this point, the ascendant forces of the Revolution began to devour their own self-defined "enemies." On the same day as Dumouriez's defection, the Jacobin Club, led by its president Marat, called, in the name of the "sovereign people," for the purging of the Convention. "Friends," he said, "we are betrayed. To arms! There is counter-revolution in the government, and in the National Convention. There, in the citadel of our hopes, our criminal representatives pull the strings of the plot they have contrived with a horde of despots coming to cut our throats!"

Paine was frightened by the power grabbing and violence. He shuddered at the paranoid talk of "betrayal" and "enemies of the Revolution"; he would surely have sweated if he had known that he was already being watched and denounced as an English meddler by the Paris-based Société fraternelle securité aux jacobins.[32] On April 20, he wrote to Thomas Jefferson describing the "extraordinary crisis" in which France now found itself. The military setbacks suffered by the republican armies were considerable. But what really alarmed and depressed him was the degeneracy of the Revolution — its violation of its own standards of the rights of man. "Had this Revolution been conducted consistently with its principles," he said, "there was once a good prospect of extending liberty through the greatest part of Europe; but I now relinquish that hope." He pointed specifically at the Jacobins, "who act without either prudence or morality," and he drew the morose conclusion that with their growing ascendancy, "the prospect of a general freedom is now much shortened," and "I begin to contemplate returning home." Depression oozed from the pages. The reasons, as the postscript to Jefferson made clear, were not only political: "I just now received a letter from General Lewis Morris, who tells me that the house and barn on my farm at N. Rochelle are burnt down. I assure you I shall not bring money enough to build another."[33]

The New Rochelle fire, sparked by spring lightning, stiffened Paine's sense of entrapment in France. But much worse news was to follow. At the time of writing to Jefferson, Paine and most other deputies were anxiously pondering Marat's claim that the Convention harbored traitors to the Revolution. Paine had smelled despotism and xenophobia in Marat's call to arms, and from a distance in Saint-Denis he quietly supported the successful move (on April 12) by Guadet, Brissot, and other Girondins to impeach Marat and order his trial before the brand-new Revolutionary Tribunal (*tribunal extraordinaire*) on the serious charge of inciting the nation to riot and anarchy. Paine found Marat pompous and ridiculously affected — he stalked about Paris dressed as a sansculotte, his hair tied back in a red cloth, clutching cockily at the pistols tucked in his belt — and Paine's dislike of him grew after Marat's loudmouthed interruptions of his address to the Convention. The men had only met socially on one occasion, and Paine had felt ill at ease. "Is it really possible that you believe in republicanism?" demanded Marat, who at that point was convinced that a constitutional monarchy was best for France. "You are too enlightened to be the dupe of such a fantastic dream."[34]

Paine reported those cutting remarks in a letter to the Jacobin Club, suggesting that Marat had for a long time harbored sympathies unfavorable to republican democracy. He sent a copy to *Le Moniteur*, the leading newspaper in Paris, but his little plan to embarrass Marat and add weight to the charge against him was overtaken in the strangest of ways. A few days before Marat's trial began, Dr. William Johnson, Paine's fellow lodger in Saint-Denis, attempted suicide. Johnson's behavior confirmed that revolutions are halls of mirrors that often stretch individuals' and groups' perceptions of reality in bizarre ways. Johnson had become so convinced by rumors that Marat's call to arms was in fact a call to massacre all foreigners in France, especially Englishmen like himself, that he decided in a state of paranoia to end his life before it was ended against his will. He made his choice melodramatically. Standing at the top of the hotel stairs, knife in hand, he stabbed himself in the chest twice and fell into the arms of his friend William Choppin. Near death, he offered Paine his blood-spattered watch and will and passed Choppin a farewell message to the world.

A local doctor arrived within minutes, quickly enough to maintain Johnson's pulse. The melodrama made good gossip. Within a matter of hours, the story had spread from the hotel to Paris. Paine spoke to Brissot, showing him the note that Johnson had written, which Brissot transcribed and passed on immediately to the editor of his newspaper, *Le Patriote français*. The whole story was then retold according to the sensationalist rules of journalistic license and printed in the issue of April 17: "Before dying, he wrote with his trembling hands these words which we have read on a paper now in the hands of an eminent foreigner: 'I came to France to enjoy Liberty, but it has been assassinated by Marat. Anarchy is even more cruel than despotism. I cannot endure the doleful spectacle of the triumph of imbecility and inhumanity over talent and virtue.' "[35]

Jacobinism Triumphant

Twelve days after his impeachment, Marat faced the Revolutionary Tribunal on charges of "advocating anarchy at the expense of liberty." Given the Jacobin ascendancy outside the Convention, it came as no surprise to anyone, least of all Paine, who attended, that much of the seven-hour trial concentrated on the juicy bits of the story of Johnson's attempted suicide. Halfway through the proceedings, the "eminent foreigner" Paine was called to the witness stand. He was asked to interpret the note written by Johnson and in his possession immediately after the attempted suicide.

Paine began by questioning the court's attempted trivialization of the issues. The court president countered by passing a copy of the note to him. Paine replied sharply, through an interpreter, that he was unable to "conceive what it has to do with the accusation against Marat." Muffled voices filled the courtroom. Paine had earned another counterrevolutionary black mark.

> *President of the Court:* Did you give a copy of this note to Brissot?
> *Paine:* I let him see the original.
> *President:* You gave it to him exactly as it is printed?
> *Paine:* Brissot could only have written this note according to what I read to him and what I told him. I observe to the court that Johnson stabbed himself twice only after learning that Marat was going to denounce him.
> *Marat* (interrupting): The young man did not stab himself because I was going to denounce him, but because I wanted to denounce Thomas Paine.
> *Paine:* For a long time Johnson had anxieties. As for Marat, I only spoke to him once, in the corridors of the Convention. He told me the English people were free and happy. I replied that they suffered under a double despotism.

Johnson was called to the witness stand shortly afterward. He admitted that he had not been well at the time of writing his last testimony and qualified his belief that foreigners living in France were endangered by the Revolution. He claimed that he had read a newspaper report that Marat intended to arrange the massacre of all deputies who had voted for a plebiscite to determine the fate of Louis Capet. Wrongly believing that Paine was among those deputies, he had decided to try to protect him by embracing martyrdom. "The friendship I had for Thomas Paine led me to want to kill myself," he said.

The explanation had an air of weak-minded melodrama about it, and although, as Paine pointed out, it had nothing directly to do with Marat's call to arms, it helped to ruin the case against him. By the time the court got around to considering the charges, Marat was in fine form, manipulating the jury with avuncular gestures and tough words. He wittily poured scorn on the accusations against him and twice paused, with great effect, to appeal to the public gallery not to interrupt his testimony with applause. The jury's verdict of not guilty came as no surprise, and everybody present in the courtroom understood the veiled meaning of the court president's radiant description of Marat as "the intrepid defender of the rights of the people." The president's conclusion was equally sinister: "It is difficult to contain our just indignation when we see our country betrayed on all sides."[36]

Marat's acquittal was greeted with a triumphant roar by the large Jacobin crowd gathered outside the courtroom. As Marat, wearing a crown of oak leaves, was shouldered through their ranks by a flying wedge of citizens brandishing pistols, Paine skulked off through the backstreets to White's Hotel, lost in thought, profoundly aware that the pseudotrial signaled the final political victory of Jacobinism and the beginning of a round of executions of its "enemies." He was especially disturbed by the thought that this turning point in the Revolution highlighted not only the huge gap between the ideals of the rights of man and the bullish tactics of the Jacobins. Those ideals, often considered by Paine since his time in England as the Archimedean point from which despotism could be criticized and overturned, were clearly being used by a minority government acting in the name of the sovereign people to justify a new species of despotism. This minority government was rash and precipitate, giddy and inconstant. These cold-blooded schemers were committing atrocious crimes *against* the people. His head rang with thoughts about the age-old prejudice of conservatives that democratic government is despotic by nature because, acting in the name of the people, it supposes itself to be the only fountain of power, against which there can be no appeal.

By the time he arrived at White's Hotel, Paine was sullen and shaken. He was hardly in the mood for the dinner party thrown by Mr. Milnes, "a gentleman of great hospitality and profusion, who usually gave a public dinner to twenty or thirty gentlemen once a week," reported a fellow guest, Clio Rickman. Paine was seated opposite a Captain Grimstone, "a stout young man about thirty," who introduced himself as a descendant of Sir Harbottle Grimstone, a member of Oliver Cromwell's Parliament and an officer in his army. Grimstone was a high-mannered aristocrat with a low reputation for having gambled himself into debt. He had escaped debtors' prison in England by fleeing to France. He was frank to the point of crassness about his royalist political beliefs, and at the end of the dinner, "when the glass had freely circulated," Grimstone "loudly and impertinently" went out of his way to pick an argument with Paine. Still depressed, Paine spoke little and softly, which threw Grimstone into a rage. "The captain became more violent, and waxed so angry," reported Rickman, "that at length rising from his chair he walked round the table to where Mr. Paine was sitting, and here began a volley of abuse, calling him incendiary, traitor to his country, and struck him a violent blow that nearly knocked him off his seat."[37]

Incivility (*incivisme*) in this form was a capital offense in the eyes of a law established some months earlier by the Convention, which also had ruled that any witness who hindered the arrest of the offender was subject to the same punishment. A recent case of assault on François Louis Bourdon de l'Oise in Orléans, and the subsequent execution of his attacker and the eight witnesses, had demonstrated the seriousness of the law. The table guests at White's Hotel called the National Guard in a flash. Paine, not wishing to add to the prevailing spirit of acrimony and revenge, did all that he could to ensure that Grimstone was released unharmed. He contacted Barère, president of the Committee of Public Safety, requesting that a passport for him be issued and safe passage out of the country be guaranteed. He even sent Grimstone enough money to cover his traveling expenses, and after several delays Grimstone was indeed released.

Paine's compassionate refusal to think in terms of friends and enemies of the Revolution seemed more like saintliness than revolutionary politics. As each spring day passed, the situation became more sinister. In an interesting letter to Danton, dated May 6, 1793, Paine calmly analyzed the deteriorating situation as he saw it. His anxiety showed: "I am exceedingly disturbed at the distractions, jealousies, discontents and uneasiness that reign among us, and which, if they continue, will bring ruin and disgrace on the Republic."

Paine made it clear that the threats to the new republic were essentially domestic: "My despair arises not from the combined foreign powers, not from the intrigues of aristocracy and priestcraft, but from the tumultuous misconduct with which the internal affairs of the present Revolution are conducted." He pointed to the dangers inherent in the present centralization of power toward Paris, including jostling and power grabbing at the center, the alienation of the departments from Paris, and, he predicted, worsening shortages and inflated prices of basic commodities subject to centralized price fixing. Paine repeated his concern about the amorality of those currently forcing the pace of the Revolution: "I am distressed to see matters so badly conducted, and so little attention paid to moral principles. It is these things that injure the character of the Revolution and discourage the progress of liberty all over the world."

The principal source of decadence, he explained, was the prevailing "spirit of denunciation." The passage is famous, the lines are moving: "If every individual is to indulge his private malignancy or his private ambition, to denounce at random and without any kind of proof, all confidence will be undermined and all authority be destroyed." Paine had in mind the recent waves of rumors and accusations that Dumouriez had plotted a dictatorship and that Danton (according to Robespierre) had offered to finance an insurrection in support of Dumouriez's planned march on the capital, as well as Marat's talk of "criminal representatives" and "a horde of despots coming to cut our throats." Paine was emphatic that in a republican democracy, such deliberate misrepresentation of others in public is contrary to the public good and therefore antidemocratic. Freedom of expression is not the same thing as freedom of denunciation, liberty of the press not equivalent to liberty to libel. The distinction ought to be legally recognized and enforced. "Calumny is a species of treachery that ought to be punished as well as any other kind of treachery," Paine wrote. "It is a private vice productive of public evils; because it is possible to irritate men into disaffection by continual calumny who never intended to be disaffected."

On the same day that he shared these anxious thoughts with Danton, he wrote a letter to Marat, which unfortunately has been destroyed or lost. It is fascinating to ponder what he might have told his opponent, especially in view of the mounting attacks on the Girondins championed by Marat and his supporters. What did Paine say to the man who, within two days of his acquittal, contributed to the drawing up of a list of twenty-two Girondin deputies "guilty of the crime of felony against the sovereign people"? We do know that one week after his letter to Marat, Paine contributed to a small if temporary defeat of Marat's calumny during the trial of Paine's Venezuelan friend and former French army general Francisco Miranda. After the disastrous defeat of the retreating French armies in mid-March at Neerwinden, east of Louvain, Dumouriez had pinned the blame on General Miranda, who had been promptly arrested, then cleared of all charges in April after being defended on the floor of the Convention by Brissot's party. But as the report exonerating Miranda was read to the Convention, it was shouted down by the Jacobins, who managed to seize the moment and reverse the decision. Miranda was re-arrested, flung into prison, and brought to trial on May 12, 1793.

Standing before a packed courtroom, accompanied by a translator, Paine, in his role as character witness, told the sansculotte jury that he was sure that Miranda was not guilty. He had first met the general ten years earlier in New York, and again in London shortly after the publication of part one of *Rights of Man*, when Miranda (unbeknownst to Paine) had been in the pay of William Pitt during the Nootka Sound affair. Paine pointed out that he had come to know Miranda especially well in the past year in France, during which time he had helped prepare plans to spread revolution to Spanish America. Paine reminded the court that just prior to his arrest, the government had been actively considering commissioning Miranda to head a military expedition to Spanish America to coincide with the invasion of Spanish holdings in North America to be led by George Rogers Clark. Paine said that he was satisfied that Miranda was not a mercenary but a trustworthy military man. Said Paine through his translator,

> It is impossible for one man to know another man's heart as he knows his own, but from all that I know of General Miranda I cannot believe that he wanted to betray the confidence which the republic has placed in him, especially because the destiny of the French Revolution was intimately linked with the favoured object of his heart, the deliverance of Spanish America — an object for which he has been pursued and persecuted by the Spanish Court during the greatest part of his life.[39]

The jury decided unanimously to acquit Miranda, who would enjoy another two months of freedom before being rearrested and imprisoned under the shadow of the guillotine. Paine was relieved by the acquittal but still profoundly depressed by the times. He would have been unspeakably miserable had he known that the stage was being set for the climax of June 2. Ever since the king's flight, the outbreak of war, and the execution of the king, power had been passing from men who believed in persuasion and compromise to men who believed in uncompromising compulsion. There had been a gradual change from decentralized and open methods of government to methods that were centralized and closed. At every turn, the Jacobin forces spied an opportunity to compass their opponents' downfall.

The final showdown came during the last week of May after a Girondin-dominated emergency committee (*commission extraordinaire*) ordered the arrest of Jacques-René Hébert and others on charges of leading a planned insurrection. On the night of May 30, the Jacobins struck back with the formation of the central committee of the Revolution (*comité central révolutionnaire*), whose aim was to organize an insurrection against the remaining Girondin stronghold in the Convention. The committee comprised comparatively unknown Parisians such as the printer Marquet, the decorator Crépin, the toymaker Bonhommet, and the ribbonmaker Caillieaux. Their detailed plan for a bloodless and orderly insurrection was precisely executed. Their first move was to organize the National Guard to seize the key positions — the Place Royale, the arsenal, and the Pont Neuf — and to close the barriers around the city. Prominent suspects, including Etienne Clavière and Mme Roland (whose husband slipped away into hiding), were then arrested, and the Convention was encircled by four hundred men and thirty-two guns. Inside the building, deputies of the Left gathered to consider an ultimatum from the commune that the Girondin deputies be arrested.

Word of the crisis quickly reached Saint-Denis. Early on Sunday morning, June 2, Paine hurried to the Tuileries to put his weight behind those working to preserve the Convention from revolutionary destruction. By the time he arrived, the Convention was meeting in camera. The building was surrounded by armed troops and gun-toting volunteers and sealed off by a vast crowd of jeering, fist-waving Parisian citizens dressed in their Sunday best. Inside, Paine was told, the spectators in the public galleries were clamoring for the resignation or arrest of the Girondin leaders. He also heard rumors that a few of the victims — Fauchet, Maximin Isnard, Barbaroux, and Paine's friend François Lanthenas — had already lost their nerve, backed down, and consented to their own suspensions.

Paine tried to enter the building by presenting his deputy's pass to François Hanriot, the tough-faced commander of the National Guard. Hanriot told him sarcastically that he might as well use it as curlpaper on his own hair. Danton, who was standing nearby, intervened in English to tell Paine that by going inside, he would risk his life by adding to the chances of his name appearing on the list of Girondin "enemies of the revolution." Paine replied that he now saw that Vergniaud had been right in likening the French Revolution to Saturn, who had devoured his own children. Danton was quick to issue his famous counterreply. "Revolutions," he snapped, "cannot be made with rosewater."[40]

Paine was stunned. Like a stake hammered into the ground, he stood motionless, watching from within the crowd the unfolding drama, shocked and speechless. From inside the assembly came the rumor that Jean Denis Lanjuinais had convinced the remaining deputies that they were no longer free agents and that they should therefore terminate the proceedings and leave the building. The crowd of eighty thousand citizens tensed and hushed. It held its breath as the trail of deputies, led by their president, Marie Jean Hérault de Séchelles, appeared at the doors. Hanriot ordered his troops to stand to arms. A few voices from the crowd called in support of the Girondins. They were immediately swamped with loud cries of "Purge the Convention! Let it bleed!" (*Purgez la convention: tirez le mauvais sang!*) At gunpoint, the same deputies were then herded back into their seats. Within minutes, in stony silence, they approved Couthon's motion for the suspension and internment of twenty-nine Girondins, together with the ministers Lebrun and Clavière. The drama was over. The Jacobin insurrection had succeeded. "The horrid days of Robespierre"[41] had begun. Like a fly before a swat, Paine's life was now threatened with extinction.

11

Prison to Dictatorship

Terror

THE EXERCISE of the right of a sovereign nation to sack its own representatives at gunpoint — what Robespierre called a "moral insurrection" — flung Tom Paine into a depression for weeks. Returning to his Saint-Denis hotel, he fell sullen, would not eat, slept badly, and drank heavily. Toward the end of June, Gouverneur Morris, still unsympathetic toward Paine, reported something of his misery: "At present, I am told he is besotted from morning till night. He is so completely down, that he would be punished, if he were not despised."[1] Unusually, Paine revealed something of his own melancholia by reporting that he and the hotel residents kept themselves occupied with "those childish amusements that serve to keep reflection from the mind, such as marbles, scotch-hops, battledores, etc., at which we were all pretty expert. In this retired manner we remained about six or seven weeks, and our landlord went every evening into the city to bring us the news of the day and the evening journal."[2]

Going into retreat made sense, for after June 2 the world beyond Saint-Denis became dangerous. Those like Paine on the fringes of state power lived increasingly in a cat's cradle of suspicion and confusion, lies and spies, fanatics and policemen. Talk of popular sovereignty, which of course did not mean doing what the people or a majority of the people actually wanted, served as a cover for convoluted plots and counterplots, denunciations and counterdenunciations. At every turn, the Jacobins pushed to quicken the pace of political events, fighting at every step against those whom they designated Girondins, bureaucrats, speculators, hoarders, monopolists, and, above all, moderates. "Those who make revolutions by halves," declared Louis Saint-Just, "dig their own grave." The Revolution could not be advanced softly, gradually, politely. It demanded swift and dramatic deeds that would intimidate and impress waverers, supporters, and enemies alike. The regeneration of humanity, the institution of republican democracy, and the majesty of its goals justified every sacrifice. Force, the midwife of achievement and the antidote to inertia, must be regarded as indispensable to the enforcement of justice and reason. Redemption required repression: the people must be made into what they should be.

The self-appointed leaders of the Revolution tried increasingly to identify the republic with their own words and deeds. They considered themselves saviors of the future, and it is not surprising that their form of government produced monsters. Pompous, crass, precocious, grandiloquent, savage, and cruel, these men quarreled like fishermen after a catch, drunk on potions of power. Long hours set their nerves on edge. Hard work ground them down. Harassed, weary, and sick, they also were frightened to the point of paranoia. The revolutionaries talked themselves into a fantasy world of black-and-white thinking and false absolutes in which, for the sake of the Revolution and its virtues, everybody should be treated as knaves. They were convinced that although the king was dead, the spirit of royalty lived on in the institutions, hearts, and minds of the country. If their fellows rejected virtue, only terror was left to combat the treason and corruption that lurked everywhere.

Paine felt hemmed in by this deadly web of paranoia. On June 21, 1793, he read a report in *Le Moniteur* that two special delegates from the city of Arras (Robespierre's birthplace), in Paine's constituency, had visited the Convention, which he no longer attended, to denounce him and the four other elected representatives. "They declare," said the report, "in the name of the citizens of the Commune of that city, that Donoux, Personne, Maignan, Vailet, and Thomas Paine, deputies to the Convention from the Department of Pas-de-Calais, have lost their confidence."[3] Understandably, the special delegates objected to Paine's withdrawal from politics. He had no longer participated in the sessions of the Convention since the Jacobin takeover. He had not signed the two petitions, presented to the assembly on June 6 and on June 19, condemning the coup as an insult to the sovereign people and a violation of the rights of man. By following this strategy of avoiding danger by keeping out of sight, however, he risked being attacked by the Jacobin leadership, who viewed political reticence with profound suspicion. Since the building of the republic required the total destruction of whatever was opposed to it, not merely traitors but also the indifferent must be punished. Turpitude was treachery. Paine was thus baptized in the same hellish dilemma posed by all subsequent regimes dependent on the use of terror. If he collaborated with the government, he would have sacrificed his principles and, given the unpredictably bizarre web of paranoia, probably been victimized and punished sooner or later by his collaborators. Yet by sitting on his hands and refusing to collaborate, as he was now doing, he faced the possibility that he would be accused of indifference, which would result in the same outcome: suspicion followed by arrest and punishment.

The dilemma stalked Paine constantly from the summer of 1793. On July 9, shortly after his denunciation in the Convention, Paine's name was linked to a rumored conspiracy against the government. The rumor was soon scotched at its source when his accuser, whose political geography was evidently poor, recommended to the Convention that Paine deserved only suspicion, not accusation: "Respect a pillar of liberty from the other hemisphere; do not condemn him, for he has been deceived."[4] To say that Paine was deceived implied either that he required rectification or, having already succumbed once, that his foolishness might again get the better of him. Paine tried to wriggle out of this insinuation by writing a formally worded letter (dated August 27, 1793) to the Convention on behalf of his Pas-de-Calais constituents, attacking "the madness of our ancestors, which has brought us to the necessity of dealing solemnly with the 'Abolition of a Phantom.'" He also offered his services to the Committee of Public Safety. On September 4, during one of his rare visits to Paris, Paine bumped into Barère on the street. Barère explained that for several days, he had been intending to contact Paine and suggested that the two go together to the nearby Bureau of Foreign Affairs, where they could speak more freely through a translator. Paine consented and sat quietly as the interpreter, Mr. Louis Otto, conveyed Barère's requests.

Barère began by flattering Paine with a request for a copy of his contribution to the committee that had drawn up the ill-fated constitution, telling him that "it contained several things which he had wished had been adopted."[5] The subsequent business revealed that the Jacobins intended to use Paine temporarily for their own ends. He reported that Barère asked "my opinion upon sending commissioners to the United States of America" and whether "fifty or an hundred ship loads of flour could be procured from America."[6] Rather than responding at once through the interpreter, which would have been tedious and time-consuming, the two men agreed that Paine would offer his opinions in writing and that Mr. Otto would translate them for Barère.

On September 5, Paine wrote a businesslike letter to Barère. He enclosed a copy of the twenty-page plan for the constitution and summarized his thoughts on contacts with the United States. He began, "The idea you have to send Commissioners to Congress, and of which you spoke to me yesterday, is excellent, and very necessary at this moment." He pointed out that Thomas Jefferson, the former United States Minister to France and currently Minister of Foreign Affairs in the American Congress, was still sympathetic to French interests and would therefore welcome a delegation of commissioners. Paine was tough on Gouverneur Morris, supposedly the Americans' agent in Paris. Although he cautioned the need to treat Morris diplomatically, given his many influential contacts, he in effect recommended sidestepping Morris, who was "badly disposed towards you," was "not popular in America," and had "set the Americans who are here against him." As for the urgently needed supplies of flour — a famine caused not by weather but by the Revolution was now threatening France — Paine pointed out to Barère that there were some forty-five idle American ships docked in Bordeaux. They could quite readily be formed into a convoy that could carry the French commissioners to America. The convoy could be safely escorted into the Bay of Biscay by French ships, leaving it free to return from America with the desperately needed flour as well as reports from the commissioners. Paine concluded politely, "I am sorry that we cannot converse together, but if you could give me a rendez-vous, where I could see Mr. Otto, I shall be happy and ready to be there."[7]

Why, given the course of the Revolution, was Paine willing to make himself available to Barère? Was he acting like a puppy dog relieved that its arrogant master was still capable of kindness?[8] Perhaps. Paine also may have been guided by his conviction that a citizen's obligation to other citizens in need always overrides political machinations, especially under threatened famine conditions. In any event, for several weeks he devoted himself to the arrangements for buying American flour for the French. Barère later reported that Paine "showed us the way to go to work, he aided in the correspondence and worked hard in the foreign office to bring about this extensive purchase of food."[9] During this period, Paine also revived his long-standing interest in saltpeter, from which France now suffered an acute shortage. He concocted a top-secret plan to occupy the British-controlled island of St. Helena, off the African coast. The French would keep the Union Jack flying, then seize the cargoes of saltpeter carried there by unsuspecting British ships docking after their long journey from India.[10]

It may be that Paine had an ulterior motive for all this hard work for the Jacobins, which served as a means of covering his tracks as he busily devised plans to leave France. That option provided his only remaining hope of escaping the developing political absurdities, although, understandably, no details were divulged in his correspondence. Only the briefest of hints was given in passing to Barère, and it carefully avoided any reference to politics. "I shall return to America on one of the vessels which will start from Bordeaux in the month of October," wrote Paine. "It will soon be seven years that I have been absent from America, and my affairs in that country have suffered considerably through my absence. My house and farm buildings have been entirely destroyed through an accidental fire."[11]

The plan to leave France never materialized. Paine ultimately judged that it was too dangerous, since it risked attracting attention and, with that, prompting the dreaded phrase "traitor to the Revolution" to be fired like a bullet in his direction. His caution was to no avail. Shortly after his meetings with Barère and the translator, twisted rumors were circulated by the Jacobin deputy François Louis Bourdon de l'Oise that Paine had been seen on the streets and in the cafés of Paris speaking English and engaging in political intrigue. On October 3, on the bloodstained floor of the Convention, the Jacobin deputy André Amar read out his name from an official list of traitors to the republic. Since the Convention now functioned as a rubber stamp of the Committee of Public Safety, the governing body that ruled by decree, the announcement was a sign that Paine had run afoul of the highest political authorities. The announcement underscored the grave trouble he was in by referring to him as an "Englishman" who in America and France had been among the strongest supporters of Louis Capet. That insinuation was double-edged. It ominously linked him to the leading military enemy of France and to the despotism of the ancien régime. The announcement concluded that Paine had "dishonoured himself by supporting the opinion of Brissot, and by promising us in his fable the dissatisfaction of the United States of America, our natural allies, which he did not blush to depict for us as full of veneration and gratitude for the tyrant of France."[12]

Paine prepared for the worst. Like an insect trapped in a spider's web, he wrote to Thomas Jefferson on October 20 to confide his belief that there was "now no prospect that France can carry revolutions through Europe."[13] Paine called on Jefferson to send an American delegation to Europe to negotiate a truce or a peace conference among the warring states. Paine's desperate hunch was that the strategy of getting the Americans involved in the European war would have a civilizing effect on all parties, the French included. The consequent easing of military pressures on the borders of France would at least have the effect of weakening the basis of the Jacobin fear of counterrevolution and treachery.

By the time the letter reached Jefferson, the Reign of Terror in France was in full sway. The Jacobin government, as it could now be called, ran amok. Ever since the murder of Jean-Paul Marat by Charlotte Corday on July 13, it had aimed its blows in every direction. The leaders of pro-federal initiatives were banned, and police control in the provinces was tightened. The Revolutionary Tribunal was reorganized. Toughly worded warnings against English intrigue were issued, and, as Paine knew well, foreigners were rounded up. Orders were issued for the deportation of the members of the Bourbon family, the trial of the queen, and the liquidation of all royal tombs. A purge within the upper echelons of the army had begun, and rebels in the Vendée were arrested. On October 15, the government unveiled a giant political show trial (the Tribunal criminel-révolutionnaire) designed to advertise its power to exterminate enemies of the Revolution.

Paine trailed reports of the trial with trepidation. He was especially anxious because on the day before proceedings got under way, he learned that his name had come up in the trial, shortly to conclude, of Marie Antoinette. A key witness, Pierre Manuel, ex-deputy to the Convention and former attorney (*procureur*) of the commune of Paris, was asked to explain his motives. He answered, "I trusted in the morality of Thomas Payne, master in republicanism. I desired like him to see the reign of liberty and equality established on fixed and durable bases; I may have varied in the means that I proposed, but my intentions were pure."[14] The Revolutionary Tribunal judge, Marie Lanne, listened carefully, but the explanation was the wrong one, and Manuel was guillotined shortly after Marie Antoinette.

It now seemed only a matter of time before Paine would suffer the same fate, especially because the key trial that had begun on October 15 was directed at the whole Girondin Party rather than at particular individuals. "We are hearing evidence as to the opinions of the accused persons," remarked the Public Prosecutor Antoine-Quentin Fouquier-Tinville, "only in order to collect and to bring out the facts which prove that they belonged to an association [*coalition* — the word used for workmen's strike unions] for the ruin of the republic."[15] This meant that individuals were to be judged "objectively" guilty of sedition without "subjectively" intending or knowing their crimes. If it were shown that they held opinions characteristic of those plotting or contemplating sedition, or knew of or kept company with the same, the presumption of guilt was to be against them individually. Driven by this aim, government witnesses were called to establish "the facts." In practice, that meant that they repeated hearsay and made up stories riddled with insinuations, lies, and half-truths. No time limit was placed on what counted as evidence. Those who currently belonged to the forces of conspiracy were deemed always to have held treacherous opinions. Those who allegedly had acted seditiously in the past, even before the Revolution had begun, were deemed guilty of crimes in the present. The acts considered criminal were defined so broadly that literally almost any deed, from opposing clerical marriage to attempting to save the life of the king to doubting the guilt of General Charles Dumouriez, was seditious — if the accusers said so.

The distinction between patriots (*les patriotes*) and faction (*la faction*) was considered so clear-cut and absolute that legal procedure was violated at every step. When the show trial opened, the documents referred to by the prosecution had yet to be placed in evidence, and their contents were not communicated to the accused. The generally worded charges against the accused often did not apply to them as individuals. And even when the accused argued back, their "voices," like those of Joan of Arc or a patient prostrate before a psychoanalyst, were deemed to have deceived them into thinking that they were acting otherwise. None of these procedural perversions mattered. The aim was to speed up proceedings and get to the point: to purge the vice of party faction from the body politic by forcing it to recognize the sovereign methods of a single party backed by the guillotine.

Paine learned from his landlord, who took his usual daily horse ride into Paris on October 30, the sixth day of the trial, that earlier that evening a unanimous verdict of guilty had been declared against every one of the accused prisoners, among whom Paine counted such friends as Claude Fauchet, Pierre Vergniaud, and Jacques Pierre Brissot de Warville. Paine was told that after the accused had been led back into court to receive their death sentences, some of them had sworn at their judges. Others had shouted, "*Vive la république!*" One of them, Valazé, had stabbed himself in the chest. Paine later learned that the day after the verdict, the condemned men had gone straight from prison to the scaffold. What he did not yet know was that Robespierre, a man who harbored a profound suspicion of foreigners and had never particularly liked Paine or his principles, had already scribbled a reminder to himself: "Demand that a decree of accusation be passed against Thomas Paine, for the interests of America and France as well."[16]

Le Siècle de la Raison

Paine tried to keep his mind off the spreading Terror by spending long hours at his desk. Ever since moving to Saint-Denis, he had been making notes in his head and rough sketches on paper on the subject of religion and politics. Paine worked fast when he worked, especially when driven by political events. By the first week of March 1793, without telling the outside world, he had composed a short pamphlet attacking organized religion. He had passed it on to François Lanthenas, who had undertaken the work of translation and publication. We do not know what hopes Paine had for the work, but we can be certain that the printed version that appeared later that month as *Le Siècle de la Raison, ou Le Sens Commun des Droits de l'Homme* proved to be the most controversial work he ever published.

Much mystery still surrounds the first edition of the pamphlet. This is partly because only one incomplete copy has survived, thanks to the small print run and the absentmindedness of posterity. The mystery is deepened by the effective measures taken to prevent its circulation by the book police, who were encouraged by Georges Couthon and his close associate Robespierre, the men responsible for supervising French religious affairs on the Committee of Public Safety. The enigma is further compounded by the odd title page of the pamphlet. Perhaps because of a printer's error, or (more likely) because, in the aftermath of the execution of Louis Capet, Paine wanted to remain anonymous, *Le Siècle de la Raison* lists the translator Lanthenas as the author, at the same time announcing to readers that it was bound with an account of "despotism and fanaticism, ancient and modern" by a "citoyen Néez," whose contribution is not included in the sole surviving copy. Further confusion stems from the fact that during the spine-chilling events of October 1793, Paine became obsessed with the task of considerably revising the already-published manuscript and republishing it under his name as a book containing several new chapters and a dedication, in effect rendering obsolete the first edition, something he had never done before.[17]

The expanded English edition, *The Age of Reason*, appeared sometime during February 1794. It has been said that the book, like its French-language predecessor, was a *pièce d'occasion*, a reflex reaction against the so-called dechristianization program of the Jacobins. That view is too simple, since Paine began his work on religion well before the onset of this program, and even before the decrees against the priesthood on March 19 and 26, 1793. Lanthenas confirmed that *Le Siècle de la Raison* "was written by the author in the beginning of the year '93 (old style). I undertook its translation before the revolution against priests, and it was published in French about the same time. Couthon, to whom I sent it, seemed offended with me for having translated this work."[18]

For a long time, Paine had privately expressed an interest in working out on paper, toward the end of his life, his religious views. In 1766, when working as a staymaker in Diss, he had reportedly sketched notes for a study of organized religion.[19] In 1786, John Hall, who had worked on the model bridge with Paine, had written to friends, "My employer has *Common Sense* enough to disbelieve most of the common systematic theories of Divinity, but does not seem to establish any for himself."[20] A decade earlier, in fact shortly after the publication of *Common Sense*, Paine recalled, he had seen "the exceeding probability that a revolution in the system of government would be followed by a revolution in the system of religion."[21] John Adams confirmed that during an evening spent at his lodgings in 1776, Paine had "expressed a contempt of the Old Testament, and indeed of the Bible at large which surprised me," and that Paine had "checked himself with these words: 'I have some thoughts of publishing my thoughts on religion, but I believe it will be best to postpone it to the latter part of my life.'"[22]

By "the latter part" of his life, Paine's thoughts on religion had become complex, not least because of the extraordinary number of different eighteenth-century religious hands that had already touched him. In Thetford, he had been born into a mixed Quaker-Anglican household, and he had later drunk deeply of Methodism, easily the best-coordinated and most dynamic body of religious opinion in England at the time. As a young man, he had regularly attended lectures given in London by Benjamin Martin and James Ferguson, who had praised the "inestimable service" of Newtonian science in destroying the foundations of what they called "Superstition" and "all kinds of Imposture" in religious matters. His stay in America during the years 1774 to 1787 had done little to shake his skepticism about organized religion, his belief in deism, and his conviction that the separation of church and state implied freedom of expression for all faiths.

His return to England several years before the outbreak of the French Revolution had reminded him of the religious bigotry he had experienced in his childhood and, consequently, of the political importance of publicly expressing views that until now he had aired in private. He had been shocked, for example, at the frequency with which royalist politicians and clergymen had tried to explain away the poverty of the poor by references to the divine will. In *Rights of Man*, he had been forced to lock horns with Edmund Burke's argument that church and state were best unified and that secular authority must always rest upon ecclesiastical and spiritual hierarchy. Since arriving in France in September 1792, he had been exposed to the furious controversy provoked by public figures such as Voltaire, Boulanger, and Guillaume Thomas François Raynal, who called for the destruction of organized Christianity as the last bastion of popular deception, social persecution, and political despotism based on the so-called divine right of kings.

But why, given these background experiences, did Paine plunge into deep concentration and intense work on the subject of religion and politics during the autumn of 1793? Without a doubt, he feared for his life. Especially after the trial and execution of the Girondins, he became convinced that his days were numbered. "I saw my life in continual danger," he recalled. "My friends were falling as fast as the guillotine could cut their heads off, and as I every day expected the same fate, I resolved to begin my work. I appeared to myself to be on my death-bed, for death was on every side of me, and I had no time to lose."[23]

Alone in his study at Saint-Denis, he meditated often, as if he were already in prison, awaiting execution. Karl Marx remarked, "Religion is the sigh of the oppressed creature, the feeling of a heartless world and the soul of soulless circumstances."[24] In Paine's case, the matter was more complicated. During these bleak autumn months, Paine was certainly conscious of standing humbly before his Maker. Feeling himself to be an exile in this world, he began to consider himself a citizen of the next. But he did not turn to religion, as the miserable turn to opium, for spiritual sustenance and physical support. His motives are not understandable through the Marxian formula because Paine in fact attempted something that many of his contemporaries (and a great number of his subsequent readers) thought to be impossible: to attack all forms of organized religion as pompous and obfuscatory, and at the same time to defend the idea of a benevolent Creator of the universe against those who were currently bent on decreeing the death of God and ensuring that "the people of France were running headlong into atheism."[25]

From the time of his arrival in Calais, Paine had watched with interest and concern the mounting attacks on the clergy. Before the outbreak of the Revolution, as Alexis de Tocqueville later noted, anticlericalism in

France had stemmed not from hostility to religion itself, but from the church's role as a pillar of the feudal system. Priests were despised because they were landed proprietors, lords of manors, and tithe owners. It was felt, consequently, that the church should be distanced from the court and aristocracy, thereby becoming purer and poorer, more concerned with the indigent and the apostolic. With the declaration against feudalism by the National Assembly on August 4, 1789, and the confiscation of church property in early November 1789, the church had lost a principal means of support — the tithe — and its political independence as well. The church had become an organ of government. In addition, the distinction between church and state, between the spiritual and temporal worlds, later said by Benjamin Constant to be at the root of "modern liberty," also came to be eclipsed by the absolute domination of the temporal.

As the Revolution gained momentum, this trend accelerated to the point where the spiritual was identified with counterrevolution. The dechristianizing movement, as it was later called, was not officially acknowledged by the Convention. It was mainly prosecuted by the revolutionary armies, Convention delegates sent to the departments, and the popular societies. The movement was fueled by the introduction of a new republican calendar, which specified that the birth of Christ was no longer the beginning of recorded time and that September 21, 1793, was the end of the First Year of the Republic. The push for dechristianizing reached a fever pitch during the months of October and November, when Paine heard daily of efforts of every sort to cleanse the capital of Christianity.

Declarations that the French people recognized no dogma except that of its own sovereignty, no privileges but those of equality and liberty under the law, were posted on walls and doors. Ministers of all sects were forbidden to practice outside their churches. Church books were sold off as packing paper to grocers. Religious paintings and icons were desecrated or burned. Lead coffins were melted down in the munitions factories. There were moves to enforce the burial of the dead of every sect in common graveyards, whose only inscription was to be an emblem of Slumber (*Sommeil*), together with the words "Death is eternal sleep." Public displays of religious emblems and clerical dress were taboo, and beggars on the streets of Paris, instead of asking for charity "for the sake of Christ" (*pour l'amour de Dieu*), now more often called out, "*Vive la nation!*" Altar linens used in chapels were made into shirts for infantrymen, and gold and pewter vessels were sent off to the mint. Proposals were heard for requiring bishops to relinquish their crosses, miters, and episcopal rings, and plans were made for demolishing church towers that stood taller than secular buildings.

At the end of the first week of November, the Archbishop of Paris abdicated, more than four hundred priests followed suit, and many churches closed. Then on November 10 came the crowning event: the renaming of that pillar of mistaken belief, Notre Dame. On that day, Jacques-René Hébert and Pierre Gaspard Chaumette of the Paris Commune organized a ceremonial procession to Notre Dame. Led by the Goddess of Reason (Mlle Maillard, a singer of the Opéra), the procession of soldiers, musicians, and young girls dressed in garlands of flowers and tricolored ribbons slowly advanced on the church. Marshaled inside, the marchers witnessed a ceremony for the purpose of renaming it the Temple of Reason, after which a hymn to Liberty composed by André-Marie de Chénier, with music by François Joseph Gossec, was sung.

Superficial readers of the manuscript Paine prepared during the autumn of 1793 have concluded that Paine wholeheartedly supported these efforts at religious cleansing. (Theodore Roosevelt's later remark that Paine was a "filthy little atheist" typifies this view.[26]) *The Age of Reason* (and its second part published during 1795) certainly savaged Christianity in militant and witty language. Attacks on Christianity were, of course, nothing new, but the plebeian style of Paine's text quickly frightened members of the clergy, who otherwise could live with the mannerly skepticism of a David Hume or an Edward Gibbon or polite deistical speculations in parlors and coffeehouses. In the earthy style for which its author was now world famous, *The Age of Reason* argued that the worst-read best-seller, the Bible, was not the word of God. It trashed the Christian doctrine of revelation as mere storytelling by "historians" who had piled "hearsay upon hearsay." Strictly speaking, Paine argued, revelation entails the direct, extralinguistic communication of something from God to humanity without intermediaries such as the Christian churches. The only thing revelatory about Christian doctrine is that the Bible is "a book of riddles that requires a revelation to explain it." Paine also likened traditional Christian beliefs to Greek mythology. He denied that monotheistic religions such as Christianity have helped to eliminate "false gods" from human affairs. In fact, Christianity perpetuates irrationalism. Thus, the old polytheistic deification of heroes is carried over into the Christian canonization of saints, while Christianity, like its mythological predecessors, rests its claims upon fabulous tales, such as that of Eve, whose tête-à-tête with a devilish snake in a garden somehow persuaded her to eat an apple and thereby ruin humanity.

The Age of Reason was particularly scathing about the disempowering effects of organized religions. Paine tried to label all of them as means to unequal wealth and power. Religion serves the avarice of priests and politicians. It is everywhere a force that crushes the life out of potential citizens. "All national institutions of churches, whether Jewish, Christian or Turkish, appear to me no other than human inventions, set up to terrify and enslave mankind, and monopolise power and profit," Paine wrote. Particularly worrisome was religion's attempt to do what no previous form of tyranny had ever done: torment individuals beyond the grave into eternity. With great energy, Paine also satirized the religious double standards of English squires and urban merchants, who were soon to fill the jury benches for the prosecutions of Paine's religious works across the Channel. "Talk with some London merchants about Scripture," he wrote, "and they will understand you mean *scrip*, and tell you how much it is worth at the Stock Exchange. Ask them about theology and they will say they know of no such gentleman upon 'Change. . . . Tell them it is in the Bible and they will lay a bowl of punch it is not, and leave it to the parson of the parish to decide."[27]

The tough language appeared compatible with the rhetoric of militant French secularists, such as Hébert and his Jacobin followers, who attacked religion as the most dangerous form of "superstition and fanaticism." Yet doubting Thomas Paine refused to accept their program of forcibly exterminating religious belief. His objection was not based on the tactical consideration that militant atheism would hurt a government in need of support from the urban and rural Catholic working class and peasantry. That cynical calculation was championed by Robespierre, for whom frontal attacks on religion were bound to trigger frontal resistance. Against the dechristianizers, Robespierre had insisted, at the same time that Paine was working feverishly on his manuscript, that the firm evidence that God exists and the soul is immortal should be put to good political use, above all because atheism was playing into the hands of counterrevolutionaries who liked to condemn the republic as irreligious and barbaric.[28]

Paine shared Robespierre's belief in God. "I believe in one God, and no more," he trumpeted in *The Age of Reason*, "and I hope for happiness beyond this life." But he denied that that same belief was simply a useful political tool. Although Paine had approved the initial French push to separate church and state — a division he considered fundamental to the establishment of a flourishing civil society — he now saw the dechristianization program as destructive of the civility and personal freedom so vital for republican democratic government. Atheism, he argued, was not aristocratic, but undemocratic. By compulsorily uprooting "everything appertaining to compulsive systems of religion," the revolutionary atheists threatened to destroy elementary human morals such as compassion, honesty, and love, replacing them with opportunism, lying, and cutthroat struggles for power. Godlessness would rule supreme.

The Age of Reason nevertheless insisted that Christianity trained people how to think without thinking and that it encouraged moral de-skilling. Paine came close to saying that if the Christian God lived on earth, virtuous people would break his windows. He agreed with William Blake that prisons are built with stones of Law, brothels with bricks of Religion. According to Paine, the Bible "is a history of wickedness that has served to corrupt and brutalize mankind." The stories it peddles deify Satan, legitimate the "moral lying" of priests, and expose their believers to exemplary tales of debauchery, cruelty, and vindictiveness. Crammed with tales of "assassinations, treachery and wars," it serves to legitimate the bloody history of Christian bigotry — its crusade against Islam, persecution of Jews and Huguenots, and enslavement of Africans, for example.

Yet in spite of all this immorality, Paine argued, Christianity keeps alive an ethical tradition vital for nurturing republican democracy. Christian commandments "contain some good moral precepts," and Jesus Christ himself "was a virtuous and an amiable man" who preached equality in the face of "the corruptions and avarice of the Jewish priests" — and paid for his integrity with his life. To destroy Christianity by force, as the Jacobins were attempting, was potentially to destroy its good moral teachings. More than that, the compulsory Jacobin struggle against "systems of religion" flatly contradicted individuals' freedom to decide where, when, and with whom they practice their belief in God. In attempting to uproot this belief, atheism substituted itself as a new dogma. Like King Canute, who tried to out-God God and his followers by telling them what to do, the dogma of Atheism implied that its own power arbitrarily to decide the shape of the world would become absolute. From its point of view, everything would become permissible. Liberty would be crushed by license. Individuals would be forced to swallow the dogma that the existence of God is a hoary superstition, that hell is a myth, and that individuals have no soul. Indecent prints and obscene books would go on sale. Moneymaking, egoism, and love of lucre would mushroom. Spying on foreigners and allegations that this or that citizen was a counterrevolutionary would proceed unchecked. Men would shout about the growth of conspiracy, talk constantly about the guillotine, and speculate endlessly about whose head would be severed next. Public virtue would be ruined.

Paine's attack on dechristianization rested upon the deist assumption that a God who let human beings prove his existence would be an idol and that the existence of God is in fact confirmed quietly each day and night by the ordered beauty of the natural world. "The creation we behold," he wrote, "is the real and ever-existing Word of God, in which we cannot be deceived. It proclaims His power, it demonstrates His wisdom, it manifests His goodness and beneficence." The deep reverence for a Maker buried in *The Age of Reason* brought frowns to the faces of militant atheists and winces to those preferring to keep their religion casual. Many of Paine's readers were confused by such passages because they appeared to be so radically at odds with his blast against Christianity. How could someone believe in God and at the same time reject Christianity?

Paine saw no difficulty in answering that question. In his view, and in the view of his many sympathizers, it revealed ignorance of the deist principles dear to his heart. Paine certainly won international support for spelling out that point in *The Age of Reason*. The greatest humiliation in life is suffered by those who work hard on something from which they expect — but fail to get — great public appreciation. Paine had escaped that fate twice before, and *The Age of Reason*, like *Common Sense* and *Rights of Man*, repeated the success. Although the impact of *The Age of Reason* in France is unknown, the two-part book rapidly became a best-seller in Britain, where the move by George III's government, supported by the evangelical Society for the Suppression of Vice, to prosecute booksellers who circulated it strengthened demand for copies produced and circulated underground. Miners in Cornwall (reported the Bishop of London) gobbled up the text. A government spy reported that in Liverpool the book "met with a welcome reception." *The Age of Reason* also was popular among London's artisans and laborers, and in late 1795 the London Corresponding Society split when several hundred furious activists renounced their membership after the executive refused to oust atheists and deists from the organization.[29]

Demand was even more feverish in America. Eight American editions appeared in 1794, seven the next year, and two in 1796. In Vermont copies were "greedily received," and at universities such as Yale and Harvard *The Age of Reason* caused a sensation. New organizations such as the New York Deistical Society and the Baltimore Theophilanthropic Society sprang up in support of Paineite principles. Thousands of copies of *The Age of Reason* were sold at auction in Philadelphia for a cent and a half, and as early as 1795 there were reportedly tens of thousands of American followers of "Mr. Paine's Reasonable Age."[30]

The book's influence was not confined to France and the English-speaking world. In the German-speaking lands, for example, the translated work was quickly published in three separate editions, adding to

Paine's wide reputation as a courageous "outlaw" and "a most original writer." According to the contemporary German historian J. J. von Eschenburg, *Das Zeitalter der Vernunft* was a huge success in the German states in part because earlier religious controversies with Hermann Reimarus and the pantheistic feuds sparked by Spinozism had helped to create an atmosphere in which the Bible and church dogma were not considered infallible.[31] Excerpts from *The Age of Reason* circulated elsewhere in Europe, for example among Hungarian-speaking Unitarians, thanks to the efforts of János Körmöczi, professor of mathematics and physics at the Unitarian college in Kolozsvár (later Cluj), and his student Mihály Kiss, a pastor in Torda. The reception was especially warm in Transylvania, where the Unitarians were at the time suffering discrimination for their attempts to democratize the Protestant church and to repudiate along deist lines the fabulous doctrine of the Trinity (which both the Lutherans and the Calvinists had adopted from Catholicism).[32] *The Age of Reason* also reached Portugal, thanks to a brilliant nineteen-year-old medical student, Francisco Solano Constâncio, whose sojourn at Edinburgh University in the mid-1790s moved him to publish a toughly reasoned defense of Paine's "weighty arguments" that lunged at the prevailing "superstition" and "despotism" in Europe and concluded, scandalously: "In Catholic countries, all who dare think are heretics; among Protestants, they are atheists."[33]

At the time, the extraordinary reception of *The Age of Reason* helped conceal the fact that some of its arguments were problematic — and at the same time more profoundly subversive than Paine or most of his followers and critics could have foreseen. Although Paine's critics reacted in various ways to his antireligious diatribe, the enormous volume of controversy arguably favored Paine's case by helping to dissolve the sacred ingredients of religious tradition. Ecclesiastical and spiritual matters once clothed in reverent silence now found themselves dragged into the public sphere, stripped naked, and forced to answer tough questions. The sheer diversity of points and counterpoints, questions and answers, undoubtedly deepened the sense of desacralized controversy. Some thought "Common Sense" had gone mad. Others, convinced that the American and French Revolutions were part of a divine scenario, soon to be followed by the return of the Jews to Palestine and the Messiah's triumphant appearance on earth, were deeply offended by Paine's scurrilous denial that the Bible was literally true. Typical of this fundamentalist response was the conclusion drawn by the leading Anglo-Jewish scholar, David Levi, that Paine's book was "one of the most violent and systematic attacks on the word of God that was ever made." Levi warned his fellow believers that *The Age of Reason* should not be handled, let alone read. The Pentateuch, he insisted, reports a series of accurate prophecies by Moses that Jews could question only at an extreme price: they would cease to be Jews.[34]

Then there were those, for instance the Baltimore Swedenborgian James Jones Wilmer, who said that *The Age of Reason* was based on "irrational principles."[35] Others (such as Hannah More, writing as "Will Chip, Carpenter, in Somersetshire"[36]) simply stated their conviction that matters of fact could not be false. Christianity was fact; therefore, it must be true. Still others, such as Paine's previous attorney, Lord Erskine, cynically recommended prosecution of publishers of the book on the ground that since organized religion was among the principal devices for ensuring commoners' faith in their masters, Paine and his cronies should be prevented from tampering with "the great anchor which alone can hold the vessel of the state amidst the storms which agitate the world."[37]

Quite a number of Paine's critics suffered panic attacks. In late-eighteenth-century England, atheism was already no bar to advancement in the church, but the hard fact was that *The Age of Reason* publicly questioned the cozy patron-client relationships binding the clergy to the one-party Georgian state. Paine's Christian enemies consequently bit to draw blood. Evangelical clergymen in England, looking to the state to save the day for the church, turned their back on cooperation with Paineite dissenters and clamored against non-Anglican Sunday schools, which were said to be seminaries of faction and infidelity. The Methodist John Prior Estlin, preaching in Bristol, joined in by roasting Paine's "uncultivated understanding" and calling for "a strenuous defence of the citadel" of Christianity.[38] Gilbert Wakefield, former Fellow of Jesus College, Cambridge, also hurled abuse at the "ignorance, misconception, effrontery, and insipidity" of *The Age of Reason*.[39] Some American clergy, turning plowshares into swords, showed no more mercy. Uzal Ogden, the first American to answer Paine, criticized him as a drunkard, saying that reasoning with him would resemble casting pearls before swine, while the American Episcopalian parson Mason Locke Weems said that *The Age of Reason* proved that Paine had "no other church but the alehouse" and that his "palsied legs can scarce bear him to that sink of vomiting and filth."[40]

Less hysterical clergy on both sides of the Atlantic reacted in various ways. Some pious figures criticized Paine's criticism of the immorality of the Old Testament. Few people nowadays would regard the massacres of men, women, and children recorded in the Pentateuch and the Book of Joshua as models of righteousness, but many of Paine's critics were offended by his impious criticism of the Israelites when, after all, the Old Testament approved of them. Among the most mild-mannered of these critics was the Bishop of Llandaff, Richard Watson, who went so far as to admit that parts of the Pentateuch were not written by Moses and that some of the psalms were not composed by David. For such concessions, the Bishop incurred the displeasure of George III and ruined any chance of a transfer to a richer see. Paine took particular pleasure in some of the Bishop's curious admissions. For example, *The Age of Reason* questioned whether God really commanded that all men and married women among the Midianites should be slaughtered and their maidens preserved. Not so, the Bishop indignantly retorted. The maidens were not preserved for immoral purposes, as Paine had wickedly suggested, but as slaves, to which Christians could not legitimately object.[41]

Also among the ranks of the calmer clergy were those who attacked Paine's false attribution of the ills of the world to Christianity. They queried, for instance, his silence about earthquakes (like the one that rocked Lisbon in 1757) and other "flaws" in the deist bible of Nature. Others scorned Paine's fabulous denial of human sinfulness and irrationality — evident in the French Reign of Terror — and objected to the way in which he placed Reason "on the throne of God" and dogmatically urged humanity to worship it as a "deity" of its own making. Still other critics tried to turn Tom against Tom by cunningly asking why it was that the straightforward revelation of God through nature had only lately, during the seventeenth and eighteenth centuries, become the privilege of deists. They also asked why, if the revelation of God could be grasped even by the simplest "untutored savage," as Paine claimed, Paine himself relied on trigonometry and other complicated Newtonian explanations.[42]

Arguably the most telling quibble came from Christian critics who challenged Paine to substantiate philosophically his belief in "one God and no more." Several pointed out that Paine's deep suspicion of language as a tricky vehicle for the expression of Christian claims to Truth should also apply to his own use of deist language. Others spotted the way in which deism rested upon humanly invented ethical claims that came wrapped in human language and were nowhere to be found in nature itself. "Will Mercury, or Venus, or Mars, or Jupiter, or Saturn; will the Sun, or Moon, or other luminary" tell us what to believe and how to live, snapped the Presbyterian Moses Hoge in a tract titled *Christian Panoply*,[43] published in 1797, the same year in which Paine's own tract sold as many as 100,000 copies in America alone.

Whether knowing it or not, Hoge and other critics, as well as Paine himself, were wrestling with the quintessentially modern dilemma of how to break the grip of religious dogma without destroying the freedom of citizens to practice the religion of their choice. Like a nest of Chinese boxes, that dilemma contained another that was to be especially pertinent in multireligious societies. The freedom of individuals to decide for themselves how they should worship — a principle essential to Paine's deism — in practice implied the need for religiously motivated citizens to minimize their daily antagonisms and ultimately to avoid bloodshed by agreeing to disagree about their respective beliefs. In practice, that implied fundamental agreement required social and political spaces within which citizens could compromise their differences and actively cooperate by suspending all religious belief. Deism implied secularism. Not only did the deist principle of freedom of religious worship implicitly require individuals to doubt the existence of a single True Revealed Faith. It also required them to recognize that civil peace forces them, on an ad hoc basis, to downplay their own particular belief in God and to cooperate with those who hold rival beliefs, no matter how unconventionally religious or even secular they might be.

This double dilemma remained unexamined in *The Age of Reason*. It concluded, simply, with an appeal for solidarity among the world's religions and pleaded for the fundamental right of all citizens to decide for themselves their religious beliefs. Paine foresaw no fundamental clash between, say, the Islamic and Christian conceptions of God. He believed that Muslims and Christians could live together harmoniously, albeit at the price of recognizing that their views about the world contained unessential, or "disposable," elements. "It is certain," he wrote, "that, in one point, all the nations of the earth and all religions agree — all believe in a God; the things in which they disagree are the redundancies annexed to that belief." The implication was clear: "If ever a universal religion should prevail, it will not be by believing anything new, but in getting rid of redundancies and believing as man believed at first. Adam, if ever there were such a man, was created a Deist; but in the meantime, let every man follow, as he has a right to do, the religion and the worship he prefers."[44]

Arrest

The words trumpeted defiantly in the face of the accelerating Jacobin attack on religion. Paine must have known that the publication of a second version of the manuscript, this time under his own name, would further soil his reputation among the Jacobins and increase the likelihood of his arrest as a foreign conspirator. Toward the end of November, Robespierre tried to slow down the pace of dechristianization by whipping up xenophobia, especially against the English, whom he personally detested. "I demand that a purifying scrutiny be held at the tribune," he shouted before the Jacobin Club, "to detect and drive out all the agents of foreign powers who under their auspices have introduced themselves into this society."[45] Within days, a warrant was secretly issued for the arrest of Paine's lodger friends Choppin and Johnson. During a bitterly cold late-November night, Paine was awakened by a loud banging at the hotel gates. He sprang to the bedroom window, startled. "I saw the landlord going with the candle to the gate, which he opened, and a guard with muskets and fixed bayonets entered. I went to bed again, and made up my mind for prison, for I was then the only lodger."[46] Choppin and Johnson were lucky, for within hours of hearing reports of Robespierre's speech, Paine managed to secure passports for them through his Foreign Ministry contacts. The passports were delivered to Saint-Denis several evenings later, and before dawn the next morning the two Englishmen had fled to Basel. Three weeks later, unannounced, the English landlord was carted off into the night.

Paine was now the last foreigner at the Saint-Denis refuge. Although the arrests seemed to be random, he suspected that he had been protected by some form of parliamentary immunity. That expired on December 23. On that day, he was singled out by Bourdon de l'Oise in a hostile speech to the Convention. After little further debate, the Convention carried a motion excluding foreigners — Paine and Anacharsis Cloots were the only two — from its ranks. Alarmed, Paine desperately put the finishing touches to the manuscript of *The Age of Reason*, and the next evening, Christmas Eve, 1793, he treated himself to a dinner with several Americans at White's Hotel. The table conversation bubbled on until after midnight, and Paine, who was tired after several weeks' hard work, decided to rent a room at the hotel to spare himself the long journey out to Saint-Denis. He slept badly, and whatever rest he had was rudely disturbed at four in the morning by a fist thumping at his door. Paine groggily unbolted his door to find five good-size policemen, two agents (*commissaires*) of the Committee of General Security (*comité de sûreté générale*), and the manager of the hotel blocking the corridor. Paine was informed, through the manager who interpreted, that the *comité* had ordered that the two foreign deputies "be arrested and imprisoned, as a measure of general security; that an examination be made of their papers, and those found suspicious put under seal and brought to the *comité de sûreté générale*."[47]

Paine played for time. After dressing, he asked to visit the room of his friend Achille Audibert, who had accompanied him from Dover to Calais and who that evening was staying in the same hotel. Paine said that he would prefer to have Audibert as his translator. Permission was granted by Commissar Gillet, and a yawning Audibert agreed. Through him, Paine explained to the government agents that his papers were with Joel Barlow, who lived in the Hotel Grande Bretagne, several miles away. At daybreak, a red-eyed Paine was escorted by the police and government commissars to see Barlow, who admitted only to having a single proof sheet and the opening thirty-one pages of the manuscript of *The Age of Reason*. The agents were immediately suspicious, instructing him "to open for us all his cupboards; which he did, and after having visited them, we . . . recognized that there existed no papers belonging to him." The agents realized that Paine had tricked them and that he clearly wanted to have an American witness and supporter present at the inspection of his papers. The arrest party, reasoning that "Citizen Barlow could be of help to us," set off for Saint-Denis, stopping en route to pick up their own interpreter, Monsieur Dessous, at the headquarters of the Committee of General Security.

At Saint-Denis, Paine's rooms were ransacked. According to the official report, the police "gathered in the sitting room all the papers found in the other rooms of the said apartment." The suspect was asked to account for them, pile by pile. Paine was quick to show them a report (subsequently lost) written at the request of Barère, "Observations on the Commerce Between the United States of America and France." After some prompting, Paine showed his captors the final forty-four manuscript pages of *The Age of Reason*, which the agents gave "the most scrupulous examination." After conferring downstairs, with Paine and Barlow upstairs under police guard, the agents decided "that no seal should be placed" upon his papers. Paine, the seasoned optimist, reported that one of the agents had even said of the new manuscript: "It is an interesting work; it will do much good." That flattery ensured that Paine was free to pass on the whole manuscript to Barlow, but it was not enough to save him. After the agents had prepared and signed a detailed report of their thirteen-hour ordeal with "thomas peine," as they referred to him throughout, the unsmiling Peine was led away, "without any difficulty," through the frosty darkness to the Luxembourg prison.

The Luxembourg

Shaking with fatigue and trepidation, Paine was processed by the prison authorities under the supervision of the prison governor, Monsieur Benoit.[48]

Around nine o'clock that evening, he was flung into a small ground-floor cell. His new home contained a palliasse, a chair, and a wooden box in which personal belongings could be stored. The cell measured ten by eight feet and contained a boarded-up window that let in slivers of light on sunny days. Being "level with the earth in the garden and floored with brick,"[49] it smelled heavily of must, its walls and floor oozing a film of water after every rainfall. The Luxembourg had certainly fallen from grace. At one time a palace, it now resembled a dilapidated luxury hotel stripped bare of its royal furnishings, its grandness dissolved by police officials, clanking keys, and the stench of death. The palace had been converted into a prison to hold the Girondin deputies accused of counterrevolution, but since their execution in October, it had become a block used mainly for detaining up to a thousand foreigners at a time.[50]

Many men and women prisoners spoke English, and Paine had little trouble finding his way around the Luxembourg. At the time of his arrival, Paine found the prison routines relatively relaxed, and his fear of the unknown gradually lifted. After breakfast, the inmates were required to spend the morning tidying and cleaning their quarters and attending to general prison duties. In the afternoon, they were free to linger with fellow prisoners in the common room, gulp chilly air in the courtyard, or lie or sit in the quiet darkness of their cells. Paine liked to meet Anacharsis Cloots for afternoon tea and discussion of religion and politics. Invariably, their conversations turned into heated arguments, with Paine resisting the militant atheism of Cloots, who regularly called himself "Jesus Christ's personal enemy" and berated Paine "for his credulity in still indulging so many religious and political prejudices."[51]

Helped by candles purchased at the prison store with the cash he had brought (all prisoners were expected to pay for their meals and accessories), Paine found quiet moments in his cell to read newspapers. Some news was repugnant. A copy of the *Sussex Weekly Advertiser*, freshly arrived from Lewes, snarled with ingratitude: "Should *Tom Paine*, for his late temporizing politicks in France, be condemned to the guillotine, his *decapitation*, we believe, would not be *so universally* lamented in this country as to cause a *general mourning*, even though it should be allowed, that for his attachment to the *Life of Royalty*, he had forfeited his head to the *Republican axe*."[52] Paine responded by picking up a quill. "Thomas Paine is in prison," reported Gouverneur Morris sarcastically, "where he amuses himself with publishing a pamphlet against Jesus Christ."[53] On January 27, one month after his detention, he had completed a one-page preface and postscript to *The Age of Reason*. Addressed "To My Fellow Citizens of the United

States," the preface contained a crisply worded defense of the obligation of all citizens to respect each other's right of freedom of expression: "I have always strenuously supported the right of every man to his own opinion, however different that opinion might be to mine. He who denies to another this right, makes a slave of himself to his present opinion, because he precludes himself the right of changing it."[54]

The decision to dedicate the work to his fellow Americans was shrewd. Paine learned from inmates that he was the third American to be imprisoned by order of the Committee of General Security and that his two predecessors, William Haskins of Boston and Thomas Griffiths of Baltimore, had both been released a few weeks after a petition had been presented to the Convention by American citizens living in Paris. Paine was told that Gouverneur Morris had been of little help in securing their release, and that, given the currently sensitive diplomatic relations between France and the United States, he had held fast to the strangely un-American view, later confirmed by President George Washington, that citizens of the United States who were temporarily or permanently resident in a foreign country and found themselves in trouble with its authorities were subject without restriction to its laws and punishments.[55] The information was confirmed by Joel Barlow, who visited Paine every few days. Barlow told him that the American community in Paris would attempt to repeat its tactic of pressuring the Convention to secure his release. Paine's reiteration of his American citizenship in the prologue to *The Age of Reason* no doubt reflected Barlow's news: it served as a reminder to both the French and American governments that he considered himself a citizen of the world and that he should not be forgotten or treated contemptuously as a puny English pawn in a power game among statesmen.

The American petitioners, who included Griffiths and Haskins, wasted no time. On January 20, eighteen of them assembled outside the Convention to request permission to address the deputies. After waiting an hour, the delegation was ushered to its seats, and President Marc Vadier gave his consent for one of the petitioners to step to the bar. "Citizen legislators! The honour of representing the French nation was extended to the most famous men of foreign nations," began the American petitioner, speaking fluent French. "Among them was the member for Pas-de-Calais, Thomas Paine, the apostle of liberty in America, a respected philosopher of profound learning, and a citizen renowned for his virtue." Without comment, the American reminded the deputies of the decree ordering the arrest of all English people resident in France and then pleaded, "in the name of the friends of liberty, your American allies, and your brothers," that Paine be unconditionally released. He continued:

We urge you: Do not allow the alliance of despots and, above all, the cowardly English tyranny which outlawed him, the pleasure of seeing him imprisoned. We remind you that the official seal on his papers has been lifted; that all of them were examined by the Committee of General Security who discovered there not dangerous propositions but nothing but the love of liberty which has characterized his whole life, that eloquence of nature and philosophy appropriate to a friend of humanity, and those principles of public morality which earned him the hatred of kings and the love of his fellow citizens.[56]

Following the speech, the petitioners offered themselves as security during the short time Paine would be in France after his release from prison, preparing his return to America, where he was considered "among the most esteemed citizens" and "one of the political authors of independence." In America, the petitioners predicted, their "fellow citizen" Paine "will be received with open arms."[57] The move was designed to disarm those hard-line Jacobin deputies convinced that Paine was a dangerous enemy of the state. The tactic failed, and the overall reception given the American petitioners was frosty. "Not a few members hissed during the reading of our memorial in which Paine's attachment to republican principles was asserted," reported Griffiths.[58] President Vadier's smooth-tongued address in reply was hardly less encouraging. He reiterated the importance of the Franco-American alliance as a means of preserving the international struggle against despotism on land and sea. He then resorted to words that chilled Paine's spine when they reached him the next day in the Luxembourg:

Thomas Payne est né en Angleterre; c'en était assez sans doute pour appliquer à son égard les mesures de sûreté prescrites par les lois révolutionnaires. On peut ajouter, citoyens, que, si Thomas Payne a été l'apôtre de la liberté, s'il a coopéré puissamment à la révolution d'Amérique, son génie n'a point aperçu celle qui a régénéré la France; il n'en a aperçu le système que d'après les prestiges dont les faux amis de notre révolution l'ont environné. Vous avez dû, comme nous, déplorer une erreur peu conciliable avec les principes qu'on admire dans les ouvrages bien estimables de cet auteur républicain.[59]

Paine's hopes for an early release were dashed by this talk of Paine as an Englishman out of step with the Revolution. That definition came from the lips of the man who doubled as head of the Committee of Public Safety and had personally signed the order for Paine's arrest. The stony silence greeting a petition on behalf of "the renowned American citizen" from Achille Audibert to the *comité de salut public* added to the ominousness.[60] A visitor to the Luxembourg brought Paine further discouraging news from his friend Sampson Perry, who reportedly had drawn the conclusion that even though "the talents, the splendid talents of Mr. Paine" warranted the highest praise, Vadier's reply "deserved respect" because "the *letter* of the decree against foreigners reached him, for he was *born in a country at war with France*."[61]

Paine refused to sit quietly. He was particularly angered by a letter passed on to him in prison without comment by Gouverneur Morris. It was written by Deforgues, the Minister of Foreign Affairs, who explained that he was "ignorant of the motives of his detention, but I must presume they are well founded." In the same letter to Morris, Deforgues reiterated the official policy of the Jacobin government first hinted at by Vadier: "Born in England, this ex-deputy has become successively an American and a French citizen. In accepting this last title, and in occupying a place in the Legislative Corps, he submitted himself to the laws of the Republic, and has by that fact renounced the protection which the right of the people and treaties concluded with the United States could have assured him."[62]

Paine bit back at Morris: "I received your letter enclosing a copy of a letter from the Minister of Foreign Affairs. You must not leave me in the situation in which this letter places me. You know I do not deserve it, and you see the unpleasant situation in which I am thrown." Paine enclosed a statement of his innocence, drafted in his cell, which he urged Morris to use as the basis for a tough reply to Deforgues. For the first time, Paine's words were desperate. Admitting that he and Morris were "not on the best terms of harmony," he begged him to inform the United States Congress of his condition and to send a letter to Deforgues. "Otherwise," wrote Paine, "your silence will be a sort of consent to his observations."[63]

The tart letter to Morris contained the suggestion that Paine had privately reached the conclusion that his detention was traceable to more than the unwillingness of either the French or the American government to let a troublemaker like him jeopardize the countries' fragile alliance. There was every reason to think that the French wanted to muzzle Paine so that he could be prevented from rocking the boat of American opinion about the course of the French Revolution. That was the force of Robespierre's memorandum to himself that the imprisonment of Paine would serve "the interests of America as well as France." A British spy noted that Morris, the American minister, had reached the same shrewd conclusion to disallow "any such fish to go over and swim in his waters."[64] But excluding the whale from American waters was only the more obvious half of the story, Paine said. In a deliberately cryptic sentence to Morris, he hinted that the Jacobin authorities were victimizing him because they too feared his literary powers of fomenting public discussion about a government that was daily becoming more arbitrary, even delirious. "They have nothing against me," he wrote, "except that they do not choose I should be in a state of freedom to write my mind freely upon things I have seen."[65] Several days after sending off his letter and testimony to Morris, Paine's suspicion was confirmed. The government responded with knife-sharp paranoia. The Luxembourg was sealed tight. "All communication from persons imprisoned to any person without the prison was cut off by an order of the police," Paine reported. "I neither saw, nor heard from, anybody for six months."[66]

Telltales and sympathizers admittedly helped to keep open some channels of communication with the outside world. Yet the reports and rumors slipping in through the cracks in the Luxembourg security system brought nothing but disturbing news. Paine began to see that France was sliding into a terrorist regime directed by moralists inspired by the ideal of a regenerated republican state backed by force and fear. The scenario had been mapped out clearly in the previous month by Robespierre. His *Report on the principles of political morality that should guide the national Convention in the internal administration of the Republic* sketched out the Jacobin utopia as a state in which "every soul grows greater by the constant sharing of republican sentiments." The republic would be a uniquely higher form of state marked by "the peaceful enjoyment of liberty and equality, and the reign of eternal justice." Robespierre was adamant that the utopia could be built only if spines were chilled and blood spilled. "If the basis of popular government in time of peace is virtue," he concluded, "its basis in a time of revolution is both virtue and intimidation. Intimidation without virtue is disastrous; virtue without intimidation is powerless."[67]

Robespierre's report both summarized what was already happening and helped accelerate the program of terror. Everyone within and around the circles of power was sucked into a vortex of accusations and arrests, interrogations and killings. Daily life within the republic resembled a bizarre game of blindman's buff, in which citizens, groping for the cap of liberty, the hand of fraternity, and the triangle of equality, were accompanied by a scythe-wielding skeleton named Death. The number of prisoners like Paine who were held without trial grew rapidly, reaching around eight thousand in Paris and perhaps eighty thousand in the country at large. In the capital, civil society, or what remained of it, trembled. The streets of Paris were almost empty of carriages, and residents no longer lingered and laughed as they went about their daily business. Above every front door hung lists of the names of lodgers, a reminder of the general program of terror as grim as the inscription "Equality or death" (*Egalité ou la mort*) daubed on housefronts and walls.

Each week brought a fresh scandal. In the middle of March 1794, as the sweetly perfumed air of another spring wafted across the country, the implementation of the Ventôse Decrees was quickly followed by the arrest and imprisonment in the Luxembourg of several dozen Hébertists. Within days, they were carried off to the guillotine along with Paine's friend Anacharsis Cloots. At the end of the month, it was the Dantonists' turn. After their arrest, they were dumped within the walls of the Luxembourg. The prisoners watched as police herded Georges-Jacques Danton and his supporters into the prison grounds after being frisked, processed, and numbered. As the cadaverous column shuffled into the common area, Paine called out to Danton, who broke ranks and walked toward him. He clasped Paine's right hand. The crowd of prisoners hushed, their eyes riveted on the most famous inmate and "giant of the Revolution."[68] Danton began: "That which you did for the happiness and liberty of your country, I tried in vain to do for mine." He paused, the traces of a smile disappearing suddenly from his face. "I have been less fortunate," he said, "but not less innocent. They will send me to the scaffold; very well, my friends, I shall go gaily."[69] He paused again, then turned toward the crowded corridor. "Messieurs," he said calmly, "I hoped soon to have got you all out of this: but here I am myself; and one sees not where it will end."[70]

Paine and those near him remained silent — with good reason. Unlike the American Revolution, whose leaders were revered and later transformed into "Founding Fathers," the French Revolution savagely cut down its heroes in their prime. Danton was no exception. After a four-day trial that concluded on the morning of April 5, he and his supporters were found guilty of treason and summarily executed. Like an illness, the terror had begun to enter its feverish phase. During April, the reorganized Office of Administrative Surveillance and Police (*bureau de surveillance administrative et de police générale*), under the personal direction of Robespierre, closed in on thousands of citizens described as aristocrats, offenders against the food laws, rebels from the regions, suspects, and dishonest or incompetent officials. The month of May saw the unveiling of the Cult of the Supreme (*culte de l'Etre Suprême*), the execution of Mme Elisabeth, and a long string of alleged assassination attempts on prominent Jacobins, scandalized in the Admiral and Renault affairs, which served to spread paranoia and embellish the drama of plots and counterplots.

Paine began to count each dawn a blessing. "The state of things in the prisons was a continued scene of horror," he reported. Each night his sleep was disturbed by the shrieking and sobbing of prisoners who were beaten and dragged away in darkness to the guillotine. The screaming and moaning continued during the daytime. "No man could count upon life for twenty-four hours," he continued. "To such a pitch of rage and suspicion were Robespierre and his committee arrived, that it seemed as if they feared to leave a man living. Scarcely a night passed in which ten, twenty, thirty, forty, fifty or more were taken out of the prison, carried before a pretended tribunal in the morning and guillotined before night."[71]

Paine somehow coped with the terror and certainty of death. Prisoners who came into contact with him noted his talent for resisting fear in quiet, undramatic ways. While others around him retreated into despair or literally crumbled, Paine was impressively calm. It was as if he waged a personal struggle to keep alive in his daily habits the republican democratic principles that the Revolution was daily destroying. A fellow prisoner reported:

> His cheerful philosophy under the certain expectation of death, his sensibility of heart, his brilliant powers of conversation, and his sportive vein of wit rendered him a very general favourite with his companions of misfortune, who found a refuge from evil in the charms of his society. He was the confidant of the unhappy, the counselor of the perplexed; and to his sympathizing friendship many a devoted victim in the hour of death confided the last cares of humanity, and the last wishes of tenderness.[72]

Paine was especially close to an English surgeon named Bond. For several consecutive weeks, each afternoon, surviving from hour to hour, not knowing when their time would be up, the two discussed politics, philosophy, literature, science, and religion in Paine's cell. Surrounded by death, it was not surprising that their conversations gravitated toward the nature of good and evil, the origin and meaning of life, and the afterlife. *The Age of Reason* was often the topic of their discussions, with Paine sometimes reading aloud passages from the copy he had brought with him to prison. Bond was unconvinced of Paine's theological and political opinions, but he deeply respected Paine's seriousness and courage under the circumstances. "Mr. Paine, while hourly expecting to die, read to me parts of his 'Age of Reason,'" reported Bond. "Every night when I left him to be separately locked up, and expected not to see him alive in the morning, he always expressed his firm belief in the principles of that book, and begged I would tell the world such were his dying opinions. He often said that if he lived he should prosecute further that work, and print it."[73]

In the evenings, with the help of candles purchased from the prison store, Paine mustered the concentration to write. Putting his thoughts on paper was an act of resistance. He drafted "Essay on the Character of Robespierre" and "Essay on Aristocracy," both of which have been lost or destroyed. For "the use and benefit of all mankind," he also revised *Rights of Man*, to which he added a new preface. The manuscript was somehow smuggled out of the Luxembourg and printed. Paine turned to poetry as well. In one effort, a pretended love poem addressed to a woman who signed her correspondence "The Little Corner of the World," the stanzas were unsophisticated, rhyming simply and expressing deep feelings for nature. "From the CASTLE IN THE AIR to THE LITTLE CORNER OF THE WORLD" was a flight of fancy, a leap from the dankness of his cell into an exotic world of rest. Paine began:

> *In the region of clouds, where the whirlwinds arise,*
> > *My CASTLE OF FANCY was built;*
> *The turrets reflected the blue of the skies,*
> > *And the windows with sun-beams were gilt.*

The spell of romanticism strengthened:

> *I had grottoes, and fountains, and orange-tree groves,*
> > *I had all that enchantment has told;*
> *I had sweet shady walks, for the GODS and their LOVES,*
> > *I had mountains of coral and gold.*

During the night, a storm blew hard through the country in the clouds. By dawn, the castle of fancy had been carried into the far distance, across fields and forests checkered with sunshine and shade. Floating high above the earth, the castle steadied, hovering over a field of serenity.

> *Like a lark from the sky it came fluttering down,*
> > *And placed me exactly in view,*
> *When who should I meet, in this charming retreat,*
> > *This corner of calmness, but YOU.*

The encounter between fancy and its desired object was sweet, but brief, as if discharged by its public display.

> *Delighted to find you in honour and ease,*
> > *I felt no more sorrow, nor pain;*
> *But the wind coming fair, I ascended the breeze,*
> > *And went back with my CASTLE again.*

G. M. Woodward's engraving
A Democrat, 1791. *(Courtesy of the
American Philosophical Society Library)*

*A Sure Cure for all Paines
or The Rights of Man has
got his Rights,* by an
unknown artist, circa
1792-93.

A Paine-like portrait from
the poetic notebooks of
William Blake, circa early
1790's. *(Courtesy of the
British Library)*

A. Schule's engraving of the Convention Member, *Thomas Paine*, from a sketch by C. Schule, circa 1793. (*Courtesy of the Thetford Town Council*)

The address of Louis the 16th at the Bar of the Convention on the 26th of December, 1792, after an engraving by Pelegrini. (Courtesy of the American Philosophical Society Library)

The Execution of Louis XVI, an engraving, from a drawing by Fioris. *(Courtesy of the Musée Carnavalet)*

The Triumph of Marat, by Duplessi-Bertaux. *(Courtesy of the Bibliothèque de l'institut d'histoire de la Révolution)*

Portrait of James Monroe, Paine's host after his release from prison. *(Courtesy of the Thetford Library)*

Tadeusz Kosciuszko, by Julian Rys. *(Courtesy of Independence National Historical Park, Philadelphia)*

A rare document, issued on November 3, 1794, by the Committee of General Safety, ordering Paine's immediate release from the Luxembourg prison. *(Courtesy of the Archives Nationales)*

An anonymous, undated engraving, *Arbitrary Imprisonment*. (*Courtesy of the Bibliothèque Nationale*)

The coup d'état of the 18th fructidor, undated, by an unknown engraver. (*Courtesy of the Bibliothèque Nationale*)

James Gillray's *Fashion Before Ease: or, A good Constitution sacrificed, for a Fantastick Form*, 1793. (Courtesy of the American Philosophical Society Library)

H. Humphrey's satirical image of English responses to French dreams of invasion, *The French Invasion: or John Bull, bombarding the Bum-Boats.* (Courtesy of the British Museum)

Paine's best friend, Clio Rickman, in French Revolutionary garb. *(Courtesy of the Thetford Library)*

James Godby's engraving *Thomas Paine*, 1805, from an original drawing by Edward Stacey. *(Courtesy of the American Philosophical Society Library)*

Mad Tom in a Rage, by an unknown artist, circa 1801.

Nineteenth-century image of Paine gazing out of the window of a house in Herring Street, now Bleeker Street, Greenwich Village. *(Courtesy of the American Philosophical Society Library)*

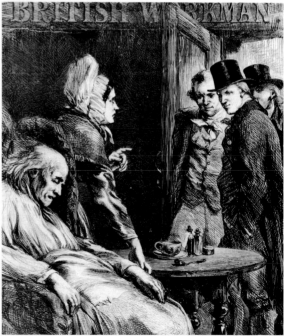

The Last Moments of Tom Paine, by John Gilbert. *(Courtesy of the Thetford Library)*

The Destroying Angel

Writing of this kind was not Paine's best — he was a lousy poet — but it provided powerful graffiti for the bleak cell walls. It transformed the space they enclosed into a mere testing ground in a long journey through a wilderness of terror to a peaceful world of freedom, equality, and solidarity. But conditions within the Luxembourg worsened in early June. The weather over Paris had been cold and wet for several weeks, bringing rising dampness and a permanently wet floor to Paine's cell. He also found himself deprived of "more than half the necessaries of life."[74] Heating fuel became scarce, most of the prison furniture having been broken up and burned, and candles, a tool so basic to Paine's peace of mind, became impossible to obtain.

Then on June 10, 1794, the Terror descended to frighten the whole of France. On that day, Georges Couthon explained to the Convention that there was a fundamental difference between ordinary crimes and crimes against the Revolution. The former hurt the individual more than society and could therefore be legally dealt with in a measured, leisurely fashion, clemency toward the accused person being extended where appropriate. Crimes of conspiring against the Revolution were different, he insisted. At stake was not merely the life of a single individual but that of an entire people. That was why judicial formality and delay must be considered positively dangerous. The guilty must be utterly annihilated, not merely punished.

With that preamble, the Law of the 22nd Prairial was introduced. It invested the Revolutionary Tribunal with virtually absolute power to punish enemies of the Revolution without regard for the ordinary safeguards of justice. The stated aim of the court was to encourage spying and denunciation and "to punish the enemies of the people." The people's enemies were defined by article 6 of the decree to include potentially everybody: those who had worked for royalism or against republicanism; reduced its food reserves; hindered the war effort; spread defeatism, false rumors, or seditious writings; or in any other way, minor or major, helped the enemies of the Revolution and hindered its friends or compromised the unity, liberty, and safety of the republic. Article 7 instructed the court to allow only two possible verdicts — acquittal or death — and articles 12–17 called for the introduction of kangaroo court procedures. The practice of subjecting the accused to preliminary questioning, which sometimes served as a loophole by enabling them to establish their innocence, was abandoned. The resort to witnesses was abolished, except in those rare cases where the court thought that there was insufficient evidence for conviction. And the accused no longer had access to counsel.

For the next forty-seven days, citizens of Paris went to the guillotine at the average rate of thirty a day. Security within the Luxembourg was drastically tightened. Lightning raids were conducted on every cell in search of sharp instruments such as knives and forks. Money was stolen from the prisoners, although Paine — whose representative's salary had been cut off from the moment of his imprisonment — had received sufficient warning to find a hiding place for his remaining coins and notes behind the lock on his cell door. Prisoners were prevented from approaching or loitering around open windows on the upper floors of the prison, two inmates having jumped to their deaths in protest at the tightening surveillance. All inmates were forbidden to use the courtyard, and conversations in the common room were broken up. Every prisoner in the Luxembourg stiffened. "There seemed to be a determination to destroy all the Prisoners without regard to merit, character, or any thing else," said Paine.[75] During one night alone, 169 prisoners were carted off, all but 8 losing their lives to the guillotine. "Domestic carnage now filled the whole year," wrote William Wordsworth: "friends, enemies, of all parties, ages, ranks, head after head, and never heads enough for those that bade them fall."[76] Paine was now surviving the Reign of Terror — and living it, daily, hourly, minute by minute. The raids on the prison by candlelight particularly unnerved him: "Many a man whom I have passed an hour with in conversation I have seen marching to his destruction the next hour, or heard of it the next morning; for what rendered the scene more horrible was that they were generally taken away at midnight, so that every man went to bed with the apprehension of never seeing his friends or the world again."[77]

During the last week of June 1794, six months into his indefinite sentence, Paine finally crumbled under the weight of nervous exhaustion. He fell into a feverish semiconsciousness, oblivious to the nightly screams and executions around him. The sickness left "a blank in my remembrance of life," Paine said. "My illness rendered me incapable of knowing anything that passed either in the prisons or elsewhere; and my comrades also made it a point all the time that my recovery continued doubtful not to inform me of anything that was passing."[78]

The intense fever lasted for more than two weeks. During that time, Paine was moved to a larger cell, which he shared with three Belgians — Michael Rubyns, Charles Bastinit, and Joseph Van Huele, who was to survive the Luxembourg and later become the mayor of Bruges. The three men devoted themselves to keeping Paine alive. They mopped his brow, fed him broth, and changed his soiled clothing and bedding. Paine also was watched over by his surgeon friend Bond and an English physician named Dr. Graham, and every several days a perfunctory examination was performed by the prison physician, Dr. Markoshi.

His condition failed to improve. The fever persisted, though less intensely, but one month after he fell ill, his comrades became convinced that he would soon die. Paine remained semiconscious, unable to speak, gesture, or concentrate on anything for more than a few seconds. His face was deathly pale, and his normally slim body had become a mere skeleton covered with blotchy flesh. He had no appetite and could not sit up or turn over in bed, let alone smile, laugh, or cry.

Meanwhile, the nightly raids on the Luxembourg continued. On July 24, the angel of death flew toward the prison, bound for Paine's cell. On that day, his name was underlined in red pencil by the Public Prosecutor, Antoine-Quentin Fouquier-Tinville. Fouquier did not know Paine personally, and indeed he was not the least bit interested in his victims. He was a quiet, hardworking, and rather dull official whose stated main ambition in life was to retain a salary sufficient to support his wife and seven children. He spent almost all his time working at his office desk at the Palais de Justice, gathering and filing evidence, compiling reports, drawing up lists of prisoners to be brought to trial, writing on average nearly a hundred letters a day, and thinking constantly about new methods of improving the cold efficiency of his work. Every evening, between ten and eleven o'clock, after his day's work was nearly done, he left his office. Accompanied by four gendarmes, he walked across the Pont Neuf to the Tuileries, where he delivered his reports to the governing committees. That evening, July 24, 1794, he submitted three lists: a provisional program for trials ten days ahead; a list of prisoners who had been tried and executed that day; and another list, which included the name of Thomas Paine, of those inmates whose time would be up the following day. Few questions were usually asked by the tired committee members, and at most a couple of minor adjustments of Fouquier's lists were made. The lists were then signed, and several copies were written up by the clerks. Instructions were sent to the prison governors, and carts were ordered for the next day's journey from the Luxembourg to the court to the guillotine. Satisfied with his hard day's work, Fouquier shook the officials' hands, wished them good evening, and went home to bed.

At six o'clock the next morning, a turnkey, carrying Fouquier's signed list, walked quietly with Death down the hushed corridors of the Luxembourg, chalking the cell doors of those inmates to be carted away later that morning. When the pair came to the door of Paine's cell, the turnkey carefully marked the number 4 on the inside of the door, signaling that time was up for Bastinit, Van Huele, Rubyns, and Paine. It was highly unusual for the turnkey to mark the inside of the door. He had done so knowing that for several weeks, Paine's comrades had been granted permission to leave open their cell door, hard against the corridor wall, to ensure that a cool breeze caressed Paine's perspiring body.

That evening, after a noticeable change of weather, the Belgians were granted permission from a different turnkey to shut their door. Knowing that the number 4 was now facing inward, they waited, breathless, with Paine murmuring on his cot. Around eleven that evening, the death squad made its way down the corridor, keys jangling, pistols drawn, lanterns trained consecutively on each door. Paine's comrades froze, pretending to be asleep. Van Huele cupped his hand over Paine's mouth. The death squad paused, then moved to the next cell, flung open its door, dragged out a petrified body, and continued down the corridor, repeating the action several times until the three Belgians could hear only muffled screams in the far corner of their prison wing. The men at first breathed more easily, then wept, their thumping hearts reminding them that they were safe — at least until Fouquier discovered the error.

The Public Prosecutor never got his chance. Paine attributed the miracle to the benevolent hand of Providence, to the lack of communication between shifts of turnkeys, and to the miraculous timing of the error. He later explained: "We . . . were four, and the door of our room was marked, unobserved by us, with that number in chalk; but it happened, if happening is a proper word, that the mark was put on when the door was open, and flat against the wall, and thereby came on the inside when we shut it at night, and the destroying angel passed by it. A few days after this, Robespierre fell."[79]

Waiting for Freedom

The attempted suicide and dramatic fall from power of Robespierre on July 27, 1794, and his execution the following day signaled the end of the Reign of Terror. It naturally boosted Paine's chances of survival, but it did not result in his immediate release. Paine hoped things would be otherwise. Ten days later, still emaciated from the illness he had at last begun to shake off, he mustered enough energy to write a letter to the Convention, a translated copy of which was forwarded to the Committee of Public

Safety. In shaky handwriting, he pleaded for his speedy release. He had not so far appealed against his incarceration, he explained, because quite aside from his brush with terminal illness, it would have been a waste of time, even dangerous, for "it is the nature of Tyranny always to strike a deeper blow when any attempt has been made to repel a former one."

He then slammed the official reason given for his imprisonment: "It is that *I am a foreigner;* where-as, the *foreigner,* thus imprisoned, was invited into France by a decree of the late national assembly, and that in the hour of her greatest danger, when invaded by Austrians and Prussians." In any case, Paine added, he was "a citizen of the united states of america, an ally of France, and not a subject of any country in Europe, and consequently not within the intention of any of the decrees concerning foreigners." He emphasized that the charge of being a foreign enemy of the Revolution was pure fabrication. It proved the point that "any excuse can be made to serve the purpose of malignity when it is in power." That malignant power was the Jacobin faction headed by Robespierre. Paine explained to the Convention that about a year earlier, Robespierre had become "my inveterate enemy, as he was the enemy of every man of virtue and humanity." He had tried to stir up resentment against Paine among the citizens of Arras, Robespierre's birthplace and regional center of Pas-de-Calais, Paine's constituency. That attempted political sabotage had initially been unsuccessful. Subsequently, that latter-day Masaniello, using what Paine called "consummate hypocrisy and the most hardened cruelties," had spread injustice throughout the country. Paine reiterated his long-standing dislike of "parties and factions" of Robespierre's kind, politely wished "fraternity and prosperity to France, and union and happiness to her representatives," and urged them promptly to restore his liberty.[80]

Prisoners in the Luxembourg were again allowed visitors and letters to and from the outside world. Paine knew from both sources that his appeal to the Convention was being morally supported from other quarters. On the same day that his letter went off to the Convention, his friend François Lanthenas appealed in writing for the release of the famous author of the recently published French translation of *The Age of Reason*.[81] Several days later, Achille Audibert petitioned Thuriot, who had heckled and interrupted Paine during the Convention debate on the fate of the king and who now served on the still-powerful Committee of Public Safety. "A friend of mankind is groaning in chains," Audibert told Thuriot. He added that Paine was among the first citizens who had "dared to say that Robespierre was a monster to be erased from the list of men."[82]

Paine waited patiently, but the Convention and the Committee kept a stone-faced silence. Then came good fortune, or so Paine thought. In mid-August 1794, still in his cell, his money having run out and his beard unkempt (all prisoners were forbidden access to sharp blades and knives), he learned that Gouverneur Morris was to be replaced by a new American minister in Paris. He checked the French newspapers circulating in the Luxembourg and found several brief news reports. James Monroe, already resident in Paris, was soon to take up his post in France. Paine was elated. On August 16, he wrote a brief letter to Monroe, congratulating him on his appointment and asking him for help. The handwriting was shaky, the tone desperate. Almost every word of the core of the letter was underlined: "I have now no expectation of delivery but by your means — *Morris has been my inveterate enemy, and I think he has permitted something of the national character of America to suffer by quietly letting a Citizen of that Country remain almost eight months in prison without making every official exertion to procure him justice,* — for every act of violence offered to a foreigner is offered also to the Nation to which he belongs."[83]

The letter, carried safely out of the prison by a friendly lamplighter, received no reply. Nor did the following day's letter, in which Paine, describing himself as "a Citizen of America," repeated his request for help, outlined to Monroe the circumstances of his invitation to France, and described the horror of his unbroken eight-month ordeal in prison.[84] The tone of the next letter to Monroe, eight days later, was decidedly nonplussed. "Having nothing to do but to sit and think," he began, "I will write to pass away time, and to say that I am still here." There were lines of self-pity: "Excluded as I am from the knowledge of everything and left to a random of ideas, I know not what to think or how to act." And words of simple humility: "*I shall be very glad to receive a line from yourself to inform me in what condition the matter stands.*" And hints that posterity might hold Monroe responsible if he did not act immediately: "There is now a moment of calm, but if through any over complaisance to the persons you converse with on the subject of my liberation, you omit procuring it for me *now*, you may have to lament the fate of your friend when its too late."[85]

The days passed slowly. There was no word from Monroe until September 4, when news worse than no news reached Paine's cell. He was informed during a visit to the Luxembourg by Peter Whiteside, his former bridge-building associate, that the reason for Monroe's silence was that the American minister had received no orders from the United States Congress, which in any case considered Paine a French citizen subject to French judicial procedures. Paine was stunned, then angry at the Washington government for its complicity with Jacobinism and with what he took to be the old-fashioned, monarchic definition of citizenship as a gift to individuals from governments. For a long time, certainly since before emigrating from England, Paine had held to the opposite view that citizenship rights and duties were established by freely consenting individuals and only ratified and protected by governments. It followed from this bottom-up definition of citizenship that individuals were not embonded (in accordance with the principles of *ius soli* and *ius sanguinis*) to any particular state and that they could belong to more than one political community at any one time — that they could, in words Paine had learned from his Irish playwright friend Oliver Goldsmith, be citizens of the world.

Paine was convinced that these elementary principles needed restating to Monroe, and during the next ten days he penned a forty-three-page letter crammed with philosophical and legal arguments. The clear prose and tough reasoning suggested that his mental powers were fully restored. He began by establishing the principle that citizenship is a contract between individuals and their governments and not a natural obligation traceable to the blood of their parents or the soil on which they were born. "Though born in England," wrote Paine, "I am not a subject of the English Government any more than any other American who was born, as they all were, under the same government, or than the citizens of France are subjects of the French monarchy under which they were born." Paine then drew a parallel between citizenship rights and the eighteenth-century practice of extending membership rights to foreigners in scientific and literary associations within civil society. "Most of the academies and societies in Europe, and also those in America, conferred the rank of honorary member, upon foreigners eminent in knowledge, and made them, in fact, citizens of their literary or scientific republic, without affecting or anyways diminishing their rights of citizenship in their own country or in other societies."[86]

There were actually two key points here, both of them unconventional in Paine's time but more familiar in ours. First, citizenship is not simply a matter of individuals enjoying entitlements and sharing duties in matters of government and politics; citizens also enjoy *civil* and *social* entitlements within the nongovernmental sphere of civil society. Second, these bundles of citizenship rights, Paine argued, are not confined to the geographic territory of a state. They are portable in that individuals, who are naturally endowed with citizenship rights, are not the property of any state. They can therefore enjoy these powers whenever they travel to or reside in another state. Paine admitted that disputes about citizenship rights and duties were ultimately a matter to be decided by elected representatives and courts referring to written constitutions. Yet he thought that citizenship is

a God-given but humanly defined privilege that governments of all nations should honor and respect. Paine put the point sarcastically to Monroe: "Why the people of one nation should not, by their representatives,
exercise the right of conferring the honour of citizenship upon individuals
eminent in another nation, without affecting *their* rights of citizenship, is a
problem yet to be solved."[87]

Monroe seemed to grasp the point, giving it an American twist. On
September 18, he wrote Paine a reassuring letter, declaring that he personally considered Paine an American and as such entitled to his services as
minister. This letter is important as the only official declaration on the
much-debated point of Paine's citizenship. "By being with us through the
revolution," Monroe declared, "you are of our country, as absolutely as if
you had been born there; and you are no more of England, than every
native of America is." Paine was considered by his fellow Americans "not
only as having rendered important services in our own revolution, but as
being, upon a more extensive scale, the friend of human rights, and a distinguished and able advocate, in favour of the public liberty."[88]

In reply on October 4, Paine thanked Monroe for his affectionate letter. Showing signs of the recovery of his health and his conceit, he attributed his imprisonment to his "literary and philosophical reputation." He
was "the victim of the principles and . . . the talents, that procured . . . the
esteem of America."[89] He reiterated that he could not understand why he
was still interned, since the system of terror had been overthrown and the
new government should have no apprehension that he would blacken the
names of its members to the world.

Nine days later, Paine showed increased signs of impatience. He had
been in prison almost ten months, two months since Monroe's arrival.
The latter circumstance, he complained, might nurture the suspicion that
his imprisonment was justified or that his reputation had been ruined in
America. Paine said that he believed that Monroe had been pressured into
accepting the French authorities' view that he would be released in the
course of time without direct interference. Again Paine insisted that Monroe claim him as an American and not rely on the promises of men whom
he did not know: "I have always been taught to believe that the liberty of
a citizen was the first object of all free governments, and that it ought not
to give preference to, or be blended with, any other."[90]

A week later, Paine wrote once more to Monroe, this time enclosing a
model letter for Monroe to submit to the Committee of General Security.
Paine came close to accusing the Committee of seeking to alienate American citizens from France and, thus, endangering the alliance between the

United States and France. So that his personal merits not be overlooked, Paine also proposed the following wording of the letter:

> Of the patriotism of Thomas Paine I can speak fully, if we agree to give to patriotism a fixed idea consistent with that of a republic. It would then signify a strict adherence to moral justice, to the equality of civil and political rights, to the system of representative government, and an opposition to all hereditary claims to govern. Admitting patriotism to these principles, I know of no man who has gone beyond Thomas Paine in promulgating and defending them, and that for almost twenty years past.[91]

Monroe, in appealing to the Committee of General Security on November 2, did not adopt Paine's proposed wording. His letter was nevertheless positively diplomatic. Monroe paid high tribute to Paine's character, but he carefully avoided all points of controversy, instead politely but firmly asking the French government to bring Paine to trial if he were guilty of any criminal offense or release him if he were not. The president of the Committee of General Security promised to communicate the contents of Monroe's letter immediately to the Committee of Public Safety.[92] The conference between the two committees took place without further delay. On November 6, Monroe received the order from the Committee of General Security for Paine's release, which he immediately put into effect.[93] That afternoon, the gray-bearded Paine, haggard and noticeably more stooped than before entering the Luxembourg, regained his freedom.

Monroe's Guest

Monroe accompanied Paine to his own home in a carriage, along the way inviting him to stay indefinitely. To James Madison more than a year later, Monroe wrote that Paine would continue to be his guest "till his death or departure for America, however remote either the one or the other event may be."[94]

Paine's physical condition was initially not bad enough to keep him indoors, and "restored to the enjoyment of his liberty" and "in good spirits" (reported Monroe), he quickly renewed contact with the Paris political scene. On December 8, 1794, he was delighted to learn that A. C. Thibaudeau, a moderate member of the National Convention, had formally requested the assembly to restore Paine to his Pas-de-Calais seat:

I appeal in favour of one of the most zealous defenders of liberty, of a man who has honoured his century by the energy with which he has defended the rights of man, who has gloriously distinguished himself by the role he has played in the American Revolution. I have never heard a single reproach uttered against Thomas Payne. Naturalized as a French citizen by the Legislative Assembly, he was named representative of the people. His expulsion from the Convention was merely the fruit of intrigue, the pretext being a decree which excluded foreigners from representing the nation. There were only two in the Convention. One is dead [Anacharsis Cloots]. But Thomas Payne, who powerfully contributed to establish liberty in a nation allied to the republic, still exists. He lives in distress. I urge that he be recalled to the Convention.[95]

Thibaudeau's motion was adopted unanimously. Shortly afterward, Paine received back pay of eighteen hundred livres, owed to him from his time in the Luxembourg. Paine, who at the time was suffering a "vicious attack of consumption," wrote to thank Thibaudeau nine days after his motion, attributing his delay in replying to the inconveniences attached to translating from one language to another. Paine told Thibaudeau that he would accept the invitation of the Convention: "I want the whole universe to know that although I have been a victim of injustice, I do not attribute my sufferings to those who were not concerned, and I am far from inclined to seek reprisals even against those who were directly responsible."[96] Since he expected to return to America in the spring, wrote Paine, he wished to be assured that returning to the Convention would not jeopardize his plans. By means of an interpreter, Thibaudeau assured him that there was no such danger and that he could even take a leave of absence from the Convention if he wished not to resign.

Paine soon received praise from the floor of the Convention. The Committee of Public Instruction had been commissioned to study means of aiding scholars and artists. One of its members, the poet Marie Joseph de Chénier, whose brother had been guillotined two days before Robespierre fell, reported to the Convention on January 3, 1795, a scheme of awarding pensions to citizens who had performed eminent literary service. Paine was first on the list, and Chénier exhorted the Convention to make amends for his maltreatment:

A caprice of tyrants banished him as a foreigner from the floor of the National Assembly. You have revoked that inhospitable decree, and we no longer see in Thomas Paine a man of genius without fortune but a cherished colleague of all the friends of humanity, a cosmopolite persecuted equally by Pitt and by Robespierre. This has been a notable epoch in the life of this philosopher, who used the weapons of *common sense* against the sword of tyranny, the *sacredness of the rights of man* against the Machiavellism of English politics, and who by his two immortal works has deserved well of the human race and consecrated liberty in two worlds.[97]

The sentiments were noble, but the odd silence about *The Age of Reason* may explain why Paine never received a penny of the proposed pension. Meanwhile, the Convention ordered a treaty of friendship and commerce between France and the United States. Monroe, thinking that something could be done for the good of both Paine and the United States, wrote to the Committee of Public Safety to propose that Paine be appointed an official envoy to carry the Convention's order to America. Monroe argued that Paine was better fitted than anyone else to serve as a confidential agent between the two republics because of his long residence in France and his close acquaintance with both countries' Revolutions and governments. The Committee replied that Paine's position in the Convention precluded his accepting such a commission. This decision, according to Paine's interpretation, was based on the fact that an application to the Convention for a passport would have made his mission public, thereby nullifying its confidential nature. That may have been so. The additional fact, however, was that some formerly terrorist members of the Committee of Public Safety mistrusted Paine, whose *The Age of Reason* was already stirring up bitter controversy in America and whose own eyes had seen such terrible things in France that he might want to tell them to other Americans — at the cost of scuppering the proposed treaty.

Paine had no option but to stay put in Paris. He successfully petitioned the executive Directory for permission to reside there,[98] after which he spent time working for the release of Mme Lafayette from prison. He also worked on getting passports for friends (like the Englishwoman Mrs. Evans) wanting to leave the country or getting the Directory's permission for friends such as Robert Smyth and the stocking manufacturer Robert Raymont to stay in Paris.[99] Paine also spent time reading "sundry Authors, as well ancient as modern," at the Bibliothèque Nationale, often accompanied by his multilingual friend Smyth, whom he described as "a man of letters and of leisure."[100]

The relaxed routine was made possible by the new political climate. Paine naturally followed with great interest every move by the conservative revolutionaries, the so-called Thermidorians, to switch off and dismantle the machinery responsible for the Reign of Terror. During 1795, the terrorist revolutionary committees of the provincial communes were suppressed and replaced by appointees of the Convention. The Committee of Public Safety, the self-perpetuating oligarchy that had been master of the Convention, was transformed into its servant, its role being confined to matters of war and foreign affairs. In Paris, the headquarters staff of the National Guard were placed under the direct control of the committees of the Convention. Meanwhile, the dreaded Paris Commune, the wellspring of terrorist dictatorship, was abolished, along with the city's administrative unity.

The package of reforms produced unintended anti-Jacobin outbursts in the countryside, especially in southeast France, where the so-called White Terror reminded everybody of the extraordinary social violence that had marked the Revolution. The 1795 reforms nevertheless had civilizing effects. They halted arbitrary arrests and ended the tyranny of the guillotine and the surveillance committees. The reforms were designed to consolidate the republic; naturally they pointed to the need for a new constitution, whose chief author was to be François Antoine de Boissy d'Anglas. The document he drew up was haunted by two ghosts: terrorist dictatorship and universal franchise democracy. Aiming to check concentrations of state power, the new constitution of 1795 established a bicameral legislature divided into a Council of Five Hundred (each male member at least thirty years of age), which initiated laws, and a Council of Elders (the Ancients), 250 men in all, each of whom was at least forty years of age and whose task was to approve or reject the laws proposed by the lower House. The administrative body was to consist of five men, known as the Directory, equipped with powers concerning war, diplomacy, police, and administration. These men, forty or older, were to be selected by the Ancients from a short list submitted by the Council of Five Hundred.

Measures for reducing popular pressure also were adopted. The new constitution sought to limit popular sovereignty, both by dividing it and, at the same time, by founding the Republic on enlightened "representation." The right of "resisting oppression" (1789) or of "insurrection" (1793) disappeared. Instead of references to the right to work, social assistance, and education, emphasis was given to obedience to the law, productive labor, and service to *la patrie*. Universal male suffrage was abolished. Priests, former émigrés, and all avowed Jacobins were specifically disfranchised. Elections were to be indirect. The right to vote for electors — who in turn chose the two-chamber legislature — was restricted to soldiers and those adult men who paid direct taxes. The ultimate aim of the new constitution was to restrict political power to the "sensible" propertied classes. "We should be governed," concluded Boissy d'Anglas, "by the best, and the best are those who are best educated and most interested in upholding the laws. With very few exceptions you will only find such men among those who, possessing property, are attached to the country containing it and the laws which protect it."[101]

Such "bourgeois" talk irritated Paine. Although he later praised the emphasis on the separation of powers and said that "a better organized Constitution has never yet been devised by human wisdom," he found various articles of the proposed Constitution "repugnant to reason, and incompatible with the true principles of liberty."[102] In early July 1795, Paine argued his case at length in a treatise submitted to the Convention under the title *Dissertations sur les Premiers Principes de Gouvernement (Dissertation on the First Principles of Government)*.

The tract followed the reasoning of *Rights of Man*. It argued for the demolition of the hereditary system and insisted that the "science of government" was comprehensible to "the meanest capacity," even though it had been traditionally enveloped in mystery "for the purpose of enslaving, plundering and imposing upon mankind." In thus treating politics as a subject that the weakest mind could master, Paine in effect called for a universal — male — franchise by following the same reasoning that the deists had applied to religion and the classical literary critics had applied to aesthetic appreciation. In politics, religion, and art, Paine said, fundamental truth is readily perceptible to all individuals when stripped of the excrescences of superstition, prejudice, and authority. For that reason alone, the attempt to link the vote to property was "dangerous and impolitic" and "always unjust." It also was ridiculous — as absurd as the idea (Paine's provocative simile was carefully chosen) that a mule owner earns the right to vote because his broodmare gives birth to a salable foal. That idea begged a question about the source of the right to vote. "Is it in the man, or in the mule?" he asked sarcastically. The answer, and the moral, were clear: "When we consider how many ways property may be acquired without merit, and lost without crime, we ought to spurn the idea of making it a criterion of rights."[103]

On July 7, 1795, Paine once more stood at the tribune of the Convention while the translation of his own speech was read aloud by a secretary. His aim was to present the substance of his tract on government and thereby to expose the contradiction between the principles of 1789 and the proposed constitution embodying property qualifications for the franchise. Paine spoke out in particular against two articles that conflicted with the "grand object of the Revolution" and the sentiments of the individuals who had accomplished it. One such article limited citizenship to those who paid direct taxes, and the other, attempting to palliate the first, conferred citizenship on every French soldier who had served in the cause of liberty. Paine argued the injustice of disfranchising all who paid indirect taxes. He also pointed out that even the soldiers would be unfavorably treated, since their families and descendants would be excluded from the rights of citizens unless they also paid direct taxes. He concluded by warning his fellow legislators: "If you dispense with principles, and substitute expedients, you will extinguish that enthusiasm and energy which have hitherto been the life and soul of the Revolution; and you will substitute in its place nothing but a cold indifference and self-interest, which will again degenerate into intrigue, cunning and effeminacy."

Cold indifference greeted Paine's plea. Only two other members of the Convention had ever advocated universal male suffrage: Paine's friend and translator Lanthenas and an obscure idealist, Julien Souhait. The Convention, dominated by men of newly acquired wealth, murmured uncomfortably. No one rose to support Paine. That was hardly a surprising outcome considering that the call for universal male suffrage smacked of Jacobinism, pushed republicanism into unfamiliar democratic territory, and confirmed Paine's willingness to nudge the spirit of the American state constitutions, almost none of which at the time conferred any broader suffrage than that of the projected constitution. Although the speech was a flop, a majority of the Convention voted politely at the end of the session to have it printed for other citizens' consideration.[104]

Agrarian Justice

The Convention shortly afterward submitted the new constitution to a plebiscite. It won just over a million votes, but the accompanying decree compelling electors to choose two-thirds of the members of the new legislative body from the ranks of the existing Convention proved unpopular. It provoked unrest, especially in Paris, where the crude attempt by the rump Convention to keep its power sparked off an uprising on October 5, 1795 (13 vendémiaire). Sixteen thousand troops commanded by a young general named Napoleon Bonaparte cordoned off the Convention and fired on angry demonstrators with muskets and cannon, leaving behind several hundred killed and wounded. The Convention was rescued, but the events of 13 vendémiaire brought the army into politics and effectively terminated Paine's position as deputy, the only publicly elected office he ever held in America, France, or (with the hybrid exception of Lewes) England. From here on, he was to be confined to civilian life. Although Paine found it impossible to live as an apolitical animal, he was forced to limit himself mainly to newspaper writing and cultivating political acquaintances in high places.

During the second half of 1795, illness crippled his plans. Jail fever (typhus) returned, adding to the constant chest pains he had been suffering from for six months. Monroe wrote in mid-September that Paine's illness was so grave that there was a danger that he would not survive more than a month or two. Rumors began to circulate in England and America that he had died.[105] According to William Cobbett, Paine was living as a helpless invalid, suffering from a type of paralysis that took away the use of his hands. "Mrs. Monroe showed him all possible kindness and attention," reported Cobbett. "She provided him with an excellent nurse, who had for him all the anxiety and assiduity of a sister. She neglected nothing to afford him ease and comfort, when he was totally unable to help himself. He was in the state of a helpless child who has its face and hands washed by its mother."[106]

One of Paine's German admirers, Carl Friedrich Cramer, translator of part of *Rights of Man* and commentator on several of Paine's writings, went to visit him in company with Joel Barlow. In a letter to Friedrich Klopstock on November 26, 1795, Cramer reported his distress at Paine's suffering "incurably from the torture of an open wound in the side, which came from a decaying rib."[107] Cramer underestimated Paine's country-bred constitution and will to live. Attended by Dessault, a well-known Paris surgeon, Paine regained full strength. His political touch also returned. During his convalescence, he even composed two works of political economy, which many of his contemporaries considered sensational. One, *Thomas Payne, à la Législature et au Directoire, ou la justice agraire opposée à la loi et aux priviléges agraires,* commonly known as *Agrarian Justice opposed to Agrarian Law, and to Agrarian Monopoly,* was a proposal for a citizen's income funded by an inheritance tax; the other, *The Decline and Fall of the English System of Finance,* predicted that the Bank of England would collapse under the pressure of excessive inflation.

Paine wrote *Agrarian Justice* in the winter of 1795–96. The decision to publish it, he said, was triggered by reading the Bishop of Llandaff's sermon praising the division between rich and poor as a sign of God's wisdom. The pamphlet had unmistakably French origins. It can be read as a protest against the class of nouveaux riches then emerging as the ruling element in the French state. Whereas the Jacobin dictatorship had preached austerity, the new Thermidoreans rediscovered private freedom with pleasure. Civil society was reborn. Salons reopened, fashion and conversation flourished. But the return to *laissez-faire* rapidly subdivided the civil society into rich and poor. With the new Directory's abolition of the old economic controls imposed by the Committee of Public Safety, government spending and inflation skyrocketed, brigandage flourished, and misery spread. Deputies and high state officials protected themselves by calculating their salaries in myriagrams of cheese, the army lived by pillage, and townspeople and villagers were rescued from starvation by food pinched from the peasantry.[108]

Paine's *Agrarian Justice* considered the widening inequality shameful. He saw it not merely as a French trend but as expressive of a central problem of modern civilization. He thought that it tended "to make one part of society more affluent, and the other part more wretched than would have been the lot of either in a natural state." He likened the division between poor and rich to "dead and living bodies chained together," but he insisted, against the apologists of poverty, that the problem was remediable. Poverty is not God's will. It is an artificial, humanly produced blight. "It is wrong to say that God made *Rich* and *Poor;* he made only *Male* and *Female;* and he gave them the earth for their inheritance."

Paine's argument was hardly original, but its plain style was distinctive. Although men and women did not create the earth originally, he wrote, God granted them the natural right to occupy it for their own use. And so they did. But the resulting inequality of occupancy rights — whose roots Paine did not explain — was marked by a growing rift between propertied and propertyless. The rich began to regard their property as an end in itself, to be held forever, as if the Creator had opened a land office issuing title deeds in perpetuity. The propertied soon began to exploit the propertyless. "The accumulation of personal property," Paine explained, "is, in many instances, the effects of paying too little for the labour that produced it; the consequence of which is that the working hand perishes in old age, and the employer abounds in affluence."

Paine attacked this practice. Private property is God-given, he agreed, but it is always subject to the primary rule that the earth is "the COMMON PROPERTY OF THE HUMAN RACE." It followed from this common ownership rule that the propertied have an obligation to help the poor, not by charity alone, but by accepting a government-administered inheritance tax system designed to redistribute and equalize income. Paine did not say what would be done with recalcitrant property owners and their families who refused to acknowledge the common property right, let alone pay their share of death duties; the problem of strikes by the wealthy against equalizing policies had to be faced by later social reformers. Paine instead sketched a plan for setting up a National Fund out of which every man and woman reaching twenty-one years of age would be eligible for a compensatory one-time payment of fifteen pounds sterling, while every person reaching fifty years of age would receive an annual citizen's pension of ten pounds.

Agrarian Justice was attacked, for instance, by Thomas Spence's *The Rights of Infants* (1797), for its failure to envisage the transformation of private property into common ownership. Subsequent interpreters of *Agrarian Justice* were wrong, however, to see it as either a reforming "bourgeois liberal" or a protosocialist tract. The anachronistic language of "capitalism or socialism" obscures Paine's concern to sketch and defend the democratic republican principle of citizens' *social* rights. Paine favored the preservation of a private-property, market-driven economy, but he argued that its self-destructive dynamism — its tendency to generate wealth by widening the income gap between classes — could be tamed by institutionalizing the basic principle of each person's entitlement to full citizens' rights. This would prevent the smothering of the poor by the rich. It also would do away with the old argument (famously outlined by Maximilian Petty during the English Revolution of the 1640s) that apprentices, recipients of alms, servants, and others should be excluded from the right to vote on the ground that since they depend on the will of their masters, they are perforce afraid of disagreeing with their masters publicly. Paine stood this old argument on its head. Instead of denying the franchise to those who currently depend politically on the rich, the dependents should be granted monetary independence. That universal guarantee of a right to a basic citizen's income would then require — contrary to the spirit of the new 1795 constitution — a universal franchise.

The Decline and Fall of the English System of Finance, published in April 1796, was an altogether different pamphlet.[109] It was an attempt by Paine to try his hand at economic forecasting. Following a notion he had already introduced in various numbers of *The American Crisis* and advised by his banker friend Robert Smyth, Paine attacked the English government through its economic system.[110] He set out to prove that within twenty years, the nation's currency would fail. England's level of foreign debt was already in excess of £400 million, even though the cash holdings of the Bank of England amounted to no more than £1 million. Paine repeated his old argument that bank notes were not worth the paper on which they are printed and added the new thought that the pound sterling would become ever more overstretched. His reasoning was based on the claimed discovery of a lawlike tendency for the national debt to rise annually in continual progression. He believed that this economic "law" was as infallible as Newton's ratio of gravitation — that laws of political economy operate parallel to those in physics and chemistry. The supposition was questionable, but the prediction came true. It happened that the Bank of England suspended convertibility of bank notes into specie the following year — with a jubilant Paine crowing that his own work had been a significant contributing factor in hastening the collapse of the Georgian monarchy.

On April 27, 1796, Paine presented copies of *The Decline and Fall of the English System of Finance* "to the French people" and to both the Council of Five Hundred and the Council of Elders. The pamphlet generated considerable discussion, especially because it predicted that the bellicose government of England was nearing collapse. A member of the Council of Elders enthusiastically proclaimed that the work should be placed under the eyes of everyone concerned with financial matters, prompting a majority of the Council to vote for its official printing and distribution. The Directory on the same day ordered one thousand copies for publicity purposes. It considered Paine's work "the most combustible weapon which France could at this moment employ to overthrow and destroy the English government."[111] The Directory seemed confident that if it were circulated in financial centers where large quantities of British funds were held, those funds would be unloaded and England "immediately reduced to the nakedness and abandonment to which she must inevitably descend." A few weeks later, the Directory arranged the printing of a German-language edition, which the translator, Dorsch, had particularly keyed to influence the financiers of Holland, Switzerland, and Germany, "whose interests are essentially linked to those of the Bank of London." The Directory sent a hundred copies of this German edition to the Ministry of Foreign Affairs to be distributed by French agents in foreign countries. Even the British government was reminded of the influence of Paine in England, where more than a dozen London editions, as well as five refutations, were published.[112] Several editions quickly appeared in America, and translations appeared in Italian (accompanied by an engraving of a curly-haired "Tomasso Paine") and other European languages, while two German authors published refutations in French.[113] One of them, S. A. Joersson — in the pay of the British — compared Paine unfavorably to Adam Smith and accused the "writer attached to the opposition" of ignoring the facts of political economy and plotting a downfall of the British government that would, in practice, reduce "an amiable and enlightened people" to French "barbarism."[114]

"A Cold Blooded Traitor"

The success of *The Decline and Fall of the English System of Finance* was quickly overshadowed by Paine's scandalous attack on George Washington. During his residence at the Monroes', Paine had become convinced that his personal bitterness toward Washington was politically justified. Something of his resentment at the president's official and private neglect had first been expressed in February 1795. During that month, Paine had composed a tart letter protesting to Washington the silence of the American government in the face of his imprisonment. He had accused Gouverneur Morris of neglecting the interests of America in France and attacked the "pusillanimous conduct of Mr. Jay in England."[115] The letter revealed disappointment over Washington's conduct, but not bitterness or outright condemnation. Monroe, seeing the letter's potential for whipping up bad feeling, had asked Paine not to send it. Paine had complied with the request for diplomacy — until September 20, 1795, when he had composed and sent off another letter, which had actually reached Washington.

In the letter, Paine accused Washington of conniving at his imprisonment, although he left open an avenue for reconciliation. "I ought not to have suspected you of treachery," Paine said, but adding, "I shall continue to think you treacherous, till you give me cause to think otherwise." Four days later, his position had toughened, as he told Monroe: "I ought not to have suspected Mr. Washington of treachery but he has acted towards me the part of a cold blooded traitor." The charge was serious, and Paine explained that he could think of only three possible motives for Washington's neglect: to keep Paine silent so that Washington and the Federalist faction might exclaim louder against the French Revolution, to restrain Paine's opposition in an attempt to dominate the American government, and to gratify the English government.[116]

Since Paine received neither apology nor explanation from Washington, his suspicions turned into firm conviction, and he determined to expose the president's perfidy to the world. Bursting with bitterness, he practiced by penning, for his friend Joel Barlow, an instruction to "the Sculptor who should make the statue of Washington":

> *Take from the mine the coldest, hardest stone,*
> *It needs no fashion, it is Washington;*
> *But if you chissel, let your strokes be rude;*
> *And on his breast engrave* Ingratitude.

Paine's sentiment would become obelized by a sword of stone hanging above the nation's capital. More words of protest soon followed. Paine left

Monroe's house sometime between January and June of 1796 and —
aside from a possible secret visit to England — he spent most of the summer at Versailles, probably at the home of Fulwar Skipwith, the American
Consul.[117] On May 13, the Directory singled out Paine for exemption
from a decree obliging all former deputies to the Convention to move
away from Paris. On July 5, Monroe reported to Madison that

> Paine having resolved to continue in Europe some time longer and knowing
> it was inconvenient for me to keep him longer in my family and wishing
> also to treat on our politics which he could not well do in my house, left me
> some time since. He thinks the President winked at his imprisonment and
> wished he might die in gaol, and bears him resentment for it; also he is
> preparing an attack upon him of the virulent kind. Through a third person
> [Dr. Enoch Edwards] I have endeavoured to divert him from it without ef-
> fect. It may be said I have instigated him but the above is the truth.[118]

Paine prepared his exposé in the form of a long open letter to Washington, eventually dated July 30, 1796, which he sent to Benjamin Franklin
Bache in Philadelphia for publication. Bache, editor of the republican-
inclined *Aurora* and grandson of Benjamin Franklin, shared Paine's bitter
distrust of Washington and was the logical man to sponsor Paine's blast
against him. In his open letter, Paine gave a detailed account of his imprisonment and said that he held Washington personally responsible for
the fact that until Monroe's arrival, he had not been considered an American citizen. Paine explained that he was making public the causes of his
personal resentment because Washington's private conduct matched the
corruption and mismanagement of his administration. In political as well
as personal relations, Washington was driven by unprincipled selfishness:
"It has some time been known by those who know him, that he has no
friendships; that he is incapable of forming any; he can serve or desert a
man, or a cause, with constitutional indifference; and it is this cold, her-
maphrodite faculty that imposed itself upon the world and was credited
for a while, by enemies as by friends, for prudence, moderation and im-
partiality." Washington's character, Paine concluded, was "a sort of non-
describable, chameleon-coloured thing called *prudence*. It is, in many cases,
a substitute for principle, and is so nearly allied to hypocrisy that it easily
slides into it."

Concluding with a reestimation of Washington's role in the American
Revolution, Paine flatly denied Washington's reputation as a skilled military commander. He summarized Washington's strategy as that of "doing

nothing," and he asserted that the great American victories were those of other commanders, backed by fearless citizen soldiers. Washington's personal campaigns were distinguished by nothing but prolonged languor. Characterizing the president as "treacherous in private friendship . . . and a hypocrite in public life," Paine warned him that "the world will be puzzled to decide whether you are an apostate or an impostor; whether you have abandoned good principles, or whether you ever had any."[119]

Washington nowhere in his correspondence alluded to receiving Paine's letter from France, but he once described the later printed version as an absolute falsehood inspired by the French propaganda machine. Washington certainly never offered any explanation of his failure to investigate Paine's imprisonment. Paine's animosity was undoubtedly fueled by a strong sense of his own importance. It may be that Washington, mindful of American neutrality, deliberately ignored Paine to avoid creating obstacles to the developing alliance with England. And it is possible that Washington did not even know about Paine's incarceration until Monroe submitted his report. Paine thought that the whole administration from the president down should have been rocked by the catastrophe of his imprisonment. But it may not have come to the attention of anyone in the administration except Edmund Randolph, Secretary of State. In turn, he may have accepted Morris's appraisal of the situation and concluded that silence was the most expedient means of dealing with Paine's plight.

Perhaps Washington was ignorant. But in any case, the striking thing about Paine's letter to Washington was the way in which the motives of both sender and receiver were quickly outweighed by the wider public controversy in America about whether or to what extent the young democratic republic needed a strong-willed, charismatic leader. Symptomatic were the dominant reactions to the reprinted version of *Letter to Washington*. Bache printed an excerpt from Paine's *Letter* in the Philadelphia *Aurora* on October 17, 1796, and on election day the next month, he printed other excerpts as propaganda in favor of the republican doctrines of Thomas Jefferson against the allegedly royalist sentiments of John Adams. Several months later, on February 6, 1797, Bache advertised the pamphlet version. It caused a sensation. Public opinion did not turn instantly against its author, as has previously been thought. Paine's letter in fact added to the mounting domestic political difficulties faced by Washington, and it is even probable that Paine had drafted his letter with the aim of forcing his old general into retirement by supplying ink to the poison-pen campaign then being waged against Washington by the Republicans.[120]

During Washington's first term, there had been public criticism of his "royal manners" and neglect of old soldiers. Receptions he had attended had been described by his critics as "monarchical parades"; when he had avoided crowds in Philadelphia and elsewhere, he had been accused of aloofness.[121] Three events in Washington's second term of office — the Genet affair, the Whiskey Rebellion, and the Jay Treaty — made him the target of a much nastier press campaign. Unfriendly newspapers asserted that the president fancied a crown and that his treatment of the French diplomat Edmond Genet showed that he regarded himself as no servant of the people. The *New York Journal* alleged that he had "aristocratical blood" in his veins, that he was a "most horrid swearer and blasphemer," and that he had been friendly to France only as long as it had had a king.[122] The treaty with England signed by John Jay multiplied the out-cries. Some attacked Washington as a pawn of Great Britain. Others in-sisted that he had "pursued the advice of wicked counsellors" and that the Jay Treaty was unconstitutional because it had sidestepped Congress and relied on Washington's authority alone. Still others insisted that the second-rate general had perpetrated war crimes, humiliated war-torn vet-erans, mortgaged public funds, produced a huge public debt, and erected a new moneyed aristocracy bent on "advancing the greatest good of the least number possessing the greatest wealth."[123]

At the heart of these criticisms of "Saint Washington" was the insis-tence that presidential infallibility was a mirage, that the American people had "spoiled their President, as a too indulgent parent spoils a child," and that he should now be impeached. The only question to be resolved, re-marked one writer, was how long Americans would "suffer themselves to be *awed* by *one* man."[124] In Swiftian language, another writer irreverently likened Washington to ambergris. "A little whiff of it . . . is very agree-able," he wrote, "but when a man holds a whole lump of it to your nose, it is a *stink* and strikes you down."[125] The smell certainly persisted until Washington left office, and odors continued even after his death.

By adding to the sardonic reactions, Paine suffered furious Federalist counterblasts.[126] They may have done more to damage Paine's reputation in America than any other circumstance of his life — more even than the Silas Deane affair or the publication of *The Age of Reason*. The reason was obvious. Although Washington's critics suspected him of counterrevolu-tionary monarchism, many Federalists considered the wooden-toothed president as sacred as Jesus Christ. Many saw him as a necessary hero, without whom the young republic could not survive. Washington had presided over the bitter quarrels within his cabinet and endured the his-toric feud between Jefferson and Alexander Hamilton, all the while struggling successfully to keep America out of European conflicts. Although there were indications that Washington's prestige was slipping among the wider public, all of his American supporters resented both the bitterness and the target of Paine's attack. An erstwhile admirer of Paine, writing in the *Aurora* on November 20, 1802, typically explained that he had read *The Age of Reason* more fervently than the Bible but that he had become Paine's bitter enemy after reading *Letter to Washington*. Washington was, after all, the "Father of His Country." Paine, a mere English commoner, was mischievously throwing stones because of a purely personal quarrel, and that was an insult to the much-loved dead.

Living with Martial Law

In the spring of 1797, as Paine was drafting the letter that ruffled so many feathers in America, he took up residence at 4 rue du Théatre Français with his young friend of long standing Nicolas de Bonneville. It was initially a "reception of hospitality" offered to Paine for a week or so. For one reason or another, the invitation was stretched out over a period of five years. Bonneville seemed unperturbed, gladly giving up his study and a bedroom to his guest. Paine nicknamed his new quarters "my work-shop"[127] and quickly resumed old habits that had not changed much since the days of the American Revolution. Amid dusty clutter, he slept late, read pamphlets and newspapers, chatted with visitors, and frequented Putode's Café on the rue des Marais. He never went out after lunch without first taking a nap, and, according to Bonneville, he never hired a coach for a journey, preferring instead to walk, thus combining exercise and economy.

The routine was soon interrupted by politics. During 1797, France witnessed a monarchist revival. Royalists emerged from hiding and trickled back across French borders. Through its envoy in Switzerland, the British government did everything to encourage the trend by pouring in money and spies. The hearts of those yearning for some form of restored monarchy fluttered with the elections of April 1797, in which the majority of new deputies to the assembly were avowed constitutional monarchists. With Directory members Carnot and Barthélemy sympathetic, it now seemed possible that monarchists would resume control of France, this time by constitutional means.

Paine grew alarmed. France was witnessing what in America was only feared: the revenge of monarchy upon republicanism. "If all this was not a conspiracy," he said, "it had at least the features of one, and was pregnant with the same mischiefs." He responded by joining a republican society called the Constitutional Club, whose members (including the famous Swiss political writer Benjamin Constant) were convinced "that the friends of the Republic should rally around the standard of the Constitution."[128] The club, which was soon declared illegal, made no headway, and in fact the designs of the crown were eventually crushed only by force of arms. On the morning of 18 Fructidor (September 4, 1797), a few months after Paine had moved in with Bonneville, Paris woke up to a military coup d'état. Barthélemy was arrested, and Carnot fled. The remaining triumvirate of the Directory, with the support of the army, took over the basic administrative functions of state, banned all opposition, and effectively prepared the way for a permanent dictatorship. A censored press, house searches, and preventive arrests became commonplace. A proclamation ordered that anyone advocating a return either to royalty or the constitution of 1793 would be shot on sight. Several hundred opponents of the dictatorship were tried before military courts, and key enemies of the state, including several hundred priests, were dispatched to the "dry guillotine," Guiana, where many subsequently perished from disease. The republic was saved, but the coup signaled the triumph of political cunning and military-conservative forces over the last vestiges of citizenship ideals and constitutional government. The coup d'état brought the revolutionary war home to France itself. With the crash of jackboots on the streets and the Directory's monopoly of all executive powers, the military dictatorship of Napoleon Bonaparte was only several paces away.

Paine reacted oddly to these events. Instead of starting at once to agitate against the revival of autocracy on 18 Fructidor, he publicly supported the new regime. "The event itself is a matter of joy," he wrote.[129] Instead of seeing the outlines of the Bonapartist dictatorship in this coup, or indeed the way in which the coup *preserved* a form of autocracy common to both monarchy and military despotism, he could see only the royalist past. Unlike Madame de Staël, the most prominent unhappy "*fructidorienne*," he did not even publicly lament the mismatch between the republican ideals of the coup and its authoritarian means. His fear of the return of the Bourbon monarchy was obsessive, but like all obsessions it had some justification. He insisted that the events of 18 Fructidor had not been precipitated by the group that had actually seized control, but by royalists and reactionary forces. A "faction" among the most recently elected members of the Council of Five Hundred had conspired to overthrow the Directory and restore the monarchy, Paine argued. The Directory had responded by assuming all powers in the name of suppressing the counterrevolutionary conspiracy.

Paine examined these circumstances in a pamphlet issued by Bonneville early in October 1797, entitled *Letter to the People of France and the French Armies on the Events of the 18th Fructidor — Sep. 4 — and Its Consequences*. Evidence that the new administration attached significance to this work — and accorded privileged status to its author — is shown in the fact that a French edition appeared several weeks later, translated by Adet, former minister to the United States. After praising the constitution of 1795 as the best ever to be devised by human wisdom (its only defect being the narrowing of suffrage), Paine justified the coup that had nullified the constitution. He was convinced that France had been haunted by the specter of monarchy. "It was impossible to go on," he wrote. "Everything was at stake, and all national business at a stand. The case reduced itself to a single alternative — shall the Republic be destroyed by the darksome maneuvres of a faction, or shall it be preserved by an exceptional act?"

The "dictatorial power" — he used the phrase in its classical sense — was depicted by him as an interim arrangement rendered necessary by counterrevolutionary plots. Paine saw 18 Fructidor as one of those rare, momentous, crisis-ridden human episodes governed by what he called "the supreme law of absolute necessity." Within these abnormal states of emergency, when time and events feel out of joint, devilish acts that would normally be considered treasonable become imperative. Swift blows against enemies become the quintessence of shrewd political leadership, and that means, paradoxically, that well-armed leaders are entitled, temporarily, to crush all opposition, even that of citizens struggling to protect their rights. Sovereign executive power must be supreme. It must be granted unlimited power and cry, with Dante, that the *maxime unum* is the *maxime bonum*.

Paine's defense of dictatorship must have raised the eyebrows of some readers. "Do not temporary dictatorships have a nasty habit of becoming permanent?" they may have asked. "Don't they invent 'emergencies' and 'enemies of the state' to justify staying in power? Don't dictatorships greatly strengthen the political hand of military and police forces and accustom citizens to dictatorial conditions by encouraging them to act in self-serving and toadyish ways?" Other readers likely wondered whether Paine's ignorance of spoken French was getting the better of him, or whether his blindness to the long-term drift toward dictatorship in French politics derived from his dogmatic conviction that the French Revolution fully embodied the "Spirit of 1776," and that France was now at the vanguard of European revolution.

Whether such doubts ever reached Paine's ears is unknown. If they did, they made no impact on his thinking. Predictably, he highlighted parallels between 18 Fructidor and the American Revolution: "At one time Congress invested General Washington with dictatorial power. At another time the government of Pennsylvania suspended itself and declared martial law." Considering the provocation of the counterrevolutionary plot and the danger of invasion from royalist despots, Paine could not see "what else, or what better, could have been done" than to save the infant republic by declaring martial law. Certainly, his faith in the general course of the French Revolution remained unshaken. "It needs no spirit of prophecy to discover that France must finally prevail," he concluded defiantly. "The sooner this be done, the better will it be for both nations, and for all the world."[130]

Paine sent copies of the work to the Directory on November 11, 1797, together with a letter advising the Directory to make a public declaration attributing to England responsibility for the breaking up of the peace negotiations at Lille. The executive director, François de Neufchâteau, answered two days later that he prized Paine's work all the more because it was "offered to him by one of the old friends of liberty."[131] Many shared that view. *Letter to the People of France* generated a steady stream of visitors to his rooms on the grand-fronted rue du Théatre Français. Paine clearly enjoyed the company. Among his frequent visitors was the English Quaker Dr. John Walker, who admired *Rights of Man* and had no antipathy toward *The Age of Reason*. Paine invited Walker to a dinner with James Napper Tandy, the famous Irish republican, and several other British exiles. Tandy, taking a glass filled with red wine, proposed a toast: "Gentlemen," he said, "may the tri-coloured flag [of France] float on the Tower of London, and on the Birmingham Tower of Dublin Castle!" Paine, joining in the toast, noticed that the teetotaling Walker refrained. "Walker is a Quaker with all its follies," Paine called out, a huge smile on his face. "I am a Quaker without them."[132]

During 1797, Paine made the acquaintance of another of the extensive circle of Irish republicans in Paris, Theobald Wolfe Tone. Tone liked Paine well enough, although he found him "vain beyond all belief." A conceited individual like Paine himself, Tone later recorded in his diary among the most penetrating summaries of Paine's conceit: "He converses extremely well; and I find him wittier in discourse than in his writings, where his humour is clumsy enough." Tone continued:

> He read me some passages from a reply to the Bishop of Llandaff, which he is preparing for the press, in which he belabours the prelate without mercy.

He seems to plume himself more on his theology than his politics, in which I do not agree with him. I mentioned to him that I had known Burke in England, and spoke of the shattered state of his mind, in consequence of the death of his only son Richard. Paine immediately said that it was the Rights of Man which had broken his heart, and that the death of his son gave him occasion to develop the chagrin which had preyed upon him ever since the appearance of that work. I am sure the Rights of Man have tormented Burke exceedingly; but I have seen myself the workings of a father's grief on his spirit, and I could not be deceived. *Paine has no children!* . . . He drinks like a fish, a misfortune which I have known to befall other celebrated patriots. I am told, that the true time to see him to advantage is about ten at night, with a bottle of brandy and water before him, which I can very well conceive.[133]

Invading England

During his residence with the Bonnevilles, Paine's spoken French hardly improved. Mme Bonneville reported that "he could not speak French; he could understand it tolerably well when spoken to him, and he understood it when on paper perfectly well."[134] Paine hardened his monolingual habits by entertaining a string of English-speaking guests and by returning to political journalism, which required only passive French. His writing, modeled on earlier American and English experiences, reiterated his old belief that the job of citizens is to keep their mouths open; the aim was to nurture public opinion and to pressure the French government to conform to its wishes. How much Paine actually wrote during this period is unknown. He certainly agitated against organized religion, and it is probable that he was a frequent contributor to *Le Citoyen français* and a close collaborator with his friend Bonneville, who from 1795 published *Le Vieux tribun et sa bouche de fer* and, later, *Le Bien informé*.[135] Since most contributions in these newspapers were left unsigned, it is difficult to know exactly which pieces Paine wrote. That uncertainty is compounded by the fact that items printed in these newspapers often reflected Paine's own views, some of which may have found their way into print on a ghost-edited basis.

The contact with Bonneville proved especially fruitful. Helped along by translations provided by Mme Bonneville, Paine contributed regularly to Bonneville's newspaper, *Le Bien informé*, from September 1797 until the government closed it down in 1799.[136] *Le Bien informé* was one of the period's more influential organs, in whose pages Paine tried his hand at numerous foreign policy topics, old and new. For example, the first issue of the newspaper (17 Fructidor, year 5) carried a letter from him on the Lille negotiations concerning the future of the Cape of Good Hope, a British possession that he argued should be converted into a free port administered by the Dutch but open to ships of all nations. Another issue (the forty-fifth) carried details of Paine's friendship with Scotsman Thomas Muir, whose Paineite activities in Britain earned him transportation to the penal colony of New South Wales, where he was the first to spread news of Paine's political philosophy and from where he miraculously escaped to the west coast of America, then to Mexico City and Havana, and eventually to France.

Paine also used *Le Bien informé* to air his views on Ireland's coming revolution. Ever since *Common Sense,* Paine had earned a reputation as the philosopher of Irish revolutionary politics. He also had established close personal ties with the flamboyant general James Napper Tandy, who had arrived in Paris in June 1797, claiming (to the annoyance of Wolfe Tone's supporters) leadership of the Irish military and political struggle against the British. Paine, excited, followed the French expeditions to Ireland in 1796 and 1798, and on October 27, 1798, he argued, in a letter to the Directory, that the lives of Irish war prisoners captured by the British could be spared if the French army retaliated by taking hostages among the Irish soldiers in the British army that had landed at Ostend, the Irish prisoners on both sides then being swapped without loss of life.

Then there were contributions to *Le Bien informé* in which Paine worked out in detail his ambitious project of a maritime descent upon the British Isles — the planning of which would bring him into personal contact with Napoleon Bonaparte and remain his major public preoccupation during the rest of his stay in France.

For a long time, Paine had believed that the principles of the rights of man would triumph over might. "An army of principles will penetrate where an army of soldiers cannot . . . it is neither the Rhine, the Channel, nor the Ocean that can arrest its progress," he had remarked in *Agrarian Justice.* Now he was convinced that principles needed platoons. He followed carefully the advance of the battle-tested French armies across the European continent. After dictating terms to Prussia, Holland, and Spain and incorporating Belgium into France, Bonaparte stepped up the French war of aggression against Austria, aimed chiefly at the conquest of northern Italy. The Austrians were defeated at Arcola in November 1796 and Rivoli in January 1797, and within the year, Bonaparte's victories had brought peace with profit through the Treaty of Campo Formio. The

Austrian emperor recognized the French annexation of the left bank of the Rhine, the former Austrian Netherlands, and the creation of the new Cisalpine Republic in northern Italy. In return, the French agreed to hand back the occupied territory of the Venetian Republic, but only after looting everything of value, including the magnificent bronze horses of St. Mark's.

The French triumph against the Austrians restored French domination in Europe on a scale that it had last enjoyed in the middle of Louis XIV's reign. Now only Great Britain had to be dealt with. It was a formidable maritime, commercial, and colonial power, a dynamic, modernizing country united around a gigantic city that was fast becoming the warehouse of the world. British power had driven the French out of North America and India with the Treaty of Paris (1763). Although France had exacted a small revenge in the American War of Independence, war had broken out again at the beginning of 1793 after Louis XVI's execution, with the British winning the colonial war in the West Indies, the treasure chest of the French slave trade. In that year, with the help of colonists hostile to the Revolution, the British had taken possession of St. Lucia, Martinique, Guadeloupe, and Santo Domingo. The spectacular revolution led by Toussaint-Louverture in the last of these isles had initially driven out the British, but the black general finally bought the independence of Haiti with a treaty (signed in 1798) favorable to British trade. Meanwhile, the British had taken advantage of Holland's transformation into a French protectorate by seizing the colonies of Guiana, the Cape of Good Hope, and Ceylon.

Faced with such facts, Bonaparte reacted soberly. He told the Directory that he personally doubted the feasibility of an invasion of England; he feared that bad weather would bring disaster, as it had in late 1796 to Louis-Lazare Hoche's attempted invasion of Ireland. Besides, Bonaparte privately dreamed of cutting the arteries of British trade with India by invading Egypt. He nevertheless showed little enthusiasm for the idea of concluding a peace treaty with Britain, despite the fact that his victories over the Austrians might now be expected to produce peace terms favorable to France. "Peace with England would seem to me the loss of the Republic," said Directory stalwart Jean-François Reubell at the time. Bonaparte agreed.[137]

Paine tried to exploit this tension within the republic's foreign policy by detailing his plan for invading England. Le Bien informé of October 31, 1797, carried an article signed "TP" urging the Directory to recognize that it should negotiate only with the representatives of a newly constituted, freely elected British Parliament. Six weeks later, on December 14-15, 1797, he published another article in *Le Bien informé* arguing that it would be easier to land ten thousand men on English shores than to send them to India. Because of its annexation of Holland, France had acquired an extensive coastline on the North Sea, admirably suited to preparing an invasion. Paine proposed that the assault be executed by means of gunboats, which could be brought right up to the English coast. In subsequent issues of *Le Bien informé* (January 15 and 29, 1798), Paine inserted passages from the republican historian Edward Gibbon to demonstrate how the early Romans attacked Britain. He insisted that the French should find invasion easier to execute since, unlike in Roman times, "the mass of the people are friends to liberty." The articles were designed to illustrate the fundamental principle that the superiority of naval forces alone could not protect the British against foreign invasion. Paine also drew up a scheme for obtaining ten million livres for constructing a minimum of a thousand gunboats. Comparing France favorably with England — where, he pointed out, William Pitt's naval budget for 1798 was fourteen times the proposed sum for French gunboats — Paine explained that new taxes were not required and that the sum could be raised by patriotic contributions. Paine himself chipped in a moderate sum. At about the same time, the representative Villiers, in a motion of order to the Council of Five Hundred, announced that various citizens wished to contribute to the descent upon England. Paine, admiring their patriotism and wishing to give something of his own, proposed a plan to allow every citizen to share in the honor of annihilating the government that, as Paine was fond of repeating, was the plague of the human race.

Paine elaborated his plans in a letter to the Council of Five Hundred on January 28, 1798. It was published the following day in *Le Bien informé* with a reply expressing the council's gratitude. "Though it is not convenient," Paine wrote, "in the present state of affairs, to subscribe to the loan toward the descent upon England, my economy permits me to make a small patriotic donation. I send a hundred livres, and with it all the wishes of my heart for the success of the descent, and a voluntary offer of any service I can render to promote it."[138]

While Paine had been living at the country home of Fulwar Skipwith in the summer of 1796, he had drawn up an elaborate document, complete with a map of the North Sea, setting forth *Observations on the Construction and Operation of Navies with a Plan for an Invasion of England and the Final Overthrow of the English Government.* Apparently intending it for the use of both the American and the French governments, Paine showed it first to

Monroe, then had it translated by Lanthenas. A copy of this version was carried by Boissy d'Anglas to Carnot in 1797, when the latter was president of the Directory, and an English version was given to Louis-Marie de La Révellière-Lépeaux, who succeeded to the presidency.

According to Paine, the Directory adopted the plan, constructed 250 ships, and then abruptly changed its policy. The plan was revised when Bonaparte was appointed commander in chief of the Army of England. He agreed in a conference at his home that Paine should be a leader of a provisional English Revolutionary Government, and that he should accompany the forces as a political adviser. "Only let us land," Bonaparte reportedly said at the time. Paine agreed. "The intention of the expedition was to give the people of England an opportunity of forming a government for themselves, and thereby bring about peace," he replied.[139]

As late as February 1806, Paine was still thinking that Napoleon Bonaparte might carry out a descent upon England to liberate the English militarily from the Georgian yoke. He hoped that the emperor would not forget "that he owes the project of a descent to an American citizen" and would therefore treat the United States favorably.[140] Quite aside from tactical military considerations, there were two basic flaws in the scheme.

Of less immediate consequence was the fact that Paine's invasion plans underestimated the way in which a century of near-constant rivalry with the French regime was ensuring, by the 1790s, that the monarchy and governing class of Britain were becoming very effectively "British" and that some of this same "Britishness" was rubbing off on the governed classes — with the consequence that considerable numbers of them were prepared to support the regime of George III in its propaganda and military struggle against the French.[141] Paine's vision of a grand uprising of the English, Welsh, and Scottish commoners sparked by an armed French invasion was arguably far-fetched — as fanciful as the lyrics of the song he wrote in the spring of 1798 for a friend, Mme Gibert:

> Blow soft ye Breezes o'er the wave;
> Soft as the thought that Love inspires,
> and safely bear, to Angleterre,
> The fleet that takes my heart's desires.
> Ye gentle Fates, if such there be,
> Who watch o'er human hopes and fears,
> O! land it Safe, and let me see
> The friends that share my anxious cares.[142]

In Paine's native land, certainly, there was a reservoir of support for an uprising, fed by the sentiments of those older men and women who had supported a Jacobite invasion of Britain during the first half of the eighteenth century, and those younger men and women who had opposed Britain's war against the Americans after 1775 or now actively supported peace with Bonapartist France. But this tradition was by no means in the ascendancy, as Paine supposed. Earlier in the century, foreign visitors to the country had often complained of hostile treatment at the hands of Englishmen. "I do not think there is a people more prejudiced," wrote César de Saussure ten years before Paine was born. "They look on foreigners in general with contempt, and think nothing is as well done elsewhere as in their own country."[143] Prejudice against France had probably deepened and widened by the end of the century. For many men and women of all classes — as James Gillray's well-known cartoon *The French Invasion; or John Bull, Bombarding the Bum-Boats, 1793* suggested — being "British" and feeling an affection for its Protestant way of life meant living as an elect nation enjoying liberty and security under a representative government and a system of common law that binds even the King. Being "British" therefore meant struggling for survival *against* the world's foremost Catholic power, a regime that was seen as decadent, militaristic, superstitious, dangerous, and unfree.

Paine's personal victimization by the growing power of French nationalism was the second, more immediate flaw in his plan for invading England. Not only were the idealistic principles that he shared with Bonneville and others too radical for the militaristic Directory, but caught in the pincers of Anglo-French rivalry, both men also were soon suspected of treachery.

Bonneville had the imprudence to print in *Le Bien informé* (September 17, 1798) a satirical report of a visit to the court of Prussia by Emmanuel-Joseph Sieyès, whom Robespierre once nicknamed "the mole of the Revolution" and who was now one of the directors. To disparage Sieyès's reputation as a constitution maker, Bonneville ridiculed his personal characteristic of taciturnity. "If there were organized at Berlin a club of mutes," Bonneville wrote, "Syeyès should be named the president, the dean of silent men." The Directory was not amused. Irritated by this jesting at the expense of one of its illustrious members, it prohibited the further publication of *Le Bien informé*. Paine immediately wrote in defense of Bonneville to the Directory. Pointing out that he had lived with Bonneville since before the 18 Fructidor, Paine described the journalist as "an honest uncorrupted Man and as firm a Patriot as any that I know." He continued, "He is besides a very industrious man — a good husband — a good Father, and a good friend." Paine stressed that his intercession was an act entirely voluntary and he hoped the ban on *Le Bien informé* would be lifted on account of the pains Bonneville had taken to establish his journal, whose subscribers were wholehearted patriots.[144] Paine's letter may have helped. Bonneville was forgiven this offense, and his printing privileges were restored. Sometime later, however, he was again arrested and sent to prison for another article in *Le Bien informé* likening Bonaparte to Cromwell.

Such was the climate of paranoia that Paine, ironically, also was accused of intriguing with British agents. The Paris police viewed him with constant suspicion and treated him as a potential source of information concerning all members of the city's British colony. On March 13, 1798, the Minister of General Police sent out an order to the Paris division instructing the apprehension of an Irish priest named Somerville or Sommers, accused of being an English spy. A letter addressed to Paine mentioning Sommers had fallen into police hands, and soon afterward the Paris bureau was instructed to interrogate Paine concerning his knowledge of British agents.[145]

Nations and Nationalism

Hostile surveillance and the generals' tightening grip on French politics made Paine miserable. The coup d'état of 18 and 19 Brumaire (November 9 and 10, 1799) was the last straw. During those late autumn days, Paine witnessed the militarization of the summits of state power. The leading player in the drama was Napoleon Bonaparte. Robed in the Nation's fears like a king and flanked by grenadiers and a staff of generals, he rode horseback to the Tuileries. After driving the "seditious" members of the Five Hundred from office, Bonaparte arranged for the nervous Ancients to vote, by candlelight, to replace the Directory with an executive commission headed by Bonaparte himself. The Nation's new leader then set the agenda of the new regime with a tough speech to his troops. "In what sort of state did I leave France, and in what sort of state do I find it again?" he asked pompously. His answer spat words in the faces of the politicians: "I left you in peace and I find war! I left you conquests, and the enemy is crossing our frontiers. I left our arsenals full, and I find not a single weapon! I left you the millions of Italy, and I find spoliatory laws and poverty everywhere!"[146]

A week after the coup d'état, Paine left Paris. He stayed briefly with a friend in Dieppe, then traveled on to Bruges, where he spent the following winter with his former prison mate, Joseph Van Huele. Paine lodged with him and his wife, Josephine de Witte, in an elegant rented *maison de maître* on Rue des Chevaliers, in the city center, amid its maze of splendid canals.[147]

Paine may have been invited to Bruges especially to attend the emotion-charged wedding, in early February 1800, of Joseph's sister-in-law Anne Marie, whose first husband, Jean-Othon Van Huele, had been shoved by police out of a third-floor window of the Luxembourg prison to his death, with Paine and his brother Joseph looking on. The two became friends for life after that macabre brush with death, and despite some political disagreements — during the early 1790s Van Huele had had strong Jacobin and atheist sympathies — Paine found infectious the energy of his thirty-five-year-old host and "very particular friend."[148] Paine happily spent the winter renewing contacts with old Bruges friends he had first met in Paris. Van Huele, former mayor of Bruges and now a tax collector and property administrator by profession, also introduced him to prominent civil servants and members of the local *Société littéraire*, and Paine also socialized with William Edwards and other members of the small English colony in the town.

At the time of Paine's sojourn in Bruges, England was attacking French troops in Holland. Paine spent a few days with his old acquaintance General Guillaume-Marie-Anne Brune, formerly a journeyman printer employed by Bonneville, hoping to witness the last of John Bull. Unfortunately for Paine, the French were defeated. In the spring of 1800, more bad news greeted Paine. Upon returning to Paris, he found himself again under police surveillance. The Consuls of the Republic, through the Secretary of State, had sent down an order to the Minister of Police dated April 15, 1800. The order directed that Paine be told "that the police are informed that he is behaving irregularly and that at the first complaint against him he will be sent back to America, his country."[149] Paine was later told by a police agent that he was under suspicion because certain political sentiments in *Le Bien informé* were considered subversive. The tough warning had some effect, for during the next eighteen months, Paine practically abandoned political writing in favor of safe obscurity.

Exchanging his quill for personal safety proved difficult. Not only had he spent much of his adult life as an opposition political writer, but the enforced withdrawal from public life and his consequent loss of trust in the Bonapartist regime were arguably more drawn out and personally vexing than would have been the case if Paine had spotted the distinction between national identity and the entirely new phenomenon of nationalism.

Paine was, of course, aware of the importance of national identity in eighteenth-century politics. *Rights of Man* was easily the most shocking and influential of the century's pleas for the right of nations to determine their own fate. That book had sparked bitter public controversies about the merits of monarchies and republics, forced Paine into permanent exile from his native England with death threats tugging at his coattails, and led to a general crackdown against Paineites — all because he had suggested that each nation is entitled to its own system of representative government. Paine had first proposed this thesis during the American Revolution, and several of his contemporaries — Sieyès and Anne-Robert-Jacques Turgot, for example — were exploring the same theme. But *Rights of Man* had examined the link between nationhood and political democracy with unprecedented intellectual fire. Paine's prose burned with the drama of the early stages of the French Revolution. Its fiery optimism also reflected the breakthroughs of the American Revolution: the declaration of the natural and civil rights of the sovereign people of a nation, including the right to resist unlawful government, and the establishment of a constitutional republic on a wholly new federal basis.

Inspired by his American experiences, Paine had spat venom at the court and government of George III and warned all other monarchic rulers that the outbreak of revolution in Europe heralded a new dawn for republican democratic principles. "Monarchy is all a bubble, a mere court artifice to procure money," he said, although he admitted that the pompous power and moneygrubbing of monarchy still trapped the world in a cage of war and rumors of war. "There are men in all countries," Paine wrote, "who get their living by war and by keeping up the quarrels of nations." He insisted, in the face of this trend, that citizens of all nations, united in their love of republican democracy, have a duty to expose despotic monarchies, understood as bellicose governments accountable only to themselves. Paine concluded that the struggle for representative government requires recognition of the right of each nation to determine its own destiny. "What is government more than the management of the affairs of a nation?" he asked. "It is not," he answered. "Sovereignty as a matter of right, appertains to the nation only and not to any individual. And a nation has at all times an inherent indivisible right to abolish any form of government it finds inconvenient and establish such as accords with its interests, its disposition and its happiness."[150]

Paine's thesis that nations and representative government are an indivisible unity subsequently enjoyed a long and healthy life. Yet it was nonetheless blind to the fact that when the winds of national feeling blow, citizens do not always, like beautiful birds, grow wings and fly their way to an independent land of liberty. The watershed experience of the French Revolution, which had inspired Paine's *Rights of Man*, should have made him rethink any such conclusion. As Paine predicted, the Revolution both destroyed forever the French faith in the divine and unchallengeable right of monarchs to govern and sparked a struggle against the privileged classes in the name of the sovereign nation of free and equal individuals. What Paine did not see — because he assumed the French events were a replay of 1776 — was that those acting in the name of the sovereign nation were ever more tempted to emphasize faithfulness to *la patrie* — that is, citizens' *obligations* to their state, itself seen as the guarantor of the nation, itself said to be "one and indivisible." The motto of the ancien régime, "*Un roi, une foi, une loi*" (One king, one faith, one law) was replaced by "*La Nation, la loi, le roi*" (The Nation, the law, the king). Thenceforth, it appeared that the Nation made the law, which the king was responsible for implementing. After the abolition of the monarchy in August 1792, the Nation had become the titular source of sovereignty. "*Vive la Nation!*" cried the French soldiers one month later at Valmy, as they flung themselves into battle against the Prussian army. Everything that had been royal had become national. The Nation even had its own emblem, the tricolored national flag, which replaced the white flag of the house of Bourbon. The new spirit of nationalism had surfaced, bringing with it a lust for the power and glory of the nation-state, which stifled the democratic potential of the Revolution. The seeds of the first nationalist dictatorship of the modern world were sown, soon to mature and bear their first fruit with the Bonapartist coup of November 1799.

The American Revolution had managed to avoid the growth of despotism fed by nationalist appeals to the Nation.[151] The utter novelty of French revolutionary nationalism can be grasped only by taking a step beyond Paine by distinguishing between national identity and nationalism. Paine saw that building a republican democracy is easier when its citizens feel themselves to be members of a nation — a people who share a language or dialect, have an affection for a defined territory, and share a variety of customs, including some historical memories. Paine sensed that national identity so defined was a specifically modern European invention whose importance for republican democracy lies in its infusion of citizens with confidence and dignity by encouraging them to feel at home. In conversations, he often pointed to the case of Poland to illustrate the point. He welcomed the Polish Revolution of May 1791, and soon after its outbreak considered applying for Polish citizenship. He knew that during the partitions of 1772, 1793, and 1795, Poland-Lithuania was carved up by the Russian Empire, the Hapsburg monarchy, and the kingdom of Prussia. And yet he also appreciated that the nobility *(szlachta)* of that country resisted the partitions by nurturing a distinctive national consciousness. Paine knew many freedom-loving Poles. During his stay in America, he had become acquainted with General Kazimierz Pułaski, who had later died heroically at Savannah, battling for the American forces. In London and Paris, during 1791–92, Paine had expressed deep admiration for King Stanislaw II Augustus, even confiding to Thomas Christie that, though an adversary of monarchy, he would be prepared to strip all monarchs of their powers and transfer them to Stanislaw II Augustus. The Polish leader of the revolt of 1794, Tadeusz Kościuszko, also was a good friend of Paine's. Kościuszko was a hero to all European republican democrats; his name was celebrated in America and even in Australia, whose highest mountain was later named after him. Especially from the time of the American Revolution, Paine noted, the Poles considered themselves (and were widely regarded as) fighters for the freedom of humanity and a nation martyred in the cause of democratic liberty. Their shared sense of nationhood enabled them to act gracefully under pressure; to be Polish, as Paine observed of Princess Izabela Lubomirska and other Polish émigrés in Paris, meant the refusal to be bullied and intimidated by unaccountable power.[152]

Paine nevertheless failed to see that the struggle for national self-determination constantly risks seduction by power-hungry nationalism. Like other ideologies, nationalism is a power-grabbing, potentially dominating form of life that feeds upon a preexisting sense of nationhood but in so doing disfigures it into a bizarre parody of itself. Nationalism is a pathological form of national identity. It has a fanatical core that destroys the heterogeneity of a nation by squeezing it into the Nation. Nationalism requires its adherents to believe in themselves and to believe that they are members of a superior community of believers known as the Nation. Nationalism tends to crash into the world, crushing or throttling everything that crosses its path, defending or claiming territory, always thinking of land as power and its native inhabitants as a clenched fist. Nationalists are driven by the feeling that all nations are caught up in an animal struggle for survival and that only the fittest survive. Nationalism revels in macho glory and fills the national memory with stories of noble ancestors, heroism, and bravery in defeat. It feels itself invincible, tracks down enemies, despises foreigners, waves the flag, and, if necessary, eagerly bloodies its hands on its enemies.

The Cosmopolitan in Retreat

Paine was certainly not a nationalist in this sense — quite the opposite, for he always argued against "the passions and prejudices of Nations."[153] He saw such dogmas as mutable, and he therefore acted in favor of a peaceful alliance of nations. During the second half of the eighteenth century, this friendship among citizens of various nations was called cosmopolitanism. It was fueled by exposure to foreign contacts in a variety of overlapping and sometimes contradictory ways: young men sent abroad to study; foreigners invited and welcomed as teachers or (like Paine) writers and political activists; involvement in European wars that took nationals elsewhere in Europe; increased travel among the "respectable" classes and regular diplomatic relations with courts; expanding commerce; and the diffusion of foreign fashions in philosophy, letters, instruction, dress, and social intercourse. A history of eighteenth-century cosmopolitanism has yet to be written, but it is clear that in the writings of Pietro Verri, Abbé de Saint-Pierre, Isabelle de Charrière, Immanuel Kant, Paine, and others, the "true cosmopolite" and the "loyal patriot" were one and the same figure. No contradiction was seen between feeling oneself to be a citizen of the wider world (note the Greek roots of *kosmopolitēs* from *kosmos*, "world," and *politēs*, "citizen") and wanting to enlighten and transform that little corner of the European world where one had been born or had been brought by destiny to live, work, love, and die.

The early modern era of cosmopolitanism soon declined. Although Paine continued until his last breath to champion the cause of republican democracy around the world and his German contemporary Kant still looked at the history of the world from a cosmopolitan standpoint (*in weltbürgerlicher Absicht*), they were among the last voices of a declining age. With the French Revolution, the era of cosmopolitanism declined, and into its place stepped nationalism, nation-state building, and nation-state rivalry. Slowly and surely, the word *patriot* became charged with all the hatred and love of modern nationalism, whereas the word *cosmopolite* symbolized an ideal political unity that could never be achieved in practice.

There is fresh evidence that toward the end of his stay in France, Paine sensed this decline of cosmopolitanism at the hands of nationalism. Despite the official banning of his work, he began to express contempt for the Napoleonic regime, either in publicly subtle or privately explicit ways. For the purpose of irritating Napoleon, he had translated and printed in Paris Thomas Jefferson's speech at the opening of Congress, "by way of contrast," he confided to Henry Redhead Yorke, "with the government of the First Consul." He took care to put it into the right hands; the copy in the Bibliothèque Nationale has inscribed on it in Paine's hand, "From Thomas Paine to his good [friend] the Citizen Grégoire."[154]

Mostly Paine limited his criticism of the Napoleonic regime to letters and private conversations. By September 1801, he was so disgruntled with the government of Napoleon and depressed about the prospects of invading Great Britain that he confided to Fulwar Skipwith, "I give up all hopes that any good will be done by France — that honour is reserved for America." About this time, a young Englishman, Lewis Goldsmith, arrived in Paris and was taken in charge by Paine and Joel Barlow. The newcomer described a dinner at Barlow's house. Among the other guests were Robert Fulton, inventor of the steamboat; Comte de Volney, a member of the Senate and author of a famous deistic work; Tadeusz Kościuszko; and Paine. During the conversation, Barlow described Napoleon as "the very butcher of Liberty, the greatest monster that Nature ever *spewed!*" He also charged the different revolutionary governments of France with plundering America. "If it had not been for us they would literally have starved, and what return have we received for our kindness?" Paine interrupted Barlow "and very jocosely observed, that 'it served the Americans right, they should have suffered the rascals to starve, slaves should not be fed by the hands of free men.'"[155]

Paine's private rethinking of the whole course of the Revolution was evidenced a few days later at a dinner party thrown by Jean-Lambert Tallien. Paine took Goldsmith along to enable his English friend to judge the character of some of the French leaders. Paine, the cicerone, sat next to Goldsmith at dinner and gave him "the nomenclature of the party." Among the guests were Louis-Sébastien Mercier, a celebrated satirist and journalist, and Antoine-Joseph Santerre, who had escorted Louis XVI to the scaffold. Paine described Mercier, a pronounced anti-Newtonian, "as a very funny, witty, old man, who had just as sound notions of liberty as he had of astronomy." Goldsmith replied that he had recently read Mercier's *Tableau de Paris* in which Tallien had been cruelly abused. He was therefore "astonished to see Mercier and Tallien visiting each other." Paine smiled. He said that "in the course of the Revolution persons dined together for the purpose of making each other talk, and then denounced the conversation to the Committee of Public Safety." Paine made similar remarks a few days later at a breakfast *à la fourchette* hosted by Goldsmith and attended by Tallien, Santerre, Merlin de Thionville, and Thomas Holcroft. During conversation, the French guests defended the doctrine that the strongest, by virtue of their strength, always deserve to dominate the weak. "Mr. Holcroft attempted to say something against this doctrine, but Paine desired him to hold his tongue, as he might as well talk of honour to a gang of thieves as to contradict revolutionary Frenchmen in their notion of right and wrong."[156]

Further evidence of Paine's hardening attitude toward the French dictatorship was provided by another young Englishman, Henry Redhead Yorke, who visited Paine in Paris just before Paine returned to America in 1802. Yorke told how Napoleon had invited Paine to dinner shortly after he had returned from Italy to be appointed commander of the Army of England. It is unrecorded how Paine reacted to the Corsican, who worked hard, ate quickly, always wore the same clothes, and hated wasting time. On this particular evening, Napoleon, as usual, looked emaciated, his youthful face devoured by huge eyes and wrapped in shoulder-length hair resembling the ears of a dog. His tongue was unusually loose. He declared that every city of the universe should erect a golden statue of Paine. Napoleon assured his guest that he always slept with a copy of *Rights of Man* under his pillow and that he would be honored to receive his future correspondence and advice.[157]

The clever, self-made dictator of the Revolution clearly had designs on citizen Paine. When a meeting of the Military Council of Paris was called to discuss the projected invasion, Paine was present by special invitation. The invasion seemed to match Napoleon's yearning for rapid troop movements, coordinated surprise attacks, and tactical prowess. Yet the majority opinion held the plan to be dangerously impractical. Its chief opponent was General d'Arcon, an engineer who had gained his reputation as organizer of the siege of Gibraltar. Maintaining that the English controlled the sea, d'Arcon argued that the invasion was doomed to failure unless supported by an uprising among the British people. Napoleon replied, "That is the very point I mean — here is Citizen Paine, who will tell you that the whole English nation except the Royal Family and the Hanoverians, who have been created Peers of the Realm and absorb the landed property, are ardently burning for fraternisation."

According to Yorke's report, Paine's reply to Napoleon's sarcasm went absolutely contrary to the opinion expressed in Paine's formally published plans for the invasion of England, which he had shown to James Monroe and presented to the Directory. Pointing out his long absence from England and adding that he could judge only by what he had known of it during his former residence, he told the First Consul that although the people were very disaffected, the British army would cut the expedition to pieces if it were able to elude the French fleet. "The only way to England," Paine allegedly said, "is to annihilate her commerce." When asked by Napoleon how long this would take, Paine answered that everything depended on peace.

From that moment, according to Yorke, the moody and impetuous Napoleon never again spoke directly to Paine. On his return from Egypt, where, treading in the footsteps of Alexander and Caesar, he abandoned his army but claimed the pyramids as French, Napoleon encountered Paine at a grand dinner honoring the generals of the republic. The First Consul reportedly wore his famous charming smile, but not for Paine, who that evening felt the full force of Napoleon's well-known bad temper, crude insults, and impatience with contradiction. After several toasts to the republic and its foreign exploits, Napoleon reportedly stared Paine full in the face while remarking in a loud voice to General Lasnes, "The English are all alike; in every country they are rascals." Subsequently, according to Yorke, Paine came to detest and despise Napoleon and to affirm that he was "the completest charlatan that ever existed."[158]

Walter Savage Landor, who also saw Paine in 1802, confirmed Paine's hostility toward Napoleon. Paine considered him "wilful, headstrong, proud, morose, presumptuous. . . . There is not on record one who has committed so many faults and crimes with so little temptation to commit them. . . . Tyrants in general shed blood upon plan or from passion: he seems to have shed it only because he could not be quiet." Perhaps these English observers — Goldsmith, Landor, and Yorke — exaggerated Paine's hostility toward Napoleon. Some surviving reports of Paine's meetings with Englishmen — such as his old friend from Diss, Thomas Manning, the first European to visit the Dalai Lama[159] — are silent about Napoleon. In several references to the Emperor in his later writings, Paine expressed no rancor, and he always defended the expediency of invading England to establish a peace-loving republic. Nevertheless, the scattered hints of hostility toward Napoleon suggest that Paine underwent some change of heart and that it finally convinced him of the need to take advantage of the peace agreement of Amiens in March 1802 to return to America.

When Paine reappeared in Paris from Bruges in the spring of 1800, his savings were exhausted. He again went to live with his friend Bonneville, paying no rent. In return, he offered Bonneville and his family a similar future asylum in the United States. When Mme Bonneville and her three children eventually decided to take advantage of this invitation, Paine promised to leave her the principal part of his property, a promise that he faithfully honored. Paine and Bonneville, meanwhile, were both in trouble with Napoleon's police, and *Le Bien informé* was soon suppressed as a consequence of the article comparing Napoleon to Cromwell. Bonneville had never been rich, and this stroke virtually wiped him out economically. Paine, penniless, resorted to lingering in local Parisian taverns, talking politics.[160] Luckily, two of his English admirers, William Bosville and Sir Francis Burdett, showed their appreciation of *Rights of Man* by presenting Paine with five hundred louis d'or to enable him to even his accounts with Bonneville and return to the United States.

Clio Rickman came from London to bid Paine farewell. After a few days together in Paris, the two friends set off for Le Havre. Resting there for another few days, the men exchanged their parting wishes, and on September 1, 1802, the winds being favorable, the *London Pacquet* carried Paine beyond the horizon toward America. "Deputy Paine, foreign benefactor of the Species . . . red carbuncled face and black beaming eyes,"[161] had left Europe forever. Rickman stayed behind on the beach, with love in his broken heart. Sensing, with tears in his eyes, that he would never see Paine again, he sketched stanzas addressed to the Atlantic:

> *Thus smooth be thy waves, and thus gentle the breeze,*
> *   As thou bearest my PAINE far away;*
> *O! waft him to comfort and regions of ease,*
> *Each blessing of friendship and freedom to seize,*
> *   And bright be his setting sun's ray.*

> *May AMERICA hail her preserver and friend,*
> *   Whose "COMMON SENSE" taught her aright,*
> *How liberty thro her domains to extend,*
> *The means to acquire each desirable end,*
> *   And fill'd her with reason and light.*

> *Tho bitter, dear PAINE, is this parting to me,*
> *   I rejoice that from EUROPE once more,*
> *From FRANCE too, unworthy thy talents and thee,*
> *Thou art hastening to join the happy and free;*
> *May the breezes blow gently, and smooth be the sea*
> *   That speed thee to LIBERTY's shore!*[162]

PART IV

America, 1802–1809

12

Growing Old in America

The Drunken Infidel

No homecoming was more inglorious than Paine's return to the United States in the autumn of 1802. For two years before his setting foot on American soil, clouds of controversy had been building up, Paine being described by his opponents as a depraved atheist, the assassin of George Washington's character, and a hack journalist who peddled his wares to the highest bidder.

The accusations began after October 1, 1800, when Paine wrote to Thomas Jefferson: "If any American frigate should come to France, and the direction of it fall to you, I will be glad you would give me the opportunity of returning."[1] Paine's request came as no surprise to Jefferson, who knew that Paine had attempted to return to America in 1795, 1797, and 1799, each time dropping his plans because of the possibility of capture by a British ship, whose captain would surely have extradited him to England and into the arms of death by hanging. Jefferson replied on March 18, 1801, only two weeks after assuming the presidency. His words were warm, their offer of support decisive, their political intention clear:

> You expressed a wish to get a passage to this country in a public vessel. Mr. Dawson is charged with orders to the captain of the Maryland to receive and accomodate you back if you can be ready to depart at such short warning. . . . I am in hopes you will find us returned generally to sentiments wor-

thy of former times. In these it will be your glory to have steadily laboured
and with as much effect as any man living. That you may long live to continue your useful labours and to reap the reward in the thankfulness of nations is my sincere prayer. Accept assurance of my high esteem and
affectionate attachment.[2]

Jefferson had supposed that the generous offer of government passage
on the warship *Maryland* was entirely proper, since Paine had worked hard
to enable the United States to become a nation-state and, thus, to have
ships flying under its flag. But Jefferson's letter to Paine was fated to become one of the most scandalous documents of the decade. It was first
publicized in a report in the *National Intelligencer and Washington Advertiser* on
July 15, 1801, the newspaper acknowledging that the story had previously
appeared in the Paris press, perhaps planted there by Paine himself to
publicize the honor. Almost immediately, the American press hostile to
Jefferson pounced on the offer as proof of his unfitness for office. The
flagship of the Federalist press in Philadelphia, the *Gazette of the United
States, and Daily Advertiser,* lumped Paine together with Jefferson and
William Duane, Jeffersonian editor of the rival Philadelphia *Aurora. General
Advertiser:*

TOM PAINE AND PAT DUANE

When the story arrived here, that the President of the United States had
written a *very affectionate letter* to that living opprobrium of humanity, TOM
PAINE, the infamous scavenger of all the filth which could be raked from the
dirty paths which have been hitherto trodden by all the revilers of Christianity, Duane, instead of attempting to refute this scandalous charge upon
the President, admits that it may be true, and even endeavours to justify it.[3]

The description of Paine as an infidel was repeated the next day, when
the same newspaper reported that it was now "probable enough that the
obscene old sinner will be brought over to America once more, if his car-
case [*sic*] is not too far gone to bear transportation." The attacks continued for several months, culminating in the suggestion that American
agriculture would gain from the return of Paine, who could be used for
manure.[4] Smearing the hyperbole on his benefactor, the *Baltimore Republican; or The Anti-Democrat* observed sarcastically that "our pious President
thought it expedient to dispatch a frigate for the accomodation of this
loathsome reptile."[5] The *New-York Evening Post* published a satirical poem
that likened Jefferson to a naive monarch and Paine to an alcoholic agitator. "Tom Paine is come from far," wrote the poet, "His coming bodes dis-

astrous times, His nose is a blazing star!"[6] The *Port Folio,* published in Philadelphia by Joseph Dennie, also poured scorn on the government-sponsored plan to bring Paine back to America. It lashed out in a vicious editorial against "the loathsome Thomas Paine, a drunken atheist, and the scavenger of faction" and described the plan as "enormously preposterous" and as "an insult to the moral sense of the nation."[7] *The Mercury and New-England Palladium,* darling of the die-hard Federalists in Boston, was even more scathing in its reaction to the news: "What! Invite to the United States that lying, drunken, brutal infidel, who rejoiced in the opportunity of basking and wallowing in the confusion, devastation, bloodshed, rapine, and murder, in which his soul delights?"[8]

Supporters of Paine — there were many — were surprised by the bitterness and rapid diffusion of rhetoric of this kind. They were especially worried that it might trigger a groundswell of protest against his return under any circumstances. The *National Intelligencer and Washington Advertiser,* which had first introduced the news to America, criticized "that intolerant spirit which is a disgrace to our country" and confessed that it had failed to anticipate "that this short paragraph would be made the mighty instrument of calumniating, and even damning, the character of the President."[9] The "calumniating" by no means subsided when word reached America that, following the Treaty of Amiens, Paine no longer needed the protection of an American warship, and that he would embark from Le Havre during the first days of September 1802 in a private vessel. If anything, the storm around Paine's head must have convinced his supporters and enemies alike that the return to America of the self-described "volunteer to the world"[10] would spark off riots when his ship eventually docked in Baltimore on Saturday afternoon, October 30, 1802. They would be disappointed. The arrival of the figure described by *The Mercury and New-England Palladium* as a "lying, drunken, brutal infidel" passed entirely without incident. The press coverage on all sides was for the most part polite, even strangely compassionate. The *American Patriot,* published in Baltimore, noted that within the large crowd that had assembled, the Federalists "were the foremost to visit him, and with smiling friendly expressions, make him welcome in the city."[11] The more militantly pro-Federalist *Baltimore Republican; or The Anti-Democrat* went out of its way to remind its readers of Paine's contributions to the Revolution. "The noted THOMAS PAIN arrived here on Saturday last," its editor noted. "It is but justice to observe that this man has some claims on our gratitude for his work entitled 'Common Sense'; for, though the motives that induced him to collect together and publish the general arguments of the day, at that time, were, as might easily be proved, those of a hireling, yet that little work was of essential service in our revolution."[12]

The same newspaper reported that a swarm of curious and excited onlookers accompanied Paine from the wharf to Fulton's Tavern, where "after sipping well of Brandy, he became somewhat fluent in conversation; and readily declared that Mr. Jefferson's invitations were the cause of his returning to this country." The *Anti-Democrat* also reported that Paine, "decently clad" but "an abominable egoist," with short gray hair and a red and carbuncled nose drooping "nearly as low as his mouth," showed off his model bridges to a gathering of forty or so people. Later that evening, in the lounge room of the tavern, Paine temporarily disarmed his critics by reciting "On a Long-Nosed Friend," a rollicking, self-mocking poem that he had written in Paris sometime during 1800:

> *Going along the other day,*
> *Upon a certain plan;*
> *I met a nose upon the way,*
> *Behind it was a man.*
> *I called unto the nose to stop,*
> *And when it had done so, ————*
> *The man behind it — he came up;*
> *They made Zenobio.*

He followed with a short speech in which he said that within several days, he intended to transport the models to Washington, then to make brief visits to "Frederic-town, Philadelphia, and New York" before returning to Washington. Paine fielded comments and questions. "I am glad to see you, Mr. Pain; I like such fellows as you," said an admirer. "How came you to write that letter to general Washington?" snapped a critic, who was visibly irritated by Paine's reply that he had a right to criticize government and that he had not changed his mind about Washington.

Republican supporters of Jefferson made political hay out of Paine's arrival. The *Philadelphia Aurora* described the warm reception given to Paine as "a circumstance honorable to the character of Baltimore" and waxed eloquent about his achievements:

Thomas Paine, the early and uniform asserter of the *Rights of Mankind*, and author of the immortal revolutionary pa[p]ers called COMMON SENSE, and the CRISIS, arrived at Baltimore on Saturday last. The arrival of this interesting man, whose history as has been well observed, is interwoven with the immortality of *two revolutions* and *three nations* of the [fi]rst distinction in human annals, was as might be expected, an object of interest and curiosity to the old who knew his services, and to the young who had heard of his fame in all the opposite modes which political sympathy or hatred could employ to express their respect or abhorrence of the asserter of freedom.

The *Aurora* went on to observe that "the writings of Mr. *Paine* on religious subjects were not even mentioned, and the right of private opinion was neither assailed, nor brought into question."[13]

Behind that remark was the deep concern of the editor, William Duane, that Paine's religious writings, especially *The Age of Reason*, might sap the popularity of the Jefferson administration, reopening by association the old wounds caused by the charges of atheism leveled against Paine personally in the months prior to his friend's election. Shortly after Paine's arrival, Duane anxiously wrote to Jefferson to explain the potential embarrassment of Paine's militant defense of quirky religious opinions: "I have tried every effort of which I am capable to persuade him against it, but nothing will operate on him. I have fairly told him that he will be deserted by the only party that respects or does not hate him, that all his political writings will be rendered useless, and even his fame destroyed." Duane told Jefferson that he had failed to persuade the culprit of his stupidity: "He silenced me at once by telling me that Dr. Rush at the period when he commenced Common Sense told him, that there were two words which he should avoid by every means as necessary to his own safety and that of the public, — *Independence* and *Republicanism*."[14]

Duane correctly foresaw that Paine's opponents would latch on to the pitfalls of deism. Admittedly, a long list of complaints was flung in Paine's direction, but they were usually traceable to a stratum of American civil society that lived its Protestantism as if it were under siege from an increasingly godless world. If Jefferson had been president during the Reign of Terror in France and had written a letter to Robespierre, praising him for his contributions to liberty and praying that he might live long to continue them, he would not have excited anything like the sense of disgust of some American Calvinists when they discovered the dalliance between their president and the deist Paine. The *Aurora* tried to head off such reaction as early as July 14, 1801: "The pretended crime of Thomas Paine, is his *Age of Reason*. We do not mean to defend that work. That has been undertaken by hundreds, and the book itself is now thrown by among other lumber. We assert however that the writing of that book, is not a proof of his impiety, nor can it be a justification of any person in attempting to asperse the man." The *Aurora* accused Paine's critics of "machiavelism" and expressed anxiety about the concerted campaign in American politics to "attack, and to destroy if possible, the reputation of every man who had an original share in the revolution and independence of America, and who did not basely desert it."[15]

Reason failed to impress counterrevolutionary bigotry. Months before Paine set foot on American soil, the din of piety had grown ever louder. In reply to Duane's earlier defense of the principle of freedom of expression, the *Gazette of the United States* screeched: "It is really an alarming thing to see almost every paper in the union which advocated the election of Mr. Jefferson, and commended his invitation to Tom Paine, now aiming their attacks, in a manner more or less direct, at the vitals of christianity."[16] The *New-York Evening Post*, announcing the arrival of Paine in Baltimore, was equally caustic about "the chief Doctor of Atheism": "We request some correspondent to inform us how Mr. Paine will obtain a permit for the landing of his baggage. For this purpose, we know it is requisite to make oath at the custom-house, upon *the Holy Evangelists,* that the trunks contain no articles for sale. If Mr. P. takes this oath, he will give the lie to all he's said against the authenticity and sanctity of the bible; and if he will not take it, we apprehend he cannot get his baggage." The report concluded, "But this is a difficulty from which Mr. Jefferson will probably relieve him, at the expense of — only a slight violation of the law."[17]

Duane's *Aurora* bit back against the covert hypocrisy and overt politicking of such sarcasm: "From the quantity of asperity employed against *Thomas Paine,* an enquiry naturally suggests itself — Is this *asperity* a criterion of *Christian piety* — or is not religion employed by hypocrites now, as in all former ages, as A MASK, to cover the attacks made on the man whose writings *vindicated America* and the *Rights of Mankind.*"[18] Paine's enemies, increasingly vocal, reacted by loading him with other accusations. A favorite was Paine's alleged private immorality — drunkenness — which drove editors and correspondents to reach for the vilest adjectives. Typical of this flank of the attack was a mock elegy written by "Stanley" and published in the *Gazette of the United States* as "Anticipated Elegy, a Parody on 'Tom Bowline'":

> *HERE the fam'd Sot lies — poor Tom Ranter*
> *The darling of our crew!*
> *No more he'll hug his dear decanter,*
> *For brandy brought him to!*
> *His face was of the manliest beauty,*
> *With carbuncles beset:*

Faithful with us he did his duty,
And kept his ashes wet.

Tom *never from his club departed;*
His prowess was so rare,
Though often led or homeward carted,
In toping he was fair.
And then he'd swear, and write so clever
Bla'phemy was his fort;
But Common Sense *is fled forever*
Since Tom *is turn'd to dirt!*

Yet shall poor Tom *not be forgotten,*
For Monticello's *Sage*
Shall rank him though with tiplers rotting,
The wisest of the age.
Thus brandy has in vain consign'd him
To death's unkind arrest;
For while an Infidel's behind him,
His memory will be blest.[19]

Talk of Paine as a hideous figure with a crimson-blotched face, fit only for foulmouthed ranting and drinking himself into the grave, was compounded by unfounded stories of his filthy personal habits. An anonymous letter published in the *Gazette of the United States* claimed satirically that Jefferson, "both a philosopher and an agriculturalist," was conducting an experiment to see whether a new use could be found for "infidel Philosophers" as a "most valuable species of manure."[20] Others adopted the moralizing tone of a stern parson. The Boston *Columbian Centinel. Massachusetts Federalist* linked the presidency to Paine's corrupt personal habits: "the importation of THOMAS PAINE, though he is clearly *a contraband article,* is most of all to be deprecated in a moral view — not on account of any ascendancy which *so notorious a drunkard,* and *so impious a buffoon* can be supposed to gain over the minds, or manners of *true Americans;* but because he comes under the sanction, and with the *co-operation* of the *highest officer* in the Union." The editor concocted the conclusion that the moral fabric of America was in danger of being torn: "Whilst these impressions lead the sober part of the community to *lament,* will they not embolden the licentious and abandoned to *rejoice,* that *the weight of presidential influence is thrown into the scale of infidelity and vice?*"[21] Then, finally, came the charge, farthest below the belt, that Paine, the infidel, was directly involved in Jefferson's promiscuous sexual relationship at Monticello with a black slave named Sally. The *Federal Ark* in Dover, Delaware, made the point bluntly:

TOM PAINE

That arch infidel, who has publicly declared to the world that he does not believe in any *creed* that he has read of, is now on a visit to

THOMAS JEFFERSON

the president of the United States, who wrote to him in France, and offered him a passage to this country in a national ship. It is said Paine has undertaken this journey to tender Mr. Jefferson his thanks for his polite letter to him while in France, and to request the *loan* of SALLY, as he has no female companion.[22]

The apocryphal story was hatched on the editorial desk of *The Recorder*, published in Richmond. The journalist alchemist, the irascible Scotsman James Thomson Callender, admitted that the drunken debauchee was "a man of superior, of gigantic, and Herculean intellect." That made him all the more politically dangerous. "As a political gladiator, his merit is of the highest kind. He knows, beyond most men, both when and where to strike. He deals his blows with force, coolness and dexterity." Then came the abuse, divinely ordained: "Powerful and formidable as Mr. Paine is, he should not expect that five millions of people are prepared to fall on their knees before him." Callender was convinced that God had predestined the public disgrace and downfall of Jefferson and that, by accepting Paine as their friend, both Jefferson and James Madison had made it plain that "they, as well as Paine, believe that the story of *the birth of Jesus Christ is an OBSCENE BLASPHEMOUS FABLE* . . . that the Virgin Mary was a woman of bad fame, and that her husband was cornuted [made a cuckold]." For such infidelity, all three would in time be punished, wrote Callender, but in the meantime Paine and his friends, who ought publicly to burn their Bibles, had performed an invaluable service to the country by clarifying the true nature of the moral decision that they and their political supporters must make: "They have no other choice than that of renouncing their saviour, or their president, the son of the Virgin Mary, or the husband of black Sally."[23]

Contrary to expectations, Paine remained silent throughout this gale of printed polemics. He obviously wanted to spend time sizing up the American scene after an absence of fifteen years. He was even amused by the hullabaloo. He was a survivor of the press controversies during the Silas

Deane affair, and the press attacks on him since arriving in Baltimore —
even talk of "the MONSTER, THOMAS PAINE" — felt benign compared to
the sinister press campaigns he had lived through and suffered under before and during the Reign of Terror in France. Paine also resolved for the
time being to "tolerate" the press nonsense and to refrain from further
ruffling feathers because he believed that a free press such as America's always contained a "decadent" element — the liberty to print licentious
opinions — which could and should never be eliminated completely without threatening the fundamental right to publish any opinion without
prior government restraint.[24]

In an essay on press freedom, Paine warned against the view, "common
with printers, especially of newspapers," that those who own and operate
a press are perforce entitled "to have more privileges than other people."
Liberty of the press, which from the days in Lewes he considered fundamental to republican government, actually refers only "to the fact of
printing *free from prior restraint,* and not at all to the matter printed, whether
good or bad." But how could the publication of bad material be mini-
mized? Paine saw several possibilities. Juries in a court of law could indeed
determine whether certain published opinions were contrary to law based
on citizens' rights. In the sphere of civil society, the cultivation of "the
manners of a nation," especially the art of making prudent judgments in
public, also could help. Finally, observed Paine, publishers' abuse of press
freedom normally backfires in a civilized society because by printing nonsense, they breed skepticism among their readers. He recalled a remark
made to him by Jefferson in another context: "The licentiousness of the
press produces the same effect as the restraint of the press was intended to
do if the restraint was to prevent things being told, and the licentiousness
of the press prevents things being believed when they are told."[25]

Pens and Parties

Paine's providentialism blinded him to the novelty and epochal significance of the newspaper campaigns waged against him. He did not see
that he was among the first modern public figures to suffer firsthand an increasingly concentrated press equipped with the power to peddle one-
sided interpretations of the world. Paine no doubt strongly favored a
competitively organized, market-based press rooted within civil society
and protected by government. He had seen the colonial press in America
transformed, often against the will and commercial interests of printers,
into a robust forum of public debate, and it had confirmed his view that a

"free press" was a basic ingredient of republican liberty.[26] It was precisely that commitment to a market-based press, paradoxically, that prevented him from understanding that the Revolution had been an exceptional period and that there was a long-term tendency in modern newspaper publishing for competition to erode competition. Paine certainly spotted the inevitable tension between citizens receiving and sending information and press owners forced by market competition to see themselves as private property owners who stay ahead of others by outcompeting them. But he did not follow through that insight to see that market-driven media are required to obey the rules of Darwinian competition that force publishers to expand in order to spread their bets and stabilize their revenues, and then to expand further — at the expense of their competitors and readers — to support the overhead generated by their original expansion. In other words, he did not see that within a capitalist economy, full freedom of the press is enjoyed only by those who own one.

The attack on Paine and Jefferson was unparalleled in the history of the young republic. Although there is no evidence that the campaign of denunciation in the Federalist press had any seriously adverse effects on Jefferson's popularity or on the long-term prospects of the Republican Party, the powerfully organized Federalist press emerged the clear victor in an ominously one-sided test of publishing strength. It was symptomatic of the tendency for communications markets to *restrict* freedom of expression by encouraging market competitors to gobble up their rivals by all available means, including sensationalism and propaganda directed at their "victims." Such a tendency was not, as is normally thought, a product of the nineteenth and twentieth centuries. Even in Paine's time, publishing was most certainly not a gentlemanly game played according to the rules of honor. Market competition had already given birth to the first great press barons — to prominents such as Charles Joseph Panckoucke in France — who struggled to monopolize the opinion market by using new techniques of production, layout, and distribution.[27] Parts of the publishing trade even resembled a form of "booty capitalism" marked by scrambling and scratching for money, reputation, and power. Publishers were plagued by pirates, spies, and rivals, and for commercial reasons they were normally much less concerned with public debate and political principles than with selling their products, if need be through bribes, counterfeit editions, false advertising, and — as Paine soon found out — apocryphal storytelling.

Press sensationalism permanently damaged Paine's reputation. With the exception of the *Philadelphia Aurora. General Advertiser,* newspapers sympathetic to him failed to counter the challenge of their opponents. Throughout the republic, there was almost no effective opposition to the clever satirical sniping of the *New-York Evening Post* and the crude frontal assaults of the *Gazette of the United States*. Matters were made worse by another novel development that shadowed Paine constantly after his return to America: the birth of open competition among political parties for control of state power.

Today we take it for granted that political parties are a vital precondition of representative democratic government, in which the exercise of power is subject to open disputation and to the consent of the governed living under a canopy of state institutions. It seems self-evident that a free and equal society supposes a competitive party system consisting of two or more democratic parties, free not only to express themselves within state institutions but also to agitate freely within the public spaces of civil society. The birth of democratic party competition of this type dates from the early years of the eighteenth century. Its subsequent growth — exemplified by the small parties that took shape in the House of Commons in England during the long reign of George III, then subsequently "exported" to the American colonies[28] — was linked with the resistance to despotism and the appearance of nascent forms of representative government.

At first, parties assumed the form of what Edmund Burke called "honourable connections" of gentlemen whose role in Parliament was to criticize, restrain, or support ministers of state in the name of the various factions of the dominant political class. Until the first quarter of the nineteenth century, these fledgling parties were located exclusively in legislatures. They neither engaged in open electoral competition nor solicited members outside the legislature. They also did not discipline themselves by means of formal party rules and regulations.

Such practices, usually associated with mass membership and competitive party systems, emerged only during the nineteenth and twentieth centuries. Yet their emergence would have been impossible without the prior crystallization of party groupings during Paine's years in America. That development had far-reaching implications for the modern world. It opened up the possibility — first realized in the nonviolent transfer of control of government office from the Federalists to the Jeffersonians in the year before Paine returned to the United States — that elections would not degenerate into acts of conquest. It also encouraged those elected to seek to retain the loyalty of the electorally defeated to the political system. Most important, perhaps, the formation of party groupings helped to activate the sense that the political spectrum was permanently splintered. It thereby weakened forever the classical republican view that parties have factious and seditious effects. That view was evident in Jefferson's remark made before assuming leadership of the Republican Party. "If I could not go to heaven, but with a party," he quipped, "I would not go there at all."[29] His friend Paine agreed.

Paine's attitude typified the almost universal mistrust and outright dislike of the fledgling political parties of this period. For a hundred years after Bolingbroke's famous early-eighteenth-century defense of a "Country Party" (a type of antiparty designed to end once and for all the corrupt patronage of government-by-party exercised by the new Whig regime of Robert Walpole[30]), early modern political thinkers, Paine included, were virtually unanimous in their dogged condemnation of parties and party conflict. A lasting political commonwealth, in which civil and political liberties were guaranteed by ordered conflict among parties, was considered a contradiction in terms — a recipe for government by faction based on passion, greedy ambition, and (as Halifax put it) "a conspiracy against the nation."[31]

This early modern prejudice understated the potential of parties to serve as addressees, protectors, and advocates of groups in civil society whose poor organization muffles their voices in the realm of political institutions. It also failed to appreciate the ability of parties to formulate sets of coherent policy programs, to recruit and nominate public officeholders, and to present them for confirmation or rejection by voting publics. Prejudice against parties also prevented the pundits from understanding the capacity of parties to aggregate social interests, thereby partly overcoming the fragmented, anarchic character of civil society and helping to mold its diverse, colliding interests into a relatively coherent (if always contingent) political coalition based on solidarity. In each respect, those afflicted with antiparty prejudice did not see that parties could help solve the peculiarly modern political problem — which Paine wrestled with constantly — of how to overcome the dangers of social faction and anarchy by political means but without succumbing to the perils of unaccountable and despotic state power. In other words, Paine and others did not see that parties are a vital mechanism for rendering "grassroots democracy" workable in a large-scale republic. They overlooked the point that by seeking to reconcile popular control and accountable government with effective and efficient state policymaking and administration, political parties could function, to borrow from Paine's friend James Madison, as representative bodies that can "refine and enlarge public views by passing them through the medium of a chosen body of citizens."[32]

In Washington

There was one crucial respect in which Paine's prejudice against parties was warranted. In his time, as now, party competition generated constant clamor within the body politic. Thanks to parties, accusation and counter-accusation, claims and counterclaims, mudslinging and backbiting became everyday phenomena. Paine was personally disgusted, but he found no easy way of avoiding the press razzmatazz produced by the emerging struggle between Republicans and Federalists. Like a monkey on his back, party politics, refracted through the press, clawed at him constantly from the time he landed in Baltimore. "You can have no idea of the agitation which my arrival occasioned," he wrote to Clio Rickman, exasperated. "From New Hampshire to Georgia (an extent of 1500 miles), every newspaper was filled with applause or abuse."[33]

The din followed him all the way to Washington, where he arrived around November 7, 1802. The applause there was sparse, but what there was of it was loud. The Washington correspondent of the faithful Worcester newspaper, *The National Aegis*, reported:

> Years have made more impression on his body than his mind. He bends a little forward, carries one hand in the other behind, when he walks. He dresses plain like a farmer, and appears cleanly and comfortably in his person, unless in the article of snuff which he uses in profusion. His address is unaffected and unceremonious. He neither shuns nor courts observation. At table he enjoys what is good, with the appetite of temperance and vigor, and puts to shame his calumniators, by the moderation with which he partakes of the common beverage of the boarders. His conversation is uncommonly interesting; he is gay, humorous, and full of anecdote — his memory preserves its full capacity, and his mind is irresistible.[34]

Newspaper reports of this kind were rare. "Calumniators" stalked him constantly from the moment he arrived in Washington, at that time a string of odd-size wooden houses with an official population of less than three hundred people, half of whom were congressmen. As if to underline the doctrine of the separation of powers, the community comprised two self-contained hamlets separated by a mile-wide mosquito-ridden swamp. In one of them, clustered around the unfinished Capitol, congressmen lodged in boardinghouses from the end of the harvest until the beginning of spring planting, which was the period when Congress normally convened. When Paine arrived, congressmen were still absent, and so he sought lodgings in the adjoining hamlet, which nestled around the executive mansion where Jefferson and his family perched "like a pelican in the wilderness, or a sparrow upon the housetop," as one observer put it.[35]

Gossip imported from the outside world traveled fast in this boring, self-contained hamlet of government officials living in the middle of a vast, bleak plain. News that Paine had left Baltimore reached Washington before him, and his arrival was greeted with considerable hostility. Doors slammed in his face. It was reported that the residents of two taverns had in advance "refused to remain in the house if Tom were admitted to the public table,"[36] and it was only with the help of a presidential aide and by registering under an assumed name that he managed to find lodgings at Lovell's, the only hotel in the hamlet. Even there he was badgered by Federalist supporters, one of whom reported, "The members who are there are not willing to acknowledge they have any society with him. He dines at the public table, and, as a show, is as profitable to Lovell as an *Ourang Outang*, for many strangers who come to the city feel a curiosity to see the creature. They go to Lovell's and call for the show — even some members of Congress have done it."[37] Paine was quick to respond. "I am become so famous among them," he quipped, "they cannot eat or drink without me. I serve them as a standing dish, and they cannot make up a bill of fare if I am not in it."[38]

Surrounded by upstarts and enemies, Paine could bite his tongue no longer. Several days after unpacking his trunk, he plunged headlong into the new party politics by completing the first of what proved to be a series of open letters called *Thomas Paine to the Citizens of the United States, and Particularly to the Leaders of the Federal Faction*. The letter was published on November 15 in Washington's *National Intelligencer*, edited by an English political exile named Joseph Gales, who in his youth had been prosecuted in Sheffield for his adherence to Paineite views. Although Paine's language was restrained, his clear attack on the divisive effects of party faction within the American republic must have been read by his opponents as a clear defense of the Jeffersonians — and, hence, as a contradiction of his antiparty views. Paine explained to his readers that the French Revolution had been thrown off course by the gales of party conflict that had naturally turned violent: "The principles of it were good, they were copied from America, and the men who conducted it were honest. But the fury of faction soon extinguished the one and sent the other to the scaffold." He went on to argue that a parallel destruction of civility and liberty was being attempted in America by the Federalists. These opponents of Jefferson had "lost sight of first principles." They were now "beginning to contemplate government as a profitable monopoly, and the people as hereditary property," and they were waging their factional struggles by means of a licentious use of the press.

Paine queried the accuracy of the label "Federalist" to describe their politics. He insisted that their principles were both antifederalist and despotic and that their practice proved the truth of the maxim "Those who abuse liberty when they possess it would abuse power could they obtain it." He predicted that the days of the Federalists were numbered, mainly because the American Revolution had produced a sizable class of prudent citizens who had already seen through the noisy nothingness of their press campaigns. These are citizens "who attend quietly to their farms, or follow their several occupations; who pay no regard to the clamours of anonymous scribblers, who think for themselves, and judge of government, not by the fury of newspaper writers, but by the prudent frugality of its measures, and the encouragement it gives to the improvement and prosperity of the country." How, then, could the recent frenzied Federalist attack on Paine himself be explained? "In every part of the Union, this faction is in the agonies of death," he answered, likening it to the epileptic behavior of a rabid dog. "My argument has struck it as with an hydrophobia, it is like the sight of water to canine madness." Lest his opponents repeat their old accusation that he was the hireling of the Republicans — that (as Moses Guest, the New Brunswick poet, told him) he had "inlisted . . . under the banners of a party" and was "adding fewel to the flaims of discord"[39] — Paine emphasized that he had no intention of seeking or accepting a government posting. Nor was he interested in making money from his writing. He had one and only one aim: to be a political writer who served ordinary citizens and the public good. "I must be in everything what I have been, a disinterested volunteer," he said. "My proper sphere of action is on the common floor of citizenship, and to honest men I give my hand and my heart freely."[40]

The disinterested volunteer saw as much of Jefferson as the president had time for. Their meetings were remarkable. Considering the vicious party politicking that followed Paine everywhere, Jefferson's frequent invitations to Paine to visit him in the presidential mansion were courageous. The invitations also revealed Jefferson's political integrity and respect for his long-standing friendship and cooperation with Paine, although their critics claimed otherwise. James Cheetham, who was at the time editor of the New York *American Citizen,* which republished Paine's writings after he returned from France until Paine quarreled with "Cheat 'em" (as Paine called him) and transferred his allegiance to the New York *Public Advertiser,* later wrote that Paine's "reception at Washington was cold and forbidding.

Even Mr. Jefferson received him with politick circumspection; and such of the members of congress as suffered him to approach them, did so from motives of curiosity. *Policy* dictated this course."[41]

Others recorded different, probably more accurate versions of the re-union of Paine and Jefferson. William Plumer recalled a visit to the presidential mansion: "Thomas Paine entered, seated himself by the side of the President, and conversed and behaved towards him with the familiarity of an intimate and an equal!"[42] Reports filtered out of Washington that Paine dined frequently at the mansion and that on fine afternoons "the two Toms" could sometimes be seen walking together, arm in arm.[43] Others reported that Paine received regular dinner invitations from members of the presidential circle, including General Henry Dearborn, Secretary of War; Robert Smith, Secretary of the Navy; and Albert Gallatin, Secretary of the Treasury. "This extraordinary man contributed exceedingly to entertain the company," a guest at a party thrown by the Gallatins related. "We had some conversation before dinner, and we sat side by side at the table. He has a red and rugged face, which looks as if it had been much hackneyed in the service of the world. His eyes are black and lively, his nose somewhat aquiline and pointing downward. It corresponds in colour with the fiery appearance of his cheeks."[44]

Paine had now outlived the average life expectancy for a man of his class by two decades — he had just turned sixty-six — but everywhere he dined he was reported in good health and spirits. He liked to recite poetry — satirizing Gouverneur Morris in stanzas of schoolboy language, for instance — and he was never short of stories to tell, his favorites being his encounter with the Native Americans of Easton in 1777, the bizarre events of the French Revolution, and his period of imprisonment during the Reign of Terror. Paine even received an invitation to dine with Jefferson's two daughters, Mary (or Marie) Eppes and Martha Randolph. Both were devout Episcopalians who had initially objected to the thought of sharing company with a loathsome atheist. Jefferson is supposed discreetly to have overruled their protests, saying, "Mr. Paine is not, I believe, a favourite among the ladies — but he is too well entitled to the hospitality of every American, not to cheerfully receive mine." Paine, the worldly conversationalist, seems to have risen to the occasion. As usual, he left a good impression. The two ladies "found his manners sober and inoffensive; and he left Mr. Jefferson's mansion the subject of lighter prejudices than he entered it."[45]

Jefferson's hospitality toward Paine profoundly irritated Federalist editors and spokesmen. "Can virtue receive sufficient protection from an administration which admits such men as Paine to terms of intimacy with its chief?" asked one of them.[46] The *Gazette of the United States, and Daily Advertiser* was less polite: "Our stomachs . . . nauseate at the sight of their affectionate embraces, and we entertain no doubt that you, as well as we, have become impatient to get out of such impious company. . . . We leave them, then, to consummate their bliss."[47] The *New-York Evening Post* printed a twenty-five-stanza poem, "Thomas Paine and the King," which ridiculed the relationship between the two men and repeated the familiar accusation that Paine was not "invited" to return to America but was actually "sent for" by King Thomas Jefferson and brought by a coach and six horses from Baltimore to his Washington court.[48] Joseph Dennie's *Port Folio* tried to put about the story that Jefferson had plotted to keep himself in power by reinforcing his meager support within the newspaper industry with Paine's quill:

> *He pass'd his forces in review;*
> *Smith, Cheetham, Jones, Duane,*
> *"Dull rascals — these will never do,"*
> *Quoth he, "I'll send for Paine."*

> *Then from his darling den in France,*
> *To tempt the wretch to come,*
> *He made Tom's brain with flatt'ry dance;*
> *And* took the tax from rum.[49]

James Thomson Callender's *Recorder* repeated the accusation. Its response to Paine's first letter to American citizens scathingly referred to him as the "*chosen vessel* of our beloved president! He sends twelve hundred leagues for an auxiliary writer, to tell his adversaries that they are *mad dogs!*"[50]

Refusing to strike back blindly at the dozens of niggling printed criticisms of their relationship, Jefferson and Paine remained loyal friends. Jefferson never uttered a bad word against the revolutionary, who brought him more political harm than good. For his part, Paine expressed pride in his support for Jefferson's republicanism and carried on drafting his weekly letters for the *National Intelligencer*. He lashed out at the Federalists, in effect for plotting a new tyranny to bring down the federal union established in 1787. Former president John Adams came in for special criticism. Paine disputed Adams's definition of a republic as an empire of laws and not of men: "As laws may be bad as well as good, an empire of laws may be the best of all governments or the worst of all tyrannies." Paine emphasized "the shallowness of his [Adams's] judgment" and accused him of "consummate vanity." He likened Adams to an ancient Chaldean ruler. After election, wrote Paine, he strutted about "in the pomp of his imagination before the presidential house . . . exulting in the language of Nebuchadnezzar, 'Is not this great Babylon, that I have built for the honor of my Majesty!'" In consequence, Paine said, switching similes, America had suffered a Reign of Terror based on lies, amorality, and the jingoistic "cry that our country is in danger, and taxes and armies must be raised to defend it."[51]

The Louisiana Crisis

America had in fact escaped the violent delirium of the French events, and the analogy Paine drew between Adams and Robespierre was far-fetched. It nevertheless revealed his interest in understanding the decadent cycles through which revolutions pass and reinforced his overriding point about the need publicly to control the exercise of political power. Fortunately, Paine argued, Adams's ballooning political vanity had been burst by citizens peacefully exercising their political right to vote. "To ELECT, and to REJECT," he wrote, "is the prerogative of a free people"[52] and certainly the unique advantage of republican democracy compared with every other form of government. Jefferson's election had put an end to the Reign of Terror that had begun toward the end of the Washington administration and now made possible a return to honest government, conducted openly before a republic of listening, reading, discussing, voting citizens.

Despite the mudslinging in his direction, Paine was determined to play the exemplary role of citizens' advocate and gadfly of government. Just before Christmas, 1802, he threw himself into the developing Louisiana crisis. Eighteen months earlier, at the Convention of Aranjuez, Napoleon had acquired control of Louisiana from Spain in exchange for installing the Spanish king's son-in-law, the duke of Parma, on the newly erected throne of Etruria. Under the earlier Treaty of San Lorenzo, signed in 1795, Spain had agreed to permit American citizens access to oceangoing vessels and the port facilities at New Orleans. The United States expected that this arrangement would continue unchanged now that the territory had passed into French hands. On October 16, 1802, Juan Ventura Morales, the acting intendant of Louisiana, ordered the closing of the Mississippi River to American traffic and announced the cancellation of the agreement without providing an alternative harbor, as had been speci-fied in the Treaty of San Lorenzo. The action caused a storm of protest among American settlers in the region. Federalists in Congress, intent on inflicting maximum embarrassment on the peace-loving Jefferson, called for a declaration of war against France.

A few evenings before Christmas Day, at Lovell's, Paine had a long and lively dinner discussion on the subject with Dr. Michael Leib, a former surgeon in the Revolutionary army and now a pro-Jefferson congressman from Pennsylvania. The Louisiana problem, Paine argued, could not and should not be resolved by force of arms. He questioned the bellicose argu-ment of Alexander Hamilton, writing as "Pericles" in the *New-York Evening Post*, that the United States should immediately seize the Floridas and New Orleans and then negotiate. Paine admitted to Leib that a stiffly worded diplomatic protest addressed to Paris and Madrid was unlikely to have any effect and that more potent means were required. Leib listened intently as Paine unraveled a proposal based on what he described as "ac-commodation." Paine continued: "Suppose then the Government begin by making a proposal to France to repurchase the cession made to her by Spain, of Louisiana, provided it be *with the consent of the people of Louisiana, or a majority thereof.*" He explained that the sum involved be fixed some-where "between the value of the commerce and the quantity of revenue that Louisiana will produce." But what guarantee, Leib asked, was there that the French would accept this buyout arrangement? Had Hamilton not insisted that there was "not the most remote probability" that Napoleon would sell the land? "The French treasury is not only empty," Paine replied authoritatively, "but the Government has consumed by an-ticipation a great part of next year's revenue. A monied proposal will, I believe, be attended to; if it should, the claims upon France can be stipu-lated as part of the payment, and that sum can be paid here to the claimants."[53]

Leib was so impressed by the originality of Paine's proposal that he urged him to submit a written proposal to Jefferson, which Paine did in the form of a hand-delivered present celebrating "*The Birthday of the New Sun,* now called Christmas Day." The next morning, he dropped in at the executive mansion to gauge the president's reaction. Jefferson seemed ret-icent, saying only that "measures were already taken in that business."[54] For reasons of foreign diplomacy and domestic party politics, Jefferson did not inform him that feelers had already been put out to the French and that Secretary of War Dearborn had quietly begun military preparations by concentrating troops on the Mississippi River just north of the Spanish border. Paine felt that he had received the cold shoulder. That evening, in a mood of despondency, he met Leib once again for dinner at Lovell's. Leib confessed to knowing much about Jefferson's plan for dealing with the French, the focus of which was the much weaker proposal to purchase only the island on which New Orleans lay and not the territory of Louisiana as a whole. Paine was annoyed. "Why then," he spluttered, "did you not tell me so, because in that case I would not have sent the note." Leib replied, "That is the reason. I would not tell you because two opinions concurring on a case strengthen it."[55]

Paine's more radical proposal was eventually adopted. He had correctly anticipated that Napoleon had abandoned the idea of a new French empire in America after failing to reclaim Santo Domingo and expecting shortly to be at war again with Britain. Napoleon regarded Louisiana as vulnerable to conquest, and, as Paine emphasized to Jefferson, the French treasury was depleted. On May 2, 1803, the French signed a treaty ceding Louisiana to the United States for the total price of fifteen million dollars. Paine could not conceal his elation at the acquisition of a territory so vast as to more than double the size of the United States and to bring the entire Missouri and Mississippi Rivers within its borders. Yet Jefferson's initially cool response sobered Paine. It served as a healthy reminder that he now stood within a force field of party-political tension that required him to be thick-skinned and that as a political writer cut off from the corridors of power, he should not assume that he would necessarily get his way with the new president.

The fate of two pieces written by Paine in the new year reinforced this conclusion. On January 12, 1803, he wrote a sharply worded note to Jefferson complaining that he had had no response to the models he had left with Jefferson shortly after arriving in Washington. "You have not only shown no disposition towards it, but have, in some measure, by a sort of shyness, as if you stood in fear of federal observation, precluded it." For good measure, to emphasize his irritation, he added, "I am not the only one, who makes observations of this kind."[56] Jefferson responded the following day, reminding him of the pressure of public business, reassuring him of his respect and friendship, and saying that he thought well of Paine's models, especially the one for planing wheels, and that he would be honored and delighted to purchase several of the machines if ever they were manufactured and sold. Paine was not completely satisfied. He tried hard to carve out a role as presidential adviser by returning to his series of letters in the *National Intelligencer* and sketching a long defense of his friend Vice President Aaron Burr. The essay amounted to a plea for Burr's exoneration from the charges of intriguing with Federalists made against him in the presidential election of 1800, a call for personal reconciliation between Burr and Jefferson, and a corresponding plea for national unity in the face of party faction. Paine was again rebuffed. Burr never regained the respect of either Jefferson or the Republican members of Congress, who subsequently dropped him from the party ticket after he killed Alexander Hamilton in a duel and was suspected, correctly, of intriguing with the British.[57]

On Religion

Beginning in January 1803, within weeks of Paine's having returned to America, his writings openly contradicted his avowed conviction that party faction was bad for the American republic. Everything he published contributed points and arguments that deepened, not healed, the existing party wounds within American society. The paradox was that, unconsciously, Paine actually contributed to the pluralization of power and identities that is now regarded as a vital feature of republican democracy. His vigorous attacks on the Federalists, which hastened the crystallization of party politics, were only one aspect of this paradox. Of greater consequence were his digs into the soil of religious assumptions binding together American civil society.

These probes hardened the hearts and toughened the resolve of Paine's critics and encouraged them to strike back against what they considered vicious cuts into the body politic. Trouble descended on Paine after New Year's Day, 1803, when he wrote a carefully worded letter to Samuel Adams on the subject of religion and politics. The previous month, Adams, then eighty years old and living quietly in retirement, had written to Paine to express his concern about his friend's atheism. Adams praised Paine's fundamental contributions to the formation of the United States: "Your Common Sense and your Crisis unquestionably awakened the public mind, and led the people loudly to call for a declaration of our national independence. I therefore esteemed you as a warm friend to the liberty, and lasting welfare of the human race." Adams's words then stiffened: "But when I heard that you had turned your mind to a defense of infidelity, I felt myself much astonished and more grieved that you had attempted a measure so injurious to the feelings and so repugnant to the true interest of so great a part of the citizens of the United States." Adams went on to remind Paine that neither religion nor liberty could long survive amid "the tumult of altercation" and "the noise and violence of faction." He concluded, "Do you think that your pen or the pen of any other man can unchristianize the mass of our citizens, or have you hopes of converting a few of them to assist you in so bad a cause?"[58]

Paine put care into his reply. He showed a draft to acquaintances in Washington and reworked it to incorporate their reactions. He considered the letter politically important and sent a copy to the *National Intelligencer* for publication, the aim being to ensure the maximum possible readership of the first reply to his critics on the subject of religion since his return to America. Throughout, Paine's tone was civil and humble. "Even error has a claim to indulgence, if not respect, when it is believed to be truth," he began, pleading for less calumny, more freedom of expression, and greater tolerance of social divisions — especially religious divisions — within the young republic. He went out of his way to repeat the key point that most critics of *The Age of Reason* had willfully ignored: that he was a firm believer in God and that the world's religions, despite their various renditions of God, actually concurred. "Do we want to contemplate His power?" asked Paine, adopting for a moment the tone of priest, scholar, and holy man. "We see it in the immensity of the creation. Do we want to contemplate His wisdom? We see it in the unchangeable order by which the incomprehensible whole is governed. Do we want to contemplate His munificence? We see it in the abundance with which He fills the earth. Do we want to contemplate His mercy? We see it in His not withholding that abundance even from the unthankful."

Paine presented a version of his belief in the possibility of global harmony among citizens of all nations by arguing that the evident diversity of life on earth is founded ultimately upon a publicly indisputable rock-solid foundation that is the wellspring of all life, the giver of meaning to all things, the First Principle of the universe. Yet in literary terms, the letter to Adams contained a strategic contradiction. The sheer energy and radicalism with which it questioned orthodox Christianity unnerved many of Paine's readers, most of whom (like Adams himself) had heard of but never read *The Age of Reason*. Intended or not, the letter to Adams felt like a knife in the heart of Christianity, which currently gripped American civil society and which, in Paine's view, made its citizens more narrow-minded and bigoted than was consistent with an open and pluralistic democratic republic. Christians, Paine told Adams, do not like to admit that the history of Christianity is the history of changing human interpretations of the meaning of Christianity. He argued that Christianity is riddled with theanthropy — the projection onto God of qualities that are alleged to be essentially derived from that Being but are in fact the artificial work of flesh-and-blood human beings who confuse and conflate the identity of God with their own temporal existence on earth. Christianity represents God in man's own image. Paine drew from this the conclusion that infidelity is an intrinsic feature of the Christian tradition and not somehow its opposite. "If we go back to your ancestors and mine three or four hundred years ago," he said, "we shall find them praying to Saints and Virgins, and believing in purgatory and transsubstantiation; and therefore all of us are infidels according to our forefathers' belief." He flung Adams an example to ponder: "The books that compose the New Testament were voted by *yeas* and *nays* to be the Word of God, as you now vote a law, by the popish Councils of Nice and Laodicea about one thousand four hundred and fifty years ago."

Paine reminded Adams that the peoples of Christian countries had paid a high price for Christians' dogmatic interpretations of their own Christianity. Latter-day Christians may well pride themselves on their reasonableness and charitableness, but the sad fact is, said Paine, that the history of Christianity has been full of dogmatism, scourged by the insistence that this or that interpretation of Christianity is absolutely true. Such dogmatism is a quintessential, not an accidental, feature of Christianity. Paine insisted that Christianity and other organized religions — if only to preserve their power over their followers, attract believers, and protect themselves against their competitors — are compelled to pretend that they are infallible. Intolerance and persecution are the inevitable results. Viewed lightheartedly, such dogmatism amounts to an absurdity. "If I do not believe as you believe, it proves that you do not believe as I believe, and this is all that it proves," he noted. Unfortunately, Paine argued, persecution and bloodshed, pushing and shoving, have been the inevitable practical consequences of dogmatism: "The world has been over-run with fable and creeds of human invention, with sectaries of whole nations against all other nations, and sectaries of those sectaries in each of them against each other." With the notable exception of the Quakers, he continued, each Christian faction has persecuted as it has been persecuted. "Those who fled from persecution persecuted in their turn, and it is this confusion of creeds that has filled the world with persecution and deluged it with blood."

The idea that Christianity, or its various sects, is a mask invented by human beings for the purpose of carrying on struggles for power over others was among Paine's most original insights. Developed (it seems) in isolation from Comte de Volney's parallel argument and well before the similar ideas of nineteenth-century figures such as Karl Marx and Friedrich

Nietzsche, it was used by Paine to explain to Adams why he considered utterly dishonest the current Federalist campaign against him and his supposed atheism. Their *"war-whoop* of the pulpit," as he called it, was being used to conceal their lust for power and to legitimate their attempts to destroy the system of federal representative institutions established during the Revolution. But Paine's argument had much broader ramifications, as many critics of *The Age of Reason* quickly spotted. By attacking the Christian tradition in the name of God, Paine, whether he knew it or not, prepared the intellectual ground in America and elsewhere for a more secular system of government and society in which, at a minimum, the freedom to believe and worship according to individual and group conscience required a pluralistic civil society, within whose nooks and crannies citizens enjoy the space in which to exercise the freedom *not* to believe and to shun the worshiping of any religion. The seeds of this subversive implication were evident in Paine's moving final sentence to Adams: "Our relation to each other in this world is as men, and the man who is a friend to man and to his rights, let his religious opinions be what they may, is a good citizen, to whom I can give, as I ought to do, and as every other ought, the right hand of fellowship, and to none with more hearty good will, my dear friend, than to you."[59]

The Traveling Infidel

By calling Christianity a bigoted fiction and emphasizing the primacy of citizenship among flesh-and-blood mortals, Paine added to the long-term pressures for the democratization of American Christianity and the secularization of American democracy.[60] Paine paid heavily for his achievement. Trouble erupted shortly after the publication of his open letter to Samuel Adams at a dinner party given in Washington by the Dearborns. Things had gone so well at table that when it came time for the ladies to retire, according to custom, Paine and other guests were invited by their hosts to converse and drink coffee. Mrs. Dearborn "intimated that the conversation would be acceptable in the drawing room." As soon as the guests had been seated, a Federalist supporter produced a letter that he claimed had been written by Dr. Manasseh Cutler of Massachusetts. The letter, a forgery, bitterly attacked Paine for his atheism. Paine reacted vehemently, as the Federalist guest had hoped. According to the half-sensationalized report that later appeared in the *Aurora*, "After dinner, Paine began to ridicule *religion,* and blaspheme the *Nazarene* in the most *shocking* manner. Mrs. D_____n, with an air of dignified authority, arose, opened the door, and *bid him Begone!* Paine and his friends feared and looked thunderstruck!" Seconds later, the room filled with silence, Mrs. Dearborn repeated her request that her infamous guest depart, "then pointing to the door commanded him to *begone that moment!* He then left the room, while the company sat in amazement!"[61]

Cutler subsequently denied that he had ever written such a letter or even said such things about Paine. The mud nevertheless stuck. Newspaper accounts of the incident and reprinted versions of the forged letter were published all over the country, laying crowns of thorns on the roads leading from Washington prior to Paine's departure a few days after the Dearborns' dinner party. The villain traveled by stagecoach to Baltimore, where he lodged overnight at the Bond Street residence of Mrs. and Captain Clark, the skipper of the ship on which he had returned to America. Next morning, outside the Clarks' home, he was accosted by a Swedenborgian minister with the news that the key to the Scriptures had been found after having been lost for nearly four thousand years. Paine was quick off the mark. "Then it must be very rusty," he said, the minister struck down in confused silence.[62]

Paine traveled on to Philadelphia, reaching the old capital on February 21, 1803. There he had hoped to renew old friendships after an absence of a quarter of a century, but the reception given him was cool. A few old friends had not abandoned their admiration for him. Charles Willson Peale, who was among the chief welcomers, excitedly showed Paine around his new museum housed in the hall of the American Philosophical Society and promised to add Paine's bridge models to the collection of model machines, dinosaur bones, and Peale's own paintings. Others with whom Paine had worked closely during the Revolution, including Benjamin Rush, refused to meet him and conveyed through messengers their disgust at the blasphemous author of *The Age of Reason.* Then there were the unexpected insults in public that wounded Paine inside. During the visit to Peale's museum, for example, Paine watched in silence as a young woman had her profile sketched with the help of a newly invented machine called a "phisognotrace." When the machine had completed its profiling work, Paine, trying to be friendly, remarked, "They take off *heads here,* with great expedition Miss." The woman snarled at Paine's wit: "Not quite so fast sir, as they once did in France." The unsmiling reply, according to an observer, "so discomfited Paine, that he turned on his heel, and walked to another part of the room." An old man standing nearby turned to the woman and whispered to her in a voice just loud enough for Paine to hear, "Excellent! excellent! young woman! The Lord is merciful, or the earth would open and swallow up that wretch."[63]

Such snubbing encouraged Paine to cut short his visit to his old hometown, as he spent only two days there before traveling on February 24 across the Delaware River to Bordentown, New Jersey, where he stayed briefly with his old friend colonel Joseph Kirkbride. There he was reunited with another set of good friends from his days in Paris, Mme Bonneville and her three children, Benjamin (whom Paine affectionately called "Bebee" and who subsequently became a general in the United States Army), Louis, and Thomas, whose group passage from France he had paid in return for the Bonnevilles' hospitality. It was a happy but fleeting moment for Paine, for controversy surrounded him again as soon as he set out for New York a few days later to visit James Monroe. Kirkbride accompanied him to Trenton, where Paine had planned to book a seat on an express stagecoach to New York. "I'll be damned if he shall go in my stage," shouted a coach owner named Voorhis when Kirkbride tried to book the seat in Paine's name. Another coach owner snorted and snuffled something to the effect that his stage and horses had once before been struck by lightning and that he refused to play with hellfire a second time. While Kirkbride and Paine were rummaging around to find a chaise, the whole town learned of Paine's presence. An angry mob quickly gathered near the stagecoach terminus to protest against him. Trenton inspectors were called as the protesting mob, led by a drummer thump-thump-thumping out the rogue's march, surrounded Paine's carriage and began to throw stones in its direction. Paine froze, waited a few seconds until the rain of missiles had stopped, and then stood before the menacing crowd and "calmly observed that such conduct had no tendency to hurt his feelings or injure his fame." The mob backed off, and Paine departed for New York, the horse pulling his carriage frightened out of its wits.[64]

The incident at Trenton indicated how less than civilized American civil society still was, inasmuch as a key measure of civility is the propensity of strangers to mingle freely without the eruption or fear of violence. New York was, by this criterion, a much more civilized place, and Paine must have heaved a sigh of relief on March 2 when he arrived among strangers who shook his hand, cheered, and welcomed him back to America. The city was full of immigrants, many of them from England, Scotland, and Ireland, and it seemed that everywhere Paine tarried, figures approached him out of nowhere to say that they had read or heard excerpts from *Rights of Man* and to wish him well. Typical was the shy approach made by Grant Thorburn, a humble seed merchant and part-time clerk in the Scottish Presbyterian Church on Cedar Street. Thorburn, hearing that Paine was staying at the City Hotel, mustered the courage to visit him without a formal introduction. "Is Mr. Paine at home?" Thorburn asked a hotel servant. "Yes, in his room," the servant replied. "Is he alone?" Thorburn asked. "Yes." Thorburn's heart thumped with trepidation. "I had no introduction," he recalled. "But I was determined now to see him. Come what will, thought I, he wrote the Rights of Man — he won't deny my right to look upon his august person, and being *alone* I will introduce myself." The servant ushered Thorburn into the large dining room. "A gentleman was at the table writing, another reading the newspaper, and at the farther end of the room stood a long, lank, coarse-looking figure, warming his hind-quarters before the fire," Thorburn recalled. Thorburn, recognizing the latter figure from book portraits, flushed with embarrassment, then asked timidly, "Gentlemen, is Mr. Paine in this room?" The room fell silent; Paine stepped forward and introduced himself, with a smile. Thorburn continued, "I held out my hand, and taking his, says I, 'Mr. Paine, and you, gentlemen, will please excuse my abrupt entry; I came from mere curiosity to see the man whose writings have made so much noise in the world.'" Paine answered, "'I am very happy in being able to satisfy your curiosity.'" Thorburn concluded, "I made a bow, something, I expect, like a goose ducking his head under water. 'Good morning, gentlemen,' said I, walked out, and shut the door behind me. They all burst out into a loud laugh, the sound of which followed me to the front steps. Thought I to myself, they may laugh that win — I have seen Thomas Paine; and, all things considered, have made a pretty good retreat."[65]

The Cedar Street Presbyterian Church later suspended Thorburn from psalm singing for three months for shaking hands with Paine. With such vindictiveness in the air, gatherings to celebrate Paine's return to New York were often boisterous. There were reports of heavy drinking bouts in his honor. "One day labourer would say, drink with me Mr. Paine; another, drink with me, and he very condescendingly gratified them all," reported a former friend and hostile biographer, obsessed with adding inebriety to Paine's reputation.[66] There were even banquets in his honor. Another early biographer reported a splendid dinner given for him by local supporters on March 18 at the City Hotel. Guests began arriving around four o'clock in the afternoon and did not leave until ten o'clock that evening, all "in perfect harmony and order," reported a local newspaper.[67] There were numerous toasts, and the guests, all of them men, raucously sang a string of patriotic songs, including "The Fourth of July," whose lyrics were written for the occasion by Paine and set subversively to the tune "Rule Britannia."

Amid the revelries, Paine found time to attend to political business. Within several hours of arriving in New York, he kept an appointment with James Monroe, whom Jefferson had recently appointed as special emissary to France and who planned to sail for that country the following day to help secure the Louisiana Purchase. Paine presented Monroe with a long memorandum outlining an interpretation of the current state of the negotiations, the difficulties working against an agreement, and what might be done to overcome those barriers. Paine urged Monroe in particular to contact upon his arrival in Paris an Irishman named Nicholas Madgett, with whom Paine was "on very friendly terms." Madgett had influence within the French government, was most knowledgeable about Louisiana, and would be sympathetic to Monroe if he knew that he had come "on the good mischief of preventing mischief." Madgett had been employed by the French Minister of Marine and Colonies to provide a report on Louisiana, and at one point during Paine's residence in Paris, Madgett had asked him to write a draft constitution for the territory, which Paine had declined to do on the ground that "it was impossible to draw up a constitution for a people and a country that one knew nothing of." Paine also warned Monroe of the urgency of getting Spain's agreement to the treaty of purchase so that if the French authorities tried to rescind the agreement, the Spanish could serve as a countervailing influence.[68] That advice proved sound. In Paris, Monroe pressed hard to secure Spanish approval of the American purchase of the territory, but Napoleon, sensing the American tactic, argued for an instant decision, thereby excluding the Spanish from the arrangement.

Campaigning

Paine spent nearly three happy weeks in New York before returning to Bordentown, where he had decided to wield his pen in support of the republican anti-Federalist forces in the New Jersey congressional and state elections. The campaign had just begun, but Paine's involvement was already controversial. Support was strong among the villagers of Bordentown, some of whom had been acquainted with him two decades earlier. Some locals even expressed affection for his quirkiness. The inhabitants of Königsberg, the east Prussian home of Immanuel Kant, Paine's German contemporary, used to set their clocks by the regular afternoon walk taken by the philosopher, whose daily life was said to resemble the most regular of regular verbs. Paine's life in Bordentown was similar. Every afternoon, rain or shine, he walked from the Kirkbrides' along country lanes into the village, observed by passersby and residents watching from curtained windows. Locals told how "in walking he was generally absorbed in deep thought, seldom noticed anyone he passed, unless spoken to, and in going from his home to the tavern was frequently observed to cross the street several times." His afternoon walk usually concluded at the Washington House tavern. There he was often surrounded by a large circle of friends and admirers, who told how "his drink was invariably brandy" and how he talked openly and relaxed "with any proper person who approached him."[69]

Beyond the close-knit circles of Bordentown, Paine was given a harder time. It was said by his critics in the state of New Jersey that he was "by the mass of the people held in odium,"[70] but, as ever, his publications magnetized large audiences and stirred up considerable controversy. After his flattering visit to New York, he felt alive, clearheaded, and full of energy. During a visit to Bordentown, his old "saintmaker" friend John Hall reported that Paine "was well and appeared jollyer than I had ever known him. He is full of whims and schemes and mechanical inventions, and is to build a place or shop to carry them into execution, and wants my help."[71] He was also in the mood for writing. Soon after settling in Bordentown, he completed his sixth letter "To the Citizens of the United States." The title was misleading, for in fact it was directed principally at his Federalist opponents in New Jersey, who were using the old tactic of playing up his association with Jefferson to win votes and gain seats in Congress. Paine's language was tough and, despite his strictures against faction, more party-political than ever before. "Religion and War is the cry of the Federalists," he began, "Morality and Peace the voice of Republicans. The union of morality and peace is congenial; but that of religion and war is a paradox, and the solution of it is hypocrisy."

Paine fiercely attacked the record of the Adams administration, accusing it in the international arena "of pulling down the little that civilization has gained upon barbarism." At home, he continued, the whole nation "was kept in continual agitation and alarm." It had introduced the Alien and Sedition Acts, whose purpose was to protect the government "within a magic circle of terror," and it had put the country to great expense. "Loans, taxes and standing armies became the standing order of the day." Paine went on to attack the current proposals of the Federalists to foment war in the Mississippi Valley and sided with those members of both houses of Congress who were calling for a public inquiry into the past and present conduct of the Federalists. Those congressmen, Paine argued, were right: "The suspicion against the late Administration is that it was plotting to overturn the representative system of government, and that it spread alarms of invasions that had no foundation as a pretense for raising and establishing a military force as the means of accomplishing that object." What should be done? Paine's basic answer had not changed since the Silas Deane affair. The Federalist abuses of public power should be examined by a public inquiry whose ultimate aim, Paine emphasized, should not be to punish them, but to discourage all future administrations from abusing the trust and power placed in their hands by citizens. "To be deceived, or to remain deceived," he wrote, "can be the interest of no man who seeks the public good; and it is the deceiver only, or one interested in the deception, that can wish to preclude inquiry."[72]

Paine's second written contribution to the New Jersey campaign was equally spirited, if more rambling and less readable. Published in *The True-American* in Trenton at the end of April, it served as the seventh and last letter "To the Citizens of the United States."[73] In it, Paine followed several overlapping lines of argument, all to do in one way or another with the split within the fledgling party system about how to resolve the Louisiana crisis.

He lashed out at the apocryphal press reports that he had tried, in 1794, to organize a French invasion force for "revolutionizing" the young American republic. The story had first appeared in the Newburyport, Massachusetts, *Herald and Country Gazette* and was republished in the *Washington Federalist* during the time Paine was living there. When no denial had been forthcoming — Paine had presumably laughed at its absurdity — the *New-York Evening Post* of February 4, 1803, published the full story, headlined "Paine's Plan, for Revolutionizing America." The editor pointed out that his newspaper considered the story "genuine," carefully adding the caveat that "should anything however at any time appear to disprove this, or even bring it into question, either from Mr. Paine or any of his friends, it shall readily have a place, and for the present we withhold all comment." This was rumormongering at its most sophisticated, for the effect of the proviso among readers hungry for scandal was to add weight to the story itself. Additional legitimacy was given to the tale by the paper's reprinting within the same story a brief note from "A Customer" that had accompanied the original story in the *Newburyport Herald and Country Gazette*. The note read: "In the '*Public Ledyard* [Ledger],' &c. of July 8, 1794, published in London, I met with a Plan proposed by TOM PAINE, to the French government, for revolutionizing the United States of America; a republication of which will oblige every friend to his country, whether Federalist or Democrat." The "Customer" quoted Paine as saying, "Should George the Third be driven from his Throne, America will be his place of refuge; there he has deposited funds; and, incredible as it may appear, there he will be King." The *New-York Evening Post* detailed Paine's "plans" for the French invasion, ending with Paine's tough-minded conclusion: "This is the only way to humble the British Lion, that now courts an alliance with the American Eagle, only to bring about its destruction."[74]

Paine said in his seventh letter "To the Citizens of the United States" that the story was a Federalist concoction, and he threatened court action if the tale persisted. The story was the product, he insisted, of "lying uncontradicted" and "all the arts hypocrisy could devise." It typified the way in which Federalists past and present relied on "outrage, coxcombical parade, false alarms, a continual increase of taxes and an unceasing clamour for war." Paine reminded his readers of the wrongheaded treaty negotiated in England by John Jay and later ratified by the Washington administration, which "had so disgracefully surrendered the right and freedom of the American flag, that all the commerce of the United States on the ocean became exposed to capture, and suffered in consequence of it." Paine contrasted the Federalist style of politics with his long-standing thesis that "commerce contained within itself the means of its own protection." To substantiate the contrast, he reprinted in the same letter the preamble and articles of the *Pacte Maritime,* in which he had sketched an alternative plan for an armed association of peace-loving, neutral nations, who would act in concert against any belligerent state by closing their ports and imposing embargoes on the commerce of the aggressor.[75]

Paine went out of his way to quote the full version of Jefferson's original letter of invitation to him. His aim in doing this was partly to defuse the continuing controversy about the relationship between the two men, which was still being fueled two years later by quotations taken out of context and by misprinted or incomplete versions of the letter. Jefferson's letter, written before he became president, also contained a long passage on American foreign policy, which Paine was convinced still had great resonance in this period of intense negotiations about the future of Louisiana. Paine quoted eagerly, underlining the whole passage:

> Determined as we are to avoid, if possible, wasting the energies of our people in war and destruction, we shall avoid implicating ourselves with the Powers of Europe, even in support of principles which we mean to pursue.

They have so many other interests different from ours that we must avoid being entangled in them. We believe we can enforce those principles as to ourselves by peaceable means, now that we are likely to have our public councils detached from foreign views.

Paine praised Jefferson's continuing commitment to "wise economy and peaceable principles" and urged his readers to keep them in mind when voting in the coming election. He warned them that "hunting after places, offices and contracts" is commonplace in democratic elections and that the best antidote to such political decadence is the commitment to moral principles such as "peace, moderate taxes and mild government." Elections, he concluded, should be about principles, not personalities: "When moral principles, rather than persons, are candidates for power, to vote is to perform a moral duty, and not to vote is to neglect a duty."[76]

It is unknown whether Paine's writing helped or hindered the campaign of the pro-Jefferson Republicans, but he must have felt at least a quiet sense of satisfaction upon hearing of their victory that spring in New Jersey. At the beginning of the congressional election campaign, Jefferson had hoped the Republicans would carry all but four states.[77] In fact, Republican candidates carried all but two states, Delaware and Connecticut, with support for Jefferson virtually unanimous in every other state, including New Jersey. The total electoral vote was 162 for Jefferson and 14 for Charles Cotesworth Pinckney, the Federalist candidate.

As spring turned into summer, Paine spent a good deal of time reading, napping in an armchair wrapped in a blanket, taking afternoon strolls, and meeting friends at the Washington House. He found traveling more tiresome these days and tried to avoid leaving Bordentown, making only one journey that summer — to New York, to be a guest of honor at his first Independence Day dinner in America since 1787. He was in excellent form, delighting his audience with a spirited recital of an extempore poem contrasting Europe and America. Paine began, his audience hushed:

> *Quick as the lightning's vivid flash*
> *The poet's eye o'er Europe rolls;*
> *Sees battles rage, hears tempests crash,*
> *And dims at horror's threatening scowls.*

The poet then turned away from the battlefields of old Europe in disgust, toward America, where freedom "holds her boundless sway." Paine's concluding stanza about liberty's triumph was crafted to raise high his audience's glasses:

'Tis here her sage triumphant sways
An empire in the people's love
'Tis here the sovereign will obeys
No king but Him who rules above.[78]

New York's torrid summer weather was not to Paine's liking, and he stayed but a few days there, returning to his comfortable routine in Bordentown's cooler country surroundings. During this period, he saw the final collapse of his long-standing dream to see built in America the bridge that he had been designing and redesigning for nearly two decades. Shortly after Congress disbanded in June, his request for a subsidy to build a prototype of the bridge having foundered, he sent off to the press a memorandum on iron bridges. The piece had been originally written to convince Congress of the merits of iron bridges. Now, he concluded, it would serve as a guide to those who would someday span America's hills and waterways with single-span arches constructed in foundries all over the country. At the end of July, the two model bridges that he had packed off to Washington to show Jefferson finally arrived in Philadelphia, where they were carefully unpacked by Charles Willson Peale and placed on display in his museum. Paine's letter to Peale on July 29, 1803, his first bit of personal correspondence for nearly five months, proved to be a final obituary on a project that had failed in America. "The model to be viewed in a proper position should be placed as high as the eye," he instructed. He then concluded with a wistful thought: "With respect to the Schuylkill Bridge, it should have been constructed in a single arch. It would then have been an honour to the state."[79]

During August, with a presidential election campaign appearing on the horizon, Paine returned to the subject of Louisiana, whose cession to the United States for the sum of fifteen million dollars had just been announced publicly. Caught up "in a retired village and out of the way of hearing the talk of the great world,"[80] he wrote to express his views about the future of the territory to both Jefferson and John Breckenridge, a Kentucky lawyer who had been elected to the Senate in 1801 and had since been actively involved in securing the Mississippi Valley and Louisiana for the United States by means other than war.[81] The two letters deserve attention because they deal with the difficult problem of how to effect a transition to republican democracy within a territory that had not experienced a revolution, that had little taste for democracy, and whose fate in effect had been determined behind its back by means of a bargain secured by an agreement among several already-existing states.

Paine dealt first with the international dimensions of the Louisiana deal. He reacted sharply against rumors that Federalist forces in Congress would try to block the deal and claim that since it was a treaty, it must be ratified by the Senate, in accordance with the second section of the second article of the Constitution, which states that the "President shall have power by and with the consent of the Senate to make Treaties provided two thirds of the Senators present concur." To Breckenridge, Paine underlined his respect for this clause: "I love the restriction in the Constitution which takes from the Executive the power of making treaties of his own will: and also the clause which requires the consent of two thirds of the Senators, because we cannot be too cautious in involving and entangling ourselves with foreign powers." But he added quickly, "I have an equal objection against extending the same power to the senate in cases to which it is not strictly and constitutionally applicable, because it is giving a nullifying power to a minority." He went on to insist that the Louisiana Purchase was a monetary exchange in which, unlike a treaty, the contracting partners have nothing more to do with each other after the sale and purchase are completed. It must, therefore, be considered simply as an item of domestic policy, which could be implemented by a congressional committee presenting to the president for his consent a bill authorizing the payment of money to the French.

As for the problem of founding a system of representative government, Paine suggested to Jefferson that Congress authorize the setting up of a provisional government initially subject to Congress's authority for a fixed period of either three, five, or seven years. From the outset, Paine explained, the population should begin to practice the art of self-government by electing their municipal governments and, later, their own state government and federal representatives. Gradually, the population could learn to become active citizens competent to run their own affairs and elect and recall their own representatives within the constitutional and political framework of the American federation. He urged Jefferson to pay a visit soon to the region to inspire this process of transition, but Paine did not fall back on the myth of the "Great Founder Hero" that peppers the entire Western tradition of political thought from Plato through Niccolò Machiavelli and Jean-Jacques Rousseau. Paine urged that, as far as possible, the adult population of the new territory of Louisiana be encouraged to develop their own skills of citizenship not only within the sphere of formal politics but also within the sphere of civil society itself.

A principal site of democratization, Paine thought, would be that of religion. As might have been expected, he recommended the principle of the separation of church and state, as well as — here he showed his opposition to the continuing grip of Catholicism on the population of the region — adherence to toleration of a diversity of religious sects. These principles would prove to be increasingly important when the first waves of new immigrants from the old United States started reaching Louisiana. "The Yankees will not move out of the road," he said irreverently to Breckenridge, "for a little wooden Jesus stuck on a stick and carried in procession nor kneel in the dirt to a wooden Virgin Mary." Paine's most original suggestion to Jefferson was that the new state constitution of Louisiana include a provision for the election of all ministers of religion by their parishioners. The antipapist and democratic intentions of this proposal, which was never adopted, were clear. "I do not make it a compulsive article," he wrote, "but to put it in their power to use it when they please. It will serve to hold the priests in a style of good behaviour, and also to give the people an idea of elective rights."

Stonington Lectures

At the end of August, drier and cooler weather swept across the eastern seaboard. Paine, whose dislike of subtropical weather was typically English, was encouraged to travel up to the tiny fishing village of Stonington, Connecticut, to stay with his friend and benefactor Captain Nathan Haley, owner of the small ship *Brutus*. During the last three years of Paine's stay in France, Haley had loaned him more than seven thousand livres to pay for things such as his board and lodgings at Dieppe, his laundrywoman, and the printing of *Pacte maritime*.[82] Paine may have come to see Haley to pay off part of his debt, either with money or courtesy, or both, but his planned brief three-week stay was extended, and then extended again, as he found himself transformed unexpectedly into an itinerant lecturer on political affairs.

Paine caused a stir from the moment of his arrival in Stonington. A steady stream of farmers, fishermen, and artisans reportedly came from as far as New London, a distance of fifteen miles, to meet him, ask him questions, and hear him talk about the vital political affairs of the month. The meetings between the local citizens and the gray-haired revolutionary perhaps smacked of worshiping sessions with a charismatic hero. But they also revealed the continuing strength of the long-term "democratic revolution" analyzed a generation later by the distinguished French writer Alexis de Tocqueville.[83] Paine brought to life the seemingly distant presidential campaign and elevated the humble citizens of the locality into the wider world of public affairs by reading and talking to them in small groups, usually in the evenings in the local tavern. Enthusiasm for Paine's lectures was heightened by the letters that he received from James Madison and Thomas Jefferson shortly after arriving in the village. Paine read the letters to his listeners, constructing before their eyes a dialogue with the government by interjecting his own views on the issues raised by Jefferson and Madison.[84]

On the subject of Louisiana, Paine explained and reiterated his view that the cession of the territory did not raise constitutional questions. He pointed out to his listeners that cession only involved extending the principles of the Constitution over a wider territory — that it did not require a constitutional amendment. Paine predicted that the satisfactory completion of the Louisiana Purchase would serve as a precedent for other territories, such as Canada and Bermuda, which would likely be incorporated into the United States if the British government continued to weaken, as Paine expected.

War had again broken out between France and England, and Paine gripped his listeners with his rich, if optimistic, interpretation of current European developments. "The English Government is but in a tottering condition and if Bonaparte succeeds, that Government will break up," he told his audience. He analyzed the news of the uprising in Dublin led by Robert Emmet in support of Napoleon's impending invasion of England. Paine did not yet know that "Emmet's Rebellion" would soon be crushed and Emmet publicly executed for his role in the movement of Irish liberation. As that was about to happen, Paine analyzed the prospects of a French landing on English shores. "I think the probability is in favour of the descent," he told Stonington's citizens. Paine confirmed that he was a supporter of the plan because the overthrow of the English government by Napoleon was "a necessary step towards the putting an end to Navies." He predicted, on the basis of his knowledge of his native Norfolk, that the French would attempt to land their forces somewhere on the North Sea coast, where there was "an open flat sandy beach for more than 200 miles" and which could be reached relatively easily by a mere thirty-six hours' rowing. Paine also told his audience, who at times must have been breathless, that if the invasion "should take place it will throw a temptation in my way to make another passage cross the Atlantic to assist in forming a Constitution for England."

Inevitably, the subject of religion surfaced during these autumn lectures. Paine was visited by a group of Baptists keen to discuss the forthcoming presidential election. Paine recalled that the leader of the group had attacked the political hypocrisy of certain American Christians. "They cry out against Mr. Jefferson," said the Baptist, "because they say he is a Deist. Well, a Deist may be a good man and if I think it right it is right to him." He continued, "For my own part, I had rather vote for a Deist than for a blue skin presbyterian." Paine nodded. "You judge right," he said, "for a man that is not of any of the sectaries will hold the balance even between all; but give power to a bigot of any sectary and he will use it to the oppression of the rest, as the blue-skins do in connection."[85]

Paine stressed to his listeners that he was opposed to religion because in the strict sense it meant thearchy — the government of individuals by a God whose supposed power derives from an oath or obligation to which those individuals are forever and unquestioningly bound. "The French use the word properly," Paine said on one of those rare occasions when he saw the need to use foreign words. "When a woman enters a convent, she is called a novitiate; when she takes the oath, she is a *religieuse*, that is she is bound by an oath." In practice, he said, the advocates of religion are required to be intolerant of dissent and doubt. They are for a single dominant belief to which the whole nation is obliged. "In Catholic countries it would mean exclusively the religion of the romish church; with the Jews, the Jewish religion; in England, the Protestant religion; with the Deists it would mean Deism; with the Turks, Mahometism." Paine argued that America reject religion in this sense of an officially sanctioned creed. Individuals' belief in God should instead be treated as a *civil* entitlement. In a civil society, all individuals should live under laws that ensure "that all denominations of religion are equally protected, that none are dominant, none inferior, that the rights of conscience are equal to every denomination and to every individual and that it is the duty of Government to preserve this equality of conscientious rights."[86]

New York

As the flaming crimson and brilliant gold trees of autumn slowly lost their dignity in gusts of chilly winds, Paine made up his mind to leave Stonington and retreat for the winter to his farm in New Rochelle. He confided his intentions to Jefferson, telling him that he wanted to arrange for a new house, including "a workshop for my mechanical operations," to be built on his farm and, while that was being done, to prepare an edition of his collected works, which he thought would run to four or five octavo volumes. He explained to his friend that the money was to come from hiring men to fell trees on his farm: "I shall be employed the ensuing winter in cutting two or three thousand Cords of Wood on my farm at New Rochelle for the New York market distant twenty miles by water. The Wood is worth $3\frac{1}{2}$ dollars per load as it stands. This will furnish me with ready money, and I shall then be ready for whatever may present itself of most importance next spring."[87] Paine packed his trunk in early December, and before the first snow fell, his head full of plans for making the best of his rural retreat, he set out by coach for New Rochelle.

Paine's intention of spending a quiet winter there, tucked away before a fire hatching building plans and preparing his collected works, never materialized. For the first time in his life, the physical hardships of aging began slowly to drag him down. Approaching his sixty-seventh birthday, he was forced to recognize that his body could not keep pace with his mind and his tongue, let alone obey the commands of his imagination. With certain activities now permanently beyond his reach, he suffered the painful experience of being startled and then hurt by hearing himself called "old man" for the first time in his life.

Within a few days of arriving at New Rochelle, Paine was struck by "a fit of gout."[88] In the eighteenth century, as today, the paroxysmal disease called gout was popularly put down to too much drink and debauchery, the shame of which added to the sufferer's pain, which was famously summarized by the seventeenth-century physician Thomas Sydenham as "violent, stretching, gnawing . . . so exquisite that it cannot bear the weight of bedclothes." Paine knew that the word *gout* derived from *gutta*, Latin for "drop," a reference to the medieval theory of the elements flowing down to the feet, where indeed he now suffered its worst effects. He had been immobilized by a gout fit twenty years before when lodging at Bordentown, but this time the pain in his inflamed joints was unbearable. He could do nothing suddenly. He found it difficult to walk more than a few feet at a time, his sleeping was disturbed, and he lost the use of both hands.

Unable to cope on his own, he accepted an invitation to stay with Captain Daniel Pelton, who kept a general store in the township of New Rochelle. His gout slowly improved, but during his two-week stay there, he was again struck by infirmity after slipping and falling on ice while puttering about the back garden. Bruised and badly shaken, Paine agreed to move to the house of one of Pelton's clerks, Mr. Staple, who offered to look after him until he recovered fully and could return to his nearby farm.

Paine was so disabled during the months of December 1803 and January 1804 that his daily routine was reduced to the simple, repetitive cycle of sleeping, reading propped up in bed, napping, poking dark yellowish brown snuff up his nostrils, eating toast and sipping tea, straining to reach his chamber pot, and hobbling to empty it when Staple was at work, followed by more sleep. Unable for a time to move his limbs, let alone walk, write, or even shave, Paine was paralyzed mentally, and he slumped further upon hearing the news, delivered by courier to New Rochelle, that his closest friend, Colonel Kirkbride, had died during November.[89] Paine killed the pain with brandy. His plans to cut several thousand cords of wood had to be abandoned, and his intention of editing and publishing his American writings from the time of *Common Sense* fell by his bedside. He simply existed.

As if to prove that death destroys a man while the thought of it saves him, Paine gradually recovered from the bruising, gout, and general debility to the point where, near the end of January, during a brief thaw, Staple was able to carry him outside to a gig and take him for a ride, wrapped in a blanket, through the network of snow-covered country lanes. Staple noted that Paine, despite aches and cramps, never lived up to the rumors that he was a drunkard, and he observed that on these afternoon excursions, he was quite uninterested in drinking either alone or in company with other passengers. Staple said that he found him "really abstemious, and when pressed to drink by those on whom he called during his ride, he usually refused with great firmness but politely." Staple encouraged him on sunny days to sit in an armchair next to others on the sheltered porch of Pelton's store, which Paine liked to do. His lively mind and polite company were certainly appreciated by customers and passersby. They always found him "the reverse of morose," Staple said, "and though careless in his dress and prodigal of his snuff, he was always clean and well-clothed." Even the local children, most of whom had been told by their parents that "*Tom* Paine must be a very bad and brutal man," seemed to take to him.[90]

Paine had always been the type whose inner sense of stability had thrived on accolades, and it was therefore not surprising that the public acknowledgment he received during this period in New Rochelle rescued him from the misery into which he had fallen. His spirits lifted, although understandably he continued to feel frustrated about the indefinite postponement of his plans. He was especially galled at his physical inability to write. Toward the end of January, for the first time in two months, he tried to sit at a desk and take quill in hand, but he had immediately to abandon the attempt in a fit of shooting pains. He was forced to resort to a scribe, to whom he dictated a draft and redraft of an essay, *To the People of England on the Invasion of England*.[91]

Reflecting Paine's continuing absorption in European politics, the essay slammed the British government for its recent invasion of Malta and predicted that the consequent renewal of hostilities between Britain and France would tempt Napoleon to revive plans to invade England, the most bellicose power in the Atlantic region. Paine heaped praise on his old enemy Napoleon, "the most enterprising and fortunate man, either for deep project or daring execution, the world has known for many ages." Paine reminded his readers of the factors favoring an invasion of England. The acquisition of Belgium by France had exposed the weakest and least defensible North Sea coastline of England, which Paine described as inaccessible to frigates and ships of the line, as suitable for flat-bottomed boats, and "as level as a bowling green, and approachable in every part for more than two hundred miles." Paine also emphasized the growing unpopularity of the English government. "There is something sullen on the face of affairs in England," he wrote. No better proof of the point was the government's resort to conscription, which "has put arms into the hands of men whom they would have sent to Botany Bay but a few months before, had they found a pike in their possession." Paine wished the English people "honor and success" and reminded them of the world-shattering originality of the American Revolution, whose specter was now haunting Europe. "The NEW WORLD is now the preceptor of the OLD," he wrote. "The children are become the fathers of their progenitors."

The essay addressed to the English people first appeared in the *Philadelphia Aurora* on March 6, two weeks after Paine had recovered enough energy to flee the end of the harsh country winter by moving to New York, where he boarded for several weeks at the City Hotel. He was soon afterward joined by Mme Bonneville and her three sons, who had been lonely and bored in Bordentown, especially since the death of Colonel Kirkbride in November. Paine was quite pleased to see them. He arranged rooms for himself and the Bonnevilles at a boardinghouse run by James Wilburn. As usual, Paine was nearly broke, this time because his woodcutting plans had collapsed. He consequently found himself worrying about debts, and, not for the first time, he was irritated by Mme Bonneville's "notions of economy." In the hotel, she ran up a bill for thirty-five dollars' worth of extra charges, which Paine refused to pay when Wilburn presented him with the bill. Wilburn immediately sued, but the court found in Paine's favor. The acquitted then took the unusual step of immediately paying the outstanding bill with borrowed money, perhaps hoping to limit the damage to his public reputation and perhaps even to ensure that the public fuss temporarily aroused by the trial would teach Mme Bonneville a lesson in the need to adopt more frugal habits.[92]

The affair quickly passed, Paine's friendship with the Bonnevilles intact. He enjoyed being back in the hustle of the city of immigrants. The sense of isolation of New Rochelle had not been to his liking. It had been exacerbated by the icing up of the eastern seaboard ports for more than two months during January and February, cutting off all communication with Europe. Paine had not received a single letter from France since leaving there, and his first letter from New York, written to his friend Fulwar Skipwith in France just as the ice was breaking up and the first ship was preparing to sail for Bordeaux, indicated how deep his feelings of isolation ran. "We have now been nearly 80 days without news from Europe," he explained. "What is Barlow about? I have not heard any thing from him except that he is *always* coming. What is Bonneville about? Not a line has been received from him."[93]

The breakup of the ice and the change of environment at the end of February boosted his energy, at least to the level required to resume a social life as vigorous as before his illness and accident. He renewed his old Bordentown habit of taking an afternoon stroll, this time around New York's rutted streets, most often locked in lengthy discussions with "enlightened citizens." Paine also was invited to a round of dinner parties, several of them given by the city's most prominent public figures. Dr. Nicholas Romayne, who was certainly the heaviest, weighing more than three hundred pounds, was his most regular and trusted host. He was one of the city's prominent surgeons, a well-read man who loved to discuss politics as much as he loved to eat good food. One evening Romayne brought together Paine and the good-humored John Pintard, knowing that the subject of religion was bound to arise during the evening's discussion. The two spent the whole evening jousting in good humor. "I have read and re-read your *Age of Reason*," Pintard told Paine at one point, "and any doubts which I before entertained of the truth of revelation, have been removed by your logic. Yes, sir, your very arguments against Christianity have convinced me of its truth." "Well, then," cracked Paine, "I may return to my couch tonight with the consolation that I have made at least *one* Christian."[94]

The Prospect

The lighthearted dinner conversation at Romayne's proved exceptional. The word *infidelity* tagged Paine whenever he moved about, adding to the weight of years now on his shoulders. Personal insults to the aging revolutionary were commonplace, becoming a near-daily occurrence on the streets of New York. Fully sober, he was often accused by passersby of yielding "to the most treacherous of monarchs, King Alcohol."[95] Every day, it seemed, insults from far and wide were sent in his direction. Typical was the case of the young poet and theater critic Thomas Paine, who petitioned the Massachusetts legislature to have his name changed to Robert Treat Paine, Jr., "assigning as a reason, that he was desirous of being known by a *Christian* name."[96]

A thick-skinned political animal, Paine tried hard to handle the insults with dignity. "Are you not, sir, the writer of my Recantation?" inquired Paine of Donald Frazer, author of the forged *Recantation of Paine's Religious Creed,* published just before he had returned to America from France. "Did you do well with the affair as a business transaction?" he asked. The accused author nodded. "I am glad," rejoined Paine, "you found the expedient a successful shift for your needy family; but write no more concerning Thomas Paine; I am satisfied with your acknowledgement — try something more worthy of a man."[97]

To counter his critics, Paine also resorted to satire, the most democratic of gestures. During the spring of 1804, he spent an evening talking over coffee with Grant Thorburn, with whom, earlier in the day, near the corner of Broadway and Leonard Street, Paine had witnessed the hanging of a convicted murderer, who had gone calmly to his death by attaching the rope around his neck to the crosspiece of the gallows. Seconds later, the cart on which he was standing alone drove from under him, leaving him to eternity. "What thought you of the scene?" asked Thorburn. "I thought the man behaved with much fortitude," replied Paine. "Mr. Paine," snapped Thorburn, "what you call the delusion of the Bible was this man's support in that trying hour." Paine retorted, "An Indian will sing his death-song while roasting at the stake, and die as bravely as that man did." "Because," Thorburn interrupted, "he believes he is going to join his kindred in the hunting grounds, where deer are plenty, and the game never fails."

Thorburn then lectured Paine for several minutes. "And so with the Turk — at death he hopes to pass into elysian fields, where he may pick up a dozen handsome wives for nothing, and swallow flagons of wine for ever without getting drunk. But you have no hope," sneered Thorburn. "Your chief ambition is to live like a dog, to die like a dog, and to find a dog's damnation." He paused, then continued:

> I would rather believe with a Turk or an Indian than in your creed; but the christian's is a reasonable and rational hope — he trusts in no less a power than in Him who made the worlds above; who counts the number of the stars and calls them by their right names; who counts the hairs on our

heads, and who takes notice of the fall of a sparrow as much as he does the crash of an empire. Thus trusting, he is supported through the troubles of life. When he breaks an arm, he is thankful it was not his leg; if he breaks a leg, he thanks God it was not his neck: this keeps him in perfect peace. But you have no peace or comfort in this life, and no hope in death. Besides, the christian has the advantage of you both ways; he has a support here, which you are ignorant of; he has a hope beyond the grave, which you laugh at. If your creed is true, he has nothing to lose; but if his creed is true, you lose your own soul.

Paine frowned, then looked Thorburn straight in the eye and said, "Why, Grant, thee had better throw away thy hammer and turn preacher: thee would make a good Methodist parson."[98]

Reactions such as Thorburn's convinced Paine of the need to respond publicly to the cacophony of voices accusing him of infidelity. When in New York, he had several meetings with Elihu Palmer, a former Presbyterian assistant minister who had founded and directed the Deistical Society of New York and, though blinded by yellow fever, edited and published together with his wife a journal called the *Prospect; or, View of the Moral World*. Palmer was a powerful public speaker who always called upon his audiences to rebel against organized religion, which he condemned as an agent of monarchy. "Kings could not exist without priests," he used to say. "Their trades exactly fit each other. First enslave the mind, and the slavery of the body follows as natural as the shadow its object."[99] Paine was attracted to such arguments, and sometime during the spring of 1804, the two men made contact and agreed that Paine should write for the journal a series of short articles on religion.

The articles are among the best-written and most intellectually powerful pieces that Paine ever wrote. He evidently enjoyed settling down for the first time for more than nine months to do some earnest writing — to "go on with my literary works, without having my mind taken off by affairs of a different kind."[100] Although he wrote steadily, he did so in short spells and with frequent breaks punctuated by naps and mugs of tea. Writing was for him more than ever a desperate act of public affirmation, an intellectual and emotional flight from a body with declining powers, an attempt to make a mark on the world despite his immobility and geographical isolation.

He particularly wanted to use the *Prospect* series to reply to his critics by blasting organized religion and trumpeting his defense of deism. He tried to accomplish this in part by playing the role of lay anthropologist. He set

to work reading and making notes from books such as Henry Lord's *Cosmogonies of India and Persia* (published in London in 1630), with the aim of
clarifying in his own mind the similarities and differences among the chief
world religions. Careful examination of their claims, argued Paine,
showed their agreement on one fundamental principle: "*The belief of a God*
is no more a Christian article than it is a Mahometan article. It is an universal article, common to all religions."[101] Such comparison served to "rel-
ativize" the particular "absolute" claims dear to each religion and, thus, to
reveal the absurdity of their dogmatic defense by their respective proponents. Paine observed:

> The Persian shews the *Zendavista* of Zoroaster the law-giver of Persia, and
> calls it the *divine law*. The Bremen [*sic*] shews the *shaster*, revealed, he says, by
> God to Brama, and given to him out of a cloud; the Jew shews what he calls
> the law of Moses, given he says, by God on the Mount Sinai; the Christian
> shews a collection of books and epistles written by nobody knows who, and
> called the New Testament, and the Mahometan shews the Koran, given, he
> says, by God to Mahomet; each of these calls itself *revealed religion*, and the
> *only* true word of God, and this the followers of each profess to believe from
> the habit of education, and each believes the others are imposed upon.[102]

Paine highlighted these conflicting religious claims with an eye to demolishing the Christian doctrine of revelation, according to which the
Bible supposedly reveals the existence of God and summarizes humanity's
obligations to Him. Paine insisted that Christians mistake revelation for history. "The bible is a history of the times of which it speaks," he said, and it
followed that Biblical stories are in every case merely human inventions.
Paine eagerly noted Saint Augustine's observation in the *City of God* that
stories such as the dalliance of Eve and the serpent in the Garden of Eden
were still considered allegories in his time (in the eighteenth century, they
had come to be considered as facts challengeable only by infidels), but
Paine stretched the point to the conclusion that the Bible was one big
jumble of concocted fables. Paine accused Christians of naively accepting
the illogicality built into their favorite allegories. "Is it a fact that Jesus
Christ died for the sins of the world, and how is it proved," thundered
Paine the empiricist. "If a God he could not die, and as a man he could not
redeem, how then is this redemption proved to be fact?" He also satirized
the wild inconsistencies among the various yarns spun by interpreters of the
Bible. "It is an established principle with the quakers not to shed blood,"
wrote Paine cheekily. "Suppose then all Jerusalem had been quakers when
Christ lived, there would have been nobody to crucify him, and in that

case, if man is redeemed by his blood, which is the belief of the church, there could have been no redemption — and the people of Jerusalem must all have been damned, because they were too good to commit murder."[103]

Paine clearly enjoyed playing the role of devil's advocate. Some essays poked irreverent fun at Christian beliefs and practices. Paine walloped the Blue Laws of Connecticut — so called not because of their subject matter, but because the statutes were printed originally on paper of that color — which specified that nobody "shall run on a Sabbath day, nor walk in his garden, nor elsewhere, but reverently to and from meeting." Paine spoofed the fanaticism of the "gloomy Calvinist" laws of rest, adding that "they oblige a person to sit still from sun-rise to sun-set on a sabbath day, which is hard Work."[104] The fable of Noah, which according to Paine contains anachronisms, elsewhere came in for some comical attention. "My opinion of this story," wrote Paine, "is the same as what a man once said to another, who asked him in a drawling tone of voice, 'Do you believe the account about No-ah?' The other replied in the same tone of voice, *ah-no.*"[105]

Other contributions by Paine had a tone of deadly seriousness, as when he told Bishop Moore, the New York vicar who administered holy communion to Alexander Hamilton just before his death, that the jumbled and illogical stories of Christianity could be made to look credible only when they relied on "priest-craft," or the art of telling lies and "keeping people in delusion and ignorance."[106] Paine's articles in the *Prospect* also argued that Christianity morally de-skills citizens by stripping them of their capacity to make moral judgments for themselves. "When men are taught to ascribe all their crimes and vices to the temptations of the devil, and to believe that Jesus, by his death, rubs all off and pays their passage to heaven gratis," wrote Paine, "they become as careless in morals as a spendthrift would be of money, were he told that his father had engaged to pay off all his scores."[107]

Worst of all, Paine argued, Christianity peddles evil. He explained this scandalous thesis in a contribution addressed to the New York Missionary Society, some of whose clergymen members had just met with the chiefs of the Osage Indians to present them with a complimentary copy of the Bible. Paine called for the outlawing of such meetings. He accused the society of hypocritically using such meetings to plan their confiscation of Native Americans' land, and he slammed its promotion of biblical ethics among Native Americans. Paine snapped:

> Will they learn sobriety and decency from drunken Noah and beastly Lot; or will their daughters be edified by the examples of Lot's daughter? Will

not the shocking accounts of the destruction of the Cananites when the Israelites invaded their country, suggest the idea that we may serve them in the same manner, or the accounts stir them up to do the like to our people on the frontiers, and then justify the assassination by the bible the Missionaries have given them?[108]

The questions typified Paine's radical suspicion of dogma and served his broader goal of defending deism. "For as a man possessed of uncontrollable power is not a proper person to be trusted with my property," he wrote, "neither is such a person proper to be the director of my judgement, who can by his power play upon my weakness, by his art impose upon my understanding, and by his tricks deceive my senses."[109] In spiritual matters, Paine argued, only deism can emancipate citizens from the crippling deception and bossy power of organized religion. Deism required no church, no tithes, no holy books. It required no bowing and scraping to prophets or preachers. It supposed only that individuals use their God-given faculty of reason to recognize the fact that "God has made of his power, his wisdom, his goodness, in the structure of the universe, and in all the works of creation."[110] That recognition implied living in truth — honoring reason as God's gift to humanity, happily using it to contemplate Him in his marvelous works, and imitating him in His ways.

There were gaping holes in Paine's reasoning in the *Prospect* papers. Like the two-part *Age of Reason*, they were silent about natural disasters and other "flaws" of Creation, and they evidently left themselves wide open to the tu quoque objection (as those suspicious of Paine's "atheism" saw) that deism was yet another example of a fabulous human concoction bottled as truth. Yet the extent to which others spotted holes in Paine's contributions to the *Prospect* is unclear, for little is known about the papers' precise effect or the extent of their readership.

It is normally thought that Paine's last years in America were victimized by the Second Great Awakening, the protracted religious upsurge that swept the country after the Revolution, reinforcing its conservative Christian instincts. It is certainly true that the wave of popular religious movements that broke over the United States in the half century after independence did more to Christianize American society than anything before or since. But that process of Christianization, curiously, had some profoundly democratic effects within America's civil society and its churches. Within civil society, rebel Methodists, Baptists, Mormons, and others offered common people, especially the poor, compelling visions of individual self-respect and collective confidence. Within America's churches, those who preached also offered what they thought commoners wanted: unpretentious leaders, down-to-earth doctrines, singable music, and lively churches in local hands.

Undoubtedly Paine was hostile to much of the Christian content of these trends and even to their form, especially the "enthusiasm" with which standard Christian tenets were preached from the pulpit. And yet he could not have failed to notice, with approval, the ways in which the Awakening profoundly questioned established structures of religious authority. The Second Great Awakening, like Methodism in Britain a generation earlier, instinctively associated virtue with ordinary folk, rather than with the clergy as a separate order of men. It exalted the vernacular in word and song, and its rituals sidestepped doctrinal orthodoxy and ignored the frowns of respectable churchmen. That emphasis on the vernacular as a means of directly communicating with and about God demonstrated that the republican democratic sensibility that had shaped the Revolution had not dropped dead with the acceptance of the Constitution. The spread of the vernacular in matters spiritual also explains why the conventional image of Paine as a loner in Christian America is, arguably, misleading. He was not a lonely deist, isolated among feverish crowds of Christianizers. In fact, Paine had numerous supporters. Among them was Lorenzo Dow, the highly intelligent, fellow-traveling Methodist who preached to more people, traveled more miles, and consistently attracted larger audiences to camp meetings than any preacher of his day.

In 1804, the year Paine was contributing to the *Prospect,* Dow barnstormed through the republic, speaking at between five hundred and eight hundred meetings, often beginning his sermons with quotations from Paine. Dow denounced inequalities of wealth and railed at priestcraft, tyranny, and the professions of law and medicine. Most who heard his sermons agreed that he was the most remarkable preacher they had ever heard. He talked like Paine and looked like John the Baptist. His magnetism had much to do with his roguish clothes, weather-beaten face, long reddish beard, hair parted down the middle like a woman, flashing eyes, crude gestures, and raspy voice. His spellbinding sermons were theatrical performances. Dow often made dramatic last-minute public appearances at preaching appointments arranged months earlier. He told sidesplitting jokes, smashed chairs to the floor for effect, moved his listeners to tears, picked on notorious sinners in the audience, singled out alleged thieves or murderers, and encouraged displays of religious ecstasy, which observers called "the jerking exercise."

"Crazy Lorenzo Dow," as he was called by his critics, refused to kowtow to any church structure, least of all to the Methodist authorities, who were forced to think twice about openly curtailing his activities because of his phenomenal success. It is unknown whether Paine witnessed Dow in action or whether he approved of his militant deism, but Dow undoubtedly helped to popularize the apparently contradictory Paineite idea that this was an "Age of Wonders," in which ever more people were recognizing that the divine permeated everyday life, and an "Age of Inquiry," in which individuals had to think for themselves and take matters into their own hands.[111] Yet Dow's successes also helped to produce a backlash against Paine's writings. There is evidence that attempts to popularize the attack on American organized religion hardened the opinions of Paine's enemies and widened his reputation in certain circles as America's most dangerous infidel.

The reputation certainly was not new. For a decade, a storm over Paine's alleged atheism — "the French disease" — had been brewing. Many American clerics found *The Age of Reason* menacing. They saw, correctly, that the author of *Common Sense* was assured an American audience. Just as he had labored to deliver Americans from political tyranny, it was said, so now he would claim to be emancipating them spiritually. That move had to be blocked, Yale president Timothy Dwight growled, for the acceptance of infidelity would surely lead America into turmoil and bloodshed. "The touch of France is pollution. Her embrace is death," he said.[112] Especially after *The Age of Reason* won wide publicity in Republican gazettes,[113] clergymen with Federalist inclinations — figures such as Jedidiah Morse — rallied with the cry that infidelity was rife, that a secret order called the Illuminati had infiltrated Democratic societies, and that Paine's *The Age of Reason* was proof of the French dangers confronting America.[114]

Such hysteria pinched and poked at Paine personally. An example occurred during November 1804, when Paine made a brief visit to New York to appear in court for the nonpayment of James Wilburn's bill for Mme Bonneville's extra charges. The stagecoach picked him up outside the post office in New Rochelle. As Paine clambered into the front of the coach and into the last empty seat next to the driver, the driver whispered rudely to other passengers, "Tom Paine, as I am a sinner." Frosty silence settled over the coach until it stopped for breakfast an hour later, when Paine initiated a conversation with the other passengers about the American Revolution. He spoke of Washington's leadership during that period, emphasizing that it had been inept. Later, back on the road, a passenger deliberately started a conversation about Alexander Hamilton, whose death at the hand of Aaron Burr several months earlier continued to be a popular topic of discussion. The passenger spoke loudly of Hamilton's merits as a political leader. "Rank nonsense," Paine snapped loudly. A young Federalist supporter in the coach grew so angry at Paine's irreverence that he blurted out that no one could soil Hamilton's great reputation, just as no one, not even Thomas Paine, had managed to soil the reputation of Washington. "Let me tell you I am that Thomas Paine," Paine replied, unaware that his identity had been divulged to other passengers as he had boarded the coach. "Well, sir," said the young man cheekily, "if the garment fits you, you are welcome to wear it."[115] For the rest of the journey, the old citizen, sitting with his back to the other passengers, continued to suffer haranguing for his political and religious views. He sat quietly, staring into the distance, sparing his energy for the court case — which he won — and the return journey to New Rochelle later that day, which passed without incident.

A Country Winter

While writing in New Rochelle, Paine turned away from his material needs, leaving them to the care of others or simply neglecting them altogether. He lived something of a saintly life, unconcerned with his possessions and wholly dependent on those around him for his food, shelter, and clothing. As someone who had spent a good part of his life traveling and living out of a well-used brown trunk, he thought of himself as well endowed. He owned three hundred acres, "about one hundred of which is a meadow land," he reported in correspondence. "I have six chairs and a table, a straw-bed, a feather-bed, and a bag of straw for Thomas," he continued, either referring affectionately to Mme Bonneville's son or poking fun at his own rural laborer's existence. He also was the proud owner of "a tea kettle, an iron pot, an iron baking pan, a frying pan, a gridiron, cups, saucers, plates and dishes, knives and forks, two candlesticks and a pair of snuffers. I have a pair of fine oxen and an ox-cart, a good horse, a chair, and a one-horse cart, a cow, and a sow and 9 pigs." His diet was correspondingly simple, though too starch-ridden and laced with snuff. "I live upon tea, milk, fruit pies, plain dumplings, and a piece of meat when I get it."[116] His meals were prepared by an unnamed black woman, who was paid to cook, wash his clothes occasionally, and do battle against the broken-down, dust-ridden mess in which he had always preferred to live.

Visitors were shocked at the squalor. "At our arrival," remarked a friend who dropped in at the cottage with a companion one morning around breakfast time, "we found the old gentleman living in a small room like a hermit, and I believe the whole of the furniture in the room, including a cot-bed, was not worth five dollars." Paine courteously invited his two callers to breakfast with him. After setting two extra places at the table, whose cloth was "composed of old newspapers," the housekeeper asked Paine whether she should boil fresh tea. Paine's friend later learned that

> the reason why the servant made this inquiry was, that Paine's general method was to re-dry the tea leaves before the fire, and have them put in the tea pot again the next time he drank tea. Our tea at that time was common bohea, and coarse brown sugar, and a part of a rye loaf of bread, and about a quarter of a pound of butter. The black woman brought in a plate of buckwheat cakes, which Mr. Paine undertook to butter; he kept turning them over and over with his snuffy fingers, so that it astonished my companion and prevented him from partaking of them.[117]

Paine's compulsiveness at the breakfast table was symptomatic of an inability to handle not only buckwheat pancakes but virtually all practical matters during this period. He was certainly incapable of keeping track of his accounts and wrote to his friend John Fellows asking him to visit New Rochelle and help sort out Paine's financial affairs. Fellows, who had fought at the Battle of Bunker Hill, had published the first American edition of *The Age of Reason*, and now ran the city waterworks in New York, obliged. In late July 1804, he quickly arranged to sell off around sixty acres of the farm to balance Paine's books. The land netted $4,020, enough to cancel some old debts and to breathe life into an old plan to rebuild the farmhouse that had been burned to the ground by lightning fire when Paine was in France. This time, Paine dreamed more modestly, sketching in his spare time a design of an extension to the cottage. "The additional part," he wrote to Jefferson, "will be one room high from the ground (about eleven or twelve feet) divided into apartments with a workshop for mechanical operations." Paine thought hard about the architectural details. His inclinations were decidedly modern:

> The upper part of this will be flat as the deck of a ship is, with a little slope to carry off the rain. It will be enclosed with a palisade all round and down to within about seven feet of the deck or floor. This part will then serve for an observatory and to live on in summer weather, and with screens, or light shrubs in light cases on casters to move easily. I can set off what rooms I like in any part, alter them and choose, and be as retired in the open air as I please.[118]

Jefferson found time to reply a few weeks later. He was interested but not greatly impressed. "I much doubt whether the open room on your second story will answer your expectations," he noted. "There will be a few days in the year in which it will be delightful, but not many. Nothing but trees, or Venetian blinds, can protect it from the sun."[119] The advice went unused because Paine had once again overstated his assets, realizing to his dismay soon after the sale of land that the profit would be gobbled up by outstanding debts. His financial difficulty was worsened, this time by the refusal of his longtime tenant to pay his back rent. After nearly eighteen years of living on the farm, the tenant had informed Paine in the spring of 1804 that he intended to leave, but "instead of paying his rent, brought Mr. Paine a bill for fencing, which made Paine his debtor!"[120] A court case ensued, with Paine receiving only his legal expenses.

Paine had as much trouble with Christopher Derrick, the new tenant who worked the farm and shared the cottage during the summer and autumn of 1804. Paine found him cantankerous and unreliable, and the two quarreled constantly. Toward the end of December 1804, Paine could stand no more of the disputation and asked Derrick to pack his bags at once. The order ricochetted. On Christmas Eve, the revengeful Derrick borrowed a local musket under false pretenses, went out rum drinking, and around eight o'clock in the evening swaggered onto Paine's property. Two friends staying with Paine for the Christmas period had "gone out to keep Christmas Eve," leaving him behind in the company of the young son of a next-door neighbor, Mr. Deane. Derrick stumbled through the snow toward the cottage, saw the outline of Paine through a curtained window, took aim with his musket, and fired. Paine recalled:

> I ran immediately out, one of Mr. Deane's boys with me, but the person that had done it was gone. I directly suspected who it was, and hallooed to him by name, that he *was discovered*. I did this that the party who fired might know I was on the watch. I cannot find any ball, but whatever the gun was charged with passed through about three or four inches below the window making a hole large enough to a finger to go through. The muzzle must have been very near as the place is black with the powder, and the glass of the window is shattered to pieces.[121]

Derrick's drunken eyes spared their intended victim, who was shaken but unharmed. Derrick was picked up the following day by the local sheriff, Mr. Shute, and after questioning was taken into custody, then released on bail of five hundred dollars, pending a supreme court trial scheduled for the following May. The trial, Paine revealed, was postponed indefinitely.[122] It materialized that Derrick owed Paine forty-eight dollars, that he had agreed some time earlier to work off the debt by building a stone fence, which he had not yet begun at the time of the incident, and that Paine had paid for more than forty pounds' worth of goods purchased by Derrick at Captain Daniel Pelton's general store. Despite these debts and the shooting, Paine refused to press charges against his attempted murderer, and Derrick went free. It may be that Paine's generosity was designed primarily to keep the peace in New Rochelle. It also was certainly consistent with his principle that violence breeds incivility, that it should be eliminated as far as possible in politics and social life, that at best it had a role in defending citizens against violent aggressors, but that it was never justified as a form of revenge.

Paine kept quiet after the incident. In mid-January, with New Rochelle cut off from the outside world by drifts of snow, he reported that he was "exceedingly well in health."[123] That same month, he immersed himself in reports of the revolution in Santo Domingo. Four years before, troops led by Toussaint-Louverture had taken possession of the capital of the island and established the first black anticolonial government in the modern world. Napoleon retaliated by sending to the island a naval fleet and a well-equipped army of twenty-five thousand men under the command of his brother-in-law General Charles Leclerc. Yellow fever decimated the French army, and on January 1, 1804, the independent black Republic of Hayti was proclaimed. From his cottage in New Rochelle, Paine wrote excitedly to Jefferson about the significance of the Santo Domingo Revolution and how to defuse the continuing tension between the new revolutionary government and Napoleon's France, which was at the time enforcing a blockade on the island. "The two *Emperors* are at too great a distance in objects and in colour to have any intercourse but by fire and sword," wrote Paine, "yet something I think might be done."[124]

Paine gently criticized the French for pursuing a policy opposed to its commercial interests. While he failed to point out the yawning gap between the ideals of the French Revolution and the current policy of French imperialism, he suggested to Jefferson that the United States had a vital role to play in pressuring the French to lift their blockade and therefore facilitate what the new revolutionary government wanted: "that France agree to let her alone, and withdraw her forces by sea and land; and in return for this Domingo to give her a monopoly of her commerce for a term of years." He thought the young American republic should seek to play the role of conciliator in the dispute. Such a policy would win the hearts of the citizens of the new Republic of Hayti. It would accord with Hayti's commercial interests and those of France, as well as benefit the American shipping industry, which would likely win contracts from both French and Haytian importers and exporters. No other power could at present play this conciliatory role, Paine argued, retrieving an image of America that he had first tried to popularize thirty years earlier and that anticipated by nearly two decades the Monroe Doctrine. The United States, he said, "is now the Parent of the Western world, and her knowledge of the local circumstances of it gives her an advantage in a matter of this kind superior to any European Nation."[125]

Paine had hoped to visit the capital city of Washington that winter to press home his plans for defusing the crisis in Hayti with Jefferson and the French minister, Louis André Pichon, whom he knew from his Paris days. Bad weather and caution about his health got in the way, as he explained in a long letter to Jefferson at the end of January. "I have given up the intention," he said, because "the present state of the weather renders the passage of the rivers dangerous and travelling precarious."[126] His spirits dipped, and, once again finding the country winter unbearable, he accepted a standing invitation to move temporarily to New York. There he stayed at the home of William Carver, a veterinarian and blacksmith, who as a young boy had cleaned the stable and brushed the mane and coat of Paine's horse when he was an exciseman in Lewes. Carver showered his old friend with hospitality, nursing him "like an infant one month old." Paine was not yet reduced to that infantile condition, but he evidently experienced ever-greater difficulty in coping with his daily and nightly routines. One day, prior to taking his afternoon nap, he warmed his bed brick himself on the stove. Not knowing that he had overheated it, he wrapped it in cloth, as Carver usually did, and creaked into bed. Within five minutes, according to one report, he was awakened by the smell of smoldering bedclothes. Seconds later, he was rescued from the small fire that quickly developed by Carver, who broke down Paine's locked door and dragged him to safety.[127]

Badly shaken, Paine carried on at Carver's for another two months, swaddled in hospitality until warmer weather enabled him to return to his cottage in New Rochelle. In the interim, he continued to make plans to publish by subscription six volumes of his works from the time of *Common Sense*. Each volume would run to around four hundred pages and cost two dollars, to be paid for on delivery. Each text would be related carefully to the context in which it was written. The political material would be given greatest emphasis. "The three first volumes will be political and each piece will be accompanied with an account of the state of affairs whether in

America, France or England, at the time it was written which will also show the occasion of writing it," he told Jefferson. The next two volumes would bring together his theological writings, while the final publication would comprise "a miscellaneous volume of correspondence, essays and some pieces of poetry which I believe have some claim to originality."[128]

Paine considered the scheme as more than a potential source of income in his old age. Although it would keep the wolf of penury from his door, it would above all serve as a candle to the American Revolution. Sixty-eight years old, hunched, and unsteady on his feet, Paine increasingly thought of his life's works as a living reminder to America's citizens and political representatives of the radical spirit of the Revolution. He also considered them as a gift to future generations, who should be encouraged, he thought, never to forget their own Revolutionary heritage. The conviction was in one sense Burkean, insofar as Paine saw the fundamental importance of cultivating traditions in a political community. But he took a giant step beyond Burke by insisting on the primacy of a republican democratic tradition, which he thought was distinguished from all others by its openness and pluralism — its support for a political culture of free and equal citizenship.

Principally because of his diminishing physical energy, Paine's ambitious publishing plan never came to fruition. Although he talked about it often with friends and visitors in New York, he was forced to busy himself with smaller, more manageable tasks. Primary among these was his renewed attacks on slavery. He reacted sharply against proposals then in circulation that black slaves should be brought to work the newly acquired Louisiana Purchase. He reported to Jefferson that ships registered in Liverpool were already beginning to transport slaves to New Orleans, and he left no doubt about his corresponding judgment of the matter. "Had I the command of the elements," he said, "I would blast Liverpool with fire and brimstone. It is the Sodom and Gomorrah of brutality."[129] He considered the slave trade immoral and, in the case of Louisiana, counterproductive in terms of improving the region's capacity to produce and trade with the other American states. Poor slaves living in wretched conditions, he explained, would have a low propensity to consume imported and locally produced articles. Hence, they would make hardly any contribution to the stimulation of local commerce and exchange. A far more effective, and certainly morally superior, approach would be to establish Louisiana as a free democratic state in which black people could become free and equal citizens. Congress, Paine proposed, could provide free passage for black families to Louisiana and arrange employment for the adults on plantations owned by whites. After a year or two, having gained experience with the soil, climate, working conditions, and markets, each black family would be allocated a tract of land, which they might eventually purchase but which in the meantime they would operate as tenant farmers, paying the plantation owners annual rent in kind.

Paine did not discuss the conditions of the enfranchisement of black tenant farmers. Nor did he examine the difficulties confronting tenant farmers under the conditions of market competition. Specifically, it remained unclear whether their initial exclusion from capital in the form of land would work against their material interests, consigning them with few exceptions to a class of relatively less wealthy and less powerful rural wage laborers condemned to live as second-class citizens of the republic. It is true that Paine was aware of the tendency of market economies to generate what he often called "self-interested speculation," but he typically thought of profiteering and other market injustices as caused by corrupt government and as controllable through wise and well-executed policies of periodically elected constitutional governments. He repeated this line of argument in *Constitutions, Governments, and Charters,* a short pamphlet written and published in the early summer of 1805, shortly after Paine had returned from New York to New Rochelle.

Brimming with energy and showing no sign of Paine's physical age, the pamphlet set its sights on the current scandal surrounding the New York–based Merchants' Bank, whose directors had recently been granted a lucrative charter after bribing several members of the state legislature. Paine insisted that such corruption resulted from the legislature's misuse of its "assumed power" of granting charters and monopolies to individuals and companies in the marketplace. He pointed out — renewing the stand he had taken during the Silas Deane affair — that such power to make decisions with long-term effects without the consent of the citizens, or at least a majority of them, was inconsistent with the spirit of the American Revolution and that the constitutions of the various states of the federation did not specifically sanction such government prerogatives. It was hardly surprising that they did not, he continued. The whole point of the Revolutionary struggle against the British had been to establish in constitutional form the principle that unchecked power corrupts both decision-makers and decision takers, whereas publicly checked power enables bad governors and bad policies to be revoked. The American revolutionaries had fought for the principle of periodically elected power "not only for the purpose of giving the people, in their elective character, the opportunity of showing their approbation of those who have acted right, by re-electing them, and rejecting those who have acted wrong; but also for the purpose of correcting the wrong (where any wrong has been done) of a former legislature."[130]

Paine here touched on a quintessential feature of modern republican democracy: it is superior to all other types of government not because it guarantees consensus or even "good" decisions, but because it enables citizens to *reconsider* their judgments about the quality and unintended consequences of those decisions. Republican democracies enable citizens to think twice and to say no, even to policies to which they once consented.[131] Paine understood that republican democracies sometimes allow majorities to decide things about which they are blissfully ignorant. But he also saw that they enable minorities to challenge blissfully ignorant majorities, to bring them to their senses, to tell them what they do not want to hear. Republican democracy is the simplest and most effective method of "taming" those who wield power by making them subject to ongoing public discussion, periodic election, and the threat of peaceful dismissal. This principle, Paine argued, definitely applied to the specific case of legislation covering "sales or grants of public lands, acts of incorporation, public contracts with individuals or companies beyond a certain amount." He proposed that after the publication of such a bill and its second reading in the legislature, the proposed measure should be shelved for the consideration, at a later stage, of a freshly elected legislature, whose political composition might well be different and possibly hostile to the bill, which might therefore not be passed, or at least not passed in its original form. That would not matter, Paine concluded, for at least the fundamental principle of accountable power would have been honored.[132]

Almost everything he wrote in the summer of 1805 reiterated this theme, but underpinning his thinking was the conviction that America was straying from its founding principles, that the memory of its origins was fading. In the eighth and final letter "To the Citizens of the United States," which Paine considered the most important, he explained the significance of the Revolution to the younger generation of Americans:

> The independence of America would have added but little to her own happiness, and been of no benefit to the world, if her government had been formed on the *corrupt models of the old world.* It was the opportunity of *beginning the world anew,* as it were; and of bringing forward a *new system* of government in which the rights of *all men* should be preserved that gave *value* to independence. . . . *Mere* independence might at some future time, have been effected and established by arms, *without principle,* but a *just* system of

government could not. In short, it was the *principle* at *that* time, that produced the independence; for until the principle spread itself abroad among the people, independence was not thought of, and America was fighting without an object.[133]

Some readers may have dismissed such passages as rootless nostalgia, as an exercise in sentimentalism of an old man who had changed countries often and whose time of glory had long passed. Paine considered such dismissals symptomatic of the problem. Partly because of his age and sensitivity to time, but partly also because of his opposition to those whom he considered unprincipled Federalists, aping English political traditions, Paine expressed growing awareness during this period that the struggle for preserving civic memories is essential in the struggle against unaccountable power. He now considered memory (along with judgment and imagination) as one of the "three great faculties of the mind."[134] Political tradition, he also thought, is made, unmade, and remade by flesh-and-blood mortals, who themselves have a propensity to forget, to bowdlerize, and willfully to destroy the memories that they inherit from the dead. That being so, votes must be extended by the living to the most disfranchised and permanently humiliated of all constituencies — our silenced republican democratic ancestors.

Exactly this work of political remembering was central to Paine's public interventions during the spring and summer of 1805. He wrote a venomous attack on the pro-Federalist Massachusetts representative John Hulbert, whom he denounced as a lying amnesiac ignorant of the virtue of "grateful remembrance."[135] Under the nom de plume "A Spark from the Altar of '76," he sided openly with Jefferson in a strongly worded two-part reply to a Virginia Federalist, Thomas Turner, whom he linked with Hulbert, and described the pair as "two skunks who stink in concert."[136]

During August, still in New Rochelle, Paine also wrote a pamphlet — the last he ever published — in support of the call for constitutional reform in Pennsylvania. He reminded Pennsylvania readers that the spirit of the Revolution was endangered in their state. Whereas their constitution of 1776 was second to none, the revised constitution of 1790 had created a form of government whose working principles were more English and monarchic than American. The state senate, whose members served four years, "is an imitation of what is called the House of Lords in England," he wrote, repeating Philip Dormer Chesterfield's scathing description of that hallowed body as "the Hospital of Incurables." The state governor, similarly, had been granted powers of veto and patronage "copied . . .

from the corrupt system of England." Paine criticized the Pennsylvania judiciary for its mimicry of the English system and called for the election of judges and greater reliance on trial by jury. He also objected to the way in which the constitution gave its blessing to "artificial distinctions among men in the right of suffrage." He roasted the old monarchic practice of voting by orders or estates and argued instead for universal suffrage — among men, at least. "We have but one ORDER in America," he said. "Why then have we descended to the base imitation of inferior things? By the event of the Revolution we were put in a condition of thinking originally. The history of past ages shows scarcely anything to us but instances of tyranny and antiquated absurdities. We have copied some of them and experienced the folly of them."[137]

At the same time as he was busily criticizing the Pennsylvania constitution and adding his voice to the ill-fated calls in that state for a constitutional convention, Paine poured scorn on the British government and heaped lavish praise on the French dictatorship. "France, at this time, has for its chief the most enterprizing man in Europe, and the greatest general in the world," he wrote in July, adding, "besides these virtues or vices (call them what you please, for they may be either), he is a deep and consummate politician in every thing which relates to the success of his measures. He knows both how to plan and how to execute. This is a talent that Pitt is defective in, for all his measures fail in execution."[138] The juxtaposition of republican democratic and nationalist revolutionary sympathies puzzled even Paine's admirers, including Clio Rickman. Paine was still convinced that the British government was the principal threat to global peace and democracy and that the French, the chief enemy of this enemy, were friends. It is possible that Paine's continuing political affection for Napoleon was clinched by Mme Bonneville, whom, together with her children, Paine saw a lot of throughout the summer. The Bonneville family traveled from New York City to New Rochelle at the end of April, but the visit went badly. Paine was often petulant. "Mrs. Bonneville was an encumbrance upon me all the while she was here," he said after her visit ended in mid-July. He complained that "she would not do anything, not even make an apple-dumpling for her own children." He concluded sourly, "It is certainly best that Mrs. Bonneville go into some family, as a teacher, for she has not the least talent of managing affairs for herself. She may send Bebee up to me. I will take care of him for his own sake and his father's, but this is all I have to say."[139]

Paine's fit of pique against Mme Bonneville's cluttering of his cottage involved more than the carping of an old man pestering a woman seen to be neglecting her mothering role, or even the frustration caused by fussing with a half-welcome guest about daily minutiae, when really he wanted nothing more than to sit quietly to think, read, and write. During the summer of 1805, his aging body again took revenge on his energy and patience with the world. In the first week of September, Elihu Palmer, the editor of the *Prospect*, visited him on the farm and reported that "his health is, I think, declining," adding the prediction that this "firm cog in the wheel of human life" would soon stop turning.[140]

Paine soon began to be troubled by money. He grew worried by the thought that his slowly crumbling body would plunge him into literary paralysis and mounting debt. At the end of September, utterly miserable, he wrote to Jefferson to remind him of the unhappy history of attempts to provide him with a government pension or stipend for his service as America's most prominent political writer. He implied that New York State's grant of land in New Rochelle was a pittance and urged the president to press Congress to "grant me a tract of land that I can make something of." The request sounded desperate, even pathetic. "Had it not been for the economy and extreme frugality with which I have lived I should at this time of life be in an unpleasant situation," he wrote, reminding Jefferson of his impeccable republican credentials. "I have been a volunteer to the world for thirty years without taking profits from anything I have published in America or in Europe. I have relinquished all profits that those publications might come cheap among the people for whom they were intended."[141]

Jefferson did not respond. On November 14, Paine wrote a sourly worded note asking why. Jefferson still kept silent. At the end of January 1806, blanketed by snow in his cottage, Paine wrote again, this time barely mentioning the request. Changing tack, he offered Jefferson his services as a special envoy to France, predicting that Napoleon would soon occupy Vienna, that this would end the war on the European continent, and that after securing a peace treaty among the Continental powers, including Russia, Napoleon's armies would then descend upon England, triumphantly. "It is as probable," he said, "he will be in London in six months as it was six months ago that he would be in Vienna." The whole letter hung on a string of misjudgments. These stemmed partly from his isolation in New Rochelle, but mainly they were caused by his newfound reverence for Napoleon, his dislike of William Pitt ("a poor, short-sighted politician — a man of expedients instead of a system"), and his general enthusiasm for seeing in his lifetime the destruction of the English government and its naval power and, hence, the establishment of peace and free commerce on the high seas. Paine ignored the news at hand that at the Battle of Trafalgar on October 21, 1805, Lord Nelson had destroyed the naval force of France and all but ruined Napoleon's plan to invade England. He thought it all nonsense. "Nelson's victory, as the English papers call it," he said, "will have no influence on the campaign nor on the descent."[142]

The letter revealed how rapidly Paine was losing his political senses. He seemed concerned mainly with reminding Jefferson that the French plan of invasion of the British Isles was his own. Lurking beneath that conceit was the fear that he was now being forgotten by America, whose citizen he now was. Jefferson responded politely. He informed Paine that it was the view of his government that negotiations were needed only with England and Spain and that qualified American envoys were already on the scene. The polite rejection added to Paine's loneliness. His spirits plummeted. He virtually stopped writing letters, hardly ate, rarely washed, and stubbornly refused to be attended by his housekeeper. It was reported that "the filthiness of his person and his intemperance had lost him his friends."[143] Enemies claimed that "the vile miscreant" was suffering from the palsy, and that "he is in daily practice of prayer for heavenly grace and reconciliation."[144] Wrapped in self-destruction, there remained only the evening company of Badeau's Tavern and long drafts of rum and water.

Several of his New York friends became concerned. In the first days of the spring of 1806, when the roads had thawed, William Carver traveled by horse and buggy to New Rochelle to comfort his friend. He was shocked to find him drunk, disheveled, and depressed. Paine had a ragged gray-brown beard, not having shaved for several weeks. His leggings were soiled, his buckle shoes filled with holes, and his ripped shirt "nearly the colour of tanned leather." His host "had the most disagreeable smell possible, just like that of our poor beggars in England." Carver set about washing and sobering up Paine. "Do you recollect the pains I took to clean you?" Carver asked. "That I got a tub of warm water and soap, and washed you from head to foot, and this I had to do three times, before I could get you clean. I likewise shaved you and cut your nails, that were like birds' claws." Paine reminded Carver of the biblical figure Nebuchadnezzar: "Many of your toenails exceeded half an inch in length, and others had grown round your toes, and nearly as far under they extended on top."[145]

The next morning, Carver proposed to his friend that he come to live permanently, or at least for a while, at Carver's home in New York City. Floundering in neglect, Paine accepted. Bathed, pedicured, and pale-faced, with tears in his eyes, he was bundled along with his trunk into Carver's buggy, unsure whether he would ever return to his farm.

New York Politics

The change of environment, from the rustic boredom of New Rochelle to the bustle of the Carvers' and the streets and shops of New York City, re-vivified Paine, at least for several months. Visitors reported him to be in reasonably good spirits. His figure remained tall and slender, said one of them, and for his age he retained "an uncommonly penetrating eye." He still had his wits about him, said another, and could argue with the opin-ions of others as clearheadedly as ever, though more slowly and less ener-getically than before. He lived modestly and loved to pass whole days surrounded by books and newspapers, sipping brandy just before bed. He had no more patience than usual for small talk and regarded people who talked to him about the weather as actually meaning something else. Sev-eral were struck by the "scorbutic eruptions" and bluish red blotches on his face. Everybody reported that although his health seemed tolerably good, Paine himself complained that he could "feel the effects of age."[146] His pride nevertheless compensated for creaking limbs, and he still had the energy to indulge his old habit of a mid-afternoon walk around New York. On July 4, 1806, a scorching hot and humid day, he even joined in the celebration of America's independence by accompanying two English visitors for a sprightly stroll "in the midst of the hustle" of poplar-lined Broadway, his companions expressing surprise that Paine lived "quite re-tired, and but little known or noticed."[147]

It was not yet true that Paine had slumped into obscurity. Through the Carvers, he met many artisans and laborers and their families, who treated the old citizen with respect. For them he was always "Mr. Paine," a friend of the people, the world-renowned author of the eighteenth cen-tury's three best-selling books. Paine also won considerable acclaim that summer for an essay on the cause of yellow fever. He had first entered the decade-long controversy as far back as September 1803 in a letter to Jef-ferson. "We are still afflicted with the yellow fever, and the Doctors are disputing whether it is an imported or a domestic disease," he began, quickly adding a new hypothesis to the dispute:

> Would it not be a good measure to prohibit the arrival of all vessels from the West Indies from the last of June to the middle of October? If this was done this session of Congress, and we escaped the fever next summer, we should always know how to escape it. I question if performing quarantine is a sufficient guard. The disease may be in the cargo, especially that part which is barrelled up, and not in the persons on board, and when that cargo is opened on our wharfs, the hot steaming air in contact with the

ground imbibes the infection. I can conceive that infected air can be bar-
relled up, not in a hogshead of rum, nor perhaps sucre, but in a barrel of
coffee.[148]

The proposal seemed wild at the time, but Paine was on the right track,
for it was shown subsequently that infected mosquitoes carried the disease
on board ships from the Caribbean to the eastern seaboard of the United
States. At the end of June, in James Cheetham's newspaper, the *American
Citizen,* Paine expanded the hunch but drew altogether different conclusions. The essay, whose arguments came wrapped in crisp language, displayed considerable care and reflection. Paine began by dismissing the
view of some American observers that the disease was indigenous to the
country. "No old history, that I know of, mentions such a disorder as the
yellow fever," he wrote. He then went on to show that the fever always
broke out during the summer, that it was not contagious, and that it was
always confined to "the lowest part of a populous mercantile town near
the water." Paine could have induced from these accurate observations, as
he had done to Jefferson before, that the disease was somehow imported
on board ships originating in the Caribbean. That might have led him to
the conclusion that the disease was imported by stowaway insects, flies, or
rodents or by some other living creature. Instead, he chose to offer an alternative interpretation: "The shores of the rivers at New York, and also
at Philadelphia, have on account of the vast increase of commerce, and
for the sake of making wharfs, undergone great and rapid alterations from
their natural state within a few years; and it is only in such parts of the
shores where those alterations have taken place that the yellow fever has
been produced."

How, then, was the disease generated? Paine answered by recalling the
experiments he had conducted with methane gas in the company of
George Washington. Yellow fever, he suggested, was somehow caused by
"inflammable air that arose out of the mud." The "pernicious vapour"
was generated from the "great quantities of filth or combustible matter
deposited in the muddy bottom of the river contiguous to the shore."
Prior to the construction of earth banks serving as wharves, this rubbish
and its vapors were diluted by the air and cleansed twice daily by tidal action. Now, with the tides and flow of air interrupted by docked ships and
solid embankments of earth protruding out into the water, the gas built up
in the summer — hence the annual outbreak of yellow fever among those
working and dwelling near the docks. The solution, Paine concluded, was
to alter the method of constructing new wharves and gradually to replace

the old earth embankments, switching to the cheaper method of building arched wharves resting on stone or cast-iron stilts, which would permit an uninterrupted flow of cleansing air and tides.[149]

The essay was reprinted widely in a number of states, especially in the South, and the reaction, even among Paine's most strenuous political enemies and critics, was generous. The Scotsman John Melish, who paid a call to Paine after its publication, reported to him that many readers had found the argument "the most intelligible account on the subject" and that Jefferson had called it "one of the most sensible performances on that disease, that had come under his observation." Paine puffed up with "a good deal of that literary vanity of which he has been accused," said Melish, but Paine was not able to enjoy the warm glow of public praise very long.[150] On the evening of July 25, after a light supper of bread and butter with the Carvers, Paine suffered a stroke while climbing the stairs to bed. "The fit took me on the stairs, as suddenly as if I had been shot through the head," he reported. He tumbled backward down the stairs into a motionless heap at the bottom. The Carvers were convinced that he had suffered a fatal fall. "I had neither pulse nor breathing, and the people about me supposed me dead," he recalled. Three weeks later, he reported that his "mental faculties have remained as perfect as I ever enjoyed them" but that he had been bruised so badly by the fall down the stairs "that I have not been able to get in and out of bed since that day, otherwise than being lifted out in a blanket, by two persons."[151]

Paine somehow bounced back. He told a visitor that he considered the stroke "an experiment on dying, and I find that death has no terrors for me."[152] To another visitor he sloughed off the brush with death that confined him subsequently to bed as "a hurt in the leg."[153] He surrounded himself with newspapers and spent much of the day pawing through their columns, napping, and eating the bird-size meals served to him. The few visitors who dropped in on him usually had their ears chewed off with opinionated talk. When Melish saw him, Paine vented his spleen about the English government. He curtly dismissed the contemporary reports of a rapprochement between France and England as patent poppycock. "The war must inevitably go on till the government of England falls," he snapped, growing red in the face when Melish suggested that the new Whig government might well right past wrongs. Paine shook his head. The English system of government "was radically and systematically wrong, and altogether incompatible with the present state of society," he snorted. Melish looked unimpressed. Paine persisted, curling his lip, repeating his old view that the age of revolution would sweep away the

British monarchy too. The system was doomed by the forces of history.
"No man, or set of men, would ever be able to reform it," he croaked.
The whole political system "was wrong, and it never would be set right
without a revolution, which was as certain as fate, and at no great distance
in time."[154]

Such dogmatic outbursts expressed more than either Paine's dreamy
belief in historical progress or his refusal to forgive the regime of George
III for its imperialism. His immobility obviously added to his testiness, as
did his growing feeling of neglect by the Carvers. He complained often
and loudly — with some justification. He claimed that on the night of his
stroke, the Carvers, for some reason, had left him unattended. He also felt
insulted at having been moved, after the stroke, into a tiny closet adjoining
the large unoccupied front room on the ground floor. The Carvers' request that he supply his own bedding added to his sense of humiliation.
When the first autumn frosts came, he added, his requests for warmth
were ignored. "I suffered a great deal from the cold. There ought to have
been a fire in the parlour," he said. The household atmosphere was
equally chilly. "In no case was it friendly, and in many cases not civil," he
noted. The awful service symbolized this. Mrs. Carver rarely brought him
his "tea or coffee till everybody else was served, and many times it was not
fit to drink."[155]

The Carvers, who suspected his "atheism," reciprocated by calling him
a stinking old troublemaker. Even before his stroke, they had grown to re-
sent the fact that he was not house-trained — that he cared nothing for
the daily routines of others — and that in the evenings, when others were
about to retire, he sometimes made matters worse by drinking himself
into a stupor, slumped in an armchair, from which he had to be carried to
bed. After the stroke, he went from being an unwanted guest to a burden.
Unable to wash, shave, or move about, he proved too much trouble, especially for Mrs. Carver, who arranged a part-time nurse, Mrs. Palmer, to
look after him. Paine instantly felt calmer. Mrs. Palmer, who was the
widow of his deist friend Elihu Palmer, came each day. With the help of
neighbors, who hammocked Paine in and out of bed, she changed his
sheets, ruffled his pillows, swept and aired the room, and served his meals.
The service lasted only for about two weeks, after which Mrs. Palmer, who
had not yet been paid for her work and who was not herself young, came
only intermittently. From then until mid-October 1806, when Paine was finally able to get out of bed, he "had a great deal of trouble. Sometimes
the room became so dirty that people that came to see me took notice of it
and wondered I stayed in such a place."[156]

He was hurt, angry, and depressed. Approaching his last days, and no longer able to wall off his ego against the world, Paine began to feel personally the social power of indifference and unchecked hostility. He had escaped the clutches of the English law of treason and the French Reign of Terror. Now he found himself confronted in America by a new form of discrimination: the hounding disapproval of his neighbors, the sense that public opinion was against him, and the feeling that it might well swallow up his very sense of self.

Paine tried in various ways to combat this "despotism of opinion," as Alexis de Tocqueville famously called it a generation later. During his waking hours, propped up in his bed, he fought back with his pen as best he could. The nearest target he could find was Stephen Carpenter, a Federalist journalist who published a New York newspaper called the *People's Friend and Daily Advertiser*. Carpenter sometimes wrote under the name "Cullen" or "McCullen" and was a prominent voice in the antigovernment chorus clamoring for the fortification of New York harbor against a possible invasion by the French. Paine interpreted Carpenter's editorials as warmongering Federalist nonsense and said so brashly in a series of six articles published in the *American Citizen*.[157]

During the evenings, Paine tried often to protect himself against the "despotism of opinion" by gathering friends around his bed to talk politics. There were three regulars: Thomas Addis Emmet, the distinguished Irish lawyer who had been imprisoned in Ireland for revolutionary activities and had recently emigrated to New York; John Fellows, the manager of the city waterworks in New York; and Walter Morton, a former customs official who now ran the Phoenix Insurance Company. Paine also was visited by strangers off the street and visitors to New York, many of them artisans and laborers. Sometimes the gatherings turned into heavy drinking sessions. In keeping with the custom of a time lacking artificial painkillers, Paine drank to kill pain, not sociably. He showed himself capable of consuming up to a quart of brandy, all the while telling story after story. According to Grant Thorburn, a teetotaling Presbyterian, most of the old citizen's bedside guests were from "among the lower orders, and most of them drunkards like himself."[158]

That Paine did more than drink himself into a stupor before his guests is suggested by Thorburn's own frequent bedside conversations with him. Although he thought of Paine as an emissary of the devil —"his countenance was bloated beyond description; he looked as if God had stamped his face with the mark of Cain" — Thorburn kept coming back to see him. He found Paine sharp, witty, and blessed with a "clear, strong head," a man who was a delight to argue with, especially about religion. Thorburn regularly brought a copy of the Bible with him and liked nothing better than to catch out the old deist with quotations from its text. He also thought that Paine could still receive God's mercy and be saved. Paine always balked at the suggestion. He called Thorburn "a young *enthusiast*," with a smile. One evening, Thorburn reacted sharply to the familiar rebuke. "Mr. Paine," he snapped, "here you sit, in an obscure, uncomfortable dwelling, powdered with snuff and stupefied with brandy; you, who were once the companion of Washington, Jay, and Hamilton, are now deserted by every good man; and even respectable deists cross the streets to avoid you." Paine calmly propped himself up on his bed, paused, looked Thorburn straight in the eye, and said, "I care not a straw for the opinions of the world."[159]

The world nevertheless continued to take an interest in him. The Christians continued their broadsides. "We are informed," reported *Relf's American Gazette,* "that the vile miscreant, *Thomas Paine,* having been visited by a second stroke of the palsy, is deeply impressed with the heinousness of a life spent in reviling all religion, and in contemning [*sic*] divine revelation; and that he is in daily practice of prayer, for heavenly grace and reconciliation."[160] Paine also found himself in political trouble. The opinions of the world crashed down especially hard on his head early in November 1806, when he had recovered sufficient strength to make a journey by stagecoach out to New Rochelle. The aim of the visit was to cast his votes for candidates in the state and congressional elections then being held. After being assisted from the coach by two local friends, Paine hobbled with their support to the post office. There he presented himself to the electoral inspectors, who were seated at a table, unsmiling even though they and Paine had for some years been acquainted. Paine, according to custom, filled out his tickets, folded them, and handed them to Elisha Ward, the supervisor.

"You are not an American Citizen," Ward said. Speechless for several seconds, Paine correctly deduced that Ward, from an old local Tory family, was objecting to Paine on party-political grounds. Ward tried to cover himself against exactly that suspicion. His subsequent lines had clearly been rehearsed: "Our Minister at Paris, Gouverneur Morris, would not reclaim you as an American Citizen when you were imprisoned in the Luxembourg at Paris, and General Washington refused to do it."[161] Paine reacted sharply. Pointing out that Ward's ruling was unjust because it rested on a lie, Paine said that he would prosecute Ward if he continued to deny his basic right to vote. "I will commit you to prison," Ward said in a rising voice, calling for a constable. Paine stood his ground. He said nothing. Several seconds passed, with the two men glaring at each other, until Ward, who had second thoughts, resumed his seat, still refusing to accept Paine's tickets.[162]

Paine left quietly that afternoon for New York. The disputed ballots were never counted, and a few days later Paine initiated legal proceedings against the Board of Inspectors. He hired Mr. Riker, a well-known district attorney, and, with the case placed on the docket for May 20, 1807, he wrote to James Madison, Joel Barlow, and Vice President George Clinton, asking each of them to forward a letter confirming Paine's status as an American citizen. Madison was asked to send a certified copy of the correspondence between James Monroe and then Secretary of State Edmund Randolph just before Paine's release from the Luxembourg prison. From Barlow he requested a brief testimonial reminding the court that Barlow and other Americans had petitioned the National Convention in 1794 for Paine's release from prison, on the ground that he was an American citizen. He asked Clinton to send a letter describing Paine's contributions to the struggle for independence. "As it is a new generation that has risen up since the declaration of independence," explained Paine, "they know nothing of what the political state of the country was at the time the pamphlet *Common Sense* appeared; and besides this there are but few of the old standers left, and none that I know of in this city."[163]

Paine was not mistaken about the spreading amnesia about the Revolution. Four decades after the outbreak of the struggle for independence, the hopes, hardships, and heartbreaks of the period seemed to many Americans tiny events buried in the past. The reaction of the judge and jury to Paine's case was symptomatic. Despite impressive factual evidence and the good work of the district attorney, Mr. Riker, Paine's case was dismissed.[164] His indignation was reinforced shortly after the trial by a demand from William Carver that he leave the house. What triggered Carver's demand remains unknown. An important factor was undoubtedly Paine's niggardliness, which had become compulsive and was by this time producing in him a tendency toward self-destructiveness. That in turn served to push him further to the margins of public and private respect.

Carver presented Paine with a bill covering Mrs. Palmer's service for twelve weeks and his own room and board for twenty-two weeks. Paine refused to pay, and the already-tense relationship with his old friend slid into outright hostility after Paine wrote Carver a letter bitterly hammering home his long list of complaints about the treatment he had received

during his five months with the Carvers. Carver responded toughly, reminding Paine of all that he had done for him in recent years and irritating him by repeating to his face a bit of malicious gossip that by now was
circulating behind Paine's back: that there was probably a "criminal connection" between Paine and Mme Bonneville and her children. When
pressed by Paine to clarify what he meant, Carver cruelly replied,
"Whether the boys are yours, I leave you to judge."[165]

There was not a scrap of evidence for the suggestion, but Carver undoubtedly grieved Paine. Others added to his misery by accusing him of
parsimony and overstaying his welcome. "Mr. Paine's extreme parsimony,
which disposes him to live on his friends while he has plenty of his own,
together with his intemperance," said one of his friends, Thomas Haynes,
"has alienated a great many of his friends who were firmly attached to
him for the good he had done for mankind."[166] Such talk hardened
Paine's conviction that he was being severely maltreated in his home
country. He continued to refuse to pay Carver for what he had understood
as an unconditional, compassionate offer of room and board during a period when he was down-and-out and could not practically cope with the
everyday world. John Fellows intervened in the dispute between Paine and
Carver, settling the bill and arranging alternative accommodations for
Paine and Mrs. Palmer in a boardinghouse in Corelear's Hook, across the
East River in Brooklyn. Paine, fearing deathly isolation, refused to go.
Only after considerable fuss did he accept an offer of accommodations at
85 Church Street, at the quarters of the painter John Wesley Jarvis.

Paine stayed there from mid-November 1806 until the following spring.
He liked the run-down bachelor surroundings and fissiparous lifestyle of
the energetic twenty-six-year-old Jarvis, who clearly took to Paine as well,
describing him as "one of the most pleasant companions I have met with
for an old man."[167] Paine had been flattered by Jarvis's oil painting of him
the previous year. Although it was one of the young artist's earliest known
works, the brushwork was assured and relied on the quite complex technique of laying on semitransparent tones. Paine was presented as a gentleman dressed in a bunched white-lace ruffle and a velvet-collared olive
cape, softly contrasted against a clear brown background. Jarvis chose to
paint his subject's flesh in Stuart-like colors, which made Paine look considerably younger than sixty-eight years and served to hide his large red
nose. Paine's cheeks looked ruddy, not inflamed with "scorbutic eruptions," and his mouth and eyes were softened. Paine's neatly brushed hair
was painted in dark brown, shot through with gray, complementing the
dark olive-gray pupils of his eyes.

Paine genuinely enjoyed Jarvis's company. He found him hardworking, honest, and fun loving. There were frequent visitors to Church Street, nicknamed Bachelors' Hall, and most found Jarvis easygoing and equipped with a wicked sense of humor. Whenever guests broached the subject of great men, he always laughed and pointed to a brass nutmeg grater on the dining room mantelpiece, saying, "There's a greater!" Paine also liked to bounce his attacks on religion off Jarvis, who remained skeptical of Paine's deism. During this period, Paine found time and energy enough to write an *Essay on Dream,* which cheekily scoffed at the Bible by pointing out its heavy reliance on the device of telling the Christian story by means of dreams.[168] The essay mostly attracted silence in the press. With a pinch of paranoia and a touch of deluded grandeur, Paine explained away the lousy reception by accusing his enemies of learning the art of cunning. "They know that if they abuse it, everybody will obtain it," he told Jarvis. The obvious move to make, replied Jarvis, was to write a sequel to *The Age of Reason* bearing an appealing title such as *Paine's Recantation.* Jarvis then became serious: "You know the time must soon come, when like Voltaire and others, you will recant all you have said on the subject of religion." Paine was not impressed. He said he did not believe the anecdote about Voltaire's deathbed confession, adding, "I do not know what I may do when infested by disease and pain. I may become a second child; and designing people may entrap me into saying anything; or they may put into my mouth, what I never said." Until that moment, Paine concluded, he would stick tenaciously, through thick and thin, to "his already written opinions."[169]

He had a chance to do just that one afternoon when his usual nap after lunch was interrupted by an unexpected guest. An old woman rapped on the door, insisting to Jarvis, who greeted her, that she wished to see Paine. Jarvis explained that he was asleep and did not wish to be disturbed. "I am sorry for that," said the stranger, "for I want to see him very particularly." Persuaded that it was important business, Jarvis broke a house rule and ushered the woman into the bedroom. Paine stirred, propped himself up on one elbow, and, "with an expression of eye that staggered the old woman back a step or two," asked her, "What do you want?" She asked, "Is your name Paine?" Paine nodded. The woman paused, then continued: "Well, then, I come from Almighty God, to tell you that if you do not repent of your sins and believe in our blessed Saviour Jesus Christ, you will be damned and" — Paine cut her short. "Pooh, pooh, it is not true. You were not sent with any such impertinent message. Jarvis, make her go away. Pshaw, He would not send such a foolish ugly old woman as you about with His message. Go away. Go back. Shut the door." Shocked by his forthrightness, the guest left, dismayed, mumbling references to the devil, her hands raised above her head.[170]

Such incidents added zest to Paine's existence at Jarvis's, but they did not compensate for his feelings of futility. As the winter slowly passed, Paine found himself ever more depressed, especially when Jarvis was absent in the evenings, which was often. Jarvis's social life was vigorous. He liked to drink and play into the wee hours of the morning, and he loved the company of unconventional women, so much so that some said that his taste for "mysterious marriages" prevented him from establishing "respectable communion with ladies." After one night of carousing, Jarvis returned home at around four in the morning to find Paine spread-eagled on the living room floor. "I have the vertigo, the vertigo," croaked Paine. "Yes," snapped Jarvis as he eyed a half-empty rum bottle on a nearby table. "You have it deep — deep."

Jarvis always insisted, against the persistent public rumors, that Paine was not a drunkard. He emphasized that whenever he was in company, he drank in moderation, if he drank at all, and that he hit the bottle only when he was feeling lonely and in pain. Jarvis's support lifted Paine, but inevitably his stiff joints and aching limbs fed his feelings of isolation, which became so acute in April 1807 that he simply could no longer cope at Jarvis's. "A convenient place to board at will suit me better," Paine confessed to his friends Binny and Ronaldson, "because it will be less trouble, than keeping house."[171] Jarvis had plans at that time to move to new quarters, so during that month Paine packed his trunk — for the third time in a year — and moved in with Zakarias Hitt, a baker, who lived with his wife and children on Broome Street, on the outskirts of the city.

The *Public Advertiser*

Paine lodged with the Hitts for the next ten months, in moderate comfort. For the sum of five dollars a week, he rented a tiny bedroom and an adjoining parlor, which contained a desk where Paine read and wrote whenever he had the energy. Few visitors made the journey out to Broome Street, and in his letters of this period Paine complained often of his enforced isolation from the world. "What are you about?" he asked Joel Barlow a fortnight after settling in at the Hitts'. "You sometimes hear of me but I never hear of you." Then followed a string of impatient requests. "What is Fulton about? Is he taming a whale to draw his submarine boat? I wish you would desire Mr. Smith to send me his country *National Intelli-*

gencer. It is printed twice a week without advertisement. I am somewhat at a loss of want of authentic intelligence."[172]

Letters from old friends and supporters were infrequent. When they did come, he was immensely cheered. Thomas Hardy wrote from England to tell him that his "labour is not altogether lost in this country for all the gloom that overshadows us. There are many who are silently reading and meditating on what you have written and lamenting that those pure principles are not put in practice."[173] Paine dealt with the prolonged isolation by indulging nightly in rum — Hitt said he always drank less than a pint each night — and pouring himself into his writing during the day.

Given his age and declining health, Paine proved to be remarkably productive with his quill during the year 1807. Just before moving to the Hitts', he had decided to switch allegiance from the *American Citizen* to the *Public Advertiser,* mainly because he had become convinced that the editor of the former paper, James Cheetham, had begun to waver in his Republican loyalties. The dispute reached the boiling point when Cheetham attempted to tamper with one of Paine's contributions. "I, sir," said Paine, "never permit anyone to alter anything that I write; you have spoiled the whole sense that it was meant to convey on the subject." Cheetham insisted on his right to edit for his readers. "It was too harsh to appear in print," he said. "That was not your business to determine," replied Paine, and with that went straight to Jacob Frank, editor of the *Public Advertiser.*[174]

It is possible that following the falling-out with Cheetham, Paine was asked to join the editorial board of the *Public Advertiser,* although the exact relationship he had with other editors is not known. That he controlled the paper — as opposition newspapers such as the *Boston Gazette* charged — is unlikely. That he was either an editorial consultant or a full member of the board of editors is suggested by his agreement with the avowed Jeffersonian leanings of the paper, the presentation of several of his pieces as editorials, and the printing of at least one contribution as an unsigned feature.

Whether Paine held any editorial post or not, he undoubtedly used the new outlet to air his political views. Many of his contributions grappled with the problem of how to protect freedom of expression against licentious use of the press. During the month of April 1807, no less than five of Paine's pieces appeared in the *Public Advertiser.* "Of Gun-Boats" called for a more imaginative debate on the future defense of New York and reiterated Paine's long-standing belief in the military flexibility and superiority of flat-bottomed boats equipped with cannon.[175] Two other essays, "Remarks, on a String of Resolutions offered by Mr. Hale, to the New York

House of Representatives at Albany" (April 3) and "Remarks on Mr. Hale's String of Resolves Concluded" (April 4), praised New York State for consolidating its impost revenues for the general benefit and commercial prosperity of the Union. In the same month, Paine addressed three indignant open letters to the state's governor, Morgan Lewis. At the time, Lewis was engaged in suing for damages against one of Paine's political allies, Thomas Farmar, who had chaired a public meeting that voted to censure the governor for his alleged pro-Federalism. Lewis was claiming the sum of $100,000, which Paine considered legally and morally absurd. The public meeting had exercised citizens' legal right of public assembly and free expression, the results of which could not legally be blamed on Farmar. "The resolves of a meeting," Paine insisted, "are not the act of the chairman." Governor Lewis's claim reeked of Federalist pomposity. "He is not governor *jure divino*," snapped Paine, "nor is he covered with the magical mantle which covers a king of England, that HE can do no wrong; nor is the governorship of the state his property, or the property of his family connections."

According to Paine, Lewis's claim was symptomatic of a bad trend in American politics in which some citizens were making a business of libel. "It often happens," he wrote, "that the prosecutor for damages is himself the calumniator. . . . As the matter stands at present, a rogue has a better chance than an honest man." Paine went on to complain that he had been publicly abused more often than any other living figure in the United States, Jefferson excepted, but that he had on principle refused to make a business of prosecuting his calumniators. "Had there been a law to punish calumny and lying by penalty and the money to be given to the poor," he said, "I would have done it. But as to damages, as I do not believe they have character of their own to endamage mine, I could claim none."[176]

In midsummer 1807, Paine's attention turned to the continuing controversy about the defense of New York harbor. "He looks better than last year," reported the English painter William Constable, who together with his brother Daniel visited Paine in mid-July. "He read us an essay on national defence, comparing the different expenses and powers of gunboats and ships of war and batteries in protecting a sea coast."[177] The Constable brothers may not have known that Paine had already taken an interest in the subject of gunboats for more than a decade and that he had always considered them as offensive weapons against the English navy. But now, in the *Public Advertiser* of July 21, 1807, he advocated the defensive use of a large fleet of small gunboats, mobile and fast, instead of bulky and clumsy warships. Gunboats required few repairs, drew little water, and, above all, were cheap to build. A fleet of seventy-four gunboats, he estimated, would cost around $296,000, whereas a single warship equipped with seventy-four guns would cost around $500,000. On top of that, wrote Paine, "gunboats, being moved by oars, cannot be deprived of motion by calms, for the calmer the weather the better for the boat." It followed that "a hostile ship becalmed in any of our waters, can be taken by gunboats moved by oars." The conclusion to be drawn was clear, if surprising: "*Gunboats in calms are the sovereign ships.*"[178]

Paine spent the late summer and early autumn elaborating these ideas. On August 6, 1807, again writing under the nom de plume "An Old Friend of '76," he discussed Benjamin Franklin's original proposal for blocking the Delaware River during the first phase of the Revolution, repeating the points on August 18 in a brief address called "To the People of New York." Four days later, he laid into James Cheetham and attacked proposals to defend New York by turning the shipping channels around the city into obstacle courses cluttered with artificially created pylons built of earth and stone. As always, Paine's contributions triggered backbiting, some of it satirical. The *New-York Evening Post* even printed a poem attacking him:

> TOM PAINE *has exploded the old-fashioned notion,*
> *That ships of the line are the lords of the ocean;*
> *And shows how a gunboat with only one gun,*
> *In a calm* can occasion a *first-rate to run;*
> *Nay more, he had prov'd (to cut the thing shorter)*
> *The gunboat can blow the first-rate out of water;*
> *Then let nations be told, who* great navies *have arm'd,*
> *The Sovereign of Ships, is a* — gunboat becalmed![179]

Cheetham also jumped on Paine, accusing him of plagiarism from the works of John Locke, political stupidity, and drunkenness. At one point, he concluded, "I advise Mr. Paine, as a friend, to write no more."[180] Paine seemed unperturbed by the attacks — it was, after all, better to quarrel than to be lonely — and he certainly gave as good as he received. "It is a great deal that may be learned from absurdity," wrote Paine in August, "and I expect to learn something from James Cheetham. When I do, I will let him know it in the Public Advertiser."[181] His words soon hardened. "Is James Cheetham an ideot [sic]," he asked a fortnight later, "or has the envy and malignity of his mind possessed him with a spirit of wilful lying?"[182] A few weeks later, in a blistering attack that appeared

anonymously in the *Public Advertiser* as "Cheetham and His Tory Paper,"
Paine accused him of "seeking to involve the United States in a quarrel
with France for the benefit of England."[183]

Pugnacious Pauper

The polemics hurled at Cheetham later cost Paine dearly, for they so personally irritated Cheetham that he was moved to publish the first vicious
biography of Paine after his death.[184] Paine did not know that Cheetham
(or "Cheat 'em," as Paine called him) was already collecting material on
his life, and, in any case, Paine was preoccupied with making ends meet.
Early in 1808, he was confronted once again with the specter of homelessness on the streets of New York after Zakarias Hitt notified him that the
charge for his room and board would rise immediately from five to seven
dollars a week.

Paine told Hitt that he could not afford to pay the increase. He said
that although he owned a farm and cottage in New Rochelle and a house
on a lot in Bordentown, he was reluctant to sell them now. Like all people
of limited means facing the end of their lives, he grew deeply apprehensive about the future. "I hold my health very well," he told James Monroe,
"but I am a great deal disabled in my powers of walking."[185] Mme
Bonneville reported that he did not want to draw on his assets yet because
although "he expected to live to a very great age, as his ancestors had before him," he also "saw his means daily diminish, while he feared a total
palsy."[186] He grew alarmed at the thought that getting about would become ever more difficult and that soon he might be permanently bedrid-
den and totally dependent on others.

For years Paine had empathized with the private troubles faced by elderly citizens. In *Agrarian Justice* and other publications, he had proposed a
public solution calling for inheritors of land to be taxed, the money being
used to establish a "national fund" to finance a scheme of old-age pensions payable annually to everyone age fifty and over, enabling these citizens "to live in old age without wretchedness, and go decently out of the
world." With schemes of this kind virtually a century away,[187] he was
forced to deal with his wretchedness privately. On January 21, 1808, he
wrote a desperate letter to Congress, asking its representatives for reim-
bursement of the costs of the trip he had made as a private citizen to
France with John Laurens during 1781. "As I never had a cent for this service," he wrote, "I feel myself entitled, as the country is now in a state of
prosperity, to state the case to Congress." He claimed that there was prob-

ably no recorded instance of a public figure in ancient and modern times who displayed such selflessness as his, adding, "All the civilized world know[s] I have been of great service to the United States, and have generously given away talent that would have made me a fortune."[188]

It was a long shot — most representatives surely would not have even known of the expedition — and it proved, after a long and painful wait, to be very wide of the mark. Paine's conceit, expressed more crudely than ever as a defense against his daily fears of falling into pauperism, probably did not help his case. Sensing that he would get nowhere with an unsympathetic Congress, he conceded, perhaps with the prompting of Mme Bonneville, that he would have to sell off at least part of the farm in New Rochelle. A buyer was found, and Paine's hopes lifted, but shortly after the contract was signed, the prospective buyer died. The agreement, which would have brought Paine ten thousand dollars, collapsed after he agreed, for compassionate reasons, to accept the widow's request to be released from the contract.

Socially isolated, unable to walk properly, and with only a few coins in his pocket, Paine had no alternative but to leave the Hitts'. A few weeks after his seventy-first birthday, he was ferried by coach with his bundle of belongings to 63 Partition Street. He lodged there for the next five months above a small, cheap tavern where each night "a sixpenny show" was put on for the rough and drunken clientele. The stench and squalor plunged the already-disheveled Paine into despair. He lost weight, cried often, and rarely washed or shaved. His room went untidied for weeks on end. On Partition Street, "he had no care taken of him," a contemporary remarked, and "he was left entirely to himself."[189]

Throughout the tavern ordeal, Paine somehow managed to keep up his correspondence with Congress. His claim for money was really a claim for dignity, and it kept him alive, furnishing him with boundaries and providing him with a measure of the hope so necessary for survival in despair. On February 14, he wrote to the Committee of Claims in the House of Representatives, which by that time had been passed his request for a stipend. He detailed his involvement in the Silas Deane affair, reminded the committee that because of his integrity during that affair, one of its predecessors, after voting him a stipend of three thousand dollars, had subsequently taken revenge on him by refusing to pay that grant. He concluded, "I prevented Dean[e]'s fraudulent demand being paid, and so far the country is obliged to me; but I became the victim of my integrity."[190] Two weeks later, he wrote a polite follow-up letter to the speaker of the House of Representatives. "It will be convenient to me to know what

Congress will decide on," he wrote, then introducing a veiled threat: "it will determine me whether, after so many years of generous services, and that in the most perilous times, and after seventy years of age, I shall continue in this country, or offer my services to some other country."[191] The threat, coming from a broken-down old man who could barely walk, was, of course, wooden, and those representatives who supported his views and knew something of his current circumstances must have felt a pang of sadness as they read his forlorn request.

Paine, always a fighter, persisted all the same. At the end of the first week of March 1808, he wrote again to the speaker of the House. This time he sounded wounded and impatient, his words laced with desperation. He complained "that the committee keep everything to themselves, and do nothing" and expressed his growing contempt for its slovenliness: "If my memorial was referred to the Committee of Claims, for the purpose of losing it, it is unmanly [unforthright] policy. After so many years of service my heart grows cold towards America."[192] His heart froze as the days, weeks, and months passed without his hearing so much as a word from Congress. On July 8, ground down by the saga, he wrote a final letter to Thomas Jefferson, which included a weakly worded request that he talk to the chairman of the Committee of Claims, David Holmes. Jefferson replied, telling him politely that the committee was likely to refuse Paine's wish. According to Mme Bonneville, the old man "was deeply grieved at this refusal."[193]

It took the Committee of Claims until February 1 of the following year to reply formally, and then in formal language more suited to a bureaucracy. It explained to Paine the several grounds on which his request for compensation had been rejected. His original memorial had been "unaccompanied with any evidence in support of the statement of facts." Moreover, the committee insisted that the journals of Congress contained no evidence that Paine "was in any manner connected with the mission of Colonel Laurens." It conceded that he had accompanied Laurens on the mission, quickly adding, however, that it did not appear from the records "that he was employed by the Government, or even solicited by any officer thereof to aid in the accomplishment of the mission with which Colonel Laurens was intrusted, or that he took any part whatever, after his arrival in France, in forwarding the negotiation." The conclusion of the committee report must have been insulting to Paine: "That Mr. Paine rendered great and eminent services to the United States, during their struggle for liberty and independence, cannot be doubted by any person acquainted with his labours in the cause, and attached to the principles of the contest. Whether he has been generously requited by his country for his meritorious exertions, is a question not submitted to your Committee, or within their province to decide."[194]

"Infinite Pain"

By the time Paine received the committee's report, he had slipped farther below the horizon of public dignity. During the early summer of 1808, his living conditions had so deteriorated that friends who visited him on Partition Street were shocked at the squalor. During July, several friends, possibly Thomas Addis Emmet and Walter Morton, took things into their own hands. Behind his back, they arranged other accommodations at the house of Mr. and Mrs. Cornelius Ryder on Herring Street in Greenwich, then a village about a mile and a half north of the city. One warm morning, they arrived in a chaise, bundled his belongings into it, and whisked him away in his nightshirt to his new lodgings, Paine grumbling all the way.

Paine quickly accepted that he was better off at the Ryders'. The care he received was adequate, and the atmosphere was friendly enough. He had a room of his own on the ground floor, and he was served several hot meals a day by Mrs. Ryder. Although the weekly rent rose from eight to ten and then to twenty dollars, Paine managed to make ends meet by agreeing, under pressure from his friends, to the sale of his house and seven acres of meadowland in Bordentown to John Oliver for the sum of eight hundred dollars. At this point in life, his elementary daily needs far outweighed money. By now his appetite even for bread and milk had waned, the strength had gone completely from both his legs, and he had to be carried to and from his bed several times a day. He "hated soap and water" (said Cornelius Ryder), required help when using his chamber pot, and shaving himself — no barber was willing to travel out from the city — proved to be a weekly trial. He spent most of his waking hours sitting in his room at a table covered with books and newspapers. He read and dozed, scribbled with his quill, and daydreamed, looking out on Herring Street and the nearby State Prison.

At times he fell into severe depression. Ryder said that he often came upon Paine in tears and that in those moods he usually craved human company and was quickly cheered by a moment's conversation, a touch of the hand on his shoulder, or a smile. Paine mostly kept his troubles to himself. He complained to almost everyone in the neighborhood — to people such as Samuel Brower, John Holdron, and Amasa Woodsworth — about his inability to walk, but he generally suffered in silence his most serious complaints about calumny, neglect, and public mistreatment. Visitors came rarely, but those who did come found him surprisingly sharp-witted for his age and circumstances. They remarked, as others throughout his life had done, on his flashing black eyes. One enamored guest said that they "were full, lucid, and indicated his true character." Another visitor, the prominent ornithologist Alexander Wilson, who arrived at the Ryders' to find Paine "sitting wrapped in a nightgown, the table before him covered with newspapers — with pen and ink beside them," was sure that his keen eyes symbolized his brilliance as a public figure. "The penetration and intelligence of his eye bespeak the man of genius and of the world," he said. Yet another guest was struck by his lingering love of political discussion. "His conversation was calm and gentleman-like," he said, "except when religion or party politics were mentioned. In this case he became irascible, and the deformity of his face, rendered so by intemperance, was then disgusting."[195]

At the end of August, Paine lunged once more with his quill at James Cheetham, whom he denounced in the *Public Advertiser* as an "imposter," a "foolish" critic of Napoleon, and a hireling of the English government, which he said he despised more than ever. Probably during the same month he pitched into Calvinist fundamentalism and its "false doctrine of the Bible." The defiantly worded conclusion was designed to scotch rumors that he was turning into a Christian. "Nonsense," he thundered, "ought to be treated as nonsense wherever it be found."[196] The crudely written attacks on Cheetham and Christianity were to be the last pieces he ever published (the latter posthumously). With the coming of autumn 1808, Paine's literary and bodily energy disappeared. He was forced to spend most of his time in bed, surrounded by newspapers, which he still loved to read but which he now found physically exhausting. During his wakeful moments, on good days, he scribbled notes to himself on various political and religious matters. Just before Christmas, sensing that his hourglass had been turned for the last time, he began to sketch out his final will. With the help of his executors, Walter Morton and Thomas Addis Emmet, it took three weeks from beginning to end to complete a final draft acceptable to Paine. He signed it on January 18, 1809, in the presence of William Keese, James Angevine, and Cornelius Ryder.

Paine had made two previous wills, saying on each occasion that "he had believed such and such one to be his friend, and that now having altered his belief in them, he had also altered his will."[197] The final will reflected the same principle that his friendships came and went and that only those close to him at present were entitled to something from his estate, if estate it could be called. To the executors, Morton and Emmet, he bequeathed two hundred dollars each, while to Mrs. Elihu Palmer he granted the sum of one hundred dollars. The money, in each case, would come from the sale of the northern section of his New Rochelle farm at present occupied by Andrew Dean. Whatever money was left over from that sale and the bequests would be divided equally between Clio Rickman and Nicolas de Bonneville. To Mme Marguerite Bonneville he bequeathed, "for her own sole and separate use," the "thirty shares I hold in the New York Phoenix Insurance Company, which cost me fourteen hundred and seventy dollars, they are worth now upwards of fifteen hundred dollars, and all my movable effects, and also the money that may be in my trunk or elsewhere at the time of my decease, paying thereout the expenses of my funeral."

The largest single item of bequest was the one-hundred-acre southern section of the New Rochelle farm. Paine instructed that it be used by Mme Bonneville to maintain and educate Thomas and Benjamin Bonneville, "in order that she may bring them well up, give them good and useful learning, and instruct them in their duty to God, and the practise of morality." Paine then explained in detail his final resting place. "I know not if the Society of people called Quakers, admit a person to be buried in their burying ground, who does not belong to their Society," he wrote, "but if they do, or will admit me, I would prefer being buried there; my father belonged to that profession, and I was partly brought up in it." His vision of the graveyard site was exact. The place where he was to be buried should be "a square of twelve feet, to be enclosed with rows of trees, and a stone or post and rail fence, with a headstone with my name and age engraved upon it, author of 'Common Sense.'" Paine concluded with a solemn summary of his earthly journey: "I have lived an honest and useful life to mankind; my time has been spent in doing good, and I die in perfect composure and resignation to the will of my Creator, God."[198]

After Paine signed the will, his condition worsened, as if he had nothing more to live for and wanted only to go quietly to his final resting place. He received constant attention from the Ryders — Walter Morton had arranged a corresponding increase in the rent — and those around him, including the physician Dr. James R. Manley, became convinced that his days were numbered. On February 25, 1809, Manley reported Paine to be "indisposed with fever and very apprehensive of an attack of apoplexy." Manley agreed to take on Paine as a patient, and from then on he examined him every day, prescribing no medicines, since none seemed more effective than a gentle chat and a check of his pulse. During the first week of March, Paine began to suffer "infinite pain." He cried out, and cried, often. His stomach swelled up, which "indicated dropsy, and that of the worst description," reported Manley. He also developed ulcerous sores on his ankles and on the toes and soles of his feet, which became badly inflamed and infected by the urine he passed involuntarily in bed.[199]

Mme Bonneville visited him every other day. The two spoke often about Paine's anxieties about the contents of his will. He worried in particular about his final resting place and said he wanted to speak to a member of the Society of Friends. On March 19, he was visited by Willett Hicks, a Quaker and neighbor of the Ryders. "I am now in my seventy-third year," Paine told him, "and do not expect to live long. I wish to be buried in your burying ground. I could be buried in the Episcopal church, but they are so arrogant; or in the Presbyterian, but they are so hypocritical."[200] Hicks conveyed Paine's request sympathetically to the local Friends, but it was refused. Hicks reported back that the society felt that Paine's own friends and sympathizers "might wish to raise a monument to his memory, which being contrary to their rules, would render it inconvenient to them." The news plunged Paine into tears. He sobbed uncontrollably and then fell into a protracted silence. He uttered not another word until the following day, when Mme Bonneville paid him a visit. She promised to arrange for him to be buried on his farm. "I have no objection to that," said Paine, calmer but not placated. "The farm will be sold, and they will dig my bones up before they be half rotten."

As Paine's discomfort worsened daily, he lost his taste for conversation. He felt utterly alone. Dying, not death, proved terrible. He confided to Manley, "I think I can say what *they* make Jesus Christ to say — My God, my God, why hast thou forsaken me?" With tears in his eyes, he pleaded on several occasions with Mme Bonneville to move to Greenwich so that she could be at his bedside constantly. She hesitated, worrying that the disruption might hasten his decline or that he might very soon die, then consented. On May 4, Paine was carried eighty yards in an armchair to the rooms she had rented at 59 Grove Street, a small house owned by John Holbron.

The move had an instant calming effect on him, as if it had prompted him into consenting to fate, rather than accepting it begrudgingly. For about a week, looked after by Mrs. Hedden, he felt strong enough to receive visitors for brief periods during part of the afternoons. Sometimes he was pleased by the company, which included William Carver, who came especially to apologize to him, and Willett Hicks, who visited every day. His friend Captain Daniel Pelton made a special trip from New Rochelle to see him. Twice a week, the gourmand physician Dr. Nicholas Romayne dropped in. Paine also was delighted to see Jacob Frank, who brought him a copy of the *Public Advertiser* of May 12, 1809, which honored Paine by reprinting *The American Crisis XIII*, explaining "that Mr. Paine had entertained a proper idea of the interests and destinies of the whole United States, while many of us were in the day of early infancy, in *other countries*, or rocked in our cradles during the period that 'tried men's souls.'"[201]

Paine was less pleased with other guests. Sometimes he was irascible. "*I am very sorry that I ever returned to this country*," he told Albert Gallatin and his wife, Hannah Nicholson Gallatin, in an unprovoked bitter outburst.[202] When Mrs. Gallatin's sister, Kitty Nicholson Few, visited him the following day, he lashed out with razor-sharp precision. He refused to shake hands. "You have neglected me," he grunted, as she began to sit by his bed, "and I beg you will leave the room."[203] She went straight out into the garden and wept. The collector of customs of New York City, David Gelston, suffered the same fate. He was ordered out of the house after he claimed to have received a letter from James Monroe insisting that Paine owed him money, which was to be collected by the officer and passed on to Monroe's children.

There were also unwanted religious visitors. Most of them were concerned to save the soul of the famous scalawag Paine by somehow extracting his precious eleventh-hour confession. A Quaker neighbor, Stephen Grellet, claimed to hear a confession from Paine, whom he reported to be in a very wretched state. The Reverend Jedediah Randall claimed to have heard the same.[204] But John Wesley Jarvis, who visited Paine several times for the same purpose, came away empty-handed. On the subject of Jesus Christ, said Jarvis, Paine "expressed a continued belief in his written opinions." And a fortnight before he died, two other visitors, the Reverends Cunningham and Milledollar, well-known Presbyterian ministers, had no luck. After being greeted at the front door by the housekeeper, Mrs. Hedden, the two men pushed their way past her, claiming that they had urgent news for Paine. Cunningham did the talking: "Mr. Paine, we visit you as friends and neighbours: you have now a full view of death, you cannot live long, and whoever does not believe in Jesus Christ will assuredly be damned." Milledollar then perorated, but Paine cut him short. Propped up in his bed by cushions, he leaned forward slightly, glanced toward the door, and said, "Let me have none of your popish stuff. Get away with you, good morning, good morning." As the men were leaving, he called out to Mrs. Hedden, "Do not let them come here again, they intrude upon me."[205]

Paine expected death, according to those around him, from around the middle of May 1809. "He was very feeble," Mrs. Hedden recalled, "quite to all appearance, exhausted. Poor man, how I felt for him! How I wished he was a Christian!" During the day, virtually every hour, she read him passages from the Bible. Those reading sessions had no religious significance, at least as far as Paine was concerned. They served instead to soothe him with language, reassuring him that he was not alone, that he was still of this world. He craved company and needed constant reassurance that there was someone in the same room. "He would be a day without speaking a word, except asking — 'is nobody in the room — who's there?'" reported Mrs. Hedden. Manley confirmed that "if, as it would sometimes unavoidably happen, he was left alone, he would scream and holler, until some person came to him."[206]

The spell of hugging the world with every last ounce of strength quickly passed. Paine soon drifted into a state of drowsiness, punctuated by wakeful moments and cries of pain. "Oh, Lord help me! Oh, Lord help me!" he called out, half twisting in vain attempts to relieve the agony caused by bedsores spreading across his body. Manley observed that the ulcers were now "excessively fetid and discoloured" and that they had "assumed a gangrenous appearance." Convinced that Paine's time on earth was nearly up, he made one final attempt, using the combined powers of medicine and organized religion, to force his patient to recant. On the evening of June 7, during one of Paine's last wakeful moments, Manley asked in slow, deliberate speech, "Mr. Paine, you have not answered my questions — will you answer them? Allow me to ask again, Do you believe, or let me qualify the question, Do you wish to believe that Jesus Christ is the son of God?"

A clock in Paine's bedroom ticked clangorously, slowly, precisely. Death dressed in pale clothes approached his bedside. Paine responded softly, "I have no wish to believe on that subject."[207] He then let go of the world. His eyes closed; his head sank into his pillow; his breathing grew heavier. Paine spent a comfortable night, dying in his sleep around nine o'clock on the overcast morning of June 8, 1809.

Notes

❧

Nearly two centuries after the death of Thomas Paine, a complete edition of his works remains to be prepared. Scholars and interested general readers currently have no alternative but to consult three different, flawed editions of his works. Moncure Conway's four-volume *Writings of Thomas Paine* (New York, 1894–1896) remains the most carefully edited. William M. Van der Weyde's nine-volume *Life and Works of Thomas Paine* (New Rochelle, 1925) is the most enthusiastic of the three efforts. Philip S. Foner's two-volume *Complete Writings of Thomas Paine* (New York, 1945) continues to be the most extensive source. Considered together, these three editions have preserved for subsequent generations of readers invaluable parts of Paine's oeuvre. Each publication is nonetheless marked by major flaws. Known items written by Paine are excluded for reasons of space or from carelessness. Some well-known publications are mistitled, improperly dated, or reprinted or translated inaccurately. Eager to boost Paine's reputation, each edition contains several items that were almost certainly not written by Paine himself.

During the preparation of this biography, these standard editions of Paine's writings served as a starting point for my efforts to locate and examine firsthand the original sources. I have managed to identify some 620 individual contributions by Paine, and the resulting bibliography is to be published as *The Writings of Thomas Paine, 1737–1809: A Guide*. The bibliography aims to help smooth the way for a meticulously researched edition of Paine's writings that, for the time being, can be called comprehensive.

The bibliography lists books, pamphlets, essays, feuilletons, published notes, letters, songs, and poems, all listed chronologically so as to highlight the recurrent themes and developing emphases in Paine's publishing career. Every item in the bibliography was consulted during the course of research for this biography. At least seventy items have not hitherto been available to or used by Paine's biographers. Most of these items are referred to in the following notes. Those works of Paine which are of doubtful authenticity, or whose actual place or time of writing are unknown, or (in the case of letters) whose addressees are anonymous, are marked with square brackets and question marks.

1. THETFORD DAYS

1. Recorded in the note by H. F. Killick, written around 1900, in Thetford Borough Council, *Early Records* (T/C1/17/31). Useful discussions of the history of Thetford include Thomas Martin, *The History of the Town of Thetford, in the Counties of Norfolk and Suffolk. From the Earliest Accounts to the Present Time* (London, 1779); Chad Goodwin, "Thomas Paine's Thetford: Eighteenth Century," in *Thetford: Antiq Burg* (Thetford, 1985), 30–33; Alan Crosby, *A History of Thetford* (Chichester, 1986), especially chapter 5. My interview with Oliver Bone, curator of the Ancient House Museum in Thetford, on January 7, 1991, also proved useful.

2. W. G. Clarke, *Notebooks Concerning the History of Thetford,* MS 125 (T131D) L7322 (a), Norfolk Record Office. See also the descriptions of the gaol in John Howard, *The State of the Prisons in England and Wales* (London, 1780), 251, 256; Vindex, *A Review of the Arguments for Removing the Lent-Assizes from Thetford to Norwich. With the Representation of the Magistrates, the Petition from the City of Norwich, and Other Documents* (Thetford: S. Mills, 1824); Lord Suffield, Henry Best, et al., "Lent Assizes, from Thetford to Norwich," *Norwich Mercury,* June 19, 1824. The following also draws upon several interviews with historian David Osborne, conducted in Thetford between January 1991 and October 1993.

3. T. L. G. Burley, *Playhouses and Players of East Anglia* (Norwich, 1928).

4. Sir William Blackstone, *Commentaries on the Laws of England. Book the Third* (Oxford, 1768), 59. Of background interest is the introductory address delivered in defense of the assize system nearly seventy years earlier by Lord Chief Justice Oliver St. John. The full version of his speech is printed as "The Introduction to My Charge att the Assises att Thetford in Norfolke the 21 March 1657," *Proceedings of the American Philosophical Society* 130, no. 1 (1986): 47–78. The remarks of François de la Rochefoucauld on the assize system also are of interest. See his *A Frenchman's Year in Suffolk, 1784,* ed. Norman Scarfe (Woodbridge, 1988), 79–91.

5. *Suffolk Mercury: or, Bury Post,* March 14, 1737.

6. *Norwich Mercury,* March 26, 1737.

7. Ian Gilmour, *Riot, Risings and Revolution: Governance and Violence in Eighteenth Century England* (London, 1992); J. S. Cockburn, ed., *Crime in England 1550–1800* (London, 1977).

8. Francis Blomefield, *An Essay Towards a Topographical History of the County of Norfolk*, vol. 2 (London, 1805), 1.

9. Robert Bloomfield, "Barnham Water," in *The Works of Robert Bloomfield* (London, 1890), 197. Years later (Robert Bloomfield to Clio Rickman, May 29, 1804), Bloomfield criticized Paine as "the vainest of all authors. My circle of friends have long ago regreted that his great mind should descend so as to disgust his readers by boasting of himself."

10. The following account of the Graftons draws upon an interview with the eleventh duke of Grafton at the Euston estate on June 20, 1992. See also Richard Barber, *Euston Hall* (Ipswich, n.d.); Sylvia Colman, *The Church of St. Genevieve, Euston* (Euston, 1986); La Rochefoucauld, *A Frenchman's Year in Suffolk*, 34–36, 39–40, 46–50, 156.

11. La Rochefoucauld, *A Frenchman's Year in Suffolk*, 156–157.

12. Daniel Defoe, *A Tour Through the Whole Island of Great Britain*, vol. 1 (1722–23; reprint, London, 1983), 91.

13. Arthur Young, *A Six Weeks Tour, Through the Southern Counties of England and Wales* (London, 1769), 50.

14. E. S. de Beer, ed., *The Diary of John Evelyn*, vol. 3 (Oxford, 1955), 591. The entry is dated October 16, 1671.

15. See Paul Langford, *Public Life and the Propertied Englishman* (Oxford, 1992).

16. K. D. M. Snell, *Annals of the Labouring Poor* (Cambridge, 1985), 107.

17. Robert Bloomfield, "Autumn," in William Wickett and Nicholas Duval, *The Farmer's Boy: The Story of a Suffolk Poet* (Lavenham, 1971), 96.

18. George Bird Burrell, Thetford Corporation, *Manuscripts* 1809, 4/1/1971, R 154D.

19. Sir E. M. Thompson, ed., *Letters of Humphrey Prideaux to John Ellis* (1875), 199–200.

20. Hamon Le Strange, *Norfolk Official Lists, from the Earliest Period to the Present Day* (Norwich, 1890), 241–243.

21. La Rochefoucauld, *A Frenchman's Year in Suffolk*, 24.

22. Le Strange, *Norfolk Official Lists*, 236. Thomas Cocke, "Comoner" and freeman of the borough, was elected to the Assembly of the Borough of Thetford on September 20, 1697. Records show that he regularly attended the Assembly from 1697. See Thetford Corporation, *Assembly Books* T/C2/6, 101 ff.

23. Francis Oldys, *The Life of Thomas Pain: The Author of Rights of Men [sic], with a Defence of His Writings* (London: John Stockdale, 1791), 3.

24. Parish of Euston, FL566/4/2, Suffolk Records Office, Bury St. Edmunds.

25. See Thetford Corporation, *Assembly Books* T/C2/6: "That upon the one & twentieth day of May in the year of our Lord 1688 William Payne of this Borough of Thetford, chordwayner, Eldest Son of William Payne of this Borough, Chordwayner now deceased who was a freeman of this Borough, was this day sworn Foreman of this Borough" (p. 74).

26. Register 3 of the vestry records at the parish church of St. Cuthbert once contained the entry "Joseph Payne (a Quaker) is buried aged 78 years. November 14th, 1786." The details are confirmed in the parish records of St. Cuthbert, PD 168/3, Norfolk Records Office, Norwich.

27. Oldys, *The Life of Thomas Pain: The Author of Rights of Men* [*sic*], 3.

28. Oldys, *The Life of Thomas Pain, the Author of the Seditious Writings, entitled Rights of Man*, 6th ed. (London, 1793), 3.

29. Cited in the parish records of St. Cuthbert, PD 168/2, Norfolk Records Office, Norwich.

30. Oldys, *The Life of Thomas Pain: The Author of Rights of Men* [*sic*], 4. Oldys continues on the same page:

> As he was not baptized, the baptism of Thomas Pain is not entered on the parish books of Thetford. It is a remarkable fact, that the leaves of the two registers of the parishes of St. Cuthbert's and St. Peter's, in Thetford, containing the marriages, births, and burials, from the end of 1733, to the beginning of 1737, have been completely cut out. Thus a felony has been committed against the public, and an injury done to individuals, by a hand very malicious and wholly unknown. Whether our author, when he resided at Thetford in 1787, looked into these registers for his own birth; what he saw, or what he did, we will not conjecture. They contain the baptism of his sister Elizabeth, on the 28th of August, 1738.

The overall hypothesis is implausible, and the passage contains several factual errors, including the date of baptism of Elizabeth. Oldys also does not explain how Paine supposedly committed a well-organized crime by getting his hands on the copies of the registers provided in the Archdeacon's or the Bishop's transcripts, which have not survived. The parish records of St. Cuthbert today read less hysterically: "The Baptismal Register before this in Book No. 1 only goes as far as May 13th 1733 AD. There is an unexplained lacuna of four years" (PD 168/2, Norfolk Records Office, Norwich). The first of the sporadic entries during Paine's first two months on earth is dated February 17, 1736–7, and there are several January births recorded where baptisms did not take place until March or April. Otherwise, the records are imperfect. I am grateful for the suggestions about how to deal with these lacunae provided by Chad Goodwin during interviews in Norwich on January 8, 1991, and in Lewes on October 24, 1992.

31. *Suffolk Mercury: or, Bury Post*, vol. 24, no. 257 (March 1737), reported that in the region or country at large (the report is unclear), there were 520 deaths during the week after Paine's birth, of which more than a third (174) were infants under the age of two. Evidence of high infant mortality rates during Paine's time is discussed in Roy Porter, *English Society in the Eighteenth Century* (London, 1990), 13.

32. The originator of this interpretation was Moncure D. Conway, who claimed that Paine "is explicable only by the intensity of his Quakerism" and that his "whole political system is explicable only by his theocratic Quakerism" (*The Life of Thomas Paine*, vol. 2 [New York, 1892], 201). The idea is repeated elsewhere, as in Moncure Conway, ed., *The Writings of Thomas Paine*, vol. 2 (4 vols., New York, 1894–1896): "Paine's political principles were evolved out of his early Quakerism" (p. 262).

33. See S. Taylor, "Sir Robert Walpole, the Church of England and the Quaker Tithe Bill of 1736," *Historical Journal* 28 (1985): 51–77; W. K. Jordan, *The Development of Religious Toleration in England* (4 vols., London, 1932–1940); Michael Watts, *The Dissenters: From the Reformation to the French Revolution* (Clarendon, 1978). The bill passed

through the Commons with the support of Walpole, only to be defeated in the Lords, where fifteen bishops, the Lord Chief Justice, and the Lord Chancellor voted against it.

34. The supposition is evident in Alison Maddock, *Thomas Paine 1737–1809* (Norwich, 1983).

35. Paine, *The Age of Reason; Being an Investigation of True and Fabulous Theology,* part 1 (Paris, 1794), 39.

36. See the document signed by J. Kendall, *Henry Fell, an Idle Vagrant Person, and a seducer of the people . . . was this, 28 day of May . . . openly whipped in Thetford affores'd, according to Law, etc.* (1671), L.7.a.3. (84), British Library.

37. Among the best studies of George Fox and the development of Quakerism are Cecil W. Sharman, *George Fox and the Quakers* (London, 1991); W. C. Braithwaite, *The Beginnings of Quakerism,* 2d rev. ed. (Cambridge, 1970); John Punshon, *Portrait in Grey: A Short History of the Quakers* (London, 1984).

38. The Forester [Thomas Paine], "Letter II. To Cato," *Pennsylvania Journal; and the Weekly Advertiser* (April 10, 1776).

39. *The Journal, and Other Writings: John Woolman* (New York, 1936), 22.

40. La Rochefoucauld, *A Frenchman's Year in Suffolk,* 66.

41. Conway, *The Writings of Thomas Paine,* vol. 4, 252.

42. R. H. Tawney, *Religion and the Rise of Capitalism* (London, 1926), 272–273. My counter-interpretation of the social attitudes of the Thetford Quakers draws upon Auguste Jorns, *Studien über die Sozialpolitik der Quäker* (Karlsruhe, 1912); Muriel F. Lloyd Prichard, "Norfolk Friends' Care of Their Poor, 1750–1850," *Journal of the Friends' Historical Society* 39 (1947): 18–32; Arthur J. Eddington, *The First Fifty Years of Quakerism in Norwich* (London, 1932).

43. Paine, *The Age of Reason,* 38.

44. Thomas Clio Rickman, *The Life of Thomas Paine* (London, 1819), 34.

45. Martin, *The History of the Town of Thetford,* 230.

46. See Nigel Heard, *Thetford Grammar School* (Burford, 1972); David Seymour, "Thetford Grammar School: The First Eight Hundred Years," in *Thetford: Antiq Burg* (Thetford, 1985), 25–27.

47. Thetford Corporation, *Assembly Books* T/C2/7, 116.

48. Paine, *Rights of Man,* part 2 (London: J. S. Jordan, 1792).

49. Francis Oldys, *The Life of Thomas Pain, the Author of the Seditious Writings, Entitled Rights of Man,* 6th ed. (London: John Stockdale, 1793), 3.

50. James Cheetham, *The Life of Thomas Paine* (London, 1817) 17.

51. Oldys, *The Life of Thomas Pain: The Author of Rights of Men* [*sic*], 5.

52. Ibid., 5.

53. Paine, *The Age of Reason,* part 1 (1794), 37. Paine's lack of interest in foreign languages is striking. In the same text, Paine, the confident modernist, wrote cheekily: "As there is now nothing new to be learned from the dead languages, all the useful books being already translated, the languages are become useless, and the time expended in teaching and learning them is wasted" (p. 32).

54. Paine, *The Age of Reason,* part 1 (1794), 32.

55. His Grace the Duke of Portland, K. G., "A Journey in the Eastern Counties, December 1737–January 1738," entry dated December 31, 1737, in P553/1040/2, Suffolk Records Office, Bury St. Edmunds.

56. Thetford Corporation, *Assembly Books* T/C2/7.

57. On the background trends in women's fashions during Paine's early years, see C. W. Cunnington and P. Cunnington, *Handbook of English Costume in the Eighteenth Century,* 3d ed. (London, 1966); Valerie Cumming, *Exploring Costume History 1500–1900* (London, 1981); A. Buck, *Dress in Eighteenth Century England* (London, 1979).

58. Oldys, *The Life of Thomas Pain, the Author of the Seditious Writings,* 4.

59. Oldys, *The Life of Thomas Pain: The Author of Rights of Men* [sic], 5–6.

60. See Crosby, *A History of Thetford,* 81–85.

61. Paine, *Rights of Man. Part the second.*

62. TP to Messrs. Binny and Ronaldson, New York, April 8, 1807.

63. Linda Colley, *Britons, forging the nation, 1707–1837* (London, 1992).

64. The eighteenth-century contours of this republican argument are examined in J. G. A. Pocock, *The Machiavellian Moment: Florentine Political Thought and the Atlantic Republican Tradition* (Princeton, N.J., 1975), chapters 12 and 13; J. G. A. Pocock, "Machiavelli, Harrington and English Political Ideologies in the Eighteenth Century," in *Politics, Language and Time: Essays on Political Thought and History* (Chicago and London, 1989). The background of the standing army controversy of the previous century is examined in Lois G. Schwoerer, *"No Standing Armies!" The Antiarmy Ideology in Seventeenth-Century England* (Baltimore and London, 1974), chapter 8.

65. Paine, *Rights of Man. Part the second,* 405.

66. (London) *Daily Advertiser,* October 16, 1756.

67. Paine, *Rights of Man. Part the second,* 405.

68. See E. P. Statham, *Privateers and Privateering* (New York, 1910); James G. Lydon, *Pirates, Privateers and Profits* (Upper Saddle River, N.J., 1970); Gomer Williams, *The Liverpool Privateers* (Liverpool, 1897); Alyce Barry, "Thomas Paine, Privateersman," *Pennsylvania Magazine of History and Biography,* C1, no. 4 (1977): 451–461.

69. Statham, *Privateers and Privateering,* 106–111.

2. THE RUINED CITIZEN

1. Paine, *Rights of Man. Part the second.*

2. *The Case of the Journeymen Taylors by the Bill now defending in the Right Honourable the House of Peers* (London, [1721?]).

3. (London) *Daily Advertiser,* October 16, 1756. "John Morris, Hanover Street, Long-Acre" was among the ninety-five master tailors and staymakers who signed the appeal against the reduction of working time.

4. Dean Josiah Tucker, *Instructions for Travelers* (London, 1757).

5. *London Chronicle* (January 18–20, 1757).

6. *London Chronicle* (February 5–8, 1757); *London Chronicle* (Feburary 15–17, 1757).

7. Paine, *Common Sense: On the Origin and Design of Government in General, with Concise Remarks on the English Constitution* (Philadelphia, 1776). The makeup of privateer crews is discussed in Lydon, *Pirates, Privateers and Profits*, 192.

8. *London Chronicle* (March 26–29, 1757). The details of the booty are listed in the Prize Assignation Books. ADM 7/352, Public Record Office, London.

9. *London Chronicle* (March 31–April 2, 1757).

10. Paine, *Rights of Man. Part the second.*

11. *London Chronicle* (April 21–23, 1757). The details of the awards are listed in the Prize Assignation Books, Public Record Office, London.

12. (London) *Daily Advertiser* (June 28, 1757).

13. (London) *Daily Advertiser* (July 5–6, 1757).

14. (London) *Daily Advertiser* (July 19, 1757).

15. Charles Wye Kendall, *Private Men of War* (London, 1931), 163–165.

16. Lydon, *Pirates, Privateers and Profits*, 124, 197.

17. From a manuscript by William Carver, quoted in Conway, *The Life of Thomas Paine*, vol. 1, 25.

18. Paine, *The Age of Reason*, part 1 (1794), 37.

19. *Present State of Republic of Letters*, vol. 16 (London, 1735), 167; Augustus De Morgan, *Arithmetical Books, from the invention of printing to the present time* (London, 1847), 68–73. See also the portrait of James Ferguson in *The Gentleman's Magazine, and Historical Chronicle* (London, 1777), 107–108, 157, 209; John R. Millburn, *Benjamin Martin, Author, Instrument-Maker, and "Country Showman"* (Leyden, 1976), especially chapter 6.

20. John R. Millburn, *Wheelwright of the Heavens: The Life and Work of James Ferguson, FRS* (London, 1988), chapter 6.

21. Ebenezer Henderson, *Life of James Ferguson* (London, 1867), 463.

22. From October 6, 1757, to February 15, 1758, Martin and Ferguson placed at least thirty-four advertisements in London's *Daily Advertiser*. A report by Mr. Haywood about Martin's lectures, which Paine attended, appeared in the same newspaper on January 16, 1758.

23. *Letter to the Abbé Raynal, on the Affairs of North America: in which the Mistakes in the Abbé's Account of the Revolution of America are Corrected and Cleared up* (Philadelphia, August 21, 1782).

24. See the preface of David Brewster, the early biographer and disciple of Sir Isaac Newton, in *Ferguson's Lectures* (Philadelphia, 1806). Also useful is Harry Hayden Clark, "An Historical Interpretation of Thomas Paine's Religion," *University of California Chronicle* 35 (1933): 56–87; John R. Millburn, "The London Evening Courses of Benjamin Martin and James Ferguson," *Annals of Science* 40 (1983): 437–455; A. Q. Morton, "Lectures on Natural Philosophy in London, 1750–1765: S. C. T. Demainbray (1710–1782) and the 'Inattention' of his Countrymen," *British Journal of the History of Science* 23 (1990): 411–434.

25. On the relationship between eighteenth-century science and ideas of republican liberty, see J. H. Plumb, *In the Light of History* (London, 1972), 9, 15–21; Eric Foner, *Tom Paine and Revolutionary America* (New York, 1976), 6–7; F. W. Gibbs, "Itinerant Lecturers in Natural Philosophy," *Ambix* 8, no. 2 (1960): 111–117; Harry Hayden Clark, "Toward

a Reinterpretation of Thomas Paine," *American Literature* 5 (1933): 133–145; Whitfield J. Bell, "Science and Humanity in Philadelphia, 1775–1790 (Ph.D. diss., University of Pennsylvania, 1947), passim; Caroline Robbins, *The Eighteenth-Century Commonwealthman: Studies in the Transmission, Development and Circumstances of English Liberal Thought from the Restoration of Charles II Until the War with the Thirteen Colonies* (New York, 1968).

26. Oldys, *The Life of Thomas Pain, the Author of the Seditious Writings*, 4.

27. Records of Sandwich Congregational Church, 1354–1937, Centre for Kentish Studies, Maidstone, N/C 323, T1/27, 28; Z 16/5; Z 16/11.

28. Conway, *The Life of Thomas Paine*, vol. 1, 9. Evidence that Wesley passed through Thetford often is cited in Cyril Jolly, *The Spreading Flame: The Coming of Methodism to Norfolk 1751–1811* (Dereham, 1972), 74–75.

29. See the note in Nehemiah Curnock, ed., *The Journal of the Rev. John Wesley, A.M.*, vol. 8 (London, 1916), 31n. The story is confirmed by an inscription inside the front cover of a copy of Wesley's *Sermons on Several Occasions*, vol. 1 (London, 1746), brought from England by the father of the well-known Methodist preacher Reverend Albert Nash (1812–1900). The copy, which may have been handed by Paine himself to Nash's father, is today held in the Methodist Archives and History Center, Drew University Library, Madison, New Jersey. Its inscription reads: "Out of this volume Thomas Paine, author of the Age of Reason, used to read sermons to the Congregations at the Methodist Chapel in Dover when they were disappointed of a Preacher. At that time he belonged to the Methodist Society in that place." See also "The White Cliffs of Dover: Methodism in a Great Fortress," *The Methodist Recorder*, August 16, 1906; George Lawton, "Matthew Bramble, Tom Paine and John Wesley," part 2, *Proceedings of the Wesley Historical Society* 33 (1961): 41–45; and John Bavington Jones, *Annals of Dover* (Dover, 1916), 200–204. Unfortunately, the South-East Kent Archives Office at the Folkestone Library contains no pre-1794 material (such as baptismal registers, circuit minutes and schedules, class books) from the Dover and Deal Methodist Circuit, which encompassed Dover and Sandwich.

30. Nehemiah Curnock, ed., *The Journal of the Rev. John Wesley, A.M.*, vol. 5 (London, 1914), 93 (entry dated September 22, 1764).

31. John A. Vickers, *The Story of Canterbury Methodism (1750–1961)* (Canterbury, 1961), 3–8. See also John Wesley's own account of the area in *A Plain Account of the People called Methodists in a Letter to the Revd Mr. Peronnet, Vicar of Shoreham in Kent* (London, 1755) and Nigel Yates, "The Anglican Establishment and its Critics 1714–1830," in Nigel Yates et al., *Religion and Society in Kent, 1640–1914* (Woodbridge, 1994).

32. This image is traceable to the thesis of Elie Halévy ("La Naissance du Méthodisme en Angleterre," *Revue de Paris*, August 1 and 15, 1906, 519–539, 841–867) that the eighteenth-century evangelical revival spearheaded by Methodism spared England from a violent upheaval like the French Revolution. Amended versions of the same fundamental thesis can be found in Victor Kiernan, "Evangelicanism and the French Revolution," *Past and Present* 1 (1952): 44–56; E. P. Thompson, *The Making of the English Working Class* (Harmondsworth, 1972), 917–923, where the Wesleyans first, and the Primitive Methodists after them, are viewed as carriers of work-discipline, and chapter 11, where Thompson states, "Methodism obtained its greatest success in serving *simultaneously* as the religion of the industrial bourgeoisie (although here it

shared the field with other Nonconformist sects) and of wide sections of the proletariat" (391); Leslie Stephen, *History of English Thought in the Eighteenth Century*, vol. 2 (1876; reprint, New York, 1962), 362, 368.

33. Quoted in Porter, *English Society in the Eighteenth Century*, 40–41.

34. *Boswell's Life of Johnson*, vol. 1, ed. G. B. Hill (Oxford, 1934), 458–459. Useful accounts of the means of communication used by the Methodists include Bernard Semmel, *The Methodist Revolution* (London, 1974); A. W. Harrison, "Why the Eighteenth Century Dreaded Methodist Enthusiasm," *Proceedings of the Wesley Historical Society* 18 (1931): 40–42; J. H. Holmes, *John Wesley and the Methodist Revolt* (Toronto, 1923); John D. Walsh, "Methodism and the Mob in the Eighteenth Century," in *Popular Belief and Practice*, ed. G. J. Cuming and D. Baker (Cambridge, 1972).

35. See the later report in *Methodist Magazine* (London, 1805), 410.

36. William Warburton [Bishop Lavington], *The Enthusiasm of Methodists and Papists Compared* (London, 1749 and 1751), especially preface; part 1, 22–26; part 2, 2–19, 43–56, 145–154; part 3, 311–341.

37. Oldys, *The Life of Thomas Pain, the Author of the Seditious Writings*, 5.

38. See William Boys, *Collections for an History of Sandwich in Kent* (Canterbury, 1792), 294, 402–404, 430.

39. A. Wilson, "William Hunter and the Varieties of Man-midwifery," in *William Hunter and the Eighteenth Century World*, ed. W. F. Bynum and Roy Porter (Cambridge, 1985), 343–369.

40. Fawn M. Brodie, *Thomas Jefferson: An Intimate History* (Toronto, 1975), 122–123.

41. Oldys, *The Life of Thomas Pain, the Author of the Seditious Writings*, 6. Paine's good friend Clio Rickman refers only in passing to Mary Lambert and her marriage to Paine in his *The Life of Thomas Paine*, 36.

42. Paine, *Letter to the People of France and the French Armies on the Events of the 18th Fructidor — Sep. 4 — and its Consequences* (Paris: Cercle-Social, 1797).

43. Paine, "A Serious Address to the People of Pennsylvania on the present Situation of their Affairs," *The Pennsylvania Packet*, December 1, 1778.

44. On the figure of the prostitute, "womanlish" behavior, and what Paine called the "manly character" of republicanism (TP to Samuel Adams [6 March 1795]), see the discussions of Linda K. Kerber, *Women of the Republic: Intellect and Ideology in Revolutionary America* (Chapel Hill, N.C., 1980), 31; Linda K. Kerber, " 'I Have Don . . . much to Carrey on the Warr': Women and the Shaping of Republican Ideology after the American Revolution," in Harriet B. Applewhite and Darline G. Levy, *Women and Politics in the Age of the Democratic Revolution* (Ann Arbor, Mich., 1990), 227–257; and Hanna Fenichel Pitkin's *Fortune is A Woman: Gender and Politics in the Thought of Niccolò Machiavelli* (Berkeley, 1984), which examines the early modern roots of the republican understanding of virtue (from the Latin root *vir*) as a male attribute that contrasts with its opposite, *Fortuna*, the personification of feminine passive unpredictability. Pitkin takes her theme from a famous passage in Machiavelli's *Il Principe:* "Fortune is a woman and it is necessary to keep her under, to cuff and maul her."

45. Written by Charles Leadbetter, a former Excise officer, *The Royal Gauger; Or, Gauging made Perfectly Easy* discussed at length the importance of "Countenance":

> If the Petitioner cannot obtain the Countenance of some Gentleman, (a Member of Parliament is best) that is personally acquainted with one of the Commissioners, frequently to sollicit and re-mind the Commissioner of his Promise, his Petition will certainly come to nothing; for notwithstanding there are several Vacancies, what by Deaths, Discharges, &c happening every Week, yet there are so many constantly applying, that those Petitioners who have the best Sollicitors always succeed soonest. (Charles Leadbetter, *The Royal Gauger; Or, Gauging made Perfectly Easy*, 4th ed. [London, 1755] 213.)

This was the first extensive manual for excisemen and appeared in seven editions during the eighteenth century. It contained a detailed account of the procedures for obtaining an Excise appointment and a lengthy exposition of the requisite skills and daily duties of excisemen. Paine may have procured a copy of the fourth edition when passing through London en route to Thetford. All citations are from this edition.

46. Quoted in Leadbetter, *The Royal Gauger*, 251.

47. Customs 47/238/47, Public Record Office, London. The relevant entry in the Board of Excise's minutes of December 1, 1762, reads: "Thomas Middleton, Officer of Holbeach Outride, Grantham Collection, being Dead, as by Mr. Thwaites Collector, his letter of 28th. ult. Ordered that the Supernumerary or proper Officer supply the vacancy and that Thomas Pain be Supernumerary on Mr. Frankland's motion."

48. Nigel Scotland, *Methodism and the Revolt of the Field* (Gloucester, 1981), 23.

49. Quoted from a report by Bartholomew Davison to the Board of Excise Commissioners dated June 15, 1775, in Customs 47/299/112–113, Public Record Office, London.

50. See George Hindmarch, "Thomas Paine: The First Excise Period" (paper, Purley, n.d.), 25.

51. Conway, *The Life of Thomas Paine*, vol. 1, 16–17.

52. The brief and bureaucratically written minute of the Board of Excise is dated August 27, 1765:

> Thomas Pain, Officer of Alford Outride, Grantham Collection, having on July the 11th stamped his whole Ride, as appears by the specimens not being signed in any part thereof, though the proper entry was shown in Journal, and the victualler's stocks drawn down in his Books as if the same had been surveyed by him that day; as by William Swallow, Supervisor's letter of the 3rd instant, and the Collector's report thereon, also by the said Pain's own confession by letter of the 13th instant; Ordered that he be discharged, that Robert Peat dropped malt assistant in Lynn Collection succeed him or &c. (Customs 47/251/98, Public Record Office, London.)

53. See the entry dated October 9, 1765, which concludes that "the said Swallow acknowledges that he had the Officer's books in his pocket while he surveyed part of the said Ride and Check; Ordered that he be reduced to be Officer of Hertford 2nd Division, Hertford Collection, that William Newton . . . be Supervisor of Horncastle District" (Customs 47/252/46–47, Public Record Office, London).

54. The dispute is mentioned in the minute books of the Board of Excise Commissioners dated May 28, 1764 (Customs 47/245/90, Public Record Office, London).

55. Eric Pursehouse, *Waveney Valley Studies* (Diss, n.d.), 197–198; A. Norfolk and J. Speirs, *Historical Notes on Diss* (Diss, 1982), 5–6. Compare the hostile account in *Historical Sketches and Tales of the Town of Diss* (Diss, 1931): n.p.

> Tom Paine, an atheist of great notability, resided at Diss for some considerable length of time, and worked as a stay-maker in a house on the terrace where the "Bee Hive" stands, in Denmark Street. This was previous to the publication of his "Age of Reason" — a book which has immortalised his name. Tom Paine wrote many works, and was the most celebrated infidel of his day. It is said that whilst employed at Diss by Mr. Gudgeon, he commenced "The Age of Reason," the greatest of his productions. Nothing need be said of the horrible end of this man, suffice it to say that though he lived a hero in the sight of the atheistical fraternity, he died a coward.

56. Blomefield, *An Essay Towards a Topographical History of the County of Norfolk,* vol. 1, 38.

57. Customs 47/255/87, Public Record Office, London.

58. Paine, *Forgetfulness. From the Castle in the Air to the Little Corner of the World* (Paris, 1794).

59. See W. T. Whitley, "Daniel Noble," *Baptist Quarterly* 7, no. 3 (July 1922), 135–138; W. T. Whitley, "Seventh Day Baptists in England," *Baptist Quarterly* 12, no. 8 (October 1947), 252–258; and Ernest A. Payne, "Tom Paine: Preacher," *The Times Literary Supplement*, May 31, 1947, 267.

60. After emigrating to America, Paine told Henry Laurens that his "particular design was to establish an academy on the plan they were conducted in and about London, which I was well acquainted with" (TP to the Honourable Henry Laurens, Philadelphia, January 14, 1779). Benjamin Rush noted, "His design was to open a school for the instruction of young ladies in the several branches of knowledge" (Benjamin Rush to James Cheetham, Philadelphia, June 17, 1809, cited in Cheetham, *The Life of Thomas Paine,* 34–40).

61. Cited in Clio Rickman, *The Life of Thomas Paine,* 37.

62. *The Gentleman's Magazine, and Historical Chronicle* 41 (1771), 523.

63. These claims are made by Oldys: "His desire of preaching now returned on him: but applying to his old master for a certificate of his qualifications, to the bishop of London, Mr. Noble told his late usher that since he was no scholar, and had no good character, he would not recommend him as a proper candidate for ordination in the church" (*The Life of Thomas Pain, The Author of the Seditious Writings,* 7).

64. Of the London poor, Wesley wrote, "I found some in their cells underground, others in their garrets, but I found not one of them unemployed who was able to crawl about the room. So wickedly, devilishly false is that common objection, they are poor only because they are idle" (quoted in Luke Tyerman, *The Life and Times of the Rev. John Wesley,* vol. 2 [London, 1870], 160).

65. Paine was appointed to Grampound on May 15, 1767 (Customs 47/258/106, Public Record Office, London). He appealed the decision on May 26, and the appeal was accepted by the Excise Board on May 30 (Customs 47/259/16, Public Record Office, London).

66. Elizabeth's baptism was recorded by the Reverend Ebenezer Johnston, who was then the local minister: "Elizabeth Ollive, Daughter to Samuel Ollive, Tobacconist, born Decemb. 16, 1749, and baptised Dec. 27, 1749." See also Walter Godfrey, "The High Street Lewes," *Sussex Archaeological Collections* 93:12.

67. Friedrich Engels, "Revolution and Counter-Revolution in Germany," in Karl Marx and Friedrich Engels, *Selected Works*, vol. 7 (Moscow, 1969), 304.

68. Audrey Williamson, *Thomas Paine: His Life, Work and Times* (London, 1973), 36. The extent of Paine's involvement in local government was first brought to light by Leslie S. Davey, *The Civil Insignia and Plate of the Corporation of Lewes* (Lewes, 1967).

69. See Colin Brent, "The Neutering of the Fellowship and the Emergence of a Tory Party in Lewes (1663–1688)," *Sussex Archaeological Collections* 121 (1983), 95–107.

70. The decine of the duke of Newcastle's power is well documented in Colin Brent, *Georgian Lewes 1714–1830: The Heyday of a Country Town* (Lewes, 1993), chapter 9.

71. See Verena Smith, ed., *The Town Book of Lewes 1702–1837* (Lewes, 1973), 55–56.

72. Ibid., 59, 61; *Sussex Weekly Advertiser; or, Lewes Journal*, November 26, 1770.

73. Smith, *The Town Book of Lewes*, 60.

74. St. Michael's Parish, *Vestry Minute Book, and Lewes Non-Conformist Registers* (1768–1773), East Sussex Record Office, Lewes.

75. Adam Smith, *Lectures on Jurisprudence, (1762–3),* ed. R. L. Meek et al. (Oxford, 1978), 331–394.

76. Interview with local historian John Houghton, Swanborough, Lewes, September 24, 1992.

77. John Cartwright, *American Independence, the Interest and Glory of Great Britain* (London, 1774), 7–8. The pamphlet was published originally as ten letters to the *Public Advertiser*. The letters appeared between March 20, 1774, and April 14, 1774, and were signed "Constitutio." Cartwright later argued to Edmund Burke that the question was whether Britain, "like an Eastern despot," would doom America "to a splendid wretchedness in his seraglio; never more to hold a social commerce with any but her hated lord; nor taste the sweets, the pure delights of liberty; and though mocked with the soothing title of Sultana, knowing too well she is no better than the slave of his lustful appetites?" (Cartwright, *A Letter to Edmund Burke, Esq., Controverting the Principles of American Government* [London, 1775], 26).

78. Quoted in Conway, *The Life of Thomas Paine*, vol. 1, 37.

79. See *Sussex Weekly Advertiser; or, Lewes Journal*, September 7, 1772; September 14, 1772; September 28, 1772; October 5, 1772; November 16, 1772; November 30, 1772; December 7, 1772; January 4, 1773. The scathing reference to the nobility as the "no-ability" later appeared in part one of *Rights of Man*. "Plain Truth" was Paine's preferred title for his pamphlet *Common Sense*. He replied to American critics of that pamphlet with the nom de plume "The Forester."

80. *Sussex Weekly Advertiser; or, Lewes Journal*, March 20, 1769; June 5, 1769; June 12, 1769; August 27, 1770. The letters of "Junius" were written about once a month between 1769 and 1772.

81. Brent, *Georgian Lewes*, 183.

82. Important studies of the Wilkes campaign include S. Maccoby, *English Radicalism, 1763–1785* (London, 1950), chapters 1–9; Miss Sutherland and G. Rudé, *Wilkes and Liberty: A Social Study of 1763 to 1774* (Oxford, 1962); Eugene Charlton Black, *The Association: British Extraparliamentary Political Organization 1769–1793* (Cambridge, Mass., 1963), chapter 1.

83. Compare the contemporary hostile remark of Dr. Samuel Johnson about the campaign's triggering of public discussion and civil resistance: "Fired with this fever of epidemic patriotism; the taylor slips his thimble, the drapier drops his yard, and the blacksmith lays down his hammer; they meet at an honest alehouse, consider the state of the nation, read or hear read the last petition, lament the miseries of the time, are alarmed at the dreadful crisis, and subscribe to the support of the Bill of Rights" (*The False Alarm* [London, 1770], 38–39).

84. *Sussex Weekly Advertiser; or, Lewes Journal,* January 13, 1794.

85. Quoted in Rickman, *The Life of Thomas Paine,* 39.

86. Ibid. William Lee, reminiscing in the *Sussex Weekly Advertiser; or, Lewes Journal* (January 13, 1794), was harsher: "He was *vain, dogmatical,* and *vindictive,* but nevertheless could render himself so agreeable, that his company was coveted by persons in much superior stations of life, who to enjoy the conviviality of the man, winked at his profession, which was that of a common Exciseman."

87. Paine's denials were highlighted by three personal enemies: John Adams, Benjamin Rush, and John Jay. That they each chose to do so suggests not only that Paine consistently concealed his early literary activities but also that he feared that their shortcomings might be flung back into his face, as indeed these (and no doubt other) critics did. See John Adams, *Autobiography,* in *The Works of John Adams, Second President of the United States: With a Life of the Author, Notes and Illustrations,* vol. 2, ed. Charles Francis Adams (Boston, 1850):

> There was one circumstance in his conversation with me about the pamphlets, which I could not account for. He was extremely earnest to convince me that "Common Sense" was his first born; declared again and again that he had never written a line nor a word that had been printed, before "Common Sense." I cared nothing for this, and said nothing; but Dr. Witherspoon's account of his writing against us, brought doubts into my mind of his veracity, which the subsequent histories of his writings and publications in England, when he was in the custom-house, did not remove. (p. 510)

Paine made parallel remarks to Benjamin Rush, insisting that an essay on slavery "was the first thing he had ever published in his life" (Benjamin Rush to James Cheetham, Philadelphia, July 17, 1809, in Lyman H. Butterfield, ed., *Letters of Benjamin Rush,* vol. 2 [Princeton, N.J., 1951], 1007). John Jay also countered Paine's denials with the thought that Paine had been "a hackney writer in London" (William Jay, *The Life of John Jay: With Selections from his Correspondence and Miscellaneous Papers,* vol. 1 [New York, 1833], 97).

88. The unfounded claim is made by George Hindmarch, "Thomas Paine: The Methodist Influence," *Thomas Paine Society Bulletin,* March 1979, 59–78. Reverend Richard Michell's contributions between the spring of 1771 and the winter of 1773–74 were eventually republished by William Lee as Reverend Richard Michell, *Fugitive Pieces*

on Various Subjects, 2 vols. (Lewes, 1787). See also Alfred A. Evans, *Richard Michell: Curate of East Dean and Friston 1779–1790* (Brighton, 1940).

89. *Sussex Weekly Advertiser; or, Lewes Journal,* April 1, 1771.

90. Humanus, "To the Printer," *Sussex Weekly Advertiser; or, Lewes Journal,* June 1, 1772. According to Colin Brent, the "passionate precision, the phrasing and sentiment" of the essay "are surely Paine's" (*Georgian Lewes,* 186). More caution is needed, if only because within the lively pages of the *Sussex Weekly Advertiser,* "Humanus" did not enjoy a monopoly on these literary qualities, and because the essay called, perhaps only rhetorically, for capital punishment of those responsible.

91. *Sussex Weekly Advertiser; or, Lewes Journal,* July 8, 1771.

92. "The Monk and Jew: A Tale," *Sussex Weekly Advertiser; or, Lewes Journal,* March 26, 1770. Using one of his most common pseudonyms, "Atlanticus," Paine later republished a versified form of the poem as "The Tale of the Monk and the Jew Versified" in *The Pennsylvania Magazine; or, American Monthly Museum,* March 1775.

93. Gilbert Vale, *The Life of Thomas Paine* (New York, 1841), 22.

94. "Farmer Short's Dog Porter: A Tale," *The Pennsylvania Magazine; or, American Monthly Museum,* July 1775.

95. Quoted in Porter, *English Society in the Eighteenth Century,* 15, 133.

96. On the Lewes Bowling Green Society, see *The Game of Bowls at the Tilting Ground, Lewes* (Lewes, 1968). On Paine's sporting activities in Lewes, see *Sussex Weekly Advertiser; or, Lewes Journal,* January 13, 1794.

97. See, for example, *Sussex Weekly Advertiser; or, Lewes Journal,* March 27, 1769; September 4, 1769; March 12, 1770.

98. The full title is *The case of the Officers of Excise; With Remarks on the Qualifications of Officers, and on the Numerous Evils arising to the Revenue, from the Insufficiency of the Present Salary: Humbly Addressed to the Members of both Houses of Parliament* (William Lee, Lewes, 1772). Copies of *A Letter concerning the Nottingham Officers* have disappeared, although its publication is confirmed in "Biographical Anecdotes of Mr. Thomas Paine," *The Literary and Biographical Magazine, and British Review,* August 1791, 82.

99. TP to Oliver Goldsmith, Excise Coffee House, Broad Street, London, December 21, 1772.

100. *Sussex Weekly Advertiser; or, Lewes Journal,* January 13, 1794.

101. Customs 47/293/21, Public Record Office, London.

102. See the notices to Ollive's creditors in the *Sussex Weekly Advertiser; or, Lewes Journal,* July 10, 1769; September 4, 1769; September 11, 1769.

103. See Thetford Corporation, *Borough Minutes,* T/C1/17/44 (dated September 27, 1769). The published list of votes for the two candidates, Mr. Arnold and Mr. Thompson, is a rare document previously unused by Paine scholars. It suggests not only Paine's early political involvement but also that there were times when the Graftons' grip on the town was controversial and even subject to public challenge. There is a chance, however, that the "Thomas Pain" listed in this document was another Thomas Pain, who in his early years, according to town records, lived with his parents in the same parish of St. Cuthbert but later moved to Wereham, twelve miles northwest of Thetford, as an apprentice tailor. See Thetford Corporation, *Joseph Williamson's Trustees 1718–1818* (T/MC1/1).

104. *Sussex Weekly Advertiser; or, Lewes Journal,* September 11, 1769.

105. *Sussex Weekly Advertiser; or, Lewes Journal,* January 30, 1769.

106. Thomas Paine Collection, Thetford Library.

107. Reprinted in "Thomas Paine's Residence in Lewes," 31. Paine was less concessionary in another letter written to the trustees on the same day concerning a separate dispute:

> GENTLEMEN, —— As I am only tenant in the house, I cannot think myself empowered to give any answer concerning the filling up of the door way which you complain of. It is no repair and consequently not even under my agreement with her. The obligation was binding on the landlord, not the tenant. As I have not even the right of objecting should Mrs. Ollive fill it up immediately, I cannot have any power to give any kind of answer in a case which is entirely her's not mine.
>
> I am, Gentlemen,
>
> on account of the other proposal,
>
> Yr. *obliged* Humble Servt.
>
> T. PAIN.

108. *Sussex Weekly Advertiser; or, Lewes and Brighthelmston Journal,* March 19, 1827.

109. *Sussex Weekly Advertiser; or, Lewes Journal,* April 11, 1774. See also the follow-up advertisement for the horse mill and odd machine parts in *Sussex Weekly Advertiser; or, Lewes Journal,* June 13, 1774.

110. From the articles of separation, dated June 4, 1774, quoted in Conway, *The Life of Thomas Paine,* vol. 1, 32.

111. Quoted in Vale, *The Life of Thomas Paine,* 24–25; and James Cheetham, *The Life of Thomas Paine* (London, 1817), 143.

112. *Sussex Weekly Advertiser; or, Lewes and Brighthelmston Journal,* July 25, 1808; *Sussex Weekly Advertiser; or, Lewes Journal,* July 8, 1793.

113. Sir William Blackstone, *Commentaries on the Laws of England. Book the First* (Oxford, 1765), 430; Mary Wollstonecraft, *The Wrongs of Woman: Or, Maria, a Fragment,* ed. Gary Kelly (London, 1980), 177. It is often claimed that Paine was the author of "Reflections on Unhappy Marriages," first published, unsigned, in *The Pennsylvania Magazine; or, American Monthly Museum* (June 1775). The claim is implausible, since Dr. John Witherspoon, who published more in the magazine than Paine, normally was the one to write on his favorite subjects: marriage, philosophy, and the education of children. If indeed Paine was the author of the essay, then its thesis — that the early passions of marriage typically give way to "coolness," "indifference," and mutual "neglect" — is evidently apologetic of men's habit of seeing things entirely from the privileged perspective of men.

3. THE EMPIRE AND THE ORPHAN

1. TP to the Honourable Benjamin Franklin Esqr, Philadelphia, March 4, 1778.

2. The details of his arrival are discussed in "TP to His Excellency General Washington," Philadelphia, November 30, 1781; Frank Smith, "The Date of Thomas Paine's First Arrival in America," *American Literature* 3, no. 3 (1931): 317–318.

3. See G. B. Keen, "Descendants of Jöran Kyn, The Founder of Upland," *Pennsylvania Magazine of History and Biography* 4, no. 3 (1880): 343–360, especially 349. See also Benjamin Franklin's note of Paine's "wretched trip across the ocean" in *Calendar of the Papers of Benjamin Franklin*, vol. 2 (Philadelphia: Library of the American Philosophical Society, 1908), 168.

4. TP to the Honourable Benjamin Franklin Esqr, Philadelphia, March 4, 1778; *Pennsylvania Evening Post*, April 30, 1776.

5. Michael Kraus, *The Atlantic Civilization: Eighteenth Century Origins* (Ithaca, N.Y., 1949), chapter 9; Gordon Wood, *The Creation of the American Republic 1776–1787* (Chapel Hill, N.C., 1969), 98–99.

6. Common Sense (Thomas Paine), *The American Crisis III* (Philadelphia, April 19, 1777).

7. See Richard Koebner, *Empire* (Cambridge, 1961), 70–85.

8. Reverend John Entick, M.A., and other Gentlemen, *The Present State of the British Empire: Containing a Description of the Kingdoms, Principalities, Islands, Colonies, Conquests, and of the Military and Commercial Establishments Under the British Crown in Europe, Asia, Africa and America* (London, 1774), 1, 4.

9. Edmund Burke, *Speech on Moving His Resolutions for Conciliation with the Colonies*, March 22, 1775 (London, 1775).

10. The classic statement of this thesis is Bernard Bailyn, *The Ideological Origins of the American Revolution* (Cambridge, Mass., 1967). For further discussion, see R. Shallhope, "Republicanism and Early American Historiography," *William and Mary Quarterly*, 3d ser., 39 (1982): 334–356.

11. See, for example, the interpretation of C. M. Andrews, *The Colonial Background to the American Revolution* (New Haven, Conn., 1924), 123–126.

12. Ian R. Christie and Benjamin W. Labaree, *Empire or Independence, 1760–1776: A British-American dialogue on the coming of the American Revolution* (Oxford, 1976), 20; Robert W. Tucker and David C. Hendrickson, *The Fall of the First British Empire: Origins of the War of American Independence* (Baltimore, 1982), 194; P. J. Marshall, "The British Empire in the Age of the American Revolution," in William M. Fowler Jr. and Wallace Coyle, *The American Revolution. Changing Perspectives*, 193–212.

13. Jack P. Greene, *Peripheries and Center: Constitutional Development in the Extended Polities of the British Empire and the United States, 1607–1788* (New York and London, 1986), ch. 4–6.

14. Bernard Bailyn, *The Ideological Origins of the American Revolution* (Cambridge, Mass., 1977), chapter 3.

15. "To the Publisher of the Pennsylvania Magazine," *The Pennsylvania Magazine; or, American Monthly Museum* I, January 1775, 10.

16. *Calendar of the Papers of Benjamin Franklin*, vol. 2, 168.

17. In a letter to James Cheetham, Benjamin Rush noted, "His design was to open a school for the instruction of young ladies in the several branches of knowledge" (June 17, 1809, cited in Cheetham, *The Life of Thomas Paine*, 34–40). Elsewhere, Rush commented, "Mr. Paine said his object was to teach a School, or to give private lessons upon geography to young ladies and gentlemen" (George W. Corner, ed., *The Autobiography of Benjamin Rush: His "Travels Through Life" Together with His Commonplace Book for 1789–1813* [Princeton, N.J., 1948], 113). Paine told Henry Laurens that his "particular design was to establish an academy on the plan they

were conducted in and about London, which I was well acquainted with" (TP to the Honourable Henry Laurens, Philadelphia, January 14, 1779).

18. "William McCulloch's Additions to Thomas's History of Printing," *Proceedings of the American Antiquarian Society*, n.s., 31 (1922): 226.

19. General subscriptions were being solicited by at least December 2, 1774, as evidenced in the letter of that date from Reverend Thomas Barton to Colonel James Burd (Thomas Balch, *Letters and Papers Relating Chiefly to the Provincial History of Pennsylvania* [Philadelphia, 1855], 241).

20. The original circular was titled *Proposals for Printing by Subscription The Pennsylvania Magazine, or, The American Repository of Useful Knowledge*, and it was reprinted in the *Pennsylvania Packet*, November 21, 1774. Notices announcing the forthcoming magazine also were published on November 23, 1774, in the *Pennsylvania Journal* and the *Pennsylvania Gazette*. See also Lyon N. Richardson, *A History of Early American Magazines, 1741–1789* (New York, 1931), 174.

21. *Parliamentary History*, vol. 18, 34 ff, quoted in Richard Koebner, *Empire*, 215.

22. See James Carey, "Advertisement," *The Works of Thomas Paine*, vol. 1 (Philadelphia, 1797).

23. "To the Publisher of the Pennsylvania Magazine," 12.

24. The account of *The Pennsylvania Magazine* provided in Conway's *The Life of Thomas Paine* makes it sound as if Paine were solely responsible for its good qualities: "For eighteen months Paine edited this magazine, and probably there never was an equal amount of good literary work done on a salary of fifty pounds a year" (vol. 1, 41–42). In fact, the poet-composer Francis Hopkinson contributed more articles than Paine (George E. Hastings, *The Life and Works of Francis Hopkinson* [Chicago, 1926], 184–192), as did Dr. John Witherspoon, who, according to Paine, also had "a concern [in] it" (TP to the Honourable Henry Laurens, Philadelphia, January 14, 1779). Paine normally used the word *concern* to mean a financial interest, and it is probable that Witherspoon played a key role in planning, developing, and funding the magazine. Unfortunately, this phase of Witherspoon's life is discussed too briefly by his biographer, Varnum Lansing Collins (*President Witherspoon*, vol. 1 [Princeton, N.J., 1925], 199), although the bibliography (vol. 2, 248–252) contains an impressive list of his published contributions to the magazine in fields such as philosophy, marriage, and the education of children. The internal and external evidence for what Paine actually wrote for *The Pennsylvania Magazine* remains confused and confusing. The most helpful analyses are Richardson, *A History of Early American Magazines, 1741–1789*, 179–196; Arnold Kimsey King, "Thomas Paine in America, 1774–87" (Ph.D. diss., University of Chicago, 1951), chapter 2; Frank Smith, "New Light on Thomas Paine's First Year in America, 1775," *American Literature* 1 (1930): 347–371. Caution should be exercised when examining positive claims that Paine wrote this or that article. Smith, for example, concluded that "any articles in which we find Quakerisms, uncommon references to English life and especially to Lewes and London, or figures of speech and turns of thought which are repeated in very much the same words in his known works of this general period" be counted as positive internal evidence of Paine's authorship of pieces written anonymously or under a nom de plume. Some of Smith's deductions are questionable, considering that Paine was not the only contributor who had an English background; that in Pennsylvania he

had no monopoly on "Quakerisms"; and that he was not alone in using "vitriolic language," "religious sanction," "rationalistic aphorisms," "parent and child" figures, and the "dream device" in his writings of this period. The use of these criteria to identify one essay as Paine's, "An Occasional Letter on the Female Sex" (August 1775), proved misleading. As Smith himself later admitted ("The Authorship of 'An Occasional Letter on the Female Sex,'" *American Literature* 2 [1930]: 277–290), the essay was in fact the first chapter of Antoine Léonard Thomas's *Essay on the Character, Manners, and Genius of Women in Different Ages* (Paris, 1772), enlarged from the French by Mr. [William] Russell, 2 vols. (Philadelphia, 1774).

25. Vox Populi [Thomas Paine], "Reflections on Titles," *The Pennsylvania Magazine: or, American Monthly Museum* (June 1775).

26. Ibid.

27. "Reflections on the Life and Death of Lord Clive," *The Pennsylvania Magazine; or, American Monthly Museum* (March 1775).

28. Benjamin Rush to James Cheetham, Philadelphia, July 17, 1809. On the contemporary interpretations of Wolfe's death, see Simon Schama, *Dead Certainties* (New York, 1992), part one.

29. Atlanticus [Thomas Paine], "Death of General Wolfe," *The Pennsylvania Magazine; or, American Monthly Muesum*, March 1775.

30. Justice, and Humanity [Thomas Paine], "To Amricans [*sic*]," *Pennsylvania Journal; and the Weekly Advertiser*, March 8, 1775.

31. Conway, *The Life of Thomas Paine*, vol. 1, 47.

32. [Benjamin Rush], *An Address to the Inhabitants of the British Settlements in America, upon Slave-Keeping* (Philadelphia, 1773).

33. Benjamin Rush to James Cheetham, Philadelphia, July 17, 1809.

34. Corner, *The Autobiography of Benjamin Rush*, 113.

35. Common Sense [Thomas Paine], *The American Crisis VII*, (Philadelphia, November 21, 1778).

36. The suspicions and rumors apparently originated from the lips of Dr. John Witherspoon, who later grew to dislike Paine. See Jay, *The Life of John Jay*, vol. 1, 97; Charles Francis Adams, ed., *The Works of John Adams, Second President of the United States, with a Life of the Author, Notes and Illustrations*, vol. 2 (10 vols., Boston, 1850–1856), 509–510.

37. Common Sense [Thomas Paine], *The American Crisis VII* (Philadelphia, November 21, 1778).

38. Ibid.

39. Bucks County [Thomas Paine?], "The Dream Interpreted," *The Pennsylvania Magazine; or, American Monthly Museum*, June 1775.

40. Hastings, *The Life and Works of Francis Hopkinson*, 268. The sermon, together with the opening prayer, were printed as Reverend Jacob Duché, *On the Duty of Standing Fast in Our Spiritual and Temporal Liberties, a Sermon* (Philadelphia, 1775).

41. A Lover of Peace [Thomas Paine], "Thoughts on Defensive War," *The Pennsylvania Magazine; or, American Monthly Museum*, July 1775, 328–329.

42. Collins, *President Witherspoon*, vol. 2, 25.

43. TP to the Honourable Henry Laurens, Philadelphia, January 14, 1779.

44. Ibid.

45. Benjamin Rush to James Cheetham, June 17, 1809.

46. Humanus [Thomas Paine], "A Serious Thought," *The Pennsylvania Journal; and the Weekly Advertiser,* October 18, 1775.

47. Josiah Tucker, *The True Interest of Great-Britain, Set Forth in Regard to the Colonies; and the Only Means of Living in Peace and Harmony with Them* (Philadelphia, 1776).

48. Adams, *Autobiography,* 363–364.

49. Worthington Chauncey Ford, ed., *Journals of the Continental Congress, 1774–1789,* vol. 1 (Washington, 1904), 75 ff.

50. See *Journal of the Votes and Proceedings of the General Assembly of the Colony of New York from 1766 to 1777* (reprint, Albany, N.Y., 1820), 112 ff; A. C. Flick, *Loyalism in New York During the American Revolution* (New York, 1901), 41.

51. Edmund C. Burnett, *The Continental Congress* (New York, 1941), 126–127.

52. Ford, *Journals of the Continental Congress,* vol. 3, 410. The general cautiousness of members of the Continental Congress during this period is underlined in Burnett, *The Continental Congress,* 80–102. The subsequent claims of various American political leaders or their biographers that they favored independence well before 1776 were normally exaggerated. An example is John Adams's claim that Paine's defense of independence "had been urged in Congress a hundred times" (*Autobiography,* 507). As has been well argued by John H. Hazelton, these leaders, to legitimate themselves as leaders, indulged the bad habit of willfully "reading back" the present into the past, thereby tailoring their own history to fit the myths of the Revolution (*The Declaration of Independence: Its History* [New York, 1906], 3–12).

53. Bernard Bailyn, *Faces of Revolution: Personalities and Themes in the Struggle for American Independence* (New York, 1990), 69.

54. Corner, *The Autobiography of Benjamin Rush,* 113.

55. Adams, *Autobiography,* 507.

56. According to William Temple Franklin, Benjamin Franklin furnished materials for Paine (*Memoirs of the Life and Writings of Benjamin Franklin,* vol. 2 [London, 1818], 13).

57. On the older European traditions of common sense philosophy, with which Paine might have been familiar, see Helga Pust, *Common Sense bis zum Ende des 18. Jarhunderts. Europäische Schlüsselwörter,* vol. 2 (Munich, 1964); Louise Marcil-Lacoste, *Claude Buffier and Thomas Reid. Two Common Sense Philosophers* (Kingston and Montréal, 1982); and S. A. Grave, *The Scottish Philosophy of Common Sense* (Oxford, 1960).

58. In the seven remaining issues of *The Pennsylvania Magazine,* Robert Aitken never even mentioned the existence of his former assistant's pamphlet.

59. The Forester [Thomas Paine], "Letter I. To Cato," *Pennsylvania Packet, or, The General Advertiser,* April 1, 1776.

4. THE BIRTH OF AMERICA

1. Homer L. Calkin, "Pamphlets and Public Opinion During the American Revolution," *Pennsylvania Magazine of History and Biography* 64 (1940): 38–40; Bernard Bailyn, *The Ideological Origins of the American Revolution,* ix.

2. "To the Public," *Pennsylvania Packet, or, The General Advertiser,* January 29, 1776.

3. "To the Public," *Pennsylvania Packet, or, The General Advertiser,* February 5, 1776; TP to [George Washington?], Philadelphia, April 21, 1783. The dispute is summarized in Richard Gimbel, *Thomas Paine: A Bibliographical Check List of Common Sense with an Account of its Publication* (New Haven and London, 1956).

4. Clifford K. Shipton and James E. Mooney, *National Index of American Imprints through 1800,* vol. 1 (Worcester, Mass., 1969), 165.

5. Jean-Paul De Lagrave, *L'époque de Voltaire au Canada* (Montréal and Paris, 1993). Shortly after arriving in Québec, Fleury de Mesplet set up a publishing house in Montreal, but he was immediately arrested and flung into prison in June or July 1776 by the British authorities. Although the congressional commission canvassed support for the American cause against British power, it was greeted with hostility by the clergy and aristocracy. Benjamin Franklin, disillusioned, set out for Philadelphia on May 11. Mesplet stayed on, to become the principal distributor of French and English editions of Paine's work in Québec. I am grateful to Jean-Pierre Boyer for clarifying these points.

6. From the entry for February 11, 1779, in Lyman H. Butterfield, ed., *Diary and Autobiography of John Adams,* vol. 2 (Cambridge, Mass., 1961), 351. From Europe, news of *Common Sense* eventually spread to other continents. After Paine's death, for example, the pamphlet had considerable influence in Chile, where Camilo Henriquez first called for the independence of that country by paraphrasing *Common Sense* in an article entitled "Exemplo Memorable" in *La Aurora,* June 4, 1812; see A. O. Aldridge, "Thomas Paine in Latin America," *Early American Literature* 3 (1969), 139–147.

7. *Gazeta Warszawska,* May 25, 1776, where *Common Sense* was said to be the work of John Adams.

8. Hans Arnold, "Die Aufnahme von Thomas Paines Schriften in Deutschland," *PMLA* 74 (1959): 366–367; Mary Bell Price and Lawrence M. Price, *The Publication of English Humaniora in Germany in the Eighteenth Century* (Berkeley and Los Angeles, 1955), 135.

9. Dragoljub Živojinović, *Americka revolucija i Dubrovačka republika* (Belgrade, 1976) analyzes the intense interest aroused by the American events among officials of the tiny republic of Ragusa, whose ruling aristocracy enjoyed something of a free press (despite the censorship efforts of the Catholic church, especially the Jesuits), unofficially opposed the British, and favored the establishment of a balance of power relationship between the Bourbons and the Britain of George III.

10. See Clara Roukshina, "Radishchev and the American Revolution," *Izvestiya of the USSR Academy of Sciences,* ser. Literature and Langauge, no. 3 (1976). Dmitriĭ Urnov, *Neistovyĭ Tom, ili poteriannyĭ prakh: povesĭ o Tomase Peĭne* [*Frantic Tom, or Lost Remains*] (Moscow, 1989), 241–247.

11. The Forester [Thomas Paine], "Letter II. To Cato," *Pennsylvania Journal; and the Weekly Advertiser,* April 10, 1776.

12. Conway, *The Writings of Thomas Paine,* vol. 4, 431.

13. William B. Reed, *Life and Correspondence of Joseph Reed,* vol. 1 (Philadelphia, 1847), 180. See also Burnett, *The Continental Congress,* 131–136.

14. The Lee Papers, vol. 1, *Collections of the New York Historical Society,* IV [1871], 252.

15. Ibid., 260.

16. See the preface to *Memoirs of the Life of the Late Charles Lee* (London, 1792).

17. Quoted in Burnett, *The Continental Congress*, 131.

18. *The Newport Mercury*, April 8, 1776.

19. Corner, *The Autobiography of Benjamin Rush*, 114–115; cf. Benjamin Rush to James Cheetham, Philadelphia, July 17, 1809.

20. William Gordon, *The History of the Rise, Progress, and Establishment, of the Independence of the United States of America*, vol. 2 (London, 1788), 275. Another contemporary historian of the revolution, David Ramsay, a participant in the events himself, agreed that *Common Sense* "produced surprising effects. Many thousands were convinced, and were led to approve and long for a separation from the Mother Country" (*The History of the American Revolution*, vol. 1 [2 vols., Philadelphia, 1789], 338–339.

21. Francis Wharton, ed., *The Revolutionary Diplomatic Correspondence of the United States*, vol. 2 (Washington, 1889), 124.

22. According to Phillip Davidson, *Common Sense* was the work of an "agitator and propagandist supreme" (*Propaganda and the American Revolution, 1763–1783* [Chapel Hill, N.C., 1941], 13–14). Similar interpretations of the pamphlet as an unoriginal work of propaganda are found in William E. H. Lecky, *A History of England in the Eighteenth Century*, vol. 4 (1892; reprint, London, 1923), 234; Charles E. Merriam, "The Political Theories of Thomas Paine," *Political Science Quarterly* 14 (1899): 389–404; E. P. Oberholtzer, *The Literary History of Philadelphia* (Philadelphia, 1906), 95–96, where the "historical and legal argument" of John Dickinson's *Letters from a Farmer* is compared favorably with the "empty rhetoric" of *Common Sense*.

23. Andrew Eliot to Isaac Smith, April 9, 1776, cited in Ian R. Christie and Benjamin W. Labaree, *Empire or Independence 1760–1776*, 271.

24. J. C. D. Clark, *The Language of Liberty 1660–1832. Political Discourse and Social Dynamics in the Anglo-American World* (Cambridge and New York, 1994).

25. Andrew A. Lipscomb, ed., *The Writings of Thomas Jefferson*, vol. 15 (20 vols., Washington, 1903–1907), 305.

26. Quoted in Foner, *Tom Paine and Revolutionary America*, 115.

27. Julian P. Boyd, ed., *The Papers of Thomas Jefferson*, vol. 1 (Princeton, N.J., 1950), 129.

28. Thomas Paine, *Common Sense: On the Origin and Design of Government in General, with Concise Remarks on the English Constitution* (Philadelphia, 1776).

29. See John Keane, "Despotism and Democracy: The Origins and Development of the Distinction Between Civil Society and the State, 1750–1850," in *Civil Society and the State: New European Perspectives*, ed. John Keane (London, 1988), 35–71.

30. Paine, *Common Sense*.

31. *Parliamentary History*, vol. 18 (February 7, 1775), 276 ff, quoted in Koebner, *Empire*, 216.

32. Ford, *Journals of the Continental Congress*, vol. 1, 49.

33. Paine, *Common Sense*.

34. Paine did not discuss *The True Interest of Britain, Set Forth in Regard to the Colonies* (Philadelphia, 1776), in which Josiah Tucker had argued that Britain itself would profit from granting independence to the colonies. According to Tucker, the former colonies would continue to find their best markets in the motherland, which would

further benefit from independence by unburdening itself of the strife and expense resulting from colonial administration.

35. Entry for January 19, 1774, in *The Journal of Nicholas Cresswell, 1774–1777*, 2d ed. (New York, 1928), 136.

36. Daniel Dulany to Robert Carter, February 1, 1776, Charles F. Gunther Collection of Historical Manuscripts, Chicago Historical Society. Such cold reactions to *Common Sense* serve as important reminders that the essay sometimes had little or no effect on the wider population. A case in point is its cool reception in Virginia, as has been argued by John E. Selby, *The Revolution in Virginia, 1775–1783* (Williamsburg, 1988), 84–85.

37. "The Diary of Colonel Landon Carter," *William and Mary Quarterly* 14 (1907): 150, 258; see also 151, 152, 155, 257.

38. Frederick W. Ricord and William Nelson, eds., *Documents Relating to the Colonial History of the State of New Jersey*, vol. 10 (Newark, 1886), 708.

39. John Drayton, *Memoirs of the American Revolution*, vol. 2 (Charleston, S.C., 1821), 172.

40. John Adams, *Thoughts on Government, Applicable to the Present State of the American Colonies; in a Letter from a Gentleman to a Friend* (Philadelphia, 1776); Bernard Bailyn, *The Ideological Origins of the American Revolution*, enlarged edition (Cambridge, Mass., 1992), 287–291.

41. Warren-Adams Letters, Being Chiefly a Correspondence Among John Adams, Samuel Adams, and James Warren, Massachusetts Historical Society Collections, LXXII, 1917, I, 204.

42. C. F. Adams, *The Works of John Adams*, vol. 2, 508.

43. John Keane, *Democracy and Civil Society. On the Predicaments of European Socialism, the Prospects for Democracy and the Problem of Controlling Social and Political Power* (London and New York, 1988); *The Media and Democracy* (Oxford, 1991); Roy N. Lokken, "The Concept of Democracy in Colonial Political Thought," *William and Mary Quarterly*, 3d series, 16 (1959), 570–580; Robert R. Palmer, "Notes on the Use of the Word 'Democracy,' 1789–1799," *Political Science Quarterly* 68 (1953), 203–226; and Russell L. Hanson, "'Commons' and 'Commonwealth' at the American Founding: Democratic Republicanism as the New American Hybrid," in Terence Ball and J. G. A. Pocock (eds.), *Conceptual Change and the Constitution* (Kansas City, 1989), 165–193.

44. C. F. Adams, *The Works of John Adams*, vol. 2, 507.

45. The Lee Papers, vol. 1, 312.

46. Ibid.

47. An Independent Whig, "To the Printer," *New York Journal, or the General Advertiser*, February 22, 1776. The remaining contributions appeared on February 29 and March 14 and 28, 1776.

48. *The True Interest of America Impartially Stated, in Certain St[r]ictures on a Pamphlet Intitled Common Sense*, by "An American" [Charles Inglis] was published several weeks later in Philadelphia by the loyalist printer James Humphreys, Jr.

49. The demonstration is reported by Samuel Loudon in Peter Force, ed., *American Archives*, 4th ser., vol. 5 (9 vols., Washington, 1837–1853), 438–440.

50. Quoted in Vernon L. Parrington, *Main Currents of American Thought*, vol. 1 (New York, 1927), 359. On the ethnic and religious politics of this period, see Wayne L. Bockelman and Owen S. Ireland, "The Internal Revolution in Pennsylvania: An Ethnic-Religious Interpretation," *Pennsylvania History* (July 1975), 125–129.

51. The bitter constitutional struggle during this period in Pennsylvania is analyzed in Paul P. Selsam, *The Pennsylvanian Constitution of 1776: A Study in Revolutionary Democracy* (Philadelphia, 1936); Theodore Thayer, *Pennsylvania Politics and the Growth of Democracy 1740–1776* (Harrisburg, Pa., 1953), chapter 13.

52. *The Ancient Testimony and Principles of the People Called Quakers. Renewed with Respect to the King and Government, and Touching the Commotions Now Prevailing in These and Other Parts of America, Addressed to the People in General* (Philadelphia, 1776).

53. Common Sense [Thomas Paine], *The American Crisis III* (Philadelphia, April 19, 1777). More generally, see Robert P. Falk, "Thomas Paine and the Attitude of the Quakers to the American Revolution," *The Pennsylvania Magazine of History and Biography* 63, 3 (July 1939), 302–310.

54. *To the Representatives of the Religious Society of the People called Quakers, or to so many of Them as were concerned in Publishing a Late Piece, Entitled* The Ancient Testimony and Principles *of the People called* Quakers *renewed, with respect to the* King *and* Government, *and touching the* Commotions *now Prevailing in these and other Parts of* America, *Addressed to the* People in General, published as an appendix to the third edition of *Common Sense* (Philadelphia, February 14, 1776).

55. "Cato"'s letters "To the People of Pennsylvania" were printed in the *Pennsylvania Packet, or, The General Advertiser* on March 11, 18, and 25 (III and IV), and April 1, 8, 15, and 29, 1776. They also appeared in the *Pennsylvania Journal, Pennsylvania Ledger,* and *Pennsylvania Gazette* during March and April.

56. See Albert Frank Gegenheimer, *William Smith, Educator and Churchman, 1727–1803* (Philadelphia, 1943), especially 177–178.

57. Cato, "Letter IV: To the People of Pennsylvania," *Pennsylvania Packet, or, The General Advertiser,* March 25, 1776.

58. Cato, "Letter VIII: To the People of Pennsylvania," *Pennsylvania Packet, or, The General Advertiser,* April 29, 1776.

59. TP to the Honourable Henry Laurens, Philadephia, January 14, 1779.

60. Ibid.

61. Ibid.

62. Arnold Kimsey King, *Thomas Paine in America, 1774–1787* (doctoral dissertation, University of Chicago, 1951), 148.

63. Philip Foner has claimed, incorrectly, that the four letters in reply to "Cato" first appeared in the *Pennsylvania Journal* on April 3, 10, and 24 and May 8, 1776. In fact, the letters appeared as The Forester, "To Cato. Letter I," *Pennsylvania Packet, or, The General Advertiser,* April 1, 1776; The Forester, "To Cato. Letter II," *Pennsylvania Journal; and the Weekly Advertiser,* April 10, 1776; The Forester, "To Cato. Letter III," *Pennsylvania Packet, or, The General Advertiser,* April 22, 1776; and The Forester, "Letter IV," *Pennsylvania Journal; and the Weekly Advertiser,* May 8, 1776.

64. The Forester, "To Cato. Letter III," *Pennsylvania Packet, or, The General Advertiser,* April 22, 1776.

65. The Forester [Thomas Paine], "Letter IV," *Pennsylvania Journal*, May 8, 1776.

66. William Duane, ed., *Extracts from the Diary of Christopher Marshall, Kept in Philadelphia and Lancaster, During the American Revolution, 1774–1781* (Albany, N.Y., 1877), 70–72.

67. *The Pennsylvania Gazette*, May 22, 1776.

68. A Watchman, "To the Common People of Pennsylvania," *Pennsylvania Packet, or, The General Advertiser,* June 10, 1776.

69. Paine, *Common Sense.*

70. The view that Paine coauthored the Declaration of Independence originated with Moncure Conway: "At this time Paine saw much of Jefferson, and there can be little doubt that the anti-slavery clause struck out of the Declaration was written by Paine or by one who had Paine's anti-slavery essay before him" (*The Life of Thomas Paine*, vol. 1, 80). The story is implausible for several reasons. Jefferson, of course, held antislavery views of his own at this time. He also informed James Madison — without dissent from Paine — that he was the sole author of the Declaration of Independence, with "neither book nor pamphlet" before him during the drafting process (see Albert Matthews, "Thomas Paine and the Declaration of Independence," *Proceedings of the Massachusetts Historical Society* 43 [1910], 241–253). Conway's view also does not explain when Paine and Jefferson first met. They were certainly acquainted in Paris during 1787, but the odd thing is that the first known correspondence between them took place during May 1788 ("TP to Thomas Jefferson on "Sir Isaac Newton's Principle," Jefferson Papers, Library of Congress, XL) and that during the next twenty years' correspondence, neither of them ever mentioned their alleged collaboration in the drafting process. Most tellingly, Paine himself denied authorship of the document. "I was myself among the first that proposed independence," he told Mr. Hulbert, "and it was Mr. Jefferson who drew up the declaration of it." ("TP to Mr. Hulbert, of Sheffield, one of the Mortified Federal Members of the Massachusetts Legislature," *Aurora*, March 12, 1805.) Despite all this nonevidence and evidence, the myth of Paine as the coauthor of the Declaration of Independence continues to resurface occasionally. Examples include Joseph Lewis, *Thomas Paine, Author of the Declaration of Independence* (New York, 1947), and a letter to me (dated February 19, 1992) from Mark Anger, who claims that "Paine was, in fact, if not the author, certainly the co-author of that wondrous manifesto."

71. *A Dialogue Between the Ghost of General Montgomery and a American Delegate, in a Wood Near Philadelphia*, which first appeared anonymously in the *Pennsylvania Packet, or, the General Advertiser*, February 19, 1776.

72. Paine's name is not included in the list of those present in *Proceedings Relative to Calling the Conventions of 1776 and 1790* (Harrisburg, Pa., 1825), 35–36.

73. Common Sense (Thomas Paine), "To the People," *Pennsylvania Packet*, March 18, 1777.

74. Compare the remark of Theodore Thayer: "Perhaps no man in Pennsylvania had more influence upon the proceedings in the Convention than did Thomas Paine" (*Pennsylvania Politics and the Growth of Democracy*, 190).

75. "To the People," *The Pennsylvania Gazette*, June 26, 1776. The address is not signed by Paine, although it is written in his characteristic style.

5. WAR

1. See the reports in *The Pennsylvania Gazette*, July 10, 1776, and *The Pennsylvania Magazine; or, American Monthly Museum*, July 1776.

2. TP to James Cheetham, August 21, 1807.

3. TP to the Honorable Henry Laurens, Philadelphia, January 14, 1779.

4. See the Fort Lee and White Plains reports dated November 2, October 25, October 26, and October 27, 1776, in *Pennsylvania Journal; and the Weekly Advertiser*, November 6, 1776; the Fort Lee reports dated November 8 and 10 in *Pennsylvania Journal; and the Weekly Advertiser*, November 13, 1776; Alexander Graydon, *Memoirs of a Life, Chiefly Passed in Pennsylvania within the Last Sixty Years* (Harrisburg, Pa., 1811), 187.

5. Quoted In David Freeman Hawke, *Paine* (New York, 1974), 58.

6. Thomas Paine, *The American Crisis II*, vol. 2, 289.

7. Hawke, *Paine*, 59.

8. The confusion generated by the retreat from Fort Lee caused the newspaper temporarily to suspend publication. Paine's report, introduced as "The Principal Events of the War Since the Reduction of Fort Washington," was therefore not printed in the *Pennsylvania Journal; and the Weekly Advertiser* until his fortieth birthday, January 29, 1777.

9. TP to John Bayard, Philadelphia, December 1776[?].

10. "The Principal Events of the War Since the Reduction of Fort Washington," *Pennsylvania Journal and the Weekly Advertiser*, January 29, 1777.

11. Originally published in the *Pennsylvania Journal; and the Weekly Advertiser*, December 19, 1776, the essay appeared in pamphlet form several days later. Christopher Marshall recorded in his diary: "21st December 1776. . . . This day the *American Crisis*, No. 1, written by T. Paine, was published" (Duane, *Extracts from the Diary of Christopher Marshall*, 108).

12. TP to Honourable Benjamin Franklin LL.D., Philadelphia, June 20, 1777.

13. All quotations are from Common Sense [Thomas Paine], "The American Crisis," *Pennsylvania Journal; and the Weekly Advertiser*, December 1, 1776.

14. For example, the first number of *The American Crisis* appeared in the *Virginia Gazette*, January 10, 1777, and in the *Boston Gazette*, January 13, 1777. It was reprinted in pamphlet form in Boston, Norwich, Connecticut, and Fishkill, New York, and several editions appeared in Philadelphia.

15. According to Paine's subsequent enemy, James Cheetham, George Washington ordered that the pamphlet be read "to every corporal's guard" (Cheetham, *The Life of Thomas Paine*, 55).

16. *The American Crisis.*

17. Quoted in William P. Cumming and Hugh F. Rankin, *The Fate of a Nation: The American Revolution through Contemporary Eyes* (London, 1975), 136.

18. Common Sense [Thomas Paine], *The American Crisis II* (Philadelphia, January 13, 1777).

19. "Minutes of the Supreme Executive Council and the Council of Safety," in *Pennsylvania Colonial Records*, vol. 9 (16 vols., Harrisburg, Pa., 1851–1853), 96, 98, 142.

20. For accounts of the Easton conference, see Reverend Uzal W. Condit, *The History of Easton, Penn'a from the Earliest Times to the Present, 1739–1885* (Easton, 1889), 59–61; Frederic A. Godcharles, *Daily Stories of Pennsylvania* (Milton, Pa., 1924), 70–71. Easton had been used as a conference site in the past. A nine-day grand council held there on November 8, 1756, between Governor Denny and the Delaware Indians had ended in an uproar when Chief Tedyuskung had stamped his foot and exclaimed, "The very ground on which we stand was dishonestly taken from us" (Frederic A. Godcharles, *Chronicles of Central Pennsylvania*, vol. 1 [New York, 1944], 185).

21. Thomas Paine, *Agrarian Justice opposed to Agrarian Law, and to Agrarian Monopoly* (Paris, 1796).

22. Richard Drinnon, *Facing West: The Metaphysics of Indian-Hating and Empire-Building* (New York, 1980), 74.

23. Thomas Paine, "On the Question, Will There be War?" in Foner, *The Complete Writings of Thomas Paine*, vol. 2, 1013.

24. Ibid. Compare Paine's earlier remark in *Common Sense* that "he who hunts the woods for prey, the naked and untutored Indian, is less savage than the king of Britain."

25. See the entry dated February 27, 1777, in Ford, *Journals of the Continental Congress, 1774–1789*, vol. 7, 166.

26. Quoted in Drinnon, *Facing West*, 70, 97–99, 102–103; Reginald Horsman, *Expansion and American Indian Policy, 1783–1812* (East Lansing, Mich., 1967). Stimulating accounts of the role of Native Americans during this period include Barbara Graymont, *The Iroquois in the American Revolution* (Syracuse, N.Y., 1972); James H. Merrell, "Declarations of Independence: Indian-White Relations in the New Nation," in *The American Revolution: Its Character and Limits*, ed. Jack P. Greene (New York and London, 1987), 197–223; Wilcomb E. Washburn, "Indians and the American Revolution," in *The Revolutionary Era: A Variety of Perspectives*, ed. John R. Brumgardt (Riverside, Calif., 1976), 26–40.

27. Quoted in Alden T. Vaughan, "From White Man to Redskin: Changing Anglo-American Perceptions of the American Indian," *American Historical Review* 87 (1982): 942.

28. Paine, *Agrarian Justice*.

29. John Hall Diaries, April 15, 1786, Journal No. 6 (February 21, 1786–April 20, 1786), Library Company of Philadelphia; Samuel Edwards, *Rebel! A Biography of Thomas Paine* (New York, 1974), 49.

30. The famous frontier soldier Robert Rogers told a London audience a decade before the Revolution that among Native Americans, "every man is free" and no one "has any right to deprive him of his freedom" (Robert Rogers, *A Concise Account of North America* [1765; reprint, New Haven, Conn., 1966], 233). Another observer during this period noted Native Americans' belief that "God made them free — that no man has the natural right to rule over another" (David Jones, *A Journal of Two Visits Made to Some Nations of Indians on the West Side of the Ohio in the Years 1772 and 1773* [New York, 1971], 73). The stimulating thesis that native peoples served as a radical symbol of independence among the American revolutionaries is argued, with some exaggeration, in Donald A. Grinde, Jr., and Bruce E. Johansen, *Exemplar of Liberty: Native America and the Evolution of Democracy* (Los Angeles, 1991), especially chapter 8. On native peoples' declarations of independence, see Gary Nash, "The Forgotten Experience: Indians,

Blacks, and the American Revolution," in *The American Revolution: Changing Perspectives*, ed. William M. Fowler, Jr., and Wallace Coyle (Boston, 1979), 29–46; Francis Jennings, "The Indians' Revolution," in *The American Revolution: Explorations in the History of American Radicalism*, ed. Alfred F. Young (DeKalb, Ill., 1976), 325–326.

31. Paine, *Agrarian Justice*.

32. Anthony F. C. Wallace, *The Death and Rebirth of the Seneca* (New York, 1969), 179–183, 196.

33. "To the People, by 'Common Sense,'" *Pennsylvania Packet, or, The General Advertiser*, March 18, 1777. Phocion, "To the Printers of the Pennsylvania Journal," *Pennsylvania Journal; and the Weekly Advertiser*, March 12, 1777.

34. Selsam, *The Pennsylvania Constitution of 1776*, 185–186.

35. Ibid., 208.

36. *The Pennsylvania Gazette*, March 26, 1777; *Pennsylvania Packet, or, the General Advertiser*, April 8, 1777:

> At a meeting of the WHIG SOCIETY, held at the Philosophical Hall the first of April, 1777, *Voted unanimously*, That Messrs. Charles W. Peale, James Cannon, David Rittenhouse, Doctor Thomas Young, and Major Thomas Payne, be a Committee of Correspondence for and in behalf of this Society, to correspond with any societies or individuals from whom they may expect to obtain information interesting to our common liberties. Extract from the Minutes, THOMAS YOUNG, Secretary.

37. Charles Coleman Sellers, *The Artist of the Revolution: The Early Life of Charles Willson Peale* (Hebron, Conn., 1939), 153–159; Robert L. Brunhouse, *The Counter-Revolution in Pennsylvania, 1776–1790* (Harrisburg, Pa., 1942), 28.

38. Common Sense [Thomas Paine], "Candid and Critical Remarks on Letter I. Signed Ludlow," *Pennsylvania Journal; and the Weekly Advertiser*, June 4, 1777.

39. Ford, *Journals of the Continental Congress*, vol. 7, 274. See also the original proposal, dated March 6, 1778, in the form of a note from "A Committee of Congress to Treasury Office, York Town" (Richard Gimbel Collection, American Philosophical Society Library, Philadelphia).

40. Butterfield, *The Adams Papers*, vol. 3, 334.

41. Loc. cit.

42. Quoted in Henry Redhead Yorke, Esq., *Letters from France; Describing the Manners and Customs of Its Inhabitants*, vol. 2 (London, 1814), 360.

43. According to the records, on June 11, 1777, Lord Richard Viscount Howe's secretary, Ambrose Serle, forwarded his superior a copy of the first number of *The American Crisis* from New York. Serle explained to Howe that Paine had lived in London as a "Grub Street Writer" and had been dispatched by Benjamin Franklin to the American colonies to cause trouble. He had emerged from obscurity in America and was now enjoying "considerable Attention." Serle concluded, "He has nothing to lose, but everything to hope, from the Establishment of the present rebellious System" (Historical Manuscripts Commission, Fourteenth Report, Appendix, Part 10, *The Manuscripts of the Earl of Dartmouth*, vol. 2, *American Papers* [London, 1895], 439; B. F. Stevens, ed., *Facsimiles of Manuscripts in European Archives Relating to America, 1773–1783*,

vol. 24, no. 2062 [25 vols., London, 1889–1898]). The intelligence networks back in Europe soon reported on Paine. "Mr. Payne should not be forgot," wrote Paul Wentworth, a British secret agent based in Paris, in January 1778 in a long report on American leaders. "He is an Englishman, was school-master in Philadelphia; must be driven to work; naturally indolent; led by his passions" (Stevens, *Facsimiles of Manuscripts in European Archives Relating to America*, vol. 5, no. 487).

44. An article published in the *Pennsylvania Packet* on December 29, 1779, was pompously signed "THOMAS PAINE, Secretary for Foreign Affairs, and Author of all the Writings under the Signature *Common Sense*." The error was later reproduced by publishers eager for sales, as in *The Works of Thomas Paine, Esq.* (London: Printed for D. Jordan, Piccadilly, 1792), where Paine was described as "Foreign Secretary to the American Congress During the War with Great Britain." Moncure Conway compounded the inaccuracy by claiming that during this period, Paine "was really the Seretary of Foreign Affairs" (*The Life of Thomas Paine*, vol. 1, 92).

45. TP to William Bingham, Philadelphia, July 16, 1777; TP to the Honourable Benjamin Franklin, Esq, Yorktown, May 16, 1778.

46. His first pay, seven hundred dollars for ten months' employment, was issued on March 6, 1778; see Ford, *Journals of the Continental Congress, 1774–1789*, vol. 8, 227.

47. TP to Benjamin Franklin, June 20, 1777.

48. Ford, *Journals of the Continental Congress*, vol. 7, 274. See the petitions to the Pennsylvania Assembly in the *Pennsylvania Packet* of May 20 and 27, 1777.

49. Common Sense [Thomas Paine], *The American Crisis III* (Philadelphia, April 19, 1777).

50. John W. Shy, "Force, Order, and Democracy in the American Revolution," in *The American Revolution: Its Character and Limits*, ed. Jack P. Greene (New York and London, 1987), 78–79. An impression of the reigning ethos of nonviolent persuasion was provided by Alexander Graydon:

> Being now independent, we had no further use for a king, or even the semblance of one; for which reason the equestrian statue of George the third in New-York, was thrown down and demolished. The head of the king was cut off by way of inflaming the public valor: but so little was the spirit of seventy-six like the spirit of subsequent eras, that the act was received with extreme coldness and indifference. Had even George himself been among us, he would have been in no great danger of personal injury, at least from the army. We were indeed, beginning to grow angry with him; and were not displeased with Paine for calling him a *royal brute*, but we had not yet acquired the true taste for cutting throats. (*Memoirs of a Life*, 141)

51. TP to William Bingham, Philadelphia, July 16, 1777.

52. TP to the Honourable Benjamin Franklin L.L.D., Philadelphia, July 9, 1777. Around this time, Paine had been reading Francis Grose, *The Antiquities of England and Wales* (published in London in 1773), which says, "The manner of using the fire-works was by throwing them from petraries or cross bows, or firing them to the great darts and arrows, and shooting them into the towns; a method . . . used with good success by the English, the last war in a naval engagement in the East Indies, between the squadron of Monsieur d'Ache and Admiral Watson" (vol. 1, London edition, 1787, 26).

53. Quoted in Christopher Hibbert, *Redcoats and Rebels: The War for America 1770–1780* (London, 1990), 158.

54. TP to the Honourable Benjamin Franklin, Esq., Yorktown, May 16, 1778.

55. TP to the Honourable Henry Laurens, Philadelphia, January 14, 1779.

56. Common Sense [Thomas Paine], *The American Crisis IV* (Philadelphia, September 12, 1777).

57. *The American Crisis IV* was reprinted, for example, in the *Virginia Gazette,* September 26, 1777; the *Boston Gazette,* September 29, 1777; and the *North Carolina Gazette,* October 17, 1777. A pamphlet edition also was printed in Fishkill, New York.

58. TP to the Honourable Benjamin Franklin, Esq., Yorktown, May 16, 1778.

59. See Worthington C. Ford, "Defences of Philadelphia in 1777," *Pennsylvania Magazine of History and Biography* 17–20 (1894–1896).

60. Following quotes are from TP to the Honourable Benjamin Franklin, Esq., Yorktown, May 16, 1778.

61. Conway, *The Life of Thomas Paine,* vol. 1, 99.

62. Timothy Matlack to TP, in Conway, *The Life of Thomas Paine,* vol. 1, 94.

63. TP to the Honourable Richard Henry Lee, Headquarters, fourteen miles from Philadelphia, October 30, 1777. Events confirmed Paine's suspicions, for General Burgoyne's troops remained in America another five years.

64. Ibid.

65. *Bucks County Provincial Tax Book, 1776* (Genealogical Society of Pennsylvania; photocopy, Historical Society of Pennsylvania), 15. The following account of Joseph Kirkbride is based on "Kirkbride Family Notes. Abstracts of Deeds, Land Drafts, etc." (Historical Society of Pennsylvania, FC/Ki); William W. Hinshaw, *Encyclopedia of American Quaker Genealogy,* vol. 2, 1007–1008; W. W. H. Davis, "Early Settlers in Bucks County," in *Bucks County Historical Society Papers,* vol. 2 (1909), 197–198; Moncure D. Conway, *The Life of Thomas Paine,* 3d ed., vol. 1 (New York, 1908), 110, 198, 267; vol. 2, 318, 325, 462, 472; W. J. Bell, Jr., "Joseph Kirkbride (1731–1803)" (manuscript, American Philosophical Society, 1974).

66. TP to the Honourable Benjamin Franklin, Esq., Yorktown, May 16, 1778.

67. TP to Benjamin Franklin, Philadelphia, October 24, 1778.

68. James Thacher, *A Military Journal During the American Revolutionary War, from 1775 to 1783* (Boston, 1823), 154 n.

69. The dispute about George Washington's military leadership is analyzed in Burnett, *The Continental Congress,* 279–297.

70. "To the Citizens of the United States and Particularly to the Leaders of the Federal Faction. Letter III," *The National Intelligencer,* November 29, 1802.

71. Christopher Marshall Diaries, February 12, 1778, Historical Society of Pennsylvania, 2nd case f1/36.

72. Colonel John Joseph Henry, *The Campaign Against Quebec* (1812), reprinted in *Pennsylvanian Archives,* 2d ser., vol. 15 (Harrisburg, Pa., 1893), 149 n. Henry's picture of Paine as a lazy, drunken atheist was written later, and it reflects that period's dominant prejudice against him.

73. Charles Evans, *American Bibliography*, vol. 5 (Chicago, 1909), 396.

74. Common Sense [Thomas Paine], *The American Crisis V* (Lancaster, March 21, 1778).

75. TP to Henry Laurens, Lancaster, April 11, 1778.

76. Common Sense [Thomas Paine], "To Governor Johnstone, one of the British Commissioners, on his late letters and offers to bribe certain eminent characters in America, and threatening afterwards to appeal to the public," *Pennsylvania Packet*, July 28, 1778. On the Johnstone affair see the "Declaration of Congress" in the *Pennsylvania Evening Post*, August 13, 1778; and Benjamin Franklin to Hartley, October 26, 1778, in A. H. Smyth, ed., *Writings of Benjamin Franklin*, vol. 7 (New York, 1905–1907), 197.

77. TP to Henry Laurens, [?], Spring 1778[?].

78. Quoted in E. James Ferguson, *The Power of the Purse, A History of American Public Finance, 1776–1790* (Chapel Hill, N.C., 1961), 120.

79. Silas Deane to Jonathan Williams, September 24, 1781, quoted in Ferguson, *Power of the Purse*, 74 n.

80. Committee of Secret Correspondence to Silas Deane, Philadelphia, March 3, 1776, in Wharton, *Revolutionary Diplomatic Correspondence*, vol. 2, 78.

81. Silas Deane to the Committee of Secret Correspondence, Paris, August 18, 1776, in Wharton, *Revolutionary Diplomatic Correspondence*, vol. 2, 112–129; Silas Deane to Pierre Augustin Caron de Beaumarchais, July 20 and 24, 1776, in Wharton, *Revolutionary Diplomatic Correspondence*, vol. 2, 102, 105–106.

82. See the oral report by Thomas Story to Benjamin Franklin and Robert Morris, October 1, 1776, and the correspondence between Mary Johnston [Arthur Lee] and Roderique Hortalez and Co. [Pierre Augustin Caron de Beaumarchais], London, May 23, 1776; Paris, June 6, 1776; London, June 14, 1776; Paris, June 26, 1776, in Wharton, *Revolutionary Diplomatic Correspondence*, vol. 2, 94, 97, 98, 151. During the summer and autumn of 1778, Lee wrote several times from Paris to the Committee for Foreign Affairs with further circumstantial evidence of the collusion between Beaumarchais and Silas Deane. He summarized his dealings with Beaumarchais before Deane's arrival in France in bold language: "The minister has repeatedly assured us ... in the most explicit terms, that no return is expected for these subsidies" (Wharton, *Revolutionary Diplomatic Correspondence*, vol. 2, 403). Beaumarchais stated the exact opposite in his communications to Congress (Roderique Hortalez and Co. [Beaumarchais] to the Committee of Secret Correspondence, Paris, August 18 and September 15, 1776, in Wharton, *Revolutionary Diplomatic Correspondence*, vol. 2, 129–131, 146–147). The literature on the disagreement is vast and includes several congressional committee reports prior to 1836 and 1842, when the heirs of Beaumarchais and Deane, respectively, were awarded some compensation. See especially Henri Doniol, *Histoire de la participation de la France a l'établissement des Etats-Unis d'Amérique, Correspondence diplomatique et documents*, vol. 4 (5 vols., Paris, 1884–1889), 1–23; Thomas P. Abernethy, "Commercial Activities of Silas Deane in France," *American Historical Review* 39 (1933–34): 477–485; Thomas P. Abernethy, "Origin of the Franklin-Lee Imbroglio," *North Carolina Historical Review* 15 (1938): 41–52; Charles Isham, ed., *The Deane Papers, 1774–1790: Collections of the New York Historical Society, 1886–1890,* 5 vols. (New York, 1891, XIX–XXIII; Charles J. Stillé,

"Beaumarchais and the Lost Million," *Pennsylvania Magazine of HIstory and Biography* 11 (1887): 1–36; Charles J. Stillé, *Silas Deane, Diplomatist of the Revolution* (Philadelphia, 1894); Elizabeth S. Kite, *Beaumarchais and the War of American Independence* (Boston, 1918).

83. Evidence that Silas Deane and Caron de Beaumarchais made unauthorized business contracts with French officers, whom they recruited to come to America, is contained in a letter from Theveneau de Francy to Beaumarchais, [?] May 14, 1778, in John Bigelow, *Letters of Theveneau de Francy to Beaumarchais, 1777–1780* (New York, 1870), cited in Thomas P. Abernethy, *Western Lands and the American Revolution* (New York, 1937), 212. During the whole Deane affair, surprisingly little was made of such contracts by Paine and others. An example of Deane's unexplained private transactions was his secret dealings across the Channel with Samuel Wharton, who in mid-February 1778 was sent 19,520 livres, perhaps in settlement of a debt arising from speculation on inside information at the time of the signing of the treaties between America and France (Isham, *The Deane Papers*, vol. 3, 28).

84. The best discussions of incipient party politics during this period include Herbert James Henderson, "Party Politics in the Continental Congress, 1774–1783" (Ph.D. diss., Columbia University, 1962), chapters 3–9; Burnett, *The Continental Congress*, 356–501; Robert A. East, *Business Enterprise in the American Revolutionary Era* (New York, 1938), 195–212; Wood, *The Creation of the American Republic*, especially 53–65, 499–506.

85. Quoted in James Thomas Flexner, *George Washington and the American Revolution, 1775–1783* (London, 1968), 335.

86. Silas Deane, "To the Free and Virtuous Citizens of America," *Pennsylvania Packet, or, The General Advertiser*, December 5, 1778.

87. Richard Henry Lee to Henry Laurens, Chantilly, August 13, 1779, in James Curtis Ballagh, ed., *Letters of Richard Henry Lee*, vol. 2 (New York, 1914), 118.

88. Quoted in Burnett, *The Continental Congress*, 364.

89. TP to the Committee of Claims of the House of Representatives, New York, February 14, 1808.

90. Common Sense [Thomas Paine], "To Silas Deane, Esq're," *Pennsylvania Packet, or, The General Advertiser*, December 15, 1778; "To the Public," *Pennsylvania Packet, or, The General Advertiser*, December 29, 1778; "Common Sense to the Public on Mr. Deane's Affair," 5 parts, *Pennsylvania Packet, or, The General Advertiser*, December 31, 1778, and January 2, 5, 7, and 9, 1779; "Common Sense to the Public," *Pennsylvania Packet, or, The General Advertiser*, January 12, 1779; "To Mr. Deane," *Pennsylvania Packet, or, The General Advertiser*, January 16, 1779.

91. TP to Henry Laurens, Philadelphia, December 15, 1778; TP to Silas Deane, Esq're.

92. See the notices and articles signed "Plain Truth" in the *Pennsylvania Packet, or, The General Advertiser*, December 17, 19, and 21, 1778. They are reprinted in Isham, *The Deane Papers*, vol. 3, 101–123.

93. "To Mr. Dunlap," *Pennsylvania Packet, or, The General Advertiser*, December 21, 1778; "Card of Thomas Paine for the *Pennsylvania Packet*," December 24, 1778, in Isham, *The Deane Papers*, vol. 3, 127–128.

94. "It gives me great pain," complained Gouverneur Morris to Congress on January 7, 1779, "to hear in the debates, both of yesterday and this morning, the word *party* made use of. This is a word which can do no good, but may produce much evil. . . . There is indeed in this house a chosen band of patriots, who have a proper respect for each other's opinion, a proper sense of each other's feelings, and whose bosoms glow with equal ardor in the common cause, but no party" (Edmund C. Burnett, *Letters of Members of the Continental Congress,* vol. 4 [Washington, 1928], 13). A more accurate account of the situation was provided by the delegate William Floyd, who sent New York governor George Clinton a copy of the *Pennsylvania Packet* on January 5, 1779, adding in an accompanying letter, "The publications of Mr. Deane, and Mr. Paine, makes a great talk in this place, and I am afraid will throw Congress and the people at large into violent parties" (Burnett, *Letters of Members of the Continental Congress,* vol. 4, 8).

95. Robert Morris, "To the Public," *Pennsylvania Packet, or, The General Advertiser,* January 9, 1779. Morris's allocation of funds to his own firm is discussed in Merrill Jensen, *The Founding of a Nation: A History of the American Revolution 1763–1776* (New York and London, 1968), 633.

96. Thomas Mifflin to Morris, January 26, 1779, New York Historical Society Collections, vol. 1 (1878), 441.

97. "Common Sense to the Public on Mr. Deane's Affair."

98. Francis Lightfoot Lee to Richard Henry Lee, December 22, 1778, quoted in Burnett, *The Continental Congress,* 367.

99. See Gérard's dispatch to Vergennes, Philadelphia, January 10, 1779, in John J. Meng, ed., *Dispatches and Instructions of Conrad Alexandre Gérard, 1778–1780* (Baltimore, 1939), no. 72, 467.

100. TP to M. Gérard, Philadelphia, January 2, 1779.

101. Ibid.

102. Gérard to the President of Congress, Philadelphia, January 5, 1779, Wharton, *Revolutionary Diplomatic Correspondence,* vol. 3, 11–12.

103. The proceedings are summarized in TP to the Committee of Claims of the House of Representatives, New York, February 14, 1808. See also Burnett, *The Continental Congress,* 373; Ford, *Journals of the Continental Congress, 1774–1789,* vol. 13, 31–36.

104. TP to the Congress of the United States, January 7, 1779.

105. Gouverneur Morris's remarks are reprinted in Jared Sparks, *The Life of Gouverneur Morris, with Selections from his Correspondence and Miscellaneous Papers,* vol. 1 (Boston, 1832), 199–202.

106. TP to the Congress of the United States, Philadelphia, January 8, 1779.

107. Ford, *Journals of the Continental Congress,* vol. 13, 36–38.

6. PUBLIC INSULTS

1. TP to the Honorable Henry Laurens, Philadelphia, January 17, 1779, vol. 2, 1165.

2. TP to His Excellency General Washington, Philadelphia, January 31, 1779, vol. 2, 1166–1167. He repeated the point in a letter written on the same day to Nathanael Greene to apologize for not having paid him a visit: "I have been out no where, and

was resolved not to go out till I had set every thing to rights" (TP to Major-General Greene, January 31, 1779).

3. TP to Benjamin Franklin, Philadelphia, March 4, 1779.

4. TP to Richard Henry Lee, Philadelphia, July 1, 1777. The reprinted passage is incorrect in Foner, vol. 2, 1134.

5. Nathaniel Scudder to Henry Laurens, March 13, 1779, in Burnett, *Letters of Members of the Continental Congress*, vol. 4, 104 n; John Armstrong to Horatio Gates, April 3, 1779, in Burnett, 136.

6. Ford, *Journals of the Continental Congress*, vol. 13, 54–55, 61–63, 70; Wharton, *Revolutionary Diplomatic Correspondence*, vol. 3, 16–17.

7. The review was published as "For the Pennsylvania Packet" in the *Pennsylvania Packet, or, The General Advertiser*, March 20, 1779.

8. Paine's irritation at Congress's silence is documented in a note by Charles Thomson (April 1779). The letters to Congress were written between March 19 and June 17, 1779. The original copies are held in Letters and Papers of Thomas Paine, Papers of the Continental Congress, Library of Congress. The list of those who voted for and against him is included in Common Sense [Thomas Paine], "To Mr. Deane," *Pennsylvania Packet, or, The General Advertiser*, April 13, 1779.

9. Francis Lightfoot Lee to Richard Henry Lee, December 22, 1778, 367.

10. Henry, *The Campaign Against Quebec*, 143–144 n.

11. "A Serious Address to the People of Pennsylvania on the Present Situation of Their Affairs," *Pennsylvania Packet, or, The General Advertiser*, December 12, 1778. This was a series (December 1, 5, 10, and 12, 1778) written after promptings by friends and was never concluded because Paine became caught up in the Deane controversy. Although articles were unsigned at the time, Paine subsequently acknowledged authorship of the four essays in "To the Printers," by "Common Sense" (*Pennsylvania Packet, or, The General Advertiser*, April 7, 1786). The Irish anecdote that follows is told by Paine in Common Sense, "To Philalethes," *Pennsylvania Packet, or, The General Advertiser*, January 21, 1779.

12. Philalethes, *Pennsylvania Packet, or, The General Advertiser*, January 19 and 23, 1779. The identity of "Philalethes" is uncertain. In Paine's reply, he speculated, "I am told that the writer or assistant writer of the piece signed Philalethes is believed to be a person of the name of *Parke*, and that he is subject at times to fits of craziness. This is not mentioned as a reproach but as an excuse for him; and being the best that can be made, I therefore charitably apply his disorder as a remedy to his reputation" (Common Sense [Thomas Paine], "To the People of America," *Pennsylvania Packet, or, The General Advertiser*, January 23, 1779).

13. *The Pennsylvania Evening Post*, July 9, 1779.

14. *The Pennsylvania Evening Post*, July 16, 1779.

15. See Jean-Noel Kapferer, *Rumeurs: le plus vieux média du monde* (Paris, 1987).

16. Cato, "The Galled Horse Winces," *The Pennsylvania Evening Post*, July 24, 1779.

17. *The Pennsylvania Evening Post*, July 22, 1779.

18. Cato, "The Galled Horse Winces."

19. As reported by Paine in "To the Public," *Pennsylvania Packet, or, The General Advertiser*, July 31, 1779.

20. Edward Langworthy to the Continental Congress, Philadelphia, July 25, 1779, in Burnett, *Letters of Members of the Continental Congress*, vol. 4, 344.

21. Whitehead Humphreys, "To the Citizens of America, and Particularly to My Friends and Fellow Citizens of Philadelphia," *The Pennsylvania Evening Post*, August 2, 1779.

22. Junius, *Pennsylvania Packet, or, The General Advertiser*, August 3, 1779.

23. See the reports in the *Pennsylvania Packet*, July 29, 1779, which also includes a letter from Paine, "To Mr. Dunlap," concerning allegations of bribery. See also the report "For the Pennsylvania Packet," signed "C. S." and probably written by Paine, in the *Pennsylvania Packet*, August 14, 1779.

24. TP to the Honourable Henry Laurens, Philadelphia, September 14, 1779.

25. TP to a Committee of the Continental Congress, Philadelphia, October 2, 1783[?]. The surviving records show that Conrad Alexandre Gérard, in a series of dispatches between December 19, 1778, and January 17, 1779, had informed Comte de Vergennes of developments in the Deane affair. On January 17, he commented on the influence of Paine's pen and concluded, "The only remedy that occurred to me was to have an offer made to M. Paine to secure him a salary by the King, in place of that lost." Gérard, wanting to be seen by the French court as working effectively, claimed, without evidence, that Paine had temporarily accepted the bribe. He repeated the claim shortly before leaving for France in a letter to President Reed: "J'aurois volontiers laissé M. Payne jouir les avantages quelconques qu'il pouvoit se promettre par la dénégation de l'acceptation qu'il avoit faite des offres de M. de Mirales et des miennes" (Gérard to President Reed, October 11, 1779, in Reed, *Life and Correspondence of Joseph Reed*, vol. 2, 156–157). Gérard attached to his letter a note confirming the substance written by M. Fooks, the official interpreter and translator for Congress. It is unlikely that Fooks, who was appointed to his post on June 2, 1779, was present at the meeting. The note has been lost. See Meng, *Despatches and Instructions*, nos. 64–74, especially 480–481.

26. "A Serious Address to the People of Pennsylvania on the Present Situation of Their Affairs," December 1, 1778.

27. The meeting with Gérard is described by Paine in "To Mr. Dunlap," *Pennsylvania Packet, or, The General Advertiser*, September 14, 1779.

28. TP to the Continental Congress, Philadelphia, April 23, 1779.

29. Henry D. Biddle, "Owen Biddle," *Pennsylvania Magazine of History and Biography* 16 (1892): 299–329.

30. Daniel of St. Thomas Jenifer to Governor Thomas Johnson, Jr., of Maryland, Philadelphia, May 24, 1779, in Burnett, *Letters of Members of the Continental Congress*, vol. 4, 232.

31. Quoted in Albert S. Bolles, *The Financial History of the United States, 1774–1789* (New York, 1879), 201. See also the discussion of inflation and its consequences in Miller, 425–477.

32. See the articles signed "A Fair Dealer" and "Mobility" in the *Pennsylvania Packet*, December 3 and 10, 1778. The latter warned merchants and speculators: "We can live without sugar, coffee, molasses and rum — but we cannot live without bread.

> Hunger will break through stone walls, and the resentment excited by it may end in your destruction."

33. "A Serious Address to the People of Pennsylvania on the Present Situation of Their Affairs," December 1, 5, 10, and 12, 1778.

34. TP to the Honourable Joseph Reed, Philadelphia, June 4, 1780.

35. Isaac Kramnick, "Religion and Radicalism. English Political Theory in the Age of the Revolution," *Political Theory*, vol. 5, no. 4 (November 1977), 527; and his "Tom Paine: Radical Democrat," *Democracy* 1, no. 1 (1981): 127–138. A similar interpretation is advanced by E. P. Thompson, *The Making of the English Working Class* (Harmondsworth, 1972). Officially approved Chinese observers agree. "Although Paine is opposed to the limitation of property regarding universal suffrage and also condemns the private property system," writes Tong Xu, "he does not propose the abolition of the private property system. Although he favours universal suffrage, he does not propose that people have the power to monitor and remove their rulers if they deem that that ruling power is abused. Therefore Paine's representative idea of a republic clearly shows his class limitation as a bourgeois political thinker." (From *The History of Western Political Thought* [Beijing, 1985], 310–311) The same thoughts appear in Hong Zhang and De Gu (eds.), *The History of Western Legal Thought* (Peking, 1990), 245–246. An East German version of the same Marxist-Leninist interpretation is defended by Horst Ihde, "Thomas Paine: Weg zum Revolutionär," *Wissenschaftliche Zeitschrift der Humboldt-Universität zur Berlin* 15 (1966), 635–640.

36. Paine's pathbreaking synthesis of pro-market and democratic republican themes may be seen as the forerunner of the later attempts by Jeffersonians to develop the Lockean ingredients of traditional republicanism by adding to it "the liberal position on private property and economic freedom," and "banishing the political distinction between the few and the many" (a development analyzed by Joyce Appleby, *Capitalism and a New Social Order: The Republican Vision of the 1790's* [New York, 1984], 48–49, 73, 99, 101).

37. William Graham Sumner, *The Financier and the Finances of the American Revolution* (New York, 1891), 301. The public meeting was reported in *Pennsylvania Packet, or, The General Advertiser*, May 27, 1779.

38. "TP (with Timothy Matlack, David Rittenhouse, Charles Willson Peale and J. B. Smith) to Robert Morris," *Pennsylvania Packet, or, The General Advertiser*, July 24, 1779. Earlier, on May 26, 1779, the committee had sent Morris a letter requiring him to appear before it to explain his actions. The letter is summarized in A. S. M. Rosenbach, *1776, a Catalogue of Autograph Letters and Documents* (Philadelphia, 1926), 70.

39. Gérard to Vergennes, Philadelphia, August 8, 1779, in Meng, *Dispatches and Instructions*, no. 147, 832. Gérard reported to Vergennes that in the election held on August 2, Paine's name was in thirty-fourth place on the ticket. Gérard concluded, "Mr. Payne, instrument of Messrs. Adams and Lee, author of the popular committees has caused all the trouble" (my translation).

40. Benjamin Rush to General Charles Lee, October 24, 1779, in *The Lee Papers*, vol. 3, 380–381.

41. TP to George Jacques Danton, Paris, May 6, 1793.

42. See the brief accounts of the committee formed to outline and defend the Citizen's Plan in the *Pennsylvania Packet, or The General Advertiser,* July 31 and September 11, 1779. See also Brunhouse, *The Counter-Revolution,* 74. The supporters of the Citizens' Plan subsequently protested loudly against the issue of paper money; see the rare letter, Tom Paine (with James Hutchinson) to General Roberdeau, Philadelphia, August 14, 1779.

43. TP to the Honourable Henry Laurens, Philadelphia, September 14, 1779.

44. TP to the Supreme Executive Council of the State of Pennsylvania, Philadelphia, September 28 and October 11, 1779.

45. Quoted in Alfred Owen Aldridge, *Man of Reason: The Life of Thomas Paine* (1959), 80. Paine's hard work impressed the Assembly, giving its members "great satisfaction" (Charles Willson Peale to Henry Laurens, March 6, 1780, Charles Coleman Sellers, *Charles Willson Peale,* vol. 1 [Philadelphia, 1947], 213).

46. TP to Henry Laurens, November 21, 1779.

47. Some surviving examples, all signed by Paine, include an official abstract of the minutes of the Pennsylvania Assembly (November 12, 1779) verifying the election of its delegates to Congress (Ford, *Journals of the Continental Congress,* vol. 15, 1263); a letter of introduction for Baron de Miklazaire directed to Colonel Peabody (Philadelphia, November 23, 1779); handwritten minutes, dated November 27, 1779, of a committee meeting to prepare articles of impeachment against two justices of the peace, Benjamin Wieser and William Atkinson (Dreer Collection, American Prose Writers, Pennsylvania Historical Society [1706–1913]); and handwritten minutes, dated May 26, 1780, of another committee decision to permit Mrs. Eliza Ferguson to live on a confiscated estate named Greame Parke (Papers of Joseph Reed, New York Historical Society). During the months of November and December 1779 and the second half of February 1780, Paine's name also appeared in virtually every issue of the triweekly *Pennsylvania Packet, or The General Advertiser.* Signed by "THOMAS PAINE, Clerk of the General Assembly," each item listed forthcoming Pennsylvania legislation covering a wide variety of matters, such as the expropriation of loyalists' property, the banning of currency counterfeiting, the prevention of "White Male persons, capable of bearing arms, from being Pedlars or Hawkers," the relief of the poor, the regulation of chimney sweeping, the protection of French citizens resident in Pennsylvania, the establishment of a High Court of Errors and Appeals, money bills, the embargoing of all exports from Pennsylvania, the supply of the Continental army, and the need gradually to abolish slavery.

48. Paine's authorship of the preamble is claimed by Moncure Conway, who reprinted the preamble twice under Paine's name (*The Life of Thomas Paine,* vol. 1, 154–155; *The Writings of Thomas Paine,* vol. 2, 29–30). Conway attempted to bolster his claim by invoking the authority of Reed (op. cit., vol. 2, 177–178, 481), who in fact ascribed the authorship of the preamble to George Bryan, on good evidence. Worried by the flimsiness of his claim, but dedicated to demonstrating its truth, Conway proposed that it "is now easily proved by a comparison of its sentiments and phraseology with the anti-slavery writings of Paine." There are indeed parallels with Paine's March 1775 essay "To Americans [*sic*]," but Conway further weakened his slim case with the extravagant conclusion that Paine, "who alone seems to have been thinking of the Negroes during that revolutionary epoch, thus had some reward in writing the first

proclamation of emancipation in America" (*The Life of Thomas Paine*, vol. 1, 154). Conway's reasoning subsequently passed into legend, repeated, for example, by Philip S. Foner (*The Complete Writings of Thomas Paine*, vol. 2, 21) who rests his case on the study of Robert L. Brunhouse (*The Counter-Revolution*, 80–81), which in fact provides no such evidence of Paine's authorship. Arnold Kimsey King doubts Paine's authorship with an equally flimsy argument: "If Paine had played an even minor role in writing the Pennsylvania Emancipation Act, the first one in America, it is safe to assume that his vanity would have led him to reveal it later" ("Thomas Paine in America," 242, note 86). Vanity sometimes got the better of Paine, it is true, but not always did he brag about his writings, his silence about his earliest texts being a striking case in point. More balanced and helpful accounts of the background to the preamble and the law include Arthur Zilversmit, *The First Emancipation: The Abolition of Slavery in the North* (Chicago, 1967), chapter 5; Gary B. Nash, *Forging Freedom: The Formation of Philadelphia's Black Community, 1720–1840* (Cambridge, Mass., 1988); Gary B. Nash and Jean R. Soderlund, *Freedom by Degrees: Emancipation and Its Aftermath in Pennsylvania* (New York, 1990).

49. Justice, and Humanity [Thomas Paine], "To Amricans [*sic*]," *Pennsylvania Journal; and the Weekly Advertiser*, March 8, 1775.

50. J. Franklin Jameson, *The American Revolution Considered as a Social Movement* (Princeton, N.J., 1926), 21–22.

51. Paul E. Lovejoy, "The Volume of the Atlantic Slave Trade: A Synthesis," *Journal of African History* 23, no. 4 (1982): 473–502.

52. Among the best studies of these efforts are Louis S. Gerteis, *Morality and Utility in American Antislavery Reform* (Chapel Hill, N.C., 1987), 8; Gary B. Nash, *Race and Revolution* (Madison, Wis., 1990), chapter 1; David Brion Davis, *The Problem of Slavery in the Age of Revolution, 1770–1823* (Ithaca, N.Y., 1975); Jean R. Soderlund, *Quakers and Slavery: A Divided Spirit* (Princeton, N.J., 1985).

53. *An Act for the Gradual Abolition of Slavery*, March 1, 1780.

54. Common Sense [Thomas Paine], *The American Crisis VIII* (Philadelphia, March 1780).

55. George Washington to the President of Congress, Morris Town, January 5, 1780, in John C. Fitzpatrick, ed., *The Writings of George Washington*, vol. 17 (Washington, 1937), 357–358.

56. Nathanael Greene to Moore Furman, January 4, 1780, in George Dangerfield, *Chancellor Robert R. Livingston of New York, 1746–1813* (New York, 1960), 120.

57. TP to [Joseph Reed?], circa January 1780.

58. George Washington to President Joseph Reed, Morris Town, May 28, 1780, in Fitzpatrick, *The Writings of George Washington*, vol. 18, 434, 439.

59. See the account in William Moultrie, *Memoirs of the American Revolution*, vol. 2 (New York, 1802), 96–97; Cumming and Rankin, *The Fate of a Nation*, 273–282.

60. TP to Blair McClenaghan, Philadelphia, May 1780.

61. TP to the Honourable Joseph Reed, Philadelphia, June 4, 1780; *A Plan for Recruiting the Army* (circa June 1780).

62. TP to Blair McClenaghan [?], Philadelphia, May 1780 [?].

63. TP to the Honourable Joseph Reed, Philadelphia, June 4, 1780.

64. *Pennsylvania Gazette,* July 5, 1780.

65. *Dissertation on Government,* vol. 2, 385. The founding of the Bank of Pennsylvania and its gradual evolution into the Bank of North America is examined in detail in William Graham Sumner, *The Financier and the Finances of the American Revolution,* vol. 2 (New York, 1892), 21–35; Bray Hammond, *Banks and Politics in America from the Revolution to the Civil War* (Princeton, N.J., 1957), 43–46; Lawrence Lewis, Jr., *A History of the Bank of North America* (Philadelphia, 1882), 2–35.

66. TP to Blair McClenaghan [?], Philadelphia, May 1780[?].

67. Common Sense [Thomas Paine], *The American Crisis IX* (Philadelphia, June 9, 1780).

68. The University of Pennsylvania Trustees' Minutes for July 4, 1780 read: "Mr. Thomas Paine being Proposed as a Proper person to receive the Honorary Degree of Master of Arts — It was unanimously agree'd to Cnfer upon him the Degree of Master of Arts, and that his Name be inserted in the Mandamus (The University of Pennsylvania Archives and Records Center, Philadelphia).

69. In *Letter to Abbé Raynal, on the Affairs of North America; in which the mistakes in the Abbes [sic] Account of the Revolution of America are Corrected and Cleared Up,* his byline reads "Thomas Paine, M.A. of the University of Pennsylvania, and Author of 'Common Sense'" (Philadelphia: Printed by Melchior Steiner and sold by Robert Aitken, 1782).

70. TP to the Honourable Henry Laurens, Philadelphia, September 14, 1779.

71. TP to a Committee of the Continental Congress, Philadelphia, October 2, 1783.

72. Paine, *The American Crisis II.*

73. TP to the Honourable Joseph Reed, Philadelphia, September 9, 1780.

74. TP to a Committee of the Continental Congress, Philadelphia, October 1783.

75. TP to the Honourable Members of the General Assembly of Pennsylvania, November 3, 1780.

76. TP to a Committee of the Continental Congress, Philadelphia, October 1783.

77. George Washington to President Joseph Reed, Morris Town, May 28 [31?], 1780.

78. Common Sense [Thomas Paine], *The Crisis Extraordinary,* Philadelphia, October 4, 1780.

79. "An order was drawn on the Treasurer in favour of Thomas Paine, Esq'r, for the amount of 360 dollars, Continental money, in State money, at 60 for one, amount of his account for ten dozen of the Crisis Extraordinary, at 36 dollars per dozen" (entry dated Philadelphia, October 10, 1780, *Minutes of the Supreme Executive Council of Pennsylvania,* vol. 12 [Harrisburg, Pa., 1853], 503).

80. TP to a Committee of the Continental Congress, Philadelphia, October 1783.

81. TP to the Honourable Senate of the United States, New York, January 21, 1808.

82. John Laurens to George Washington, December 23, 1780, in Sara Bertha Townsend, *An American Soldier: The Life of John Laurens* (Raleigh, N.C., 1958), 164.

83. John Laurens to his father, February 9, 1778, in David D. Wallace, *Life of Henry Laurens,* 122.

84. TP to Robert Morris, Esquire, February 20, 1782. On John Laurens, see "Sketch of the Life of Lieutenant-Colonel John Laurens," in Wallace, *Life of Henry Laurens,*

463–494; Flexner, *George Washington and the American Revolution*, 257, 341, 409, 432; Townsend, *An American Soldier*, passim; *Army Correspondence of Col. John Laurens, 1777–78*, with a memoir by William Gilmore Simms (New York, 1867).

85. Marquis de Chastellux, *Travels in North America in the Years 1780, 1781 and 1782* (Bowling Green, Ohio, 1910), 419–420.

86. TP to a Committee of the Continental Congress, Philadelphia, October 1783.

87. Sarah Franklin Bache to Benjamin Franklin, January 14, 1781, photocopy, The Gimbel Collection, American Philosophical Society, Philadelphia.

88. See the report of the proceedings in *The American Philosophical Society Year Book, 1943* (Philadelphia, 1944), 72–73. Twenty-one names were proposed, and seven were elected, including "the Marquis de la Fayette" and "the Chevalier de Chatelleux." Mr. John Nancarrow, proposed by Colonel Lewis Nicola, was struck off the list along with Paine, who had to wait another four years before the American Philosophical Society finally voted for his admission; see the *Pennsylvania Packet*, February 2, 1785.

89. TP to a Committee of the Continental Congress, Philadelphia, October 1783.

90. TP to Major-General Nathanael Greene, Philadelphia, January 10, 1781.

91. On the departure of the *Alliance*, see Gardener W. Allen, *A Naval History of the American Revolution*, vol. 2 (2 vols., Boston and New York, 1913), 547; M. I. J. Griffin, "Commodore John Barry," *Annual Report of the American Historical Association* (Washington, 1895), 356.

7. THE FEDERALIST

1. TP to James Hutchinson, L'Orient, March 11, 1781. Other descriptions of the voyage of the *Alliance* include Allen, *A Naval History*, vol. 2, 547; John Laurens to the President of Congress, L'Orient, March 11, 1781, Wharton, *Revolutionary Diplomatic Correspondence*, vol. 4, 279.

2. TP to James Hutchinson, L'Orient, March 11, 1781.

3. Ibid.

4. *Annual Report of the American Historical Association*, 356.

5. TP to James Hutchinson, L'Orient, March 11, 1791.

6. Jonathan Williams to Benjamin Franklin, Nantes, April 18, 1781, Franklin Papers, vol. 5, no. 20, University of Pennsylvania Library, Philadelphia.

7. See Durand Echeverria, *Mirage in the West: A History of the French Image of American Society to 1815* (Princeton, 1957).

8. Winslow C. Watson, ed., *Men and Times of the Revolution; or, Memoirs of Elkanah Watson* (New York, 1856), 108–110.

9. Evidence of these clerical activities include an undated letter to Benjamin Franklin Bache (circa April 1781) requesting "some commercial information" for John Laurens and a letter to Ralph Izard, probably written during May 1781. The letter, subsequently lost, is mentioned by Paine in TP to a Committee of the Continental Congress, Philadelphia, October 1783. The background of Paine's stay in Passy is sketched in Major William Jackson, "Embassy of Lieut. Col. Laurens to France in

1781," in Alexander Garden, *Anecdotes of the Revolutionary War in America* (Charleston, S.C., 1826), 12–18; "The Mission of Col. John Laurens to Europe in 1781," *South Carolina Historical and Geneaological Magazine* 1, nos. 1–4 (1900), 2, nos. 1, 2 (1901), passim.

10. John Laurens to the President of Congress, Philadelphia, September 2, 1781, in Wharton, *Revolutionary Diplomatic Correspondence*, vol. 4, 686.

11. TP to a Committee of the Continental Congress, Philadelphia, October 1783.

12. Conway, *The Life of Thomas Paine,* vol. 1, 171.

13. TP to Robert Morris, Esq., February 20, 1782.

14. TP to a Committee of the Continental Congress, Philadelphia, October 1783.

15. TP to William Temple Franklin, Paris, May 1781, in Franklin Papers, vol. 57, no. 126, American Philosophical Society, Philadelphia.

16. TP to Nathanael Greene, Philadelphia, September 10, 1781; cf. John Laurens to the President of Congress, Philadelphia, September 2, 1781, 692.

17. The arrival of the convoy was reported in *Pennsylvania Journal; and the Weekly Advertiser,* September 12, 1781. The report noted, "Among other articles, it is said, they contain twenty thousand suits of cloaths, and at least three million of livres, on account of the United States. Col. Laurens, who has had the honour of transacting this important business at the Court of Versailles, came passenger, accompanied by Mr. Paine, the celebrated author of *Common Sense.*"

18. See Gaillard Hunt, ed., *Journals of the Continental Congress, 1774–1789,* vol. 21 (Washington, 1912), 932. The minutes of September 4, 1781, state: "That all the money shipped by the order of Mr. Laurens, for the use of the United States, be upon its arrival delivered to the order of the superintendant of finance, who is hereby empowered and directed to take charge of the same." See also Merrill Jensen, *The New Nation: A History of the United States During the Confederation* (New York, 1950), 61–62.

19. Compare the buoyant tone of John Laurens to the President of Congress, Philadelphia, September 2, 1781, 685–692.

20. Chastellux, *Travels in North America.*

21. TP to a Committee of the Continental Congress, Philadelphia, October 1783.

22. Ibid.

23. TP to His Excellency General Washington, Philadelphia, November 30, 1781.

24. TP to a Committee of the Continental Congress, Philadelphia, October 1783. During this period, others became "interested" in his case. On December 11, 1781, John Laurens wrote to a member of Congress, Thomas Bee, urging him to raise the matter of financial support for Paine in the legislature (Papers of Thomas Bee, Manuscripts Division, Library of Congress).

25. On December 14, 1781, Chevalier de La Luzerne wrote to Comte de Vergennes to inform him that he had "engaged Paine to write a few articles on the advantages gained by the United States through the Alliance" (quoted in William E. O'Donnell, *Chevalier de la Luzerne, French Minister to the United States, 1779–1784* [1938], 212). The arrangement was kept strictly secret, and during the next two years it earned Paine more than a thousand dollars. According to O'Donnell, who perused a private collection of La Luzerne's files containing his correspondence with Vergennes

and most of the quarterly expense accounts rendered during the years 1779 to 1784, Paine was paid 1,530 livres ($306) in 1782 and 2,400 livres ($480) in 1783. La Luzerne's expense accounts for March 1782 were nowhere to be found in the files, and it is possible that Paine received an additional payment during that period.

26. Robert Morris Diary, September 18, 1781, in John Catanzariti and E. James Ferguson, eds., *The Papers of Robert Morris 1781–1784*, vol. 2 (Pittsburgh, 1975), 290.

27. TP to the Honourable Robert Morris, Esq., Philadelphia, September 20 1781[?]; "Extracts from the Papers of General William Irvine," *Pennsylvania Magazine of History and Biography* 5 (1881): 269.

28. TP to Jonathan Williams, Merchant, Philadelphia, November 26, 1781.

29. Robert Morris Diary, January 26, 1782, in Catanzariti and Ferguson, *The Papers of Robert Morris*, vol. 4, 115–116.

30. TP to Jonathan Williams, Merchant, Philadelphia, November 26, 1781.

31. See the memorandum written by Gouverneur Morris, Agreement with Robert R. Livingston and George Washington, Philadelphia, February 10, 1782, in Catanzariti and Ferguson, *The Papers of Robert Morris*, vol. 4, 201.

32. Robert Morris Diary, Memorandum on Thomas Paine, Philadelphia, February 1782, in Catanzariti and Ferguson, *The Papers of Robert Morris*, vol. 4, 327–328.

33. See Gouverneur Morris, Agreement with Robert R. Livingston and George Washington, Philadelphia, February 10, 1782, 201. See also Robert Morris Diary, February 19, 1782, in Catanzariti and Ferguson, *The Papers of Robert Morris*, vol. 4, 262.

34. Joseph Reed to Nathanael Greene, March 14, 1783, in Reed, *Life and Correspondence of Joseph Reed*, vol. 2, 393.

35. TP to Robert Morris Esq., February 20, 1782.

36. Alexander Hamilton, "The Continentalist, No. II," *New-York Packet, and the American Advertiser,* July 19, 1781. Others in the series were published on July 12, 1781 (No. I); August 9, 1781 (No. III); August 30, 1781 (No. IV); and April 18, 1782 (No. V). The essays are reprinted in Harold C. Syrett and Jacob E. Cooke, eds., *The Papers of Alexander Hamilton*, vol. 2 (26 vols., New York, 1961–1979), 649–674. The evolution of arguments about congressional weakness is traced in Greene, *Peripheries and Center,* chapter 9; Peter S. Onuf, *The Origins of the Federal Republic: Jurisdictional Controversies in the United States, 1775–1787* (Philadelphia, 1983).

37. The first two letters, titled "Messieurs Hall & Sellers," appeared in the *Pennsylvania Gazette* on June 30 and July 14, 1779; the third appeared as "Common Sense on the Fisheries, Concluded from Our Last" in the *Pennsylvania Gazette* on July 21, 1779. They were in reply to articles in the same journal written by "Americanus" (see Burnett, *Letters of Members of the Continental Congress,* vol. 4, 276–278), who was in fact Edward Langworthy, a former delegate to Congress from Georgia who was probably employed by Gérard. In the third letter to the *Pennsylvania Gazette* (July 21, 1779), Paine attacked the "Gallican Party" in Congress and offered them some good "Anti-Gallican" advice on how to handle Gérard, whom they mistakenly treated "as if that gentleman was *our* Minister instead of the Minister of his Most Christian Majesty. . . . And we seem in some instances to forget, that as France is the great ally of America, so America is the great ally of France."

38. The Articles of Confederation, Article 9, in Merrill Jensen, *The Articles of Confederation* (Madison, Wis., 1940), 266–269. See also Abernethy, *Western Lands;* F. J. Turner, "Western State-Making in the Revolutionary Era," *American Historical Review* 1 (1895).

39. The advertisement, placed by publisher James Davidson, appeared in *Pennsylvania Packet, or, The General Advertiser,* December 30, 1780.

40. The reaction of James Madison appeared in a letter to Thomas Jefferson, reprinted in William T. Hutchinson and William M. E. Rachal, eds., *The Papers of James Madison*, vol. 4, 155.

41. The accusation of bribery by "Caractacus" appeared in *The Freeman's Journal: or, The North-American Intelligencer,* April 24, 1782. The latter accusation appeared in articles published in the *Maryland Journal,* April 2, 1782, and in Richmond's *The Virginia Gazette and Weekly Advertiser,* April 6, 1782. It was perhaps no accident that they appeared at the same time as Thomas Jefferson, George Mason, Edmund Randolph, Arthur Lee, and Thomas Walker were preparing a written reply to a congressional committee report favoring the land companies; see Kate Mason Rowland, *The Life of George Mason,* vol. 2 (New York, 1892), 21 ff; Turner, "Western State-Making," 85. The allegation that Paine was in the employ of the land companies was made by Arthur Lee in a sixteen-page handwritten manuscript titled "A Concise View of the Title of Virginia to the Western Lands in Refutation of the Pamphlet Called Public Good" (Lee Family Papers, Alderman Library, University of Virginia). George Mason described Paine as a "mercenary party scribbler" in a letter to Edmund Randolph on October 19, 1782 (Rowland, *The Life of George Mason,* vol. 2, 29).

42. Private Papers of Simon Gratz and Anderson Gratz, 2d ser., vol. 1, 105, from a private manuscript collection mentioned in Albert T. Volwiler, *George Croghan and the Westward Movement, 1741–1782* (Cleveland, 1926), 317.

43. Common Sense [Thomas Paine], "For the Freeman's Journal," *The Freeman's Journal: or, The North-American Intelligencer,* May 1, 1782.

44. TP to Honourable Robert Morris, Esquire, Philadelphia, February 18, 1782.

45. The commentary on the speech George III delivered at the opening of Parliament on November 27, 1781, was published as "On the King of England's Speech." It appeared under the pseudonym "Common Sense" in two installments. The first was published in the *Pennsylvania Packet* on February 19, 1782, and reprinted in the *Pennsylvania Gazette* on February 20, 1782, and the *Pennsylvania Journal* on February 23, 1782. The second installment was published simultaneously in the *Pennsylvania Gazette* and the *Pennsylvania Journal* on February 27, 1782 and reprinted in the *Pennsylvania Packet* on February 28, 1782. Both installments were published together in *The Freeman's Journal* on February 27, 1782. The myth that these writings were intended by Paine as the tenth number of *The American Crisis* originated in the edition prepared by W. T. Sherwin (London: Printed and sold by W. T. Sherwin, 1817). The claim was repeated by Moncure Conway and Philip S. Foner (*The Complete Writings of Thomas Paine,* vol. 1, 189–207). The introductory note of the first edition of Paine's collected works (*The Writings of Thomas Paine* [Albany, N.Y.: Charles R. and George Webster, 1792]) had already scotched this possible interpretation: "No. 10, the publishers have not been able to procure after the most diligent search and enquiry in the principal cities and towns etc. in America." Paine confirmed in his will that he

was the author "of the several numbers of the 'American Crisis,' thirteen in all." Each one of these was numbered by Paine, with the exception of the tenth, which appeared on October 4, 1780, titled *The Crisis Extraordinary*, by "Common Sense" (Philadelphia, October 4, 1780).

46. Written under the name of "Common Sense," "To the People of America" was published in the *Pennsylvania Gazette* on March 6, 1782, and reprinted in the *Pennsylvania Packet* on March 7, 1782, and *The Freeman's Journal* on March 13, 1782.

47. See TP to Honourable Robert Morris Esquire, Philadelphia, April 7, 1782; Robert Morris Diary, April 8, 1782, and April 10, 1782, in Catanzariti and Ferguson, *The Papers of Robert Morris*, vol. 4, 537–538, 552.

48. An Alliance Man, *Hints on the present Condition of Foreign Commerce, Pennsylvania Packet*, April 11, 1782.

49. Common Sense [Thomas Paine], "To the People of America," *The Pennsylvania Gazette*, April 3, 1782. The article appeared simultaneously in *The Pennsylvania Journal*, April 3, 1782.

50. See the sniping remarks in Hawke, *Paine*, 124–126.

51. See Murray Forsyth, Unions of states: the theory and practice of confederation (Leicester, 1981).

52. Joshua Miller, *The Rise and Fall of Democracy in Early America, 1630–1789: the legacy for contemporary politics* (University Park, Pennsylvania, 1991), for example, critically examines Paine's political thought as a "liberal" contribution to Federalist efforts to centralize power and distance it from "the people" by the eventual passage of the 1787 Constitution.

53. [Paine], "To the People of America."

54. "To Sir Guy Carleton," *Pennsylvania Gazette*, June 5, 1782. This article was reprinted by Conway as "A Supernumerary Crisis" (*The Writings of Thomas Paine*, vol. 1, 355–359).

55. TP to His Excellency General Washington, Bordentown, September 7, 1782.

56. The following is based on a letter from Benjamin Rush to Elizabeth Graeme Ferguson, Philadelphia, July 16, 1782, in Butterfield, *Letters of Benjamin Rush*, vol. 1, 278–282. On La Luzerne, see Brissot de Warville, *Travels in North America*, vol. 1, 179; William Stinchcombe, *The American Revolution and the French Alliance* (New York, 1969), 82; O'Donnell, *Chevalier de la Luzerne*.

57. Quoted in Stinchcombe, *The American Revolution*, 83.

58. Benjamin Rush to Elizabeth Graeme Ferguson, Philadelphia, July 16, 1782.

59. TP to a Committee of the Continental Congress, Philadelphia, October 1783. The same point was made in TP to Robert Morris, Bordentown, September 6, 1782, where he explained that "one of my principal designs . . . was to give it the chance of an European publication."

60. *Letter Addressed to the Abbé Raynal, on the Affairs of North America. In which The Mistakes in the Abbe's Account of the Revolution of America are Corrected and Cleared up. By Thomas Paine, M.A. of the University of Pennsylvania, and Author of the Pamphlet and other Publications, entitled, "Common Sense."* The argument of Darrel Abel that the pamphlet marked the "stage where Paine actually ceased to think in nationalistic terms and became a practical internationalist" is misleading ("The Significance of the Letter to the

Abbé Raynal in the Progress of Thomas Paine's Thought," *Pennsylvania Magazine of History and Biography* 65 [1942]: 177). Paine had never been, nor was he ever, a nationalist in the strict sense. The modernist plea of *Letter to the Abbé Raynal, on the Affairs of North America* for the right of self-determination of nations, contradicts the claim of Hannah Arendt that "Paine wanted no more than to recapture the old meaning of the word 'revolution' and to express his firm conviction that the events of the time had caused men to revolve back to an 'early period' when they had been in possession of rights and liberties of which tyranny and conquest had dispossessed them" (*On Revolution* [New York, 1963], 38).

61. Charles Evans, *American Bibliography*, vol. 6 (Chicago, 1910), 180–181; Joseph Sabin, *Bibliotheca Americana. A dictionary of books relating to America*, vol. 14 (New York, 1884), 127, 129.

62. See Daniel of St. Thomas Jenifer to Gouverneur Morris, Annapolis, September 6, 1782: "I thank you for Common Sense's Letter to the Abbe Raynal, it is well wrote [*sic*], and will be of Service to any person, that may hereafter Publish a History of the American War" (Catanzariti and Ferguson, *The Papers of Robert Morris*, vol. 6, 330).

63. Letter by "An American gentleman in France," February 3, 1783, *Journal of Annual Literature*, quoted in Frank Smith, *Tom Paine, Liberator* (New York, 1938), 100. See also Echeverria, *Mirage in the West, A history of the French image of American society to 1815* (Princeton, N.J., 1957).

64. La Luzerne to Vergennes, August 27, 1782, quoted in O'Donnell, *Chevalier de la Luzerne*, 57 n; Jared Sparks Historical Manuscripts, European MSS (Harvard University Library, Cambridge, Mass.), vol. 1, no. 32, p. 77.

65. Common Sense [Thomas Paine], "The Crisis, No. XI. On the Present State of News," *Pennsylvania Gazette*, May 22, 1782. This essay probably drew upon information about the alliance supplied by La Luzerne, who wrote to Vergennes on May 14, 1782, reporting that he had employed Paine to write a few articles; see O'Donnell, *Chevalier de la Luzerne*, 217, and the earlier confirmation of the same point to Vergennes by Marbois, La Luzerne's secretary (O'Donnell, 190).

66. "To the Earl of Shelburne," *Pennsylvania Gazette*, October 30, 1782.

67. George Washington to Marquis de Lafayette, Verplanks Point, October 20, 1782, in Fitzpatrick, *The Writings of George Washington*, vol. 25, 281.

68. "To the Earl of Shelburne," *Pennsylvania Gazette*, October 30, 1782.

69. Nathanael Greene to Thomas Paine, November 18, 1782, quoted in Conway, *The Life of Thomas Paine*, vol. 2, 437.

70. Quoted in a letter of Benjamin Vaughan to the Earl of Shelburne, December 26, 1782, cited in Hawke, 132.

71. Ibid.

72. Examples of the "Country" ideology include A Countryman, *Providence Gazette*, September 21, 1782 (reprinted in *The Freeman's Journal*, November 6, 13, and 20, 1782, initially under the pseudonym "A Citizen of Rhode-Island" and then under the original pseudonym); A Freeholder, "A Vindication," *Providence Gazette*, October 26 and November 9, 1782; and the unsigned "Thoughts on the Five Per Cent," *Providence Gazette*, October 19, 1782, supplement (reprinted in the *Pennsylvania Packet*, December 12 and 14, 1782). These writings were directly or indirectly a response to the

articles written by James Mitchell Varnum, a later collaborator of Paine's and a former Rhode Island delegate, who wrote in favor of the congressional tax during March 1782 under the psuedonym "A Citizen"; see Irwin H. Polishook, *Rhode Island and the Union, 1774–1795* (Evanston, 1969), 66–75. On the English roots of Country ideology, see H. T. Dickinson, *Liberty and Property: Political Ideology in Eighteenth-Century Britain* (London, 1979), especially chapter 5.

73. On the controversy, see Ferguson, *The Power of the Purse*, 152–154. Paine's role in the controversy is well analyzed by Polishook, *Rhode Island*, 66–75.

74. TP to the Honourable Robert Morris Esquire, Philadelphia, November 20 [28?], 1782.

75. Thomas Paine, "Letter I, in Answer to the Citizen of Rhode Island on the Five Per Cent. Duty," *Pennsylvania Packet, or, The General Advertiser,* November 23, 1782. This letter was reprinted in the *Pennsylvania Gazette* on November 27, 1782, and in the *Providence Gazette* on December 21, 1782.

76. Thomas Paine, "Letter II, in Answer to the Citizen of Rhode Island on the Five Per Cent. Duty," *Providence Gazette and Country Journal,* December 28, 1782.

77. Robert Morris Diary, December 7, 1782, Catanzariti and Ferguson, *The Papers of Robert Morris,* vol. 7, 180; TP to the Honourable Robert Morris Esquire, Philadelphia, December 7, 1782; Catanzariti and Ferguson, *The Papers of Robert Morris,* vol. 7, 81–82.

78. Thomas Paine, "Letter 3, in Answer to the Citizen of Rhode Island on the Five Per Cent. Duty," *Providence Gazette,* January 4, 1783.

79. See A Freeholder, "A Vindication of Rhode-Island for Not Granting the Five Per Cent. Impost," *Providence Gazette,* January 9 and 11, 1783; a letter signed "A Lover of Liberty" and A. C., "On the Five Per Cent. Impost," *Providence Gazette,* January 25, 1783; T.P., "In the Name of Common Sense, Amen," *Providence Gazette,* February 1, 1783. Articles supporting Paine were rare. An example was the praise for "the necessity of some constitutional coercive powers, to oblige the states to contribute their proportions of the public expences" (Tullius, *Three Letters Addressed to the Public* [Philadelphia, 1783], 19–20.

80. David Howell to Benjamin Rush, February 8, 1793, Rush Papers, Library Company of Philadelphia, Pennsylvania.

81. TP to the Honourable Robert Morris Esquire, Providence, January 23, 1783.

82. Thomas Paine, "Letter IV: On the Five Per Cent. Duty," *Providence Gazette,* January 11, 1783. On Paine's attempts to split rural interests from the mercantile opponents of the impost, see Polishook, *Rhode Island,* 69–75, 77–78.

83. Thomas Paine, "Letter V: On the Five Per Cent. Duty, Addressed to Such of the Citizens of the State of Rhode-Island as Have Opposed the Measure," *Providence Gazette,* January 18, 1783. The letter was reprinted in the *Salem Gazette* on February 6, 1783.

84. Thomas Paine, "Letter VI: On the Five Per Cent. Duty," *Providence Gazette,* February 1, 1783. The letter was reprinted in the *Boston Evening Post* on February 15, 1783.

8. THE WOES OF PEACE

1. "To the Citizens of the United States and Particularly to the Leaders of the Federal Faction. Letter II," *The National Intelligencer and Washington Advertiser,* November 22, 1802.

2. Robert Morris Diary, March 24, 1783, Catanzariti and Ferguson, *The Papers of Robert Morris,* vol. 7, 180.

3. Merrill Jensen, *The New Nation: A History of the United States during the Confederation, 1781–1789* (New York, 1950), 68.

4. Common Sense [Thomas Paine], *The Crisis, No. XIII: Thoughts on this Peace, and the Probable Advantages Thereof* (Philadelphia, April 19, 1783). The pamphlet was widely reprinted. It appeared in the *Pennsylvania Gazette,* April 23, 1783; *Maryland Gazette,* May 1, 1783; *Providence Gazette,* May 2, 1783; and *Boston Gazette,* May 19, 1783.

5. TP to [?], Philadelphia, June 26, 1783; TP to [the Honourable Robert Livingston?], Borden Town, May 19, 1783. Although the addressee of the letter is not indicated, Paine's reference at the end of the letter to the "repossession of your City" suggests that it was written either to Gouverneur Morris or Robert Livingston, both of whom were close friends from New York. In a letter to George Washington (TP to His Excellency General Washington, Bordentown, September 21, [1783?], Paine enclosed a copy of an earlier letter written to Livingston explaining the need "in rendering my situation permanent." An endorsement on the original copy of the letter is in the handwriting of Robert Morris, which suggests that even if it was not originally addressed to Livingston, it was intended for private circulation among Livingston, Robert Morris, Gouverneur Morris, and Washington, his federalist friends and patrons.

6. TP to a Committee of the Continental Congress, Philadelphia, October 1783. Although the Cincinnati was open to both French and American officers and headed by such prominent figures as Washington, Lafayette, and Rochambeau, its formation stirred up considerable controversy and bred such spiteful attacks as the Comte de Mirabeau's *Considérations sur l'Ordre de Cincinnatus* (London, 1784), with which Paine may have been familiar.

7. TP to [Robert Livingston?], Borden Town, May 19, 1783.

8. TP to His Excellency Elias Boudinot, President of Congress, Bordentown, June 7, 1783.

9. See Varnum Lansing Collins, *The Continental Congress at Princeton* (Princeton, N.J., 1908). The signatories are listed on pages 263–269. Evidence that Paine wrote the petition is contained in TP to Doctor Benjamin Rush, Philadelphia, July 13, 1783 (misdated as June 13, 1783, in Foner, vol. 2, 1219–1220).

10. All of the above is from "Report of Mr. Clark, Mr. Peters, Mr. Hawkins on letters from T. Paine, October 31, 1783," in *Papers of the Continental Congress,* Item 19, vol. 5 (The National Archives, Washington, D.C.), 3, 5.

11. To a Committee of the Continental Congress, Philadelphia, October 178[3?].

12. TP to Robert Morris, October 14, 1783. His illness is also discussed in a letter of the previous day, TP to [George Washington?], Bordentown, October 13, 1783.

13. *The Cause of Yellow Fever, and the Means of Preventing It in Places not yet Infected with it. Addressed to the Board of Health in America* (New York, June 27, 1806).

14. The stolen coat episode is related in John Hall to John Coltman, May 16, 1788, Hall Manuscripts.

15. See Flexner, *George Washington and the American Revolution*, 524–526.

16. Colonel Benjamin Tallmadge, *Memoir of Colonel Benjamin Tallmadge*, ed. Henry Phelps Johnston (New York, 1904), 95–98.

17. TP to James Duane, New York, December 3, 1793.

18. Common Sense [Thomas Paine], "To the People of America," *Pennsylvania Gazette*, December 17, 1783. Conway misleadingly titled this piece "A Supernumerary Crisis" (*The Writings of Thomas Paine*, vol. 1, 376–380). See also TP to George Clinton, December 19, 1783.

19. TP to General Lewis Morris, Bordentown, February 16, 1784.

20. See Chevalier de La Luzerne's quarterly report of extraordinary expenditures to Comte de Vergennes (January 1, 1784), cited in O'Donnell, *Chevalier de la Luzerne*, 58.

21. TP to General Lewis Morris, Bordentown, February 16, 1784.

22. The complaint is recalled in TP to Mr. Hyer, New York, March 24, 1804.

23. TP to [?], Philadelphia, June 26, 1783.

24. Interview with Tom Hocter, New Rochelle, New York, July 27, 1991.

25. Quoted in Frank Smith, *Tom Paine, Liberator*, 107.

26. TP to His Excellency General Washington, New York, April 28, 1784.

27. TP to [?], Paris, [Feburary 1802?]; TP to His Excellency General Washington, New York, April 28, 1784.

28. George Washington to James Madison, Mount Vernon, June 12, 1784, Fitzpatrick, *The Writings of George Washington*, vol. 27, 420–421. On the same day, Washington wrote to Richard Henry Lee (Fitzpatrick, 422–423) and Patrick Henry (Fitzpatrick, 421–422).

29. James Madison to Thomas Jefferson, Richmond, July 3, 1784, in James Madison, *Letters and Other Writings of James Madison, Former President of the United States*, vol. 1 (Philadelphia, 1865), 89.

30. John Dickinson to the Pennsylvania Assembly, circa June 12, 1784.

31. John C. Fitzpatrick, ed., *Journals of the Continental Congress 1774–1789*, vol. 29 (Washington, 1933), 662–663. The full text of the resolution reads:

> *Resolved*, That the early, unsolicited and continued labours of Mr. Thomas Paine, in explaining and enforcing the principles of the late revolution by ingenious and timely publications upon the nature of liberty and civil government, have been well received by the citizens of these states, and merit the approbation of Congress; and that in consideration of these services, and the benefits produced thereby, Mr. Paine is entitled to a liberal gratification from the United States.

32. TP to the Continental Congress, New York, August 13, 1785.

33. TP to the Congress of the United States, September 27, 1785.

34. TP to a Committee of Congress, September 1785.

35. Recalled by Paine in TP to the Committee of Claims of the House of Representatives, New York, February 14, 1808.

36. TP to My Dear Father and Mother, New York, September 11, 1785.

37. The song, which I have not been able to identify, is mentioned in TP to His Excellency General Washington, New York, April 28, 1784. Paine's choice of subject illustrates the way in which legendary figures of antiquity often served as powerful, symbolic models for political conduct in the young American republic (a point reiterated by Carl J. Richard, *The Founders and the Classics: Greece, Rome, and the American Enlightenment* [Cambridge, Mass., 1994]). In 458 B.C., Lucius Quintilius Cincinnatus was summoned from the plow on his farm and appointed Dictator, to rescue a Roman army that had become surrounded by the Aequi. Cincinnatus accomplished his mission in fifteen days, then relinquished his dictatorial power to return to his plow, to serve the republic through honest toil and domestic virtue.

38. See Hammond, *Banks and Politics in America*, 48–64; Janet Wilson, "The Bank of North America and Pennsylvania Politics, 1781–1787," *Pennsylvania Magazine of History and Biography* 66 (1942): 3–28; Brunhouse, *The Counter-Revolution*, 173–175, 182–183; Alfred Owen Aldridge, "Why Did Thomas Paine Write on the Bank?" *Proceedings of the American Philosophical Society* 93, no. 4 (1949), 309–315.

39. Quoted in Hammond, *Banks and Politics in America*, 50.

40. The original letter to Fitzsimmons, dated April 19, 1785, was published in the *Pennsylvania Gazette*, December 21, 1785.

41. The letters so far identified include "For the Pennsylvania Packet," signed "C . . . S . . . ," *The Pennsylvania Packet* (March 18, 1786); "To the *Pennsylvania Packet:* On the Bank," by "Common Sense," *Pennsylvania Packet* (March 25, 1786); "For the *Pennsylvania Packet and Daily Advertiser*," by "Common Sense," *Pennsylvania Packet* (March 28, 1786); "To the Printers," by "Common Sense," *Pennsylvania Packet* (April 4, 1786); "To the Printers," by "Common Sense," *Pennsylvania Packet* (April 7, 1786); "To the Public, Number III," by "Common Sense," *Pennsylvania Packet* (April 20, 1786); "On the Advantages of a Public Bank," *The Pennsylvania Packet and Daily Advertiser* (June 20, 1786); "Number VI," by "Common Sense," *Pennsylvania Packet* (November 7, 1786); "Addressed to the Opposers of the Bank," by "Common Sense," *The Pennsylvania Gazette* (March 7, 1787). Prior to these letters, he published *Dissertations on Government; the Affairs of the Bank; and Paper Money* (Philadelphia, February 18, 1786).

42. Common Sense [Thomas Paine], "To the Printers," *Pennsylvania Packet and Daily Advertiser*, April 7, 1786.

43. Paine, *Dissertations on Government*.

44. James Wilson, *Considerations on the Bank of North America* (Philadelphia, 1785).

45. Common Sense [Thomas Paine], "For the Pennsylvania Packet and Daily Advertiser," *Pennsylvania Packet, and Daily Advertister*, March 28, 1786.

46. *Pennsylvania Packet*, April 4, 1786.

47. The debate is reported in Matthew Carey, ed., *Debates and Proceedings of the General Assembly of Pennsylvania, on the Memorials Praying a Repeal or Suspension of the Law Annulling the Charter of the Bank* (Philadelphia, 1786).

48. Carey, *Debates and Proceedings*, 116.

49. "On the Advantages of a Public Bank," *Pennsylvania Packet, and Daily Advertiser*, June 20,

1786. The letter also appeared in *The Freeman's Journal: or, the North-American Intelligencer,* June 21, 1786.

50. Common Sense [Thomas Paine], "To the Printers," *Pennsylvania Packet, and Daily Advertiser,* April 7, 1786.

51. "On the Advantages of a Public Bank." Three years later, Paine told Thomas Jefferson that he owned "one thousand dollars stock in the bank of Philadelphia [*sic*] and two years interest due on it last April" (TP to Thomas Jefferson, Rotherham, July 13, [1789?]).

52. Paine, *Dissertations on Government.*

53. Atticus [John Smilie], "Letter the First," *Pennsylvania Packet, and Daily Advertiser,* April 25, 1786); "Letter the Second," May 8, 1786); "Letter the Third," May 22, 1786; "Letter the Fourth," June 28, 1786.

54. TP to Mr. Claypoole, March 22, 1786, and TP to Mr. Claypoole, April 1786[?]. Foner (*The Complete Writings of Thomas Paine,* vol. 2, 1254) misdates the second letter and neglects both the first and others. See TP to Mr. Claypoole, March 1786[?]. TP to Mr. Claypoole, March 29, 1786.

55. Quoted in Sister Mary Chrysostom Diebels, S.S.N.D., *Peter Markoe (1752?–1792: A Philadelphia Writer* (Washington, 1944), 99.

56. John Hall Diaries, February 25, 1786, Journal No. 6 (February 21, 1786–April 20, 1786.

57. TP to the Honourable Thomas Fitzsimmons, Bordentown, November 19, 1786.

58. The argument is chronicled in John Hall Diaries, November 19, 1786, Journal No. 11 (November 17, 1786–January 14, 1787.

59. Brunhouse, *The Counter-Revolution,* 196–197.

60. T. I. Wharton, "Memoirs of William Rawle," in *Memoirs of the Historical Society of Pennsylvania,* vol. 4, part 1 (Philadelphia, 1840), 25. On the Society for Political Inquiries, whose members included Benjamin Rush, George Clymer, and Gouverneur Morris, see *Rules and Regulations of the Society for Political Inquiries* (Philadelphia, 1787); and Paul W. Conner, *Poor Richard's Politicks. Benjamin Franklin and His New American Order* (New York, 1965), 105–106.

9. RIGHTS OF MAN

1. Jennifer Tann, ed., *Selected Papers of Boulton and Watt,* vol. 1 (London, 1981), 179–180. On Hall's working experiences, see H. W. Dickinson and R. Jenkins, *James Watt and the Steam Engine* (Oxford, 1927), 280, 284–285; A. H. John, ed., *The Walker Family* (London, 1951), 55–76; S. Smiles, *Boulton and Watt* (London, 1904), 223–224.

2. John Hall Diaries, November 16, 1785, Journal No. 4, Library Company of Philadelphia.

3. John Hall Diaries, December 12, 1785, Journal No. 4: "With much pains drawd the board in at Hanna's chamber window to work Mr. Pain's bridg on. . . . I pinned 6 more arches together whitch makes the whole 9. I sweat at it. Mr. Pain gave me some wine and water as I was verry dry."

4. John Hall Diaries, March 10, 1786, Journal No. 5:

> Before 7 Oclock a brother saint-maker [John Fitch] came with a model of a masheen to drive boats against the stream. Poor man had

tears in his eyes as he had communicated his scheme to [William Henry] Hollingworth some time past and he had made some alterations in his principles and a company had agreed to put it in Execution by a model and would not admit him a partaker of the profits by taking him in as a partner. So he fully explained the model to me and Mr Pain and his calculations upon it. And would fain have given it to Mr. Pain or me, but I a stranger refused and Mr. Paine had enoug hobys of his own. . . . Gave him a breakfast, and after Mr Pain pointed out a mode to simplify his aparatus greatly.

5. TP to His Excellency Benjamin Franklin, Borden Town, June 6, 1786.

6. Quoted in J. G. James, "Thomas Paine's Iron Bridge Work 1785–1803," *Newcomen Society Transactions* 59 (1987–88): 192.

7. TP to a Member of the Pennsylvania Council, June 1786; TP to John Hall, Bordentown, September 22, 1786.

8. TP to Mr. John Hall, Bordentown, October 1786 [?].

9. TP to the Honourable Thomas Fitzsimmons, Bordentown, November 19, 1786.

10. John Hall Diaries, December 14, 1786, Journal No. 11.

11. John Hall Diaries, December 28, 1786, Journal No. 11.

12. John Hall Diaries, December 26, 1786, Journal No. 11. The description of the other viewers is cited in Conway, *The Life of Thomas Paine,* vol. 2, 467. Conway presents this as an entry in Hall's diary of January 1, 1787. No such entry exists, and I therefore presume that he quotes from a subsequently lost letter written by Hall.

13. John Hall Diaries, October 19, 1786, Journal No. 10.

14. TP to His Excellency Benjamin Franklin, March 31, 1787.

15. The letters of introduction by Franklin are reprinted in Albert H. Smyth, ed., *The Writings of Benjamin Franklin,* vol. 9 (New York, 1905–1907), 565–567.

16. John Hall Diaries, April 20, 1787, Journal No. 14.

17. TP to Benjamin Franklin, Paris, June 22, 1787.

18. Elisabeth Badinter and Robert Badinter, *Condorcet (1743–1794): Un intellectual en politique* (Paris, 1988), 255.

19. TP to George Clymer, Paris, August 15, 1787.

20. TP to Thomas Jefferson, Paris, August 18, 1787.

21. The original report is in the Archives de l'Académie des Sciences, *Procès Verbaux* (Paris, August 29, 1787).

22. See J. G. James, "Iron Arched Bridge Designs in Pre-Revolutionary France," *History of Technology* 4 (1979): 63–99; B. Lemoine, "L'Origine des Points Métalliques en France," *Annales des Ponts et Chaussées* 3e trimestre, no. 19 (1981): 44–52.

23. Archives de l'Académie des Sciences, *Procès Verbaux.*

24. J. R. Perronet, "Report on Monpetit's 200-foot span wrought-iron arch design, with two appendices of calculations," Ecole des Ponts et Chaussées, MSS 2219 (undated, probably late 1779 or early 1780), cited in James, "Iron Arched Bridge Designs," 63–99.

25. M. Charon [Migneron de Brocqueville], *Mercure de France,* January 26, 1788, 183–186.

26. TP to My Dear Father and Mother, New York, September 11, 1785. Elizabeth Hustler was the wife of the recently deceased (March 13, 1787) Samuel Hustler, whom Paine mentions in his letter, and who had been a prominent grocer in the town of Bury St. Edmunds, an owner of a nearby small farm, and who had been active in local affairs; see Suffolk Record Office 441/26.1; 441/26.6; 441/26.2; 586/43; 1627/208-211 (1784).

27. TP to the Right Honourable the Marquis of Lansdowne, Thetford, September 21, 1787.

28. TP to George Clymer, Esquire, Paris, December 29, 1787.

29. TP to Edmund Burke, Broad Street, London, August 10, 1788. Paine had for some time carefully monitored the Philadelphia Convention. The Marquis de Lafayette reported (Lafayette to Henry Knox, February 4, 1788, quoted in Louis Gottschalk, *Lafayette Between the American and the French Revolution, 1783–1789* [Chicago, 1950], 374) that in Paris he, Jefferson, and Paine had debated the new Constitution "in a convention of our own as earnestly as if we were to decide upon it." Although Paine shared Jefferson's concern for the Bill of Rights, he was decidedly in favor of adopting the Constitution, despite its flaws. His views evidently had not changed from the remark made to Washington summarizing his views from the early 1780s. "Thirteen staves and ne'er a hoop will not make a barrel," he told Washington, drawing the conclusion that "considerable advantages must arise from the Federal hooping of the States" (TP to George Washington, July 30, 1796).

30. TP to Edmund Burke, Broad Street Buildings, London, August 7, 1788; TP to Thomas Jefferson, London, September 9, 1788.

31. The original, handwritten patent application is titled, "Arches and Vaulted Roofs on a New Construction: Paine's Specification," dated September 25, 1788, Public Record Office, London, C73/18/22985.

32. TP to Thomas Jefferson, London, September 9, 1788.

33. TP to Thomas Walker Esquire, London, January 16, 1789. On Billy Yates and the Walkers, see J. G. James, "The Cast-Iron Bridge at Sunderland," *Newcastle upon Tyne Polytechnic Occasional Papers in the History of Science and Technology,* no. 5 (1986).

34. TP to Thomas Jefferson, London, February 16, 1789.

35. TP to Thomas Jefferson, London, December 16, 1788; TP to Thomas Walker, Esquire, London, February 26, 1789. Paine had prepared the way for further contacts with Burke by writing him a friendly letter, recently discovered (Thomas Paine to Edmund Burke, Paris, August 1787), urging him to join hands in working for peace between Britain and France. Around the time of Burke's inspection of the Masborough experimental arch, Paine also accepted Burke's invitation to stay with him for a week.

36. TP to John Hall, London, November 25, 1791.

37. TP to Sir Joseph Banks, Rotherham, May 25, 1789. This letter was reportedly read to the Royal Society on May 28, 1789. (TP to Sir George Staunton, Rotherham, May 25, 1789, Library of the Royal Society of Arts.) Attached to the letter is a note written by Staunton, dated April 30, 1790: "The enclosed very interesting letter was too late for the Society's Volume of last year. I hope it will be inserted in the Volume now preparing for the Press. The Subject is highly curious and the writer, whose

name is already celebrated in the Political World, seems to possess a Genius for Mechanics that promises much benefit to Mankind."

38. John Byng, *The Torrington Diaries, containing the tours through England and Wales of the Hon. John Byng,* vol. 2 (London, 1935), 23.

39. TP to Thomas Jefferson, London, June 17, 1789.

40. TP to Thomas Jefferson, Rotherham, July 13, [1789?]; compare the earlier, similarly worded account in TP to Thomas Walker Esquire, White Bear Inn, Piccadilly, April 7, 1789.

41. Ibid.

42. TP to Thomas Jefferson, London, September 18, 1789.

43. TP to His Excellency George Washington, London, May 1, 1790; TP to His Excellency George Washington, London, May 31, 1790.

44. Conway, *The Life of Thomas Paine,* vol. 1, 275–276.

45. TP to Thomas Walker Esq., April 7, 1789.

46. TP to Thomas Walker, Esquire, Lisson Green, August 8, 1790.

47. TP to Thomas Walker, Esquire, Lisson Green, August 30, 1790; TP to Thomas Walker, Esquire, Lisson Green, September 27, 1790.

48. Thomas Walker to Earl Fitzwilliam, September 28, 1790, Wentworth Woodhouse Muniments, no. F127/29, Sheffield City Library.

49. The diary entry, dated April 23, 1791, is cited in A. C. Todd, *Beyond the Blaze: A Biography of Davies Gilbert* (Truro, 1967), 208.

50. The undated eleven-page manuscript was probably written toward the end of September 1791 and is titled "Observations and Remarks on the Bridge proposed to be built over the River Wear at or near Sunderland," Sir John Soanes Museum, Draw 79, Set 1, 57A, Lincolns Inn Fields, London.

51. C. Hutton, "History of Iron Bridges," *Tracts on Mathematical and Philosophical Subjects* 1, tract 6 (London, 1812): 144–166.

52. A. Rees claimed that after the Walkers reclaimed the Lisson Green bridge, "the malleable iron was afterwards worked up in the construction of the bridge at Wearmouth" ("Bridge," in *The Cyclopaedia* (London, 1805).

53. TP to John Hall, London, November 25, 1791.

54. Ibid.

55. TP to Kitty Nicholson Few, London, January 6, 1789. On Paine's "American" perceptions of French events, see Ann Thomson, "Thomas Paine, représentant de l'Amérique républicaine," *Frontières* 4 (1993): 70–82.

56. TP to [George Washington?], London, October 16, 1789; TP to Thomas Jefferson, London, December 16, 1788.

57. TP to the Right Honourable the Marquis of Lansdowne, Thetford, September 21, 1787.

58. TP to Benjamin Rush, Paris, March 16, 1789.

59. Edmund Burke, *A Letter from Mr. Burke, to a Member of the National Assembly; in answer to some objections to his book on French affairs* (London, 1791).

60. TP to Edmund Burke, Paris, January 17, 1790.

61. TP to His Excellency George Washington, London, May 1, 1790. On the process of retreat, see John Keane, "The Politics of Retreat," *Political Quarterly*, vol. 61, 3 (July-September 1990): 340-352.

62. TP to the Right Honourable the Marquis of Lansdowne, Thetford, September 21, 1787.

63. TP to Thomas Walker, Esquire, London[?], February 26, 1789.

64. Ibid.

65. Badinter and Badinter, *Condorcet*, 244-245, 256.

66. See Aldridge, *Man of Reason*, 126-133.

67. See, for example, Owen Connolly, *French Revolution/Napoleonic Era* (New York, 1979), chapter 3. On Lafayette's career, see G. Michon, *Essai sur le parti Feuillant, Adrien Duport* (Paris, 1924); Louis Gottschalk and Margaret Maddox, *Lafayette in the French Revolution*, 2 vols. (Chicago, 1969-1973).

68. Robespierre's activities during this period are discussed in Jacques-Pierre Brissot, *Correspondance et papiers*, ed. Claude Perroud (Paris, 1911), 241; P. J. B. Buchez and P. L. Roux, *Histoire parlementaire de la Révolution française, ou Journal des Assemblées nationales depuis 1789 jusqu'en 1815*, vol. 3 (40 vols., Paris, 1834-1838), 213. On the emergence of the grass-roots democratic movement in Paris, see M. Genty, "Mandataires ou représentants: une problème de la démocratie municipale, Paris 1789-1790," *Annales historiques de la Révolution française*, no. 207 (1972): 1-27; Gary Kates, *The Cercle Social, the Girondins, and the French Revolution* (Princeton, N.J., 1985), 17-71; R. B. Rose, *The Making of the Sans-Culottes: Democratic Ideas and Institutions in Paris, 1789-1792* (Manchester, 1983); Jack Richard Censer, *Prelude to Power: The Parisian Radical Press, 1789-1791* (Baltimore, 1976).

69. The manuscript of Condorcet's speech is located in the Archives de la Seine (Paris), VD12, 48-57. It was first published in Bonneville, *Cercle Social*, letter 8 (February 1790), 57-75, and is considered in Marcel Dorigny, "Les Girondins et la droit de propriété," *Bulletin de la Commission d'histoire économique et sociale de la Révolution française* (1980-81): 15-31.

70. Sigismond Lacroix, ed., *Actes de la Commune de Paris pendant la Révolution. Première série, 25 juillet 1789 à 8 octobre 1790*, vol. 3 (7 vols., Paris, 1894-1898), 520-560. The responses of the democratic activists later associated with the Girondins are examined in Marcel Dorigny, "La Presses Girondine et les mouvements populaires: necessité et limites d'une alliance," *Mouvements populaires et conscience sociale* (Paris, 1985), 519-527.

71. TP to Edmund Burke, Paris, January 17, 1790. The changing relationship between Paine and Burke is well examined in R. R. Fennessy, *Burke, Paine and the Rights of Man: A Difference of Political Opinion* (The Hague, 1963); Thomas W. Copeland, *Our Eminent Friend Edmund Burke. Six Essays* (New Haven, Conn., 1949), 146-182. Compare the more recent interpretation of Paine's support for the Fayettistes, for example in Gary Kates, "From Liberalism to Tom Paine's *Rights of Man*," *Journal of the History of Ideas* 50, no. 4 (1989): 574-575. Kates writes, "Rights of Man was begun in January 1790 as an apology for Lafayette at the very instant when that statesman was under attack for his anti-democratic policies" (p. 574).

72. Burke's slowly rising hostility toward the French Revolution is analyzed in Carl B.

Cone, *Burke and the Nature of Politics: The Age of the French Revolution* (Lexington, 1964), 294–302.

73. *A Discourse on the Love of our Country, delivered on Nov. 4, 1789, at the Meeting-House in the Old Jewry, to the Society for commemorating the Revolution in Great Britain* (London, 1789). For the English background to Dr. Richard Price's sermon, see Derek Jarrett, *The Begetters of Revolution: England's Involvement with France 1759–1789* (London, 1973); Stuart Andrews, "'Insects of the Hour': Dr Price's 'Revolutions,'" *History Today*, May 1991, 48–53.

74. TP to [Thomas Christie?], London, April 16, 1790.

75. *The General Evening Post* (London), March 8, 1790.

76. TP to [Thomas Christie?], London, April 16, 1790.

77. TP to His Excellency George Washington, London, May 1, 1790.

78. See William B. Todd, "The Biographical History of Burke's *Reflections on the Revolution in France*," *The Library*, 5th ser., 6 (1951–52): 100–108.

79. *Substance of the Speech of the Right Honourable Edmund Burke in the Debate on the Army Estimates in the House of Commons, on Tuesday the 9th day of February, 1790* (London, 1790).

80. W. S. Lewis, ed., *Horace Walpole's Correspondence*, vol. 11 (New Haven, Conn.: 1944), 131–132.

81. R. Blunt, ed., *Mrs. Montagu "Queen of the Blues," Her Letters and Friendships from 1762 to 1800*, vol. 2 (2 vols., London, 1923), 249.

82. Quoted from an undated petition postmarked "Oxford 90. DE. 9," Collections of the Fitzwilliam Museum, Cambridge, England.

83. Edmund Burke, *Thoughts on the Cause of the Present Discontents* (London, 1770). Burke's suspicion of abusive power is well examined in Conor Cruise O'Brien's *The Great Melody: A Thematic Biography and Commented Anthology of Edmund Burke* (London, 1992). It is worth noting that Paine was attracted from the outset to Burke's reputed mistrust of power, and it is surely the key reason why Burke once humorously remarked to a mutual friend, "We hunt in pairs." Unfortunately, O'Brien's cursory dismissal of Paine both neglects the significance of this remark and fails to examine the anti-despotic sentiments that each author found attractive in the other's writings. Consequently, O'Brien's treatment of the breakdown of Paine's complex but close friendship with Burke is as shoddy as his hero's subsequent rash denunciation of "the ignorant flippancy of Thomas Paine" (540–541).

84. Quoted in Frank L. Lucas, *The Art of Living: Four eighteenth-century minds* (London, 1959), 156.

85. Samuel Rogers, *Recollections of the Table Talk of Samuel Rogers*, ed. A. Dyce (London, 1856), p. 76.

86. Quoted in Fennessy, *Burke, Paine and the Rights of Man*, 190.

87. The "Norman Yoke" tradition in English political literature, to which Paine belonged, is discussed in Christopher Hill, *Puritanism and Revolution* (London, 1958), chapter 3, especially pp. 99–109.

88. All quotations are from Edmund Burke, *Reflections on the Revolution in France and on the proceedings in certain societies in London relative to that event* (London, 1790).

89. All citations are from either part one, Thomas Paine, *Rights of Man: being an answer to Mr. Burke's attack on the French Revolution* (J. Johnson, London, 1791), or *Rights of Man. Part the second* (J. S. Jordan, London, 1792).

90. *Rights of Man* (London, 1791).

91. Ibid.

92. F. Sheldon, "Thomas Paine in England and in France," *The Atlantic Monthly* 4 (1859), 694.

93. The most outstanding is James T. Boulton, *The Language of Politics in the Age of Wilkes and Burke* (Westport, Conn., 1975 [1963]), chapter 8, especially pp. 143–146.

94. *Rights of Man* (London, 1791).

95. Ibid.

96. Ibid.

97. See Peter T. Manicas, *War and Democracy* (Cambridge, Mass., and London, 1989).

98. *Rights of Man* (London, 1791).

99. Friedrich von Schiller, *Wallenstein, ein dramatisches, Gedicht* (Tübingen, 1800).

100. *Rights of Man, Part the second.*

101. Cited in Moncure Conway, *The Life of Thomas Paine*, vol. 1, 238.

102. The emergence of various forms of *Polizeistaat* prior to the eighteenth century is examined in Adam Smith, *Lectures on Jurisprudence,* vol. 6 (Oxford, 1978 [1763]), 331–394.

103. *Rights of Man. Part the second.*

104. William Godwin, *Memoirs of Mary Wollstonecraft* (London, 1927), diary entry dated May 14, 1791.

105. William Wordsworth, *Descriptive Sketches,* line 653, in Thomas Hutchinson ed., *Poetical Works* (Oxford, 1969), 479.

106. Georg Forster to C. F. Voss, Mainz, June 4, 1791, *Werke im vier Bänden,* vol. 4 (Frankfurt, 1967–1970), 661; cf. Georg Forster to C. G. Heyne, Mainz, February 21, 1792, *Werke im vier Bänden,* vol. 4, 695. A Yiddish translation of *Rights of Man* was also published in Amsterdam during 1795; see J. S. Da Silva Rosa, *Gescheidenis der Portugese Joden te Amsterdam* (Amsterdam, 1925), 129.

107. József Kovács, *Az Író és a Forradalmár Thomas Paine* (Budapest, 1983), 7–8.

108. Charles Harrington Elliot, *The Republican Refuted in a series of biographical, critical and political strictures on Thomas Paine's Rights of Man* (London 1791), 2; Sir Brooke Boothby, *Observations on the Appeal from the New to the Old Whigs, and on Mr. Paine's Rights of Man* (London, 1792), 106 n, 273–274.

109. See Thomas Spence, "The Rights of Man for Me," reprinted in *Essays in honour of William Gallacher* (Berlin, 1966), 340.

110. Isaac Hunt, *Rights of Englishmen. An antidote to the poison now vending by the Transatlantic Republican Thomas Paine* (London, 1791), 85.

111. *The Monthly Review,* May 1791, 93.

112. Samuel Romilly to M. Dumond, April 5, 1791, in Samuel Romilly, *Memoirs of the Life of Sir Samuel Romilly,* vol. 1 (London, 1840), 317–318.

113. Lewis, *Horace Walpole's Correspondence*, vol. 11 (New Haven, Conn., 1973), 239.

114. Ibid., 318.

115. Raymond Williams, "Notes on English Prose," in *Writing in Society* (London, 1980), 69–70.

116. E. P. Thompson, *The Making of the English Working Class*, 117.

117. Quoted in D. Craig, *Scottish Literature and the Scottish People: 1680–1830* (London, 1961), 77.

118. Quoted in Elbridge Colby, *The Life of Thomas Holcroft*, vol. 1 (London, 1925), xli.

119. *The Oracle* (London), March 25, 1791.

120. Thomas Bayly Howell, *A Complete Collection of State Trials and Proceedings for High Treason*, vol. 25 (London, 1809), 116.

121. Batley to Wyrill (April 14, 1792), quoted in Fennessy, *Burke, Paine and the Rights of Man*, 228.

122. *The Gazetteer and London Daily Advertiser,* April 27, 1791.

123. This claim has been made by Hawke, *Paine*, 223.

124. Colby, *Life of Thomas Holcroft*, vol. 1, xli.

125. Howell, *A Complete Collection of State Trials*, vol. 22, 381.

126. TP to His Excellency George Washington, London, July 21, 1791.

127. George Washington to TP, May 6, 1792, Fitzpatrick, *The Writings of George Washington*, vol. 32, 38–39.

128. *Letter Addressed to the Addressers on the Late Proclamation.*

129. Ibid., 215–216; cf. TP to His Excellency George Washington, London, July 21, 1791, where Paine wrote that he intended to "make a cheap edition, just sufficient to bring in the price of the printing and paper, as I did by *Common Sense*."

130. Beatrix Cary Davenport, ed., *A Diary of the French Revolution by Gouverneur Morris*, vol. 2 (London, 1939), 159, 163.

131. Etiènne [Pierre Joseph] Dumont, *Recollections of Mirabeau, and of the two first Legislative Assemblies* (London, 1832), 261–262.

132. Davenport, *A Diary of the French Revolution.*

133. *Morning Chronicle,* May 29, 1791.

134. Rickman, *The Life of Thomas Paine*, 84–85.

135. *Morning Chronicle,* June 29, 1791; a different version of the same remark is reported in Rickman, *The Life of Thomas Paine*, 84.

136. Rickman, *The Life of Thomas Paine*, 84.

137. Edmund Burke, *Reflections on the Revolution in France.*

138. George Rudé, *The Crowd in the French Revolution.*

139. TP to Messieurs Condorcet, Nicolas de Bonneville and Lanthenas (Paris, June 1791).

140. Quoted in J. M. Thompson, *The French Revolution* (Oxford, 1964), 214.

141. *Reasons for Preserving the Life of Louis Capet* (January 1793). A French translation of this was read to the National Convention on January 15, 1793. On the Société des républicains, see *Le Républicain, ou le Défenseur du gouvernement représentatif* (July 3, 1791), 5; and Hélène Delsaux, *Condorcet journaliste (1790–1794)* (Paris, 1931), 49–61.

142. "A Republican Manifesto," *Le Républicain,* July 1, 1791.

143. *Gazette Nationale, ou Le Moniteur Universal,* circa July 10, 1791. Translated as "The Explanatory Note of M. Syeyes, in Answer to the Letter of Mr. Paine, and to Several Other Provocations of the Same Sort," *The London Review,* August 1791, 129–133. Paine's reply was published as "Lettre de M. Thomas Paine à M. Emmanuel Sieyès," *Gazette Nationale, ou Le Moniteur Universel,* July 16, 1791, and reprinted in *Le Républicain, ou le Défenseur du gouvernement représentatif* 3, July 16, 1791.

144. Quoted in J. M. Thompson, *The French Revolution,* 216.

145. "Lettre de M. Thomas Paine à M. Emmanuel Sieyès."

146. Davenport, *A Diary of the French Revolution,* vol. 2, 212–213.

147. The report is dated July 12, 1791; see MSS 3998, no. 47, Czartoryski Library, Krakow.

148. TP to His Excellency George Washington, London, July 21, 1791.

149. Ibid.

150. *An Impartial Sketch of the Life of Thomas Paine* (London, 1793[?]).

151. Rickman, *The Life of Thomas Paine,* 100–101.

152. Ibid., 102–103.

153. TP to John Hall, London, November 25, 1791.

154. *Address and Declaration at a Select Meeting of the Friends of Universal Peace and Liberty. Held at the Thatched House Tavern, St. James' Street, August 20, 1791* (London, 1791).

155. Edmund Burke, *An Appeal from the New to the Old Whigs, in consequence of some late discussions in Parliament, relative to the Reflections on the French Revolution* (London, 1791).

156. TP to William Short, London, November 2, 1791.

157. TP to John Hall, London, November 25, 1791.

158. TP to William Short, London, November 2, 1791.

159. TP to John Hall, London, November 25, 1791.

160. Howell, *A Complete Collection of State Trials,* vol. 22, 400–401; *An Interesting Collection of Modern Lives; with Observations of the Characters and Writings* (London, 1792), 6.

161. *Rights of Man, Part the second.*

162. Howell, *A Complete Collection of State Trials,* vol. 22, 401–403.

163. Ibid.; *An Interesting Collection of Modern Lives,* 8.

164. Edmund Frow and Ruth Frow, "Thomas 'Clio' Rickman, Poet, Bookseller and Radical Publisher," *Thomas Paine Society Bulletin* 2, no. 1 (1992): 3–5.

165. TP to Thomas Jefferson, Secretary of State, London, February 13, 1792.

166. Davenport, *A Diary of the French Revolution,* vol. 2, 368.

167. R. R. Palmer, *The Age of the Democratic Revolution: A Political History of Europe and America, 1760–1800,* 2 vols. (Princeton, N.J., 1959).

168. *Rights of Man, Part the second.*

169. *An Interesting Collection of Modern Lives,* 8; Christopher Wyvill, *Political Papers,* vol. 5 (York, 1804), 1, 51.

170. TP to the Chairman of the Society for Promoting Constitutional Information, May 18, 1792. (Misdated by Foner, *The Complete Writings of Thomas Paine,* vol. 2, 1324.)

171. Society for Promoting Constitutional Information, May 18, 1792, 47.6.12.143, British Museum.

172. TP to the Chairman of the Society for Promoting Constitutional Information, London, May 1792. Foner includes two versions of this letter, the second of which (*The Complete Writings of Thomas Paine*, vol. 2, 1325–1326) is misdated and contains a serious typographical error related to the year in which Paine last resided in Lewes.

173. Francis Place Manuscripts, Add. MSS, 27,814 fol. 178, British Museum.

174. W. Roberts, *Memoirs of . . . Mrs Hannah More*, vol. 2 (London, 1834), 424–425.

175. E. P. Thompson, *The Making of the English Working Class*, 117–118; Freda Knight, *The Strange Case of Thomas Walker* (Manchester, 1957), 117.

176. Memorandum on Clubs, October 1792, Home Office Papers, ser. 42.22; see also D. Davies, *The Influence of the French Revolution on Welsh Life and Literature* (Carmathen, 1926).

177. *Gazette Nationale, ou Le Moniteur Universel*, December 1, 1792.

178. *Gazette Nationale, ou Le Moniteur Universel*, November 26, 1792.

179. Interview with James Green, the Library Company of Philadelphia, April 1992.

180. *Boston Gazette*, September 7, 1789.

181. *Boston Independent Chronicle*, January 17, 24, and 31, 1793; *Boston Gazette*, January 21–February 4, 1793; *Columbian Centinel*, January 26 and 30, 1793; *Massachusetts Mercury*, January 30, 1793.

182. Thomas Jefferson to William Short, [?] July 28, 1791, Boyd, et al., *The Papers of Thomas Jefferson*, vol. 20, 692, 693. See also Dumas Malone, *Jefferson and His Time*, vol. 2 (Boston, 1948–1981), 351–370; Michael Lienesch, "Thomas Jefferson and the American Democratic Experience," in *Jeffersonian Legacies*, ed. Peter S. Onuf (Charlottesville, Va., 1993), 320–321.

183. R. D. Altick, *The English Common Reader. A social history of the mass reading public, 1800–1900* (Chicago, 1957), 69–73.

184. *Prospects on the Rubicon: Or an Investigation into the Causes and Consequences of the Politics to Be Agitated at the Next Meeting of Parliament* (London, August 20, 1787).

185. J. L. McCracken, "The United Irishmen," in T. Desmond Williams, *Secret Societies in Ireland* (New York, 1973), 62; see also Ann Thomson, "Thomas Paine and the United Irishmen," *Etudes Irlandaises*, June 1991, 109–119.

186. W. Benjamin Kennedy, "The Irish Jacobins," *Studia Hibernica*, vol. 16 (1976), 109–121; T. Pakenham, *The Year of Liberty: The Story of the Great Irish Rebellion of 1798* (London, 1969); B. Inglis, *The Freedom of the Press in Ireland 1784–1841* (London, 1954); H. L. Calkin, "La propagation en Irlande des idées de la Révolution française," *Annales historiques de la Révolution française* 27 (1955), 152–155. According to Theobald Wolfe Tone, Paine's later friend, *Rights of Man* quickly became the "Koran of Belfast" (cited in T. A. Jackson and C. D. Greaves, *Ireland Her Own* [London, 1971], 119).

187. Quoted in A. Aspinall, *The Early English Trade Unions* (London, 1949), 4–5.

188. House of Commons Proceedings, May 25, 1792 (London, 1792).

189. Quoted in E. P. Thompson, *The Making of the English Working Class*, 118.

190. Public Record Office, Chatham MSS, G.D. 8/229.

191. See R. Phillips, *Original Papers Published in the Leicester Herald &c.* (Leicester: Leicester Gaol, 1793).

192. E. P. Thompson, *The Making of the English Working Class*, 124–125.

193. *Times* (London), July 12, 1792.

194. *Intercepted Correspondence, from Satan to Citizen Paine* (Leicester Fields: J. Aitkin, [1792?]); cf. "A Word or Two of Truth," 47.6.12.60, British Museum.

195. *Brother Fustian's Advice to the Inhabitants of Manchester and Salford*, December 10, 1792, 47.6.12.100, British Museum; cf. the identical passage in Job Nott, Framework-knitter, "Advice to Sundry Sorts of People," 47.6.12.98, British Museum.

196. A Poor Man to his Equals, *Liberty and Equality: treated of in a Short History* (London, 1792), 39.

197. John Bull to his Brethren (London, [1792?]), Political Broadsides, 648.c.26, British Museum.

198. F. Paine to "Dear Daughter," Thetford, July 27, 1774, 47.6.12.105, British Museum.

199. Henry Gunning, *Reminiscences of the University, Town and County of Cambridge, from the Year 1780*, vol. 1 (London, 1854), 256–279.

200. R. I. and S. Wilberforce, *Life of William Wilberforce*, vol. 2 (London, 1838), 1–5. Reports of symbolic violence against Paine streamed in from outside the country as well, including from Barbados (*Columbian Centinel* [Boston], April 10, 1793).

201. James Woodforde, *The Diary of a Country Parson, the Reverend James Woodforde*, vol. 4, ed. John Beresford (London, 1929), 2.

202. Quoted in E. P. Thompson, *The Making of the English Working Class*, 122–123.

203. Frank Peel, *Spen Valley: Past and Present* (Heckmondwike, 1893), 307–308.

204. J. H. Priestley, "John Howarth, Lawyer," *Transactions of the Halifax Antiquarian Society*, 1949; *Morning Chronicle*, March 11, 1793. Further details of anti-Paine demonstrations are listed in Michael Weinzierl, *Freiheit, Eigentum und keine Gleichheit. Die Transformation der englischen politischen Kultur und die Anfänge des modernen Konservatismus 1791–1812* (Munich/Vienna, 1993), 37–56; Gregory Claeys, *Thomas Paine: Social and Political Thought* (Boston, 1989), 139–146; and Alan Booth, "Popular loyalism and public violence in the north-west of England, 1790–1800," *Social History* 8 (1983), 295–313.

205. Frank Peel, *Spen Valley: Past and Present*, 307–308.

206. John Knowles, *The Life and Writings of Henry Fuseli*, vol. 1 (London, 1831), 374–375.

207. Oldys, *The Life of Thomas Paine, the author of Rights of Man* (London, 1793), 158.

208. Address to the Jacobin Club, May 27, 1792, reprinted in Moncure Conway, *Thomas Paine (1737–1809) et la Révolution dans les deux mondes* (Paris, 1900), 210–212.

209. *Letter Addressed to the Addressers on the Late Proclamation.*

210. TP to the Attorney-General, [May 1792?].

211. TP to Mr. Secretary Dundas, London, June 6, 1792.

212. The original Romney painting is sometimes thought to have been lost, although the engraving by Sharp has survived. See Alon Bement, "Some Portraits of Thomas Paine," *Antiques* (July 1949), 34–35. During the nineteenth century, the Romney portrait was often said to be from the brush of John Wesley Jarvis, in whose house Paine lived in 1806. Moncure Conway, who lent the picture for a time to London's National Portrait Gallery in 1897, considered it to be the original portrait of Paine by Romney. His reasons are summarized in the *Athenaeum* (June 26, 1897), 848. The same painting is reproduced on the front cover of the American edition of this biography, with courtesy of the Thomas Paine National Historical Association.

213. (London) *Times,* May 28, 1792. Paine's editorial role in the prestigious *La Chronique du Mois* is examined in Gary Kates, *The Cercle Social, the Girondins, and the French Revolution,* 188, 202–209. Paine was appointed to the editorial circle of the journal after the resignation of Collot d'Herbois. Nominated by Nicolas Bonneville, the journal's producer and leading contributor, Paine joined the company of a group of prominent Girondin political workers who had been writing, socializing, and politicking together since before the Revolution. It may be that the purpose of Paine's appointment was to heighten his chances of election to the forthcoming Convention. Of the nine editors of *La Chronique du Mois* who were subsequently elected to the Convention during the summer of 1792, all nine were Girondins: Jacques-Pierre Brissot; Jean-Antoine-Nicolas Condorcet; Jean Dusaulx; Jean-Philippe Garran-Coulan; M. E. Guadet; Armand-Guy Kersaint; François Lanthenas; Sébastien Mercier; and Thomas Paine. Paine's first contribution to the journal ("Résponse de Thomas Paine a quatre questions sur les pouvoirs législatif et exécutif," *La Chronique du Mois,* May 1792, 85–88) reveals the impact of Pennsylvanian and wider American politics upon his political thinking. It proposed the establishment in France of a bicameral legislature. Each chamber would be empowered to debate the same proposed legislation, but not at the same time. While one chamber debated, the other would listen. After the second chamber had debated the same questions, both chambers would meet as a single legislative body to decide the matter at hand. During the summer of 1792, Paine also published *Sermons civiques adressés au peuple, par Thomas Paine* (Paris, 1792). Presented as the first number of a periodical, the essay condemned ignorance, opposed the bullying by governments of their subjects, and emphasized the importance of citizens using their powers of reason and judgement to contribute to the formation of public opinion.

214. Vindex [Thomas Paine?], *Old Truths and Established Facts, being an answer to A very new pamphlet indeed!* (London, 1792[?]). Responding to *A very new pamphlet indeed* by "Truth," Vindex denounced "that horrid traffick in human kind; which, in spite of the boasted refinements and the extensive philanthropy of an enlightened age, remains, though I trust not indelibly, to be its disgrace" (3–4).

215. TP to Onslow Cranley: Lord Lieutenant of the County of Surry; on the Subject of the Late Excellent *Proclamation: — or* the *Chairman* Who Shall Preside at the Meeting to be Held at Epsom, June 18 (London, June 17, 1792); and TP to Onslow Cranley: Lord Lieutenant of the County of Surry; on the Subject of the Late Excellent *Proclamation: — or* the *Chairman* Who Shall Preside at the Meeting to be Held at Epsom, June 18 (London, June 21, 1792).

216. TP to the Chairman of the Society for Constitutional Information, London, July 4, 1792.

217. Blanchard Jerrold, ed., *The Original,* vol. 1 (London, 1874), 41.

218. John Hall Diaries, September 6, 1792, Journal No. 30 (August 12–December 10, 1792).

219. G. E. Bentley, Jr., *Blake Records* (Oxford, 1969), 530.

220. *Gazette Nationale, ou Le Moniteur Universel,* September 23, 1792; cf. the accounts published in *The London Chronicle,* September 18–20, 1792. Paine's account of the episode that followed is found in TP to Mr. Secretary Dundas, London, June 6, 1792.

221. See J. Mason to J. B. Burges, September 13, 1792, in J. B. Fortescue, *The Manuscripts of J. B. Fortescue, Esq., Preserved at Dropmore,* vol. 2 (10 vols., London, 1892–1927), 316–317.

10. EXECUTING A KING

1. TP to Mr. Secretary Dundas, Calais, September 15, 1792.

2. To the English Attorney-General, on the Prosecution Against the Second Part of Rights of Man, Paris, November 11, 1792.

3. *The Celebrated Speech of the Hon. T. Erskine in Support of Liberty of the Press*, Edinburgh, 1793.

4. John Frost to Horne Tooke, September 20, 1792, in Howell, *A Complete Collection of State Trials*, vol. 24, 535; Richard Carlile, *The Life of Thomas Paine, Written Purposely to Bind with His Writings*, 3d ed. (London, 1820), 14–15; William Lindsay to Lord Grenville, September 27, 1792, in Fortescue, *The Manuscripts of J. B. Fortescue*, vol. 3, 472; and the report of Paine's Calais reception in the *Columbian Sentinel* (Boston), January 5, 1793.

5. J. M. Thompson, *The French Revolution*, 313.

6. Paine was nominated by the departments of Pas-de-Calais, Puy-de-Dome, Aisne, and Oise. See the *Gazette Nationale, ou Le Moniteur Universel*, September 8, 11, 13, and 15, 1792.

7. John Frost to Horne Tooke, September 20, 1792, 535; Carlile, *The Life of Thomas Paine*, 14–15; William Lindsay to Lord Grenville, September 27, 1792, 472.

8. John Frost to Horne Tooke, September 20, 1792.

9. Check the accounts in Gouverneur Morris to Charles Pinckney, September 23, 1792, in Davenport, *A Diary of the French Revolution*, vol. 2, 555; TP to James Monroe, Paris, September 14, 1794 (misdated by Foner as September 10, 1792).

10. Quoted in J. H. Thompson, *The French Revolution*, 317.

11. Material on Anacharsis Cloots is found in A. Tuetey, *Répertoire général des sources manuscrites de l'histoire de Paris pendant la Révolution* (Paris, 1912), vol. 10, no. 2482; vol. 11, preface. On the socio-political composition of the Convention's members, see Allison Patrick, *The Men of the First Republic: Political Alignments in the National Convention of 1792* (Baltimore, 1792).

12. Davenport, *A Diary of the French Revolution*, vol. 2, 555, 566.

13. Quoted in Albert Mathiez, *The French Revolution* (London, 1964), 229.

14. *Morning Chronicle*, October 4, 1792.

15. *Lettre de Thomas Paine au Peuple françois* (Paris, September 25, [1792]). During the same period, pursuing the same themes, Paine may have written the unsigned "Essai antimonarchique à l'usage des nouveaux républicains," *La Feuille villageoise* 49, September 6, 1792, 4–12.

16. TP to James Monroe, Paris, August 18, 1794.

17. I am presuming that this undated letter was written to Danton, since he was the only colleague on the drafting committee who read and spoke English fluently. It is located in the Danton Files, item no. 5, AF II 49, Dossier 380, Archives Nationales, Paris.

18. Quoted in J. M. Thompson, *The French Revolution*, 323–324.

19. An annotated copy is held in the Gimbel Collection, the American Philosophical Society Library, Philadelphia.

20. Quoted in Conway, *Thomas Paine et la Révolution*, 442; see also Davenport, *A Diary of the French Revolution*, vol. 2, 587.

21. Quoted in Frank Smith, *Tom Paine, Liberator*, 200.

22. Quoted in J. M. Thompson, *The French Revolution*, 331.

23. *Gazette Nationale, ou Le Moniteur Universel*, January 17, 1793. See also the accounts given in Conway, *The Life of Thomas Paine*, vol. 2, 4–5, and Frank Smith, *Tom Paine, Liberator*, 188–190.

24. See the summary of proceedings in *Gazette Nationale, ou Le Moniteur Universel*, January 18, 19, 1793; speech giving reasons for wishing to preserve the life of Louis Capet, *Gazette Nationale, ou Le Moniteur Universel*, January 23, 1793.

25. Quoted in John King, *Mr. King's Speech, at Egham, with Thomas Paine's Letter to Him on it, and Mr. King's Reply, as they all appeared in The Morning Herald* (London, n.d.).

26. Rickman, *The Life of Thomas Paine*, 129–130.

27. Ibid.

28. See the descriptions of these meetings in K. W. Cameron, ed., *Shelley and His Circle 1773–1822*, vol. 1 (London, 1961), 125–126, and in Conway, *The Life of Thomas Paine*, vol. 2, 66.

29. Georg Forster to Therese Forster, Paris, May 17, 1793, in Forster, *Werke in vier Bänden*, vol. 4, 861.

30. Rickman, *The Life of Thomas Paine*, 131–132.

31. Thomas Paine, *Forgetfulness. From the Castle in the Air to the Little Corner of the World*.

32. See the surviving extract from the minutes, dated April 1793, BB/3/72, 105, Archives Nationales, Paris.

33. TP to Thomas Jefferson, Paris, April 20, 1793.

34. Antoine Claire Thibaudeau, *Mémoires sur la convention, et le directoire*, vol. 1 (2 vols., Paris, 1824), 111.

35. *Le Patriote français*, April 17, 1793; see also the letter concerning the affair of Sampson Perry, W/269/16, Archives Nationales, Paris; and the report in *Gazette Nationale, ou Le Moniteur Universel*, May 3, 1793.

36. A full report of the trial was published in *Gazette Nationale, ou Le Moniteur Universel*, May 3, 1793. See also Conway, *The Life of Thomas Paine*, vol. 2, 50; Eloise Ellery, *Brissot de Warville: A Study in the History of the French Revolution* (Boston and New York, 1915), 334; and the document written by Sampson Perry, item no. 16, W 269, Archives Nationales, Paris.

37. Rickman, *The Life of Thomas Paine*, 151, 152.

38. TP to George Jacques Danton, Paris, May 6, 1793.

39. Miranda's trial is summarized in *Archivo del General Miranda*, vol. 12 (15 vols., 1929–1938), 170–172. The trial is analyzed in Aldridge, *Man of Reason*, 198–199. Paine's own thoughts on Miranda are sketched in TP to a Gentleman in Philadelphia, New Rochelle, March 20, 1806, and published in the *Philadelphia Aurora*, April 3, 1806; his description of the expedition against Louisiana is found in TP to Doctor James O'Fallon, Passy, February 17, 1793.

40. Lewis Goldsmith, *Antigallican Monitor*, February 13, 1814, quoted in Aldridge, *Man of Reason*, 201.

41. *Lettre de Thomas Paine au Peuple françois*.

11. PRISON TO DICTATORSHIP

1. Gouverneur Morris to Robert Morris, June 25, 1793, Davenport, *A Diary of the French Revolution*, vol. 2, 48.

2. "Forgetfulness. From the Castle in the Air to the Little Corner of the World" (Paris, 1794).

3. *Gazette Nationale, ou Le Moniteur Universel*, June 21, 1793.

4. Frank Smith, *Tom Paine, Liberator*, 201.

5. Recalled in TP to James Monroe, Paris, October 21, 1794.

6. *Loc cit.*; another version of the events, written by Paine, appears in Moncure D. Conway, "Newly discovered writings of Thomas Paine," *The Athenaeum*, n.d., 291–292.

7. TP to Citizen Barère, September 5, 1793.

8. Hawke, *Paine*, 288–289.

9. Bertrand Barère, *Memoirs*, vol. 2 (1897), 114–115.

10. See the anonymously addressed and undated letter, TP to Citizen Barère[?], September 5, 1793 [?]. The timing and addressee of the proposal are divulged in TP to James Monroe, Paris, October 21, 1794.

11. TP to Citizen Barère, September 5, 1793.

12. See Conway, *The Life of Thomas Paine*, vol. 2, 94; Aldridge, *Man of Reason*, 206.

13. TP to Thomas Jefferson, October 20, 1793.

14. The original documents related to Manuel's interrogation and trial are in W/295/246, Archives Nationales, Paris.

15. Quoted in J. M. Thompson, *The French Revolution*, 370.

16. *The Age of Reason, Part the second,* preface. The French text reads: "Demander que Thomas Paine foit decreté d'accusation, pour l'interêt de l'Amérique autant que de la France."

17. The copy is located in the Gimbel Collection, American Philosophical Society Library, Philadelphia, and is briefly described in Richard Gimbel, "The First Appearance of Thomas Paine's The Age of Reason," *Yale University Library Gazette* 31 (1956): 87–89. *Le Siècle de la Raison* differs substantially from its English-language sequel, *The Age of Reason; Being an Investigation of True and Fabulous Theology* (Paris: Printed by Barrois, 1794). The phrasing of words, sentences, and paragraphs in the French text is often different; it concludes with four pages of "Maximes républicaines," which do not appear in the English text; and, significantly, the latter's opening jeremiad about "the total abolition of the whole national order of priesthood, and of every thing appertaining to compulsive systems of religion, and compulsive articles of faith" does not appear in *Le Siècle de la Raison*.

18. Lanthenas to Thionville, F7 4774 64, Archives Nationales, Paris. Paine confirms that the manuscript was completed early in the year in a letter to Daniel Isaac Eaton,

who republished it as part of an advertisement in *Morning Chronicle*, December 19, 1795.

19. *Historical Sketches and Tales of the Town of Diss.*

20. Quoted in Harry Hayden Clark, "An Historical Interpretation of Thomas Paine's Religion," *University of California Chronicle* 35 (1933): 84.

21. *The Age of Reason. Being an Investigation of True and Fabulous Theology.*

22. Quoted in Clark, "An Historical Interpretation of Thomas Paine's Religion," 83–84.

23. TP to Samuel Adams, Federal City, January 1, 1803.

24. Karl Marx, "Towards a Critique of Hegel's Philosophy of Right. Introduction," in Lloyd D. Easton and Kurt H. Guddat, *Writings of the Young Marx on Philosophy and Society* (Garden City, N.Y., 1967), 250 (translation altered).

25. TP to Samuel Adams, Federal City, January 1, 1803, 1436.

26. Theodore Roosevelt, *Gouverneur Morris* (New York, 1888), 289. Roosevelt added: "There are infidels and infidels; Paine belonged to the variety . . . that apparently esteems a bladder of dirty water as the proper weapon with which to assail Christianity" (ibid.).

27. *The Age of Reason. Being an Investigation of True and Fabulous Theology.*

28. Robespierre, *Oeuvres complètes de Maximilien Robespierre*, vol. 10, M. Bouloiseau and A. Soboul (10 vols., Paris, 1910–1967), 193–199.

29. Gregory Claeys, *Thomas Paine: Social and Political Thought*, 190.

30. Robert Michie to David Watson, May 9, 1795, quoted in "Letters from William and Mary, 1798–1801," *Virginia Magazine of History and Biography* 29 (1921): 134–135. See also Richard H. Popkin, "*The Age of Reason* versus *The Age of Revelation.* Two Critics of Tom Paine: David Levi and Elias Boudinot," in *Deism, Masonry, and the Enlightenment: Essays Honouring Alfred Owen Aldridge*, ed. J. A. Leo Lemay (Newark, N.J., 1987), 166; James Turner, *Without God, Without Creed: The Origins of Unbelief in America* (Baltimore, 1985), 1–113.

31. See the German translator's introduction to Thomas Paine, *Untersuchungen über wahre und fabelhafte Theologie* (Deutschland [Lübeck], 1794), 8, 3. J. J. von Eschenburg's remarks appear in *Annalen der brittischen Geschichte*, vol. 13 (Tübingen, 1796), 313–314.

32. The title of the manuscript of the late 1790s was *Vizsgálódás a Mesés és ğaz Vallásról Paine Tamás Amerikai Philosophus által* [An Examination of the Fabulous and True Religion by the American Philosopher, Thomas Paine]. Further details are provided in József Kovács, *Az Iró és a Forradalmár Thomas Paine* (Budapest, 1983), 134–135.

33. *Hélio Osvaldo Alves*, "One Wonder and the Rest: Watson, Solano Constâncio and *The Age of Reason*" (unpublished lecture, Universidade do Minho, Portugal, January 1994). The chief work referred to here is F. S. Constâncio, *Watson Refuted* (Edinburgh, 1797).

34. See Popkin, "*The Age of Reason* versus *The Age of Revelation*," 158–170.

35. James Jones Wilmer, *Consolation: Being a Replication to Thomas Paine and Others on Theologics* (Philadelphia, 1794).

36. Hannah More ["Will Chip, Carpenter, in Somersetshire"], *A Country Carpenter's Confession of Faith: with a Few Plain Remarks on the Age of Reason* (London, 1794).

37. Lord Erskine, *On the Limitations of Free Speech, Delivered in 1797 on the Trial of Williams for the Publication of Paine's "Age of Reason,"* in *Representative British Orations*, ed. Charles Kendall Adams (New York and London, 1884), 293. According to one story (ibid., 307–308), Erskine partly redeemed himself by subsequently abandoning the case against Thomas Williams, a London publisher and bookseller accused by the Society for the Suppression of Vice and Immorality of printing copies of *The Age of Reason*. Erskine "was one day walking in a narrow lane in London when he saw a woman in tears and emaciated with disease and sorrow. The woman pulled him forward into a miserable hovel where in a room not more than ten or twelve feet square were two children with confluent small-pox and the wretched man whom he had just convicted. The man was engaged in sewing up little, religious tracts, which had been his principal employment in his trade. Erskine was convinced that Williams had been urged to the publication of Paine by his extreme poverty and not by his will. The advocate was so deeply affected by what he saw and heard that he believed the cause for which he had pleaded would best be subserved by the policy of mercy. He wrote to the Society in whose behalf he had been retained by the crown urging such a course. His advice, after due consideration, was rejected, whereupon Erskine abandoned the case and returned the fees he had received."

38. John Prior Estlin, *Evidences of Revealed Religion, and Particularly Christianity, Stated, with Reference to a Pamphlet Called The Age of Reason* (Bristol, 1796), 10, 13.

39. Gilbert Wakefield, *An Examination of The Age of Reason, by Thomas Paine* (London, 1794), 67.

40. Uzal Ogden, *Antidote to Deism: The Deist Unmasked*, vol. 1 (Newark, N.J., 1795), 16 n; Mason Locke Weems, *His Words and Ways in Three Volumes, a Bibliography Left Unfinished by Paul Leicester Ford*, vol. 1 (New York, 1929), 70.

41. Richard Watson (Bishop of Llandaff), *An Apology for the Bible; in a series of letters addressed to Thomas Paine, Author of . . . The Age of Reason, Part the second, being an investigation of true and of fabulous theology* (London, 1796).

42. Moses Hoge, "Sophist Unmasked," in *Christian Panoply* (Shepherd's Town, Virginia, 1797), 253.

43. Ibid., 254.

44. *The Age of Reason; Being an Investigation of True and Fabulous Theology.*

45. Quoted in R. R. Palmer, *Twelve Who Ruled: The Committee of Public Safety during the Terror* (Princeton, N.J., 1941), 122. On the rising tide of xenophobia during this period and such bizarre proposals as the compulsory wearing by foreigners of armbands bearing the name of their country and the word "hospitality," see Julia Kristeva, *Strangers to Ourselves* (New York, 1991), chapter 7.

46. "Forgetfulness."

47. The original report of Paine's arrest and imprisonment, signed by Paine and Barlow, is located in F7/4774/61, Archives Nationales, Paris. Paine recalls the events in *The Age of Reason, Part the second* (H. D. Symonds; London, 1795), *v–viii*. Other discussions include Conway, *The Life of Thomas Paine*, vol. 2, 104–107; Hawke, *Paine*, 295–297; and Moncure D. Conway, "Newly discovered writings of Thomas Paine," *The Athenaeum*, n.d., 291–292.

48. See the note written by Benoit, Concièrge, 8. Nivose, l'an 2, F7/4774/61/6, Archives Nationales, Paris.

49. "To the Citizens of the United States and Particularly to the Leaders of the Federal Faction, Letter III," November 29, 1802.

50. General conditions within the Luxembourg are described in Helen Maria Williams, *Letters Containing a Sketch of the Politics of France*, vol. 1 (2 vols., London, 1795), passim; Frank Smith, *Tom Paine, Liberator*, 230; Aldridge, *Man of Reason*, 214.

51. Williams, *Letters Containing a Sketch of the Politics of France*, vol. 2, 176. See also Clootz's first biography by Georges Avenel, *Anacharsis Clootz, L'Orateur du genre humain, Paris! France! Univers!* (Paris, 1865).

52. *Sussex Weekly Advertiser; or, Lewes and Brighthelmston Journal*, January 13, 1794.

53. Quoted in the appendix to Thomas Paine, *The Age of Reason* (New York, 1898), 183.

54. "To My Fellow Citizens of the United States of America," January 27, 1794. The postscript, which narrates the events leading to Paine's arrest and includes an extended reply to Bourdon de l'Oisè, who had denounced him in the convention just prior to his arrest, is cited in Moncure D. Conway, "Newly discovered writings of Thomas Paine."

55. George Washington to the Acting Secretary of State, September 23, 1795, in Fitzpatrick, *The Writings of George Washington*, vol. 34, 312.

56. *Gazette Nationale, ou Le Moniteur Universel*, January 29, 1794, 326. The original petition, dated 12 Ventose and signed by eighteen Americans, including Thomas Griffith, John Billopp, Joel Barlow, and William Hoskins, is in F7/4774/61, Archives Nationales, Paris.

57. F7/4774/61, Archives Nationales, Paris.

58. Thomas W. Griffith, cited in Elizabeth Wormeley Latimer, *My Scrap-Book of the French Revolution* (London, 1898), 51.

59. *Gazette Nationale, ou Le Moniteur Universel*, February 1, 1794. A translation of Vadier's reply appears in Conway, *The Life of Thomas Paine*, vol. 2, 109–110: "Thomas Paine is a native of England; this is undoubtedly enough to apply to him the measures of security prescribed by the revolutionary laws. It may be added, citizens, that if Thomas Paine has been the apostle of liberty, if he has powerfully co-operated with the American Revolution, his genius has not understood that which has regenerated France; he has regarded the system only in accordance with the illusions with which the false friends of our revolution have invested it. You must with us deplore an error little reconcilable with the principles admired in the justly esteemed works of this republican author."

60. The petition by Achille Audibert, dated 2 fructidor, l'an 2 de la République, is in F7/4774/61, Archives Nationales, Paris.

61. Sampson Perry, *The Argus* (1796), 559.

62. Deforgues to Gouverneur Morris, quoted in Faner, *The Complete Writings of Thomas Paine*, vol. 2, 1338–1339, note 236.

63. TP to Gouverneur Morris, Luxembourg Prison, February 24, 1794.

64. Quoted in the preface to Paine, *The Age of Reason* (New York, 1898), iv.

65. TP to Gouverneur Morris, Luxembourg Prison, February 24, 1794.

66. TP to George Washington, July 30, 1796.

67. Quoted in J. M. Thompson, *The French Revolution*, 497.

68. Thomas Carlyle, *The French Revolution: A History*, vol. 3 (1837; reprint, London, 1888), 217.

69. Quoted in Conway, *The Life of Thomas Paine*, vol. 2, 129.

70. Quoted in Carlyle, *The French Revolution*, 217.

71. TP to George Washington, July 30, 1796.

72. Williams, *Letters Containing a Sketch of the Politics of France*, vol. 4, 55–56.

73. Rickman, *The Life of Thomas Paine*, 194.

74. TP to James Monroe, Luxembourg Prison, October 13, 1794; compare the rare letter, TP to Citizen Lebrun, Luxembourg Prison, September 26, 1794.

75. TP to James Monroe, Luxembourg Prison, August 17, 1794 (misdated by Foner as August 18, 1794).

76. William Wordsworth, *The Prelude*, in *Poetical Works*, 566.

77. TP to James Monroe, Luxembourg Prison, August 25, 1794.

78. From a statement deposited in W 189, Archives Nationales, Paris.

79. "To the Citizens of the United States and Particularly to the Leaders of the Federal Faction. Letter III." Compare the similar account in Carlyle, *The French Revolution*, vol. 2, 412.

80. TP to the French National Convention, Luxembourg, August 7, 1794 (19 Thermidor, l'an 2). The English original and the French translation were accompanied by a note; see F7/4774/61, Archives Nationales, Paris.

81. François Lanthenas's appeal, dated 18 Thermidor, l'an 2 de la Revolution, is located in F7/4774/61, Archives Nationales, Paris.

82. Audibert's appeal is printed in Conway, *The Life of Thomas Paine*, vol. 2, 139.

83. TP to James Monroe, Luxembourg Prison, August 16, 1794 (misdated by Foner as August 17, 1794).

84. TP to James Monroe, Luxembourg Prison, August 17, 1794.

85. TP to James Monroe, Luxembourg Prison, August 25, 1794.

86. TP to James Monroe, Paris, September 14, 1794.

87. Ibid.

88. James Monroe to TP, Paris, September 18, 1794.

89. TP to James Monroe, Luxembourg Prison, October 4, 1794.

90. TP to James Monroe, Luxembourg Prison, October 13, 1794.

91. TP to James Monroe, Luxembourg Prison, October 21, 1794 (misdated by Foner as October 20, 1794).

92. James Monroe to the Secretary of State [Edmund Randolph], Paris, November 7, 1794.

93. A certified copy of the original is held in Archives Nationales, F7/4774/61, Paris. The events leading up to Paine's release are described in James Monroe to the Secretary of State [Edmund Randolph], Paris, November 7, 1794.

94. James Monroe to James Madison, January [June–July?] 20, 1796, in Stanislaus Murray Hamilton, ed., *Writings of James Monroe*, vol. 2 (7 vols., 1898–1903), 440.

95. Antoine Claire Thibaudeau, *Mémoires sur la Convention et le Directoire,* vol. 1 (2 vols., Paris, 1824), 108–109.

96. TP to A. C. Thibaudeau, Paris, December 17, 1794. Paine's illness is described in TP to Citizen Barère [?], Paris, January 15, 1795. Six weeks later (TP to Citizen Pelet de la Lozère, Paris, February 27, 1795) Paine complained of a chest abscess that "continues to be very bad and causes me much pain."

97. Marie Joseph Chénier, *Oeuvres,* vol. 5 (8 vols., 1823–1827), 180–181.

98. See the permission signed by Barras, Carnot, and Révellière-Lépeaux, dated 24 floréal, an 4, in AF/III/1808, p. 80, and the note by Lanthenas in AF/III/369, 1808, p. 79, and AF/III/369/1805, p. 28, Archives Nationales, Paris.

99. See TP to Citizen Pelet de la Lozère, Paris [February 1795?]. Evidence of Paine's efforts to secure the release of Mme Lafayette is contained in her letter to Paine, quoted in W. E. Woodward, *Tom Paine: America's Godfather, 1737–1809* (New York and London, 1945), 280. See also the plea for a passport for Mrs. Evans in TP to Citizen Pelet de la Lozère, Paris, February 27, 1795; TP to [Directory?], Paris, 23 floréal, 4th year, a petition on behalf of the wife and three children of Robert Smyth, a banker, whom Paine said "likes neither the Government nor the climate" of England (AF/III/369/1808, p. 80, Archives Nationales, Paris). Paine's defense of the stocking manufacturer Robert Raymont is found in TP to [Barras], Paris, 24 floréal, l'an 4 de la Republic [*sic*]), AF/III/369/1808, p. 115, Archives Nationales, Paris.

100. TP to [Directory?], Paris (23 floréal, 4th year).

101. Quoted in Alfred Cobban, *A History of Modern France,* vol. 1 (London, 1990), 250.

102. *The Constitution of 1795 . . . Speech in the French National Convention* (July 7, 1795).

103. *Dissèrtations sur les Premiers Principes de Gouvernement.*

104. *The Constitution of 1795;* on the American franchises, see Jackson Turner Main, "Government by the People. The American Revolution and the Democratization of the Legislatures," *William and Mary Quarterly* 23 (July 1966), 391–407.

105. See *The Last Dying Words of Tom Paine, Executed at the Guillotine in France on the 1st of September 1794* (n.d.), and the announcement of Paine's death due to prison fever in the *Philadelphia Aurora General Advertiser,* January 14, 1796.

106. James Monroe to Joseph Jones, Paris, September 15, 1795, quoted in *The Life of Thomas Paine,* vol. 2, 166; Cobbett-Bonneville Manuscripts, in ibid., 441.

107. K. F. Cramer to Friedrich Klopstock, Paris, November 26, 1795, reproduced in Hermann Tiemann, "Neues aus Paris Anno 1795. 'Cramer der Krämer' berichtet an Klopstock," in *Der Vergleich. Literatur — und Sprachwissenschaftliche Interpretationen* (Hamburg, 1955), 167–183.

108. Georges Lefebvre, *La France sous le Directoire 1795–1799* (Paris, 1984).

109. A translation of *The Deline and Fall of the English System of Finance* by François Lanthenas appeared as *Décadence et chute du système de Finances de l'Angleterre* (Paris, 1796).

110. Robert Smyth's involvement in the project is mentioned in TP to Directory [?], Paris, 23 floréal, 4th year.

111. The Directory's call for the pamphlet's promotion is dated 8 floréal (1796), AF/III/374, p. 19, Archives Nationales, Paris.

112. Among the published replies were R. Broome, *Observations on Mr. Paine's . . . "Decline*

and Fall of the English System of Finance" (London, 1796); S. Pope, *A Letter to the . . . Lord Mayor . . . in Reply to Paine's "Decline and Fall of the English System of Finance"* (London, 1796); Lieutenant-Colonel Chalmers, *Strictures on a Pamphlet . . . by T. Paine, on the English System of Finance* (London, 1796).

113. See, for example, *Decadenza del sistema di Finanze del'Inghilterra di T. Paine* (Venice, 1796), with a note, possibly written by Domenico Alberto Azuni; and *Sinken und Untergang des englischen Finanzsystems* (Hamburg, 1796). The rare Italian engraving of "Tomasso Paine," published during this period, was adapted from C. W. Peale's original portrait, and is today held in the Gimbel Collection, the American Philosophical Society Library.

114. S. A. Joersson, *Adam Smith and Thomas Paine, A Critical Essay Published in All Languages* (Germany, 1796).

115. TP to George Washington, February 1795; compare Aldridge, *Man of Reason*, 242.

116. TP to George Washington, September 20, 1795; TP to James Madison, Paris, September 24, 1795.

117. Given Paine's ill health and the grave security risks involved, the possibility of a secret visit to England during this period is slim. But on August 29, 1796, "Mr. Thomas Pain, Authour of the rights of man" is reported to have attended (with fourteen other "gentlemen") the last meeting of Hambledon Cricket Club, later renowned as the cradle of cricket ("Hambledon Cricket Club 1772–1796: Minutes and Accounts," Hampshire Record Office, Winchester, 4M85). During this period, cricket was not yet part of a bourgeois moral culture (as it became during Victorian England). It was played by aristocrats and the lower-middling classes (to which Paine originally belonged), and it may be that Paine himself first indulged the game during his time in Lewes, where cricket (and its attendant gambling, of which Paine would not have approved) was certainly popular during the summer months. But why, given that Paine never once mentions the sport in his writings, he should have risked everything to travel across the Channel prior to the Hambledon meeting is unclear. How did he travel? Whom did he meet in England, and for what purpose? Although full details of the signatories to the meeting are unavailable, it is most likely that the August 29 meeting was a meeting of radicals — an irony in itself, considering cricket's later conservative image — who aimed to test the patience or humor of local Hampshire magistrates, who were empowered by the prevailing Sedition Act to dissolve such assemblies. I am grateful to Tom Nairn for providing the details of this Hambledon mystery.

118. James Monroe to James Madison, Paris, July 5, 1796, in Stanislaus M. Hamilton (ed.), *The Writings of James Monroe*, vol. 3, 20–21.

119. TP to George Washington, Paris, July 30, 1796.

120. See James Alton James, "French Diplomacy and American Politics 1794–1795," *Annual Report of the American Historical Association*, vol. 1 (1911), 153–163.

121. Rufus Wilmot Griswold, *The Republican Court, or American Society in the Days of Washington* (New York, 1856), 289.

122. *New-York Journal*, December 7, 1793; cf. *Gazette of the United States*, September 6, 1794.

123. See "Hancock" in the *Philadelphia Aurora General Advertiser*, August 21 and September 3 and 8, 1795. Similar criticisms were printed in the *Boston Independent Chronicle*,

September 7, 1795; *Jersey Chronicle,* October 10, 1795; "Belisarius" in the *Philadelphia Aurora General Advertiser,* September 15, 1795; and *Greenleaf's New York Journal,* December 2, 1795.

124. See the contribution by "An Old Soldier" in the *Philadelphia Aurora General Advertiser,* June 30, 1796.

125. *Boston Independent Chronicle,* July 23, 1798.

126. Among the most bitter were the attacks on Paine in the *Baltimore Federal Gazette,* January 4, 1797, and in the *Columbian Centinel,* January 18, 1797, where Paine was denounced as "a traitorous scribbler, saturated with brandy." See also Mary Elizabeth Clark, *Peter Porcupine in America: The Career of William Cobbett, 1792–1800* (Philadelphia, 1939), 77–78; Donald H. Stewart, *The Opposition Press of the Federalist Period* (Albany, N.Y., 1969), 528.

127. TP to Robert R. Livingston, Paris, December 16, 1801.

128. *Letter of Thomas Paine to the People of France, and the French Armies . . . on the Events of the 18th Fructidor — Sep. 4 — and Its Consequences* (Paris [October 1797?]).

129. Ibid.

130. Ibid.

131. AF III/478/2955, Archives Nationales, Paris.

132. John Epps, *The Life of John Walker* (London, 1831), 133.

133. Theobald Wolfe Tone, *The Life of Theobald Wolfe Tone, Edited by His Son* (Washington, 1826), vol. 2, 348.

134. Conway, *The Life of Thomas Paine,* 3d ed., vol. 2, 339. Paine's lack of ease with the French language is confirmed in Benjamin Franklin's letter to M. Le Veillard, April 15, 1787, in *Benjamin Franklin's Works,* ed. A. H. Smyth (New York, 1906), vol. 9, 562.

135. Gary Kates, *The Cercle Social, the Girondins, and the French Revolution,* 274–275. During this period, Paine's writings on religion and politics include *Lettre de Thomas Paine sur les Cultes* (Paris, July 21, 1797), a rejoinder to Camille Jordan, a church-minded legislator who had petitioned the Council of Five Hundred to reinstate the ringing of church bells in France. Paine denied that any organized religion had the right to be a public nuisance, and insisted that legislators should concentrate on developing the *social* rights of citizens: "It is a want of feeling to talk of priests and bells while so many infants are perishing in the hospitals, and aged and infirm poor in the streets from the want of necessaries." *A Discourse Delivered by Thomas Paine to the Society of the Theophilanthropists at Paris, 1798* (London, 1798) is a philosophical defense of the Society, whose aims of propagating "God, Love, and Man" Paine publicly supported — in opposition to both organized religion and atheism. The same pamphlet was also published by J. Johnson under the title, *Atheism Refuted; in a discourse to prove the existence of a God* (London, 1798).

136. Evidence of Paine's contributions is discussed in Henry Redhead Yorke, *France in Eighteen Hundred and Two,* ed. J. A. C. Sykes (London, 1906), 224; A. O. Aldridge, *Man of Reason,* chapter 22; Ann Thomson, "Thomas Paine, représentant de l'Amérique républicaine," *Frontières* 4 (1993), 69–82.

137. Cited in François Furet, *La Révolution Française. De Turgot à Napoléon,* vol. 1 (Paris, 1988), 347.

138. TP to the Conseil des Cinq-cents, printed in *Le Bien informé* 149, January 29, 1798.

139. TP to Thomas Jefferson, New Rochelle, January 30, 1806. A confidential British secret service document of 1798 reported Bonaparte's plan that "the Directory in England is to comprise Paine, Tooke, Sharpe, Thelwall, Landsdown" (cited in Bernard Vincent, *Thomas Paine ou la religion de la liberté* [Paris, 1987], 343).

140. Aldridge, *Man of Reason*, 262.

141. Colley, *Britons*. Great care should be taken in charting the rise of "Britishness" during this period, if only because of considerable fluctuations through time and space. Developments in the county of Suffolk, where Paine had relatives and where he hoped French troops would land, are a case in point. At the end of 1792, shortly after Paine had been hunted into exile, local militia were formed, often through the enlistment of artisans; effigies of Paine were torched; and in Sudbury, a week before Christmas, "109 leading townsfolk put their name to a resolution declaring their support for the government, and their determination to suppress all seditious and treasonable meetings, publications and writings tending to undermine or destroy the constitution as established at the Glorious Revolution of 1688" (Allen W. Berry, *Eighteenth Century Sudbury* [Ipswich, 1992], 64). By 1795, there is considerable evidence that the predominant ultraloyalism had begun to lose ground to the widespread opinion that the government of George III was repressive, that radicalism and disorder were not synonymous, and that the ongoing acute food shortages in the county urgently needed to be remedied (Grant J. Bage, "A provincial reaction to the French Revolution: radical politics, social unrest and the growth of loyal opinion in East Anglia at the end of the eighteenth century, with special reference to the county of Suffolk," unpublished M. Litt. thesis, University of Cambridge, 1984).

142. *On the Descent Upon England, Written at the desire of a Favourite* (Criel [?], near Chantilly, May 10, 1798).

143. César de Saussure, *A Foreign View of England in the Reigns of George I and II* (London, 1902), 177.

144. TP to the Executive Directory, Paris, 1798[?], AF/III/544/3620/9. Archives Nationales, Paris. Evidence that Bonaparte's regime had for some time considered Bonneville (and by implication Paine) "as an enemy of the government" is found in the Archives Nationales document F7/8083/1196.

145. F7/6152/PLAQ 2/dossier 868 B.P., Archives Nationales, Paris.

146. François Furet, *La Révolution Française*, vol. 7, 368.

147. The following paragraphs draw heavily upon the author's correspondence with Andries Van den Abeele. See also his "De filosoof Thomas Paine en zijn Brugse vriend Joseph Van Huele," *Brugge die Scone* 4 (1993), 7; *In Brugge onder de Acacia* (Brugge, 1987), chapter 10; and "Jean-Othon Van Huele, een revolutionaire ééndagsvvlieg in Brugge," in André Vanhoutryve, *Liber Amicorum* (Brugge, 1990), 195–205. See also Paine's account of the visit in Thomas Paine to Citoyen Skipwith, American, Paris, September 29, 1801, in which Van Huele is described as "a Merchand by profession, writes the most correct English of any foreigner I am acquainted with, and French also and is a man of property."

148. TP to Citoyen Skipwith, Paris, December 14, 1801.

149. AF 194, 41–42, Archives Nationales, Paris.

150. *Rights of Man. Being an Answer to Mr. Burke's Attack on the French Revolution.* Paine's failure to appreciate the rise of modern nationalism is elaborated in John Keane, "Nations, nationalism and citizens in Europe," *International Social Science Journal* 140 (June 1994), 169–184.

151. Here I dissent from the anachronistic claim that the American Revolution was an aggressive colonial challenge to British authority fueled by a powerful, if at the time unacknowledged, nascent American nationalism. See Robert W. Tucker and David C. Hendrickson, *The Fall of the First British Empire* (Baltimore, 1982).

152. Thomas Christi do króla, May 22, 1791. See also Zofia Libizowska, "Tomasz Paine a Polska stanisławowska," *Annales Universitatis Mariae Curie-Skłodowska* 29, no. 10 (1974), 105–115; M. Haiman, *The Fall of Poland in Contemporary American Opinion* (Chicago, 1935), 38–62.

153. TP to [?], St. Honoré, Paris, August 11, 1787.

154. Thomas Jefferson, *Discours pour l'ouverture de la dernière session du Congrès* (Paris, 1802); 8Pb.1761, Bibliothèque Nationale, Paris.

155. Lewis Goldsmith, *Antigallican Monitor,* September 27, November 1, 1812, and February 6, 13, 1814.

156. Ibid.

157. Rickman, *The Life of Thomas Paine,* 164.

158. TP to Citoyen Skipwith, American, Paris, December 29, 1801.

159. Norfolk and Speirs, *Historical Notes on Diss,* 6.

160. In the summer of 1802, Abraham Raimbach, a noted British engraver, reported a meeting with Paine: "He was at this time constantly to be seen at an obscure *cabaret* in an obscure street in the Fauxbourg St. Germain (Café Jacob, Rue Jacob). The scene, as we entered the room from the street — it was on the groundfloor — was, under the circumstances, somewhat impressive. It was on a summer's evening, and several of the tables were occupied by men, apparently tradesmen and mechanics, some playing at the then universal game of dominos, others drinking their bottles of light, frothy, pleasant beer, or their little glass of liqueur, while in a retired part of the room sat the once dreaded demagogue, the supposed conspirator against thrones and altars, the renowned Thomas Paine! He was in a conversation with several well-dressed Irishmen, who soon afterwards took their leave, and we placed ourselves at his table. His general appearance was mean and poverty-stricken. The portrait of him engraved by Sharp from Romney's picture of him is a good likeness; but he was now much withered and care-worn, though his dark eye still retained its sparkling vigour. He was fluent in speech, of mild and gentle demeanour, clear and distinct in enunciation, and his voice exceedingly soft and agreeable. The subject of his talk being of course political, resembled very much his printed opinions; and the dogmatic form in which he delivered them seemed to evince his own perfect self-conviction of their truth." (*Memoirs and Recollections of Abraham Raimbach, . . . including a Memoir of Sir David Wilkie,* ed. M. T. S. Raimbach [London, 1843], 78–80).

161. Thomas Carlyle, *The French Revolution: A History,* vol. 3, 59.

162. Rickman, *The Life of Thomas Paine,* 171–172.

12. GROWING OLD IN AMERICA

1. TP to Thomas Jefferson, Paris, October 1, 1800.

2. Thomas Jefferson to Thomas Paine, March 18, 1801.

3. *Gazette of the United States, and Daily Advertiser,* July 21, 1801.

4. *Gazette of the United States, and Daily Advertiser,* July 22 and September 28, 1801.

5. *Baltimore Republican; or The Anti-Democrat,* October 18, 1802.

6. *New-York Evening Post,* January 10, 1803.

7. *Port Folio,* July 18, 1801, 231.

8. Quoted in Woodward, *Tom Paine,* 309.

9. *The National Intelligencer and Washington Advertiser,* July 29, 1801.

10. TP to Thomas Jefferson, New Rochelle, September 30, 1805.

11. Quoted in Aldridge, *Man of Reason,* 273.

12. Reprinted in the *New-York Evening Post,* November 3, 1802, and *The Connecticut Courant,* November 15, 1802. The hostile *Columbian Centinel,* November 27, 1802, claimed that Paine had been arrested in Baltimore by a "Mr. O'Maly," an "honest Irishman . . . for the debt of 50 guineas."

13. *Philadelphia Aurora. General Advertiser,* November 3, 1802.

14. Worthington C. Ford, ed., "Letters of William Duane, 1800–1834," *Proceedings of the Massachusetts Historical Society* 20 (1906–07), 279.

15. *Philadelphia Aurora. General Advertiser,* July 14, 1801.

16. *Gazette of the United States, and Daily Advertiser,* September 28, 1801.

17. *New York-Evening Post,* November 4, 1802.

18. *Philadelphia Aurora. General Advertiser,* November 8, 1802.

19. *Gazette of the United States, and Daily Advertiser,* September 25, 1801.

20. *Gazette of the United States, and Daily Advertiser,* September 28, 1801.

21. *Columbian Centinel. Massachusetts Federalist,* August 22, 1801.

22. Reprinted in *The (Richmond) Recorder,* December 15, 1802.

23. *The (Richmond) Recorder,* December 8, 1 and 8, 1802.

24. *The Mercury and New-England Palladium,* September 6, 1801.

25. "Liberty of the Press."

26. According to Michael Schudson, American colonial newspapers scrupulously avoided controversy up to the decade before the Revolution, when writers like Paine dragged printers, against their will and commercial self-interest, into taking sides with the patriots or the loyalists ("Was There Ever a Public Sphere? If So, When? Reflections on the American Case," in *Habermas and the Public Sphere,* Craig Calhoun, ed. (Cambridge, Mass., and London, 1992), 143–163.

27. Suzanne Tucoo-Chala, *Charles-Joseph Pancoucke et la librairie française* (Paris, 1977). The market pressures leading to franchising and concentration of ownership in publishing and bookselling in the papal enclave of Avignon, which was unaffected by French government regulations on printing and censorship and therefore operated as a major exporter of counterfeit and clandestine works, are examined in René Moulinas, *L'Imprimerie, la libraire, et la presse à Avignon au XVIIIe siècle* (Grenoble, 1974).

28. See Lewis B. Namier, *The Structure of Politics at the Accession of George III*, 2d ed. (London and New York, 1957); Lewis B. Namier, *Monarchy and the Party System* (Oxford, 1952); Harvey Mansfield, Jr., "Party Government and the Settlement of 1688," *American Political Science Review* (1964), 937, 945; Eric J. Evans, *Political Parties in Britain, 1780–1867* (London, 1985). The emergence of parties in the United States is best analyzed by Richard Hofstadter, *The Idea of a Party System: The Rise of Legitimate Opposition in the United States, 1780–1840* (Berkeley, Calif., 1970); William N. Chambers, *Political Parties in a New Nation: The American Experience 1776–1809* (Oxford, 1963).

29. Quoted in Benjamin R. Barber, "The Undemocratic Party System: Citizenship in an Elite/Mass Society," in *Political Parties in the Eighties*, ed. Robert A. Goldwin (Washington, 1980), 34.

30. "A Dissertation upon Parties," in *The Works of Lord Bolingbroke*, vol. 2 (Philadelphia, 1841), 11, 21, 167.

31. See Erwin Faul, "Verfemung, Duldung und Anerkennung des Parteiwesens in der Geschichte des Politischen Denkens," *Politische Vierteljahresschrift* (1964), 60–80; Caroline Robbins, "'Discordant Parties': A Study of the Acceptance of Party by Englishmen," *Political Science Quarterly* (1958): 505–529; John Keane, *Democracy and Civil Society* (London and New York, 1988), 101–151.

32. *The Federalist Papers*, no. 10 (New York, 1964), 82.

33. TP to Thomas Clio Rickman, New York, March 8, 1803.

34. *The National Aegis*, December 15, 1802.

35. James Sterling Young, *The Washington Community, 1800–1828* (New York, 1966), 41.

36. Rufus King to William V. Murray, November 12, 1802, in Charles R. King, *Life and Correspondence of Rufus King*, vol. 4 (6 vols., New York, 1894–1900), 182.

37. Manasseh Cutler to Dr. Joseph Torrey, Washington, January 3, 1803, in William Parker and Julia Perkins Cutler, *Life, Journals and Correspondence of Rev. Manasseh Cutler, LL.D.*, vol. 2 (Cincinnati, 1888), 119.

38. "To the Citizens of the United States and Particularly to the Leaders of the Federal Faction. Letter III," *The National Intelligencer*, November 29, 1802.

39. Moses Guest to TP, Philadephia, December 1, 1802, reprinted in *Journal of the Rutgers University Library* 14 (1950), 28.

40. "To the Citizens of the United States and Particularly to the Leaders of the Federal Faction. Letter 1," *The National Intelligencer*, November 15, 1802.

41. James Cheetham, *The Life of Thomas Paine* (New York, 1809), 227.

42. William Plumer to Judge Smith, December 9, 1802, in William Plumer, Jr., ed. *Life of William Plumer, by His Son, William Plumer, Junior* (Boston, 1856), 242.

43. John Bach McMaster, *A History of the People of the United States, from the Revolution to the Civil War*, vol. 2 (8 vols., New York, 1883–1913), 620.

44. "Dr. Mitchill's Letters from Washington," p. 745, quoted in Hawke, *Paine*, 359.

45. Randall, *The Life of Thomas Jefferson*, vol. 2, 644.

46. William Plumer to Judge Smith, December 9, 1802, 242. According to Plumer's son, his father "had read his 'Age of Reason' with unqualified disapprobation of its tone

and temper, its coarse vulgarity, and its unfair appeals to the passions and the prejudices of his readers."

47. Reprinted in the *New-York Evening Post*, October 15, 1802.

48. *New-York Evening Post*, January 10, 1803.

49. Reprinted in *The (Richmond) Recorder*, April 6, 1803.

50. *The (Richmond) Recorder*, December 8, 1802.

51. See the second, third, and fourth letters, "To the Citizens of the United States," *The National Intelligencer and Washington Advertiser*, November 22 and 29 and December 6, 1802.

52. "To the Citizens of the United States and Particularly to the Leaders of the Federal Faction. Letter III."

53. TP to Thomas Jefferson, Christmas Day, 1802.

54. TP to Thomas Jefferson, New York, January 25, 1805.

55. Ibid.

56. TP to Thomas Jefferson, January 12, 1803.

57. "To the Citizens of the United States. Letter the Fifth," *The National Intelligencer and Washington Advertiser*, February 2, 1803. On Aaron Burr, see Noble E. Cunningham, Jr., *The Jeffersonian Republicans in Power: Party Operations, 1801–1809* (Chapel Hll, N.C., 1963), especially 38–43.

58. Samuel Adams to TP, November 30, 1802, printed in *Letters from Thomas Paine to the Citizens of America, After an Absence of Fifteen Years in Europe* (London, 1804), 36.

59. TP to Samuel Adams, Federal City, January 1, 1803.

60. Nathan O. Hatch, *The Democratization of American Christianity* (New Haven, Conn., and London, 1989).

61. *Philadelphia Aurora. General Advertiser*, February 17, 1803.

62. Quoted in William M. Van der Weyde, ed., *The Life and Works of Thomas Paine*, vol. 10 (New Rochelle, N.Y., 1925), 143. Another account of crowd attacks on Paine is provided in "Old Letters: New Understanding," *Social Studies* 61 (January 1950).

63. The story was printed originally in *Port Folio*, and reprinted in *The (Richmond) Recorder*, April 16, 1803.

64. The incident was originally reported in the *Trenton True American* and is cited in Conway, *The Life of Thomas Paine*, vol. 2, 327 n.

65. *Reminiscences of Grant Thorburn*, 75–76.

66. Cheetham, *The Life of Thomas Paine*, 233.

67. [William James Linton], *The Life of Paine* (London, 1841), 38; *American Citizen*, March 16, 1803.

68. The memorandum is titled "Louisiana" and was likely written in Bordentown during the last week of February 1803 — that is, just prior to Paine's departure for New York City — and not July 1803, as is claimed by Foner, *The Complete Writings of Thomas Paine*, vol. 2, 1502.

69. E. M. Woodward and John F. Hageman, *History of Burlington and Mercer Counties*, N.J. (1883), 471.

70. Ibid.

71. John Hall Diaries, Journal Number 52, entry of "Tuesday, April 19, 1803."

72. "To the Citizens of the United States. Letter VI," Bordentown, March 12, 1803; published in the *Philadelphia Aurora. General Advertiser,* May 14, 1803.

73. "To the Citizens of the United States. Letter VII," Bordentown, April 21, 1803, published in the *Trenton True-American,* April 1803.

74. *New-York Evening Post,* February 4, 1803.

75. Thomas Paine, *Pacte Maritime, adressé aux nations neutres. Par un neutre* (Paris, 1800).

76. "To the Citizens of the United States. Letter VII."

77. Thomas Jefferson to James Monroe, January 8, 1804, in Paul L. Ford, ed., *The Works of Thomas Jefferson,* vol. 10 (New York, 1904), 61.

78. Thomas Paine, *Lines Extempore* (July 1803). See the reports of the dinner in the *American Citizen,* August 9, 1803; Foner, *The Complete Writings of Thomas Paine,* vol. 2, 1102; and Conway, vol. 2, 2329 n.

79. TP to Charles W. Peale, Bordentown, July 29, 1803.

80. TP to John C. Breckenridge, Bordentown, August 2, 1803.

81. TP to Thomas Jefferson, Bordentown, August 2, 1803; TP to John C. Breckenridge, Bordentown, August 2, 1803.

82. See the memorandum titled "N. Haley's Account Against Thomas Paine," Gimbel Collection, American Philosophical Society Library, Philadephia.

83. Alexis de Tocqueville, *De la démocratie en Amérique* (2 vols., 1835–1840; reprint, Paris, 1981).

84. TP to Thomas Jefferson, Stonington, Connecticut, September 23, 1803.

85. TP to Thomas Jefferson, New York, January 25, 1805.

86. TP to Thomas Jefferson, Stonington, Connecticut, September 23, 1803.

87. Ibid.

88. TP to Mr. Hyer, New York, March 24, 1804.

89. TP to Anthony Taylor, New Rochelle, November 20, 1803.

90. Quoted in Vale, *The Life of Thomas Paine,* 145–146.

91. "To the People of England on the Invasion of England," *Philadelphia Aurora. General Advertiser,* March 6, 1804.

92. Vale, *The Life of Thomas Paine,* 146–147.

93. "TP to Citizen Skipwith," New York, March 1, 1804.

94. John W. Francis, *Old New York: or, Reminiscences of the Past Sixty Years* (New York, 1866), 139.

95. Ibid., 143.

96. Joseph T. Buckingham, *Specimens of Newspaper Literature: With Personal Memoirs, Anecdotes, and Reminiscences,* vol. 2 (Boston, 1850), 250.

97. Francis, *Old New York,* 139.

98. *Reminiscences of Grant Thorburn,* 81–82.

99. Quoted in John Fellows, "Memoir," in *Posthumous Pieces by Elihu Palmer* (London, 1824).

100. TP to Colonel John Fellows, New Rochelle, July 9, 1804.

101. A Member of the Deistical Congregation, "To the Rev. John Mason, One of the Ministers of the Scotch Presbyterian Church, of New York; with Remarks on His Account of the Visit He Made to the Late General Hamilton," *Prospect; or, View of the Moral World*, August 18, 1804.

102. "Of the Religion of Deism Compared with the Christian Religion, and the Superiority of the Former Over the Latter," *Prospect; or, View of the Moral World*, June [July] 7, 1804. Compare the call for the systematic study of the world's "cosmogonies" in "Hints towards Forming a Society for Enquiring into the Truth or Falshood of Ancient History, so Far as History Is Connected with Systems of Religion Ancient and Modern," *Prospect; or, View of the Moral World*, July 21, 1804.

103. "Remarks on the Foregoing Sermon," *Prospect; or, View of the Moral World*, February 18, 1804.

104. An Enemy to Cant and Imposition, "Of the Sabbath-Day of Connecticut," *Prospect; or, View of the Moral World*, September 15, 1804.

105. "To the Editor of the Prospect," *Prospect; or, View of the Moral World*, March 10, 1804.

106. A Member of the Deistical Church, "To Mr. Moore, of New-York, Commonly Called Bishop Moore," *Prospect; or, View of the Moral World*, August 4, 1804; "Of the Religion of Deism Compared with the Christian Religion."

107. "Of the Religion of Deism Compared with the Christian Religion."

108. "To the Members of the Society, Stiling Itself the Missionary Society," *Prospect; or, View of the Moral World*, September 1, 1804.

109. English Writer [TP?], "Miracles," *Prospect; or, View of the Moral World*, April 7, 1804.

110. "Of the Word Religion, and Other Words of Uncertain Signification," *Prospect; or, View of the Moral World*, March 3, 1804.

111. See Lorenzo Dow, *History of Cosmopolite: or, The Four Volumes of Lorenzo's Journal* (Wheeling, W. Va., 1848), which reveals his familiarity with "deistical writings" and "T. P _____'s Age of Reason" (270) and contains many paraphrases of Paine's arguments (419–470); Charles Coleman Sellers, *Lorenzo Dow: The Bearer of the Word* (New York, 1928); Richard Cawardine *Transatlantic Revivalism: Popular Evangelicalism in Britain and America, 1790–1865* (Westport, Conn., 1978), 104–107, 134–135.

112. *National Gazette*, January 16, 1793.

113. See, for example, *Farmer's Weekly Museum*, October 10, 1794; *Western Star*, November 18, 1794, and March 1, 1796; *Massachusetts Mercury*, March 13, 17, and 20, 1795.

114. See James King Morse, *Jedidiah Morse: A Champion of New England Orthodoxy* (New York, 1939), 51–52, 55–56; Charles Roy Keller, *The Second Great Awakening in Connecticut* (New Haven, Conn., 1942), 19–20; G. Adolf Koch, *Republican Religion: The American Revolution and the Cult of Reason* (New York, 1933), 253–254; Vernon Stauffer, *New England and the Bavarian Illuminati* (New York, 1918), 128, 228–236.

115. F. Smith, *Tom Paine, Liberator*, 317–318.

116. TP to John Fellows, New Rochelle, July 31, 1805.

117. Cheetham, *The Life of Thomas Paine*, 246–247 n.

118. TP to Thomas Jefferson, New Rochelle, April 20, 1805.

119. Thomas Jefferson to TP, Washington, June 5, 1805, Albert Ellery Bergh, ed., *The Writings of Thomas Jefferson*, vol. 11 (Washington, 1907), 81.

120. Quoted in Cobbett-Bonneville Manuscripts, 447.

121. TP to William Carver, New Rochelle, January 16, 1805.

122. TP to [Clio Rickman?], New York, July 12, 1806.

123. Ibid.

124. TP to Thomas Jefferson, New York, January 25, 1805. Paine's comments on the Santo Domingo revolution are scarce, if mainly enthusiastic, and further research on his attitude to the events would therefore be welcome, as has been argued by Ann Thomson, "Thomas Paine, la lutte anti-esclavagiste et la révolution de Saint-Domingue," paper presented to the conference "La Révolution française et Haïti," Port-au-Prince, December 1989.

125. TP to Thomas Jefferson, New Rochelle, January 1, 1805.

126. TP to Thomas Jefferson, New York, January 25, 1805.

127. William Carver to TP, December 2, 1806, quoted in Cheetham, *The Life of Thomas Paine*, 267.

128. TP to Thomas Jefferson, New York, January 25, 1805.

129. Ibid.

130. Common Sense [Thomas Paine], *Constitutions, Governments, and Charters*, June 21, 1805.

131. The reversibility of decisions by democratic procedures is analyzed in John Keane, *The Media and Democracy* (Oxford, 1991).

132. *Constitutions, Governments, and Charters.*

133. "To the Citizens of the United States and Particularly to the Leaders of the Federal Faction. Letter VIII," *Philadelphia Aurora. General Advertiser*, June 7, 1805.

134. *An Essay on Dream* (New York, 1807).

135. "To Mr. Hulbert, of Sheffield, One of the Mortified Federal Members of the Massachusetts Leglislature," *Philadephia Aurora. General Advertiser*, March 12, 1805.

136. "Another Callender — Thomas Turner of Virginia," *American Citizen*, July 23 and July 24, 1805.

137. *Thomas Paine to the Citizens of Pennsylvania on the Proposal for Calling a Convention* (Philadelphia, August 1805).

138. "Remarks on English Affairs," *Baltimore Evening Post*, July 8, 1805.

139. TP to John Fellows, New Rochelle, July 31, 1805.

140. Elihu Palmer to Robert Hunter, September 6, 1805, New York Public Library.

141. TP to Thomas Jefferson, New Rochelle, September 30, 1805.

142. TP to Thomas Jefferson, New Rochelle, January 30, 1806; and TP to Thomas Jefferson, New Rochelle, March 15, 1806.

143. Journal of Daniel Constable II, August 2, 1807.

144. *Relf's American Gazette*, December 1, 1805.

145. William Carver to TP, December 2, 1806. Carver's visit to New Rochelle must have been after May 1, 1806, since on that day a traveller, Dr. J. McDowell, wrote from New Rochelle to Mrs. Henrietta McDowell in Stamford, Connecticut: "The infamous Tom Paine resides in this village, & lodges at present in the tavern at which we

stopped. He was not in" (Gratz Manuscripts, case 8, box 38, Pennsylvania Historical Society, Philadelphia).

146. John Melish, *Travels Through the United States of America, in the Years 1806 & 1807, and 1809, 1810, & 1811* (Philadelphia, 1818), 61–62; Conway, *The Life of Thomas Paine*, vol. 2, 388.

147. Grant Thorburn, *History of Cardeus and Carver or the Christian and Infidel Family: A Contrast* (1847), 32.

148. TP to Thomas Jefferson, Stonington, Connecticut, September 23, 1803.

149. *The Cause of the Yellow Fever, and the Means of Preventing It in Places not yet infected with it* (June 27, 1806).

150. Melish, *Travels Through the United States*, 150.

151. TP to Andrew Dean, New York, August 15, 1806. According to the widow of Elihu Palmer, Paine collapsed on July 27; see her letter to [?], September 3, 1806, New York Public Library.

152. TP to Andrew Dean, New York, August 15, 1806.

153. Melish, *Travels Through the United States*, 61.

154. Ibid., 61–62.

155. TP to William Carver, November 25, 1806, in Cheetham, *The Life of Thomas Paine*, 255–256.

156. Ibid., 255.

157. See Investigator [Thomas Paine], "Communications," *American Citizen* (September 23, 1806), which calls Carpenter a "lunatic" whose "cry is war! war!"; the anonymous contribution, "Communications," *American Citizen* (October 11, 1806), which attacks Carpenter and insists that "the press is free for the discussion of principles but not for lying"; Thomas Paine, "A Challenge to the Federalists to Declare their Principles," *American Citizen* (October 17, 1806); Thomas Paine, "Communications. The emissary Cullen otherwise Carpenter," *American Citizen* (October 28, 1806), where the point is reiterated that "*lying* is so naturally the mother tongue of an emissary that *truth* is to him like a foreign language"; Common Sense [Thomas Paine], "Communications," *American Citizen* (November 5, 1806), which attacks "the continual abuse and blackguardism in Cullen's infamous paper against the French nation, the French government, and the French minister at Washington"; and Common Sense [Thomas Paine], "Notifications respecting the Impostor Cullen, alias Mc Cullen, alias Carpenter, the associate of the federalists of New York," *American Citizen* (November 19, 1806), where Carpenter is denounced as "a British subject, and not a citizen of the United States."

158. Thorburn, *History of Cardeus and Carver*, 32.

159. Ibid., 102–104.

160. *Relf's American Gazette*, December 1, 1805.

161. TP to James Madison, New York, May 3, 1807.

162. TP to George Clinton, New York, May 4, 1807.

163. Ibid.

164. It was only in July 1945, 139 years after the trial, that New Rochelle officially granted Paine "full citizenship and the rights thereof of this city."

165. William Carver to TP, December 2, 1806.

166. Thomas Haynes to Robert Hunter, October 30, 1807, New York Public Library.

167. Jarvis to C. B. King, Harold E. Dickson, "The Jarvis Portrait of Thomas Paine," *New-York Historical Society Quarterly* 34 (1950): 9. See also Harold E. Dickson, *John Wesley Jarvis: American Painter 1780–1840, with a Checklist of His Works* (New York, 1949).

168. Thomas Paine, *An Examination of the Passages in the New Testament, quoted from the Old and called Prophecies concerning Jesus Christ. To which is prefixed an Essay on Dream, shewing by what operation of the mind a Dream is produced in sleep, and applying the same to the account of Dreams in the New Testament. With an Appendix containing my private thoughts of a Future State. And Remarks on the Contradictory Doctrine in the Books of Matthew and Mark* (New York, 1807). The essay on dreams, is further discussed in TP to Andrew Dean, New York, August 15, 1806.

169. Quoted in Dickson, *John Wesley Jarvis*, 97–104.

170. Ibid.

171. TP to Messrs. Binny and Ronaldson, New York, April 8, 1807.

172. TP to Joel Barlow, New York, May 4, 1807.

173. Thomas Hardy to TP, October 15, 1807, New York Public Library.

174. Quoted in Aldridge, *Man of Reason*, 308.

175. "Of Gun-Boats," *New York Public Advertiser*, March 11, 1807.

176. "Letters to Morgan Lewis on his Prosecution of Thomas Farmar, for One-Hundred Thousand Dollars Damages. Letter First," *New York Public Advertiser, National Aurora* (April 27, 1807); "Letters to Morgan Lewis on his Prosecution of Thomas Farmar, for One-Hundred Thousand Dollars Damages. Letter Second," *New York Public Advertiser, National Aurora* (April 27, 1807); "Letters to Morgan Lewis on his Prosecution of Thomas Farmar, for One-Hundred Thousand Dollars Damages. Letter Third," *New York Public Advertiser, National Aurora* (April 27, 1807).

177. Quoted in Conway, *The Life of Thomas Paine*, vol. 2 (1892), 389–390. Compare *Journal of Daniel Constable II* (June 28, 1807–March 21, 1808), July 21, 1807: "We found the old philosopher look better than when we left N. York last year, — he presented me with a copy of his last publication." A recently discovered watercolor profile of Paine from this period is believed to have been completed by William Constable (interview with Richard Maass, White Plains, New York, June 1993). Unfortunately, the *Journal* contains no account of the portrait.

178. "Of the Comparative Powers and Expence of Ships of War, Gunboats, and Fortifications," *New York Public Advertiser*, July 21, 1807. A few weeks earlier, on June 1, 1807, the same argument had been broached in the *Public Advertiser* in a piece written by Paine and bearing the signature "One Who Knows England."

179. *New-York Evening Post*, September 25, 1807.

180. Quoted in "Farewell Reprimand to James Cheetham," *New York Public Advertiser*, September 5, 1807.

181. *New York Public Advertiser, National Aurora*, August 21, 1807.

182. "Reprimand to James Cheetham," New York, September 5, 1807.

183. "Cheetham and His Tory Paper," *New York Public Advertiser, National Aurora*, September

26, 1807. The contribution was published anonymously, not under Paine's name, as Foner claims in *The Complete Writings of Thomas Paine*, vol. 2, 1017–1018.

184. Cheetham, *The Life of Thomas Paine* (London 1817), 148.

185. TP to James Monroe, New York, December 30, 1807.

186. Cobbett-Bonnevill: Manuscripts, 450.

187. In Paine's native England, so-called death duties were not levied on land until 1894, while old-age pensions were not introduced until January 1, 1909.

188. TP to the Honourable Senate of the United States, New York, January 21, 1808.

189. Cheetham, *The Life of Thomas Paine*, 287.

190. TP to the Committee of Claims of the House of Representatives, New York, February 14, 1808. The letter was printed in *Annals of Congress*, 10th Cong., 2d sess., 1783–1784.

191. TP to the Honourable Speaker of the House of Representatives, New York, February 28, 1808.

192. TP to the Honourable Speaker of the House of Representatives, New York, March 7, 1808. The letter was printed in *Annals of Congress*, 10th Cong., 2d sess., 1783–1784.

193. Cobbett-Bonneville Manuscripts, 450.

194. *Annals of Congress*, 10th Cong., 2d sess., 1780–1781.

195. T. Adams, *Democracy Unveiled; in a letter to Sir Francis Burdett* (London, 1811), 293. See also Aldridge, *Man of Reason*, 314–315. On Paine's residence in the village of Greenwich, see the remarks and map drawn by John Randel, "Residence of Thomas Paine," in D. T. Valentine, *Manual of the Corporation of the City of New York* (New York, 1864), 841–846.

196. "Predestination. Remarks on Romans, IX, 18–21, addressed to the Ministers of the Calvinistic Church, *Public Advertiser, National Aurora*, August 25, 1808.

197. Cobbett-Bonneville Manuscripts, 451.

198. "The Will of Thomas Paine."

199. Quoted in *Memoirs of the Life and Gospel Labours of Stephen Grellet*, ed. Benjamin Seebohm, 2d ed. (London, 1861), 125.

200. Ibid., 295.

201. Cobbett-Bonneville Manuscripts, 451. Paine's premonition proved correct. In 1819, one of Paine's most zealous converts, William Cobbett, exhumed his bones and shipped them in a box to Liverpool, England, where he hoped to raise enough money to erect a monument to "the common sense of the great man." The project failed for want of money. After Cobbett's death, Paine's bones passed from hand to hand; all trace of them has been completely lost.

202. Ibid., 453.

203. Rickman, *The Life of Thomas Paine*, 174–175.

204. "Paine's Last Moments," *The British Workman*, London, 1861.

205. Rickman, *The Life of Thomas Paine*, 184.

206. Quoted in Cheetham, *The Life of Thomas Paine*, 304.

207. Rickman, *The Life of Thomas Paine*, 189.

Index